Innovation Management

Dr. C.S.G. Krishnamacharyulu
Professor (Retd), Department of Management Studies,
Sri Venkateswara University, Tirupati.
&
Director, RVS Institute of Management & CA,
Karaikal.

and

Dr. Lalitha R.
Professor & Head, Department of Management,
&
Centre Head,
Pondicherry University, Karaikal Campus,
Karaikal.

Himalaya Publishing House
ISO 9001 : 2015 CERTIFIED

First Edition : 2008
Second Revised Edition : 2013
Reprint : 2023, 2024, 2025
Reprint : 2026

Published by : Mrs. Meena Pandey
for **HIMALAYA PUBLISHING HOUSE PVT. LTD.,**
Vishal Industrial Estate, 1st Floor, Office No. 63/64,
Bhandup Village Road, Subhash Nagar (Opp. CEAT Tyres),
Nahur (W), Mumbai - 400 078. **Phone:** 022-35131464/65/66/67
E-mail: himpub@bharatmail.co.in; **Website:** www.himpub.com

Branch Offices :

New Delhi : "Pooja Apartments", 4-B, Murari Lal Street, Ansari Road, Darya Ganj, New Delhi - 110 002.
Phone: 011-23270392, 23278631; Fax: 011-23256286

Nagpur : Kundanlal Chandak Industrial Estate, Ghat Road, Nagpur - 440 018.
Mobile: 09325409992, 09325908881

Bengaluru : Plot No. 91-33, 2nd Main Road, Seshadripuram, Behind Nataraja Theatre,
Bengaluru - 560 020. Phone: 080-41138821; Mobile: 09379847017, 09379847005

Hyderabad : No. 3-4-184, Lingampally, Besides Raghavendra Swamy Matham, Kachiguda,
Hyderabad - 500 027. Phone: 040-27560041, 27550139

Chennai : No. 34/44, Motilal Street, T. Nagar, Chennai - 600 017. Mobile: 09380460419

Pune : "Laksha" Apartment, First Floor, No. 527, Mehunpura,
Shaniwarpeth (Near Prabhat Theatre), Pune - 411 030.
Phone: 020-24496323, 24496333; Mobile: 09370579333

Cuttack : Plot No 5F-755/4, Sector-9, CDA Markat Nagar, Cuttack - 753 014,
Odisha. Mobile: 09338746007

Kolkata : 3, S.M. Bose Road, Near Gate No. 5, Agarpara Railway Station,
North 24 Parganas, West Bengal - 700109. Mobile: 09674536325

DTP by : **Sri Siddhi Softtek**
Bengaluru

Printed at : Geetanjali Press Pvt. Ltd., Nagpur. On behalf of HPH (P).

We dedicate this book to

The divine mother

Goddess Padmavathi at Tiruchanoor

and

Mother (mother-in-law)

Late Srimathi Goda Nancharu

PREFACE TO THE SECOND REVISED EDITION

The progress of a nation and its organizations today depend on the innovative capacities and achievements. Foreseeing this development Peter F. Drucker wrote:

A Latin American slogan is "Countries are not under developed: they are under managed". The fact that management is an organ of the business embodies a major responsibility for creative action. Management is not just a creature of the economy; it is a creator as well. Emphasis on, and drive for workmanship produces innovations and advances in every area of management."

Accordingly organizations are focusing on innovation function and developing structures, strategies and systems for promoting creativity and innovation. Also, they are recruiting people with creative talents.

Institutes of management and universities are quick to recognize the importance of offering a course on innovation management and started including it in their curricula. While there are a variety of books dealing with concepts, theories and skill exercises, the lack of comprehensive text book on the subject is felt by instructors. To fill this gap, The present text was conceived and the contents were designed to meet the requirements of both students and executives. It aimed at supplying knowledge and skill inputs required for strategizing innovation as well as promoting employee creativity.

The revision of the book focused on streamlining the description of processes and techniques on making presentation simpler. The structure is also changed to make it more focused. In the place of 5 parts, now the book has 8 parts. One chapter is added to raise the number of chapters from 23 to 24.

Part – I introduces innovation management and its functions

Part – II discusses the planning and strategy dimensions of innovation management covering environment and strategy dimensions.

Part – III deals with issues relating to structure and dynamics of creative organization

Part – IV elaborates the operational issues of innovation functions and projects.

Part – V focuses on innovation skill development of employees.

Part – VI presents a wide array of creativity techniques useful for individuals and groups.

Part – VII explains managerial aspects of product and process innovations, their diffusion and protection.

Part – VIII examines innovative characteristics of entrepreneurs and explores the path of progress of India as an innovative nation.

The attractive features of the book are:

- Simple, objective and lucid presentation of the knowledge.
- Clear explanation of tools and techniques.
- Chapter- end summaries for a quick understanding of the essential concepts and issues.

- Chapter -end questions and exercises for reinforcing knowledge through tests and practical applications.
- Chapter -end cases for improving analytical and evaluative thinking in varied situations.

To make it a comprehensive textbook, we have drawn material from different sources and acknowledged them carefully. Certainly, we do not claim any originality. We are indebted to many researchers, executives and thinkers who made creativity and innovation a discipline of interest and practice.

We are thankful to our students, who by their inquiries about the progress of the book sustained our interest in writing this book. We are grateful to our colleagues, family members and friends who have encouraged us in our project. Our special thanks are due to Dr C. Madhavaiah (Pondicherry university) and Sri Sivaji Ganesan (KBN College, Vijayawada) for their support.

Finally, our word of appreciation is to our little ones - Sri Krishna and Sri Valli -who by their incessant innovations in life please us in many ways.

C.S.G.Krishnamacharyulu

Lalitha R.

BRIEF CONTENTS

DETAILED CONTENTS

PART – IV: MANAGING INNOVATION PROJECTS

PART – V: MANAGING CREATIVE PEOPLE

PART – VI: CREATIVITY PROCESSES AND TECHNIQUES

Chapter 1

Innovation and Creativity

Learning Objectives

After you have studied this chapter, you will be able to...

- Understand the concept of innovation and creativity
- Identify the characteristics and components of innovation
- Know the sources of innovation
- Explain the process and impact of creativity

Structure

- Introduction
- Concern for Innovation
- Concept of Innovation
- Characteristics of Innovation
- Components of Innovation
- Sources of Innovation
- Types of Innovations
- What is Creativity?
- Creativity Process
- Impact of Innovation
- Summary
- Questions
- Exercises
- Case: Innovation – A New Driver

INTRODUCTION

Conventional business organizations think traditionally and abide by the old rule of thumb and view competition as an inevitable threat. Modern organizations view competition as an opportunity to excel. They seek to maintain a competitive edge by constantly spotting and adjusting to developing trends in market and advances in technology. Innovation has been playing an extraordinary role in business triumph today.

CONCERN FOR INNOVATION

The National Knowledge Commission survey confirms the rising innovation activity and awareness in India. The following findings, explain the innovativeness of Indian firms:

- **Innovation a Priority:** About 17% of the large firms rank "Innovation" as the top strategic priority and 75% rank it among the top 3 priorities. All the large firms agree that innovation has gained importance as being critical to growth and competitiveness since the start of economic liberalization in India.
- **Investment Rising:** All the large firms, agree (of which nearly half strongly agree) that they cannot survive and grow without investment in Innovation. An overwhelming 96% of large firms have reported rise in their Innovation spending over the next 3-5 years.
- **Objective of Innovation:** For large firms Innovation has the most significant impact on competitiveness, while for SMEs, innovation has the most significant impact on increase in market share.
- **Focus Areas and Types of Innovation:** For large firms, Innovation is most highly concentrated in operations and sales and marketing. 37.3% of large firms have introduced breakthrough innovation, while 76.4% have introduced incremental innovation, which may be an indication that large firms in India are still in the mindset of incremental Innovation as compared with breakthrough Innovation.
- **Innovation Project Time Frame:** The average timeframe (from idea generation to market) of Innovation projects for half of the large firms is 1–3 years. Innovation projects in manufacturing firms have longer gestation period than in services.
- **Benefits of Innovation:** More than half of the increase in market share, competitiveness, profitability and reduction in costs due to Innovation has occurred in SMEs due to three types of Innovation – new products, new processes and new services.
- **Large Firms are More Innovative:** About 42% of the large firms and 17% of the SMEs are 'Highly Innovative' firms (i.e., firms who have introduced 'new to world' innovations during the course of business in the last five years).
- **Facilitators for Innovation:** Innovation Intensity is higher in case of privately and publicly owned firms (than government owned firms), foreign ownership firms (than Indian ownership firms) and MNCs (than non-MNCs), firms with their primary market in India (those in abroad) and in industries where Innovations are patented (than those not having patenting facilities).

- **Strategic Approach:** Firms maintaining a specific Innovation department, allocating funds, rewarding innovative employees, forecasting probabilities of success, formalizing processes and systematic attempts, maintaining physical locations for Innovation and constituting cross-functional teams all lead to firms being more innovative. Further, firms with greater R&D spending, Innovation spending and strategic prioritization for Innovation are also more likely to be more innovative.

The advertisement of Toyota (Box 1.1) succinctly explains the kind of commitment, firms in Indian market display.

Box 1.1: Toyota – a Trust Worthy Company

Two pillars of the Toyota way, "Respect for people" and "Continuous improvement" are practiced in all our operations. Our "Customer first philosophy" drives us to develop safe and high quality products and services. Our widespread and customer friendly dealer network helps us to get closer to our customers. We focus on building and maintaining sound relationships with our customers, dealers, suppliers, employees and all other stakeholders.

We believe that the success of a business comes from each individual's creativity and good teamwork. We stimulate the personal growth of our employees through "mutual trust and responsibility".

Source: *The Hindu*, October 11, 2010, p.18.

CONCEPT OF INNOVATION

The word innovation appears to have its origins in the Latin word innovare meaning "to renew, to make new, or alter". The definition by Everett M. Rogers (1995) is similar to this view.

Innovation is an idea, practice or object that is perceived as new by an individual or other unit of adoption.

NKC defines Innovation in the following manner:

Innovation is defined as a process by which varying degrees of measurable value enhancement is planned and achieved, in any commercial activity. This process may be breakthrough or incremental, and it may occur systematically in a company or sporadically; it may be achieved by:

- Introducing new or improved goods or services and/or
- Implementing new or improved operational processes and/or
- Implementing new or improved organizational/ managerial processes

Is Invention an Innovation?

Joseph Schumpeter was the first to draw the distinction between Invention and Innovation. According to him, invention is a new combination of preexisting knowledge, whereas innovation represents use of new procedure or system or production of good or service, new to an organization. In this view invention-if present-is a part of innovation.

Viewed in this way, innovation represents a change process at two levels:

- ❖ Creation of technological or other type of change new to both the enterprise and economy (e.g.: production of personal computer by Apple).
- ❖ Diffusion of the change in to the economy and its adoption by the firms (adoption of computers for word processing and office automation).

Is it Creativity?

Creativity is coming up with ideas whereas innovation is bringing ideas to life and making them productive and profitable. The differences between Creativity and Innovation are succinctly stated in the following words.

Innovation is anything that somebody thinks is a great idea. At a minimum, creativity can be defined as problem identification and idea generation whilst innovation can be defined as idea selection, development and commercialization.

Innovation often means that outside decision-makers have to get involved as complete development and commercialization commonly requires the competencies and knowledge of a team. Different competencies, structures, processes, resources and time-scales are required.

Is it an Improvement?

A change in product or process that provides benefits to adopters and sustainable competitive advantage to the firm is called innovation. As such the following improvements are not innovations:

- ❖ An improvement that only meets the market standard or reacts to innovation of competitors is not innovation. It's playing catch-up.
- ❖ An improvement that does not significantly differentiate you from your competitors is not innovation. It's a routine, or evolutionary progressive action.
- ❖ An improvement that may give you a competitive advantage but can be easily copied by your competitors is not innovation. It's just a temporary advantage.

CHARACTERISTICS OF INNOVATION

The following description identifies the main features of innovation –

- ❖ **Tangible in Outcome:** An innovation is a tangible product, process or procedure within an organization. A new idea may be the starting point for an innovation, but cannot be called an innovation in itself.
- ❖ **New to Society:** An innovation must be new to the social setting within which it is introduced (e.g., work group, department or whole organization) although not necessarily new to the individual(s) introducing it.
- ❖ **An Intentional Activity:** An innovation must be intentional rather than accidental. If a factory reduced its production because of the effects of a heat wave on staff and equipment, this

would not be an innovative action. If, however, the factory took the same action in order to improve product quality or decrease staff sickness, we could describe it as innovative (so long as it also met the above criterion of novelty).

- **A Change Initiator:** An innovation must be a challenging change. The appointment of a new member of staff to replace one who had retired or resigned would not be considered an innovative change. The creation of an entirely new post-would.
- **Beneficial to Adopters:** An innovation must be aimed at predicting benefit to the organization, some subsection of it, and/or the wider society (whether it succeeds in so doing is another matter). Intentionally destructive actions such as sabotage or purely whimsical changes are excluded from the definition.
- **Pubic in Effects:** An innovation must be public in its effects. If an individual introduces a change to his or her work, which has no discernible impact on, or implications for, other people in organization, it would not be considered an innovation.

COMPONENTS OF INNOVATION

All innovations are not fully tangible. Innovations like television, computer, mobile phones etc., are more tangible and others like TQM, virtual learning process, tele-medicine are less tangible. The following three components are universally present in all innovations but in varying degrees, as shown in Table 1.1.

Table 1.1: Components of Innovation

Component	Computer	Quality circle
Physical, material or hardware	Semiconductors, transistors, keyboard, etc.	Recording systems
Functional or process mechanism	Computer software	Discussions
Knowledge component	Operator manual	Ideas for improvement

TYPES OF INNOVATIONS

Competitive success results from pursuing an appropriate amalgam of different types of innovation. There numerous ways in which innovations can be categorized. We will discuss some of the approaches.

(i) Based on Company Point of View:

Innovations are classified based on the company point of view as those which are – (i) new to the world and new to the company and (ii) ultimate and instrumental.

Base	Classification	Description
Newness	New to the world	Totally new and never tried before.
	New to the company	New to the company introducing it.
Nature of action	Ultimate	Introduced as an end in itself.
	Instrumental	Introduced as a means to facilitate the adoption of a further innovation.

(ii) Based on Consumer Point of View:

The two ends of the innovation spectrum are: Radical or discontinuous innovation and Incremental or continuous innovation. Continuous innovations refer to gradual, evolutionary improvements in product or technology whereas discontinuous innovation refers to dramatic, revolutionary changes.

- ❖ Incremental (Sustaining) innovations take the existing product or offering and make small-step improvements to the original technology and design. Incremental improvements add up to produce a great deal of change in an offering overtime.
- ❖ Radical innovations can create an essentially different kind of product or offering with a new combination of types of value produced. The new products and services would require customers to radically change their past behavior with the promise of gaining equally dramatically new value. They are disruptive technologies that permit entire industries and markets to transform or even disappear.

Classification	Description
Major/Radical	Represent radical technological advance like Polaroid's instant camera, cell phones, calculator and computers. Change is both novel and risky.
Minor/Continuous/ Incremental	Modification in existing products/services. E.g.: Gel tooth pastes, E.Sandal Life-buoy.

(iii) Based on Source of Development:

Innovations can be classified based on the source of ideas and development.

Classification	Description
In-house	Developed within the organization.
Out-sourced	Acquired from another innovative organization.
Emergent	Innovations based on ideas emerging from within the organization itself
Adopted (Imported)	Innovations copied from other similar organizations, often with subsequent modifications
Imposed	Innovations which an organization has been forced to make by some external regulatory or legislative power.

(iv) Based on managerial planning:

Innovations in organizations may occur when a decision is taken to introduce new products or processes thorough acquisition, mergers or licensing or alliances. On the other hand, innovation may be made a planned decision of idea generation and development.

Classification	Description
Programmed innovation	Planned or scheduled in advance through research and development.
Non-programmed innovation Slack	When there is a slack in the organization in the form of availability of more resources than are presently needed, the slack resources are then used for innovation purpose.
Non-programmed innovation Distressed	When a crisis is perceived and new actions are taken, there is a forced innovation.
Proactive	Where an individual or group tries to draw the organization's attention to an area where the need for change has not been previously recognized.

(v) Based on design:

Innovations can be classified based on the design approaches. The developers may adopta modular or architectural approach to innovation creation.

Classification	Description
Modular	Significant changes in elements of products, organizational practices and technologies without significant changes in existing configuration of the elements. Eg.: Digital telephone and Quality circles.
Architectural	Reconfiguring the existing organizational practices or technologies Eg.: Plain paper copiers and Just-in-time.

(vi) Based on area of application:

In which domain of organization, innovation is causing a major change? The specific area of impact can be a basis for classifying innovations.

Classification	Description
Product	The development of a new or improved product such as mobile phones with multiple features like calculator, internet, photography etc.
Process	The development of a new elements in service operations or manufacturing process such as Pilkington's float glass process.
Technical	Technology based innovations like steam/diesel/electric trains.
Social	Social improvements like management, installment buying, etc.

Classification	Description
Organizational (structure)	A new venture division, a new internal communications system, introduction of new accounting procedure
Management	Related to basic functions like planning etc., and in different functional areas like production (TQM), Finance (Demat), marketing (Internet selling), human resources (360 degree feedback).

INNOVATIONS BASED ON APPLICATION

We will take a look at the different types of innovations.

Product Vs. Process innovations

In organisations, product innovations occur at a greater speed and frequency than process innovations. Damanpour and Gopalakrishnan (2001) show that in a large sample of US banks (n=101), product innovations are introduced at a higher rate and speed than process, which they explain in terms of managers' perceptions that the former will confer greater competitive advantage. However, firms will be much more successful when they coordinate both process and product innovations.

Today we find banks, insurance and health organizations are innovating both products and processes. Computerization has given a big push to process innovations in them.

Technical Vs. Social innovations

Technical innovations refers to the product of new technology like machines, cameras and computers. Social innovations refer to functioning of the organizations in education, healthcare, government, politics, etc. Few technical innovations can compete in terms of impact with such social innovations as the newspaper or insurance or installment buying. Wherever, introduced, it changed the economy from supply driven to demand-driven.

With the advent of Information and Computer Technology (ICT), a new generation of academic entrepreneurs innovated Internet based learning systems. Most of these distance-learning schools seem to differ little from the older institutions in their curriculum. But they were deliberately designed for a new and different "market" for people in mid-career rather than for youngsters fresh out of high school.

Similarly, the advancements in telemedicine in medicare systems, e-governance in public administration and electronic voting system in politics, are results of not only technology advancements but also cultural shifts.

Organization Vs. Management innovation

Management refers to the process of design and maintenance of an internal environment where individuals working together in groups can perform effectively and efficiently toward the achievement of organizational goals. The process which consists of planning, organizing, leading and controlling is improved from time-to-time by new approaches and tools.

Organization is the structure within which people work to accomplish goals. Several structures are evolved over the years. The line, line-staff, committee, project, matrix and the latest virtual organization are innovations in design of structures.

The innovation in management in most of the cases requires structural innovations too.

Take the case of McDonald. It did not invent anything, to be sure. Its final product was what any decent American restaurant had produced years ago. But by applying management concepts and management techniques (asking, what is "value" to the customer?), standardizing the "product," designing process and tools and by basing training on the analysis of the work to be done and then setting the standards it required, McDonald's both drastically upgraded the yield from resources and created a new market and a new customer. It has developed a chain of restaurants which are run with an emphasis on quality and customer satisfaction. It has improved it door delivery system to make it competitive.

RADICAL VS. INCREMENTAL INNOVATION

A useful distinction should be made between Radical innovation and Incremental innovation. A first-approximation evaluation of the difference between Radical and Incremental innovation may lead to the following Table 1.2. It highlights the sources, determinants and outcomes of both types of innovations:

Table 1.2: Radical Vs. Incremental innovation

Feature	Radical innovation	Incremental innovation
Significance	Major novelty (e.g. entirely new products)	Minor improvements in existing products and processes
Approach	A fresh look on old problems.	Determination in solving problems within a given framework
Typical people triggering innovation	1.Critical individualists 2. Mission-oriented teams	Front-line workers
Knowledge base	New Knowledge. Diversified, with unprecedented use of analogy and tools developed in other industries/contexts	New technology. Specific knowledge.
Organization where the innovation takes place	Outsiders and new entrants	Within an organization.
Outcome factors	New knowledge and /or technology. Gain of long-term competitive advantage. Fulfillment of law requirements. Availing of tax benefits and other incentives.	New applications. Adoption to immediate competition, utilization of research advances within a firm. Adoption to business cycle fluctuations. Adoption to consumer interests.
Determinants (Causal /source factors)	Long-term investment in R&D, Strong R&D (infrastructure and researchers), S&T institutions and linkages, Changes in demographics (Population composition, Education patterns, Materialistic values in society, dynamic consumption patterns). Firms desire to be unique.	Short-term investments in R&D, Integration of R&D and other functions, Competition, Changing consumer interests, Entrepreneurial spirit of firms, Unexpected success, incongruity and gaps (needs).

Jamshyd Godrej observes

Disruptive Innovation is not something that can happen easily and quickly. To make it happen, you have to change the mainstream culture so that it is suitable for nurturing Disruptive Innovation initiative. The other important thing to remember is that Disruptive Innovation is not only about the product. It's about finding new ways to do business, build new distribution channels, finding new ways to advertise…the disruptiveness must be built into the system, services and everything else.

WHAT IS CREATIVITY?

Joseph Campbell, the great mythographer, sees creativity as a journey. Creativity involves exploration. It involves looking beyond the boundaries of our normal thinking and experience. To be creative, we must venture into areas we don't know well. This is why creativity is often described as "scary", "chaotic", "disorientating" and "elusive" – but also "thrilling" and "intriguing". On the contrary, normal thinking is stable, orderly, focused and deterministic.

Definitions on creativity

Most commonly, creativity is conceived of as a mental process. It is associated with creating a new product or problem solving. Product has wider meaning-it can be either a tangible or an intangible one. We will now view different definitions on creativity.

The Penguin Dictionary of Psychology (Reber,1985) defined:

Creativity refers to mental processes that lead to solutions, ideas, conceptualizations, artistic forms, theories or products that are unique and novel.

Harmon (1955) stated.

Creativity is any process by which something new is produced – an idea or an object, including a new form or arrangement of old elements.

Barron (1975) argued.

Creativity does not mean only exploring, inventing or discovering new things or relations, rather it means, to make a new combinations from already existing objects and elements.

Torrance (1988) defined creativity as –

The process of sensing difficulties, problems, gaps in information, missing elements, something askew; evaluating and testing these guesses and hypotheses; possibly revising and retesting them and finally communicating the results.

CREATIVITY PROCESS

In a lighter vein, the creativity process can be stated as follows, prefixing a letter in alphabetical order to the word old to get meaningful stages.

OLD idea – BOLD challenge and discussion – COLD storage – FOLD it up and forget – GOLD idea is struck – HOLD it in reality – SOLD to interested – TOLD to every one by world.

Graham Wallas identified four stages in creativity process as shown in Table 1.3.

Table 1.3: Process of creativity

Stage	Description	Guidelines
Preparation	The individual turns his or her attention to a task or problem, examining relevant information from his or her own experience and the task environment.	Work hard until exhausted. Investigate in all directions. Allow intuition to take over.
Incubation	Conscious work on the problem ceases; the individual may turn his or her attention to another problem, or simply relax. During this period, Wallas claims that some degree of unconscious and involuntary (or fore-conscious and fore-voluntary) work on the problem occurs.	Let the problem go off conscious mind, Sleep on it, Forget it, Take a break, Allow intuition to work.
Illumination	The classic '*Eureka*" moment when the core (or even the whole) of the problem solution suddenly springs into awareness.	Allow discontinuity or break in patterns, a quantum leap, radical change in perception and enlightenment.
Verification	The individual uses logical and rational thought processes to turn the sudden insight into a correct or appropriate solution, apparent as such to others.	Attempt logical evaluation, justification and implementation.

An elaborate description of creativity as a 7-step process is given under.

1. Preparation:

As Louis Pastuer said, "*Chance favors the prepared mind*". Look for stimuli-both internal and external. It may be a random and planned. It may be in response to a problem or an opportunity. What ever may be the source of stimulus, prepare your mind by identifying the problem and defining it in relationship with the environment.

For example, the ruined paint job observed by Dick Drew stimulated the thinking that eventually led to masking tape.

More recently, conventional thinking about the performance limits of silicon-based semiconductors inspired IBM researcher Bernard Meyerson to experiment with a silicon germanium alloy. In so doing, he managed to break through the theoretic computing speed barrier and produce a far superior product.

2. Saturation:

It is the process of investigating the problem in all directions to become familiar with in its setting, causes and effects. Information gathering is carried out extensively with reference to the problem/ decision issue. As more and more information is gathered, decision maker becomes familiar with problem and situation.

3. Deliberation:

Ideas do not fall from heaven, they emanate from mind. Imagine a new, different world and think for new ideas. It is the process of mulling over these ideas, analyzing and challenging them, viewing them from different optics. Through discussion, the information relating to a particular problem, can be analyzed, models developed and constructs evolved. Quite your Voice Of Judgment (VOJ) and go deep in your analysis. *If you want jewels you have to go deep into the sea.*

4. Incubation:

It is the process of relaxing, switching off, and turning the problem over to the unconscious mind. It's based on the fact that the usual, the normal is a weak stimulus for thinking. If the construct is not found valid, the outcome is frustration. The good thing is to set aside a thing and relax. Return afresh to work. If the construct deserves attention, even then relax. *"Be in the world, but guidance comes down as lightly as falling snow. Make the big decisions with heart and little ones with your mind*". Accept the mysterious sub-conscious that nurtures your thoughts into ideas.

A quick way to get this technique to pay-off is to change your routine. Take a new way to or from work. Eat lunch in a new area. Listen to a new radio station. Watch a television show that's not in your native language. Love interior design? Read a magazine about boxing. You might consider having your new-ideas session in a new location, one not usually associated with your business meetings. Think of the following locations and actions-amusement park (riding), beach (relaxing), boat (rowing) and fitness center (Jacuzzi).

John J. Moran a laboratory technician made fortune by inventing automatic blood analyzer in 1965. Moran worked for months on the problem before giving up in frustration and setting out on a long postponed excursion. But on his first day out, as the sun's rays filtered through the hotel window on to his face, he saw in his mind's eye a detailed diagram of a finished machine. Recognizing it as the long sought solution to the problem, he sprang from the bed, hastily sketched it on hotel stationary and flew home, where he spent the next few months building a prototype from the sketch. The prototype worked perfectly and Moran built around it a company called Hycal, Inc., which he sold to a West Germany conglomerate for $40 million.

5. Illumination:

It is a process, which leads to flashing of ideas. The illumination happens all of a sudden. The subconscious acts as filter and screens out the wild and useless ideas. When restraints of rational thoughts are relaxed, new combinations emerge. That is we move from telescopic and microscopic examination to that of kaleidoscope. Then there is emergence of answers-dramatic, perhaps off beat, but fresh and new.

6. Verification:

It is the process of clarifying and flushing out the idea, testing it against criteria of appropriateness. Let your voice of judgment speak out. Challenge your ideas yourself. Play angel's and devil's advocate.

7. Accommodation:

It is the process of trying out the new idea introducing to different people at different places and gaining acceptance. It is made a part of our life. In this process, try to redefine the limits.

IMPACT OF INNOVATION

Innovation is a pervasive phenomenon, whose effects are often ambivalent, i.e. leading to opposite direction, depending on the goals of the innovator, the technological opportunities as well as the society constraints. In particular, innovation can exert an impact on several spheres of society as shown in Table 1.4. Some effects are based on the asymmetry between the Innovator and his Competitors. Others depend on the large diffusion of the innovation.

Table 1.4: Impact of innovations

Sphere	Variables
Company	Costs-Process innovations and product substitutes (e.g. energy savings),
	The quality of the produced good/service.
	Sales since new needs could be matched the new good / service.
	Product differentiation.
	Profitability, potentially both through lower costs than competitors and higher quality.
Legal	Fulfillment of law requests (e.g. about environmental protection.
Social	The required skills of manpower (ambivalently both in the directions of standardization / simplification / reduction or of empowerment.
	Employment structure, thus the relative weight of social groups and productivity.
Economic	Exports when the new good is desired also abroad and there has no adequate substitutes
	Variety of the goods/services available to both consumer and business user.
	Patterns of consumption.
	The number of firms operating in the market, ambivalently multiplying it if innovation is due to young start-up or reducing it if incumbents dominate the innovation trajectory, which becomes a barrier to entry.
	Investments of successful innovator leading to more investments by imitators explain - at least in part - the strong and violent fluctuations in the aggregate investment.
	When innovative products become affordable to the general public there is an equitable distribution of knowledge and income.
Technological	Spurs more investments on R&D and innovation.

SUMMARY

Managers in the industrialized as well as the developing world, in business or in government, are today facing challenges imposed by unprecedented demands. They are considering innovation as strategic resource for sustainable competitive advantage and crafting strategies reinforced by innovation and for innovation. Innovation is the conversion of new knowledge into new products, new processes and new services. Its characteristics include: tangibility, newness and intentional process, challenging and beneficial to public. Its components are physical, functional and knowledge. Innovations can be classified in many ways; process, product, social, technical, administrative like that. Creativity process involves preparation, saturation, deliberation, incubation, illumination, verification and accommodation. Innovation impact is multi fold –affects individuals, organizations and society.

QUESTIONS

1. What is innovation? Explain the characteristics and components of innovation.
2. How do you classify innovations? What are the approaches to innovation?

EXERCISES

Visit websites and prepare a note on 'Innovation for Excellence'.

CASE: INNOVATION – A NEW DRIVER

"Our business is innovation". Said G.V. Prasad CEO of Dr Reddy's Laboratories. In India, where the investment in Research & Development (R&D) makes up a mere 0.8 per cent of the GDP (1.23 per cent for China), innovation is a relatively new concern. But how ready are Indian firms to make innovation an integral part of their growth strategies?

Business Today and Monitor Group jointly surveyed more than 75 senior executives across sectors on their innovation-related attitudes, beliefs and practices.

Meaning – At Marico, for example, innovation is referred to as "uncommon sense". According to Ameya Naniwadekar, Marico's Head of Strategy, "Uncommon sense is a mindset that seeks to create and unlock new value by challenging prevailing rules of the market." According to ICICI: "Innovation is the ability to identify opportunity and seek new growth horizons continually using people, processes and delivery mechanisms as the platform."

Importance – More than 90 per cent of CEOs surveyed said that innovation is "very important" to achieving their organisations' goals and is an explicit part of their corporate strategies. Bharti Airtel, for one, has established the Future Factory— a "center of innovation" that aims to develop innovative applications specifically targeted at individual customer segments. Wipro has established an "Advisory Board" and "Innovation Council" to invest in and manage innovation projects. Tata Motors has initiated a "New Product Introduction" process that defines business processes for new products — tackling everything from understanding customer requirements to commercialisation and everything in between.

Less satisfied – However, more than 73 per cent of CEOs are unsatisfied with the current level of innovation in their organisations. CEOs repeatedly said that their organisations had too many competing priorities, faced difficulty in cross-functional coordination, were overly focussed on short-term results and faced resource constraints that make innovation difficult.

Google, for example, started as a search engine but realised that it had to do more than that or else risk falling behind some upstart company. Today, Google's leadership has ensured that innovation is an integral part of the company's strategy, systems, processes and culture. Marissa Mayer, Head, Google's Idea Factory, searches for the best ideas, talent and resources and then drives them to commercialisation.

The result is visible to all: with remarkable products like AdSense, Google Earth, Google Checkout and Google Notebook, Google towers over its competitors.

Facilitators – Most organisations in India rely on the CEO or a team of directors to drive innovation. Most CEOs also say that they spend more than 10 per cent of their time on innovation-related projects. At companies like TCS, Dr Reddy's Laboratories and Ranbaxy, the CEO spends more than 30 per cent of his time on innovation-related activities.

A company's CEO and board of directors must set stretch growth targets to drive breakthrough innovation. Global innovation leader 3M has the "35 per cent Rule": 35 per cent of the company's revenues must come from products and services that have been introduced in the last four years. Similarly, at the US aluminium giant Alcoa, stretched cost-reduction targets are used to drive out-of-the-box ideas and partnerships and employees are compensated far more handsomely for meeting stretch targets than they are for meeting planned targets.

Indian firms also need to create a role for individuals or teams to operationalise the innovation agenda, build innovation capabilities and support business units' innovation efforts. All of these goals can be accomplished more readily when a firm designates one individual who is accountable for the company's innovation agenda. Global giants such as CEMEX, Frito-Lay and Hitachi have already created the Chief Innovation Officer (CIO) position, which reports directly to the CEO. These officers ensure that there is enough focus on innovation programmes and help link innovation efforts to the firm's strategy and growth. They ensure that innovation is an integral part of the company and get innovation projects executed to ensure that stretch targets are met.

Questions:

1. Explain the concern for innovation among Indian companies as presented in the case. Is the situation same or different now?
2. How can a company promote innovation? Develop a list of guidelines.

Source: *India's most innovative companies - Business Today - Business News businesstoday.intoday.in/ ../indias... innovative-companies.../1875.ht...*20 Apr 2008.

Chapter 2

Innovation Management

Learning Objectives

After you have studied this chapter, you will be able to…

- Explain the concept, scope and characteristics of innovation management
- Know about systems management
- Trace the evolution of innovation management
- Know the significance of innovation management
- Understand how to measure performance of innovation management
- State the principles for effective innovation management

Structure

- Introduction
- Concept
- Scope
- Characteristics of Innovation Management
- Systems Approach
- Evolution of Innovation Management
- Significance
- Performance Evaluation
- Effective Innovation Management
- Summary
- Questions
- Exercises
- Case:You Can't Innovate Like Apple

INTRODUCTION

Successful firms value the slogan, "innovate or perish". In the dynamic, knowledge economy of today, innovation is considered as a strategic resource for sustainable competitive advantage and consumer acceptance for the products and services. The major task of competitive organizations therefore is developing strategies for innovation, designing creative organizations, nurturing creativity among employees and allocating resources for experimentation and commercialization of ideas. In nut shell, it can be said that, management of innovation has become an enterprise-wide function and a Key Result Area (KRA) in modern organisations.

CONCEPT

Innovation management may be defined in different ways as given under.

Innovation management is concerned with planning, organizing and controlling innovation effort, and fostering creativity among individuals and groups to achieve the goals of an organization.

Innovation management is a socio-psychological process of generating ideas and a techno-economic process of converting the ideas into profitable products and services.

SCOPE

Innovation management is concerned with four key functional areas for decision-making as shown in Table 2.1.

1. ***Strategy*** – Managing organic nature and responsiveness of organization to environment and evolving strategies to achieve environment and organization fit.
2. ***People*** – Managing the dynamics of organization that involves fostering and promoting creative spirit and skills among employees
3. ***Projects*** – Managing innovative projects, right from idea generation to product or process development and application.
4. ***Commercialization*** – Patenting, innovation diffusion and marketing.

Table 2.1 Innovation Management – Key Areas

Level	Aspects	Decision areas
1	Organization and environment	What kind of strategies can a firm develop? Is there an ideal structure, climate and culture for innovation? What kind of policies and procedures are required to promote innovations and make it a way of life in the organization?
2	People	How is individual creativity related to organizational innovation? What are the characteristics of innovative persons? What are the characteristics of innovative work groups? How should organizations select individuals for creativity? What type of training enhances creative performance at work? How effective are team-building initiatives for promoting innovation?

Level	Aspects	Decision areas
3	Projects	Does the innovation process develop in clearly defined stages? What are the pros and cons of using different techniques of creativity?
4	Commercialization	How do innovators protect innovations from imitation by rival firms? How can innovations be diffused?

CHARACTERISTICS OF INNOVATION MANAGEMENT

The following features characterize innovation management:

Knowledge based – Innovations within an organization are not random; they occur in relation to the past and present conditions of the organization. Different kinds of knowledge representing different aspects within an organization, such as 'know why', 'know what' and 'know-how' are essential. 'Know why' is the theoretical understanding, 'know what' is the strategic understanding and 'know-how' is the practical understanding.

It is important to note that organizational innovation is not a one-time product of knowledge creation and application. Innovation is a continuous process of utilizing current and future knowledge and formal and non-formal knowledge.

Culture based – The source of innovation in an organization is the value based behavior and attitudes. If experimentation and discovery are given importance, there will be cumulative experiences and articulations of individuals and groups relating to search for new order. Appreciation of participation and team work in the decision to innovate tends to raise the commitment of organization members towards the innovation. A higher level of commitment is associated with more successful innovation.

Need based – Necessity is the mother of invention. The urge to innovate is strengthened when the inventor or inventive organization identifies a specific need. Consider the invention of Xerography.

Carlson was a patent attorney who was motivated to find an easier way to make copies of his patent applications. Because of Kodak's strong patent position in photographic processes Carlson deliberately looked for solutions to document copying in non-traditional fields. The result was Xerography, which had an invincible patent position and, as history has demonstrated, was an optimum solution to the problem.

Many inventions have been made under compulsive necessities of war.

The Germans developed rocketry and ballistic missiles to destroy England. America made the atom bomb to crush Japan. The allies developed radar and sonar to protect themselves.

All these inventions turned out to be quite beneficial in peace time. Rocket and missiles opened the way for space exploration and epochal landing of man on the moon. Atomic power is now being used for power generation and other purposes.

Entrepreneurial and Intrapreneurial – In US, the subject of innovation management is often covered in terms of entrepreneurship. Entrepreneur is described as a person who starts a new venture associated with risk. Thus he is considered as a risk taker and innovator and his job is described as innovation management. Innovation is the specific tool of entrepreneurs, the means by which they exploit change as an opportunity for a different business or a different service.

The entrepreneurship approach has become a necessity for even existing organizations and managers have become strategists and intrapreneurs for survival and success. In light of this, today we speak about entrepreneurial management and learning organization.

Science and art – Peter F. Drucker observed that innovation cane be systematic and scientific. He wrote:

Before 1880 or so, invention was mysterious; early nineteenth-century books talk incessantly of the "flash of genius". The inventor himself was a half-romantic, half-ridiculous figure, tinkering away in a lonely garret. By 1914, the time World War I broke out, "invention" had become "research", a systematic, purposeful activity, which is planned and organized with high predictability both of the results aimed at and likely to be achieved.

Something similar is happening to innovation. Innovation is capable of being presented as a discipline, capable of being learned, capable of being practiced. Entrepreneurs (and managers) need to search purposefully for the sources of innovation, the changes and their symptoms that indicate opportunities for successful innovation. They need to know and to apply the principles of successful innovation.

Risky – Innovations manifest in new processes and new products which are profitable. Of course, there is a risk; they may not succeed. It is true that many innovations have failed. On the other hand, there are many organizations around whose success rate rejects the universal belief that innovation is risky.

IBM, in a fast-moving high-tech field, that of the computer and in competition with the "old pros" in electricity and electronics, has a record of successes.

Procter & Gamble, the well-known producer of branded and packaged consumer goods, similarly has had a near-perfect record of successful innovations.

3M in St. Minnesota, a "middle-tech" company, which has created around one hundred new businesses or new major product lines, has been successful four out of every five times in its venture.

There is evidence to reject the view that innovation is risky. Innovation is "risky" mainly because many of the organizations do not know what they are doing. They lack the methodology. They violate elementary and well-known rules.

Economical and social – Innovation is an economic or social rather than a technical term. Classical economists like J.B. Say defined entrepreneurship (and innovation) from supply side, as changing the yield of resources. Modern economists defined it in demand terms, as changing the value and satisfaction obtained from resources by the consumer.

The shift from logistics to Supply Chain Management (SCM), the move from MRP (Materials Requirement Planning) to ERP (Enterprise Resource Planning) and the shift from in-house production to outsourcing are best described and analyzed in supply terms. The end product, the end uses and the customers are the same, though the costs are substantially lower.

But the call centers, mobile service vans, cell phones with cameras and internet like features, though "technical", are better described or analyzed in terms of consumer values and consumer satisfactions, as are such social innovations as the news magazines developed by Henry Luce of Time-Life-Fortune in the 1920s.

SYSTEMS APPROACH

Systems approach provides *holistic view* of the innovation by identifying the various components in the innovation function. It emphasizes the following information and action:

- ***Components*** – Knowing the components that make up the system (Innovators, Innovation process and effort, organizational factors like size, systems, culture and climate, management factors like leadership and supervision and external environmental factors).
- ***Inter-relationships*** – Knowing the interrelationships between the components.
- ***Effectiveness*** – Knowing the ways to make each component effective in relation to other. components in the system and with reference to the goals set for accomplishment.
- ***Whole*** – Knowing how to make the whole system effective and efficient in achieving the goals.

Rationale of the approach

Systems approach has been adopted by many organizations across the world. It is considered necessary for managing business operations.

- ***Non-linearity*** –.Managing innovations is quite different from managing operations.

  Operations are characterized by a greater degree of certainty and rely on familiar deterministic models. Operational management is more orderly and disciplined. It involves mostly logical, convergent thinking. It enforces conformity in thinking, actions and results.

  Innovation, on the other hand, requires a spirit of relentless growth that keeps fresh ideas flowing and reinvigorating the organization. Innovation requires non-linear process and it is more critical and complex. Hence, the need for systems approach is quite obvious.

- ***Uncertainty*** – Innovations create *tomorrow's opportunities*, while operations generate today's value. Managing *uncertainty* inherent in innovation requires specific tools and thinking.
- ***Learning Process*** – Innovation is a *learning process*, the product of which is new applied knowledge. The process of innovation is a rhythm of search and selection, exploration and synthesis, cycles of divergent thinking followed by convergence.
- ***Coordination*** – Innovation requires *managing knowledge workers*, who think differently and exhibit low tolerance levels. To keep all these independent thinkers pointed in the same direction and working towards same goal is a tough challenge.
- ***Expanded Scope*** – Innovation has an *expanded scope* now. Until recently innovation is equated with commercially successful products or services. Today, innovation goes beyond requiring improvements in process, structures, systems and products. There is convergence of different sources and technologies, forming a wide spectrum of applications in markets and management functions.

Benefits

The application of systems model for innovation gives the corporate management many tangible benefits.

- ***Establishes a framework*** – It helps in streamlining the innovation process and identify its driving forces. It helps capture the practices of market champions and understand what makes them so successful and unique.
- ***Understand dynamics*** – It helps identify the core elements of innovation, their behavior and interactions. Such an understanding helps locate strong and weak links and take actions to strengthen the process.
- ***Integration within*** – A functional integration for cross functional teamwork is essential for innovation. This need can be effectively fulfilled only when various functions in the organization and forces in the external environment are integrated.
- ***Extends focus beyond the firm*** – Innovation arises from complex interactions between Individuals, Organizations and their operating environments. The integration extends organizational focus beyond R&D to engage sources outside environment.

EVOLUTION OF INNOVATION MANAGEMENT

Innovation and entrepreneurship had been focal points of discussion among the economists since the 1880s. Figure 2.1 shows the changes in emphasis of business managers during the last six decades. From the scientific management of F.W Taylor who focused on innovations in shop floor management by providing functional organization and principles of efficiency management, there is a progression in management. Different foci points are added – focus on people and performance, focus on strategy, focus on quality, focus on technology and focus on knowledge and innovation. The science of management developed to supply the knowledge and skills and books and research papers on creativity and innovation management flooded the market.

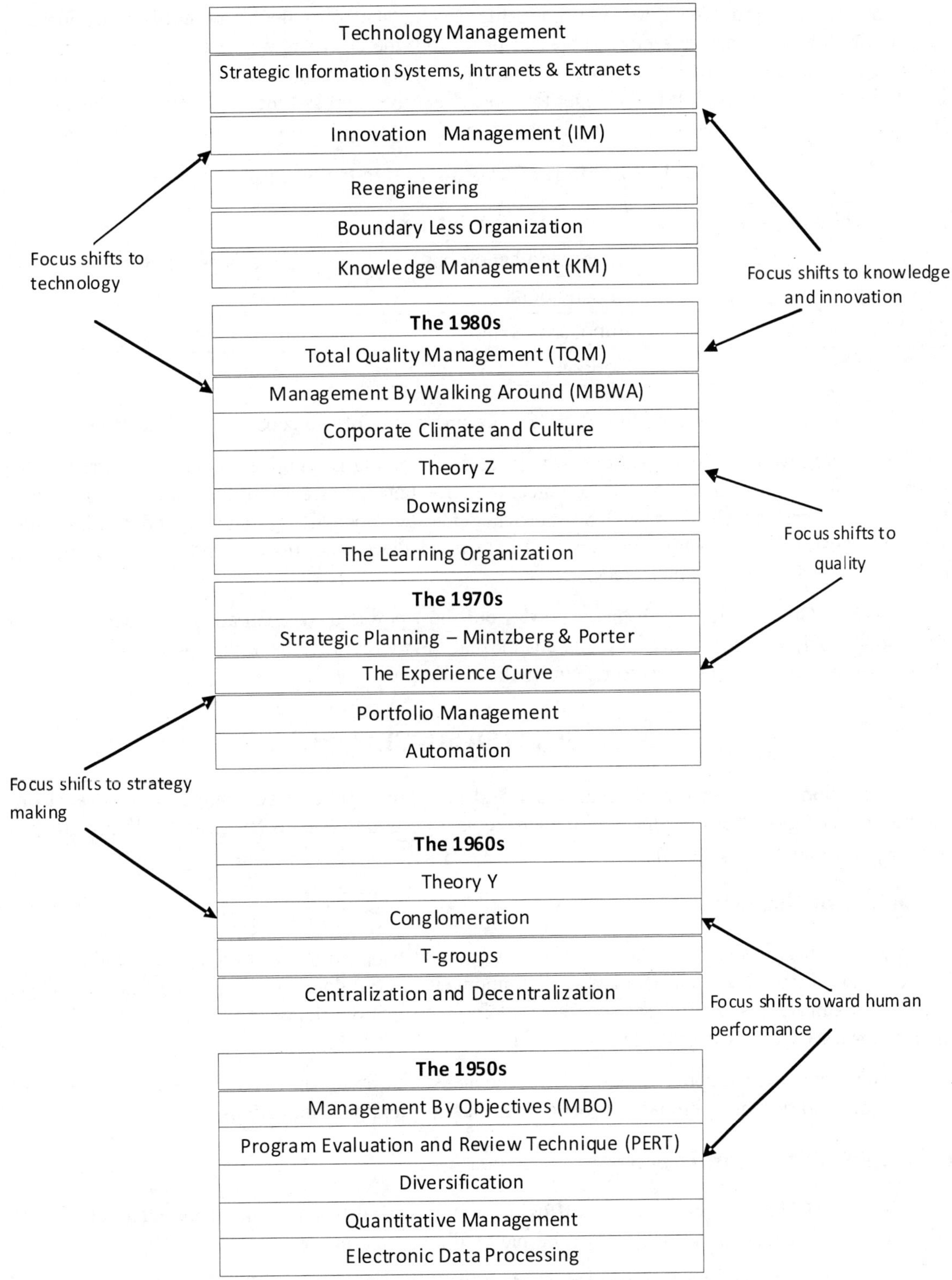

Figure 2.1 Emergence of innovation management

The evolution process led to another notable development. It is the adoption of innovation as a regular function in corporate sector. Table 2.2 brings out the emergent approach to innovations. The thinking is no longer linear, it is systematic. The innovation is no longer focused on technical aspects; it is entire business focused. It is no longer technologists driven; cross-functional teams are the drivers. It is led by cross-functional leaders and is continuous.

Table 2.2 Different approaches to Innovation

Thinking style	Linear thinking	Systemic thinking
Target	Technological process	Entire business wheel
Drivers	Technologists	Cross-functional teams
Lead innovator	Functional expert	Cross- functional synergist
Process	Periodic	Continuous

To appreciate the fact that innovation has become a way of life consider the case of Godrej.

At Godrej, we have developed our own process of creating Disruptive Innovation. Currently, the Disruptive Innovation process is used for unlocking large untapped market at the bottom of the income pyramid and fostering inclusive growth by improving their livelihood, living standards and their lifestyles. Thus, the Disruptive Innovation journey will help us to meet aspirations of millions of people and making a huge difference to their lives.

Navroze Godrej said, "With innovation as our most powerful weapon and a brighter future our most noble goal, we need to act now and ensure that in ten years we have the whole world asking - How did you find it in yourselves to rise up to the challenge?"

SIGNIFICANCE

Innovation is needed for survival and for strategic competitive advantage in this world of competition and globalization. Innovation management generates excellence, ensures better quality of life and meets human aspirations.

(i) Driver of change:

Innovation is a spark that keeps organizations and people moving ever onward and upward. Without innovation, new products, new services and new ways of doing, business would never emerge, and most organizations would be forever stuck doing the same old things the same old way.. As Jack Welch, former CEO of General Electric, puts it.

"The operative assumption today is that someone, somewhere, has a better idea and the operative compulsion is to find out who has that better idea, learn it and put into action-fast".

(ii) Engine of economic growth:

The speed and efficiency of the diffusion of innovation through the economy is critical to productivity and economic growth. It can be pictured as a cascade process.

Innovation created by a firm is adopted, developed, improved and diffused.

As such the impact on the economy of an innovation is many times greater than that brought about by the first application of the innovation.

An entrepreneur brings to market an innovation forcing established enterprises to respond to the change. It is Nirma of Karsan Bhai Patel that forced Hindusthan Unilver to become more innovative. It is Maruti of Maruti Udyog that unleashed competition and paved way for more innovative cars.

Encouraging the emergence of new firms is a strong force for innovation in many sectors.

(iii) Provides sustainable competitive advantage:

Sustainable Competitive Advantage (SCA) is created when firms possess and employ resources and capabilities that are *valuable, rare, hard to copy and non-substitutable*. Competitive advantage occurs when an entrepreneur or manager is implementing value-creating strategy not simultaneously implemented by current or potential competitors. Resource based theory recognizes six types of business resources called **PROFIT** factors. Table 2.3 presents the factors with characteristics.

Table 2.3 Strategic resources outline

Resources	Valuable	Rare	Hard to copy	Non-substitutable
Physical	Yes	Some times	Not usually	Some times
Reputational	Yes	Yes	Yes	Yes
Organizational	Yes	Yes	Yes	Yes
Financial	Yes	Some times	No	No
Intellectual	Yes	Yes	Usually	Some times
Technological	Yes	Some times	Some times	Some times

Source: Marc J. Dollinger (2003), *Entrepreneurship,* Pearson Education, New Delhi, p. 38.

(iv) Creates Profits and productivity:

The profits of a firm are result of three forces working together. They are: knowledge, innovation and technology as shown in Figure 2.2. Innovation contributes to more efficient and effective functions that raise productivity levels of a firm. Process improvement can lead to dramatic cost reduction in non-core processes far beyond what can be accomplished through traditional cost-cutting efforts. Thus innovation reduces costs and increases profit margins.

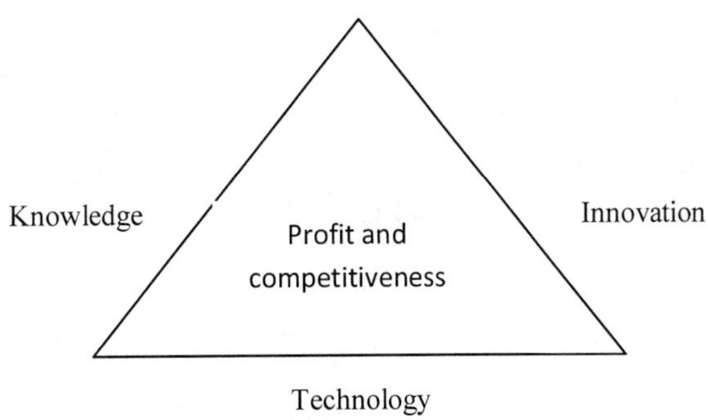

Figure 2.2 Business Triangle

(v) Revolutionizes the industry:

In fact, innovation destroys. More than a half-century ago, economist Joseph Schumpeter described the economic, sociological and organizational impacts of innovation and its "*winds of creative destruction.*" Those winds sweep away both old ways of doing things and the enterprises and institutions that cling to them.

Innovation valued by the marketplace has long been recognized as *creator and sustainer of enterprise.*

Every time Intel's engineers produce a new generation of computer chips that its customers value, its fortunes are renewed. Immediate customers such as Dell, IBM, Toshiba, and other personal computer makers quickly snap up the new chip and, by doing so, offer faster and more powerful machines to their customers.

(vi) Survival and excellence:

Within the core business process, the innovation effort is usually aimed at reaching the "best in class" and attaining competitive parity with those who have in the past set standards and laid the rules of the competition. However, for some it is a survival *mantra.*

Shift to the new knowledge based economy combined with a dramatic increase in highly capable global competition, created a new world of business- a fierce contest set in truly global context, with more capable players, higher stakes and vastly different rules of engagement from those that firms have enjoyed to date. Those who innovate-create, find and/or combine knowledge into new products, services and distribution methods faster than competitors lead this new economy.

(vii) Achieves business-market fit:

Markets are dynamic. Business organizations have two options in relation to markets, to be reactive or proactive. Innovations, which fulfill a felt and manifest need will have , immediate market acceptance. Innovations that are ahead of time, attempt at changing the market as they represent latent needs of target market. In either case, the aim to maintain business –market fit.

(viii) Enhances motivation and potential of employees:

By managing creativity it is possible to enhance motivation. There is a significant positive correlation between Creativity and Intrinsic motivation. Creative people are intrinsically motivated. This means that they see inherent value in what they are doing, as opposed to extrinsic motivation, which causes them to engage in an activity to fulfill ulterior goals. Some extrinsic motivation is useful (adequate financial reward is a form synergistic extrinsic motivation, upto a point).

Creative people enjoy what they are doing (they tend to describe themselves as passionate). As a result, they tend to behave more positively towards their colleagues, customers and people they come into contact with.

(ix) Improves quality of life:

Scientific inventions and discoveries lead to creation of mechanisms and artifacts which improve or make our living conditions much more comfortable and convenient.

The alarm clock in place of a cock, toothpaste in place of ash, automobile in place of a man-or animal pulling cart and television in place of radio, for instance, show how human life has become more pleasant and humane.

PERFORMANCE MEASURES

Innovation is a desirable phenomenon, though its effects are often ambivalent. Research has attempted to identify the positive influence of innovation on performance and progress of organization and society. For instance, Yamin et al. (1999) found a positive relationship between Innovativeness and Increased performance, though highly innovative firms may not outperform moderately innovative firms in all measures of effectiveness.

What can be the appropriate measures? There are no guidelines available that assist researchers to find an appropriate performance measure for innovation management. Innovation provides differentiation to the innovator and benefit of product or service experience to users and increase in market share and profits to innovator by diffusion.

The impact of innovation can be measured by taking measures of two types (quantitative and qualitative) and in two spheres(micro and macro) as given in Tables 2.4, 2.5 and 2.6.

Subramanian and Nilakanta (1996) suggest using either (or both) an efficiency measure, which has a cost-benefit focus, or an effectiveness measure, which has a revenue generation focus. These are measured by indicators such as financial ratios, market share, sales etc. Atuahene-Gima (1996) used a 12-item scale where respondents were asked to rate the degree of success of an innovation. This is a method that relies on the subjective judgement of managers. Increase in employee motivation in the case of a process or operational innovation is considered as another useful measure.

Table 2.4 Micro (organization) – Quantitative Measures

S.No	Areas	Measures
1	Cost measures	• Cost advantage (mainly if process innovation).
2	Output measures	• Increased volume of output • Increase in number of people served
3	Quality measures	• Quality improvements in the produced good/service
4	Marketing advantage	• Product range - Variety of the goods/services available to both consumer and business user. • Sales, since new needs could be matched the new good / service
5	Organization goals	• Productivity • Profitability, potentially both through lower costs than competitors and higher quality

Table 2.5 Micro (organization) – Qualitative Measures

S.No.	Areas	Measures
1	Practice improvements	• Standardization / simplification • Increase in skills and empowerment of people. • Economical use of inputs (e.g. energy savings)
2	People management	• Employee satisfaction
3	Product positioning	• Product differentiation • Quality improvements in the produced good/service
4	Organization goals	• Compliance with law (good citizen) • Image • Customer satisfaction

Table 2.6 Macro (society) – Measures

S.No.	Areas	Measures
1	Consumption	Changes in patterns of consumption Improved quality of life
2	Investment	Expansion of industry with the number of firms operating in the market.
3	Employment	Increase in employment
4	Savings	Consumer savings due to economy goods Cost savings in production
5	Global relations	Exports, when the new good is desired also abroad and there are no adequate substitutes.
6	Income	Growth in economy and high GNP.

EFFECTIVE INNOVATION MANAGEMENT

Entrepreneurial innovation will be as important to management as the managerial function…and will be more important in the years to come." So says well-known business author Peter Drucker in Technology, Management and Society.

However, corporations face substantial obstacles to innovation. If management is not vigorous enough at encouraging and stimulating innovation, it is unlikely to occur. The features of an effective innovation management are given here to help make innovation function more effective.

1. Starts from the top: Top management considers innovation as an essential process for keeping up with new trends, thoughts and tools. Creativity is expected to result in new, improved products, streamlined procedures and waste reduction. They communicate their commitment and provide direction for innovations. They encourage their employees, but stay out of the creative process. They are aware that it is their subordinates' job to develop, plan and execute products and ideas-and they respect their subordinates' ability.

Andrew Grove, the president of Intel, is a good example. A busy man running a very successful company, he values creativity, entrepreneurship and peak performance. He believes in his people. He coaches them, prods them, and helps each of them fulfill his or her potential. He knows that his role is to make decisions and provide general direction. He also understands that his employees do the work, know the ropes and are eager to demonstrate their competence.

During its 15 years of existence, Intel has been extremely successful. The company invented both the memory chip and the microprocessor, among other innovations. Obviously, Grove is doing something right. His attitude creates a culture, which says, Okay, folks, we're good and we know it, but we can be better. If we all work together we can create, invent, succeed and surpass. It'll be exciting to do it.

2. Balances innovation and stability: Rapid growth increases an organization's complexity and the number and seriousness of its change-related problems. Inherent in large systems is the tendency for order and prediction to crush flexibility and creativity. Good management needs to balance innovation and organizational stability. Unfortunately, it is just when they need creativity most, during an unstable or fluctuating economy, that companies are likely to sacrifice creative activities for projects with a fast return. Unless it also recognizes and exploits creativity, the organization will quickly be left behind by its competition. Farsighted, progressive and open-minded management can maximize creativity by understanding and recognizing what it is, nurturing it and capitalizing on it.

***3. Makes Planned effort*:** Good management takes creative, planned, long-term determination and emphasis to generate the innovative results. It assumes the responsibility for studying, understanding, and implementing the opportunities and techniques of innovation.

4. Demands best outcomes: Innovations occur when there are targets and deadlines; when there is demand for the best. In innovative culture good management says,

We want to be the best. And to be the best, we've got to be innovative, stay ahead of the competition and be creative and entrepreneurial. If we are to accomplish our goals, we can't stand-still. We need new ideas, new products and new processes. Our ultimate objective is to be the best, and to have fun doing it.

***5. Shows bias for action*:** Good management has a "bias for action." They know that problems require careful analysis, but they don't overanalyze. They're willing to test, on a small-scale, any idea that seems good to the person who developed it. If the idea pass out, that's great; on to the next stage. If it doesn't, then they go back to the drawing board. You never really know unless you try. Good managers do all those things, by being open and supportive, but also by being demanding and goal-directed. As the saying goes, "If you don't know where you're going, you'll probably end up somewhere else." Good management no bones about the organization's direction, nor about its belief in the abilities of its members.

6. Develop skills: Good management seeks to develop skills. Management training curricula should pay more attention to courses designed to sharpen the skills of leadership in the area of technological innovation.

*7. **Responds to ideas spontaneously:*** Within a framework that demands quality, good managers get excited about ideas, developments, concepts, theories and products. They realize that innovation demands experimentation and show genuine excitement for ideas, before and after they are tested, whether or not they work. When an employee brings an idea, the response by manager is: "That's great! I'm behind you all the way!". Creativity and entrepreneurship demand the spontaneity that excitable management generates.

*8. **Values originality***: Good management values every idea in its search for originality. In effect nothing is sacred. Everything's up for discussion, every idea has merit and every concept is worth exploring. Sure, most ideas will fall through the cracks, But, every once in a while, some champion will burst forth from his or her cocoon with a "*Eureka*!" that rattles the rafters. That's what makes it all worthwhile.

*9. **Supports innovators:*** Good management listens. Creative and entrepreneurial people need sounding boards-people to present ideas to help put things into perspective, and to support them. People to gently guide them, to listen to their problems and help translate their ideas into usable formats, to acknowledge their successes, and to put failures into perspective.

*10. **Encourages experimentation:*** Good management knows that innovation, entrepreneurship, and creativity only thrive in an open environment. There is freedom to experiment, explore, test and create without fear of punishment or embarrassment.

Ask 3M about this concept. It works because each of us, deep down, has a great idea we'd like to try-a feeling that we can do something better than anyone else. We just need an opportunity to let it out without fear. Once we do, it's like a fountain-creativity just bubbles up.

*11. **Understands mistakes:*** Fletcher Byrom once said that to be successful, you should make sure you generate a reasonable number of mistakes. Andrew Grove likens management to sports-over time, he says, we're bound to lose 50 per cent of our games. Good management should learn to win through failures. It should expect that the reward for one success far outweigh the cumulative failures. A company that has a positive attitude toward failure will find people willing to take intelligent risks.

*12. **Rewards success***: Good managers create a supportive environment for the innovators and acknowledge their contributions, both in public (in the form of recognition and promotion) and in private (in the form of higher pay).

*13. **Builds pride***: As Macdougall says, "Good managers seem to have a consistent style that somehow makes everyone involved with their business feel like one of the Chosen Few." They are quick to give credit to specific individuals. When they don't like something, they criticize the development, not the people who worked on it. Most importantly, they generate mutual respect.

SUMMARY

Innovation management deals with innovative behavior at individual, group and organizational level. Innovation management is knowledge based, culture based, need based, entrepreneurial and intrapreneurial, science and art, risky, social and economical. A systems approach will be beneficial in many ways. Innovation management has evolved over the years. Innovation is constantly needed to create competitive advantage, as suggested by Michael Porter through *low cost advantage, differentiation and value addition, and focus.* Innovation management generates excellence, ensures better quality of life and meets human aspirations. Innovation management can be measured at micro-level by production and profits and at macro-level by quality of life. To make innovation effective principled approach is necessary. Top management initiative, balance between Stability and Innovation, plan and expect best outcomes are some of the principles.

QUESTIONS

1. What is innovation management? Examine its nature, scope and significance.
2. Trace the evolution of innovation management.
3. Do you advocate systems approach to innovation management?
4. Explain the principles that make innovation management effective.

MINI-PROJECT

Visit websites and prepare a note on 'Innovation for Excellence'.

CASE: YOU CAN'T INNOVATE LIKE APPLE

Nearly everyone believes the equation Apple = Innovation is a fundamental truth. It is clearly the "Most Admired," the "Most Innovative," and the "Master at Design".

Apple thinks good design is a present – Apple "wraps great ideas inside great ideas," and the whole experience is linked as the present concept traces concentric circles from the core outward.

Pixel-perfect mockups are critical – This is hard work and requires an enormous amount of time, but is necessary to give the complete feeling for the entire product. For those who aren't familiar with the term, pixel perfect means the designers of a piece of Apple software create an exact image—down to the very pixel (the basic unit of composition on a computer or television display) — for every single interface screen and feature. Doing this detailed mockup removes all ambiguity—everyone knows and can see and critique how the final product looks.

10 to 3 to 1 – Apple designers expect to design 10 different mockups of any new feature under consideration. By using specified criteria, they narrow these 10 ideas down to three options, which the team spends months further developing…until they finally narrow down to the one final concept that truly represents their best work for production.

This approach is intended to offer enormous latitude for creativity that breaks past restrictions. But it also means they inherently plan to throw away 90 per cent of the work they do. For many organizations this would not be an acceptable ratio. The CFO would probably declare, "All I see is money going down the drain."

Paired design meetings – Every week, the teams of engineers and designers get together for two complementary meetings.

- *Brainstorm meeting* – This meeting involves free thinking with absolutely no rules.
- *Production meeting* – The absolute opposite of the brainstorm meeting, where the aim is to put structure around the crazy ideas and define the how to, why and when.

These two meetings continue throughout the development of any application.

Pony meetings – These meetings are scheduled every two weeks with the internal clients (senior managers) to educate them on the design directions being explored and influence their perception of what the final product should be. The meetings give a sense of control to senior management, so that they have visibility into the process and can influence the direction. Again, the purpose of this is to save the team from pursuing a line of direction that ultimately gets tossed because one of the decision-makers wasn't on board.

Guidelines

To succeed at innovation as Apple has, you need the following:

You need a leader who prioritizes new product innovation – The CEO needs to be someone who looks out to the horizon and consistently sets a vision of innovation for the organization that he or she is willing to support completely with people, funds and time.

You need to focus – A cohesive vision describes the storyline for your products and services. That storyline needs to state decisively what is in bounds and what is out-of-bounds over an 18-month to 3-year period. Everyone in the development process who matters must be in lockstep with this vision, which means you need to have open lines of communication that are regularly and consistently managed.

This storyline or strategic vision needs to be revised according to market changes and the evolution of your new product pipeline. It helps to develop the "total solution" rather than just loosely joined components.

Obviously, the other focus is to make a profit, since that is what supports the continued efforts to design the next great product. When every one of the major products is a moon shot, they have to work to ensure it meets exacting standards – to do everything they can to ensure success.

You need to know your customer and your market – Jobs and team can get away with not doing market research. Most technology companies also believe they can get away with this—and most technology companies get it wrong.

Do not ask your customers what they want. If you ask that question in the formative stages, then you're doing it wrong. The point is to go immerse yourself in their environment and ask lots of "why" questions until you have thoroughly explored the ins and outs of their decision making, needs, wants, and problems. At that point, you should be able to break their needs and the opportunities down into a few simple statements of truth.

You need the right people, and you need to reward them – The designers at Apple are paid 50 per cent more than their counterparts at other organizations. These designers aren't working at Apple simply because they're paid more. They stay at Apple because of the amazing things they get to do there. Rewards are about salary and benefits, but they are also about recognition and being able to do satisfying work that challenges the mind and allows the creative muscles to stretch. Part of this also comes down to ensuring your teams are passionate about innovation and dedicated to the focus of the organization. As Jobs says, he looks for people who are crazy about Apple. So you need to look closely at the people you are hiring and whether you have the right team in the first place.

Questions:

1. Identify the reasons that have made Apple innovative.
2. Can a FMCG company adopt the approach of Apple and be successful in becoming an innovative company?

Source: *Alain Breillatt, You Can't Innovate Like Apple — Pragmatic Marketing, world's most ... www.pragmaticmarketing.com/.../6/.../you_cant_innovate_like_apple*

Chapter 3

Functions of Innovation Management

Learning Objectives

After you have studied this chapter, you will be able to…

- Understand how the style of management at top affects innovation.
- Know the functions of management in relation to innovation.

Structure

- Introduction
- Top-down Function
- Planning
- Organizing
- Staffing
- Leading
- Controlling
- Summary
- Questions
- Exercises
- Case: Innovation Assessment Survey

INTRODUCTION

Proper management of innovation is perhaps the most potentially rewarding challenge facing business today. Innovation and creativity do not happen in a vacuum or in a predictable order. Innovation is not like most other business functions and activities. There are no reliable templates, rules, processes, or even measures of success. In a sense, each act of innovation is a unique feat, a leap of the individual or the collective – imagination that can be neither predicted nor replicated. Planning, organizing, staffing, leading and controlling the creative processes in an organization takes courage, the same courage found in the truly creative individual-a personal courage of mind and spirit.

TOP-DOWN FUNCTION

The encouragement of innovation is a management function and it has to be a 'top-down' effort. Different researchers have pointed out that Management support for an innovative culture is the most important determinant for innovatio as shown in Table 3.1

The twelve determinants identified in the qualitative research are:

1. MS - Management support for an innovative culture
2. CF - Customer/market focus
3. CN - Communication/networking – internal & external
4. HR - HR strategies that emphasize innovation
5. TM - Teams and teamwork
6. KN - Knowledge management, development and out-sourcing
7. LS - Leadership
8. CD - Creative development
9. SP - Strategic posture
10. FS - Flexible structures
11. CI - Continuous Improvement
12. TE - Technology adoption

Table 3.1 Research on determinants of organizational innovation

Authors	MS	CF	CN	HR	TM	KN	LS	CD	SP	FS	CI	TE
Atuahene-Gima (1996)	x	x		x	x							
Balbontin et al.(1999)	x	x	x				x	x				
Spivey et al. (1997)	x	x	x	x	x							
Tang (1999)	x		x			x	x					
Sirilli & Evangelista (1998)		x										x
Ozsomer et al. (1997)									x	x		
Soderquist et al. (1997)		x									x	

Cho (1996)			x	x	x					x		
Zhuang et al. (1999)	x							x				
Hurley & Hult (1998)	x								x			
Keogh (1999)				x		x						
Shaw (1998)		x	x			x						
Birchall et al. (1996)	x	x	x								x	
McGourty et al. (1996)	x			x								
Zien & Buckler (1997)	x	x	x		x							
Totals	9	8	7	5	4	3	2	2	2	2	2	1

Source: Anthony Read, (2000), Determinants of Successful Organisational Innovation: A Review of Current Research, *Journal of Management Practice*, 3(1), p.106.

Style at the Top : Adaptive Vs. Innovative

Top management has an onerous task of matching the creative styles to organizational strategy.

The ability of a firm to generate internal changes in procedures, to produce new products or to react to new competitive situations is often essential to its long-term survival. Change may take the form of radical departure from the organization's established operations, or it may involve less sweeping modifications in behavior of and in the organization. There are some situations in which stability is highly valued and others in which flexibility is essential.

For example, six categories of managerial personalities (management archetypes) have been identified for six basic strategic directions. For three of these directions-Explosive Growth, Expansion, and Retreat-Reposition-a flexible, divergent individual with an innovative bent is desired. For the other three-Continuous Growth, Consolidation, and Harvest-a stable, adaptive personality is more appropriate (Kuhn, 1970). Similarly, the stage of the company's life-cycle may influence the requisite capabilities of a management team, with entrepreneurial (that is innovative) skills and administrative and integrative (that is, adaptive) abilities shifting in importance at various stages (Wissema and Vander Pol, 1980).

Though they differ in styles, both the innovative and the adaptive contributions are creative. The truly creative firm is one where both types of creative input are encouraged in those situations in which it is appropriate. By recognizing the potential contributions of both of these creative personality styles, organizations can build balanced, creative management teams and enhance organizational effectiveness.

PLANNING

Managers of innovative organizations take a long-term perspective and develop long-range objectives and policies for areas of internal growth and innovation. They act with a challenging vision of the future.

Become aware of innovation opportunities:

Mangers search for opportunities from different sources of innovation and identify the right ones to pursue. They will employ environmental intelligence and environmental scanning procedures for this. Also they encourage idea generation processes within the organization. Many successful organizations have kept their main focus on Customers and Engineering people.

*1. **Customers are carefully screened to identify new ideas:*** User groups and customer conferences are continually held to identify customer reactions, problems, ideas and innovative suggestions. Hewlett Packard and Wang Laboratories have institutionalized these procedures.

*2. **Engineers and research scientists are encouraged to meet the customer:*** A recent survey of high technology firms noted that business unit managers in successful, high technology companies encourage their product development engineers to get out into the field. These managers want their designers to meet users directly in their own environment rather than having user's needs communicated to designers via the marketing department.

Set goals for innovative achievement:

Setting up clear-cut goals is the next step in planning innovative effort. The goals should be objective and measurable in respect of current innovations. However, in case of long-term innovative effort they can be broad and qualitative.

At 3M, for instance, every division is expected to get 25 per cent of its sales each year from products that did not exist five years earlier. As Daniel J. Mac Donald, general manager of 3M's Occupational Health and Safety Products Division, comments: "Our top executives are never interested in what you've already got on the market. They want to know what's new."

Decide protection policies:

Examine corporate policy concerning pre-invention disclosure agreements and post-invention patenting. Limit the agreements to company business or to the direct work assignments given to an individual. When in doubt, examine the patent laws used in India and other countries like USA, Germany, Great Britain, Scandinavia and Japan.

In a knowledge economy, the ability of an organization to impose ownership on the result is becoming harder, not easier.

Mr Hammer, who in turn adapted the idea from the research of a work-study manager at ICI in the 1950s, created BPR as a concept. The concept was turned into a product by CSC Index, a small consultancy headed by James Champy, who went into partnership with Mr Hammer. The concept made a fortune for them and the consultancy in the early 1990s. But there was nothing CSC Index could do to stop other consultancies producing their own versions of it. Andersen consulting (now renamed Accenture), in particular, was able to eat rapidly into CSC Index's market because it could undercut on price by using economies of scale. Disillusioned, Mr Hammer left the consultancy, as did Mr Champy.

Make resource allocation:

Funding the innovation efforts is a ticklish issue. Resource allocation cannot rely on quantitative reasoning; it requires intuitive skills to promote high risk, less certain innovative projects.

(a) Prioritizing projects:

The following guidelines will be of help in prioritizing innovation projects:

(i) **Use capital budgeting models:** Most modern corporations calculate their investment opportunities in new activities with concepts that involve the time value of money such as net present value, internal rate of return or profitability indeed. Although the concepts are good, it is difficult to get accurate input data, so these calculations should be used primarily as a guide to sort out the real "dogs." If too much weight is given to these computations, only fast payback projects will pass the test and a large corporation will inadvertently kill its long-range growth potential.

(ii) **Rely on intuition of innovators:** Successful entrepreneurs always have a gut feel about new areas of growth. If your corporation is lucky enough to have an entrepreneur with the drive and desire to undertake new and challenging projects, try to keep that individual and use the financial-analysis models as a cross-check.

Remember that most film companies felt that the instant pictures were an insignificant market. It took a man with guts and persistence like Dr. Land of Polaroid Corporation to prove that the instant picture market was real.

(iii) **Fund long-term innovations:** People working on long-range new products are generators of future profit and growth. Such funding is particularly important to companies that are in medium to high technology areas. For historically they tend to grow in greater proportion to the money spent in development than others. Statistically, in the long-term, a policy of developing long-range new products is also a hedge against inflation.

Time horizons in successful innovative enterprises were longer than those common in their fields. Bell, Xerox, and IBM all had planning and advanced systems groups looking decades ahead and their top managements began major innovative programs even when product lines appeared solidly positioned for seven to ten years into the future. Pilkington was privately held, was not concerned about short-term stock movements, and was headed by a vigorous chairman in his mid-forties. Each company was willing to absorb the fiscal drains associated with significant developments. Pilkington, for example, experienced negative cash flows for eleven years on its float glass introduction.

(iv) **Balance growth and regulatory needs:** In these days of regulation, it is necessary for a growth-oriented company to keep its perspective. In many industries development funds must be expended on regulatory activities to keep the company out of court and in compliance with regulations. If, however, all growth funds are used in regulatory activities, new business development will cease. Thus a balance between Regulation and Development is necessary. Where the proper balance rests is dependent on one's industry segment.

For example, high technology requires more development funds than medium technology. In determining what should be the balance between Regulation and Development, be guided by the old saying, "Render unto Caesar that which is Caesar's, and render unto God that which is God's."

(v) **Allocate special funds for innovation:** Special unrestricted funds are made available to explore innovative ideas without upper-level approval.

For instance, Texas Instruments has a program called IDEA, which allows forty program representatives throughout the company to finance long-short projects without any higher-level approval.

(vi) Have benchmarking: Fund the innovation projects on a coherent industry basis. Bear in mind that generalizations based on all industry averages are useless, since each industry segment has specific requirements based on product life-cycles, competition, customer needs and resource requirements. Remember, too, that one-product companies go out of business when their product becomes obsolete, so a good rule of thumb is the introduction of three successful new products per product life-cycle.

(vii) Accept risks: For large-scale innovations to reach fruition, management should accept risks. At IBM, Messrs. Watson and Learson, successive chairmen of the company, were behind the 360 development and maintained close contact with both the program and its potential customers during crucial periods. Pilkington established a special Directors' Float Glass strategy committee at the Board level to coordinate float's introduction.

(b) Financing projects:

In financing innovation projects, corporate managers may employ one of the following approaches:

(i) Unlimited Access Concept: Most corporate managers approach the planning budgetary process as if they were rationing a limited available stock of capital or resources. Venture capitalists and financial houses take another approach-that there is no real limit to available capital. They simply seek ideas or business opportunities of sufficient quality to attract capital at the current price. When Corporations develop an "unlimited access" attitude the real task, is producing high quality ideas directed toward its goals and market needs.

(ii) Opportunity Planning: To accomplish this, the whole planning process must be converted from a "resource rationing" process into an "opportunity seeking" process. It involves the following steps:

- Defines its major areas of expertise and interest broadly.
- Encourages proposals to achieve these
- Conducts feasibility analysis. In the same way a venture capitalist does, evaluate the proposals first in conceptual terms only, using very broad figures and then through a careful appraisal of the individual or team making the proposal.
- Considers the company's capacity to support the concept if it is successful in the appraisal process.
- Makes more detailed numerical analysis to determine requirements of funds. Purposely allocate resources to major new innovations as a portion of a "total portfolio". For example, the organization can protect itself by investing the bulk of its resources in traditional, less risky, cash-generating ventures. But overall strategy could purposely define a portion of its total portfolio as investable in longer-term, higher-risk ventures and thus yield new concepts.

(iii) Portfolio Planning: Portfolio planning is an effective way to break out of the short time horizons and risk-averse tendencies of normal control systems. It is done as follows.

- Corporation's total product/business strategy is broken out into its most important thrusts.
- Each of these thrusts is defined as a coordinated "mission" cutting across all of the several groups or divisions, which must support it. For example, the development of a

second generation of products might require support from marketing, production, engineering, research and development, and/or specific geographical groups.

- Make coordinated planning in each of several existing divisions to accomplish "mission goals." Planning within each of the functional groups must insure that sufficient resources are committed behind each mission and that these commitments are coordinated laterally among divisions.
- Some missions, such as technical work to build the quality leader for a product line or to take care of anticipated environmental requirements, might have negative or very low present values for specific divisions or functional groups. Nevertheless, these investments might be crucial to the success of the total strategy. In short, the requirements of the major missions with a strategy must override the ROI or PV rankings of projects within a particular function or division. Otherwise, "current product lines" and "cash cows" obtain all of the organization's attention. Long-term, developmental and growth-related activities will be systematically driven out of the technical mixture and the future of the enterprise can be jeopardized.

(c) Select many to win at least a few

Finally, managements must allow a sufficient number of projects and a long enough lead time for the "one in twenty" success ratio to have effect. Initially, entrepreneurial managers may need to undertake projects with somewhat lower risk ratios in order to build management confidence. Once top managements develop "comfort factor" with a few entrepreneurial investments, they tend to be more willing to accept venturesome risks farther from traditional approaches and innovation flourishes.

Innovative companies had at risk millions to billions of dollars. However, when successful, IBM or Xerox had achieved powerful positions in their expanding fields; Pilkington could make millions in royalties and control access to important world markets; and Bell-AT&T could defend its monopoly position and expand its revenue base.

Exhibit 3.1 and 3.2 show the thinking tools in planning.

Exhibit 3.1

Idea: .... **Date:**

Generated by:...................

Innovation (what form the idea will take):

Sources of Support What sources of assistance or support are needed to carry out this innovation?	
Who	Why Needed
What (money, resources, etc)	

Ways to gain and strengthen support	
Sources of Resistance	
What are the sources of resistance—people to policies, procedures and so forth that could impede the process of innovation?	
Who	Why
What (for example, organizational policy)	
Ways to overcome or minimize resistance	

Exhibit 3.2

Planning for Innovation:

Immediate Goals and Action Planned	
Goal/Action	Completion Date
Measures of Success	
1.	6.
2.	7.
3.	8.
4.	9.
5.	10.
Target Long-Term Actions	
Action	Completion Date
Source: HMM Managing for Creativity and Innovation.	

Source: Harvard Business Review, How to Promote Innovation, *Indian Management*, October 2002, Vol. 41, Issue 7, pp.58-64.

ORGANISING

Organizing for innovation takes different routes like establishing separate units and providing supportive roles.

Skunk Works:

Many companies have found that a most effective way to stimulate truly innovative development is to place a highly talented team of engineers, technicians and model builders "in a shed" where they can work closely and informally together-without the formal procedural structures of larger units.

This was the approach used by Cray at Control Data, the Pilkington float glass development team, Kelly Johnson at Lockheed, Issogonis at British Motor Corporation, Bruekner at KMS and numerous other successful innovative groups in large companies.

The approach tends to orient the group toward its tasks, rather than toward organizational promotion. It speeds turn-around time, increases the number of experiments and encourages all technical, design, and shop personnel to join in the venture as productive coequals.

Promote supportive roles:

Michel Syrett and Jean Lammiman have identified five roles in idea development in innovative organizations. Awareness of the roles (Table 3.2) and providing training and opportunities for the energetic play of the roles is essential for successful innovation effort.

Table 3.2: The Five roles in ideas development

Role	Definition	Often undertaken by
Spark	Someone who "sparks" the creative process by spotting or coming up with the idea, creating the vision or defining the need.	Anyone employed by or associated with the organization; often comes from the least expected area.
Sponsor/ Champion	Someone who promotes the idea or project inside the organization, ensuring that it is not dismissed, and who sustains interest during difficult or lean times.	Senior line managers, members of the board, and non-executive directors
Shaper	Someone who makes the idea or project "real", using their own creativity to flesh out the premise and/or find practical means to achieve the objective	Members of the project team appointed to implement the idea, process-oriented consultants, and R&D staff from principal suppliers.
Sounding board	Someone outside the project whose objectivity and broader knowledge can be drawn on to inform and validate the premise or to comment on the practicalities.	Informal or formal members of personal or professional networks, trusted colleagues or company mentors, strategy-oriented consultants, appointed academics or researchers in the field.
Specialist	Someone who draws on their specialist skills to shape the idea or project from a specific standpoint and uses the opportunity to break new ground in the field.	Members of the project team, consultants (process and strategy), academics and researchers, and R&D staff from principal suppliers.

Source: Roffey Park Institute, 2000.

STAFFING

One of the most critical tasks for any organization is that of matching the skills of people to the demands of the jobs they are to perform. Considerable attention is devoted, therefore, to screening, testing, interviewing and evaluating both potential and current employees to select those whose aptitudes best suit them to the requirements of particular jobs. This matching process is not less important in the case of managers, whose skills, especially in communication and problem solving, are deemed of critical importance. It is no easy matter, however, to identity the salient characteristics of managers or potential managers.

Job requirements:

One has keep in mind the fact that all people are not highly creative and also all the jobs do not require breakthrough creative talent. Creativity style may prove to be especially important to certain positions; for example, in product development. Innovative problem solvers may be ideally suited to the task of creating and developing new products, where the emphasis is upon novel solutions or ideas. Adaptors may be better suited to administering existing product lines, where the usual demands involve maintenance, administration and improvement of existing systems.

Recruiting:

Organizations must then recruit people with the necessary entrepreneurial, inventive outlooks. Often, in recruiting, research-technical groups squander enormous time checking the applicant's course work, publications and detailed technical knowledge and neglect the question of whether he might really invent something or have the will to see it introduced. The organization must make clear that its major objectives include innovation and the directions toward which those innovations should lead.

Retain talented:

Organizations assemble first-rate people and supplying them with a leader possessing extensive knowledge about programs and their underlying art in order to maintain high expertise and research discipline. Non-performers are removed from programs.

Bell Laboratories, for example, conducted peer reviews of its highly selected basic researchers' performance and over a decade some nine out of ten of these researchers moved on to other tasks. IBM reassigned its most talented technical people to head its 360 programs and systematically weeded out non-performers.

Training:

Training to encourage teamwork, improve creative skills and create change orientation is essential in innovative organizations. Intense training on creativity is not necessary for all employees. An awareness of the adaptation/innovation continuum may help tailor organizational training programs to meet specific needs of employees. Adaptors can be encouraged to introduce greater novelty in their problem solving; innovators, on the other hand, can be encouraged to develop more systematic ways of approaching problems and implementing solutions.

Appraisal:

Goal oriented appraisals like MBO will create performance orientation as they encourage individuals to come up with standards they would like to maintain. Innovation can be a part of the standards and goals, along with the routine job standards.

LEADING

The success of innovative organizations largely depends on the kind of leadership provided to guide the innovation effort. Leadership function is concerned with supervising the creative people (individuals and groups) and facilitating the innovative efforts through proper systems of communicating, training, appraising and motivating.

People and innovation oriented style:

Innovation promoting leadership style is characterized by the following:

Loose-Rein" Management Style: In this style, operations tend to be decentralized, autonomous and independent. Idea people are given freedom to choose, pursue problems and discuss ideas. Management tolerates and expects risk taking as they do not run an "extremely tight ship".

Attention to Highly Creative Personnel: As far as possible, the creative persons are partly isolated from daily operating pressures. An environment conductive to study and work is provided. . Work is assigned carefully by stressing how the work meets the objectives of both the individual and the company.

Time to Think: Time to think is provided. Slack time provides the opportunity to think and engage in creative work. This time may not be possible in a constrained setting or when employees are continually engaged in handling crises or immediate problems.

Communication for innovation:

Communication promotes understanding of objectives, fosters teamwork and encourages the spirit of achievement.

Communicate innovation Plans – Communicate innovation plan, with specific objectives laid out. This is only one way to make innovation attractive to managers; a systematic policy of abandoning whatever is outworn, obsolete and no longer productive.

- First, it helps focus on managerial vision on opportunity. People see what is presented to them; what is not presented tends to be overlooked. And what is presented to most managers are "problems" – especially in the areas where performance falls below expectations-which means that managers tend not to see the opportunities. They are simply not being presented with them.
- Second, such a plan ensures that the innovation budget is adequate.

Communicate innovation expectations: A clearly defined need is specified in economic/technical performance terms for the whole system, each important subsystem and the interaction of various subsystems. Great care is taken at the outset not to define these needs in terms of particular technologies or solution sets.

IBM and Bell at first defined their needs in terms of "user needs." "functions to be performed" "systems architecture," or "black boxes" of input/output characteristics. Pilkington decided early that, to be introduced, its float process must "perform to obsolete existing plate technologies."

Identification with goals: Goals must appeal to and stimulate technical people. Organization must seek to promote identification with these goals by ensuring that employees: 1) participate in goal establishment, 2) make their own proposals for specific technical approaches and 3) are measured and rewarded against challenging performance goals. The more people can understand, identify with and internalize stimulating goals, the more likely they are to work productively on their own, create in relevant directions and follow through to ultimate uses of their results.

Open Communication: Creative success usually builds upon the work of others. This building depends on the free flow of information and access to data. Contact with outside sources should be encouraged. Blocking communications seriously hampers creativity.

Supervision:

Most authorities would agree that the crucial aspect in managing creative people is good supervision. Therefore the relationship of creative persons with the immediate supervisor is most important. A manager should strive to build an atmosphere, which encourages change and new ideas. Design a positive individualized approach to stimulate and encourage creativity. Give recognition for all new ideas and special thanks when deserved.

With proper handling and supervision, the creative individual's peculiarities, which are often diagnosed as symptoms of a problem employee, can be highly productive. If the supervisor understands how vital time and freedom are to the employee, the manager and the company can reap the harvest of innovation.

Encourage teamwork:

Innovation needs teamwork. It needs many minds at different stages of its evolution. Alexander Graham Bell has very rightly said:

Great discoveries and improvements invariably involve the cooperation of many minds. I may be given credit for having blazed the trail, but when look at the subsequent developments, I feel the credit is due others rather than to myself.

Freedom at work:

Providing a creative atmosphere both emotionally and physically can foster freedom at work. Pressure should be specially directed towards attaining goals. Tread a middle ground between Firmness and Permissiveness to enable a creative employee to work at his or her own pace, but give the individual definite goals to accomplish and an approximate deadline to meet. Allow him or her some time alone for intense concentration, reflection and insight.

Interactions:

Encouraging an employee or simply listening sympathetically can foster interactions. Help him or her verbalize his or her thinking and reach conclusions. Always let him or her know just how he or she stands and evaluate work quickly. Individuals need constructive criticism and praise. They also need to know the results of their work so that they can either move on or elaborate on what they've already done.

Relationships:

Leaders attain mutual respect and encouragement by defending a creative employee from unnecessary attacks by others. He respects his or her outside activities and sources of stimulation. Some creative individuals keep unusual time schedules or outside associates. Leaders may tolerate some shortcomings, as long as they don't interfere with work.

Support innovation enhancing roles:

Ideas for breakthrough initiatives are not confined to highly paid scientists or R&D staff. A lack of innovation usually indicates that managers at all levels lack the awareness or motivation to spot the potential of the ideas floating around their organization. They may see original thinking as a threat and therefore discourage or even stifle it.

- **Sparks** – Kvaerner, a Norwegian shipbuilding conglomerate, has for many years promoted the circulation of ideas around the business, encouraging front-line staff to participate through such mechanisms as competitions and ideas Olympics. The innovations that resulted are generating substantial savings for the company. Arne Svensson, a welder, was awarded a prize of $3,800 in 1991 for an idea on how to automate the welding of an important component, which resulted in Kvaerner's subsidiary, Kamfab, saving $45,000 a year.
- **Sponsors** – Ideas need people to promote them inside the organization to sustain interest during difficult or lean times. The higher the level of the sponsor the more impact the sponsorship would have. However, a project succeeds only when it is "sponsored" at every level of management and in all areas that it touches.
- Texas Instruments requires supervisors and line managers at its factories to assess and follow up all ideas suggested by their staff and to make this an integral part of their personal performance appraisal.
- **Hewlett** – Packard allows, and often helps fund, staff to travel, take sabbaticals, formulate their own research programs and even nominate the academic collaborators with whom they would like to work. There is also encouragement to staff to publish papers, take part in conferences and involve themselves in the formulation of industrial standards. Furthermore, the company may reward staff for published work that is original and that it is felt will enhance Hewlett-Packard's reputation.
- **Shapers** – These are the people who make the idea or project real, adding their own creativity, fleshing out the initial premise and/or finding the practical means to meet its objectives. Members of a project team working with the originator may perform the role.
- **Sounding boards** – These are people outside the project whose objectivity and broader knowledge of the field can be drawn on to inform and validate the premise or to comment on the practicalities. The role can be performed by any number of sympathetic but disinterested individuals, including personal or professional friends and contacts, trusted colleagues, company-appointed mentors, consultants, academics or researchers in the field.

- **Internal and external support** – Large corporations will have own experts in organizational behavior, facilities management, training and information technology. However, there may not be time for specialists to share time with all the innovators. To provide expert support, corporations look to external consultants who, in effect, play the role of sounding boards.

Motivation:

Paradoxically, both achievement and security needs are important in motivating creative people. Recognizing creativity both publicly and monetarily can fulfill achievement need. Security need can be met by tolerating failures. Tolerate failures-failures may eventually lead to success. Nothing kills true initiative faster than fear. You could inadvertently be handing over to your competitor your best employee by unnecessarily dismissing him or her for failure.

Reward-punishment system:

There should be a system of rewarding the successes and supporting the failures.

At International Harvester, inventors are given large cash bonuses and lavish praise. An $ 11,000 banquet was thrown for one inventor.

In well-managed innovative firms, failures are accepted as part of the game. Managers and researchers often are given a second and third chance by companies; which realize that even the most effective innovator faces a high risk of failure in the extremely complex and competitive business of innovation.

In most corporations and government laboratories, the motivation for research and development personnel quickly becomes the completion of publishable papers, the expansion of budgets and "the carrying out of investigations". Rarely do such organizations make their technical entrepreneurs into millionaires or give them other perquisites representing success. A few conglomerating concerns, however, have learned that they need to reward richly the people who headed their intended growth divisions, or those people will grow similar enterprises elsewhere. Similarly, outstanding technical entrepreneurs have been recognized, even if belatedly, by some large enterprises. Although admittedly tricky to implement, such awards do have stimulating effects.

Competition and parallel development:

Multiple competing approaches are to be encouraged at both the basic research and development levels. This technique serves different purposes in large company development programs.

- Creates a positive competitive spirit among the people on each program team.
- Stimulates 'scientists' and 'engineers' commitment to their programs.
- Instills a sense of urgency to the work.
- Allows the discipline of knowledgeable people critiquing each other's approaches.
- Encourages people to invent and to use basic research knowledge to improve their approach to the problem.
- Prevents premature commitment to any single approach. Final system choices can be made as late as possible consistent with the information available.

Multiple competing approaches, by being more effective, ultimately end up being more efficient. For such reasons, almost all large-scale innovating companies consciously encouraged parallel development.

Morale-discovery Mode

High morale occurs when team members intensely share a common goal. "Making more profits" rarely achieved such identity in larger organizations. But creating a significant technical advance did prove energizing.

For example, at Pilkington, "people would literally work until they dropped of fatigue and then come back for more" because they saw their innovation as exciting, challenging and capable of making St. Helens "the creative center of their industry."

In successful programs there was fervor to solve a problem, to genuinely invent, or to create something new for a purpose. Challenging goals stimulated people to look beyond the feasible to the possible.

CONTROLLING

Innovation effort will be successful in terms of efficiency, economy and effectiveness only when it is regulated. Some of the monitoring techniques are detailed below:

Feedback and review:

Feedback from expectations to results – on a continual basis is necessary. Feedback ensures quality and reliability of both innovative plans and innovative efforts.

User evaluation:

User guidance and participation in programs insured that specifications remained current and that people who would manufacture, install, service or use the system had a hand in its development. This interface occurred at all levels of the organization, not just at the technical or top level alone. To facilitate this interface, development groups were placed in physical proximity to research, production, and, when appropriate, marketing groups. People were often moved to locations where face-to-face contacts could more easily occur.

Performance evaluation:

Clearly, the control system must be adjusted to measure performance of innovation projects. Performance indicators may include – fulfillment of strategy requirements, profitability, expansion of portfolio of products etc. The control system should be dominated by the strategy. It must ensure that all of the important goals of the enterprise are served in the patterns intended, not just current profitability. With sophistication and care, this end can be accomplished.

Innovation audit:

Develop a systematic review of innovative efforts all together. Judge the company's total innovative performance against the company's innovative objectives, against its performance and standing in the market and against its performance as a business altogether. It is indeed true that there are some areas in which no one can, or should, decide the degree of relative importance. Which is more significant, current improvements or breakthrough in basic research. Every few years an entrepreneurial management looks at all the innovative efforts of the business. Which ones should receive more support at this stage and should be pushed? Which ones have opened up new opportunities? Which ones, on the other hand, are not doing what we expected them to do and what action should we take? Has the time come to abandon them, or, on the contrary, has the time come to redouble our efforts-but with what expectations and what deadline?

Controls for results:

It will be improper if controls are report oriented. Concentration on weekly or monthly reports or making frequent program reviews or performance appraisals is not real controlling. Management's role should be to remove roadblocks, expedite effort, provide resources and enhancing encouragement. Management itself should be innovative and learn how not to impede creative effort.

Create corporate memory:

To ensure continuity and innovation, it is desirable to maintain a record of innovation processes. Firms often have to cut costs and lay-off staff, but most could do much more to retain and sustain the corporate "memory" that will keep the innovations of recent years fresh in people's minds. The plethora of new technologies at their disposal – intranets, electronic brainstorming software and video-conferencing-makes it possible for the first time to record the cognitive processes that lead to innovative breakthroughs as they occur and in the spontaneous language used at the time.

SUMMARY

Proper management of innovation is perhaps the most potentially rewarding challenge facing business today. Top management has an onerous task of matching the creative styles to organizational strategy. There are some situations in which stability is highly valued, and others in which flexibility is essential.The truly creative firm is one where innovative and adoptive types of creative input are encouraged in those situations in which it is appropriate.

Managers of innovative organizations take a long-term perspective and develop long-range objectives and policies for areas of internal growth and innovation. They act with a challenging vision of the future. In financing innovation projects, corporate managers may employ one of the following approaches-Unlimited access concept, portfolio planning or opportunity planning.

Organizing for innovation takes different routes like establishing separate units (Skunk works), and providing supportive roles (Sparks, sponsors, shapers, sounding boards and specialists). One of the most critical tasks for any organization is that of matching the skills of people to the demands of the jobs they are to perform. Innovative problem solvers may be ideally suited to the task of creating and developing new products, where the emphasis is upon novel solutions or ideas. Adaptors may be better suited to administering existing product lines, where the usual demands involve maintenance, administration and improvement of existing systems. Innovation can be a part of the standards and goals, along with the routine job standards. Leadership function is concerned with supervising the creative people (individuals and groups) and facilitating the innovative efforts through proper systems of communicating, training, appraising and motivating. With proper handling and supervision, the creative individual's peculiarities, which are often diagnosed as symptoms of a problem employee, can be highly productive.

Paradoxically, both achievement and security needs are important in motivating creative people. Recognizing creativity both publicly and monetarily can fulfill achievement need. Security need can be met by tolerating failures. Innovation effort will be successful in terms of efficiency, economy and effectiveness only when it is regulated. Some of the monitoring techniques are: Feedback review, User evaluation, Performance evaluation, Innovation audit, Controls for results and Corporate memory.

EXERCISES

Using the exhibits conduct survey in local companies to find out how good the companies are favorable to innovation.

Exhibit -1 Checklist of Organizational Characteristics that Support Creativity and Innovation:

Here is a checklist of the characteristics that support and encourage creativity and innovation. The converse of these characteristics actually discourages both. Consider these characteristics and how your company or your operating unit stands relative to them. Is it strong? Is it weak? If it's weak, what can be done to change the situation?

Characteristics	My Company's Rating	
	Strong	Weak
Risk taking is acceptable to management		
New ideas and new ways of doing things are welcomed		
Information is free flowing—and not controlled by managers		
Employees have access to knowledge sources: customers, benchmarking partners, the scientific community and so forth		
Good ideas are supported by executive patrons		
Innovators are rewarded		

Source: *Managing Creativity and Innovation,* Harvard Business School Press: Boston, p.101.

Exhibit -2 Top Management visibility and involvement:

Statements here describe typical behaviors of top management towards innovation. Write Yes or No against each statement that represents your view of top management behavior in your organization.

1. Spend only a very small percentage of my time on the innovation front.
2. Leave early design decisions to low-level personnel who may not understand the big picture of the business.
3. Insulate from the technological issues shaping our business.
4. Involve so late in the process that their only interest is in whether a project will clear financial hurdles.

5. Keep friends and yes-men off the board. Like to have unvarnished advice as they consider investing in innovative ideas.
6. Surround themselves with people who have complementary skills and different approaches to analyzing issues and making decisions.
7. Listen to suggestions and arguments, even if they disagree.
8. They believe that to win any game, they must participate.
9. They always double-check the assumptions since, what looks rosy can be a disaster if those assumptions are not realistic.

CASE: THE INNOVATION ASSESSMENT SURVEY

Designed to assess the "environment for innovation" in order to facilitate innovation improvement, an innovation assessment survey was administered to 249 managers and other technical professionals employed in the R&D and technical planning departments of more than 30 "Fortune 100" companies. They had been with their current companies for an average of 11 to 15 years; they were, on the average, between 36 and 40 years old; and the majority was second and third level managers. Data from the instrument, a self-administered questionnaire, were collected over an eight-month period. The survey defined innovation as "seeking new of better work methods, products, processes, or service."

Questionnaire:

Respondents were asked how important thinking innovatively and devoting time to innovative projects" were to

- their superiors' evaluation of their job performance,
- their personal satisfaction on the job,
- their status among their peers, their potential for advancement,
- the demands of their job, and
- the continuing success of their organization.

In addition, four items were included that asked respondents to judge how often they were encouraged to innovate and/or discouraged from innovating. A number of open-ended questions asked for suggestions on how "improve the level of innovative processes and products" and for the respondents' impressions of their organizations' strength and weaknesses in encouraging innovation. Finally, a series of demographic items examined length of tenure with the organization, time spent in the current job, as well as age, management level and company type.

Findings:

1. An examination of mean scores for the items dealing with the importance of innovation clearly demonstrates that the respondents personally value innovation more than they felt it was valued in their organization. Means for the questions, "How important is thinking innovatively and devoting time to innovate projects in your personal job satisfaction" and "in the continuing success of your organization"

were 4.3 and 4.2 respectively, out of a possible score of 5. This is what might be expected in today's innovation-conscious corporations. But what one might not foresee is the relatively low value that these same respondents see others in their environment placing on innovation. The importance of innovation is given under

- their superior's evaluation of their job performance,
- their status among their peers,
- their potential for advancement and
- the demands of their jobs

This implies that corporations are not doing a particular good job of taking advantage of their employee's innovative fervor. Employees find innovation personally satisfying and important to their companies' futures, but see themselves as "island of innovation", with neither their bosses nor their peers recognizing their efforts. They see their organizations as unwilling to build innovation into the advancement timetable or into the specific demands of particular job assignments. Organization may not be satisfying or meeting the potential for innovation that their employees seem to processes. Responses to the questions about communication may hold some explanation.

When asked how often they are "explicitly encouraged to approach (their) job responsibilities innovatively", only one-third of the respondents said frequently or always, while nearly the same number responded never or rarely. The mean response was 3.0, or "sometimes". Implicit encouragement was experienced somewhat more frequently ($x = 3.2$). Thirty per cent of the respondents said that they were frequently encouraged toward innovation. This not only lends empirical support to the argument that informal communication is as important, if not more so, than formal communication; it may also on innovation than do their organizations. The implicit channels may be stoking the fires to a greater degree than the more visible official channels, leading to a belief that the organization is less interested in innovation.

While only 48 per cent of the sample said that they were frequently explicitly encouraged (none said always), 36 per cent said that they were frequently implicitly discouraged from innovation (again, no one said always). Responses to the open-ended questions helped highlight this phenomenon.

Answers were analyzed in terms of their emphasis-that is, did they stress communication, organization, educational, managerial, policy or environmental concerns. The following Table lists the number of times each concern was raised in response to the question, "What do you think is your firm's greatest asset in encouraging innovation?"

Area	Greatest strength for encouraging innovation	Greatest weakness for encouraging innovation
Communication	7	7
Organization	18	26
Education	8	1
Management	12	22
Policy	5	8
Environment	24	16

It demonstrates that when environmental and organizational factors are good, they are seen as important assets to a firm's innovative potential. When these factors are bad, they are seen as major inhibitors (along with management). What should be obvious here is that these employees view these organizational and environmental problems as a responsibility of management and consider the eradication of these problems to be desirable.

In case of demographic indicators of innovation , only two variables – managerial level and length of time with the firm-showed any relationship with attitudes toward innovation. In fact, while statistically significant, these relationships were relatively weak.

- Managerial level was positively related to the importance of innovation in personal satisfaction and to the importance of innovation in the demands of their jobs. This seems reasonable in as much as the challenge of particular position would be expected to increase with its height on the organization ladder.
- Length of tenure with a firm was negatively related to the frequency of implicit encouragement toward innovation. The longer individuals were with their current organization, the less frequently they experienced implicit encouragement. This may be due to the fact that their organizations were paying less attention to them as innovators.

What this demographic/ innovation attitude relationship signifies is that organizational design and environment are keys to fostering innovation? This view is borne out in the company-by-company analysis of the data. Although there was no pattern suggesting that certain industries were better managers of innovation than others, individual companies did show unique "innovation profiles" that varied considerably from the picture drawn from the aggregate data. Specific corporate culture of climate is important for innovation. The firms that seemed most successful in the realm of innovation to achieve and a willingness to experiment with and reward innovation. They offered their people a sense of personal involvement in innovative activities and made them feel appreciated for their efforts. They are companies that have made best use of informal channels to communicate about, reinforce, and reward innovation.

Returning to this study's overall data, however, it appears that management has generally not done as well as it would like in the realm of innovation. Business and government leaders, as well as the popular and professional press, have all expressed how important it is for companies to strongly support innovation. The managerial challenge is to translate that desire to innovate into an organizational environment. Our survey results, however, suggest that top management's stated commitment to innovation has yet to be successfully infused into organization structure and environment.

Questions:

1. Highlight the major findings and their implications to management as given in the case.
2. Develop a plan of action for making the companies innovative.

Source: Barab Stanley, Zandan, Peter and Vanston, John H., How effectively are we managing innovation, *Research Management*, Industrial Research Institute, 1985.

Chapter 4

Innovation Environment

Learning Objectives

After you have studied this chapter, you will be able to...

- Identify the originators and key drivers of innovations.
- Examine the environmental factors influencing innovation.
- Explain, how innovation can be nurtured in e-business.

Structure

- Introduction
- Originators of Innovation
- Key drivers of Innovation
- Factors Influencing Innovation
- Nurturing Innovation in e-business.
- Summary
- Questions
- Exercises
- Case: Environment for Innovation

INTRODUCTION

Creativity and innovation are critical for business effectiveness, but firms generally struggle with realizing them in their business and translating them into everyday life. The vexing questions for managers are: What makes an organization innovative? Is it internal factors like culture and competences within an organization? Is it situational and environment driven? A general observation in this context is: innovativeness is based on the symbiotic relationship between the Environment and Organizations.

ORIGINATORS OF INNOVATION

There are two conflicting views on the sources of innovation –

(i) The social deterministic school argues that innovations are the results of a combination of external social factors and influences. The argument is – when the conditions were right, innovations would occur.

(ii) The individualistic school argues that innovations are the result of unique individual talents and as such innovators are born.

Innovation is internal driven:

The vie argues that innovations are results of the trials and tribulations of some innovators. The belief that innovators are born cannot be ruled out. Most discoveries are the result of people who have had a fascination with a particular area of science and technology. They have made persistent efforts on their part, against several odds, with a passion to succeed, though the external environment was hostile. Galileo was imprisoned and Copernicus was burnt to death for their discoveries . Table 4.1 shows some of the inventions of individuals.

Table 4.1 Notable Innovations of Individuals (1600-1950)

Inventor	Country	Invention	Year
Nicolas Cugnot	France	Car (Steam)	1769
Benjamin Frankllin	U.S.A.	Bifocal lens	1780
Jacques Nicolas Conte	France	Pencil	1792
Alessandro Volta	Italy	Battery (Electric)	1800
Kirkpatrik Macmillan	Britain	Bicycle	1840
Alexander Bain	Britain	Facsimile Machine	1843
Lewis E Waterman	U.S.A.	Fountain Pen	1884
Rudolf Diesel	Germany	Diesel Engine	1895
Rudolf Dieself	Germany	Diesel Engine	1895
Roentgen. W.K.	Germany	X-ray	1895
W.L. Judson	U.S.A.	Zip fastner	1891
Orville & Wilbur Wright	U.S.A.	Aeroplane	1903
Willem Kolff	Netherlands	Artificial Heart	1957

Innovation is external driven:

External factors have propelled innovations in business and service sectors across the globe. Industrial revolution and subsequent advancements have brought about a radical change ushering in an era of competition among industrial firms. Industrial firms started investing in R and D. Table 4.2 shows the innovation in recent past, associated with organizations rather than individuals.

Table 4.2 Organizational innovations

Year	Innovator	Innovator
1945	Ballpoint pen	Reynolds International Pen Corporation
1950s	Floating glass manufacturing	Pilkington
1970/80s	Photocopying	Xerox
1980s	Personal computer	Apple computer
1980/90s	Windows 95	Microsoft

KEY DRIVERS OF INNOVATION

How is organizational innovation stimulated and achieved? Different writers have explained the innovation behaviors of organizations. Table 4.3 shows the chronological development of the models. We will now discuss the important models.

Table 4.3 Chronological Development of models of Innovation

Date	Model	Characteristics
1950/60s	Technology push	Simple linear sequential process. Emphasis on R & D. The market is a recipient of the fruits R & D.
1970s	Market pull	Simple linear sequential process. Emphasis on Marketing. The market is the source for directing D. R & D has a reactive role.
1980s	Coupling model	Emphasis on integrating R & D and marketing
1980/90s	Interactive model	Combinations of push and pull.

Innovation process has been viewed as a sequence of separable stages. There are two basic variations of this model of innovation, based on where the trigger for the idea or need was initiated. Figure 4.1shows the linear model of innovation.

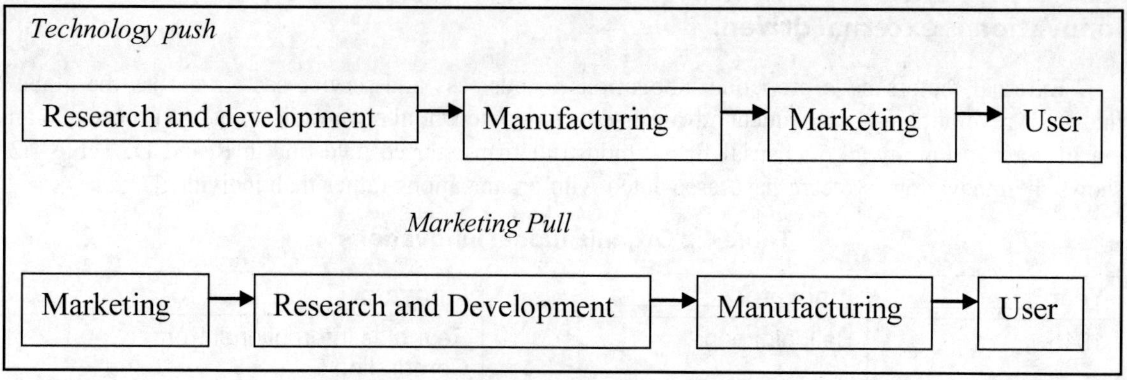

Figure 4.1: Linear models of Innovation

The technology push model assumes that scientists make unexpected discoveries, technologists apply them to develop product ideas and engineers and designers turn them into prototypes for testing. Manufacturing makes the products efficiently and marketing offers them to the consumers. The customers – driven model emphasizes the role of marketing as an initiator of new ideas resulting from close interactions with customers. The product ideas are conveyed to R and D, which creates new product designs and then to manufacturing for production. The interactive model represents the latest approach to creative behavior in organizations. It suggests:

(i) Modern organizations have communication that is simultaneous with feedback. It is transactional and spiral not linear and one-way.

(ii) There is integration of functions by linking mechanisms like cross-functional teams and common goals.

Innovation process therefore can be regarded as a logically sequential, though not necessarily continuous process, that can be divided into a series of functionally distinct but interacting and interdependent stages (Rothwell and Zegveld, 1985). It is a system with external and internal linkages. Figure 4.2 shows the interactive model of innovation.

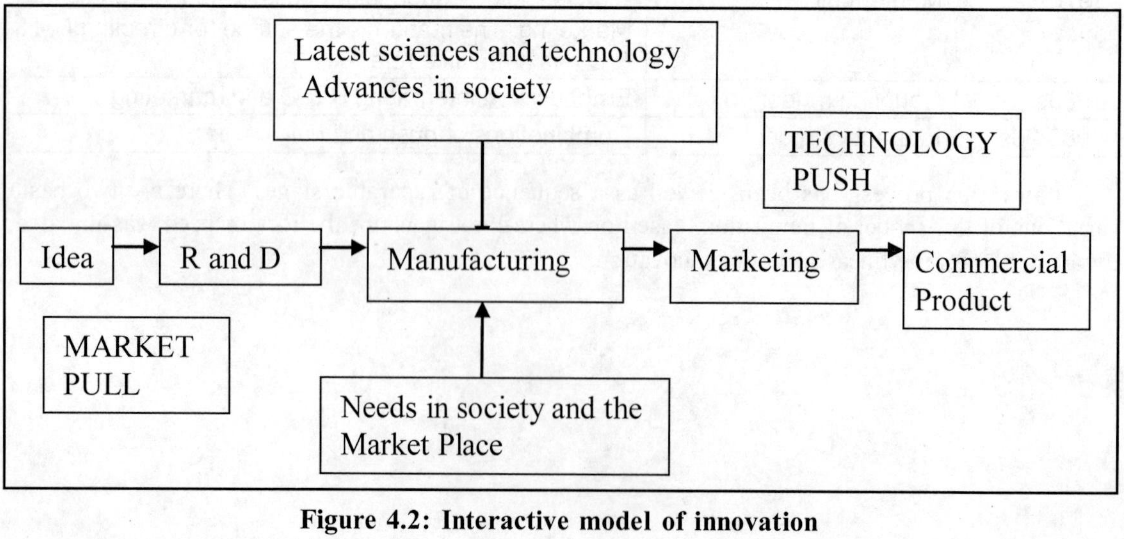

Figure 4.2: Interactive model of innovation

Suitability:

Which model better explains innovate behavior of organizations?

- Pharmaceutical industry characterizes much of the technology push model.
- Food industry is better represented by market pull model.
- Many industries have a mixture of both the models.

FACTORS INFLUENCING INNOVATION

Figure 4-3 presents the model presenting interaction between organization and environment.

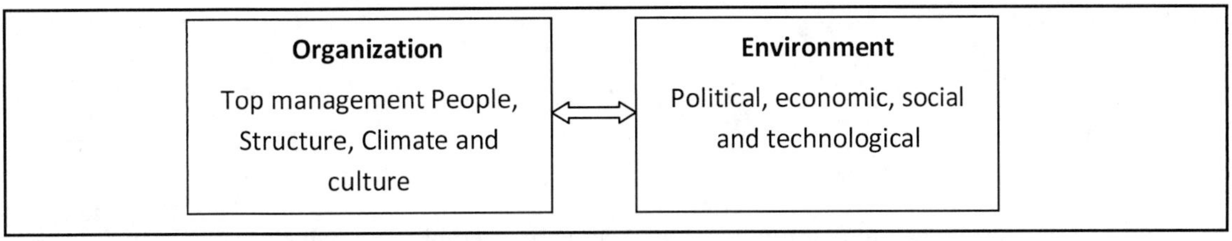

Figure 4.3 Organization and environment dynamics

Morgan (1986) argues that some organizations fail to innovate because they have a rigid view of themselves as entities separate from their environment.

He gives the example of typewriter manufacturers who failed to take account of changes in computer technology, which led to the development of word processors because they did not see micro processing technology as being part of their environment. To have done so would have required a change in the way they perceived themselves.

In reality, people within organizations simultaneously exert influence on and are influenced by the 'outside world'. Organizations are innovative either because they are innovative or environment is encouraging or compelling them to be innovative. When the environment is stable or placid and the competition is marginal, companies are assured of success and may lay more emphasis on efficiency. On the other hand, when going is tough, firms may search for ways to win and lay emphasis on creativity and innovation.

The two factors, which influence innovation behavior of firms, are:

(i) Quality of interaction with the environment.

(ii) The posture a firm takes in relation to the environment.

Interaction with Environment

Much research has examined how the quantity and quality of communication with the environment influences the organization's ability to innovate. Employees sensitive to environment and acquiring professional attitude and skills can become good innovators.

Studies have shown innovativeness to be associated with the existence of boundary – spanning roles within the organization (Tushman, 1977) and with professionalization of organizational members

(Draft, 1978). In both cases, the relationship with innovativeness can be understood in terms of *organizational knowledge* of innovations.

Individuals in roles, which cross-organizational boundaries and professionals who have access to formal and informal networks of fellow professionals, have the opportunity to come across new ideas that could be applied within their own organizations.

Postures:

The extent to which an organization engages in an active search of the environment for new ideas to adopt (commonly referred to as 'environmental scanning') depends on its perceptions of its own relationship with its environment. Such perceptions have been used as the basis for classifying organizations into 'strategic types'. Miles and Snow (1978) identify four strategic types:

- Defenders
- Prospectors
- Analyzers
- Reactors

The first two are innovation facilitators. Defenders are organizations, which see their environment as essentially, stable and therefore are concerned with the efficiency of existing operations in order to dominate their market niche. Prospectors in contrast see their environment as uncertain and turbulent, and therefore place a high value on innovation.

Meyer (1982) looked at the responses of American hospitals of different strategic types to a crisis caused by a doctors' strike. He observed that the prospector-type hospital responded to the crisis by defining it as a 'good experiment' and increased its innovative activity, whilst the defender-type hospital fell back on its financial slack to carry on business as usual.

Analyzers and reactors are more inward looking and slow in response to environment. They operate more or less within an existing framework. As such they impede innovation initiatives.

Environmental Factors

The innovation is environmentally propelled and performance-gap driven. It is determined by the nature of the environment and the gaps in performance. Table 4.4 presents a summary of external environmental factors.

Table 4.4 External factors influencing innovation

Environment	Factors
Social	❖ Interaction with users and the implicit knowledge in the marketing departments. ❖ Education and learning. ❖ Social rules. ❖ A pluralistic, multi-polar, open society. ❖ Change orientation. ❖ Desires for quality of life.
Economic	❖ Venture capital financing. ❖ Large and diversified human capital. ❖ Entrepreneurial spirit both in business and the academy. ❖ Wide consumption. ❖ Past investment in S&T. ❖ Current investment flows in S&T. ❖ Intensity of competition. ❖ Innovators among consumers.
Politico-legal	❖ Tax laws. ❖ Intellectual property rights and patent protection. ❖ Incentives for technological achievements. ❖ Globalization and trade relations.
Technological	❖ Research & Development expenditure, both in public and private institutions. ❖ The number of researchers. ❖ Lab/machinery endowments - in short, tangible and intangible investment. ❖ Application of creativity and proper methods (e.g. *kaizen*) to normal production processes (learning-by-doing, innovation-by-doing). ❖ Progress level of basic research. ❖ Knowledge sharing facility. ❖ Current innovations.

(i) Socio-cultural Environment

People grow up in a particular society that shapes their basic beliefs, values, and norms.

- ***Attitude towards new ideas*** – People in theological and economically backward societies may be unwilling to look for new ideas. They discourage innovation and change. On the contrary, people in materialistic societies, in which economic development is progressive, welcome change and innovation. The number of innovations in US and Japan compared to other countries substantiates this point.

- ***Changing Work Ethic*** – The traditional work ethic is highly focused on fair day's work and fair day's pay and quality of life. This survival focus has been a barrier to innovation. Now it is undergoing significant change. Personal desires such as job satisfaction, freedom of dissent, achievement and discretionary time are becoming essential items in the minds of the employees.

Business managements are increasingly paying attention on teamwork, job enrichment and employee participation to satisfy the needs of their employees. This development is favorable to innovation.

- ❖ ***Increasing Female Representation*** – Females are considered to be more innovative than men. As such lack of such innovative resource has been a negative point so far. Now the impact of more women in work force will continue to cause favorable changes. Management and scientific ranks in the male-dominated technological industries are now prime areas for female participation. The effect of women on the innovation activity in the corporations in such industries is likely to be quite significant. How to take maximum advantage of these new inputs for the process of innovation is still another challenge in the management of change?

(ii) Economic Environment:

Economic incentives and a favorable economic environment can be regarded a sufficient condition for innovativeness.

- ❖ ***International Competition*** – A nation's prosperity will be tied more strongly in the future to how well its corporations can compete internationally, either as multinational partners or entrepreneurs in world markets. This trend requires appropriate risk-benefit analyses and innovations. Competitive advantage can be gained only by innovations. As such international competition encourages, in fact, compels innovations. On the other hand, nations with domestic outlook tend to be slow in innovations.
- ❖ ***Shortage of resources*** – The resources shortage problems are being more acute. Naturally available land, water, and air are also going to become major concerns as population growth is alarming. Innovations for preserving natural resources and improving quality of life are essential.
- ❖ ***Social responsibility concerns*** – Firms have to decide on the balance between satisfying desirable social goals and Achieving the necessary economic competitiveness. The funding of high social goals drains too many of country's resources away from technological innovation. Conversely, this may promote social innovations. Social responsibility may trigger new innovations in the social arena improving the quality of life of people.

(iii) Technological Environment:

Technology and innovations have interacting relationship.

- ❖ ***High R&D emphasis*** – Technological environment with high R&D budgets helps accelerate the technological changes and provide unlimited innovational opportunities. On the other hand, mere concentration on minor improvements rather than on major discoveries and increased regulation of technological change may have adverse effect on innovation spirit.
- ❖ ***Technological progress*** – The progress rate of technology determines the innovation rate. Today technological progress is rapid, leading to convergence. Convergence refers to the coming together of two or more technologies to create a new system with greater benefits than the original technologies alone.

In the case of e-commerce we observe the Internet, television, radio and telephone are being combined into single technology.

(iv) Politico-legal environment:

This environment is composed of laws, government agencies and pressure groups that influence and limit various organizations and individuals in society.

- *Policies* – Government export-import policies, tax concessions, laws relating to wages, etc, have significant impact on business management in general and on innovation management, in particular. Governmental policies can encourage or discourage innovation. It has been rather clearly demonstrated that Japanese governmental policies, including tax, trade and regulatory policies were better coordinated and more conducive to innovation than those of the United States. The result was rapid and intense innovation by Japanese business firms.
- *Government Business Interaction* – Increased government regulation of business is causing disturbing changes in the general business environment. Business leaders are becoming reactive instead of proactive. When industry expects that government will impose more rules and regulations, they adopt short-term tactics. In this process, the longer range is neglected. Innovation survives, only when a better balance of long- and short-term considerations is achieved.
- *Patent laws* – Legal protection to innovative processes and products is a potent motivating factor for business and service organizations. The expenditure incurred on R&D to create innovations can be recovered and future investments can be made when innovations are profitable.

NURTURING INNOVATION IN E-BUSINESS

Although innovation is important for all organizations, it's absolutely critical for e-businesses. As John Chambers, CEO of Cisco Systems, states so clearly,

"The first company to capitalize on an innovation reaps the greatest rewards and most improved operating margins. When competitors start to use the same technologies, your competitive advantage of differentiation gets commoditized. Then it's time to move on to the next new thing."

The statement "innovate or lose" takes on added urgency in an e-business world.

The e-business world is definitely a white-water rapid environment. Change is continual, unpredictable and sudden. In this type of environment, how can managers nurture the innovations that are so vital to success?

The structural characteristics of e-businesses are almost always organic in nature, which is exactly what innovation needs to take root and thrive. There is a high level of flexibility and openness. Employees can easily collaborate with others both inside the organization and outside. Also, easy access to information facilitates knowledge sharing among employees throughout the organization, which is critical for stimulating and nurturing innovative efforts.

For instance, the loose structure at Tivoli Systems, a fast-moving software division of IBM, allows employees to share ideas and critique each other's efforts openly. Tivolians (as they like to call themselves) are comfortable with taking stands, speaking their minds and challenging authority.

The cultures of e-business organizations are critical to the nurturing of innovation. From encouraging experimentation, risk and conflict to accepting ambiguity, the cultures of e-businesses must value the pursuit of imagination, experimentation, and agility. That culture begins with a compelling vision. Innovative e-businesses must have a clear and inspiring vision that serves as the motivation for people to come up with big ideas. Then the values embodied in the organization's culture need to support the pursuit of those ideas.

Take General Electric, for instance, where former CEO Jack Welch fashioned a vision of GE as a nimble Web-savvy competitor even in its traditional, old-fashioned industries. Welch's vision established a cultural environment of innovation in which GE's employees continually share best practices and transfer knowledge among units.

Finally, human resource variables are important to innovation in e-businesses. Because of the hyper dynamic and competitive forces of the e-business world, everyone must play the role of idea champion. It's unrealistic in the fast changing world of e-business to think that only a few people could be champions of change. It's imperative for success and survival that everyone in e-businesses be actively engaged in searching for innovative products of services and innovative ways of doing work. It's fast paced and it's frenetic. The brutal realities of working in this type of setting will drive out those individuals who can't deal with hyper change. But on a more positive note, those individuals who thrive in this type of environment tend to be those who are willing to try the new, the untested, the innovative. That's exactly the type of people e-businesses need.

SUMMARY

Innovation has been called the most precious capability that any organization in today's economy must have and nurture. Innovativeness is based on the symbiotic relationship between the Environment and Organizations. There are two conflicting views on the sources of innovation. The social deterministic school argues that innovations are the results of a combination of external social factors and influences. The argument is – when the conditions were right, innovations would occur. The individualistic school argues that innovations are the result of unique individual talents and as such innovators are born.

In organizations innovation can be technology push or market driven or both. In thetechnology push model manufacturing makes the products efficiently and marketing offers them to the consumers. The customers – driven model emphasizes the role of marketing as an initiator of new ideas resulting from close interactions with customers. The interactive model represents the latest approach to creative behavior in organizations.

Various factors within and outside the organization (politico-legal, socio-cultural, economic and technological) exercise influence on the type and number of innovations.

QUESTIONS

1. Explain the concept and significance of innovation.
2. Describe the different models of innovation in society and organization.
3. Discuss various factors that influence innovations in organizations
4. What are the outcomes of innovation? How do you nurture innovation in e-business?

EXERCISES

Study any three of the latest innovations and identify the factors that have prompted their introductions.

CASE : ENVIRONMENT FOR INNOVATION

The small and informal business sector, a mix of manufacturing and service activities, is an important feature of the urban economy of the developing countries. This sector emphasizes the development of small entrepreneurs and intermediate technology. Being an important source of income and employment, it provides an important linkage between the modern manufacturing and the rural economic sector. In Bangladesh, this sector is believed to employ about two-thirds of the urban population but contributes only 4.5 per cent to GDP. The small and informal business sector, therefore, needs to become innovative. Poor innovation coupled with other adverse factors resulted in several hundred sick Small and Informal Business Enterprises (SIBEs).

Study Objectives

- To investigate the relevant issues and environmental challenges in the process of innovation in terms of growth of S&IBEs in Bangladesh.
- Finding suitable remedial measures to overcome the problems in implementing innovation programmes.

Methodology

The study is conceptual as well as explorative in nature. The relevant and supporting data have been collected through desk study. Besides primary data on the prevalence of innovative process in S&IBEs have been collected through a structured questionnaire in the light of the objectives of the paper.

The sample size comprises 500 S&IBEs of Bangladesh, selected on the basis of random sampling, engaged in 20 types of products and services, such as production of food and allied products, ready-made cloth selling, small-stationery retailing and shoe-repairing Data Regarding innovativeness were also connected from entrepreneurs, managers and owners of these enterprises through questionnaire and direct interview methods. The survey results regarding innovativeness are shown in Table-1.

Table 1: Survey Results on Innovativeness

Nature of Response	Number of Sample	Frequency in percentage
Innovative process followed to some extent	35	7
No innovative process followed	435	87
No response	30	6
Total	500	100

Source: Field Survey

Table1 portrays that only 7 per cent of the sample respondents claimed to have followed innovative process to some extent. It further reveals that 87 per cent of the sample entrepreneurs/managers have not innovated.

We asked them to point out the major factors that adversely affect the operational environment, and to rate the factors on a five-points scale. A score of 2 or more would indicate very adverse impact, and score falling between 1 and below 2 would indicate moderate adverse impact. Table 2 shows the score thus obtained.

Table 2: Average Score on Factors Adversely Affecting Environment

Adverse Factors	Average Score	Remarks
Social Environment		
Lack of proper education/training of entrepreneurs/manager	1.7	Insignificant
Apathy to work	1.8	Insignificant
Dominance of fate in the attitude of entrepreneurs towards life	2.1	Significant
Inadequate commitment to the profession	1.6	Insignificant
Economic Environment		
Inconsistent commercial policy	1.8	Insignificant
Inadequate fund for expansion and modernization	2.1	Significant
Server competition in home and abroad for marketing of products/services	2.6	Significant
Cost inflation	2.7	Significant
Unstable fiscal policy	1.9	Insignificant
Political Environment		
Absence of political stability	1.9	Insignificant
Red-tapism of supportive agencies	2.2	Significant
Frequent changes of national policies	2.0	Significant
Political philosophy of ruling party	1.8	Insignificant
Technological Environment		
Lack of scientific quality control system	1.8	Insignificant
Scarcity of skilled human resources	2.0	Significant
Outdated technology	2.2	Significant
Lack of R&D activity	2.1	Significant
Inefficient system management	1.9	Insignificant

Source: Field Survey

Table 3 depicts the opinions expressed by the samples processed through 7-points Likert type summated scale system satisfaction and +1 least satisfaction and on the contrary, -3 indicates complete dissatisfaction, -2 moderate dissatisfaction and –1 least dissatisfaction.

Table 3: Options of Sample Respondents About Adequacy and Efficacy of Package Assistance

Variables	Average Score	Remarks
Stimulatory activities:		
Motivational training for innovativeness is purposeful	1.9	Insignificant
Techno-economic information is available	1.8	Insignificant
Planned publicity for innovative entrepreneurial opportunities is effective	2.0	Significant
Innovative entrepreneurial education is adequate	1.7	Insignificant
Counselling and guiding serve the desired purpose	1.6	Insignificant
Supportive activities:		
Arrangement of adequate fund for innovative process is satisfactory	1.7	Insignificant
Provision of materials, power etc. are adequate	1.6	Insignificant
Guidance of government agencies is significant	1.6	Insignificant
Management consultancy is effective	1.5	Insignificant
Granting tax relief is regular	2.0	Significant
Sustaining activities:		
Marketing facilities are adequate	1.9	Insignificant
Quality improvements are ensured	1.6	Insignificant
New avenues for marketing the products is created	1.7	Insignificant
Programme of diversification of products/services is regular	1.5	Insignificant
Guidance in diagnosing the cause of failure is effective	1.6	Insignificant

Source: Field, Survey.

Questions:

1. Is environment for innovativeness of S& IFBEs encouraging?
2. What kind of measures do you suggest to promote innovativeness?

Source: Mohammed Solaiman and A.K.M.Tafzal Haque (1997), Innovation Management in Small and Informal Business Enterprises in Developing Countries: Case of Bangladesh, *South Asian Journal of Management,* Vol. 4, No.2, pp.43-50.

Chapter 5

Innovation Opportunities

Learning Objectives

After you have studied this chapter, you will be able to...

- Identify the major sources of innovations.
- Know the determinants of innovation.
- Explain the analytical and forecasting tools of innovation.

Structure

- Introduction
- Sources of Innovation
- Innovation Behavior
- Opportunity Identification Tools
- Opportunities Analytical Tools
- Forecasting Tools
- Summary
- Questions
- Exercises
- Case : Tool Kit Marketing

INTRODUCTION

Innovation is the activity of people and organizations to change themselves and the environment. It means breaking routines and dominant ways of thinking, introducing new things and behaviors, and launching new standards. Identifying the sources of innovation and forecasting the developments that stimulate innovations is an important task of managers. There are tools and techniques which help managers to assess and forecast.

SOURCES OF INNOVATION

The stimulants to innovations can be classified as given under based on the sources of innovation mentioned by Peter F. Drucker (1991).

Unexpected:

It may be the unexpected success, the unexpected failure or the unexpected outside event. One should be ready to identify *unexpected success* opportunities. IBM had twice succeeded by taking the unexpected into its fold (Drucker, 1991).

In the early 1930s, IBM developed electro-mechanical book keeping machine, meant for banks. However, due to depression, American banks did not buy new equipment. A chance meeting of Thomas Watson, Sr., the founder, with the director of the New York Public Library; opened up new segment for the product.

IBM designed a computer for scientific purposes. But when they found that businesses were buying for the most mundane of purposes, such as payroll, they sacrificed the design and developed a suitable one. Within four years IBM had attained leadership in the computer market.

Incongruity:

An incongruity is a discrepancy, a dissonance, between what is and what "ought" to be, or between what is and what everybody assumes it to be. Incongruity arises by changes within an industry, a market, or a process. There are several kinds of incongruity.

- ***Economic realities*** – The gaps between expected demand and actual demand might force organizations to find ways to succeed.

  Holiday resorts and premium goods like ₹ 1 lakh TV and ₹ 5,000 shoes were expected to succeed in late 1990s as middle-income groups started showing signs of high purchasing power. But it did not happen. Then the industry realized the power of value-for-money proposition in India and started offering products of that kind.

- ***Reality and assumptions*** – The role of an industry in serving needs of society may be improperly defined based on wrong assumptions.

  In India, for a long time, the FMCG companies fought their battles in urban market. It was on the assumption that rural markets are not only uneconomical but also not accessible. The assumptions are now changed. They have seen a great opportunity in rural markets and redefined their role. They are adopting development marketing strategies and packaging innovations to gain rural share.

- ***Efforts and 'values and expectations'*** – Producers and marketers almost always misconceive what it is the customer actually buys. They believe that what is value for them is also value for the customer.

  One of the important reasons for the failure of many products in India is the direct and insensitive adoption of product forms, which have been popular elsewhere. Examples are Rothmans cigarettes, which was once a coveted brand, English Leather and Yardley cosmetics, Rayban sunglasses, Reebok shoes, Maxwell House coffee and so on. Brooke Bond, a major player in the beverages market, had repeatedly attempted to launch a different flavor of coffee in South India and failed. Brooke house is one such brand that comes to mind. Lipton's launch of a range of noodles with a very British sounding brand name, supermum, which too sank without trace, is yet another instance.

Gap:

An old proverb says, "Necessity is the mother of invention." Gap analysis makes possible a process by supplying the "missing link". It is task-focused rather than situation-focused. It perfects a process that already exists, replaces a link that is weak, redesigns an existing old process around newly available knowledge.

In India, every student has to apply to more than one college to be sure of admission into a professional course. The students and their parents know the inconvenience in taking too many examinations of different colleges or universities. The Common Entrance Test (CET) procedure has minimized the inconvenience. The Internet has minimized the problem of waiting for results or receiving applications.

Changes:

Changes in industry structure or market structure that catch everyone unawares may lead to innovation.

- ***Industry structure*** – Change in industry structure by the entry or exit of organizations offers opportunities to outsiders and threats to the insiders. The outsiders who innovate can thus become a major factor in an important industry or area quite fast and at relatively low risk.

  The automobile industry dominated by Ambassador of Hindusthan Motors had experienced a visible change ever since the Maruti redefined the rules of competition. Economic reforms intensified competition from foreign companies. The middle-income group emerged as a major segment by seizing opportunities of installment buying and low cost loan facilities offered by banks.The introduction of Nano by Tata is a new challenge to car makers.

- ***Demographics*** – Of all external changes, demographics-defined as changes in population, its size, age structure, composition, employment, educational status and income are the clearest. Now India has more youth and their number is on the rise. This provides opportunity for education and life-style products.

- ***Social attitudes*** – When society changes to become more optimistic, enterprising and materialistic, enterprises find an opportunity to innovate. In addition we find new products created by users who turned into entrepreneurs.

Eric Von Hipple of the MIT Business School made many studies of the sources of innovation in the electronics industry and concluded that more than 70% of the product innovations came from the users, who initially can't find the tools or equipment they need on the market and are forced to develop them in-house.

Edward Land was taking pictures of his family while on a vacation trip in the Southwest. His young daughter asked, "Why do we have to wait to see the pictures?" and Land thought to himself "good question!" sketched out some ideas and tried them after he returned to his lab in Boston. The Polaroid Camera and the science of instant photography appeared soon thereafter.

- **Knowledge and technology changes:**

  Knowledge-based innovation is the "super-star" of enterprises. The knowledge can be technical or social. Social innovations based on knowledge can have equal or even greater impact. New technology turns into products, processes or services in the marketplace.

  Bell was inspired to start development of the telephone when he read an account, written in German, describing an invention, which he thought, had the function of a telephone.

  A social innovation is ushered in when society learn to empower women. As women entered into work force supported by changes in social attitudes and values, innovations in work life balance have become necessary.

  Innovations gain pace by adoption and convergence. Successful innovations in one industry may also gain applications in other industries.

  - From military to civilian applications (e.g., GPS technology)
  - From professional/scientific to consumer uses (e.g., digital imaging)
  - From early-adopter "techies" to lagging adopters who are non-technical and use the innovation in non-technical ways (e.g., personal computers)

  By convergence, the mobile technology has revolutionized the life of people making some products less necessary (cameras, landlines, music systems, etc).

INNOVATION BEHAVIOR

Systematic innovation is a feature of a complex national system. Thus, to large extent, long-term elements prevail on short-run macroeconomic fluctuation.

Regularities in innovation:

Although innovations can often be seen as a punctual artifact or event, Giovanni Dosi has underlined that a flow of innovations tends to self-organize along technological trajectories, i.e., tendencies of improvement along certain product features/performances by repeatedly using similar heuristics (e.g., the trend of faster and more powerful computer chips by miniaturization).

In some cases, it is even possible to forecast future developments of the successive waves of technologies by relying on past quantitative trends (e.g., the Moore's Law of doubling the speed every 18 months). Innovations tend to cluster in time and space, since there is often a strong interdependency and complementarity among them. Silicon Valley is a typical example.

Long-term trends:

Across countries, the determinant of differences in income and wages can be traced back to productivity and innovation. Thus, it is exactly when and if useful innovative products become affordable to the general public that we can say that growth has taken place. This requires adequate level of per-capita GDP and a reasonably equitable distribution of knowledge and income.

Business cycle behavior:

Nonetheless, firms choose the timing of putting innovation on the market and in the production lines. The adoption of cost-reducing process innovation and low cost products takes place during recessions, whereas higher-performance expensive innovative products are sold during boom phases.

OPPORTUNITY IDENTIFICATION TOOLS

Opportunities for innovation can be found within a firm or in external environment.

1. Environment analysis:

Analysis of the business environment includes four processes as given under.

- Scanning to detect change.
- Monitoring to track development.
- Forecasting to project the future.
- Assessing to interpret data.

Scanning:

Scanning the environment is the process by which the entrepreneur first identifies the key elements and their characteristics. It is a surveillance system for early detection. The goal of scanning is to detect change that is already underway. Successful scanning catches important changes early, giving the new venture enough lead-time to adapt. Scanning gives the entrepreneur a sensitivity to environmental conditions that sometimes looks like intuition.

Monitoring:

Monitoring is the process of tracking the evolution, development and sequence of critical events that affect the survival and profitability of the future new business. Data from the scanning process are input into the monitoring process. Specific trends and events identified for the new venture are monitored in real time to confirm or disprove predictions about how they will affect the firm. Monitoring is less general and, therefore, more focused than scanning. The entrepreneur follows specific periodicals, consults selected experts and even convenes focus groups. The outcome of the monitoring process is a detailed model of how various elements in the macro-environment influence and affects the firm. The model, however, is not reality, but a workable version of cause and effect.

Forecasting:

Forecasting enables the entrepreneur to develop plausible projections for the future. These can be projections for elements such as the level of prices, the direction of interest rates or future scenarios for cause and effect; for example, a typical forecast might be – if the money supply grows at above-target rates, then inflation will occur. Thus inputs for forecasts are the data from monitoring. Forecasting uses a series of techniques to provide insight into the future. The specific techniques chosen for a task should correspond to the type of data used as input and the nature of the desired forecast.

Assessing:

Assessing the environment is the most difficult and important of the four tasks of environmental analysis. Here the entrepreneur has to answer the most difficult of question: "What does it all mean?" Interpretation is an art form, and so is assessment. In assessing most entrepreneurial opportunities, there are few facts that people would agree can be generalized. One of the useful tools in analyzing the trends in technological developments is S-curve.

Although the four-part process we just described seems quite analytical it actually takes place overtime in a mode that would appear to be more intuitive than rational. This is what is sometimes called "entrepreneurial insight" or "vision."

2. Organization analysis:

A study of innovation opportunities inside depends on a firm's core competencies and needs. One useful tool to analyze is Business X-ray. Others are Buyer –utility map and S-curve.

Business X-ray:

Every three years or so, the enterprise has to take a "Business X-ray". It must put every single product, process, technology, market, distributive channel, not to mention every single internal staff activity, on trial for its life.

The Business X-ray furnishes the information needed to define how much innovation a given business requires, in what areas, and within what time frame. Michael J. Kami developed the best and simplest approach to this. In this approach a company lists each of its products or services, but also the markets each serves and the distributive channels it uses, in order to estimate their position on the product life-cycle.

How much longer will this product still grow?

How much longer will it still maintain itself in the market place?

How soon can it be expected to age and decline-and how fast?

When will it become obsolescent?

This enables the company to estimate where it would be if it confined itself to managing to the best of its ability what already exist. This then shows the gap between what can be expected realistically and what a company still needs to do to achieve its objectives, whether in sales, in market standing or in profitability.

The Business X-ray of the existing business, its products, its services, its markets, its technologies; and the definition of innovation gap and innovation need-these together enable a company to formulate a plan with objectives for innovation and deadlines.

Buyer utility map:

W. Chan Kim and Renee Mauborgne (2000) have described a method called the buyer utility map (Figure 5.1) that indicates the likelihood that customers will be attracted to a new idea or product. Kim and Mauborgne believe in focusing on an innovation's utility—how it will change the lives of customers? The buyer utility map, shown in figure, helps innovators to think about two things:

(1) the levers they can pull in delivering utility to customers.

(2) the various stages in the "buyer experience cycle," which runs from purchase to disposal. Each stage encompasses a wide variety of specific experiences. An innovator can use this map to identify the utility offered by the new product or service at various stages of the buyer experience cycle.

Ask yourself the following questions:

- Where can we create the greatest utility for our customers? Does our idea fill this space?
- Is that utility higher or lower than the utility created by the products or services offered by our competitors?
- Which of these utilities matters most to customers?
- How could we redesign our product or service idea to offer the greatest utility to customers in the areas that matter most to them?

In answering each question, you can get a good sense of the business potential of an innovative idea.

The Buyer Utility Map

		The Six Stages of the Buyer Experience Cycle					
		Purchase	Delivery	Use	Supplements	Maintenance	Disposal
The Six Utility Levers	Collective Productivity						
	Simplicity						
	Convenience						
	Risk						
	Fun and Image						
	Environmental Friendliness						

Source: W. Chan Kim and Renee Mauborgne, 'Knowing a Winning idea When You See One," *Harvard Business Review,* September-October, 2000, pp.129-138.

S-curve:

The course of successful technological innovation is often described through an S-shaped curve (Figure 5.2). The horizontal axis shows time and investment, while the vertical axis indicates some particular dimension of product performance or cost competitiveness.

The S-curve of the established technology is on the left in Figure 5.2, and the curve of its newer rival is on the right. The performance of the established technology has improved overtime, at first rapidly and then at a modest pace. By the time the rival technology first enters the picture (T1), the established technology is much improved and approaching its maturity. With maturity, the pace of improvement slows. Years of experimentation and incremental improvements have exhausted most of the opportunities to improve cost and performance. Every incremental improvement is more and more costly.

Typically, the newly emerged rival technology is crude when compared with the established technology, with many issues yet unsolved — that's what we see at T1 in the figure. These weaknesses cause established companies to write it off as "not a real threat." Most customers likewise ignore the new technology because it lacks the performance or cost characteristics they require — at least at the moment.

The first-generation roll film cameras developed by George Eastman late in the Nineteenth Century fit this description. The images produced by Eastman's roll film couldn't hold a candle to the superb images produced by chemically coated glass plates, the technical standard of that era. Therefore, the professionals and serious amateurs who constituted the market overwhelmingly rejected Eastman's product.

The same can be observed with respect to many of the innovative high-tech products introduced over the years.

The first-generation Apple's word processor, was not better than the typewriter. It had only uppercase letters, and the printers available at the time were expensive and produced low-quality output. History tells us that the first typewriters were even less satisfactory. Samuel Clemens (also known as Mark Twain) was one of the first typewriter owners and complained often about its shortcomings.

Many of the problems first associated with a new technology, however, are gradually solved over time. Manufacturing process improvements and large-scale production cause costs to fall. Thus, the performance/cost characteristics of the new technology improve with time and investment. That movement is typically slow in the beginning, but picks up speed. At a certain point (T2), the new technology matches its older rival in performance or cost features or both. But unlike the established technology, the new one has plenty of opportunities for continued improvement. If all goes well, it will improve to the point that its older rival will be displaced from the main marketplace.

Consider the plight of chemical-based photography today as it faces the challenge of digital imaging. The low and medium-hanging opportunities for film improvement have been exploited. Those that remain will be costly and difficult to exploit. Meanwhile, digital imaging can look forward to many years of technical improvements. It's already happening. Digital cameras are now available for professional and consumer applications. Prices are dropping and performance gets better every year. It's very conceivable that digital photography will eventually dominate, with film photography surviving only in a number of specialized niches.

Where does a firm stand on a S-curve? Figure 5.1 and Table 5.1 provides answers.

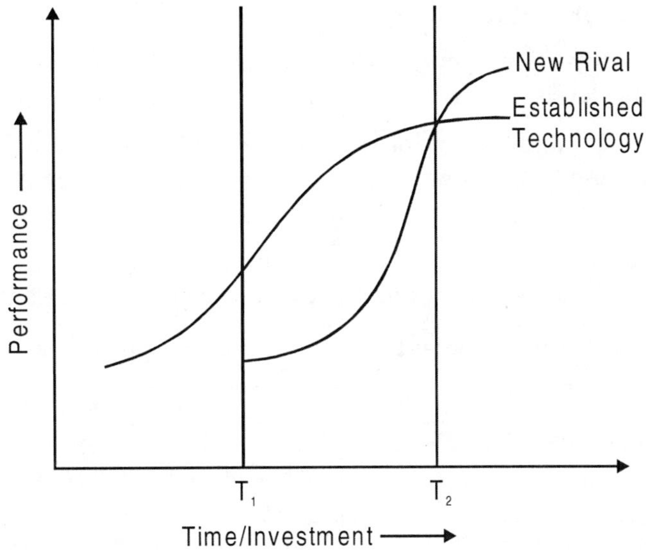

Figure 5.1: S-Curve

Source: Adapted from James M. Utterback, (1994), *Mastering the Dynamics of Innovation, Boston: Harvard Business School Press, p. 158.*

Table 5.1 Where Do You Stand on the S-Curve?

Situation	Position	Action
My company is at the point where every incremental improvement to the products, services, or technology is more and more costly to produce and less and less important to customers.	You're at or near an end-game situation.	Get on board the rival technology—perhaps by acquiring the innovator company. Leapfrog the rival technology with something better. Look for a breakthrough that will give your technology a new lease on life. Stick with your current technology, but expand it into different markets.
Rival company is challenging by a new technology and my company is not enjoying performance or cost advantages.		

Forecasting tools:

When forecasting is used to help search for new business opportunities and to uncover potential macro-environmental constraints on these opportunities, the following "five-step process is suggested."

1. Choose the macro-environmental variables that are critical to the new venture. These will probably relate to the resource base of the firm.
2. Select the sources of data for the forecast. These will probably be those you have been monitoring.

3. Evaluate various forecasting techniques.
4. Integrate forecast results into your plan for the creation of the new venture. These will probably concern resource levels and availability and sales forecasts.
5. Keep track of the critical aspects of your forecast. This will mean comparing actual results with forecasted results. If and when a gap appears, it is time for another forecast, beginning at step1.

Table 5.2 furnishes forecasting techniques relating to each of business activity. Table 5.3 summarizes the costs and benefits of six quantitative and judgmental forecasting techniques.

Table 5.2 Forecasting techniques and purposes

Purpose	Forecasting techniques
Searching for relevant scenario	Expert opinion, Panels, Brainstorming, Delphi technique, Technology monitoring, Scenario development.
Searching for trends among parameters	Extrapolation, Growth curves, Substitution
Searching for alternative among various choices to reach a goal	Relevance Tree, Morphology, Cross impact analysis, Dynamic modelling & Simulation
Identifying implications for action	Expert consultation, Sçenario building, Modelling & Simulation

Use of a combination of methods will generally be more reliable than dependence on a single parameter or single forecasting method. Also, it may be useful to have the user of a technology, generator of technology, manufacturers, suppliers and designers involved in an integrated exercise to shape the combined perspective into a forecast

Table 5.3 Quantitative and Judgmental Forecasting Methods for Emerging Industries, New Ventures, New Products

Method	Description	Cost	Complexity
Sales force estimate	A bottom-up approach that aggregate unit demand	Low	Low
Juries of executive opinion	Forecasts jointly prepared by experts in a functional area.	Low	Low
Customer survey, Market research focus groups	Learning about intentions of potential customers and final users	Medium	Medium
Scenario development	Effects of anticipated conditions imagined by forecasters.	Medium	Low
Delphi method	Experts guided to consensus.	Low	Medium
Brainstorming	Idea generation in a non-critical group situation	Low	Medium

Source: Adapted from J.Pearce and R.Robinson, *Strategic Management*, 4th ed. (Homewood, IL:Irwin, 1991

Pitfalls in forecasting and analysis:

Following is a list of common mistakes and pitfalls in forecasting and analysis:

(i) Failure to use appropriate data:

(a) Use of unreliable and inconsistent data

(b) Failure to use valid, available data due to the use of wrong technique

(c) Use of imprecise and incomplete data with a sophisticated techniques etc.

(ii) Mistakes in selecting appropriate methodology:

(a) Use of inappropriate technique

(b) Inability to handle intrinsic uncertainties

(c) Reliance on single expert

(d) Overemphasis on quantitative techniques, etc.

(iii) Lack of imagination in the form of:

(a) Failure to distinguish between Signals and Noises

(b) Acceptance of trends as rigidly continuing

(c) Reliance on limited information

(d) Neglecting uncertainty, etc.

(iv) Biases introduced by personal factors

(a) Vested interest of the forecaster

(b) Unwillingness to alter other previous commitments

(c) Over optimism or pessimism

(d) Avoiding unpleasant courses of action, etc.

Suitable one:

The choice of selecting an appropriate technique for a particular forecasting exercise is a complex problem. The methodology that is adopted depends on the purposes for which a forecast is being prepared. The approach to be used depends on the following factors:

(a) Purpose for which the forecast is being made

(b) Reliability needed for the forecast

(c) Precision of the available data

(d) The time frame for the forecast

However, a general comparison of the major approaches of forecast (on a 1-10 scale; 1 being lowest and 10 highest is given in Table 5.4 below:

Table 5.4 Comparisons of Techniques of Forecasting

Technique	Use of intuition	Complexity	Resource requirements	Identification of alternatives
Individual Expert	10	1	1	Yes
Delphi	10	3	3	Yes
Trend Extrapolation	4	1	1-2	No
Growth Curves	4	4	3	No
Technology Monitoring	1	2	6	Yes
Relevance Tree	7	8	4	Yes
Morphological Analysis	7	8	4	Yes

Source: S.C. Wheelright and S. Makridakis, (1973). *Forecasting Methods for Management,* Wiley, New York.

The ultimate test of goodness of a forecast is whether it is accepted and used in the decision-making process. The forecast must be understandable, credible and meaningful to the decision-maker.

SUMMARY

Environment analysis of the business environment includes four processes as given under-Scanning to detect change, Monitoring to track development, Forecasting to project the future and Assessing to interpret data. A study of innovation opportunities inside organization depends on a firm's core competencies and needs. The useful tools to analyze are Business X-ray, Buyer –utility map and S-curve. Forecasting tools helpful to envisage innovation opportunities include the survey techniques and statistical methods.

QUESTIONS

1. What are the sources of innovation? Explain with examples.
2. Identify the determinants of innovation. How do you forecast innovation potential?
3. What are the tools for identification of innovation opportunities?
4. Explain analytical tools useful in analyzing innovation opportunities.

EXERCISES

Identify six innovations and classify them into radical and incremental. Based on them identify the innovation opportunities. If necessary, undertake a market survey.

CASE – TOOLKIT MARKETING

An intriguing idea (which is all but self-evident) has emerged recently about managing corporate innovation. User toolkits are considered to be the best bet for optimum customization of a product obviating the risks of customer dissatisfaction or a sense of supplier futility.

Double Innovation:

Innovation is basically an iterative or looping process. A key feature of the new innovation process is that it involves the concurrent development of two products – (1) the base, general purpose product to be delivered to the customer and (2) the toolkit which would help the customer to effect the required "customerization" to the base. The base product, consisting of shared components, helps to achieve economies of scale in a core module. Meanwhile, the toolkit facilitates the achievement of economies of scope in terms of the variety of markets served by means of swappable components. Hence we term this a double-loop innovation process and propose that, in future, PD will take the double-loop form.

Currently, the best example of customer toolkits is available in the semiconductor industry where the toolkit is actually a suite of electronic design automation software tools for purposes such as circuit simulation, detailed layout, design verification, testing, etc. These enable circuit designers in customer companies, who are not specialists in the semiconductor manufacturing process, to design products that are compatible with this process. The customer purchases the design software and carries out the design activities. Typically, the customer has access to electronic libraries of tried and tested design elements which can be combined, expanded, edited, etc., to complete new designs. The software helps to analyze designs proposed by the customer to verify that the underlying design rules or constraints are satisfied. Verified designs become the subject of a production contract with the semiconductor manufacturer (Leachman and Leachman, 2001).

Commercial toolkits sold to competitors ("users") for their own developmental purposes may have to be distinguished from customer ("end-user") toolkits discussed here.

Arguments against:

However, it becomes necessary to evaluate a potential drawback which might negate the prospects of the double-loop process at this stage. This lies in the observation that:

- With the transfer of design work from firms to their customers, there would be a decline of design in the supplier firms.
- With a tendency for "followers" to simply replicate toolkits developed by "leaders," the double -loop process would get pre-empted.

To bypass this, the additional category of "strivers" is proposed, especially given the obvious shortcoming of relying on a "one best way" philosophy.

Arguments for:

The argument goes that instead of devoting scarce resources in-house to mass customization, suppliers should make toolkits available to users to effect the customization themselves on a base product (Thomke and von Hippel, 2002). Such toolkits, if well thought out, promise to increase customer satisfaction ad provide companies with a long-term competitive advantage by ultimately catering to customer needs for self-expression and the creation of a distinct identity.

The toolkit approach is not something new. In fact, in the semiconductor industry it has evolved over a couple of decades and has spurred volume growth (of logic chips) to about $15 billion levels (Thomke and von Hippel, 2002).

Provided customer designs generated by the toolkit are within the suppliers' operational capabilities, they can be produced and delivered to the customer according to its specifications without undue quality, cost and delivery problems. Of course, this places a premium on the supplier's flexibility and the currency of its capabilities, subject to the overall limits placed by its strategy.

Besides the toolkit proper, customization toolkits would also include supplementary elements such as education, training and familiarization programmes and other instructional materials (such as manuals). Ideally, the use of the toolkit should be intuitive and require minimum involvement of the supplier. Perhaps this would be related to the level of sophistication of the customer and the design of the product.

For the vast majority of products, the toolkit concept may only be an "ideal" to be approached persistently. This would, nevertheless, prove invaluable in the Product Development (PD) process by inducing an acute understanding of mainstream as well as new stream customers and thus providing a long-term competitive advantage. Ultimately products themselves may benefit from being viewed as toolkits which maximize customer freedom along particular dimensions. Thus, we envisage the emergence of a new-look innovation process in future.

Finally, a historical perspective reveals that the precedent for the double-loop process can be found in two areas of Concurrent Engineering (CE) (viz. of product and process technologies) and in the concurrent evolution of markets for innovations. All three are clubbed together as "CE" and all three emphasize rapid knowledge transfers (including on global basis) and rapid problem-solving (including via simulation). Thus, CE, along the three foregoing dimensions, provides a quasi-analytical framework for shaping the emerging double-loop innovation process.

Scope:

A priori, applicability of the approach could be limited to a class of product termed "customerizable" (which goes beyond conventionally "customizable") products. In general, customerizable products would be those where the number of variants required in a time unit are relatively large while the production volumes of each in the same period are relatively small. Thus, a need for customer toolkits may be manifested by shrinking customer segments (Thomke and von Hippel, 2002).

In the past, CE has helped expand markets for a variety of developed-country products such as cars and computers mostly in developed country markets. Thus, it is believed that CE II will help boost business in the so-called "Base-Of-Pyramid" (BOP) markets around the world.

The software and services industry of India may be well placed to apply the customer toolkit concept. This is because:

- It basically involves the extension of existing practices in the computer industry.
- There is a huge global need for lower cost, lower complexity software applications that need to be customized.

Software toolkits should thus help leverage scarce personnel resources in the software industry as well as accelerate customization in other industries worldwide.

In this situation, the Indian software industry is envisaged to play a key role. But it means that the traditional neglect by the global software industry of the ultimate end user (as opposed to a "client") perspective, apparently due to software's growing complexity and the need to ship packages which work "somehow" rather than work "well" (Tepper, 2002) has to be overcome. This only underlines the importance of the toolkit approach as an "ideal" if not a reality in most industrial situations.

The Indian software services industry may be very well placed to spearhead the required attack globally. Thomke (2002) of Harvard Business School confirms that "the Indian software industry may be in a strong position to create tools for simpler applications development. In part this is due to a huge market for lower cost, lower complexity software application that need to be customized." Hence, more emphasis than ever before will have to be given to software toolkits not only for internal development purposes (so as to leverage scarce human resources) but also, to the extent possible, for the required customization around the world.

Questions:

1. Explain the double-loop innovation process and discuss its merits and demerits.
2. To what extent do you think, Indian software industry will benefit from this innovative idea?

Sources:

1. Philip S. Thomas, (2003), Double-Loop Process: The Next Innovative Paradigm, *Vikalpa*, Vol. 28, No. 1, January – March, pp 83-89.
2. Leachman, R C and Leachman, CH, (2001), "E-commerce and the Changing Terms of Competition in the Semiconductor industry," in *BRIE-IGCC Economy Project, Tracking a Transformation*, Washington DC: Brookings Institution Press, pp. 214-228.
3. Thomke, S, (2002), Personal e-mail correspondence, dated December 30.
4. Thomke, S, and Von Hippel, E (2002). "Customers as Innovators: A New Way to Create Value," *Harvard Business Review*, April.
5. Von Hippel, E and Katz, R, (2002), "Shifting Innovation to Users via Toolkits," *Management Science*, Vol. 48, No. 7, pp. 821-83.

Chapter 6

Strategising Innovation

Learning Objectives

After you have studied this chapter, you will be able to...

- Appreciate innovation as a strategy component of organizations
- Know-how to develop an innovation strategy
- Identify various types of strategies for innovation

Structure

INTRODUCTION

A study by Towers Perrin and his team (2001) indicated that the technology-induced new business environment has made innovation the most important element in competitive strategy. Their research indicates that by 2003, globally organizations will have to emphasize on innovation, new markets, new products and services and finally e-commerce sales and solutions. Today we observe that, the major concerns of modern organizations are innovation, productivity and competitiveness.

INNOVATION AS A STRATEGY COMPONENT

A corporate or business strategy that intends to "change the rules of the industry or marketplace, almost always needs to pursue breakthrough or disruptive innovation and to be proactive rather than reactive". The goals of the strategy makers and the circumstances of the business environment dictate how aggressive the company needs to be in this pursuit. In any case, the business strategy sets the innovation context within which the marketer has to operate.

DEVELOPING INNOVATION STRATEGY

The steps involved in general, in developing and managing an innovation strategy are as follows:

1. Identify the mission, vision and goals:

In order to compete in today's highly competitive markets, companies do not only have to be efficient and competent in what they do. They have to offer uniqueness, whether it is in the form of service benefits or technical attributes or more usually a combination of these. Hence, innovation has become one of the major areas of pursuit. Peter. F. Drucker has identified eight areas in which, performance and results are vital for the success of any organization.

Profitability	Innovation	Manager performance and development	Physical and financial resources
Productivity	Market standing	Worker performance and attitude	Public responsibility

Innovation is one such key area. As such, innovation has become an integral part of corporate strategy.

2. Know the firm's posture:

Is company interested in a conservative or aggressive innovative policy (reactive)? Is it interested in a defensive or offensive (proactive) strategy? At one extreme, firms are not interested in innovations. They simply emphasize the existing offerings. They react to new innovations continuously and pursue an imitation strategy. At the other extreme, firms are proactive and try to be innovation leaders following the path of steady and continuous innovations. They sense the market and technology developments, devote substantial time and funds, make structural arrangements and establish system for innovations. Table 6.1 shows these positions.

Table 6.1 Innovation continuum

Action	Continue with existing	Imitation (Copy cats)	Incremental (Improvements)	Radical (Unique-never before)
Posture	Inactive	Reactive	Active	Proactive
Risk	High risk	Low	Medium	High risk

The field has come to distinguish two ends of the innovation spectrum in terms of *radical* or *discontinuous innovation* and *incremental* or *continuous innovation*. Continuous innovations refer to gradual, evolutionary improvements in product or technology where as discontinuous innovation refers to dramatic, revolutionary changes. They are *disruptive technologies* that permit entire industries and markets to transform or even disappear. Table 6.2 shows the nature and implications.

A corporate or business strategy that intends to "change the rules of the industry or marketplace, almost always needs to pursue breakthrough or disruptive innovation and to be proactive rather than reactive. The innovation strategy is to be designed keeping in mind the requirements of the firm and various hurdles in the way of success. Here, the analytical tools like SWOT analysis, Portfolio models like BCG matrix and Product life-cycle and S-curve will be of help

Table 6.2 Strategy approaches

Strategy	Decision	Actions	Implications
Incremental innovation	Take the existing product and offering and make small-step improvements to the original technology and design. Incremental improvements add up to produce a great deal of change in an offering overtime.	Analyzing expanding customer needs. Analyze customer use patterns, combinations of products, new uses, etc. Making brand or product extensions.	Require change in customer perception and usage patterns.
Discontinuous innovation	Replacing one's own successful product or service with new technology or process or product, providing greater customer value.	Identify competitive threats or break-through technologies. Consider new product possibilities. Choose new technology. Create new-to-the-world technology and new forms of customer value.	Require customers to radically change their past behavior. Get ready for the current business demise.

3. Align innovation strategy with corporate strategy:

The firms spending most on R&D are not always the successful ones. The frequent winners are the firms managing prudently their innovative processes by integrating R&D strategy with corporate strategy. R&D is long-term process of creating science and technology. As such, it should be an integral part of corporate strategy aiming at long-range corporate strengths and opportunities for growth.

Top management of high-tech companies may develop a 'strategic intent'. Strategic intent represents an ambitious target that a firm is pursing over the coming decade and emphasizes the distinctive competencies that must be developed to achieve this desired competitive position (Hamel and Prahlad, 1985). A firm may have to revise the strategic intent in light of changing environment. The need for a change in the strategic intent can be identified through intelligence system and sales force reports. The point that signals a change is referred to as strategic inflection point. Burgelman and Grove (1996) explained Strategic inflection point as the giving way of one type of industry dynamics to another; the change of one winning strategy into another; the replacement of an existing technological regime by a new one. Strategic gaps refer to deficiencies in firm's market alignment. To fill the gaps, firms may create new business or change market character (discontinuous innovation).

4. Establish innovation charter:

By identifying key areas in innovative effort and clarifying company position, innovative strategy will help the firms to achieve maximum benefits with less effort. The major decision areas in an innovation charter areas given in Table 6.3.

Table 6.3: Key Areas in Innovative Effort

S.No.	Decision area	Aspects
1	Nature of new products to be developed (level of innovativeness, level of quality, etc).	New products can be categorized as follows depending upon the degree of their innovativeness: • New/original products • Improved products by R&D • Modified products by engineering and production
2	Nature of technology used	Existing Vs. New Related Vs. Unrelated
3	Frequency of new products	Time gap between one innovation and another.
4	Expenditure levels of projects	Present and future Investment in rupees
5	Benefits expected	Competitiveness Synergy within firm
6	Risk involved	High Moderate Low

5. Apply portfolio thinking:

Only the smallest firms deal with one or two development projects. In contrast, big firms may have dozens of funded projects in play at any given time. Some may be low-risk, short-term projects that aim to incrementally improve an existing product. Others may represent a radically new concept that aims to create new markets. Still others may fall between these two extremes. Because incremental and radical projects entail substantial differences in risk levels, time frames and potential payoffs, management must employ portfolio thinking in dealing with them. Portfolio thinking helps managers to see a collection of ongoing projects in terms of its overall risk/return characteristics. Once they understand those characteristics, they can shape and mange the portfolio to achieve the right balance of risk and potential return.

As a first step toward portfolio thinking, it is often helpful to map ongoing projects onto a two-dimensional matrix like the one in Figure 6.1. Here, the horizontal axis indicates the maturity or "newness" of market or technology factors. The vertical axis indicates rising levels of technical challenge, uncertainty, and economic opportunity. Each circle in the matrix represents a project and the size of each circle indicates the magnitude of resources dedicated to it.

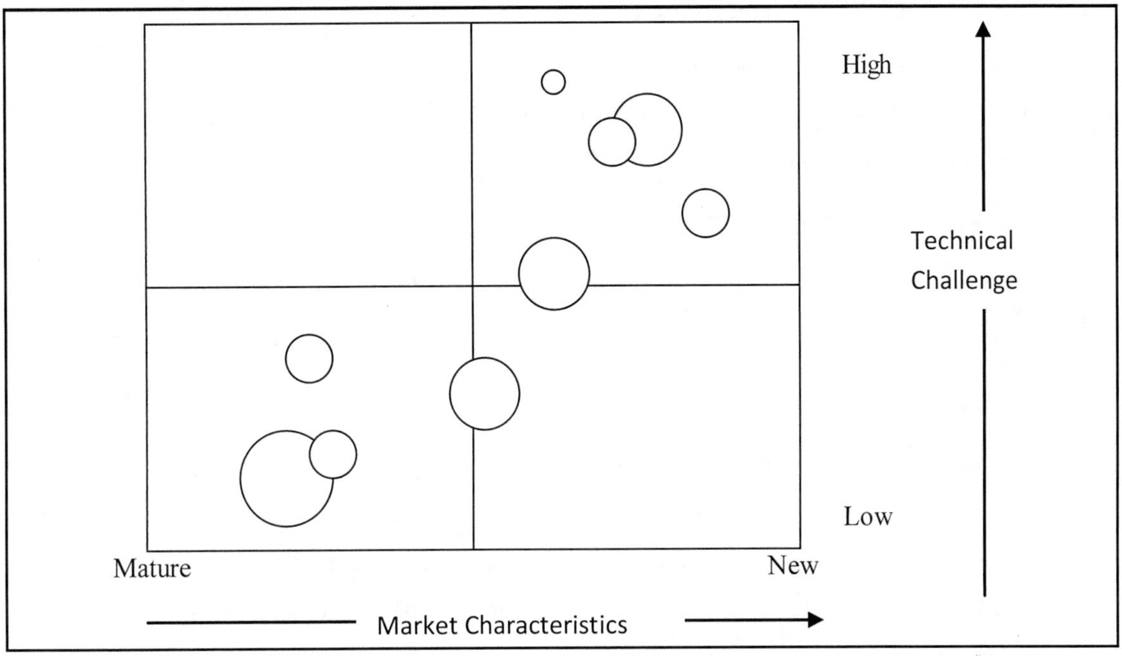

Figure 6.1: Innovation Portfolio Matrix

Source: *Managing Creativity and Innovation*; HBS Press: Boston, 2003. p.125.

As this matrix indicates, the biggest projects are cautious ones. They have mature technical and market characteristics. Like wise, these projects are among the less technically challenging and involve the least risk and potential opportunity for the company. Many small projects populate the upper-right quadrant. These involve higher technical risk and address new markets, but they also hold the prospect for greater economic opportunity for the company.

Try constructing a similar matrix for your company. Once you've mapped out your current projects, what does it tell you? If most projects and resources are located in the lower-left quadrant, your company is being very risk averse and may be doing too little to address future opportunities, new technologies and new markets. On the other hand, if most projects and resources are in the upper right quadrant, it is being very aggressive. What would constitute a suitable risk/reward balance for your company? Who could articulate that balance?

6. State objectives of innovation:

Top management must establish broad as well as specific objectives to innovation. Take the case of new products. They should assign to the new products specific strategic roles, which may vary from being a bread winner to merely line filler. The objectives of new products development may be one or more of the following:

- Maintain the image of product innovator.
- Defend own market share in a competitive market.
- Prevent entry of new competitors.
- Exploit available technology in a new way.
- Utilize idle capacities in product and distribution.
- Gain control on market.

7. Make aggregate project plan:

In aggregate project plan is a mechanism to ensure accomplishment of development goals. Three basic steps in constructing such a plan are: (Wheel Wright and Clark, 1992).

- ❖ Mapping the varying kind of development projects.
- ❖ Making capacity decisions.
- ❖ Making provision for gaining critical skills and capabilities.

Projects may be mapped on two dimensions:

- The extent of product change (i.e., derivatives, enhancements and new core products)
- The extent of process changes (incremental change to new core processes)

Based on outputs, projects may be arranged as follows:

(1) **Derivative projects** – are initiatives that realize small advances in firm's products or processes such as cost reduction features, product line extensions, etc.

(2) **Platform projects** – are in the middle of the development spectrum. They are further improvements over derivatives or 'naked solution' for a new core product.

(3) **Breakthrough projects** – generate new core products/processes.

(4) **Research and Advanced Development (RAD) projects** – aim at inventing new science and know-how for application.

(5) **Alliances and partnership projects** – are those done in conjunction with one or more outside firms. The project may be RAD or commercial type.

8. Organize for innovation:

A company can add innovations to its portfolio mainly in two different ways:

(i) By acquisition.

(ii) By development: in-house or outsourcing.

For instance, the acquisition of a new product from an innovator company can be done in three ways:

- ❖ Buy patents and pay royalty for making a new product.
- ❖ Buy a license to make that company's product or service.
- ❖ Take a franchise to make and sell the product.

Product development route can take two forms:

- Within the company (in-house) or
- Contracting with independent research agencies (out sourcing).

For development in-house, consistent and committed effort is necessary. Further, the spirit of innovation should pervade the whole organization and permeate all levels. Incremental innovations can be managed with less structural changes like-committees and taskforces whereas radical innovations require separate organizational set up.

In case of new product development, organizational arrangements vary as follows:

- ❑ New product division
- ❑ New product department
- ❑ Venture team
- ❑ New product committee
- ❑ New product manager

For the existing business to be capable of innovation it has to create a structure that allows people to be capable of innovation, it has to create relationships that center on innovation and creativity. It has to make sure that its rewards and incentives, its compensation, personnel decisions and policies, all reward the right entrepreneurial behavior and do not penalize it.

There has to be a special locus for the new venture within the organization, and it has to be pretty high up. Even though the new project, by virtue of its current size, revenues and markets, does not rank with existing products, somebody in top management must have the specific assignment to work on tomorrow as an entrepreneur and innovator.

This need not be a full-time job; in the smaller business, it very often cannot be a full-time job. But it needs to be a clearly defined job and one for which somebody with authority and prestige is fully accountable.

Innovative efforts, especially those aimed at developing new businesses, products or services, should normally report directly to this "executive in charge of innovation" rather than to managers further down the hierarchy. They should never report to line managers charged with responsibility for ongoing operations.

9. Lead the innovative effort:

Whatever may be the choice of organization, the important considerations in leading for innovation are:

(i) *Innovation climate:* First, the organization must be made receptive to innovation and willing to perceive change as an opportunity rather than a threat. It must be organized to do the hard work of the innovator.

(ii) *Innovation culture:* There must be clear understanding throughout the organization that innovation is the best means to preserve and perpetuate that organization and that it is the foundation for the individual manager's job security and success. Innovative thinking should become a way of life.

In some companies the practice is conducting meetings with managers in which a senior manager elicits opinions of participants. They are an excellent vehicle for upward communications, the best means to enable juniors and especially professionals, to look up from their narrow specialties and see the whole enterprise. They enable juniors to understand what top management is concerned with, and why. In turn, they give the seniors badly needed insight into the values, vision and concerns of their younger colleagues. They provide innovative ideas to senior mangers. However, the yield of entrepreneurial ideas from all this may not be its most important product. The most valuable achievement may well be entrepreneurial vision, receptivity to innovation, and "greed for new things" throughout the entire organization.

(iii) *Right people*: Determine how many people are needed, with what abilities and capacities. Only when people with proven performance capacity have been assigned to a project, supplied with the tools, the money and the information they need to do the work and given clear and unambiguous deadline, innovations become possible.

(iv) *Research as a team effort*: Innovations are more in firms that encouraged cross-fertilization of ideas through teams of diverse disciplines. A good interaction between R & D, engineering, manufacturing and marketing personnel is essential for successful innovations.

(v) *Have Product champions:* A product champion is a company-oriented manager who inspires subordinates to find better ways of doing things and lends support to conversion of a product idea into a marketable product. Theodore Leavitt (1981) maintains, **"Creativity without action – oriented follow-through is a barren form of behavior".**

(vi) *Evaluation*: Systematic measurement or at least appraisal of a performance as manager and innovator is mandatory. Measures on learning and innovation along with measures on efficiency and effectiveness should be included in the appraisal.

In some companies, the operating report has two "first pages" the traditional one lists the problems: the other one lists all the areas in which performance is better than expected, budgeted or planned for. The gap as well as the unexpected success is important symptoms of innovative opportunity. Typically, in companies that are managed for innovation, there are therefore two meetings on operating results, one to focus on the problems and one to focus on the opportunities.

10. Evaluate the innovative effort:

A well defined measurable criteria/standards are essential to assure benefits from innovation effort.

(a) Time Standards:

In how many years a new product is to be introduced? A company may aim at exploiting a technology in a new way may allow one or two years. In case of new technology, it may have to allow about 10 years. Breakthrough occur in different ways. Some take very long time others take very short time.

(b) Budget Standards:

How much to budget for a new product development? The size of resources allocation and approaches vary from firm-to-firm.

(i) Some companies may encourage more number of projects with a hope to hit one or two (Open end budget).

(ii) Some companies may decide the frequency of new product introductions and work back (Objective –task method).

(iii) Some companies may relate the investment to their sales. (Percentage of sales method)

(c) Idea Generation Standards:

How many new product ideas are to be generated in a year? It requires creativity or innovativeness to generate new ideas. Every new idea generated cannot become a new product. In 1970s, it took 58 new product ideas to yield one good one. In 1980s, *one out of seven ideas* was successful (Booz, Allen & Hamilton, 1980).

INNOVATION STRATEGIES

Peter F. Drucker (1986) observed that there are four innovation strategies.

1. Being Fustest with the Mostest.
2. Hitting Them Where They Ain't.
3. Finding and occupying a specialized "ecological niche".
4. Changing the economic characteristics of a product, a market or an industry.

We will now discuss the first three and examine the last one with reference to market and environment based strategies.

Being Fustest with the Mostest:

Being "Fustest with the Mostest" requires an ambitious aim; otherwise it is bound to fail. It always aims at creating a new industry or a new market.

The word processor is not much of a "scientific" invention. It hooks up three existing instruments: a typewriter, a display screen, and a fairly elementary computer. But this combination of existing elements has resulted in a genuine innovation that is radically changing office work. Dr. An Wang was a lone entrepreneur when he conceived of the combination some time in the mid-fifties. He had no track record as an entrepreneur and a minimum of financial backing. Yet he clearly aimed from the beginning at creating a new industry and at changing office work-and Wang Laboratories has, of course, become a very big company.

Hitting them where they ain't:

Two different strategies are identified –*Creative imitation and entrepreneurial judo.*

Creative imitation:

Creative imitation has the following features:

- It satisfies a demand that already exists rather than creating one. As such it starts out with markets rather than with products and with customers rather than with producers. It is both market-focused and market-driven.
- Creative imitation is a strategy aimed at market or industry leadership, if not at market or industry dominance.
- It is much less risky. By the time the creative imitator moves, the market has been established and the new venture had been accepted.
- There is usually more demand for it than the original innovator can easily supply.
- The creative imitator does not invent a product or service; he perfects and positions it. It may be additional product features. It may be segmentation of product or services so that slightly different versions fit slightly different markets.

When semiconductors became available, everyone in the watch industry knew that they could be used to power a watch much more accurately, much more reliably and much more cheaply than traditional watch movements. The Swiss soon brought out a quartz-powered digital watch. But they had so much investment in traditional watch making that they decided on a gradual introduction of quartz-powered digital watches over a long period of time, during which these new timepieces would remain expensive luxuries. Meanwhile, the Hattori Company in Japan had long been making conventional watches for the Japanese market. It saw the opportunity and went in for creative imitation, developing the quartz-powered digital watch as the standard timepiece. By the time the Swiss had woken up, it was too late. Seiko watches had become the world's best sellers, with the Swiss almost pushed out of the market.

IBM's personal computer is practically indistinguishable from the Apple in its technical features, but IBM from the beginning offered the customer programs and software. Apple maintained traditional computer distribution through specialty stores. IBM in a radical break with its own traditions-developed all kinds of distribution channels, specialty stores, its own retail stores, and so on. It made it easy for the consumer to buy and it made it easy for the consumer to use the product. These, rather than hardware feature, were the "innovations" that gave IBM the personal computer market.

The success of creative imitation is assured when (i) there is a rapidly growing market and (ii) imitation is in high-tech areas.

High-tech innovators are least likely to be market-focused and most likely to be technology and product-focused. They therefore tend to misunderstand their own success and fail to exploit and supply the demand they have created.

Entrepreneurial judo:

This strategy is based on sensing the opportunity, not properly utilized by the innovator and exploiting it. There are in particular four common bad habits that enable newcomers to use entrepreneurial judo against the established companies. Table 6.4 presents four judo tactics.

Table 6.4 Entrepreneur judo tactics

S.No.	Bad habits	Description	Innovation
1	NIH ("Not Invented Here")	What others find out is useless. Belief in themselves.	Competitors come up with ideas and create new products and services
2	Cream a market	Skimming the cream to get high-profit.	Competitors focus on the bottom of the market and come up with low price products.
3	Quality confidence	Customers pay for the quality	Competitors develop reasonable quality products and occupy vacant positions in the market.
4	Maximize rather than optimize	Trying to satisfy every single user through the same product or service.	Competitors make products that cover the gaps left by the leader.

Ecological niche strategy:

The ecological niche strategy aims at making its successful practitioners immune to competition and unlikely to be challenged. There are three distinct niche strategies, each with its own requirements, its own limitations and its own risks:

- ***The toll-gate strategy*** – Developing a product or service that is critical in making some products or offering services.
- ***The specialty skill strategy*** – Developing a specialized skill and offering a service based on it for specific category of clients.
- ***The speciality market strategy*** – Making products or services that cater to the needs of a specific segment of market.

MARKET STANDING BASED STRATEGIES

Based on market standing companies can be categorized into five types as shown in Table 6.5.

Table 6.5 Market standing based strategies

S.No.	Position	Description	Innovation strategies
1	Leader	Companies associated with the established technology and large market share.	• Leapfrog attacker's technology, • Acquire attacker, • Strengthen existing business and wait for emergence of new business
2	Attacker	Companies that champion the emerging technology to gain leadership position	• Invest in R&D and innovation by setting autonomous units
3	Defender	Companies that look for alternate technology or market to save market position from the onslaught of leader.	• Divest • Hold • Mixed strategy

S.No.	Position	Description	Innovation strategies
4	Followers	Companies that adopt the new technology with imitations or licensing from leader.	• Imitation • Franchising
5	Nichers	Companies that find a small market and offer unique products.	• Unique product or process innovation

Strategies of leader:

Leaders in one generation of technology are seldom leaders in the next.

The phenomenon has been observed in many other industries. Here are a few examples:

- ❖ In the mid-1950s, leading firms in electronics included companies as RCA, Sylvania, Raytheon, and Westinghouse. Yet from 1955 to 1982, there was a remarkable shakeout brought on by the advent of the transistor.
- ❖ When mini-computers came along, upstart Digital Equipment became the leader, not IBM, the then-dominant computer company.
- ❖ Hindusthan Motors was leader with its ambassador in market till Maruti came into the market.

Leaders can face this challenge, according to Richard Foster, employing the following strategies:

- ***Leapfrog the attacker's technology*** – If the attacker is a small company with limited resources, full development of innovation may be slow in coming. The competitor with greater resources has an opportunity to get ahead of the innovating firm by spending more resources.
- ***Acquire the attacker*** – If the attacker's new technology appears poised to eat up your business, consider buying the attacker. If you follow this course, however, be sure to give the acquired company the autonomy it needs to succeed. Alternatively, consider licensing the attacker's technology.
- ***Wait for emergence of innovation*** – The company can continue to operate the existing business and serve current customers as the new business develops.

Strategies of Defender:

Companies that live off an established technology may choose one of the following options:

1. *Divest* – Abandon the business they already own, with all its cash flow and certainty and invest in the rival technology.
2. *Hold* – Work hard to make existing business better or useful to more customers.
3. *Mixed strategy* – Hold onto the existing business and begin investing in the new technology as a hedge against the future.

The third option seems logical, but it has practical problems:

- ❖ The company may not have the competencies to develop the new technology.
- ❖ The culture of the organization may not welcome the new technology.
- ❖ Existing customers may pressure the company to stay in the old business.

In many cases the best solution to these practical problems is for the established enterprise to develop the new technology within a separate subsidiary or operating unit.

Strategies of attackers:

Attackers are active in developing new technologies and innovative business models.

Hewlett Packard, DEC, Intel, Apple, Microsoft, Amgen, Southwest Airlines, Dell, Sun and eBay all set up innovation centres as small autonomous units and invested resources for developing innovations.

Follower strategy:

The three behaviors of the strategy are – (i) to upset the cart, (ii) to get noticed and (iii) to hitch-a-ride.

- ***First is to upset the cart.*** It means create innovations that the market leaders must address. The tactic is to force the leaders to change their standards to match with your innovations. This is exemplified by Google(TM). They are forcing the market leaders to change their perspective.
- ***Second, to get noticed introduce innovations.*** This tactic is often used by startups to position them for purchase by a market leader or to become a market leader by instilling new customer desires into the market.
- ***Finally is the hitch-a-ride strategy.*** They typically don't innovate nor challenge the industry with new ideas. They just plod along taking what they can get, changing very little and running along with every one else.

Nicher strategy:

It is the strategy of selling smaller quantities of a wider range of goods, designed to resonate with consumers' preferences and earn higher margins. In US, to support its decision to become a cost leader, JetBlue created a cost structure that would support low fares, without lowering service standards. JetBlue adopted a number of innovative measures on its flights. It decided not to serve meals on its flights, no matter what the distance or duration. An important factor in JetBlue's success was that it operated in a niche market, where it had no competition.

Suzuki unveiled a green version of its luxury sedan, Kizashi—the EcoCharge Concept, that works on gasoline and electricity. The Kizashi EcoCharge Concept is an innovative, eye-catching four-door sedan that illustrates Suzuki's global eco-mobility story and establishes the brand's effort to provide clean motoring technology.

ENVIRONMENT BASED STRATEGIES

Organizations facing uncertainty have two major dilemmas:

- Efficiency Vs. Creativity.
- Stability Vs. Uncertainty.

Organizations operating in stable environment encourage specialization, standardize outputs and increase their turnover. Thus they attain high levels of productivity and profitability and compete effectively with other firms. On the other hand, organizations operating in a dynamic environment experience high stress in responding to external and internal events, some of which are unpredictable and beyond their control. Managing uncertainty is the central feature of the management of these organizations.

In managing uncertainty, Pearson's (1991) uncertainty map shown in Figure 6.2 offers useful guidelines. Pearson divided uncertainty into two separate dimensions.

- ❖ Uncertainty about ends (What is eventual target of the activity or project?)
- ❖ Uncertainty about means (Process-how to achieve this target)

Based on the division he identified four strategies of innovation as explained in Table 6.6.

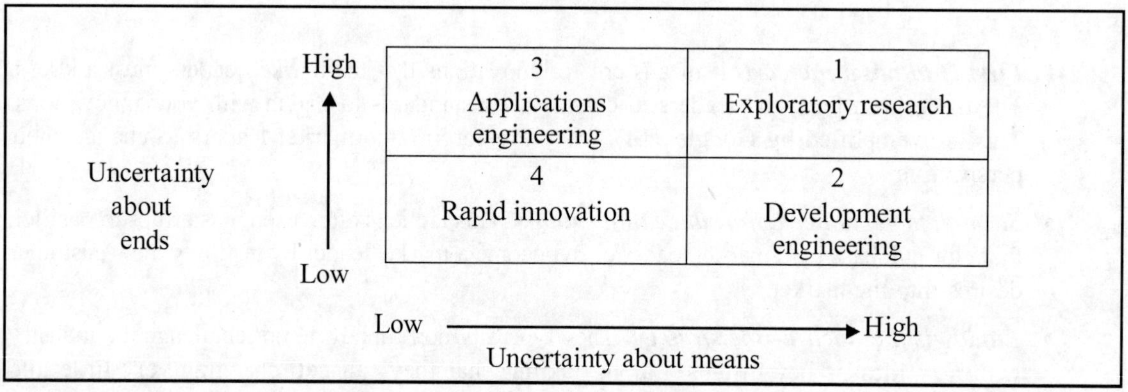

Figure 6.2 Pearson's Uncertainty map

Source: Narayanan, V.K, (2005), *Managing Technology and Innovation for Competitive Advantage,* Pearson Eduction (Singapore) Pte. Ltd. Delhi.

Table 6.6 Innovation Strategies based on environment

Base	Rapid innovation	Application engineering	Development engineering	Exploratory research
Environment	Stable	Less certain	Less uncertain	Uncertain
Orientation	Market	Market	Market	Laboratory
Managerial Needs	Matching technology with market	Create new Markets	Serving known Markets effectively	Exploration
Philosophy	Differentiation	Incrementalism	Incrementalism	Radical change
Technology (Process)	Known	Known	Unknown	Unknown
Output	Known	Unknown	Known	Unknown
Duration	Short	Long	Long	Very long
Critical aspect	Project management	Project management	Project management	Project choices

Exploratory research:

Also called 'blue sky' research because the work some times seems so far removed form reality that people liken it to working in the clouds. This is largely the domain of university and research laboratories. Large organizations, with adequate resources may fund this type of research. For them, the key question is: how to evaluate research in this area? Technical managers and commercial managers may hold different views on the value of a project. Continual and informal discussions are usually the best way to explore all possibilities fully and decide which one to drop and which one to support. There are many examples of wrong decisions in this regard.

Development Engineering:

Companies may initiate different projects centered on different technologies or different approaches to:

- ❖ Convert a new product concept into a real product.
- ❖ Improve existing product features and functional capabilities.
- ❖ Reduce costs of production and improve efficiency.

Thus the ends are clear. Only the means are uncertain. This is an ongoing activity in many firms. This activity requires special project management skills.

Application engineering:

It involves exploring the potential uses of known technology and serving new markets. The key questions are:

- ❖ What are the potential applications of the known technology?
- ❖ Which are ineffective due to cost or performance?
- ❖ Which are feasible?

For application engineering, also special project management skills are essential.

Rapid innovation:

In this situation, based on the existing technological capability existing products are improved or new products are created to tap market opportunity. Speed of development is critical because competition is both proactive and reactive. The key questions are:

- ❖ What are the emergent market expectations?
- ❖ Which of the expectations can be met by existing technology?
- ❖ How much time is needed for the innovation?

For this activity, scientists should have market-orientation. The development of new products and processes has enabled many firms to continue to grow in a competitive environment. A wide range of alternative innovative strategies is open for firms to choose depending on their resources, their heritage; their capabilities and aspirations. Four such strategies are described below. Table 6.7 explains them in the context of a PC industry.

- *Leader/offensive* – Companies having monopoly of the technology adopt this strategy. It requires a significant R&D activity and substantial marketing resources to promote the new product.
- *Follower/defensive* – This strategy is followed by companies, which have a substantial technology base and are agile in manufacturing, design and development and marketing. Followers imitate leaders and may develop improved version of the original.
- *Cost minimization/Imitative* – This strategy is based on imitation and low cost operation. Obviously, exceptional skills and capabilities in production and process engineering are required. Technology is often licensed from other companies, as the companies do not have a well-developed technology base.
- *Market segmentation specialization* – This strategy is based on meeting the precise requirements of a particular segment or niche. There is less need for changes in products. For example: Scottish Whisky manufacturers.

Table 6.7 Innovative strategies in the personal computer industry

Strategy	Characteristics	Examples of companies	Products
Leader/ offensive	Science/technology Intensive; High risk	Intel	Microchip
Follower/defensive	Strong technology Base. Agility in design and manufacturing	Apple	Macintosh and graphical-user Interface operating system personal computer (leader in mainframe)
		IBM	Regarded as market leader largely due to its range of PCs and additional features
Cost	Low-cost manufacture	Compaq	Low-cost PC
Minimization/ Imitative	Limited technology base	Research machines	Focus is on assembly of component parts
Market segmentation (Specialization)	Niche market	Research Machines Apple	Graphic design and education markets

PRINCIPLES

For aligning innovation and creativity to competitive strategy, it is important to consider the following aspects:

❖ **Strategic alignment** – Innovation and creativity need to be aligned to organizational values, which provide broad guidelines for adoption of principles, vision, mission and strategies.

- **Policy definition** – There should be a clear documented policy about innovation and creativity. Like how it is captured, how one should reward the best innovative ideas and the process of implementation.
- **Need focused** – Innovation should be focused and need-specific. The creativity must be directed to understanding and meeting the current and future needs of customers.
- **Talent based** – Innovation and creativity cannot be outsourced; hence emphasis should be on in-house talent. If it is outsourced, it loses its competitive strength as others can replicate it.
- **Idea generation** – All innovative ideas should be subjected to brainstorming and, if acceptable, should first be tried in pilot projects.
- **Benchmarking** – For risk hedging, innovative ideas can be benchmarked with other organizations. HLL may succeed in repositioning their 'Lifebuoy' by changing its attributes (from carbolic soap with an inbuilt health essence in it). Colgate is trying desperately to retain market share by increasing product variety. Each organization pursues a different way to win.
- **Implementation** – Implementation should be closely monitored, preferably by calculating Return On Investment (ROI), and should be institutionalized only after one sees success in pilot projects.

SUMMARY

Today we observe that, the major concerns of modern organizations are innovation, productivity and competitiveness. The business strategy sets the innovation context within which the marketer has to operate. Strategy making steps include: identify the mission, vision and goals, know the firm's posture, align innovation strategy with corporate strategy, establish innovation charter, apply portfolio thinking, state objectives of innovation, make aggregate project plan, organize for innovation, lead innovation effort and evaluate it. Innovation strategies as given by Drucker are: being fustest with mostest, hitting them where they ain't, finding and occupying a specialized ecological niche and changing economic characteristics of a product, market or industry. In addition we find market based and environment based strategies.

QUESTIONS

1. Examine, how innovation can be viewed as a strategy component?
2. Explain the process of developing innovation strategy.
3. Elaborate the four strategies suggested by Drucker.
4. Discuss the market standing based strategies of innovation.
5. Describe the environment based strategies of innovation.

EXERCISES

1. Form a group of four members. Visit local organizations – one retail shop, one manufacturing organization, one commercial bank and one educational institution. Inquire how they are strategizing to increase their profits. Compare their strategies with those of their close competitors and identify the innovative elements in them.

   Prepare a report for discussion in classroom.

2. Visit website of a company of your choice and find out their innovations. Gather further data from magazines and journals. Also write to the company and find out their innovative strategies. Make a report and present it in classroom.

CASE : TATA METALIKS: ORDINARILY EXTRAORDINARILY

Tata Metaliks is a company not willing to fall into the trap of viewing innovation as something that simply happens one fine morning, galvanizes a company and takes it to a higher level.

We define innovativeness as small — at times incremental, at others breakthrough — changes brought about with the involvement of all the employees all the time. "It comprises a large number of people making small improvements in what they are doing, instead of being confined to the research and development department or product development cell," says Harsh K. Jha, Managing director, Tata Metaliks.

Mr Jha believes that it is this approach that has opened many new business avenues and opportunities for the company whose primary product is pig iron.

When we recently exported our first consignment to Japan, the customer opened the container, had one look at the product and emailed us immediately. He was delighted with the consignment. "This Japanese customer has signed a long-term contract to be our exclusive agents," says he.

Tata Metaliks is the most profitable Mini Blast Furnace (MBF) operator in the country, it is also economic value-added positive. It was way back in 1999-2000 that Tata Metaliks decided to free itself from the commodity cycles. The management planned to make one-third its production in a niche that would not be dependent on these ups and downs.

"Once you are wedded to me on a certain product which meets your specific requirement exactly, you are unlikely to move out in a hurry," says Harsh Kumar, vice-president, marketing.

Product:

Keeping this in mind, Tata Metaliks has come up with product innovations that make customers stick with them. For the aluminium industry, it makes pig iron with very high levels of phosphorus. While most manufacturers take the level of phosphorus to 0.1, 0.2 or 0.25 per cent. Tata Metaliks takes it up to a whopping 1.6 per cent. As the company is probably among two or three entities to offer this mix, it has presence in markets like Egypt and Dubai, among others.

Similarly, as ultra-high silicon product is good for making softer and less brittle iron, Tata Metaliks offers a silicon percentage of 3.5, compared to the usual 2.5 or 2.7 per cent. "Smelters inform us that hardly anyone in the country does this," says Mr. Kumar, Tata Metaliks also offers to bundle other products that meet the customers' requirements along with the pig iron.

If what the customers consume coincides with what we ourselves buy, we supply it along with the pig iron? "That way we become a one-stop shop for them," says Mr. Kumar.

The company uses economies of scale in its own favour to purchase limestone and coke, which the company requires as well and offers these as a package to its customers.

Service:

It has also gone beyond product offerings to providing solutions for the foundries. It is helping the casting manufacturers optimize their charge mix in such a way that either their cost or their rate of rejections is reduced. It helps the customers improve the melt rates in their cupola and to decrease the SPN level or pollution. This is a first in the Indian pig iron industry. Most of the foundries the company caters to are small and operate on primitive technology. Tata Metaliks makes it its business to assist them with their technical inputs and problem solving.

We are transferring know-how to them free of cost. If the operator calls on us with a problem, we send our people down to debug it. "We have already built up a reputation for this service with our bigger customers," says Mr. Jha.

Interestingly, the MBF operator did not itself have the expertise to operate a foundry but has acquired it from consultants. Tata Metaliks also supports the foundry operator in the design of castings using software tools and computer simulations. The company is, in fact, planning ahead and even hiring foundry professionals. In the near future the company will look at building foundry parks, which can bring down manufacturing cost substantially for the foundries located close to the plant. Bundling product and service attributes together has also proved an effective and unconventional branding route for Tata Metaliks.

Operations:

Thinking laterally is, of course, not the reserve for product or service alone, but all areas of operations. Introduced electronic cheque writing in the accounts department and the entire activity is out sourced the entire activity to an international banker. Tata Metaliks is also ahead of competitors in the alertness and speed with which it tracks market intelligence.

For instance, if some MBF operator closes down, we can make a killing by being there to fill in the space he vacates," says Mr. Jha. "Thus, each of us has to think about how we, who have been doing this job for many years, can do it differently," says Mr. Ghosh.

Human resources:

For employees to become innovative, they have to be brought out of their burrows and shown the big picture. "Therefore, we decided that each and every employee would see all the steps of activity in the entire supply chain — from raw material to the customer's end," says Mr. Jha.

This process orientation to create knowledge employees started in April 2003 and ended in May 2004. The company has spent almost 2.5 times the usual amount on training and development. This is crucial in the context of the future for which the company is gearing up.

"The employee has to believe he can achieve all that we set out to do," says Mr. Jha. The company's objective is to 'reach tomorrow first'.

Tata Metaliks is not insecure about other entities catching up with it because it does not look at earth-shattering innovations but implementation and on constantly thinking on its feet for success. As long as there are many Archimedeses in this Metaliks pool, it is going to remain a '*eureka company*'.

Questions:

1. Examine the salient features of the competitive strategy of Tata Metaliks.
2. Can it be a "*eureka company*' in future if it continues the same strategy?

Chapter 7

Innovative Organization Structures

Learning Objectives

After you have studied this chapter, you will be able to...

- Describe organizational theories and structures suitable for innovation.
- Identify the traits of innovative organization.
- Know the factors influencing organizational design for innovation.

Structure

- Introduction
- Concepts
- Organizational Structures and Innovation
- Traits of Innovative Organization
- Organizing for Innovation
- Current Trends
- Factors Influencing Organizational Design
- Size Decisions
- Summary
- Questions
- Exercises
- Case Rallis : The Spectrum of Success

INTRODUCTION

During the first half of the Twentieth Century, managers viewed work specialization and efficiency as an important source of increased productivity and competitive advantage. Accordingly, organizations were structured on line, line-staff and committee bases. Managers in contemporary organizations are finding that these traditional hierarchical designs are unsuitable in the current environments of change and challenge. Market place demands are today for lean, flexible, responsive, learning and innovative organizations.

CONCEPTS

The importance of an organization structure in its ability to innovate has long been a major theme in the literature. Work groups don't exist in isolation. They are part of a larger organization.

A research team in Reddy Labs, for instance, must live within the rules and policies dictated from the division's headquarters and corporate offices.

What is meant by an organizational structure? Organization is a framework within which coordination takes place for the accomplishment of common goals. The challenge for managers is to design an organizational structure that allows employees work not only for effectiveness and efficiency but also for excellence.

ORGANIZATIONAL STRUCTURES AND INNOVATION

The organizational design is broadly influenced by the management view of how organization should be. Ever since Fredrick Winslow Taylor introduced scientific management in 1905, management has begun evolving with new concepts, tools and approaches. Three different philosophies that governed organization structure and their innovative capabilities are shown Table 7.1.

Table 7.1 Schools, organization structures and innovation capability

School	Tenets	Organization	Innovative ability
Classical	Division of work, specialization, centralization, chain of command and cooperation	Functional organization, (mechanistic and bureaucratic)	Rationalization. Operational improvements by study and experimentation.
Behavioural	Competences participation and empowerment of people	Committee, decentralization (partly organic)	Conformity for operational efficiency and creativity for incremental innovation organization wide.
Systems and contingency	Adaptation, integration, elaboration and coordination	Project and matrix (organic)	Emphasis on innovation as a key for growth

Strategic choice perspective:

The strategic choice perspective argues that, in any context, organizations can choose to be innovative or adaptive.

Jacob's study of four pairs of Indian organizations indicates that organizational design for innovativeness is a strategic choice of the management (1988). Each pair shared the same industry or activity or parent organization and yet one in the pair displayed relatively high innovativeness (corporate creativity) while the other one displayed a distinctly lower innovativeness. A striking difference was within a pair of advertising organizations, both based in Ahmedabad. The Reliance business group set up Mudra Communications in 1980; Bidhan Advertising, started a decade earlier, was a proprietorship. Mudra was highly entrepreneurial; Bidhan found a niche early in its life and stuck to it tenaciously.

Organizations may adopt a variety of structural designs depending upon the strategic choices they make. Strategic options may include growth options like innovation, diversification, integration and internationalization of operations or survival strategies like turnaround, cost minimization and limitation.

Table 7.2 shows the structural options for mangers of the different strategic choices . Innovators need the flexibility of the organic structure, while cost minimizers seek the efficiency and stability of the mechanistic structure in order to maintain tight controls and low costs in their current activities, while imitators create organic subunits to pursue new undertakings.

Table 7.2 The strategy-structure relationship

Strategic choices	Structural option
Cost minimization, productivity and efficiency	**Mechanistic:** Tight control. Extensive work specialization, High formalization, High centralization.
Imitation	**Mechanistic and organic**: Mix of loose with tight properties. Tight controls over current activities and looser controls for new undertakings.
Innovation	**Organic:** A loose structure. Low specialization, Low formalization, Decentralized.

Mechanistic Vs. Organic structures:

What are the characteristics of mechanistic and organic structures? How do they differ?

Burns and Stalker (1961) placed mechanistic and organic structures on a continuum. Table 7.3 shows the differences between them.

Table 7.3 Characteristics of mechanistic and organic structures

Mechanistic organizations	Organic organizations
Hierarchical structure, with stable divisions and departments based around functions	Flat structure with temporary workgroups/teams based around specific projects.
Narrow span of control and unity of command	Wide span of control
Vertical communication dominates	Lateral communication dominates

Mechanistic organizations	Organic organizations
Rigid job definitions set by senior management	Flexible job definitions, defined by individuals through interaction with colleagues.
Power and authority based on seniority in hierarchy	Power and authority changing with changing circumstances, based on individual skills and abilities.
Highly specialized groups	Cross-functional teams
High formalization and centralization	Low formalization and decentralization.
Suitable for less stress-threat situations, Routine and recurring problem solving for which solutions are often those used before	Suitable for high stress-threat situations, non-recurring and unprecedented problem solving for which solutions are novel.

TRAITS OF INNOVATIVE ORGANIZATION

Several studies have shed light on the organizational design needed for innovativeness.

Some of the studies are cited here.

Khandwalla (1985) studied 75 companies and found that pioneering innovative organizations are 50 per cent faster than the group of companies that were traditionally managed. There is emphasis on innovation and experimentation in all the operations of the organization, entrepreneurial risk taking, operating flexibility and hiring of creative youngsters with considerable operating responsibility and autonomy:

Khandwalla (1995) studied 90 Indian companies and identified three top management styles – entrepreneurial, organic and participative decision-making styles had the largest co-relations with the organization's rated innovativeness. The bureaucratic and the altruistic styles of management that stressed accountability have the largest number of significant correlations with organizational aids for implementing innovations and changes.

An American study on141 pairs of projects conducted by Teresa Amabile and associates (Amabile et al., 1995) found that 'creative' projects significantly outscored the 'uncreative' projects on the following aspects of workplace practices:

1. Greater challenge provided in work.
2. Greater encouragement to creativity.
3. Greater work group support to individuals.
4. Greater sense of autonomy as well as of ownership.
5. Greater encouragement provided by superiors to subordinates.

In another study, it was found that when people jointly identified work-related problems, there was not only greater feeling of participation but the solutions individuals found to problems tended to be more creative (Plunkett, 1990).

In a profile of innovative companies, Business Week noted how P&G, faced with a flat top-line, created a new innovation structure, with a vice-president for design, innovation and strategy and supplemented it by asking people from various design houses to sit on its "design boards", interact with divisional heads and, finally, consumers. This process reaped rich dividends, Swiffer, the dry mop being one good example. Who could have thought that the humble mop could be innovated upon? Noticing that standard wet mops created a mess and that dry rags offer better electrostatic attraction, designers created a radically new ergonomic and attractively colored design that gave P&G the next $1 billion potential winner.

Based on the above discussion , we can say that in designing the organizations for innovation and creativity, managers have to make sure that they are organic, flexible and lean. The organizational characteristics that facilitate innovation process can be summarised as shown in Table 7.4.

Table 7.4 Traits of innovative organization

S.No.	Trait	Description
1	Growth orientation	A commitment to long-term growth rather than short-term profit.
2	Vigilance	The ability of the organization to be aware of its threats and opportunities.
3	Commitment to technology	The willingness to invest in the long-term development of technology.
4	Acceptance of risk	The willingness to include risky opportunities in a balanced portfolio.
5	Cross-functional cooperation	Mutual respect among individuals and a willingness to work together across functions.
6	Receptivity	The ability to be aware of, to identify and to take effective advantage of externally developed technology (ideas and innovations).
7	Slack	An ability to manage the innovation dilemma and provide room for creativity.
8	Adaptability	A readiness to accept change.
9	Diverse range of skills	A combination of specialization and diversity of knowledge and skills.
10	Enthusiasm for knowledge	A respect and encouragement for accumulation of knowledge as a legitimate undertaking.
11	Drive to stay ahead	A commitment to stay ahead of capabilities. This drive to access the latest knowledge keeps people listening, another absolutely critical skill.
12	Tight coupling of complimentary skill sets	A respect for a knowledge basis other than one's own and enables flow of knowledge from research organizations into product development, whether the researchers reside inside a firm's laboratories or are outside entities such as think tanks or national laboratories.
13	Alternation in activities	A continual reexamination of assumptions through experimentation and further divisions. There is a "try it and learn it" attitude to counteract the arrogance of excellence.
14	Higher order teaming	A continual self-examination to discover insights within one activity that may be transferred to other activities within the firm. For example, firms often use project teams as mechanisms to generate higher-level process learning.

ORGANIZING FOR INNOVATION

Four different organizational mechanisms for stimulating and sustaining innovation are:

- Research organisations.
- Separate units for innovative activity.
- Project-based organization.
- New venture division.

Research organizations:

The creation of an R&D department or a central research laboratory is one of the common forms of promoting innovations.

For example, during the 1970s, Monsanto's vehicle for entry into the biotechnology sector was through the setting up of a corporate research and development facility in St. Louis.

The advantages of such mechanism are:

- *Commitment to innovation* – Such a set up signals that a firm is committed to building technological capability in pursuit of competitive advantage.
- *Innovation intelligence and research* – Helps trace the science and technology developments that could pose a threat or opportunity for the firm and establishes a means to gather, synthesize, and transfer scientific and technical information from the scientific community.
- *Focused effort for innovations* – Conducts focused research both basic and applied that is strategically aligned with the firm's efforts.
- *Generates Innovations* – Creates radically new process and product technologies that could be developed into new products and services.

Separate entrepreneurial unit:

Why an autonomous organization? Clayton Christensen put it this way in an interview about his book *The Innovator's Dilemma.*

With few exceptions, the only instance in which mainstream firms have successfully addressed a disruptive technology those in which the firm's managers set up an autonomous organization charged with building a new and independent business around the disruptive technology. Such organizations, free of the power and influence of the mainstream company's customers, can align themselves with a different set of customers — those who want the product of the disruptive technology.

Dangers:

The business formed around the disruptive technology faces the danger of being killed, undermined, or sold by internal rivals and nay Sayers. The reasons may be as follows:

❖ The concerns of the established business and of the new business are poles apart.

- The new business will be evaluated by mangers of the mainstream business by their standards, which are profits and efficiency. The new business typically fails to meet any of the standards of the mainstream business.
- The day-to-day concerns of these managers are diametrically opposed to those required by the innovative business.

As a result, the mainstream managers may say, "This is draining investment funds from our profitable businesses. It has potential, but not for us. Let's find a buyer."

Another danger, is that these autonomous operations will be absorbed back into the parent organization as soon as they show signs of success — before they reach a point of self-sustaining development.

Benefits:

Though entrepreneurial firms are generally weak in terms of brand recognition, manufacturing, and financing in their early stages, they often enjoy substantial advantages. Here are the most important:

- *An undivided focus* – Managers of upstart companies spend little time on internal operations and people issues: There are very few of either. Instead, they devote most of their attention to development of the technology or business model.
- *An ability to attract talent* – Capable technical and managerial talents are often attracted to new ideas with promising futures, especially when stock options are a significant portion of compensation.
- *They are not captives of powerful customer* – Many established companies fail to make the leap to the new technology because powerful customers persuade them to continue doing what they are doing. This is what happened to Goodyear Tire and Firestone when radial tire technology appeared. Not wanting to change their suspension design, the Big Three U.S. automakers urged their suppliers to stick with bias ply tires. Michelin, which had no supplier relationship with the Big Three, pressed forward, establishing leadership in the field. Attackers are seldom the pawns of customers.
- *Little bureaucracy* – Almost by definition, small entrepreneurial companies are unencumbered by the bureaucracy that burdens their larger rivals. That makes them fast and flexible.
- *No need to protect investments in unrelated skills or assets* – Established companies can find many reasons to not adopt new technologies or business models: "We can't sell it though our existing distribution network." "It would cannibalize our current sales." "We just invested $50 million in facilities to manufacture our current product." "Our salespeople wouldn't understand it; they'd have to be retrained." Attackers seldom have such concerns.

Project Organization:

Companies engaged in the tasks of creating new products or embedding new technologies in the value chain, usually take the form of projects. Projects require team efforts, because they need to bring together technical talent from diverse disciplines (as in the case of building the space shuttle) or functions (as in the case of the cross-disciplinary teams in new product development processes).

Project set up can be either *ad hoc* or permanent. Projects are in general initiated on an *ad hoc* basis for creating a specific innovation. However, some projects may become permanent to sustain innovation. There are two forms of permanent project organizations utilized by firms: (1) matrix organizations and (2) quasi-structure.

Matrix Organization:

During the late 1950s and 1960s, the project organization called the matrix structure evolved within the aerospace industry, partly stimulated by the Department Of Defense (DOD). Having been enormously impressed by the performance of the DOD project control system during the 1950s, DOD began to require that all defense contract proposals be accompanied by a similar project control system.

Some projects require high level of technical skills and undivided focus on innovation effort. This meant that an organization that shared a dual focus had to be developed. Matrix organization was a natural response. It is a combination of the project organization with functional organization. It handles more easily project control than a functional organization, because matrix managers can focus exclusively on project progress without worrying about developing technical skills.

Quasi-structure:

High-tech firms prefer quasi-structure, as they have to continuously innovate for survival.

Firms such as Intel, National Semiconductor, Texas Instruments, Hewlett-Packard and Motorola have found that matrix organizations often tend to create more problems than they solve. Hence, they have reverted to an organizational form with clear organizational reporting relationships. These firms maintain a formal structure as well as quasi-formal structure.

There are four major characteristics of quasi-structures:

1. *Stable formal structure* – It provides guidance to the employees. The defined, explicit reporting relationships maintain internal predictability in the midst of frequent product and manufacturing process changes.
2. *Frequent reorganization* – Innovating organizations reorganize frequently and employees have come to regard structural change as a part of life in these companies.
3. *Participative changes* – The process by which this reorganization is accomplished is substantially participative. Although the members of the top-management team may sketch the major skeletal changes in the structure, the group and the division levels detail the reorganized structure jointly.
4. *Temporary structures* – There is an extensive use of committees, task forces, teams and dotted-line relationships.

New Venture Division:

Firms often create a New Venture Division (NVD). The NVDs are desirable for the following reasons:

- *To locate radical innovations* – Radical product innovations sometimes coming out of R&D departments and central research units cannot be linked to existing departments. To alleviate this problem, NVDs decouple the new ventures from the established spheres of business operations and seek to move their development to a congenial place.

- *To pursue innovation with vigor* – The NVD provides an internal-to-the-firm environment in which new business opportunities can be explored, incubated, turned into projects and provided with the opportunity to demonstrate economic viability.
- *To create innovation climate* – Generally, NVDs are staffed and managed differently from the regular operating organization. NVDs allow more entrepreneurship and attract more risk-takers; the rewards are based on the success of the venture, not on predictable milestones as in an operating division. Table 7.5 provides differences between NVD and operating division.

Table 7.5 Differences between New Venture Division and Operating division

Dimensions	NVD	Operating Division
Span of control	Wide	Narrow
Job descriptions	Loose	Detailed
Controls	Loose	Tight
Planning Frequency	Frequent	Infrequent
Planning Detail	Low	High
Time Frames	Long	Short
Size of Reward	Large	Small
Compensation	Deferred	Current
Performance Criteria	Innovation and risk taking	Current profits

Merits and demerits:

The three models of organization – Separate units, Project organization and New Venture Divisions – have their own merits and demerits as given in Table 7.6.

Table 7.6 Merits and Demerits of Three Innovative Organizations Types

Organization	Merits	Demerits
Separate	Easier to manage, given the clarity of relationship.	Less efficient and flexible. Attention is required to develop customer focus and integration with business operations.
Project	Achieves efficiency and stability. Quasi structures accomplish greater customer focus and integration.	Dual authority and lack of clarity in relationships in matrix type. Quasi-structures need to be supported by strong cultures.
NVD	High degree of customer focus and business integration.	Relatively less flexible. They can focus only on the markets for which they are conceived.

CURRENT TRENDS

Constant innovations in information and computer technologies combined with the globalization of markets have created a chaotic world. As a result, many of the earlier principles and mechanisms no longer apply. Successful organizations of Twenty first Century must be able to learn and respond quickly. They must be capable of innovating to meet the diverse needs of people in different cultures. In this direction, new trends in organizing are found. We will discuss three new forms of organizing.

- Virtual organization.
- Boundary less organization.
- Learning organization.

Virtual Organization:

Virtual organization is also known as network *or modular organization.* It is typically a small, core organization that out sources major business functions. In structural terms, the virtual organization is highly centralized, with little or no departmentalization. A virtual organization creates networks of relationships that allow it to contract out manufacturing, distribution, marketing or any other business function where management feels that others can do it better or more cheaply. Companies like Nike, Reebok, Liz Claiborne, Emerson Radian and Dell Computer are just a few of the thousands of companies that have found that they can do hundreds of millions of dollars in business without owning manufacturing facilities.

The major advantage to the virtual organization is its flexibility. For instance, it allows someone with an innovative idea and little money, such as Michael Dell and his Dell Computer firm, to successfully compete against large companies like IBM.

Boundary less Organization

General Electric chairman, Jack Welch, coined the term boundary less organization to describe his idea of what he wanted GE to become. By removing vertical boundaries, management flattens the hierarchy. Status and rank are minimized. The organization looks more like a silo than a pyramid, where the grain at the top is no different than the grain at the bottom. Cross-hierarchical teams (which include top executives, middle managers, supervisors and operative employees), participative decision-making practices and the use of 360-degree performance appraisals (where peers and others above and below the employee evaluate his or her performance) are examples of what GE is doing to break-down vertical boundaries.

Functional departments create horizontal boundaries. The way to reduce these barriers is to replace functional departments with cross-functional teams and to organize activities around processes.

For instance, xerox now develops new products through multidisciplinary teams that work in a single process instead of around narrow functional tasks. Similarly, some AT&T units are now doing annual budgets based not on functions or departments but on processes such as the maintenance of a worldwide telecommunications network.

Another way management can cut through horizontal barriers is to use lateral transfers and rotate people into and out of different functional areas. This turns specialists into generalists. When fully operational, the boundary less organization also breaksdown barriers to external constituencies and barriers created by geography. Globalization, strategic alliances, supplier-organization and customer-organization linkages and telecommuting are all examples of practices that reduce external boundaries.

Coca-Cola, for instance, sees itself as a global corporation, not a U.S. or Atlanta company. Firms like NEC Corp., Boeing and Apple Computer each have strategic alliances or joint partnerships with dozens of companies.

These alliances blur the distinction between one organization and another as employees work on joint projects. The one common technological thread that makes the boundary less organization possible is a networked computer. They allow people to communicate across intra-organizational and inter-organizational boundaries. Electronic mail, for instance, enables hundreds of employees to share information with senior executives. Inter-organizational networks now make it possible for Wal-Mart suppliers like Procter & Gamble and Levi Strauss to monitor inventory levels of laundry soap and jeans, respectively, because P&G's and Levi's computer systems are networked to Wal-Mart's system.

Learning Organization:

A learning organization is an organization that has developed the continuous capacity to adapt and change. Just as individuals learn, so too do organizations.

Xerox, Coming, Federal Express, Ford, General Electric, Motorola, and Wal-Mart, are among those firms, which have learning focus. Many leading IT companies like Wipro, Satyam and Infosys in India are having knowledge management focus and learning resources centers to enhance learning of their employees.

Most organizations engage in what has been called single-loop learning. When errors are detected, the correction process relies on past routines learning. When an error is detected, it is corrected in ways that involve the modification of the organization's objectives, policies and standard routines. Double-loop learning challenges deep-rooted assumptions and norms within an organization. In this way, it provides opportunities for radically different solutions to problems and dramatic jumps in improvement.

Box 7.1 and Figure 7.1 present the characteristics of a learning organization. It's an organization where people put aside their old ways of thinking, learn to be open with each other, understand how their organization really works, form a plan or vision that everyone can agree upon and then work together to achieve that vision.

Box 7.1 Characteristics of a Learning Organization

1. There exists a shared vision, which everyone agrees on.
2. People discard their old ways of thinking and the standard routines they use for solving problems or doing their jobs.
3. Members think of all organizational processes, activities, functions and interactions with the environment as part of a system of interrelationships.
4. People openly communicate with each other (across vertical and horizontal boundaries) without fear of criticism or punishment.
5. People sublimate their personal self-interest and fragmented departmental interests to work together to achieve the organization's shared vision.

Source: Based on P.M. Senge, *The Fifth Discipline* (New York: Doubleday, 1990).

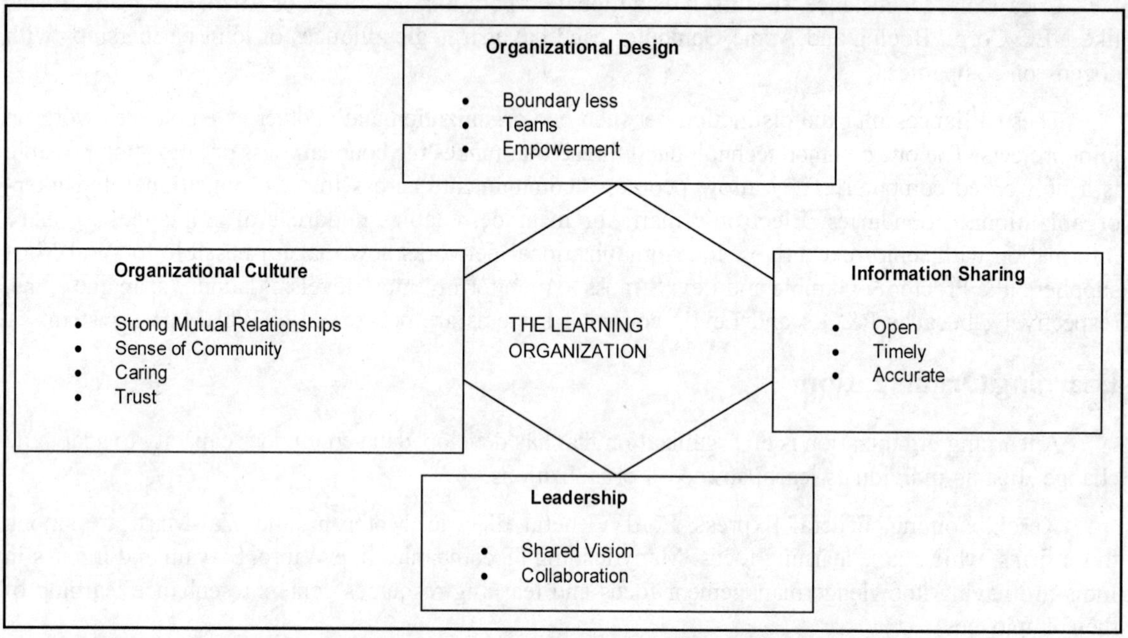

Figure 7.1 Characteristics of a Learning Organization

Source: Based on P.M. Senge. *The Fifth Discipline: The Art and Practice of Learning Organizations* (New york: Doubleday.1990): and R.M. Hodgetts, F.Luthans and S.M. Lee. "New Paradigm Organizations: From Total Quality to Learning to World Class." *Organizational Dynamics*. Winter 1994. pp.4-19.

The differences between Learning organization and Traditional organization are highlighted in Table 7.7.

Table 7.7 Traditional Vs. Learning organization

Aspect	Traditional organization	Learning organization
Operational focus	Specialization. It fragments different functions into independent and often warring fiefdoms.	Cross-disciplinary learning resulting in integration.
Relations	Competition oriented. Reduces opportunities for collaboration.	Collaboration for synergistic outcomes.
Response	Reactiveness leading to problem solving.	Proactiveness leading to innovative solutions.
Values	Risk moderation, closed approach and stability.	Risk taking, openness and growth.
Conflict	Encourages conformity and resolves conflict to enhance cohesiveness.	Supports the importance of disagreements, constructive criticism and other forms of functional conflict
Leadership	Transactional. States Vision for others to know and Controls others.	Transformational. Shares Vision with others and enables others.

Aspect	Traditional organization	Learning organization
Attitude toward change	If it's working, don't change it.	If you aren't changing, it won't be working for long.
Attitude toward new ideas	If it was n't invented here, reject it.	If it was invented or reinvented here, reject it.
Main fear	Making mistakes.	Not learning, not adopting
Competitive advantage	Products and services.	Ability to learn, knowledge and expertise.
Responsible for innovation	Mainly R&D.	Everyone in organization.

FACTORS INFLUENCING ORGANIZATIONAL DESIGN

The organizational design is influenced by environmental, strategic and economic and globalization factors.

Environmental factors:

The organization should be sensitive to the more salient of the two environmental sectors: Market and Technology. Figure 6.2 shows the choices under different conditions.

- When the technology sector is more salient, that is, technological developments lead to later market development; corporate research centers seem to be appropriate.
- When market development is the salient activity, especially in the case of mature technologies, new venture divisions can serve as appropriate organizational mechanisms.
- When both market and technology assume saliency, the traditional matrix may be appropriate, especially when the rate of change in the technology and market sectors is relatively moderate.
- Quasi-structures seem to have amassed in high-technology industries where, in addition to technology the market dynamics have been relatively fast.

MARKETSALIENCE

TECHNOLOGY SALIENCE	*High*	*Medium*	*Low*
High	Quasi-Structures Separate unit for innovative activity	Matrix Separate unit for innovative activity	*Ad hoc* project teams Separate unit for innovative activity
Medium	NVD Separate unit for innovative activity	Matrix/NVD R&D units	*Ad hoc* teams
Low	Strategic business unit	*Ad hoc* teams	*Ad hoc* project teams

Figure 7.2 Organizational choices under different market and technology situations.
Source: V.K. Narayana(2001), *Technology and Innovation for Competitive Advantage*, Pearson Education (Singapore) Pvt. Ltd., New Delhi.

Strategy factors:

Corporate strategy of a firm has a major influence in the overriding organizational framework that it adopts for its functioning.

1. *Innovation mix:* When a firm decides to carry out basic and applied research, the development may be carried out in an operating division and basic research in a central facility. Process development may, in turn, be carried in close proximity to the manufacturing centers of the firm.

2. *Diversification:* When a firm diversifies it may opt for decentralization of R&D, with R&D being relocated within the various divisions.

3. *Radical innovations:* When a firm chooses to pursue radical innovation strategy, it opts to set up a separate unit for research.

Economic factors:

Large multidivisional corporations or large companies with multiple product lines, face the question of where they should locate their innovative activity: Should the activity be decentralized and located in the divisions or centralized and located in a central research facility? The arguments for centralization and decentralization are given in Table 7.8.

Table 7.8 Merits of Centralization and Decentralization

Factor	Centralization	Decentralization
Economies of scale and scope	High	Low
Infrastructure economies	More	Less
Internal communication links	Good	Average
Long-term focus	Yes. Can pursue original ideas. Undertake long-term basic research.	No. Preoccupation with short-term. Responsive to local needs.
Networking with other research agencies	Better chances. Can tie-up with universities and other labs.	Fewer chances.
Focus	Overall.	Tailor-made to actual needs of a division.
Location benefits	No.	Yes. Can tap into government aid and incentives.
Special talented people	May not be encouraged.	Can be encouraged.
Competitive surveillance	General.	Specific to certain localities.

However, these benefits of centralization need to be weighed against the benefits of decentralization. With the developments in communication technology (e-mail, video-conferencing, etc.) and the growing emphasis by firms on commercially oriented research a decentralized pattern of innovative activity is preferred.

Globalization factor:

Globalization has led to multinational operations and corporations have begun to locate research facilities abroad. The reasons for these decisions are obvious.

- To tap into pools of scientific and technical labor.
- To have low-cost research basis.
- To secure cross-cultural integration.

Hoechst's establishment of overseas R&D activities was the result of their desire to benefit form the balance of foreign chemists and pharmacologists as well as the need to be part of those communities at the forefront of pharmaceutical research.

The three ways in which R&D laboratories have been set up abroad are:

1. The direct establishment of a research facility on a site on its own or with existing corporate facilities.
2. Indirectly through the acquisition of an overseas company.
3. As an evolutionary process associated with overseas manufacturing and other facilities.

The coordination among the research centers set up in different nations can be accomplished by two means:

1. *Cross – border teamwork* – This involves the research staff located at two or three different countries working on the same project.
2. *Use of information and communication technologies* – The increasing use of shared databases, electronic mail, media conferencing and workstation technology has enabled companies to explore ways in which research and innovation can be undertaken between separate sites.

SIZE DECISIONS

One important aspect concerning organizational design is size decision. There are plenty of large companies that have done well as entrepreneurs and innovators.

- In the United States, there is Johnson & Johnson in hygiene and health care, 3M in highly engineered products for both industrial and consumer markets. Citibank, America's and the world's largest non-governmental financial institution, well over a century old, has been a major innovator in many areas of banking and finance.
- In Germany, Hoechst-one of the world's largest chemical companies and more than 125 years old by now-has become a successful innovator in the pharmaceutical industry.
- In Sweden, ASEA, founded in 1884 and for the last sixty or seventy years a very big company, is a true innovator in both long-distance transmission of electrical power and robotics for factory automation.

However, some companies believed that innovative effort require different policies, rules and measurements in many areas.

The earliest example of this was set up more than one hundred years ago, in 1872, by Hefner-Alternexk, the first college-trained engineer hired by a manufacturing company anywhere, the German Siemens Company. Hefner started the first "research lab" in industry. Its members were charged with inventing new and different products and produces. But they were also responsible for identifying new and different end uses and new and different markets. They not only did the technical work; they were responsible for development of the manufacturing process, for the introduction of the new product into the marketplace and for its profitability.

Johnson & Johnson (J&J) has developed a remarkable record for developing new products by structuring itself more like a small entrepreneurial firm. "We don't view ourselves as a big company," says its chairman, Ralph Larsen. "We view ourselves as 160 small companies."

In case of large organization, the obstacles to innovation stem from the following difficulties:

Resistance to change:

Very large organizations foster resistance to change. A large corporation is a formalized structure, which maintains and manages the successes of the past. Procedures have been designed to achieve efficiency in "doing what we do best." Innovation disrupts the stable state of corporate society, interfering with the corporation's vigorous and continuing efforts to be efficient at what it does. Innovation thus meets a wall of resistance to change.

Threat to current success:

Innovation may become a threat to the current successes. New products often cannibalize the existing one. As such, large corporations are reluctant to innovate in areas, which would compete with their already existing products, markets, and/or technologies.

Conservative subordinates:

In the rigid hierarchy the relationship of boss and subordinate may lead to conservatism. Subordinates who take risks are exposed to the possibility of bad outcomes. Since bosses tend to spend more time worrying about problems than thinking about successes, bad outcomes are more likely to be noticed and remembered than good outcomes. At higher levels, where subordinates and bosses have even less frequent contact, negative consequences of risk-taking by subordinates may be more pronounced. The innovative people are not as likely to be promoted and rewarded in a large corporation, as are their more conservative counterparts. As a result, large corporations tend to develop and foster conservatism.

Confined to limited area of business:

Large organizations manage by MBO and if innovation is not included in the list of goals, it will be avoided for good. When development work goes on within a corporate divisional structure, may division business charters sometimes cut off potentially successful innovations because they do not match the current narrow objectives of that division.

Separate functional identities:

Functional integration is essential for innovation. In large organizations, a tendency to build functional empires is not uncommon. For instance, marketing and production are usually separated in large organizations because specialization is believed to enhance efficiency. It leads to a "propose and dispose syndrome," where each function is free to propose something which must be disposed of or acted upon, by the other function. It is difficult for one function to sell its idea to the other. The result is conservative moves that satisfy the minimal vision of both functions.

Politics:

The politics of large organizations can lead to compromises that decrease the effectiveness of attempts at innovation. The balance of organizational power can lead to other difficulties, ones exemplified by the old adage that "a camel is a horse designed by a committee." V. Stefflre observes that new product champions sometimes try to form a coalition of committed advocates to a project by delegating out selected something that they personally want.

Short-term focus:

The largest firms tend to develop short-term focus for two reasons.

- *Annual financial performance measures* - Large organizations use management control systems which emphasize financial measures-profits, ROI and soon on yearly basis. But the payoff from innovation is typically at least five or more years.
- *Short-run perspective of executives* - The rotation system of training managers at large corporations develops a short-run perspective in managers. Assignments for fast track, bright managers are seldom made for more than two years. Thus, these individuals do not see innovations as being within their horizons on any particular assignment.

Failure to see opportunity:

Frequently, large corporations view a given market opportunity as too small to be interesting. However, these small market niches sometimes mushroom into sizable markets over time when proper market development is practiced. Spin-off firms are often started by individuals who leave a large firm because it does not allow them to pursue an innovative project. Sometimes these spin-offs become very successful.

The Control Data Corporation is a prime example. CDC was a spin-off from the Univac division of Sperry Rand in 1957; now CDC dwarfs its parent organization.

Incrementalism:

Large firms have marketing departments that follow, rather, than lead, the market. Too much reliance is placed on market surveys, consumer questionnaires and test panels for new product ideas, the tendency is to develop incremental product improvements or changes in existing products rather than to develop new products for which there may be no readily perceived or existing market.

Acquisition focus:

Equipped with vast resources, large organizations take acquisition route for growth. Such a strategy discourages innovation in-house.

SUMMARY

The importance of an organization structure in its ability to innovate has long been a major theme in the literature. Market place demands are today for lean, flexible, responsive, learning and innovative organizations. Organic structures that are loose and decentralized structures with low specialization and low formalization are desirable for innovation. Organizational design is established as a critical strategic choice of managers. In designing the organizations for innovation and creativity, managers have to make sure that they are organic, flexible and lean. Three different organizational mechanisms for stimulating and sustaining innovation are: Separate units for innovative activity, Project-based organization and New venture division. In the direction, new trends in organizing are found. Such of the three new forms of organizing are: virtual organization, boundary less organization and learning organization. The organizational design is influenced by environmental, strategic economic and globalization factors. One important aspect concerning organizational design is size decision. There are plenty of large companies that have done well as entrepreneurs and innovators. However, in case of large organizations, the obstacles to innovation stem from the following difficulties: resistance to change, threat to current success, conservative subordinates, confined to limited area of business, separate functional identities, politics, short-term focus, failure to see opportunity, incrementalism and acquisition focus.

QUESTIONS

1. Explain, how innovation is valued in the three major organizational theories?
2. Explain the traits of an innovative organization. How do you organize for innovation?
3. What are the latest organization structures? Do they facilitate innovation?
4. Examine the factors that influence organizational design for innovation.
5. 'Large organizations cannot compete with small ones when it comes to innovation'. Do you agree?

EXERCISES

Take any four organizations of your choice like Wipro, Infosys, Dell and Sony and study their innovations. Also find out their organization structures and relate them to their innovative capabilities.

CASE RALLIS : THE SPECTRUM OF SUCCESS

Any manager will tell you that a company needs to plan quantum leaps in product, process and profit to be on the growth path. To this end, and in order to stay ahead of competition, Rallis India has celebrated many successes and also derived many well-learnt lessons from its failures.

"We introduce at least two new products every year, apart from concepts in marketing and production to stay on top of the development curve," says Dr.Mithyantha, Vice-president (R&D), Rallis Research Center. "Invention and exploitation is innovation," he says.

People power:

To get the formula right, innovative marketing and problem solution practices are captured through Innogate, an HR initiative, which in itself is innovative. Rallis India devised Innogate, to encourage people to generate, capture and implement new ideas in marketing and production. The system aimed at inspiring the organisational community to innovate, which in turn enhanced the organization's capability of sharing knowledge and ensured proper recognition of idea originators. The system operates in a networked environment and is user-friendly.

In the last two years since its implementation, a series of suggestions have been posted by employees. These concepts are filtered through an Innogate manager before presenting them to the board," says Mithyantha. "These suggestions have affected cost reduction, improved delivery systems and developed existing products.

The company, one of the agro majors in the country, operates in a highly competitive market. Products and operations are bound by statutory requirements of the government. This necessitates evolving strategies to counter the competition and also to comply with the regulations. The various options include introducing new products regularly.

To meet this challenge, Rallis embarked on New Product Development (NPD). The systematic introduction of the product with the combined efforts of employees across the company enables cost reduction and compression of time without compromising on the quality of the product. The products identified are taken through the conceptual 'innovation funnel,' which critically reviews the products to check various aspects such as market potential, cost efficiency, techno-feasibility, bio-efficacy, safety of the product to humans and the environment, etc.

Innogate also acts as a bonding exercise across the company. The essence of Innogate is capturing and prioritizing development of new products and services to add value to the customer. "By addressing the needs of the customer, the practice enables creating satisfied and loyal customers, which in turn helps the company in the market place," adds Mithyantha.

Lessons from experience:

Rallis carried out successful product innovations, the important ones being *Hexaconazole* and *Imidacloprid.* Rallis' foray into *rodenticide* with *Bromadiolone*, however, proved unsuccessful. *Thiophante-methyl,* a fungicide, was also a failed enterprise by Rallis. Rallis derived an important learning from this experiment. The company now understood importance of product positioning. It was erroneous to position Thiophante-methyl as a substitute to Captafol. "We learnt to work from the field backwards," says Mithyantha. "The failure was the result of a lack of marketing feedback to R&D. Since this experiment, the marketing and R&D units began working closely. Today a product is conceptualized and critically examined by the marketing department before it is put on the market development".

Questions:

1. Examine the organizational arrangements for innovation in the firm.
2. Suggest ways to improve organizational effectiveness in delivering more innovations.

Chapter 8

Making Organization Creative

Learning Objectives

After you have studied this chapter, you will be able to...

- Know the characteristics of innovative organization
- Identify the creativity crushers
- Explain, how innovation can be fostered in organizations

Structure

- Introduction
- Characteristics of Creative Organization
- Creativity Crushers
- Creating Creative Organization – 7S Framework
- Summary
- Questions
- Exercises
- Case: Institutionalized Learning to Compete

INTRODUCTION

Creativity does not occur easily and automatically. The choice and design of right structure is the starting point for making an organization creative and pioneer in innovative products and processes. The major task of management is making people in the organization strive for excellence by way of creative thinking and innovative practices. As such, establishing enterprising and challenging environment and leadership is essential to nurture and foster creativity in organizations.

CHARACTERISTICS OF CREATIVE ORGANIZATION

Peters, Waterman (1982), in a study of successful US companies, discuss the attributes that characterize the innovative companies.

- *People*: Autonomy and entrepreneurship, a bias for action, for getting on with it. Productivity through people. Respect for individual.
- *Attitude*: Value-driven, hands-on, leadership and management support.
- *Organization*: Simple form, lean staff, centralized and decentralized.
- *Market*: Stay close to the customers, stick to the knitting. Stay close to the business you know.

CREATIVITY CRUSHERS

There exist several forces that negate creativity. The principal ones relate to the values and attitudes of managers and employees.

Management is science:

Management is still regarded as a science-in the old-fashioned Newtonian or Aristotelian sense of the word-by most of the people who practice it. This dictates that there is a right or wrong answer to everything, that the solutions to management problems are reached by rigorous examination and analysis, and that everything is understandable over time and therefore ultimately controllable. This attitude feeds into not only high strategy but also day-to-day work. It creates a culture in which individuals do not open their mouths.

Pressure of today:

Drawing inspiration from the world outside is important to employees. But the opportunity to reflect on and tap into these influences is constrained or cut-off altogether by workplace stress, over-long hours and a form of presenteeism that is being extended from the office to the home by mobile phones and home computers linked into office e-mail systems. The higher an individual rises in the organization, the more these pressures grow and in terms of an individual's creative capability, they are proven killers.

Apathy of employees:

Companies face the risk of psychological withdrawal or "work to rule". It seems obvious, that people cannot be ordered to think on behalf of the company. At times of particularly focused change-a merger, a relocation, a global expansion –in which their roles or jobs are likely to be under review, individuals may either be too stressed to think creatively (psychological withdrawal) or too calculating to pass on ideas that might be put to better use elsewhere (psychological work to rule).

Friendships

Friendship is nowadays increasingly work-based. It may fuel more productive creative exchanges, underpinned by trust and openness. Yet as some cases show, division of loyalties, particularly in projects involving a number of suppliers or stakeholders, can result in the slow downs.

CREATING CREATIVE ORGANIZATION: 7S FRAMEWORK

Making creativity an organizational resource implies redesigning the components of an organization for innovation. Mckinsey's 7-s framework (Peters and Waterman, 1982) will be useful for deciding on the kind of initiatives to be taken. Table 8.1 shows them.

Table 8.1 Creating Creative organization

No.	Subsystem	Innovative features
1	Structure	Organic, that evolves and grows. Flexible, that accommodates new approaches and systems. Flat, that provides opportunity for teamwork and participative style of management. Decentralized, that gives autonomy for individual decision-making. Open, that has symbiotic relationship with environment. Fragmented, that divides into small groups (like quality circles
2	Strategy	Innovation strategies-radical and incremental (Product, process ,value chain and administrative
3	Systems	Planning systems that highlight innovation needs and priorities and allocate funds for experimentation. Communication systems that keep every one aware of innovation goals, policies and facilitate mutual exchange of information on innovation efforts. Information and knowledge systems that provide free access to gain awareness and knowledge in areas of interest. Appraisal systems that give value to innovation effort and outcomes. Motivation systems that reward and encourage innovators. Control systems that evaluate ideas and projects on a continual basis to ensure desired results. Authority systems to give go or no-go signals to ideas and projects at different levels.

No.	Subsystem	Innovative features
4	Shared value-	Being the best. The importance of people as individuals. Superiority of quality and service. Organizational members as innovators. Importance of informality to enhance communication. Importance of economic growth and profits. Change is law of life. Originality and newness are valuable.
5	Styles	High orientation towards work excellence among the organization members. High orientation towards duty among the organization members. High orientation towards cooperation among the organization members in the performance of their tasks, based on mutual trust and regard.
6	Staff	Hard working and entrepreneurial type of persons. Work force diversity.
7	Skill	Lateral and divergent thinking skills. Integration skills.

DESIGN RIGHT STRUCTURE

1. Create Ambidextrous Organization:

Operations and creative pursuits are two very different games and few companies play both games well. Success in the current business is usually driven by certainty, efficiency and cost control; the future business, on the other hand, is the product of an innovation process that is uncertain, inefficient and costly. Not many executives can operate successfully in these two very different worlds. Most are so absorbed with the current business that the future business is treated as a stepchild.

Michael Tushman and Charles O'Reilly propose that successful leaders of innovation create "ambidextrous" organizations—that is, organizations that can "get today's work done more effectively and also anticipate tomorrow's discontinuities."

2. Minimize Bureaucracy:

For ideas to become innovations, create an open, less bureaucratic organization.

The open, decentralized organization created by founders William Hewlett and David Packard had been highly encouraging to innovators and had put the company at the forefront of many emerging product categories. But the retirement of the founders, new management and enormous business growth resulted in a more centralized and bureaucratic organization. People with innovative ideas now found that they had to gain approvals from many layers of committees before they could move forward. The result was marked slowdown in new product introductions and plummeting profits. Thankfully, the company's aging founders intervened, broke up the bureaucratic tangle and returned HP to its characteristic idea-friendly ways. A huge leap in new product introductions followed—as did profits.

3. Right Structure for Collaboration:

David Falvey Executive director of the British Geological Survey, which has its headquarters in Keyworth, Nottingham, United Kingdom, observed that organization structures should facilitate collaboration. Narrating his experience he says:

When I joined the British Geological Survey in 1998, I found a hierarchical organization structured around the various disciplines and sub-disciplines in geology. These had developed into competing empires and collaboration on creative approaches to a customer problem was, at worst, unthinkable, and at best, forced.

I created a matrix structure. A programme, headed by a manager, would be responsible for a range of projects. But the people working on those projects would come from a human resource pool whose allegiance would be to the mission of the organization rather than to a specific programme. The structural change, in addition to eliminating internal competition, heightened our external competitive focus, which fostered increased innovation.

DEVELOP RIGHT STRATEGY DIRECTION

1. Establish strategic direction:

Setting strategic direction is the first responsibility of senior leaders. Since both creative energy and money are scarce commodities, it makes sense to encourage idea generation within boundaries defined by company strategy.

For example, if you're a consumer product marketer, you may wish to encourage ideas that fall within the boundaries of "providing better linkages with customers and providing fast and accurate order fulfillment." Within those strategy-related boundaries, new ideas for improving customer intelligence, order processing and logistics would be welcomed.

Having decided the strategic direction, communicate it to all of your employees clearly and often. It's rare to find an organization whose employees can clearly articulate company strategy—particularly employees at lower levels. "I just do my job," they'll say.

2. Align resources with strategy:

People follow the money. Once they see ideas that fall within stated boundaries being funded for development, they'll channel their creative energies in that direction. Senior management should also review its existing development projects and place their emphasis on those, which have a strategic fit.

3. Align objectives with ideals:

Daniel Vasella, (Chairman and chief executive officer of Novartis, a pharmaceutical company based in Basel, Switzerland) observes: "One way we try to foster innovation – both the technological innovation that leads to new products and the organizational innovation that improves the way we do business – is to align our business objectives with our ideals".

Novartis complemented their goal of economic value creation with another goal: good worldwide corporate citizenship. Having recognized that many ailments pervading the poorest countries are neglected diseases, with few R&D resources dedicated to finding treatments. With this in mind, Novartis founded a research center in Singapore that focuses on developing drugs to treat diseases such as dengue hemorrhagic fever and tuberculosis. In all likelihood, such drugs will be barely profitable at best.

These activities have a deep meaning for the employees and unleash their energy and enthusiasm. With regard to their breakthrough cancer drug *Glivec* (called *Gleevee* in the United States), for instance, their researchers overcame every obstacle to develop the drug and their production teams worked around the clock to produce enough supply for clinical trials.

4. Network for innovation:

Larry Keely (President of Doblin, an innovation strategy firm with offices in Chicago and San Francisco) says: "Companies miss out on all sorts of opportunities for innovating because they focus so closely on their competitors. You can actually spend less and make more money in innovation if you pay attention to the valleys, those places your competitors have overlooked." Make employees see that there are actually many types of innovation – product innovation is one type, but so is innovation in customer service, in business models, in networking and so on.

Consider the Chrysler minivan. Chrysler developed it at a time when the company was on the verge of bankruptcy. It created the van as a platform and depended on a network of suppliers to develop family-oriented advances that could be plugged into the platform – video games, removable seats, integral baby seats that fold down so beleaguered parents don't have to wrestle with them. The suppliers had to bear the cost of the R&D. That's an example not of product innovation but of networking innovation.

DESIGN SOUND SYSTEMS

1. Allow free exchange of information:

Information can stimulate thinking, which leads to idea generation. Many creative ideas are outcomes of cross-fertilization.

For example, Harold was working on vehicle steering systems; Maude was an expert in electromechanical application. When these two communicated and shared information, they got an idea for an electronic steering system.

In hierarchical firms, information is often hoarded as a source of organizational power. Information flows are controlled and channeled through the chain of command. Managers can encourage the free flow of information in many ways: through e-mail, the physical co-location of team members, joint work sessions, and regular brown-bag lunches.

2. Provide Access to knowledge sources:

Organizational innovation is not a product of hunches and magic. It is knowledge based. It is triggered by an idea that goes beyond what is known. To know the unknown, one has to learn existing knowledge and move beyond the boundaries of it seeking to discover new knowledge. If employees have free-flowing lines of communication between one another, they gain access to sources of knowledge—both inside and outside the organization and share it with others. Formal approaches to create knowledge sources are:

- *Internal* - Libraries, databases training centers and creation of communities of interest. A community of interest is an informal group whose members share an interest in some technology or application.
- *External* - Professional and scientific meetings, Visits to customers and benchmarking partners, discussions, lectures, workshops and consulting outside experts.

3. Improve the Idea-to-Commercialization Process:

Like cultural change, improving the innovation process is a job for senior management. It's one of the most important jobs they will ever handle. Scrutinize the innovation process continually for improvement opportunities. Make sure that your process has the following features:

- Generates a sufficient number of good ideas. If it's not generating enough good ideas, find the root cause and fix it.
- Is free of the bottlenecks that impede development and frustrate innovators?
- Is free of politics?
- Encourages calculated risk taking.
- Is non-arbitrary?
- Creates cheap failures.
- Channels resources to the most worthy projects.
- Involves people who understand the company's capabilities, its strategy and its customers.

Some companies have deliberately shaped their organizational practices and policies to support employee creativity and innovation.

4. Design participative systems:

Nonhierarchical organizations in which people are accustomed to and value collaborative work is suitable for creative explorations. Employee Suggestion Scheme and Quality Circles are the some of the structural arrangements for creativity.

5. Set high standards and expect people to meet them:

The act of stating high standards creates dissatisfaction with the current level of performance and spurs creativity. There should be the use of more creative language and report writing with high expectations.

6. Provide counseling to reduce stress:

Following ten years of research, Cary Cooper, a professor of organizational psychology at Manchester Business School, has found that employees' ability to think effectively is directly related to the level of stress they experience. Cooper also points out that much of the output of knowledge working –ideas, new approaches and new concepts-is linked to IT based delivery systems. Coping with these systems is a constant source of stress to older workers that might undermine the very creativity it was supposed to facilitate.

7. Establish Reward System:

Creativity will not flourish in the absence of a reward system that encourages individuals to stretch beyond the bounds of normal work. Motivating rewards can either be intrinsic or extrinsic. An intrinsic reward appeals to a person's desire for self-actualization, curiosity, enjoyment or interest in the work itself. An extrinsic reward appeals to a person's desire for attainment distinct from the work itself: a cash bonus, a promotion or stock options. These two sources of motivation work hand in hand.

ADOPT RIGHT LEADERSHIP STYLES

1. Be visible and involved:

Innovation and R&D are the crucibles within which the future company is being formed today. Leaders cannot make good decisions if they operate in a vacuum or think of innovation as a mysterious force. They need an understanding of the technical and behavioral issues relating to projects that are in the pipeline at any given time. Some of the useful approaches are:

- Visit the research and innovation centers on a regular basis.
- Have lunch with project teams.
- Get to know key people one-on-one.
- Try to understand the technical hurdles the stand between Appealing ideas and their Commercialization.

Some of the best and most successful executives were happiest and most effective when they were down in R&D lab rubbing elbows with bench scientists and technicians. Bill Hewlett, David Packard and Motorla's Bob Galvin fit this description. So does Bill Gates today.

If organizational leaders are visible and personally involved in the early stages of the innovation process, the following four important benefits can be obtained:

- It sends a powerful signal to employees that innovation matters.
- It provides senior management with opportunities to articulate the strategic direction of the firm and the boundaries within which innovation should be pursued.
- It gives senior management a direct hand in the design of products and services that will define the company in the future.
- It educates leaders on technical and market issues and prepares them to act as recognizers and patrons of good ideas.

2. Maintain open and receptive environment:

The worst environment for creativity is one that is unwelcoming to new ideas.

Some senior managers are so bound up with the status quo that they have no enthusiasm for anything that's new or different. They say: *We've been successful over the years by doing things this way, so why should we change*? An organization with this attitude is heading for trouble. Of course, there may be times when management is compelled to shoot down good ideas. Two such instances are:

- When the ideas lack a strategic fit with the business.
- The organization lacks the resources to pursue them.

In these cases, however, management has a responsibility to communicate its reasoning to employees.

Even when there is a good team of creative people, results cannot be amazing when condemned to operate within an organization that's unfriendly to new ideas. The experiences of Xerox Corporation's Palo Alto Research Center (PARC) during the late 1970s and early 1980s and Hewlett-Packard around 1990, substantiate this viewpoint (Managing Creativity and Innovation, Harvard Business Press, 2003).

PARC was (and remains) a cornucopia of innovative thinking. Its brainy scientists and engineers had conjured up many of the technologies that would eventually power the emerging era of desktop computing: Ethernet connectivity, the mouse and a user-friendly operating system. Xerox management, however, was not receptive to those innovations, which were not going to produce financial returns in the time frame required by the company. Many of PARC's innovations found their way into personal computers developed by Apple.

3. Design congenial physical workplace:

A congenial work environment encourages creativity. Organizations that have been wellsprings of creativity over many decades (companies such as 3M, Ciba-Geigy, Corning, Siemens, Sony, Hewlett-Packard, Merck, Motorola, Nokia, and Procter & Gamble) show interest in design of the workplace environment.

When an environment is filled with many types of stimuli and when it provides physical and electronic links between individuals, it encourages people to see new connections and to think more broadly.

Some specific ways to encourage the interactions that lead to information sharing and creative ideas are:

- Physical stimuli (for example, books, videos, art on walls, journals).
- Accessible, causal meeting space. Conversations and spontaneous meetings often occur in public areas: canteen, corridors and around water coolers. So make these spaces into comfortable gathering places where people will linger and share ideas.
- Place whiteboards and flip charts in places where people naturally congregate. This will allow them to sketch out their ideas during spontaneous discussions. Provide e-mail facility for interactions.

- Institute a weekly lunch at which people take turns telling their coworkers about their ideas and soliciting feedback.
- Give teams "idea rooms" in which they can meet, plan, post-information, and display competing ideas.
- Space for quiet reflection. Game or relaxation areas.
- "Employee only space" for solitary thinking and reflection.

4. Develop cross-functional teamwork:

Innovation efforts require cross-fertilization of ideas and collaboration of individuals and groups. Team culture and cross-disciplinary experiments enhance innovation outcomes.

The two cases given under substantiate the argument.

Spectrography originated by searching for a cross-disciplinary solution. Bunsen, a chemist, used the color of a chemical sample in a gas flame for a rough determination of the elements it contained. He described the technique and its shortcomings to Kirchhoff, who, being a physicist, immediately suggested using a prism to display the entire spectrum and thus get detailed quantitative information. This led to the science of spectrography and, following application to measurement of the absorption spectra of the stars, to the modern science of cosmology.

Artificial Intelligence (AI) researches went off on a dead-end track for years by trying to design around a single processing level in neural networks. Eventually it was found that multiplayer processing eliminated this fundamental barrier. By asking a biologist they would have quickly and easily learned that the image processing cells in the eye exist in three distinct layers.

5. Provide support to innovation roles:

Senior executives are not necessarily more clairvoyant than other managers, and they sometimes place their bets on the wrong ponies. Nevertheless, research points to executive patronage as an important contributor to radical innovation. Organizations need people in high places who will champion good ideas and provide them with moral support and protection as they travel the bumpy road toward commercialization.

Leifer and colleagues in their study observed a form of executive patronage in each of the radical innovation projects they studied. They concluded, for example, that IBM's silicon germanium computer chip project would not likely have survived without the implicit protection of two senior IBM executives, who over a period of years provided under-the-table resources to keep that project alive. They observed the same at General Electric, where a now-successful digital x-ray technology would have died on the vine had it not been for the backing of two high-placed executives—one being then-CEO Jack Welch.

6. Encourage participation in idea generation:

The leader has another important role – that of a facilitator for employees to generate new ideas.

At uWink, for example, we have regular "compost" sessions to come up with new game ideas. We don't debate their value. Our priority is simply to get as many ideas as possible out of individuals' heads and into the group's heads. The ideas then become collective problems or puzzles that percolate through out the group. And a couple of months later, someone – very often not the person who came up with a particular idea – has a breakthrough insight that allows us to move forward. In software, especially, the best ideas lose their owners and take on lives of their own.

Chevron Corporation, a leader in the petroleum industry, used 'Direct Participation' (DP) by involving employees in innovative thinking for designing and implementing change. In the DP process, a variety of stakeholders meet (for two to three days) to address a problem or issue that calls for change and produce detailed outputs, which are quickly implementable. It brings multiple perspectives relating to the problem and facilitates an identification of the changes required to resolve.

7. Set firm deadlines:

Nolan Bushnell (CEO of uWink, an entertainment and game network located in Los Angeles) opines that firm deadlines and tight budgets keep people focused on creating viable products and getting them to market as soon as possible. He observed that at uWink they have very fast product lifecycles. So they believe in a tough love approach to new product development. If too much time is given a project can become a breeding ground for internal politics. Likewise, too much money can become a crutch for creative thinking. There's no substitute for getting something on the shelves and hearing what customers have to say. The true test of any innovation is how the marketplace responds.

EMPLOY THE RIGHT STAFF

1. Hire right people:

Hiring creative people and grouping them into well-crafted teams, is an essential step toward producing greater creativity and useful innovation. Every innovative organization has to strengthen its selection and recruitment systems and see the process as a critical issue. Every hiring opportunity is to be utilized to populate the organization with people whose special training, experience or personal interests are aligned with the strategic direction of the company.

Potential R&D managers should

- have a good feel for the trajectories of technologies important to the company.
- have practical experience in dealing with customers.

The general climate for innovation can be improved if executives hire the right middle managers.

In her study of innovative middle managers, Rosabeth Moss Kanter found a number of common characteristics. Such managers

- ❖ Were comfortable with change.
- ❖ Viewed unmet needs as opportunities.
- ❖ Selected projects with great care.
- ❖ Adopted long time horizons and viewed setbacks as bumps on the road to success.
- ❖ Were always prepared and professional in making presentations.
- ❖ Understood organizational politics and where they could get support when needed.
- ❖ Practiced participative management.

These managers could operate with these characteristics, in Kanter's view, because they worked in organizations whose cultures supported collaboration and teamwork and where people were encouraged to "*do what needs to be done*".

2. Employ diverse workforce:

The right step is to recruit workers with a broader range of backgrounds and perspectives. Different outlooks from the outset lead to previously unlooked-for avenues of thought.

"*Diversity is about individuals*," says Susan Lax, diversity manager for McDonalds in the UK. By valuing different life experiences, backgrounds and ideas, she believes companies will reap rewards in wholly new ways in their markets, customers and future growth-and she is not alone in this belief.

DEVELOP SKILLS

1. Set up Learning mechanisms:

Arrangements for instruction and training of personnel in the functional areas, communication skills and creativity process and techniques are to be made.

- Invite skilled practitioners of creativity, both internal and external experts.
- Encourage sharing of knowledge experience and problem solving successes.
- Hold frequent meetings, seminars and workshops.

PROMOTE SUITABLE SHARED VALUES

In the absence of a supportive culture, creativity and innovation are like seedlings planted in arid, rocky. They simply won't germinate and grow. The following tips for changing organizational culture may be considered. Box 8.1 narrates culture at 3M.

1. Communicate vision:

Create an appealing and shared vision of the future. People won't buy into the pain and effort of change unless they can see a future state that is tangible better—and better for them—than the one they have at the moment. Successful change leaders form such a vision and communicate it in compelling terms.

2. Develop good language:

There is a strong link between Language and Creativity. People are inspired by language more than any other medium, except perhaps music. Roos sees organizations as "systems of language". They have their own sets of phrases and analogies and ways in which these are used, and this usage is not transferable from one organization to another.

- *Update language regularly* – If it is in line with the times and the organization's current circumstances, Roos argues, it will be better able to cope with change.

- *Helps capture vision* – Language helps capture the vision and inspiration behind an idea. It also determines whether it will last after the initial spark to go into the hands of shapers.
- *Heritage* – Without a set of documents, e-mail exchanges or memos that enable the "mythology" or "legend" to become embedded in the firm's corporate memory, there will be nothing to be picked up and built on by succeeding generations.

3. Create trust:

With the best intentions in the world, many firms inadvertently send out conflicting signals to their workers. They say that they want their staff to experiment and be inventive, but at the same time they may behave in ways that inhibit the generation of ideas. Inhibiting factors can include a fear and zero tolerance of failure. As Kenneth Labiche, a senior of Fortune, an American business magazine, wrote in 2000.

Your workers haven't been evincing much energy and talent? Maybe that's because they don't trust the company to reward these qualities and perhaps that's because the company doesn't trust the workers to exhibit them.

4. Retain scientific skepticism:

Some people will "pitch" their ideas to leaders and look for support and resources. The leader has to approach these encounters with a balance of open-mindedness and scientific skepticism. That means two things: (1) demonstrating an interest in new ideas, even when they challenge the company's current products and ways of operating and (2) simultaneously maintaining scientific skepticism.

5. Promote risk taking attitudes:

Progress and risk are inseparable companions. Management must recognize the risk/reward relationship and find organizational mechanisms for handling it. It must communicate a clear understanding that reasonable risks are acceptable, since they are the handmaidens of progress. Cheap failure is the second method for dealing with risk. A cheap failure is a project or experiment that is terminated with the least possible outlay of resources—just enough to tell mangers that "*This isn't going to work*".

6. Have tolerance for failures:

Esther Dyson told readers of Harvard Business Review.

"Be open to experimentation and philosophical about things that go wrong. My motto is, 'Always make a new mistake.' There's no shame in making a mistake. But then learn from it and don't make the same one again. Everything I've learned, I've learned by making mistakes."

7. Sustain spirit of innovativeness:

Creating the right spirit is important for the success of an organization. The spirit of innovativeness can be crated in the following ways:

Celebrate milestones - Celebrating the achievement of each milestone recognizes progress and reenergizes commitment.

Interact with employees - Top management, according to Beer, often fails to understand why employees are not as concerned about innovation, customer service, or costs as they are. Too often this is because management has failed to put employees in touch with the relevant data. Creating dialogue on the data is more productive. Dialogue should aim for a joint understanding of company problems. .

Establish hot line - In some cases, top management is out of touch with the weaknesses of the business or emerging threats-things that frontline employees understand through daily experience on the factory floor or in face-to-face dealings with customers. A hot line would improve communications between top management and front-line people.

Story telling - Storytelling, for example, has always been an important part of culture of 3M, which has often been cited as one of the most innovative companies in the world. As one of its senior executives commented:

At 3M, we tell stories constantly. We tell stories about how we failed with our first abrasive products and stories about how we invented masking tape and wet and dry sandpaper. More recently, we've been telling a story about one of our scientists who, while singing in the choir, wished he had bookmarks that wouldn't fall out of the hymnal-and later created Post-It Notes.

8. Merge Patience and Passion:

John Talley (Vice-president of drug discovery at Microbia in Cambridge, Massachusetts.) explaining the need for patience and passion he narrates his experience:

"Look at what happened when we worked on Celebrex" Ever since aspirin was introduced in the United States at the end of Nineteenth Century, chemists have been trying to make better non-steroidal anti-inflammatory compounds. One problem everyone encountered was that the enzyme that causes painful inflammation also helps protect the stomach lining from digestive acids. So when a painkiller blocks inflammation, it also can cause serious gastrointestinal problems.

A few colleagues had evidence that the form of the enzyme that induced inflammation was slightly different from that which protected the stomach. So we set out to find a molecular compound that would block only the form that induced inflammation. We went down so many fruitless alleys. We combed through mountains of literature. Sure enough, we found a compound created in the early 1980s that partially inhibited this enzyme. But we were now about two per cent of the way there; we still had to find out how to turn the compound into a safe and effective drug. When we put the drug into clinical trials, we didn't expect to know for years whether it would make it to market.

In fact, Celebrex had an almost record journey from the lab bench to the pharmacy shelf: seven years from the time we started work on the project. In an environment with these kinds of timeframes, you need passion to sustain you. Nevertheless, it's important that your passion does not blind you to the fact that sometimes you need to kill a project. Before our chemistry team began working on what turned out to be Celebrex, we were working on a blood pressure drug. Although it was clear that research ultimately wouldn't yield a product, some people on the team had emotional attachments to the technology and had a hard time letting go. "But if we hadn't moved on, we wouldn't have Celebrex"

Box 8.1 3M Culture of Innovation

3M has evolved from a maker of sandpaper to a manufacturer of hundreds of different products, including adhesives, films, and fiber optics. In almost a century, it has commercialized over fifty thousand products. Its success as an innovator is generally attributed to its corporate culture, which very deliberately fosters creativity by giving employees the freedom to take risks and tinker with new ideas. That culture is a legacy of William L. McKnight (1887-1978). McKnight joined 3M in 1907 as an assistant bookkeeper but rose rapidly through the ranks, becoming president in 1929 and board chairman in 1949. During his tenure he worked to create a culture that put employees in direct contact with customer problems and that encouraged initiative and innovation. His philosophy was to listen to anyone who proposed an original idea and to let him or her run with that idea through "experimental doodling." As he wrote in 1948:As our business grows, it becomes increasingly necessary to delegate responsibility and to encourage men and women to exercise their initiative. This requires considerable tolerance. Those men and women, to whom we delegate authority and responsibility, if they are good people, are going to want to do their jobs in their own way. Mistakes will be made. But if a person is essentially right, the mistakes he or she makes are not as serious in the long-run as the mistakes management will make if it undertakes to tell those in authority exactly how they must do their jobs. Management that is destructively critical when mistakes are made kills initiative. It's essential that we have many people with initiative if we are to continue to grow.Today the company backs up McKnight's management philosophy with a number of creativity-supporting practices. Here are just a few: McKnight's notion of experimental doodling is institutionalized into 3M's unofficial "15 per cent Rule," which allows technical and scientific employees to use that percentage of their time to pursue ideas unrelated to their official assignments. The 15 per cent Rule has spawned a number of commercially successful products over the years. The work of outstanding technical employees is recognized by admission to the prestigious Carlton Society, which opens its doors to a few remarkable innovators each year. Their peers in recognition of their outstanding contributions to new technologies and 3M products choose the individuals. Teams that create products that earn $4 million or more in profitable revenues receive the Golden Step award. Employees can choose between management and Technical career ladders. Not everyone is cut out to be a manager and not all who are qualified for management want to leave the laboratory.These organizational features are part of 3M's culture of innovation and they help account for the company's success in producing new and useful products decade after decade. That culture is changing with new management and a new competitive environment, so there is no guarantee that it will remain a culture of innovation.

Source: *Managing Creativity and Innovation* (2003), Harvard Business School Press, Boston, Massachusetts, p.106.

SUMMARY

Establishing inquisitive, investigating, enterprising and challenging culture and leadership is essential to nurture and foster creativity in organizations. Creative organizations are made up of people who have autonomy and entrepreneurship, value driven attitudes, lean structures and market orientation. Several forces that negate creativity include: management practiced as science, pressures of today, apathy of employees and friendships.

Initiatives that foster creative culture and environment are to be build around 7S-structure, strategy, systems, style, staff, skills and shared values.

QUESTIONS

1. Explain the need for creative organization and its characteristics.
2. How do you analyze a creative organization using 7S Framework.
3. Identify the factors that inhibit creativity in organizations. State the principles for fostering creativity.
4. How do you establish innovation climate and culture in your organization?

EXERCISES

Visit a local company having concern for creativity and assess the adequacy for innovation and identify improvements needed.

CASE : INSTITUTIONALISED LEARNING TO COMPETE

Nachiket Urdhwareshe, Chief Executive Officer, SoftJin Infotech Pvt. Ltd., observed:

We exist in the highly technology-intensive and competitive EDA tools and design flow consulting and solutions space. To us, the choice thus was between pursuing a beaten path, which is not relevant to creating a new one from scratch or one where either the rules of the game are not there or they are yet being written. We chose the later and are happy to see the success Technoforum enjoyed. Another impact of this has been the reiteration of SoftJin as a progressive HR practices company. I hope, with the support of the team, to push ahead and look at newer initiatives as we move forward in this space.

The company:

Bangalore-based SoftJin Infotech Pvt. Ltd., incorporated in December 2000 is a unique growth venture specializing in contract R&D services in the highly competitive EDA tools and design flow space.

The company has a proven track record of executing complex, high performance EDA software development projects across the spectrum of electronic design flow. Its flexible software delivery process ensures highest quality and timely delivery while protecting intellectual property. SoftJin caters to a gamut of customers including but not limited to companies in System Design, EDA product, FPGA Vendors, Platform Providers, Design Services Companies – Fujitsu Laboratories of America, PACT, Ball, Semiconductor Inc, Tharas Systems to name a few. SoftJin Info Tech currently has employee strength of over 70 with a majority of them belonging to India's premier technology education brand – the IITs.

The Problem:

In the business context of SoftJin, the specific problems the teams work on, are typically the problems for which no off-the-shelf standard solutions are available, since these problems were related to cutting edge and upcoming technologies. In order to service the requirements of such new and upcoming domains, it was imperative for SoftJin to be a learning organization. While there have been previous attempts by companies in technology industry and outside to find a way to do that, SoftJin found that these really did not apply to the company's context. This led SoftJin to look internally at developing a system or process that would enable the creation of a seamless and sustained learning environment and an institutionalized learning culture. This resulted in the "Technoforum" initiative, which is already successfully running at SoftJin.

Issues in Designing:

How to keep adequate balance in terms of efforts spent on Technoforum activities so that live projects are not impacted? The deliberation to find this perfect balance gave rise to other questions.

- What is the ideal frequency of the Technoforum presentation?
- How do terms select topics to research? What should be the ratio of the research component and how much should be the survey in the study undertaken by the team?
- How to keep the teams motivated over extended periods of time especially in the face to deadline and other usual project related pressures?

Design decisions:

(i) *Objective:* Technoforum was begun with the objective of nurturing and encouraging employees to develop and share expertise related to SoftJin's domain of operation.

(ii) *Focus:* It induces a process of continuous exploration and drives the hunger to know more. Here, groups of engineers spend efforts on understanding latest technology challenges and possible solutions for them. More importantly, these challenges are not related to the project at hand, but are chosen in anticipation of new problems and challenges. The outcomes of these studies are presented in a systematic manner, are evaluated and best contributions get recognition and rewards.

(iii) *Frequency & Balance:* Technoforum in SoftJin is a bi-annual event celebrating learning.

(iv) *Topic Choices:* It was decided to make it compulsory. However, people were given initial choice to choose the topics as well as join the topic of their choice.

(v) *Motivation:* The rewards program was designed to ensure that all teams did get benefits based on their efforts, in addition to certain awards which carried much higher benefits on the average compared to "rewards". The idea behind this scheme was that the effort of all would be rewarded, but the best ones will get more recognition and more benefits.

There were incentives for individual performance as well. The reward and the award points were given to a team, which internally had the choice of sharing the spoils equally or otherwise, thus giving an opportunity for key contributors to be recognized.

Implementation:

With defined and clear solutions to key issues, the management decided to kick-start the idea of such a unique platform. Technoforum thus was launched as a continual learning platform in April 2004. Says Sheetalkumar R. Mehta, Senior Software Engineer.

"I think the Technoforum was a very positive step taken by the management to place emphasis on learning. Sometimes, we engineers have tough deadlines to meet and this means that on our own initiative, we may not have the time to read and keep abreast of new and emerging technologies. This fact is more pronounced in the case of a niche domain like EDA. Technoforum helps people to share knowledge, and this is what I like the most. The questions asked by the panel members at the end of the presentation, make us think about the entire topic from a different perspective and help us to look at newer dimensions of the topic, thereby gaining more in-depth knowledge. The fact that the whole process had awards and rewards, motivated us even more. It gave us an opportunity to work with people who we do not interact with on a regular basis for project purposes and this was fun. When the process of knowledge sharing is incentivized and fun, we have a great process in place."

The proof like they say is in the pudding. Earlier 4 teams of 4 people led the vision, today it is a much larger team of 4-7 and 8 teams working on content further subdivided to 2 topics per group, thus ensuring better and in-depth coverage of the topic. Another very definite pointer of the growing success of the scheme has been the adoption of the deadlines. The first Techno forum event was re-scheduled to accommodate project schedules. However, the second Techno forum was held on the day scheduled, thus showing that the employees had planned their preparation keeping in mind their project schedules and Techno forum is now a part of their goals. The main challenge going forward would still be the ability to keep the people motivated especially in view of the growing size of the organization.

Evaluation and Reward Structure:

The evaluation process consisted of both review of a white paper developed by the teams on the subject as well as live audience presentation made by the team. Getting into the specifics of the evaluation scheme, each white paper was to be evaluated for 25 points on content only and a penalty of 10% and 20% of points won respectively for groups that submit 1 or 2 days later than specified timelines. The final white paper score was weighted with 25% towards the final team score.

The presentation carried the remaining 75% weightage and the evaluation criteria was broadly as follows:

1. Relevance of presentation to the topic
   (a) Cover all aspects of the topic being presented.
   (b) Convey the current state-of-art, state-of-market and challenges in the field.
2. Clarity of content/communication
   (a) Understanding and explanation of technical terms.
   (b) Provide insights into the inferred topic rather than presented from another source.
3. Slides/Illustration with examples
   (a) Reference to tools in the market/projects done in SoftJin.
   (b) Use of diagrams and visuals effectively.
4. Delivery of presentation/interactiveness
   (a) Presentation style.
   (b) Effective handling of questions and answers.

The panel was chosen from senior technical staff within SoftJin, academicians and senior industry experts. Each member of the panel was to score each team on a scale of 0-100 based on the above criteria. The average score of the panel for each team will be calculated as the panel score for the team.

Each member of the panel would also rate the top two teams/individuals in the following categories.	For an effective evaluation the audience are encouraged to rate both individuals and teams on
▪ Best Team-Technical Content ▪ Best Team-Presentation ▪ Best Individual Presenter	▪ Best Team-Presentation ▪ Best Individual Presenter ▪ Best Team-Technical content

The panel composition is also something Soft in was categorical about ensuring that they were independent and had adequate knowledge of the topic presented to judge fairly and accurately.

A total of 60,000 points were up for grabs across multiple categories with it being a ratio of their panel team scores. The awards were based on the combined ratings of the panel and the audience, with a 50% weightage given to the panel ratings. This mixing up ensured transparency and balance were inbuilt into the process making it unquestionable and logical. This audience score was incorporated to ensure that the audience keenly participated in listening to the other teams' presentations in addition to theirs. The awards were given out based on the below point structure:

Best Team-Technical Content [Winner]-	25,000 points
Best Team-Technical Content [Runner-up]	12,500 points
Best Team-Presentation [Winner]	10,000 points
Best Team-Presentation [Runner-up]	5,000 points
Best Individual Presenter [Winner]	5,000 points
Best Individual Presenter [Runner-up]	2,500 points

Questions:

1. Identify the key factors that have led to the success of Techno forum.
2. How do you sustain motivation of the employees in view of the growing size of the organization?

Source: *Human Capital*, March, 2005, pp.38-41.www.humancapitalonline.com.

Chapter 9

Research & Development Management

Learning Objectives

After you have studied this chapter, you will be able to...

- State the meaning, objectives and significance of R&D.
- Know the prerequisites of successful R&D and approaches to technology development.
- Explain the process of R&D.
- Describe the role of small industry in promoting R&D.
- Examine the status and progress of R&D in India.

Structure

- Introduction
- Meaning
- Objectives
- Significance
- Prerequisites
- Technology Development Approaches
- R&D Process
- Management of R&D
- In Source to Open Source Movement
- R&D in Small Industry
- Summary
- Questions
- Exercises
- Case : Patenting and Pharma

INTRODUCTION

Research & Development (R&D), enables technological innovations and contributes to the competitive strength of nations. Innovative capacity is the determinant of industrial competitiveness and economic progress for nations in this era of globalization. In this context, it is believed that the future economic growth and industrial performance of developing countries will largely depend on the R&D management at macro-and-micro levels. Accordingly the measures taken by the government and industry players to promote research and development have drawn the attention of policy-makers and analysts.

MEANING OF R&D

The following descriptions make the meaning of R&D clear:

Back (1997) observed:

R&D are the use of resources, to create new knowledge and to develop new and improved products or more economic methods of production. Research is the part devoted to discovering new knowledge; Development is the part devoted to bringing new ideas to the stage where production for the market can start. This includes devising methods of making the products and testing that they work reliably and do not create hazards for health and safety.

Gibson, (1981) maintained:

Research is that exploratory activity that seeks to discover the principles of nature. Development is the application of existing scientific principles, along with economic and other constraints, to the design of devices and processes that meet the needs of human kind

OBJECTIVES

Corporate R&D projects may have the following objectives:

(1) To support current business.

(2) To promote new business ventures.

(3) To explore possible new technology basis.

SIGNIFICANCE

R&D has a vital role to play in the advancement of different sectors of the economy (industry, trade, services and agriculture). R&D and technological innovations play a decisive role in industrial development because they facilitate industries to bring out a large proportion of the new and improved materials, products, processes and systems, which are the ultimate source of industrial advancement. The production stimulates consumption; encourages investment and employment. Thus the economic cycles expand leading to higher GNP and better quality of life.

TECHNOLOGY DEVELOPMENT APPROACHES

Technology development can take several routes.

In-house R&D:

Technology development activities are generally carried out through setting up of separate in-house R&D units within the corporation, managed and headed by a well qualified and experienced chief, directly reporting to the top management. This unit will have close interactions with other departments within the company and there could even be exchange of personnel among the different departments. The strength and facilities in the in-house R&D unit would depend upon the technology policy of the company and the nature of the business. In large companies, there are sometime R&D labs for each department and a central R&D lab for major R&D projects. Industrial R&D is mostly product or process oriented with specific objectives and time schedule; and not basic research. Incremental developmental efforts or import substitution efforts are generally common in most of the industries in developing countries including India, while emphasis is on new technologies or new applications of technologies in advanced countries.

Cooperative R&D:

A group of companies in a particular industrial sector promotes an R&D centre as a society or a non-profit making company. The expenses for R&D efforts are met from the contributions of the participating companies (as a fixed percentage of their turnover) as well as grants from the governments. This centre undertakes R&D as per the requirements of the companies in their larger interest and set up expertise and facilities of common nature and which are usually expensive. A company can also sponsor specific projects to this centre. Cooperative research facilities are normally utilized for the projects which are not of secretive nature from the business point of view .The first substantial part of the R&D can be done at the centre and the remaining part involving finer details or critical technological aspects affecting the competitiveness is done at the in-house R&D division of the company. National Council of Building Materials (Cement) at New Delhi and Textile Research Centre at Ahmedabad (ATIRA), are example of this type in India.

Contract Research:

A company may contract components of technology development to suitable R&D organizations, academic institutions or consultants or experts. The in-house R&D unit may coordinate the progress of the activities, to develop the desired technologies. This approach usually requires considerable internal technical and managerial capabilities coupled with a strong S&T information base.

R&D collaboration:

Different types of collaborations are becoming common.

- A company may collaborate with another company in areas of common interest. Such inter-firm collaborative R&D efforts are becoming common in developed countries mainly due to high costs and shorter technology life cycles, in areas such as micro-electronics, materials, information technologies, bio-technologies and so on.

- A firm may also collaborate with the public funded or privately funded R&D institutions on case-to-case basic where R&D results are shared mutually and so are the expenses.
- A company in India may even collaborate with another company or R&D institution abroad, on mutually agreed terms. The Government of India encourages such collaborations. In such cases, relative advantages of the collaborative partners are the main guiding factors and are one of the ways to avoid large technology payments in future.

Research Societies:

Large corporations or industrial houses may set up independent research societies, in addition to their in- house R&D units. Such societies may undertake R&D activities mostly relating to the broad interests of the promoting companies in line with the national interests. They will also take advantage of those facilities for the activities/programs in their in-house R&D unit. Governments usually encourage such societies and provide several tax concessions and fiscal incentives.

Research Companies:

Large corporations of technology innovative entrepreneurs may promote research companies, specifically for conducting research and development of technologies for others on commercial basis. The development costs and reasonable profits are recovered from the sale and transfer of technologies.

Prerequisites:

Successful R&D and technological innovations are seen as outcome of the intellectual exercises of researchers in science and technology in response to new knowledge developments or identified needs of people in the society. As such there are two models of innovation process: Market pull (need based) and Technology push (knowledge based).

Therefore, technological innovation presupposes the existence of three elements.

- Scientific and technological capability
- Market demand.
- An agent that transforms this capability into goods and services, which satisfy the demand. The agent is the industrial firm or more precisely, the entrepreneur.

It is the variations in technological capability, market opportunities and quality of management by agent which will explain the varying research intensity of sectors and nations. Other things remaining the same, technology infrastructure such as R&D institutions and laboratories and R&D personnel have been as the major indicators of R&D intensity of nations.

R&D PROCESS

The steps in R&D process vary based on the model that is applicable for an innovation.

(a) Market (Need) pull

Basically, one can consider the R&D process as having four distinct stages as shown in Figure 9.1. Recognition of a need for innovation is one of the motivations for R&D. "Research" on existing knowledge for satisfying identified need helps in idea generation.

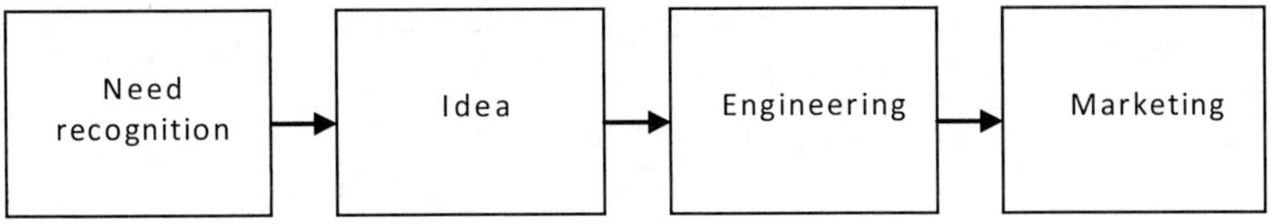

Figure 9.1 Market pull innovation development

(b) Technology push

The other primary motivation for R&D is to find potential applications for advances in knowledge as shown in Figure 9.2 . "Research" on existing activity for introducing new knowledge also helps in idea generation.

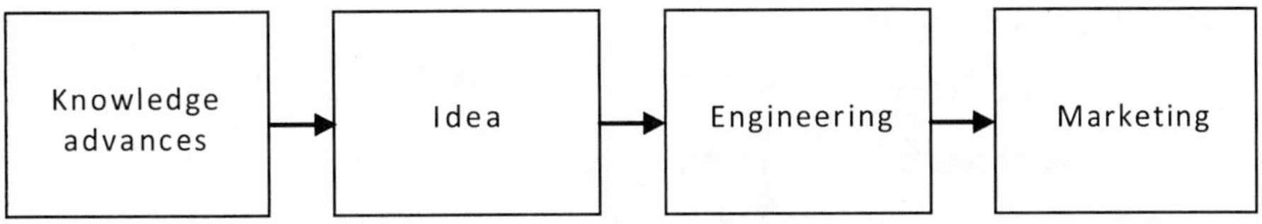

Figure 9.2 Technology push innovation development

In both the models "Development" includes engineering (creation, design and production) and marketing (first use and diffusion) of the generated idea. Through the entire process it is ideas and knowledge, which are being pursued, and the process is not complete until the new idea is converted into a marketable product or service (a hardware of software intensive technology). As explained earlier, the R&D projects tend to go through the stages given in Table 9.1.The stages are explained elaborately in the next chapter.

Table 9.1 Stages in R&D

Aspect	Stages
Research	Basic research and invention
	Applied research and functional proto-type
	Engineering proto-type and testing
Development	Production proto-type and pilot production
	Product testing and modification
	Initial production and sales

MANAGEMENT OF R&D

Managing R&D requires special skills and covers a wide variety of issues ranging from technical matters to management techniques and overall business environment at national and international levels. R&D can be seen as a system with an integration of three elements: inputs, process and outputs, that functions with a set of predetermined goals (Figure 9.3).

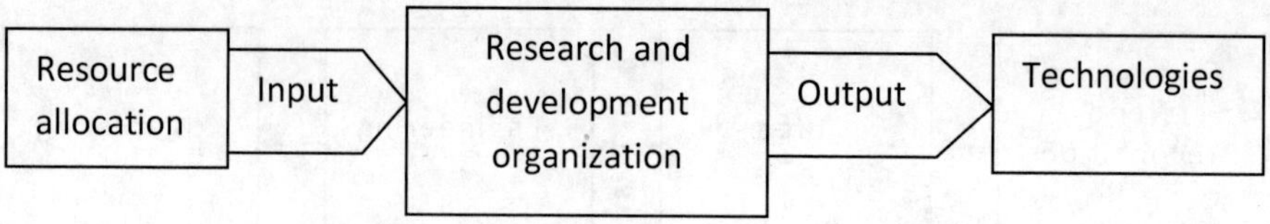

Figure 9.3 Systems model of R&D

Planning:

The first phase of management is concerned with identification of goals and resources required for innovation.

(i) **Goals** – The goals of R&D projects may be one or more of the following:

- To fulfill human needs.
- To achieve self-reliance in technology.
- To increase productivity of industry, agriculture, etc.
- To promote international trade by finding new products or processes.

(ii) **Resources acquisition** – The input resources are the traditional inputs such as money, materials, facilities, energy, labour and management and the intelligence based inputs such as science, knowledge, skills, information and existing technologies. Funding is as such critical for the initiation of R&D project.

Organising:

In Indian industry or corporate sector, it is generally observed that the research personnel occupy secondary place to finance, marketing and production personnel and are not given due importance in decision-making at corporate level. Sometimes, inefficient personnel from other departments are posted or transferred to R&D department, thereby indicating a complete neglect of R&D concept. Such management attitudes need to be changed in the overall interest of the company.

Leading:

Personnel are also critical part of any R&D project, since the talents, creativity, dedication and problem solving ability of the personnel are essential to the success of any R&D project. Training and development of the people is a critical area for the success of the project.

Controlling:

Managing R&D projects requires attention to performance, timing, cost and personnel.

The performance parameters must be defined for an R&D project in order to determine how successfully the goals of the project are attained. Progress in R&D projects can be watched by monitoring:

- **Time** - Timing is important to the success of a project, since lead-time created from timely innovation provides a competitive advantage. Milestone and PERT charts are useful in identifying the necessary tasks and sequencing to accomplish the R&D project.

- **Cost** – Costs of the project are essential to its commercial success, for R&D costs must be recovered as part of the investment costs in the new product or process.
- **Output** – The output is a new technology embedded in a product or process or service. The effectiveness of any R&D is determined in terms of the 'usefulness' of the technologies it produces with respect to the overall objectives of the corporation.

Top management support:

The quality of resource leadership and commitment of the top management for research is extremely important.

IN SOURCE TO OPEN SOURCE MOVEMENT

These are the two models Eric Raymond contrasts in his book on open source – *The Cathedral and The Bazaar*. The '*Cathedral*' is how Microsoft develops software – a traditional closed R&D model where it takes charge of the innovation and controls the intellectual property. Then, there is the 'B*azaar'*, where you buy innovation off the open market. This is what Cisco and a lot of pharma companies do.

Cathedral:

Under this traditional notion, a proprietary process residing within the firm drives innovation. Knowledge is selectively imported into the firm via customer surveys or supplier inputs and then the firm manages the innovation process. This is a limited way to think about innovation and an incomplete way to tap into the expertise that resides outside the firm.

In the cathedral, one is limited by his creativity and reach. It is too structured, too ritualistic and closed to fresh ideas and creativity of people outside the firm.

In 1970, Xerox set up the Palo Alto Research Centre (PARC) to get a 10-year head start in new markets. The model of locating innovation outside the core organization has become the dominant model for corporate innovation. However, Xerox's managers felt that most of the PARC's output did not do much for existing customers. In fact, it benefited the savvy competitors, rather than Xerox. Microsoft also tried to manage their R&D in-house.

Companies encourage on the job creativity by recognizing good ideas and encouraging innovators.

Hallmark sends some of their creative people to exotic places that on the surface appear to have nothing to do with greeting cards, but when these people witness a sunrise over an incredible mountain landscape they tend to get a heightened appreciation for emotional experiences. They are often able to tap into creativity that they were unable to tap into back at office.

Networking:

The company should have long-term R&D ties with a variety of companies across many different industries. The company should make reciprocal and substantive participation in research consortia, joint ventures and partnerships. All participants in the joint research project enter as equals and each assumes a responsibility for contributing a certain expertise.

Keen to tap India's intellectual capital, technical and scientific expertise more fully, P&G plans to establish collaborations with Indian individuals and companies to enhance its global R&D strength and help create and introduce new products more cost effectively. These collaborations will tie in to P&G's '*Connect+Develop*' strategy, which seeks to accelerate its internal R&D efforts by leveraging ideas, talents and innovation assets of individuals, institutes and companies from around the world. Through this model, P&G aims to build a global innovation network that could well be the source of ideas for the next generation of products and technologies. A team of scientists and managers from P&G's Cincinnati offices has been touring India and selling the concept among Government organizations and research set ups and have signed on CSIR labs to participate.

Bazar model:

In 1991, an alternative model, termed as open source model emerged. The bazaar model sits at the other extreme. The idea here is that managers of a firm cannot get all these ideas on their own; therefore they go out and buy them. It relies too much on chance.

In 1991, Linus Torvalds released the Linux kernel on line and invited other hackers to help him create a free operating system. This collaborative approach between Torvalds and a voluntary army of part-time programmers represented a brand new way of managing distributed innovation.

Communities of interaction:

The social aspect of knowledge creation is missing in the above models. Sometimes, these external entities(customers, partners, suppliers) can become so central to innovation that the locus of innovation moves outside the firm, into the network. That is the essence of communities of creation. Innovation need not occur with in the firm. An excellent example of this is the open source movement. What this community of developers has created is not owned by any firm or individual. A community with a joint purpose and a coordinated mechanism created it.

Take Texas Instruments. One of its design engineers was working on a new calculator the T1-92. As lots of these calculators are used in high schools, he thought he should test the prototype with teachers. He registered about 30,000 high school teachers and posted the design specifications and asked for feedback. That sparked off a fairly detailed and sustained debate. The new calculator based on the specifications was a huge success. What's more, the teachers also had a sense of ownership for the product? When a rival copied the new features of the T1-92, there were messages on the discussion board like: "Someone has ripped off our design."

Pharmaceutical firm Eli Lilly puts up unsolved chemistry problems that crop up during its R&D at *www. Innocentive.com.* It offers bounties on every problem. Over 7,000 scientists have registered at the site from all over the world to bid for these problems. What is amazing is that Lilly's in-house staff of chemists numbers just 300? The total number of chemists employed by the big pharmaceutical companies worldwide is about 5,000 less than the human capital available to Lilly within 18 months of launching the site. Thus, Lilly is tapping global expertise to solve the problems they work on.This shows how R&D can now extend across the world, tapping into networks of intellectual capital one had no access to earlier.

The application of this model is not limited to high-tech industries only. Involving the customer as co-creators transcends industry context.

- ❖ Take Kraft. It has developed the "Kraft Interactive Kitchen" to suggest recipes to consumers and to get ideas from them. The site gets over a million people every month.
- ❖ Another excellent example is Italian motorcycle firm Ducati. They have created communities of motorbike enthusiasts on their Website. These are mined for new products ideas.

The leadership has to move away from the traditional command and control structure. Profiting from the wisdom of the community requires humility, an attitude of collaboration and an open mind.

Table 9.2 summarizes the features of the three models.

Table 9.2 INNOVATION MANAGEMENT MODELS

Type	Closed Hierarchy model	Partially Open	Open Market
Characteristics	Xerox Parc	Eli Lilly's Innocentive	IBM Alphaworks
Governance mechanism	Hierarchy	Community	Market
Rigidity of boundaries	Closed system	Emergent system	Open system
Degree of structure	Basically structured	Self-organizing	Basically unstructure
Degree of order	Order	Creative tension	Disorder
Degree of change	Stasis	Edge of chaos	Chaos

Open market innovations:

This open-market approach, which includes the communities of interaction and Bazar model, has its own merits and dangers. Besides merits, this approach has its own demerits.

Merits:

The positive outcomes of open market innovations areas are as given under:

More ideas - It improves speed, cost and quality of innovation. It lets companies set realistic market values for their internal ideas.

Tetrapak took help from outsiders in developing its breakthrough product, Tetra Recart, which makes it possible to sterilize paperboard containers filled with soups, sauces, fruits and vegetables. Tetrapak collaborated with its paper and polymers supplier to make the paperboard package capable of withstanding high temperatures, humidity and rigors of commercial sterilization. It worked with another company with expertise in sterilizing hospital equipment to help it figure out how to sterilize the food inside the package. The company could move fast by outsourcing crucial elements of the new product and thus saved many years of development time.

Motivates creative employees- Exporting ideas adds urgency to the innovative process and creative people feel motivated with the knowledge that their good ideas will not be discarded but may be commercialized by some outside company, which is interested in it.

IBM earns a huge amount of revenues in royalties from the patent it exports. People in IBM understand that if they do not act fast on a promising idea it will be offered to outsiders, even competitors.

Bellsouth, the telecommunications company, sells its technologies to its competitors because it understands that they are going to develop it anyway.

Know the value of innovation - When outside laboratories do not show interest, the company knows there is not much potential in the compound. Free markets tell what a product or technology is worth. A company may be very upbeat about a technology but when it takes it to the market, no one may want it. The company is able to save lot of money and effort it would have expended on the technology.

Eli Lily offers licenses for compounds underdevelopment, when the therapeutic and business value of the drugs is still unclear.

Clarify capabilities – Companies often believe that their core business is broader than it really is. A sustainable core competency lets the company produce something at a lower cost or at higher quality than other companies in the open market can. When a company tries to weigh its capabilities relative to competitors, it discovers that it is strong in some areas, which it should pursue whereas it should with draw from the rest as others have more capabilities in them.

Boeing discovered that its true comparative advantage lay in system integration and not in manufacturing. Large suppliers were much better in manufacturing bust boeing understood the design and integration complexities of airplane components better than anyone else. It became designer and system integrator of its planes as well as many of the systems that go in them and withdrew from manufacturing.

Dangers:

But there are real dangers in sharing innovations.

Xerox gave away a stream of innovations from computer mouse to the graphical user interface and other companies capitalized on them.

Whether to share?

Companies need not be dismissive of the open-market innovation approach.

Buyers take time to innovate - The buyer of an innovation takes time to bring the idea to market and by that time the seller can introduce the next generation of the innovation. Buyers may not be able to capture the full value of innovation transfers.

Disney has developed a superior service model and it is so confident that its system for delivering service cannot be copied by competitors. It makes money by sharing its innovations with them.

Competitors anyhow innovate - Even when an innovation is not shared there is very little chance that competitors will not be able to come up with a similar innovation by reverse engineering. A tweak here and there will save them from risks of patent infringements.

Sharing is better than suing - An innovator will generally make more money and build more mutually beneficial relationships by licensing an innovation than by suing for patent infringements. The real risk in sharing innovations is in the structuring of the deals. If Xerox had structured their transactions to adequately share in the upside of its innovations, it could have reinvested that money in additional research.

When suitable?

The approach is suitable when unpredictable situations arise that require new competencies fast and when it is not clear as to which direction the technology would evolve.

Linux development effort drew thousands of independent software writers to its help.

Cisco explores multiple product strategies with outside partners until one emerges as the most likely.

A scientist from Bangalore was able to provide a solution to a problem facing Procter & Gamble (P&G), through *Innocentive*, an online forum for a global community of 18,000 scientists.

This approach also makes sense when innovations from disparate sources must come together to bring promising idea to market.

A joint venture between Cartgil and Dow has been set up to make plastic from renewable crops.

R&D IN SMALL INDUSTRY

Do we find R&D in small industry? If yes, what are the facilitators? What kind of R&D takes place there?

More Innovative:

In fact, small enterprises are often regarded as being more innovative than large ones.

The reasons are:

- The innovation activities of individuals form an important part of the innovation activities of small firm because the influence of the manager/owner is especially strong in small firms.
- The flexibility and willingness to adopt any new approach.
- Concentration and internal communications, which would facilitate efficient matching of market demand and R&D decision-making.

Informal R&D:

Empirical studies have brought out that small industries in the developed world, in general, carry out R&D informally (Freeman and Soete, 1999 and OECD, 1971). In a sample of 1358 units, 716 units have some kind of R&D. Of them, only 72 units have formal (exclusive) R&D departments within their premises and out of these only 12 units have got recognition from the Department of Scientific and Industrial Research (DSIR), Government of India. About 644 units carry out R&D activities informally (Bala Subrahmanya, *et.al.*, 2002).

Influencers:

It is found out that competition is the major factor, which prompted about 70 per cent of the 716 units to go for R&D, followed by technological change and customer needs. Self-motivation is the other important factor, which drove 360 units to engage in R&D, among others. On the whole, it is the external factors, which prompted majority units to go for R&D in Karnataka.

Objectives:

Since the major driving forces for R&D in SSI are competition, technology change and customer pressure, the major objectives of carrying out R&D are to improve quality (88%), reduce costs (79%) and meet customer needs (71%). Majority of the units aim at either changing product quality, solving common problems or changing product designs to suit customer needs or develop new processes or a combination of these.

Going solo:

What is more significant is that as many as 91 per cent of the 716 units carry out R&D activities independently, with self-efforts. The role of national and international agencies was found to be negligible. Parent companies are an important source of R&D for their ancillaries (about 9% of 716 units).

Staff and expenditures:

To carry out these activities, 396 units did not employ any full-time labour and 136 units did not incur any expenditure.The 320 units, which have employed at least, one full-time labour for R&D, together had 1336 full time R&D employees, which accounted for about 10 per cent of their total employees. The 580 units, which have incurred one or the other form of R&D expenditure, spent a total of ₹ 123.1 million on R&D activities. The R&D intensity of 539 units (which provided data both on R&D expenditure and total value of output) stood at 0.79 per cent. This is much less than that observed in France (2.5 per cent) and UK (2.3 per cent) (Chanaron, 1998).

Achievements:

What did they achieve out of R&D? Out of 716 units that carried out R&D, 590 units claimed to have improved quality, 474 units succeeded in reducing the rate of rejection of output and 372 units improved the process of production.

Less intensive R&D:

This brings out that small industries, in general, are engaged in "incremental innovations" and not "radical innovations" which bring out new products. This is substantiated by the fact out of 716 units, which are into R&D, only five units have obtained patents from their R&D and innovations.

This also explains why R&D intensity of SSI in India is substantially lower, absolutely as well as relatively.

SUMMARY

Research & Development (R&D), which enables technological innovations, contributes to the competitive strength of nations. Research is that exploratory activity that seeks to discover the principles of nature. Development is the application of existing scientific principles, along with economic and other constraints, to the design of devices and processes that meet the needs of human kind.

The objectives of R&D may be – to support current business, to promote new business ventures and to explore possible new technology basis. Successful R&D and technological innovations always require the existence of three elements, namely, scientific and technological capability, market demand, and an agent that transforms this capability into goods and services, which satisfy the demand.

Technology development approaches include – In-house R&D: Cooperative R&D, Contract Research, R&D collaboration, Research Societies and Research Companies. Steps in research include: basic research and invention, applied research and functional prototype, engineering prototype and testing. Development involves, production prototype and pilot production, product testing and modification and initial production and sales.

R&D or technology generation involves many other aspects such as monitoring and evaluation of R&D projects, funding of R&D, training and development of resource personnel, interactions at all levels, management policies and support, the availability of support structures and incentives at government level, and timely collection and interpretation of technical and other information's, etc.

Open market innovations are gaining ground in recent times. There are two models which Eric Raymond contrasts in his book on open source – *The Cathedral and The Bazaar*. The '*Cathedral*' is how Microsoft develops software – a traditional closed R&D model where it takes charge of the innovation and controls the intellectual property. Then, there is the '*Bazaar*', where you buy innovation off the open market. This is what Cisco and a lot of pharma companies do?

QUESTIONS

1. State the meaning, objectives and significance of R&D.
2. Know the prerequisites of successful R&D and approaches to technology development.
3. Explain the process of R&D.
4. Describe the role of small industry in promoting R&D.
5. Examine the status and progress of R&D in India.

EXERCISES

1. Visit two local manufacturing organizations and inquire how much they spend on R&D, how is the budget utilized, what kind of research and development work is in progress and what were their accomplishments during the last five years? If local organizations are not available, undertake the study through mail questionnaire selecting nearby organizations.
2. Visit local university and find out how much research in the direction of new applications is taking place. Identify the linkages they have with different S&T organizations of government and industry.

CASE : PATENTING AND PHARMA

A study was undertaken aimed at ascertaining the impact of product patents on Indian pharmaceutical industry with the following specific objectives:

- ❖ To study the present practices in pharmaceutical industry.
- ❖ To understand the impact of patenting.
- ❖ To know the strategies adopted by the companies to cope with the change in post-2005 patenting regime.

For the purpose of the study, the following five pharmaceutical companies which are into the exports of bulk drugs and formulations and practice patenting for their products were selected:

(i) Ranbaxy Laboratories Limited, New Delhi.

(ii) Indswift, New Delhi.

(iii) Morepen Pharmaceuticals Limited, New Delhi.

(iv) Orchid Chemicals and Pharmaceuticals Limited, Chennai.

(v) Alembic Limited, Chennai.

Top management and senior managers/executives of the above-mentioned companies were personally interviewed to collect the primary data.

Competition:

The rapid growth of pharmaceutical industry has witnessed an increase in the number of companies leading to intense competition in the domestic market.

Table 1: Competition (Domestic)- Present Scenario

Parameters	Number of Responses	Companies
Large number of players	4	Indswift, Morephen, Alembic, Orchid
Presence of large number of off-patent drugs	1	Ranbaxy
Effect of Patenting in 2005		
More-off within existing products	4	Indswift, Morephen, Alembic, Orchid
More-off patent products	1	Ranbaxy
Ways to Deal with the Change		
Reduce costs	3	Orchid, Alembic, Indswift
Have own molecules	2	Alembic, Morepen
Spend on Research & Development	2	Alembic, Indswift
Brand building	1	Ranbaxy
Niche marketing	1	Orchid

Companies felt that at present there are a large number of players in the domestic market due to growing needs of the industry for new drugs and molecules.

The international market has undergone drastic changes due to the implementation of both process and product patents in different countries. As shown in table.2, Alembic and Indswift feel that in the international market the main competition is from established MNCs, which have comparable resources to compete with these companies.

Table 2: Competition (International) – Present Practices

Parameters	Number of Responses	Companies
With multinational Companies	2	Alembic, Indswift
Active Pharmaceutical Ingredients exports	2	Orchid, Ranbaxy
Generics	2	Ranbaxy, Morepen
Effect of Patenting Post-2005		
Increase competition	2	Alembic, Indswift
Increase in business	2	Ranbaxy, Morepen
More tie-ups	1	Orchid
Ways to Deal with the Change		
Generics	2	Orchid, Ranbaxy
Develop own molecules	2	Ranbaxy, Morepen
Strategic alliances	1	Orchid
Contracts	1	Indswift
Global brands	1	Ranbaxy
Subsidiaries	1	Alembic

Competitive Edge:

The competitive edge of most of the companies lies in stronger R&D base and new molecule development followed by exports and manufacturing of drugs.As shown in Table-3, in order to increase the competitive edge, maximum number of companies are looking forward to increase investments in R&D and focus on New Drug Development and Research (NDDR). Other areas where the companies are finding avenues for increasing competitive edge are strategic decisions related to marketing and finance, mergers and acquisitions and consolidations.

Table 3: Competitive Edge – Present Practices

Parameters	Number of Responses	Companies
Research and development	4	Ranbaxy, Morepen, Orchid, Alembic
Developing New Molecules	4	Ranbaxy, Morepen, Orchid, Alembic
Exports	2	Ranbaxy, Orchid
Manufacturing	2	Morepen, Orchid
Plans to Increase Competitive Edge		
Going for Research and development	4	Ranbaxy, Morepen, Orchid, Indswift
New Drug Discovery Research	4	Ranbay, Alembic, Orchid, Indswift.
Strategic decisions related to marketing and finance	3	Morepen, Ranbaxy, Orchid
Mergers & Acquisitions	2	Alembic, Orchid
Consolidation	1	Ranbaxy

Drug Research:

For the purpose of drug research, three practices were considered important by the companies, i.e., development of new molecules, orientation towards bulk drugs and process development for Active Pharmaceutical Industry (API). Only one company, Ranbaxy focuses on developing dosage forms.

Table 4: Drug Research – Present Scenario

Parameters	Number of Responses	Companies
Development of new molecules	2	Alembic, Indswift
Orientation towards bulk drugs	2	Alembic, Morepen
Process development for API	2	Ranbaxy, Orchid
Dosage forms	1	Ranbaxy
Effect of Patenting in 2005		
Increase in R&D spend	5	Morepen, Orchid
Introduce own patented products	2	Alembic, Ranbaxy
Form strategic alliances	1	Morepen
Focus on alternate routes of off-patent drugs	1	Indswift
Focus on regulated market	1	Morepen
Focus on brand building	1	Alembic

Product patenting in 2005 is going to affect the way the companies deal with the drug research as many new drugs and molecules will come in Indian market due to entry of more multinational companies. All the companies say that patenting in 2005 will lead to increase in expenditure in R&D. As shown in table-4, this will also lead to companies introducing their own-patented products for longer market presence and to meet the competition from other multinational companies, plans to focus on strategic alliances, alternate routes of off-patent drugs, export to regulated markets like U.S., Europe, Canada, Japan and Korea and foucs on brand building.

Drug Development:

Drug development refers to the post-research activities, which include the developing of the drug through technology to make the drug effective and unique. Out of the total sample only two companies, i.e., Indswift and Alembic presently develop drugs by emphasizing on developing new molecules through conventional or combinational synthesis and two companies that are Ranbaxy and Orchid focus on off-patent products and are tapping the generics market. Only one company, Morepen, develops drugs as per the requirements of the market. The main effect of patenting, which most of them feel, would be an increase in prices of drugs as they will be patented and it will be difficult to obtain them. Uncommon medicines are likely to become unaffordable. As a result companies have started implementing plans to face the changes and to survive. Indswift, Morepen and Orchid plan to focus on Novel Drug Delivery System (NDDS) and New Drug Development Research (NDDR). Ranbaxy and Indswift will increase their expenditure in R&D whereas Alembic prefers to form alliances with other companies.

Table 5: Drug Development – Present Practices

Parameters	Number of Responses	Companies
New drug development	2	Indswift, Alembic
Going-off patent strategy	2	Ranbaxy, Orchid
Based on market needs	1	Morepen
Effect of Patenting in 2005		
Increase in prices	3	Indswift, Alembic, Morepen
Difficulty in getting new products	1	Ranbaxy, Orch
Ways to Deal with the Change		
NDDS* & NDDR**	3	Indswift, Morepen, Orchid
Increase in R&D	2	Ranbaxy, Indswift
Alliances	1	Alembic

*Novel Drug Delivery System **New Drug Development Research

Formulations:

Formulation is the composition of a dosage form,.including the characteristics of its raw materials and the operations required to process it.

Table-6 indicates that Ranbaxy and Orchid focus on generics in order to gain formulations of the drugs which are going off-patent. Indswift and Morepen concentrate on molecules, which require complex chemistry and several reaction steps. Alembic wants to meet the increasing competition by focusing on formulating new drugs in therapeutic segment, as this is a very profitable segment with a lot of scope for growth. It was revealed that there will be no change in the formulations due to the patenting regime and the companies will follow the same strategies and will keep on finding new ways to increase their market share. But to meet the competition, companies have plans to focus on various areas. Orchid and Morepen have plans to form alliances with other companies in order to grow their base and expand. Indswift will have contracts with other companies for formulating new molecules.

Ranbaxy will increase its share in generics market and launch new brands in less regulated markets like China, Brazil, Russia and East European countries. Alembic has plans to explore untapped markets with potential, like, exploring new avenues, which would provide desired growth level and increase the market share. They also have plans to work as contract manufacturer in order to become more competitive for patented products as the costs in India are less and thus, this will provide a good route to increase revenues.

Table 6: Formulations

Parameters	Number of Responses	Companies
Generics	2	Ranbaxy, Orchid
Concentrate on Molecules	2	Indswift, Morepen
New products through therapeutic segments	1	Alembic
Effect of Patenting in 2005		
No change	5	Ranbaxy,Orchid, Alembic, Morepen, Indswift
Ways to Deal with the Change		
Forming alliances	2	Orchid, Morepen
Contracts	1	Indswift
Increase share of generics	1	Ranbaxy
Launch brands in less regulated markets	1	Ranbaxy
Explore untapped potential	1	Alembic
Contract manufacturing	1	Orchid

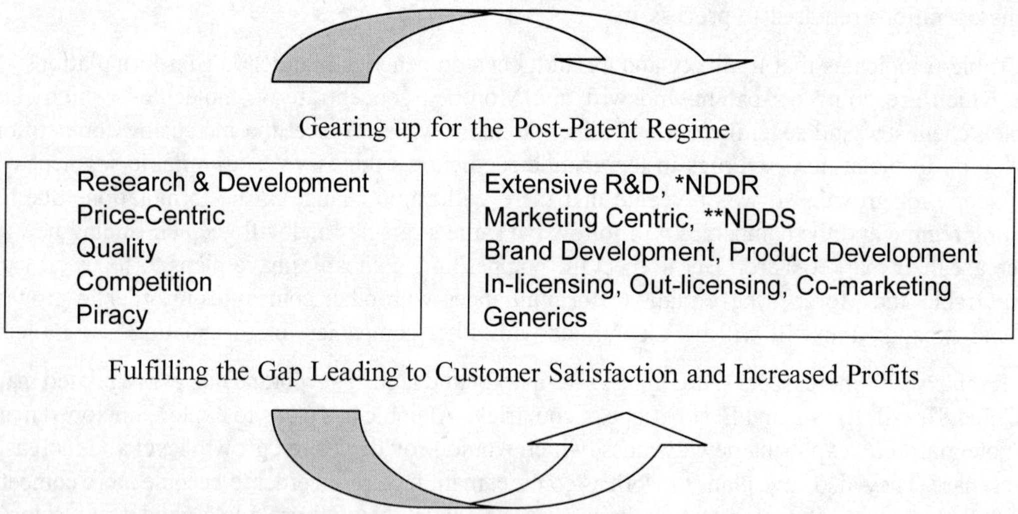

Figure 1

*New Drug Discovery Research ** New Drug Development System

There are two opportunities that Indian companies can capture well. One is the generic market. Many products are going of patent. Second is the research led play, which most of the companies have started and this will have an impact beyond 2005. the demand for better products will become a norm after 2005. This demand can be fulfilled if the companies follow the stringent quality control methods. Along with this there will be need to rely on Intellectual Property Rights to safeguard the inventions. Also the changing scenario will see an increased opportunity with the growth of markets and also increase in competition in international as well as domestic markets.

Thus, to gain from the changing scenario Indian companies need to attain the right product-mix for sustained future growth. The future of the industry will depend on how well it markets its products, its R&D, its consolidation through mergers and acquisitions and co-marketing. Core competencies will play an important role in determining the future of many Indian pharmaceutical companies in the post-product patent regime. The Indian pharmaceutical industry also needs to take advantage of the recent advances in biotechnology, contract research, clinical testing, contract manufacturing, discovery services and bio-informatics.

Questions:

1. Analyze the impact of patenting on Pharma companies.
2. Evaluate the strategies followed by the companies and make your own suggestions.
3. What kind of strategies do you suggest to boost export operations?

Source: Dipti Chadha, Gagandeep Banga and Babita Kumar (2004), Implications of Patenting on Major Pharmaceutical Companies in India – An Empirical Study. *Indian Management Studies,* Vol. 8, No. 2, October 2004, pp. 1-19.

Chapter 10

Innovation Project Management

Learning Objectives

After you have studied this chapter, you will be able to...

- Appreciate the importance of innovation
- Understand the differences between Disruptive and Incremental innovation
- Explain the innovation cycle and process models
- Know the principles of successful innovation management

Structure

- Introduction
- Innovation Cycle
- Innovation Project Stages
- Key Areas for Success
- Ideas Management
- Managing Critical Roles
- Managing Resources
- Summary
- Questions
- Exercises
- Case : Escotel's Quality Journey

INTRODUCTION

Most CEOs recognize the strategic potential of innovation and it remains a key strategy to lever competitive advantage. It is no surprise that in an Accenture study, 83 per cent of senior executives surveyed said innovation was vital to the future success of their company. But the surprising point, as another Accenture survey of the readers of Chief Executive magazine showed, most companies are able to commercialize less than one in five promising ideas; only one in eight executives felt strongly that their companies excelled at implementing innovative ideas.

INNOVATION CYCLE

The major steps involved the technology based innovation processes are shown in Table 10-1.The process is not linear; it is iterative. The stages often overlap and frequently recycle. Each stage and activities require a different mix of people skills and behaviors.

Table 10.1 Technology based innovation process

Stage	Activity
Preproject	Recognizing opportunities. Scientists, engineers and marketing people engage in intelligence activity and discussions to know the developments. Engage in technical problem solving. Ideas are discussed in rough-cut ways.
Project possibilities	Generating a new technical ideas The ideas are tested for feasibility by considering the views of customers
Project initiation	Examining economic, technical and operational feasibility. Acting as a sounding board to emerging project group.
Project execution	Project leader undertakes planning, leadership, controlling efforts. Others provide support.
Project outcome evaluation	When the technical effort seems complete, the development is evaluated based on prior expectations. The invention/discovery is transferred to manufacturing or other functions for further development.
Project transfer	The project transferred is subjected to further processing until successful innovation is achieved.

Minnesota model:

Vande Ven *et.al* (1999) conducted longitudinal studies of 12 firms and identified innovation process as a step 3- model. Table 10.2 shows the process observations from the Minnesota innovation Research Program.

Table 10.2 Innovation process at Minnesota

Stage	Activity
Initiation period	1. Most innovations have a long *gestation* period prior to initiation as search for ideas goes on. 2. Internal or external '*shocks*' trigger initiation. 3. *Plans* are developed, more to 'sell' the idea than as realistic scenarios for development.
Development period	4. The initial idea *proliferates.* 5. *Setbacks* and mistakes are frequently encountered. 6. *Criteria* of success and failure often change during the process. 7. Organizational members *participate* in the innovation in highly *fluid ways.* 8. *Senior managers* and/or investors intervene in the process throughout development. 9. *Relationships with other* organizations develop during the process and shape its course. 10. Innovation participants often work with external organizations and agencies to build *infrastructure*s for their innovations.
Implementation/Termination period	11. During the innovation, the *'new' and 'old' are linked* and integrated. 12. The innovation process stops at implementation or is *terminated* through lack of resources. 13. *Attributions* of success or failure are made, though are often misdirected.

Planned growth model:

Success is never guaranteed, but it is more easily attained through "planned growth." It's method, not magic, that brings creativity to new product strategy. Here's how one tried and true method works. It consists of four steps, as explained by Caresh Calish Gagliano (1985).

1. **Preparation:** Developing criteria and identifying opportunities.
2. **Creation:** Identifying concepts.
3. **Evaluation/qualification**: Bridging the gap between Ideas and Commercialization.
4. **Commercialization**: Taking the product or service to market.

INNOVATION PROJECT STAGES

We will now discuss various stages in an innovation project based on the planned growth model.

Phase I: Preparation

Kick-off meeting – This process begins with daylong kick-off meetings attended by as many as eight people. The officials –"growth problem owners" –would represent each of the company or division's primary functional areas and should be expected to contribute to the solution. The responsibility of the task force is to develop a preliminary draft of criteria. Here's possible agenda for such a group discussion:

1. **Goal parameters:** Setting objectives for revenue/volume, return on investment, profit, general program and development time. Goal parameters also should include a company's individual needs and desires.
2. **Implementation parameters:** Identifying company's assets and limitations. E.g.,: Leverageable company assets; investment/development/money available; technical/physical capabilities; marketing/distribution.
3. **Policy parameters:** Understanding how a company runs its business. Policy specifications in regard to degree of proprietariness; corporate fit; quality/image; market; and unit economics-such as cost, price/volume, value added.

Criterion review meeting – Review takes place at a subsequent meeting of the "growth problem owners" in which criteria are reformulated. Criterion statements must be realistic, concise and specific and provide a framework for judging candidate ideas. One of the simplest ways to rank each criterion is to assign rating of "M" for must, "D" for desirable, or "B" for bonus. Smit's team, for example, identified 24 criteria for considering opportunities. Here is the top 4.

- Exploit Smit's present capabilities in its key technologies.
- First commercial sale should occur by mid-1986.
- Should generate a cumulative pretax profit of at least 3 million Dutch guilders by 1988.
- Limit total investment to 6 million Dutch guilders.

Opportunity area identification session – After the final criteria are agreed upon, a company should seek assistance from objective outside experts to help identify new product opportunities. A company should look for "horizontal" experts: people with a broad overview of trends and activities in a specific area. Those experts usually are editors, academics, consultants or industry and government workers. A trained moderator can be used during the meeting to ensure that ideas are added to or built upon, not judged. All of the information from the briefing documents and the session tapes should be pulled together. That data must be studied and organized into "opportunity areas," which can be examined by secondary research.

Opportunity areas evaluation session – The company team of "growth problem owners" meets to evaluate the areas of opportunity identified by the panel of experts. The team enhances those ideas based upon their knowledge and expertise. Then they correlate them with the final criteria. Secondary market research, user panels, etc. should be used to supplement those considerations.

Strategy review meeting – The same group takes part in the strategy review meeting to finalize the strategy (opportunities to be exploited). A company should distribute to those participants:

- The finalized criteria (complete with "musts", "desirables" and "bonuses").
- The opportunity areas on which they are to concentrate their efforts.
- An identification of expected trends and changes.
- Additional research results.

Figure 10.1shows the steps in opportunity identification.

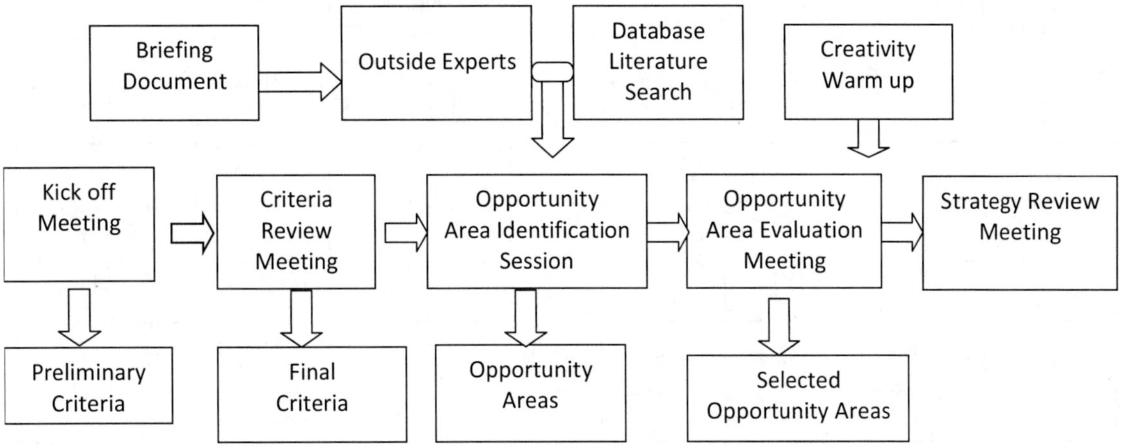

Figure 10.1 Phase 1: Opportunity Identification

Phase 2 : Creation

Having selected the best area of opportunity, it is time for concept generation and development.

Creative session – It begins with a second meeting of outside experts. But this time, the expertise needed is vertical in nature. A company should remember, however, to select a team to "surround" the area of interest not just hit it on the head. A briefing document stating the new objective and additional information on the company and current trends should be given to participants. It should encourage members to generate ideas rather than conduct straight analysis.

Fine tune meeting – Based on the literature survey, most promising ideas are found out form the ideas generated in the previous session.

Creative session – It also should use some creative technique to get the participants to think about the relationships of known elements.

Fine tune meeting – The output of this second, more focused session also will need to be organized to present at yet another team meeting. At that meeting, inside experts should once again build on each other's ideas before those ideas are evaluated against the criteria.

Figure 10.2 presents steps in concept generation and development.

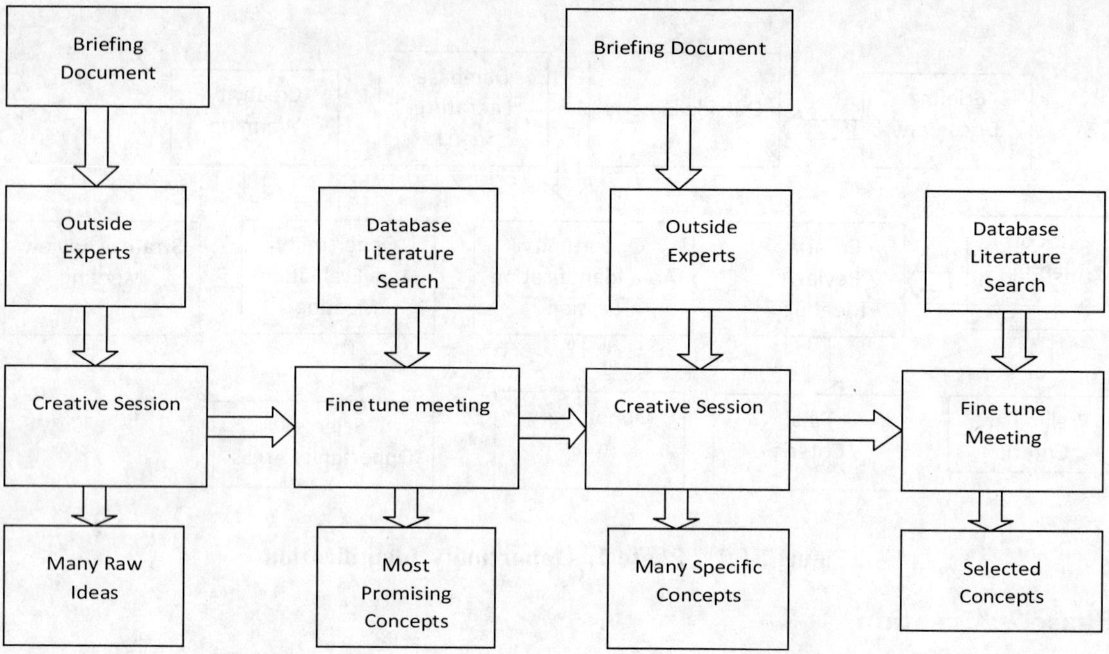

Figure 10.2 Phase 2: Concept Generation & Development

Phase 3: Evaluation /Qualification

Evaluation – In this stage, the company team must evaluate the most promising new business, product or service ideas and decide which ones will be commercialized. To make that decision, the company must conduct feasibility studies, engineering studies, potential customer interviews and focus groups. Because phase 3 ends with a new product concept, nothing should be left to chance.

Task meeting – A "mini meeting" attended by the company team kicks off Phase 3. Various tasks are identified and responsibilities assigned. Here's a sample of some task assignments that might be made if the company is searching for a new product:

- Prepare renderings and/or models of the most promising new product ideas or new applications.
- Identify "authorities" in the appropriate fields; then gather opinions and recommendations through personal interviews and/or panel discussions.
- Set up individual or group interviews with potential customers.
- Begin engineering studies.
- Obtain relevant preliminary market information from available secondary data.
- Perform competitive analysis.
- For consumer products or services, obtain primary market data by conducting one or more focus groups drawn from relevant segments. For non-consumer products, obtain primary market data from selected large prospective users and/or purchasers, either through phone interviews or through industrial focus groups.

If a company is searching for new applications for a material or technology, here are some typical task assignments:

- Prepare an outline/description for each of the most promising ideas.
- Identify and contact design engineers in leading firms in appropriate industries.
- Prepare a questionnaire asking for technical and market information to be mailed to design engineers.
- Identify pertinent trade and professional organizations and trade publications.

Idea Champion – While groups are terrific for generating new ideas, individuals make those ideas happen. Thus, at the beginning of phase 3, one person should be assigned to spearhead the activities and be responsible for turning the new idea into reality.

The Final Countdown – The company team should hold at least two additional meetings once the assigned tasks are completed. During those meetings, team members review and narrow down the available options. Evaluating good ideas is difficult. And sometimes when all other methods of evaluation fail, gut feelings are best. What's needed, therefore, are evaluation techniques that help clarify those gut feelings? Here are some tips:

1. All ideas should be collected and numbered sequentially (I).
2. The top seven or eight factors should be selected to evaluate the ideas: (F).
3. Each idea should be rated against each factor by assigning it one of the following values:

   3 = a good fit with F.

   1 = needs some modification to fit F.

   0 = can't decide.

   -1 = needs major refinement to fit F.

After evaluating each idea against each factor, a check should be put above any number that triggers a positive response or gut feeling, for the idea it represents.

- Those ideas that scored well but did not win on gut feeling should be examined.
- Also those factors where the idea fared poorly should be examined.
- Evaluation should be performed with ideas that won on gut feeling but elicited weak responses to one or more factors.

What part of those ideas needs to be changed or modified? The idea should be revised to reflect your new insights. Many companies are fearful of entering unknown territories, such as putting a new product on the market. Many new products have died during the planning stage because of that last-minute fear of the unknown. Making companies feel comfortable about the money they are investing, therefore, is the purpose of phase 3.

Timing – It's difficult to pinpoint the best time to act. The process, however, tends to drive itself home when information has been gathered and enough facts analyzed. The staff unites to fulfill the promise of the best ideas.

Figure 10.3 depicts steps in pre-commercialization.

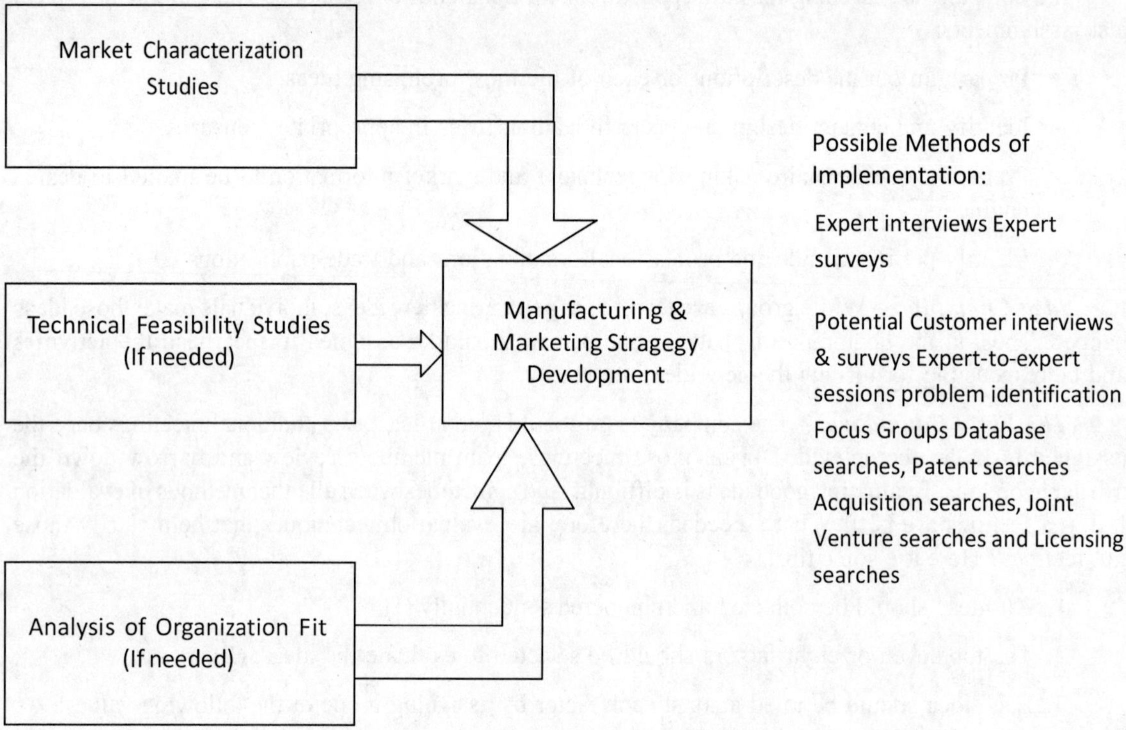

Figure 10.3 Phase 3: Pre-Commercialization

Phase 4: Commercialization

Project leader undertakes development work or implementation of idea approved. Planning, leadership and controlling efforts commence with the support of tools like PERT and work breakdown structures. Managers in other functional areas provide support. When the engineering or technical effort seems complete, the development is evaluated based on prior expectations. The invention is transferred to manufacturing for production or other functions.

The product or process so created is marketed to reach end users, through innovation diffusion process. The success of innovation is measured by market acceptance and revenues generated by the innovation.

KEY AREAS FOR SUCCESS

There's no magic formula for ensuring success. About eight of 10 new products introduced today fail. But a company certainly can improve those odds by enlisting outside experts, proceeding systematically and carefully from one point to the next and by leaving little to chance. Success is never guaranteed, but it is more easily attained through application of techniques and following principles. We will discuss the key areas in the innovation project management.

(i) Managing ideas.

(ii) Managing critical roles.

(iii) Managing resources.

IDEA MANAGEMENT

The ideas management from opportunities to implementation is the most crucial task in successful innovation. Ideas are like babies; they should be protected and nurtured. We will examine the progress of ideas through different stages of innovation and suggest tips to ensure their healthy development. Table 10.3 highlights the key questions in promoting an idea.

Table 10.3 Promoting an Idea: A Checklist

Dimension	Evaluative questions
Strategy fit	How will this idea serve the mission or objectives of my organization? Does the firm have core competencies needed for the innovation?
Resources	What assets do I have to champion this idea? What resources do I have to promote the idea? What do I need to promote the idea?
Supporters	Who will be affected if the idea is implemented? Who can become my ally? Why should they support me? Who could I add to my band of supporters? How do I convince them?
Opposition	Who can I trust for reliable feedback? Who will be my opponents? What resources do my opponents have to oppose me? What resistance can I anticipate? How can I minimize its impact?
Competitors	Who are our competitors in this area? What are they doing?
Testing	How could I test or pilot this idea with minimum risk?
Attachment	Why do I like this idea so much? What aspects of my idea, am I willing to alter or sacrifice?

Recognizing Opportunities:

Recognizing the opportunity associated with an innovation is usually chancy.

Use multiple sources -In short, to work, innovation must be a collaborative initiative in which top management takes conspicuous ownership. According to Bart,

At Reckitt Benckiiser, innovative ideas are generated from consumers, from suppliers, from creative shops. In fact, everybody in this organization is there to generate ideas as well and to bring them to the table. The more ideas I have, the better my chances of finding a winner.

Organizations are finding innovative ways to get ideas. Consider the case of Hilton given in Box 10.1.

Box 10.1 Hilton's challenge

Hilton Hotels Corporation is always seeking new approaches to increase the sense of community for its guests. In 2005, the organization wished to target a group of forward-thinking individuals who were familiar with the Hilton brand and family of hotels. Additionally, Hilton desired a broad range of concepts from a geographically diverse group of future business leaders. Finally, Hilton wanted to have access to all ideas through a web-based interface and have the ideas pre-screened by a qualified group of innovation professionals to understand which ideas held the most promise.

A solution:

Idea Crossing invited Hilton to submit its question in the 3rd Annual Innovation Challenge. Idea Crossing marketed the event, managed contestant registration and communication, accepted structured submissions, recruited judges and facilitated the judging process through its web-based application (Challenge Accelerator™).

This allowed the company to engage nearly 400 bright MBAs from around the world to tackle this issue. Students were encouraged to visit a local Hilton or franchise hotel, research the company's current efforts to foster a community among its guests, compile their most innovative thoughts, and submit their best concept for judging. Hilton's only task was to define a challenge question and await results.

Benefits to Hilton:

Ideas: Hilton retained ownership of over 80 new approaches to develop a sense of community among its guests.

Expert evaluation: Each plan was graded with both a quantitative score along with a set of individualized comments, which shed additional light on each concept's viability, strengths and weaknesses.

Emotional connection: Participants immersed themselves in the Hilton brand for several weeks while constructing their submissions and every student felt the effect of the Hilton Hotels Corporation on their MBA experience.

Encourage employees – Norman R. Baker, Stephen G. Green, Alden S. Bean, suggested the following practices to enhance and sustain idea generation and submission by employees:

- Telling the potential sources of first suggestion, especially R&D staff, those new project ideas are desired.
- Telling them what kinds of ideas are desired.
- Communicating goals, objectives, needs, priorities, etc.
- Making idea generation and submission a part of the job description.
- Making idea generation and submission part of the performance appraisals.
- Rewarding individuals who do well at idea generation and submission.
- Exerting time pressures—set short-term goals and expectations for idea generation.
- Periodically updating and communicating the information that the R&D staff must have in order to: (1) assess whether the idea will be positively and enthusiastically received by management and (2) evaluate the nature and quality of rewards likely to be received if the idea

is a winner and the losses if it is not. Minimize the extent to which relevance is seen as reviewer dependent.

- Positively recognizing idea generation and submission when they occur and publicly recognizing ideas when they become a project or part of a project.
- Allowing for and considering the submission of incompletely developed ideas by providing the support necessary to develop them more fully.
- Rewarding the idea originator when the project results in value to the organization.
- Providing, when possible, the idea originator with the opportunity to research, develop, transfer, and implement the project and its consequences.

Idea screening – Innovative companies must eliminate unpromising ideas as quickly as possible, before they absorb significant resources. The identified opportunity areas are to be evaluated using techniques that are objective as well as subjective.

Kill quick-Kill right – Quick kills have the virtue of making more resources available for the handful of ideas that have real merit. However, killing focus may cause loss of some good ideas, which may look unpromising in the embryonic stage.

Use techniques for evaluation – Every company must have a method for sorting good ideas from bad ones. Screening techniques should be objective and rigorous. At the same time the value of intuition should not be ignored.

(i) Rough-cut business evaluation:

A rough-cut business evaluation of opportunities is another non-quantitative screen that separates good ideas from all the rest. It asks three fundamental questions:

1. Does the innovation have a strategic fit with the company?
2. Does the company have the technical competencies to make it work?
3. Does the company have the business competencies to make it successful?

If you get positive answers to all three, the idea has potential.

(ii) The Idea Funnel:

The funnel has a wide mouth into which many undeveloped and roughly screened ideas are poured. As the funnel narrows, the criteria for staying in the funnel become progressively more rigorous. The process encompasses "tinkering," experimentation, market research and prototyping. Some ideas survive this winnowing process longer than others, but only a few pass entirely through the funnel toward commercialization.

The funnel concept raises a number of important issues for innovators:

- What should the criteria be for staying in the funnel?
- How long will development and experimentation be allowed to progress before someone pushes the "kill" button?
- How should the kill decision be made?

(iii) Stage-Gate Systems:

Robert Cooper developed the stage-gate system in the late 1980s. It is an alternating series of development stages and assessment "gates" that aims for early elimination of weak ideas and faster time-to-market for potential winners. Here's how it works in practice

- *Stages:* Phases of the process in which development work is done. For example, a system would have stages for developing the raw idea, technical specifications, a prototype and so forth. Commercialization is the final stage.
- *Gates:* Checkpoints at which people with decision-making authority determine if the project should be killed, sent back for more development or advanced to the next development stage. Gates may be used at various points to determine strategic fit, whether the project passes technical and financial hurdles, whether it's ready for testing or launch and so forth.

The system has some merits.

- It is an improvement over one that is either *ad hoc* or arbitrary.
- Superior to a system in which managers must curry favor with powerful executives to keep their projects alive and moving forward.
- Prevents projects of dubious value from hanging on and soaking up scarce resources that could be applied profitably elsewhere.

The effectiveness of a stage-gate system, however, is no better that the decision-making teams that control each gate. These teams should have the following features:

- Be experienced with innovation and product development.
- Have expertise in the discipline required at their particular gate (e.g., marketing or financial analysis).
- Have the authority to extend or withdraw funding.
- Be very clear about company strategy.
- Be objective and unencumbered by political pressure.

The first gate in any stage-gate system is the screening of what appear to be promising ideas. Screening is the most important gate and screeners should do the following:

- *Seek a balance between Errors of acceptance and Rejection* – Don't be so conservative that only "sure things" are accepted, and don't be so lax that the company must spread its limited development funds too thinly over many projects.
- *Learn to live with ambiguity and uncertainty* – Reliable data and quantitative measures are almost never available at this early stage.
- *Use decision criteria that reflect the company's objectives* – Also consider the goals of the new product program.

The problem, some companies find, is with the screeners and the go/kill criteria they apply. If a company kills every idea that cannot demonstrate value for existing customers or large existing markets, then few radical ideas will survive. This practically guarantees that the company will not be on the leading edge of the next wave of innovation that washes through its industry. Persistent killing of radical ideas will also signal employees that the company is not interested in doing anything substantially different from what it has done in the past. In other words, "Wasting our time and resources with far-out ideas won't help our career at this firm." One antidote to this problem is to set up a parallel evaluation system to deal with innovations that fall outside of a company's current markets and technologies.

Idea evaluation:

At the end of this process you should have a solution that is novel, attractive and feasible. Managers and innovators must eventually confront the financial issues bound in new ideas as those ideas move closer and closer to commercialization.

❖ **Novel:**

Has it been tried before?

Has it been put into practice anywhere else (by other teams; by the competition; in similar organizations)?

Is it radically new or superficially new?

❖ **Attractive:**

Is the idea simple? Does it seem obvious? Is it too clever, ingenious or complicated?

Is it direct and uncomplicated?

Can you write a simple, clear and concise statement of it?

Can it be understood by anybody working in the field?

Is the idea exciting? Does it 'explode' in people's minds? Does it provoke cries of: "Why didn't I think of that?" if it doesn't quite explode, could you simplify it?

Do we like the idea?

Is it compatible with human nature? Could anyone accept it as reasonable?

Is it likely to be attractive to the organization?

Will it solve the problems that the organization considers most significant?

What are the specific benefits (cut costs; streamline operations; provide new markets; take us into a new product sector; improve our image with our customers)?

How will it fit our strategy, vision, culture or style?

Is it timely? Would it have been better six months ago? What's the point of pursuing it now? Will it be better six months hence? Can you afford to wait?

❖ **Feasible:**

Is there any flow or inherent inconsistency in the idea? Could it work? Could we imagine it happening here, in this organization?

Make business evaluation:

The questions in evaluation are:

- ❖ How much would it cost to bring the idea to market?
- ❖ What price would we ask?
- ❖ How many units could we expect to sell at that price?
- ❖ What would be our costs of marketing, production and service?

In its early stages, a radical idea is usually too raw and unformed to examine in terms of these questions. If the idea represents something truly new to the world, any answers would have to be based on sheer guesswork—hence, they would be useless.

In case of incremental innovations, the cost of developing the new idea, launching it, and filling orders can often be estimated from experience with related products. Thus, innovators and managers can often apply financial tools as they determine which ideas should move forward, be killed, or be sent back for additional development. Two of those tools are:

- ❖ Breakeven analysis.
- ❖ Discounted cash flow analysis.

Examine Cannibalization issues:

Innovators and managers must confront the cannibalization issue as they assess the value of their new technologies and products. In most cases they will conclude that the wisest course is to displace their current products and services; otherwise, competitors will step in to do the job.

Make prototypes to save costs:

In many sectors, such as pharmaceuticals, car manufacture and IT, firms know that they need to manage carefully the economic costs of experimentation. The expenditure they need to invest in people, research, prototyping and training required to test and refine unproven ideas is to be guided properly. It requires an ability to recognize projects that are "no hopers" and those that may have a future hopes. But such decisions are not easy to make and may lead technical and research staff to be risk-adverse.

Mindful of this, BMW has built into its R&D centre at Munich a system that minimizes the financial costs of failure. Traditionally, for example, new components require expensive prototypes to be made that have to be discarded if the project is abandoned. This can prevent experiments getting beyond the blueprint stage, because researchers want to be sure that the cost of designing and manufacturing these prototypes is justified and that the project has a high probability of succeeding. BMW developed a robust plastic that can be molded at comparatively little cost to a high precision by lasers. The resulting prototypes are sufficiently durable and finely molded to enable researchers to refine and test their designs to their heart's content.

Idea implementation:

Project leaders/innovators often face difficulties in promoting the idea at different stages. The typical nagging questions one would face in different stages of an innovation project are shown in Table 10.4 :

Table 10.4 Dilemmas in different stages

Stage	Dilemmas
Screening	How to sell an idea to my manager?
Development	How to gain the team's commitment to a new procedure? How to convince the Board to allocate funds for the project?
Implementation	How to win regional office's approval for a new distribution system? How to interest an awkward client in a new product?

The following guidelines will be helpful:

- Think about implementation as early as possible. Clarify your goal. Ask yourself: "What do I want to do? What's stopping me?"
- **Find a sponsor:** Somebody who can give your idea powerful support in the organization.
- Identify the people who will help to implement the idea? How will they need to change their behavior? How soon can you involve them? How will you motivate them to do what you want them to do?
- Set milestones for yourself. They will help to motivate you. Reaching each milestone is a sign of progress and an opportunity to pat yourself on the back.

Use tactics to sell ideas:

It is pointless to suppose that if a solution is correct then there is no need to sell it – that its truth will shine for all to see. No one is obliged to accept anything he disagrees with. **[Edward de Bono]**

There are two main reasons why implementation or getting acceptance to new ideas is so difficult- *Ego attachment* ('I and my idea') and *Tendency to reject other's ideas*(I am Ok –you are not OK). Table 10.5 lists the idea killers.

1. **Detach your self** – You must sacrifice your attachment to your idea: to let it go out into the world and fend for itself. Like any anxious parent, we find it difficult to relinquish ownership of ideas that we have nurtured from birth. But we must.
2. **Know reasons for resistance to accept new ideas and act** – Making an idea work involves influencing other people. They must be convinced that it is a good idea, and that it can work. Experience suggests that people will be ready with lots of reasons not to be convinced. One may have to use political pressures or rational tactics to gain acceptance and support from others.

Table 10.5 Idea Killers

Reaction mode	Descriptive statements
Rejection	We don't have the resources /staff/ money/ time/ expertise. It'll never work. We tried it before and it failed. It's not relevant to our current strategic plan. It's a bit too radical for this company. It'll cost too much.
Suggestion	Hm. Now supposing we just changed this little bit and that piece...

Reaction mode	Descriptive statements
Cold reception	What's the point? That reminds me…
Criticism	You'll never do the way we do things round here. You haven't thought it through. Of course, that's just the sort of idea we might expect from you. Not practical. Too complicated. What about the intangibles? It'll never catch on.
Evasion	Let's wait a bit I like the idea, but my manager… Good idea. We'll appoint a committee to look into it.

Locate a sphere of influence:

Implementing a new idea involves as much liaison and networking as it does influence and command. You will need to find the sphere of influence that is relevant to your idea. It may not be a conventional centre of power. Identifying and evaluating spheres of influence is a more complicated issue.

- ❖ Who is making all the important decisions these days?
- ❖ What issues or concerns are driving the organization at the moment?
- ❖ What parts of the organization address those concerns most directly?
- ❖ How relevant is our idea to those concerns?
- ❖ In what directions do we want influence to move in the organization?
- ❖ What kind of authority would give our idea credibility (financial/technical/marketing/personnel)?

Find a sponsor:

Finding the right sponsor is an important and tricky matter. Begin by asking:

- ❖ Who owns the problem?
- ❖ Who owns the solution?

The problem owner will certainly have an interest in sponsoring our solution. But we will also want to win over the future owner of the solution.

- ❖ Who would control the budget for implementing this idea?
- ❖ Who has access to the people and resources we will need?
- ❖ What is the nature of their authority in the organization?
- ❖ Are they likely to stay in the organization long enough to see our idea through?
- ❖ What is their past record on implementing ideas?

The most powerful sponsor will be the person who can do most to help us to implement the solution. We will recognize them, not only by their position in the organization (and the size of their budget!) but also by their innate authority and ability: their capacity to influence others, their status, the value others place on their expertise – and their past record as people who '*make things happen*'.

Know the sponsor:

Having chosen the sponsor, find ways of persuading him/her to support the idea. To do this, we need to exercise empathy, projecting ourselves into their mind.

- ❖ How do they see the organization and their place in it?
- ❖ What are their goals – immediate and long-term?
- ❖ How can our idea help to achieve those goals?
- ❖ What are their needs – and how can our idea address them?
- ❖ What are their prevailing mindsets?
- ❖ What are their systems of values?
- ❖ What style of management do they operate?

Gain support – Having known about the sponsor, the next task is making a convincing presentation.

- *Present the idea in their terms* – In their language, locating it in their network of priorities and plans.
- *Present the prism of truth for them to see* – Arguing the case for an idea is not a good way of selling it. Give somebody logical reasons for doing something and they will immediately start to find arguments for not doing it.
- *Demonstrate* – In advertising jargon '*the eye buys'* If at all possible, demonstrate your idea. Build a prototype or a model; create a worked example; apply your idea to a real situation and show the benefits. Better still, asks your sponsor to 'do it themselves'.
- *Create images* – If a practical demonstration is not possible, do the next best thing: create an evocative image in your sponsor's mind, which will make an immediate, lasting impression and stimulate their imagination. Search for ways of bringing the idea alive, of personalizing it, of making it concrete. Search for the following:
  - ❖ Examples from experience.
  - ❖ Anecdotes.
  - ❖ Analogies.
  - ❖ Metaphors.
  - ❖ Symbols.
- *Rely on oral communication* – Do not rely on selling your idea on paper. Memos, reports and proposal documents are useful for supporting your idea with detailed evidence; by themselves, they are unlikely to be persuasive. Find a way to talk about the idea, either informally in conversation or in a more formal presentation.
- *Keep your message simple* – Your task is to inspire: to create a shared vision of a future. You will do this most effectively by planting images in your audience's mind that will stimulate their imagination. You could create a set of fancy slides or overhead projections; but the most powerful images are those that you conjure up in your audience's mind.

MANAGING CRITICAL ROLES

Michel Syrett and Jean Lammiman have identified five roles in idea development in innovative organizations: Spark, sponsor/champion, shaper, sounding board and specialist. Robert and Fusfeld identified five roles: idea generating, entrepreneuring and championing, project leading, gate keeping and sponsoring/coaching. Awareness of the roles and providing training and opportunities for the energetic play of the roles is essential for successful innovation effort. Table 10.6 discusses the roles by integrating the views of both the writers. Table 10.7 identifies the contribution by each role and the rewards appropriate to each role.

Table 10.6 Roles in ideas development

Role	Personal characteristics	Definition	Often undertaken by
Spark /idea generating	Expert in one or two fields. Often will work alone. Enjoys doing innovative work.	Generates new ideas and tests their feasibility. Searches for the breakthroughs.	Anyone employed by or associated with the organization.
Sponsor/ Champion/ Entrepreneuring	Strong application interests. Possesses a wide range of interests. Energetic.	Promotes the idea or project inside the organization, ensuring that it is not dismissed. Sustains interest during difficult or lean times. Gets resources. Takes risks.	Senior line managers, members of the board, non-executive directors.
Shaper/Project leading	Focus for information and decision-making. Ability to integrate. Leadership.	Provides the team leadership and motivation. Plans and organizes the project. Achieves functional coordination. Ensures progress of project.	Project leader and project team.
Sounding board/Coach	Possesses experience in developing new ideas. Good listener.	Provides encouragement, guidance and acts as a sounding board for the project leader and others. Helps the project team to get what it needs from the others parts of the organization.	Often a senior person who knows the organizational ropes.
Specialist	Strong research and project management capabilities.	Someone who draws on their specialist skills to shape the idea or project from a specific standpoint and uses the opportunity to break new ground in the field.	Members of the project team, consultants (process and strategy), academics and researchers, R&D staff from principal suppliers.
Gatekeeper	Possesses high technological competence. Is approachable and personable.Enjoys face to face contact of helping others.	Passes information on to others about developments inside and outside. Serves as an information resource for others in the organization. Provides informal coordination among personnel.	Engineers, scientists or marketing people with technical background.

Table 10.7 Measuring and Rewarding Critical Function Performance

Dimension	Contribution for appraisal of performance	Appropriate rewards
Idea Generating	Quantity and quality of ideas generated.	Opportunities to publish. Recognition from professional peers through symposia, etc
Entrepreneuring or Championing	Ideas picked up; per cent carried through.	Visibility, publicity and further resources for project.
Project Leading	Project technical milestones accomplished. Cost/schedule constraints met	Bigger of more significant projects. Material signs of organization status
Gatekeeping	People helped; Degree of help.	Travel budget. Key "assists" acknowledged. Increased autonomy and use for advice.
Sponsoring or Coaching	Success in developing staff. Extent of assistance provided.	Increased autonomy. Discretionary resources for support of others.

Source: Roberts, Edwards B. and Fustfeld, Alan, R, Staffing the Innovative Technology Based Organization, *Sloan Management Review,* 1961.

Appointing a project "champion" to take charge during the preparation and creative phases of the planned growth process is desirable. But it becomes essential during the evaluation/qualification stage.

There are certain problems found in general in respect of the persons playing different roles. Steps are to be initiated to make them positive contributors. Table 10.7 outlines the problems and possible measures. The failure to play roles effectively comes out of their egos, biases and attitudes. They can be corrected by taking the following measures:

- Creating positive innovation climate in the organization.
- Conducting periodical reviews of the roles and contributions of the different persons playing the roles.
- Rewarding good effort.
- Organizing training programs periodically to refresh and recreate the innovative and supportive mind.

Table 10.7 Problems with critical role players and measures

Role	Problems	Measures
Spark /idea generating	Have a lack of team spirit (not worried about the views of the group). Be nonconformist in a way that may irritate others (even though they may at first sight seem conventional in their appearance and outlook). Be reserved in a team or group situation. Be uninterested in gaining commitment if compromise is the price.	Allow them freedom to think and experiment. Train them to work in teams. Make them realize the innovation needs of organization and emphasize their importance.
Sponsor/ Champion/ Entrepreneuring	Be too detached to convince. Suffer from the law of diminishing returns, if too attached to the role, as they end up seeming a professional champion.	Train sponsors to be professional. Periodically evaluate their roles and contributions and reward.
Shaper/Project leading	Become too task-oriented, concentrating on achieving pre-set milestones rather than sticking to the original vision. Be willing to submit to pressure from the top on issues such as timing and cost. Be tempted to take too much credit for the idea because they came up with a practical way forward or added a subsequent dimension that was not there before. They may even take over.	Top management should be careful in demanding project completions. Project leaders should be given Principled leadership training.
Sounding board/Coach	Take too much of a helicopter view. Demonstrate a lack of insight of the practicalities. Seem arrogant or aloof.	Encourage teamwork. Train them to be practical in outlook and cooperative with idea generators.
Specialist	Place their own speciality out of proposition in the list of priorities connected with implementing the idea. Lapse into jargon or assumed knowledge. Let technical issues or considerations act as a constraint in achieving goals.	Periodical review of specialist's role in developing a project is essential.
Gatekeeper	Lack of information systems	Strengthening information systems

MANAGING RESOURCES

The last key ingredient for a successful innovation management is the resources to carry it out-the funds, staff time, space, equipment or materials. Not all significant improvements involve large capital allocations, but even for small investment prospects, the time and money have to be found, especially because innovations, almost by definition, are likely to go beyond a formal budget allocation.

There are legendary stories, of course, of important innovations largely supported at first on "bootlegged" funds pulled creatively out of budget lines or by using after-hours labor: *people at Xerox talk about its development of liquid crystal applications in this way*. But companies where innovation is common try to keep extra resources locally accessible and there are likely to be many sources of uncommitted funds to tap.

Other companies find ways to make resources accessible outside the hierarchy, beyond normal budgetary channels. Companies like 3M have "*innovation banks*" to make "*venture capital*" available internally for development projects, a system supported by a project focus and an emphasis on small-scale operating units to keep approval points close to a manager's home base. Another high innovation company group has experimented with a top management steering committee to which any employee could bring proposals to fund a special project team.

SUMMARY

Most CEOs recognize the strategic potential of innovation and it remains a key strategy to lever competitive advantage. Edward B.Roberts and Alan R.Fusfeld explain technology based innovation process in terms of behavioral functions such as: preproject, project possibilities, project initiation, project execution, project outcome evaluation and project transfer. Vande Ven *et.al* (1999) identified innovation process as a step3- model: Initiation period, development period and implementation period. Planned growth model has four steps: Preparation, Creation and Evaluation/qualification and commercialization. Successful innovation management consists of three steps: Managing ideas, managing critical roles and managing resources.

The ideas of management from opportunities to implementation is the most crucial task in successful innovation. Recognizing the opportunity associated with an innovation is usually chancy. For better results, Use multiple sources and Encourage employees. The identified opportunity areas are to be evaluated using techniques (rough –cut evaluation, idea funnel and stage-gate systems) that are objective as well as subjective. At the end of this process you should have a solution that is novel, attractive and feasible. Innovators and managers can often apply financial tools as they determine which ideas should move forward, be killed or be sent back for additional development. Two of those tools are: Breakeven analysis and Discounted cash flow analysis. Implementation is made easy by the following guidelines: Think about implementation as early as possible, Clarify your goal, Find a sponsor, Identify the people who will help to implement the idea and set milestones for yourself.

Michel Syrett and Jean Lammiman have identified five roles in idea development in innovative organizations: Spark, sponsor/champion, shaper, sounding board and specialist. Robert and Fusfeld identified five roles: idea generating, entrepreneuring and championing, project leading, gate-keeping and sponsoring/coaching. Awareness of the roles and providing training and opportunities for the energetic play of the roles is essential for successful innovation effort. The last key ingredient for a successful innovation management is the resources to carry it out-the funds, staff time, space, equipment, or materials. Bootlegged funds, innovation banks or steering committee are the ways in mobilizing resources.

QUESTIONS

1. Explain the importance of innovation and distinguish between Disruptive and Incremental innovation.
2. Describe the innovation cycle and Minnesota model of innovation process.
3. Describe the key issues in innovation management.
4. What are the critical roles in innovation management and problems faced by them?
5. Discuss the steps to be taken in managing ideas for innovation from generation to implementation.

EXERCISES

Form a team of 10 members. Set the objective of innovating a new system (say, education) or product (say, projector) or process (say, learning). Now manage the project and document the experiences of your team. Present them in class for discussion.

CASE - ESCOTEL'S QUALITY JOURNEY

At Escotel, the quality journey was launched from inception of company in 1996. In the year 2000, the company focused in aligning quality with the business and ensured that it was internalized in each management activity, i.e., strategic planning, recruitment, people development or front-end service like sales, customer service or collection. The initiative aimed at internalizing quality contributing to bottom line of the company by facilitating radical changes as well as help internalizing a change culture in the organization.

Six-sigma philosophy:

After detailed study of various change methodologies the company decided to launch the Six Sigma philosophy in the company. The success of Six Sigma concept in companies like GE and Wipro gave them confidence of meeting their requirement by addressing need for facilitating objectives like customer satisfaction, people development and profitability. Intensive participation sessions were held across the company to define the vision, mission and values of the company. Six Sigma was to fill the gap from "as is state" to the actual accomplishment of company's vision and mission, evolving with extensive deliberations and discussions with the top team.

Structure:

The structure that they have created is in line with the business structure of the company. The sponsor of project is decision-maker, approver in the organizational hierarchy and thus a member of leadership team. The coach is the functional head at the head office and thus provides special knowledge, canalizes energy of the project team on value creating process and facilitates management support. The process champion is an individual who manages processes on day-to-day basis and thus has knowledge of best practices and is one who achieves maximum benefit with improvement of process.

Select application areas:

At the launch of concept, Six Sigma processes were taken up for internalizing Six Sigma in chosen areas of mobile sales; network performance; activation; customer complaint and query management process; billing and bill delivery; and collection. These were chosen since they are points of direct interface with customers-'moments of truth' in Escotel's business.

Training:

The intensive education plan for Six Sigma team members, champions and sponsors included white belt training for member, green belt training for champions, coaches and black belt training for champions who have completed two projects. Each project team was launched with lot of excitement, communications personally driven by he CEO and member of the top management team. A review process was evolved and coaches participated in at least one meeting of the project team each month, progress of the projects is reviewed by the circle leader as well as sponsor, at least once in a month during operation review committee meeting.

Outcomes:

At the end of two years, member, champions began to realize specific benefits. Operations management skills using facts and data were getting developed. People were acquiring team management skills for change execution. Knowledge of process beyond the functional domain was increasing. There was more networking across layer and boundaries of the organization. Employees were able to relate their contributions to the larger purpose of the company. These benefits, which were expressed in a feedback survey and gave satisfaction of initiatives being in line with change facilitative dimensions.

Reward and recognition scheme:

Reward and recognition schema created a lot of excitement as well as competition amongst team member. Project gets recognized at three levels.

1. At the first level or Level-1, a project gets an opportunity to make presentation to the circle management group and is given a token gift for participation. Each team gets an opportunity to make presentation to top management team member.
2. Selected teams participate and make presentation at Level -2. Each member of the participating team gets a decent financial reward; two teams from each of the locations get an opportunity to participate in the annual Six Sigma event.
3. At Level-3 in a convention teams make presentations to the chairman. Best Six Sigma project team members and runner up becomes member of the CEO's club for the year. Best Six Sigma team goes for a trip abroad. Each member of the team is also assessed separately for contribution made to Six Sigma at the time of annual appraisal. Rewards include gifts, beside additional weightage for promotions, compensations and benefits enhancement.

Creativity enhancement process:

Another challenge in a knowledge-based company is to create opportunity for each employee to intellectually participate in the improvement process. Creativity Enhancement through Participation (CEP) is one such program where individuals submit ideas, individuals and teams work on idea of their choice as projects. The process is IT enabled and enables individuals to participate in the improvement journey of the company and get recognized for the same. CEP is a step towards creating opportunities for employees to challenge products, processes, approaches, existing market segments and develop them, modify them for improving quality, cost, delivery and service. CEP is a program launched to help acquire the habit of challenging the paradigms and improving continually.

Employees who take initiatives to set-forth their ideas are the backbone of success of the company. It is essential to have good ideas supported by commitment to make them happen. Participation and creativity are crucial to unleash talents of a firm's most valuable resource-it's human asset. Participation encourages people to take ownership and responsibility for business results. Recognition and praise reinforces creativity about employees and hence make them realize their enormous potential. Active involvement in a program heightens employee morale, retains top talent and motivates individual to contribute to the success of the business. An environment permitting free flow of ideas, empowering individual to champion change is considered. A culture is developed where unseen layers do not restrict mind, boundaries of hierarchy and functions. It is this feeling of being an important part of the large company which facilitates in creating a positive work culture. There is a dramatic change. Initially, when CEP was launched in February 2003, the company was getting 30 ideas per month. Now they receive 300 ideas per month, i.e., one idea per employee in two months.

Excellence in execution:

To align human processes with strategy and operational plans so as to achieve excellence in our operations, we have put together a process of "Excellence in Execution" in our company. The concept covers the dimensions of leadership, creating a shared need, shaping a vision, mobilizing commitment, making change last, monitoring progress and changing systems and structures to achieve high degree of creativity, innovations and excellence in whatever we do. These projects are reviewed and evaluated by the top team periodically. Initiatives that are critical in line with business objectives are being taken up as Excellence in Execution project. Besides adopting the methodology and project work, a conscious attempt is being made to internalize dimensions of achieving excellence in execution. The purpose is to ensure a culture to facilitate radical change gets internalized across the company.

Benefits abound:

There are many non-tangible benefits of the initiative like change in perspective from function to system, change in paradigm from efficiency to effectiveness. Tangible benefits have led to a contribution of ₹ 12 crores in the year 2002-03. Changes, which have contributed to it, include:

- Improving delivery in terms of time and 99.7% age of bills are delivered.
- Radical enhancement of collection by due date, radical reduction in bad debt. Improvement in sales process with more referral business.
- Radical improvement of call center processes and thereby complaint resolution and query handling.
- Redefining customer activation process and there by reduction of Activation time by 24 times for 65% of subscribers.
- Implementation of measurements and prebilling verification. As a result, there is delivery of bill on time by avoiding rework.

Questions:

1. Analyze the efforts of Escotel to achieve quality and excellence.
2. Are there any shortcomings in their approach?
3. How can they integrate creativity with quality achievement?

Source: Rajan Dutta and Arun Malik, Scaling heights with quality, *Human Capital*, November, 2003, pp. 31-35.

Chapter 11

Individual Creativity

Learning Objectives

After you have studied this chapter, you will be able to...

- Make an inventory of traits and beliefs of a creative person
- Understand the motives of creative persons
- Explore relationship between Ego states and Creativity of persons
- Know the blocks to creativity of people
- Evolve strategies for unblocking creativity

Structure

- Introduction
- Traits of Creative Persons
- Beliefs of a Creative Person
- Motivation to Creativity
- Creativity – An Adult Function
- Creative Styles
- The Uncreative - Traits and Blocks
- Strategies for Unblocking Creativity
- Summary
- Questions
- Exercise
- Case : Travel Agency

INTRODUCTION

Creative societies are complex of myriad organizations, which are creative. Similarly creative organizations are characterized by the existence of creative groups and creative persons. The basic unit being individual in societies and organizations, the challenging task is creating creative personalities. A surprising fact is that creativity is the ability that everyone possesses. It is to the individual to use it or not. May be the person is not aware of presence of this wonderful aspect of personality.

TRAITS OF CREATIVE PERSONS

Personality is a set of distinctive characteristics of the individual that one manifests is a variety of situations. Creativity depends upon novel and varied responses on the test task.

Research studies have brought out various characteristics of creative individual. Table 11.1 presents sme of the research findings.

Table 11.1 Research on Qualities of Creative Person

S.No	Research	Year	Qualities
1.	Tripathi	1995	High intelligence. High IQ not essential
2.	Bowenfled	1952	Sensitivity, fluency, flexibility, originality, redefinition, abstracting, synthesis and organizing.
3.	Torrance	1962 & 1965	84 qualities, sensitive to objects, ideas, problems and gaps.
4.	Robbins	1980	Dissatisfaction with the status quo, lack of imagination, practicability,logic and order in thought, less anxiety, more autonomy, dynamism, less authoritarianism, acceptance of inner-impulses, achievement orientation, and responsiveness to moderate level of conflicts.
5.	Coleman	1969	Openness to experience, independence in thought and action, unusual capacity to record and retain, ability to relate to store of knowledge and experience, fluency in scanning thoughts and producing those that serve the problem to solve.
6.	Butcher J.	1970	More in the following: autonomous, self-sufficient, independent in judgement, open to irrational in them, stable, feminine in interests and characteristics, dominant, self–assertive, complex, self-accepting, resourceful, adventurous, radical, self-controlled, emotionally sensitive and introverted.
7.	Barron	1963	Less concerned about what others think of them, free in thinking, thinks wide range of possibilities and original in ideas.
8.	Sharma	1979	Adventure, Altruism, naïve, versatile, awareness of others, attraction towards disorder, attraction towards mysteries, attempting at difficult jobs, constructive in criticism, courageous, defiance of convention of courtesy, desire to excel, determination, intuitive, differentiated value hierarchy and discontented.

S.No	Research	Year	Qualities
9.	Board and others	1971	Extrovert, intelligence, constructive capacities, relative ideas of form and depth, perception of chromatic values and achromatic shades, verbal acuity, confidence, sociability, spontaneity, eccentricity and absorbing nature.
10.	Ray Choudhary	1965	Preference for complexity, high in dominance, independence, gentle, patient, helpful, sympathetic, introvert, high tolerance for ambiguity, open to inner-experience, arouse intrinsically.
11.	Dasgupta	1977	High creatives exhibit disturbed parental relationships, and more involved in their own beliefs and attitudes.
12.	Upadhyay	1977	More intelligent, socially bold, less tense stronger self-sentiment.
13.	Berkshire	1995	Speculative thinking, empowerment involving attentiveness, being organized, collaboration, cohesiveness, a willingness to change, acknowledgement, clarifying, commitment and a sense of history.
14.	Drucker	1985	Perceptiveness, self-efficacy, risk taking, openness to ambiguity, self-confidence, evaluation with the help of positive chances, operacy (skill of getting things done), proactive self-awareness, willingness to Confront Vs. Blind faith and Rule bounds Vs. Idea based decision.

We will now discuss the following distinctive characteristics of the creative people based on the list of traits mentioned above.

Sensitivity	Flexibility	Perseverance	Courage
Idea fluency	Imaginativeness	Tolerance of ambiguity	Novelty
Openness	Curiosity	Confidence	Constructive discontent
Ability to suspend judgment and criticism			Optimism

Sensitivity to surroundings and problems:

Sensitivity to surroundings is an ability to see things, note problems or areas of need and be aware of promising situations. There is a knack for making unusual and detailed observations.

Problem sensitivity refers to the ability to recognize that a problem exists. The easiest way to improve your problem sensitivity is to keep in mind nothing is ever as well done as it could be. Every man made thing can be improved and some day will be.

Idea fluency:

It is the ability to pile up a large number of alternate solutions to a given problem in a given time. Fluency development is possible. First, remember that it is quantity that you are after. Second, don't mix evaluating with your idea gathering. Third, use the following aids – Making notes, picking your time and location to be creative, set a dead line for idea generation and give you a quota for ideas.

Openness:

The creative mind is never a closed one. It shows mobility as related and unrelated data and ideas are rearranged, modified and redefined. When *no significant thoughts* occur for a problem, the creative person *stops and relaxes.* Creative person welcomes the pause. The pause gives time to recall many forgotten facts and associations, which may provide the keys to solving a current problem.

Flexibility:

The creative mind considers a *wide variety of approaches* to a problem. Rather than obstinately freezing onto one particular idea, or a single approach to a problem, the flexible person starts out by remembering that if one solution won't work, he can always approach the problem from another angle. This is also called '*creative expectancy*', meaning, the creative person expects to solve the problem no matter how many failures temporarily delay the solution. *Adjustments to new developments* and changes are quickly made.

Imaginativeness:

Creative people are comfortable with imagination and with thinking so-called weird, wild, or unthinkable thoughts, just for the sake of stimulation. Creative thinking involves the addition of imagination. The secret is to be able to combine imagination with knowledge. During brainstorming or just mental playfulness, all kinds of strange thoughts and ideas can be entertained. The mind will probably find something useful in it all. The following quotes indicate how imagination help see things differently.

Curiosity:

It is the ability of finding new ways to vary existing conditions or new ways to adapt existing ideas to new conditions etc.

There is an intensive curiosity about everything. Creative people want to know things—all kinds of things— just to know them. Knowledge does not require a reason. The question, "Why do you want to know that?" seems strange to the creative person, who is likely to respond, "Because I don't know the answer." Knowledge is enjoyable and often useful in strange and unexpected ways.

For example, Krishna was once attempting to repair something, without apparent success, when an onlooker asked testily, "Do you know what you're doing?" Krishna replied calmly, "No, that's why I'm doing it."

Curiosity can be stimulated by the questioning ability. Charles Kettering call it 'systematically challenging the obvious'. Questions like: Why is this made this way? Why do we follow this procedure? How can we improve the way we do this? One may use checklists to questions every aspect of the object.

Perseverance:

Most people fail because they spend only nine minutes on a problem that requires ten minutes to solve. Creativity and problem solving are hard work and require fierce application of time and energy. How many filaments Edison tried before he found a working one? How many aircraft designs failed in the attempt to break the sound barrier? There is no quick and easy secret. Perseverance is required to succeed.

Tolerances of Ambiguity:

Creative people tolerate uncertainty, complexity and apparent disorder since these conditions may produce desirable answers. There is little need to impose a premature simplified structure.

Confidence:

Creative people keep trust in their abilities. As Lu Yockum, a man who has had a lot of jobs and is now a top executive of Westing house Electric Corp., said:

"I never worried what job they gave me. If I didn't like it, I always changed it into one I did like. It isn't hard, if you learn to trust your own ideas."

Possibly the most important single element in bringing an on-the-job idea into being is simply believing in it-and hanging on to that belief. The story of Kietman who started Edutran is an example for confidence. Box 11.1 briefly presents it.

Box 11.1 Edutran

Matt Kiernan, an aggressive young salesman of business education courses for a New York management association, got his golden idea during his daily two-hour commute from port Jefferson on the Long Island Rail Road he proposed to his employer that they hire rail road car and present their courses to the commuters. Management couldn't see it "at that time." But everyday, Matt watched all those people sleeping, reading newspapers, wasting precious hours; the idea gnawed at him and he proposed it several more times. Finally, he resigned his job, rented a railroad car, built two classrooms in it, and formed a company call "Edutran." Now he needed academic support and he got it from Adelphi University, which supplied professors, books and curriculum as well as 55 commuting graduate students. Matt's programs has been expanded to two other Eastern railroads and 200 students, one of whom has received a master's degree. Fifteen more will do so in the near future.

Courage:

Creative people have courage to face problems. For creative thinkers, problems are interesting and emotionally acceptable. Many people confront every problem with a shudder and a turn of the head. They don't even want to admit that a problem exists—with their car, their spouse, their child, their job, their house, whatever. As a result, often the problem persists and drives them crazy or rises to a crisis.

As stated long ago, "*It takes courage to be creative. Just as soon as you have a new idea, you're a minority of one.*" There is a willingness to be different and deviate from past practices even if it means standing alone against pressures to conform. Risks are taken if they appear to be worth chancing failure. Mistakes are viewed as situations from which better ideas may arise.

Novelty:

Curious people like to identify and challenge the assumptions behind ideas, proposals, problems, beliefs and statements. Many assumptions, of course, turn out to be quite necessary and solid, but many others have been assumed unnecessarily and in breaking out of those assumptions often come a new idea, a new path and a new solution.

Consider this Problem. We make brandy and for this special edition of our finest kind, we want a fully-grown pear in one piece inside each bottle. The bottle is narrow necked. How can we do it? As you think, watch for the assumptions you are making. Possible solutions:

- *Assuming fully-grown pear:* close the neck or bottom after insertion, use a plastic bottle like heat-shrink tubing, change to a wide mouth bottle.
- *If we do not assume a fully-grown pear:* grow the pear from a bud inside the bottle.

Constructive discontent:

Constructive discontent is a positive, reflecting thought, "Hey, I know a way to make that better." One of the hallmarks of the constructively discontented person is that of a problem-seeking outlook.

Constructive discontent is necessary for a creative problem solver. If you are happy with everything the way it is, you won't want to change anything. Only when you become discontent with something, then you see a problem, will want to solve the problem and improve the situation. The more problems you find, the more solutions and therefore improvements you can make. Even previously solved problems can often be solved again, in a better way. A constructively discontent person might think.

"This is an excellent solution, but I wonder if there isn't another solution that works even better (or costs less, etc)."

Ability to suspend judgment and criticism:

Recall the proverb, *"A crank is a genius whose idea hasn't yet caught on"*. Many new ideas, because they are new and unfamiliar, seem strange, odd, bizarre and even repulsive. Only later do they become "obviously" great.

Remember that – (1) an idea may begin to look good only after it becomes a bit more familiar or is seen in a slightly different context and (2) even a very wild idea can serve as a stepping-stone to a practical, efficient idea.

By too quickly bringing your judgment into play, these fragile early ideas and their source can be destroyed. The first rule of brainstorming is to suspend judgment so that your idea-generating powers will be free to create without the restraint of fear or criticism. You can always go back later and examine—as critically as you want—what you have thought of.

Optimism:

Creative thinkers see good in the bad. When faced with poor solutions, they don't cast them away. Instead, they ask, "What's good about it?" because there may be something useful even in the worst ideas. However little that good may be, it might be turned to good effect or made greater.

How can we get college students to learn grammar better? Solution: Spank their bottoms with a hickory stick. This isn't a good solution, partly because it's probably illegal. But should we just toss it out? Why not ask what's good about it? (1) It gives individual, attention to the poor performers, (2) It gives them public attention, (3) It motivates other students as well as the student being spanked and (4) It's easy and costs nothing. The next question is, Can we adapt or incorporate some of these good things into a more acceptable solution, whether derivative of the original or not?

In the above example, changing the physical spanking to verbal spanking changes the entire aspect of the solution while keeping all the good points we identified.

BELIEFS OF A CREATIVE PERSON

The beliefs of a creative person are given below:

Problems can be solved - Problems are solved by a commitment of time and energy and where this commitment is present, few things are impossible.

Problems lead to improvements - Problems lead to search for solution that lead to improvements.

A problem can also be a solution - A fact that one person describes as a problem can sometimes be a solution for someone else. Creative thinkers also look at problems and ask, "Is there something good about this problem?"

3M chemists were experimenting with adhesives and accidentally came up with one that was so weak you could peel it right back-off. A glue that won't hold? Quite a problem. But this problem was also a solution, as you now see in Post-It Notes.

Mistakes are welcome.

Actually failure is an opportunity; mistakes show that something is being done. So creative people have come to realize and accept emotionally that making mistakes is no negative biggie.

Sir Francis Pettit Smith, one of the early developers of the screw propeller, tried one design in 1836. During the test, half of it broke off—what a failure—but then the boat increased in speed substantially, revealing the efficiency of a new design, formed from a mistake.

MOTIVATION TO CREATIVITY

Pradeep N. Khandwalla has identified the following motives for creativity:

1. Hedonism or materialism – desire to live with pleasures and amass wealth.
2. Career success – to gain achievements and progress in career.
3. Desire for original achievement – to accomplish something novel in one's life time.
4. Power and authority – to exercise authority, to have status and to be the key person in decision-making.
5. Self-actualization or personal development – to become what one wants to be.
6. Affiliation – to have relationships with people of his or her choice.

7. Altruism – believe in helping others and doing good.
8. Security – protection of interests of life–assurance of need fulfillment.

CREATIVITY – AN ADULT FUNCTION

Though it is argued that creativity is more of a child characteristic, it is proved by some research studies that it can be an adult function.

Age and Creativity:

The general argument is children are more creative than adults. It may not be true.

When a group of university psychologists tested creativity in various age groups, it found that about 2% of the 45 year olds tested out as creative according to the criteria set. When they tested a 44 year old group, the figure was the same as it was for those of 43 years of age. But when the same test was given to children, the number of 7 year olds ranked highly creative jumped to 10% and of 5 year old to 90%. The psychologists concluded that nearly everyone is born creative, but somehow this spark is lost in growing up process.

Ego States and Creativity

Research has shown that critical parent and adaptive child are not creative where as other ego states contribute fairly well to creative pursuits. Table 11.2 summarizes the findings of Sanjot Pethe (2003).

Table 11.2 Ego States and Contribution to Creativity

Ego state	Description	Contribution
Critical Parent	Controlling, critical, traditional, rules, regulations, policies	Negative
Nurturing	Caring, nurturing, protecting, encouraging, guiding	Positive
Adult	Rational, evaluative, positive perceptiveness, self-confidence sense of priority, risk taking	Positive
Natural Child	Curiosity, initiative, fearlessness probing	Positive
Little Professor	Divergent thinking, innovativeness	Positive
Adaptive Child	Adjustment, acceptance	Negative

Source: Sanjyot Pethe, Study of Relationship between Managerial Creativity and Ego states of a Manager, *South Asian Journal of Management,* Vol. 10. No.1, Jan-Mar. 2003, pp. 5, 8, 9.

CREATIVE STYLES

Insight into the influence of personal characteristic as on creativity comes from Michael Kirton's (1976) research into the nature of the creative process. Basically, Kirton posits a continuum of decision-making styles with Adaptors on one side and Innovators on the other.

- ***Adaptors*** - Are those who seek to solve problems by "doing things better." They prefer to resolve difficulties or make decisions in such away as to have the least impact up on the assumptions, procedures and values of the organization; they seek to improve the existing framework and do not "rock the boat."
- ***Innovators*** - Those inclined to "do things differently." They are likely to see the solution to problems in the alteration of the basic approaches and framework of the organization; a certain amount of disruption may contribute positively to the achievement of the organization's goals.

Individuals differ, then, not only in their levels of creativity but also in the form that creative expression takes. Thus there are both qualitative and quantitative differences in individual styles and levels of creativity. Table 11.3 summarizes some of the characteristic of adaptors and innovators. In reality, of course, most people do not fall strictly and exclusively into one of these two personality types.

Table 11.3 Two approaches to problem solving

Basis	Adaptor	Innovator
Method orientation	Employs disciplined, precise, methodical approach.	Approaches task from unusual angles.
Problem definition	Is concerned with solving, rather than finding, problem?	Discovers problems and avenues of solutions.
Change orientation	Attempts to refine current practices.	Questions basic assumptions related to current practice.
Mean orientation	Tends to be means oriented.	Has little regard for means.
Routine orientation	Is capable of extended detail work?	Has little tolerance for routine work.
Consensus	Is sensitive to group cohesion and cooperation?	Has little or no need for consensus; often insensitive to others.

Source: Adapted and modified version of Michael Kirten, Adaptors and Innovators: A description of measure, *Journal of Applied Psychology*, 61, No.5, (1976), p. 623.

Each of these basic problem-solving styles has its own strengths and weaknesses and makes its own contribution to the function of the organization.

Strength: For some problems the methodical, detailed application of the existing organizational methods yields the most effective result. Some problems, on the other hand, cry out for the original, innovative solution that gives the organizations totally new direction.

Weakness: Adaptors and innovators may not see eye-to-eye and may not understand that their differences lie at a fundamental psychological level. Thus, the potential for considerable interpersonal conflict arises, with both individuals and organizations paying the price. To adaptors, innovators may seem to be neurotics, grandstanders and misfits, bent on upheaval and destruction within the organization. Innovators, on the other hand, may view adaptors as dogmatic and inflexible "organization types" who serve as insurmountable obstacles to fundamental change in the organization. Although objectively in accurate, such pejorative stereotypes tend to polarize decision-makers and prevent objective evaluation of the merits of individual ideas.

THE UNCREATIVE – TRAITS AND BLOCKS

Various traits and barriers to creativity are identified and discussed here.

(i) Less creative Traits and Behaviours:

Traits judged by experts as farthest to form ideal creative personality include the following.

Passive:	**Attractive to others:**
Timid Reserved Bashful Quiet	Sophisticated Courteous Talkative Popular, well-liked by peers Altruistic Obedient Willingness to accept judgement of others
Abrasive:	**Active:**
Haughty and self-satisfied Domineering Stubborn Negativistic	Physically strong Does work on time

Berkshire (1995) categories of behavior that encourage creativity include:

Speculative thinking, openness, empowerment, involving, attentiveness, being organized, collaboration, cohesiveness, a willingness to change, acknowledgement, clarifying, commitment and a sense of history.

Those that hinder creativity include:

Controlling, being non-committed, competitive, blaming, disagreeing, discounting, not being organized, not being attentive, defensive, fearing reprisal, poor sense of history, rationalizing, routine thinking, and no cohesiveness.

(ii) Barriers:

Table 11.4 notes some of the findings of researchers on barriers to creativity. They include attitudes and myths. Some of the barriers are described here.

Table 11.4 Barriers to Creativity

Researcher	Findings/views
Khandwalla, (1988)	Fear of failure, allergy to ambiguity, touchiness (fear of humiliation and rejection), conformity, resource myopia, starved sensibility and rigidity.
Hurlock (1978)	Non-intellectual factors like inappropriate education and vocational goals, fear of criticism, poor economic status and other unresolved problems in diverting even the intellectually gifted creative children from full expression of their talent.
Pareek (1997)	The prescriptive style of manager with not-OK Critical Parent dominating. People with this style are critical of the behaviour of others; they develop rules and regulations and impose them on others. Mangers using this style make quick judgments and insist that all the subordinates follow certain norms.

(iii) Attitudes as blocks:

Basically it is the attitudes that determine the behavior of the people. The following negative attitudes seem to restrict the creative problem solving.

Natural resistance - Some people avoid or deny problems until it's too late, largely because these people have never learned the appropriate emotional, psychological and practical responses.

Laziness - Some people prefer status quo and the comfort associated with it. This attitude is, in effect, surrendering before the battle. By assuming that something cannot be done or a problem cannot be solved, a person gives the problem a power or strength it didn't have before. Giving up before starting is, of course, self-fulfilling.

Lack of confidence - Some people think, that the problem can be solved by some expert, but not by them because I'm not smart enough, not an engineer, or an expert, etc. Everyone is creative to some extent. Most people are capable of very high levels of creativity. The problem is that this creativity has been suppressed by education. All you need to do is let it come back to the surface.

Consider the following:

- Wright brothers invented an airplane. They are not aviation engineers. They were bicycle mechanics.
- The ballpoint pen was invented by a printer's proofreader, Ladislao Biro, not a mechanical engineer.
- Major advances in submarine design were made by English Clergyman G. W. Garrett and by Irish schoolmaster John P. Holland.
- That well-known attorney and tutor, Eli Whitney, invented the cotton gin.
- A captain of militia, George Manby, invented the fire extinguisher.

So on. In fact, a major point made by recent writers about corporate excellence is that innovations in industry almost always come from individuals (not research groups) outside of the area of the invention.

Fear of ridicule - The constant emphasis we see in society is toward the ruthlessly practical and conformist. It is common practice to criticize or laugh at unusual or different ideas before determining whether they are good or not. In our effort to appear always mature and sophisticated, we often ridicule the creative, playful attitudes that marked our younger years. Isn't play a lot of fun? Even the wild fashions, from those in Vogue to punk rock, are narrowly defined, and to deviate from them is considered wrong or ridiculous.

Solutions are often new ideas and new ideas, being strange, are usually greeted with laughter, contempt or both. That's just a fact of life, so make up your mind not to let it bother you.

Opponent within one's head - Once again, it is important to recognize that inner-reality may be inhibiting the choice. The opponent within one's own head, to use Timothy Gallwey's phrase, can be a powerful censor.

"It can't be done."
"We can't do it like that."
"They would never agree to it."
"It will be too expensive."
"Altogether too risky/disruptive/complicated/radical..."
"I don't have the time."
"That's already been tried – and look what happened."
"I might fail."

Inventors like Thomas Edison worked with a desire to succeed. As such they learnt from failures. Remember the proverb: *Mistakes aren't fun, but they sure are educational.*

Thomas Edison, in his search for the perfect filament for the incandescent lamp, tried anything he could think of, including whiskers from a friend's beard. In all, he tried about 1800 things. After about 1000 attempts, someone asked him if he was frustrated at his lack of success. He said something like, "I've gained a lot of knowledge — I now know a thousand things that won't work."

Prejudice - The older the people, the more the preconceived ideas they have about things. These preconceptions often prevent them from seeing beyond what they already know or believe to be possible. They inhibit us from accepting change and progress. Consider the problems and prejudices given under. Box 11.2 presents a few cases which demonstrate the viewpoint.

Box 11.2 How prejudice works?

Problem: How can we connect sections of airplanes with more ease and strength than using rivets?

Solution: A modern solution is to use glue—glue the sections together. We probably wouldn't think of this solution because of our prejudice about the word and idea of glue. But there are many kinds of glue, and the kind used to stick plane parts together makes a bond stronger than the metal of the parts themselves.

Problem: How can we make lighter weight bulletproof windows? Thicker glass is too heavy.

Solution: Use plastic. Again, we are prejudiced against plastic. But some plastics are not flimy at all and are used in place of steel and in bulletproof windows.

Problem: Make a ship's hull that won't rust or rot like steel or wood.

Solution: Use concrete. Our prejudice is that concrete is too heavy. Why not make lightweight concrete? That's what's done

Problem: How to divide a piece of cake equally between two kids so they won't complain that one kid is preferred over the other: "You gave him the bigger piece; you like him better! Waaaah!"

Solution: Put the kids in charge of dividing the cake. Our prejudice is that immature, selfish kids can't do the job. But the solution, one cuts the cake; the other has first choice of pieces, works very well.

Learned helplessness - This is the feeling that you don't have the tools, knowledge, materials, and ability, to do anything, so you might as well not try. We are trained to rely on other people for almost everything. We think small and limit ourselves. But the world can be interacted with.

Functional fixation - Sometimes we begin to see an object only in terms of its name rather in terms of what it can do. Thus, we see a mop only as a device for cleaning a floor and do not think that it might be useful for clearing cobwebs from the ceiling, washing the car, doing aerobic exercise, propping a door open or closed and so on.

There is also a functional fixation of businesses.

The big calculator companies Dietzgen or Pickett were among the biggest makers of slide rules. But when electronic calculators began to rise, they didn't know what business they were in. They thought they were in the slide rule business, when they were really in the calculator business. They didn't adapt, they didn't accept the challenge of change and opportunity and they fell.

Disregard for some solutions - Some solutions are not considered or are rejected simply because our reaction to them is "Yuck." But icky solutions themselves may be useful or good if they solve a problem well or save your life.

When doctors noted that some unsophisticated natives were using giant ant heads to suture wounds, they imitated this pincer-closing technique by inventing the surgical staple.

Navy commandos in Vietnam overcame their blocks and put on women's panty hose when they marched through the swamps and jungle. The panty hose cut down on the friction and rubbing from the plants and aided in removing the dozens of leeches after a mission.

(iv) Myths as blocks:

Some of the myths held by people who fail to be creative are.

Myth-1: Every problem has only one solution (or one right answer):

The goal of problem solving is to solve the problem and most problems can be solved in any number of ways. If you discover a solution that works, it is a good solution. There may be other solutions thought of by other people, but that doesn't make your solution wrong. What is THE solution to putting words on paper? Fountain pen, bal point, pencil, marker, typewriter, printer, xerox machine, and printing press?

Myth-2: The best answer/solution/method has already been found:

Look at the history of any solution set and you'll see that improvements, new solutions, new right answers, are always being found.

What is the solution to human transportation? Is it the ox or horse, the cart, the wagon, the train, the car, the airplane, the jet? Is that the best and last? What about pneumatic tubes, hovercraft, even Star Trek type beams?

What is the best way to put words on paper? The word processor? Is that the last invention? How about voice recognition, or thought wave input?

Why do shoelaces still exist, when technology has produced several other, better ways to attach shoes to feet (like velcro, elastic, snap buttons, and so on)?

Myth -3: Creative answers are complex technologically:

Only a few problems require complex technological solutions. Most problems you'll meet with require only a thoughtful solution requiring personal action and perhaps a few simple tools. Even many problems that seem to require a technological solution can be addressed in other ways.

For example, what is the solution to the large percentage of packages ruined by the Post Office? Look at the Post Office package handling method. Packages are tossed in bins when you send them. For the solution, look at United Parcel. When you send a package, it is put on a shelf. The change from bin to shelf is not a complex or technological solution; it's just a good idea, using commonly available materials.

As another example, when hot dogs were first invented, they were served to customers with gloves to hold them. Unfortunately, the customers kept walking off with the gloves. The solution was not at all complex: serve the hot dog on a roll so that the customer's fingers were still insulated from the heat. The roll could be eaten along with the dog. No more worries about disappearing gloves.

Note by the way what a good example of changing direction this is. Instead of asking, "How can I keep the gloves from being taken?" the hot dog server stopped thinking about gloves altogether.

STRATEGIES FOR UNBLOCKING CREATIVITY

Strategies for unblocking creativity start with creation of awareness and lead to goal setting.

(1) **Awareness -** Identify blocks. As Johari Window points out people may not be aware of their block. Introspection and discussion with people with whom one interacts helps in getting factual information about the blocks.

(2) **Analysis and diagnosis** - Understand the blocks fully. Reading books on psychology, discussing with people who have similar blocks and exchanging information with known people help in understanding the block in-depth.

(3) **Help from credible source** - A little guidance and encouragement is needed. It is better consult and expert in the field or a person whom you trust.

(4) **Inoculation** - It helps to get rid of a block in stages. Move from less risk to high risk situation.

(5) **Reward -** It is better to join an organization, which rewards overcoming blocks.

(6) **Goal setting** - After some success at unblocking, it may be useful to set some goals and pursue.

SUMMARY

The basic unit of creative organizations is creative persons. The challenging task therefore is creating creative personalities. Researches have been done to bring out various characteristics of creative individual. Among the distinctive characteristics of the so-called creative people are the following: Sensitivity to surroundings and problems Idea fluency, originality, flexibility and openness, imaginative, curious and inquisitive, perseverance, tolerance of ambiguity, originality, courage and confidence, constructive discontent, ability to suspend judgment and criticism and optimistic.

The beliefs of a creative person are: problems can be solved; problems lead to improvements; a problem can also be a solution and mistakes are welcome. Pradeep N. Khandwalla has identified the following motives for creativity: hedonism or materialism, career success, desire for original achievement, power and authority, self-actualization or personal development, affiliation, altruism and security. The psychologists concluded that nearly everyone is born creative, but somehow this spark is lost in growing up process.

Kirton posits a continuum of decision-making styles with adaptors on one side and innovators on the other. Traits judged by experts as farthest to form ideal creative personality include: passivity, abrasive, active and active to others. Barriers to creativity include: negative attitudes (natural resistance, laziness, lack of confidence, fear of ridicule, opponent within one's head, prejudice, functional fixation and disregard for some solutions. Some of the myths held by people who fail to be creative are: every problem has only one solution (or one right answer);the best answer/solution/method has already been found and creative answers are complex technologically. Strategies for unblocking are: Awareness, Analysis and diagnosis, Help from credible source, Inoculation, Reward and Goal setting.

QUESTIONS

1. Give inventory of traits and beliefs of a creative person.
2. Highlight the motives of creative persons.
3. Examine the relationship between Ego states and Creativity of persons:
4. What are the blocks to creativity of people? Describe strategies for unblocking creativity.

EXERCISES

Conduct a study and test the following hypotheses employed by Sanjyot Pethe. Ego state scale of Jongeward and Sayers was standardized on a Indian sample (Reliability 0.9. and validity : 0.89). Managerial creativity scale is that of Pethe and Guptha (1997). You may use correlation and regression analysis.

Hypothesis 1 Nurturing Parent has a positive relationship with managerial creativity

Hypothesis 2 Adult has a positive relationship with managerial creativity.

Hypothesis 3 Little Professor has a positive relationship with managerial creativity.

Hypothesis 4 Natural Child has a positive relationship with managerial creativity

Hypothesis 5 Critical Parent has a negative relationship with managerial creativity.

Hypothesis 6 Adaptive Child has a Negative relationship with managerial creativity.

Hypothesis 7 Nurturing Parent promotes managerial creativity.

Hypothesis 8 Adult promotes managerial creativity.

Hypothesis 9 Little Professor promotes managerial creativity.

Hypothesis 10 Natural Child promotes managerial creativity.

Hypothesis 11 Critical Parent and Adaptive child do not promote managerial creativity.

Hypothesis 12 Critical Parent and Adaptive child inhibit managerial creativity.

CASE : TRAVEL AGENCY

Kiran Software Developers developed a product to Kirsha Travel Agency, which was aggressively engaged in ticketing and traveling business. A study of the customer interface process, revealed major inadequacies. For instance, in response to a customer query about alternative prices and airlines for traveling from Delhi to London, the travel agency gave the fares for Air India and British Airways. There are some glaring gaps in such a response. The entire gamut of alternatives (other airlines) was not given to the client. The lowest cost alternative was not provided. And the alternative of flying to a closer and then taking a subway or bus to reach the final destination (if lowest cost alternative is required) was not suggested. As a possible solution, user-friendly database management system using Fox-Pro was conceptualized.

Using the new system, the travel agency can adequately modify its response to clients.

Customer needs can be satisfied more quickly and effectively. Information regarding the lowest cost alternative, information regarding key hotels in the destination, city and their room rates and information regarding foreign exchange can be made available.

Operational needs could have been satisfied much better. The travel agency was earlier dependent on two or three people for providing relevant and comprehensive information to customers. In case the proposed innovation is adopted, any company employee would be able to provide the requisite information to customers.

Given the benefits like increase in productivity, improvements in customer service and decrease in dependence on personnel, there should have been an eagerness to implement the innovation. However, that was not to be the case. The chronological sequence of events that took place are given below:

Event 1: The innovation demo was shown to the managing director and some key personnel of the travel agency. They liked the innovation and gave the go-ahead for development.

Event 2: The developed product was shown to the managing director and another employee who in the organization was considered to be a prized employee because of his being the prime source of airline travel related information. Though he was not opposed to the innovation, he raised two objections. First one is, the inputting of database, which would take a huge amount of effort and time. Second, since updating from airlines regarding ticket prices is frequent, the system would not be of much use.

Event 3: This was basically a non-event. The travel agency did not try out the system. Though the travel agency never rejected the innovation proposal, it slowly went into oblivion.

Kiran and his associates are worried about this outcome. To avoid such disappointments they have decided to be more careful in the future. They discussed probable reasons for such failure and listed the following causes:

- Lack of mental patterns related to innovation and its benefits among the decision-makers and implementers in the implementing organization.
- Lack of a structure to implement innovation and give it specific focus.
- Resistance from the organization and interest in maintaining status quo.
- Lack of innovation strategy and commitment to innovation on the part of the key decision-makers.

- Lack of the skills of selling an innovation in the skill innovation developers. They should be able to convert objections into an opportunity to present the benefits of implementing the innovation.

Questions:

1. What in your view are the reasons for not implementing the innovation?
2. What suggestions do you make to innovation developers to make their innovations acceptable to the clients?

Source: Sanjiv Narang (2001), The Death of Good Ideas, *Human Capital*, June, pp.54-55.

Chapter 12

Group Creativity

Learning Objectives

After you have studied this chapter, you will be able to...

- Identify the factors influencing group creativity.
- Explain, how group creativity can be promoted in an organization.

Structure

- Introduction
- Factors Influencing Group Creativity
- Promoting Group Creativity
- Summary
- Questions
- Exercises
- Case: Innovation Delays

INTRODUCTION

Creativity for corporations, like vitamins for people, is essential for good health and growth. Though older businesses involved in slowly changing markets or technology need not take seriously the creativity cure, companies whose share of the market is constantly shifting or those that are dependent on high technology ought to take creativity seriously. The task of contemporary managers therefore is fostering creativity in individuals and groups. In so doing, managers can build a balanced creative management teams and enhance organizational effectiveness.

FACTORS INFLUENCING GROUP CREATIVITY

People in organizations are likely to identify with a range of reference groups, some more strongly than others. How they react to innovations introduced by the organization and how well they perform as innovators themselves, will be heavily influenced by these identifications and by the type of interaction between Groups within the Organization.

There has been sufficient research to enable some conclusions to be drawn about factors, which tend to inhibit or encourage innovation. We will now discuss some of the factors that have influence on group creativity.

Group conformity	Group decision-making	Social identity	Minority influence	Leadership
Group composition	Group structure	Group climate	Group longevity & development	Group norms

Group conformity:

There is good empirical evidence that conformity with the majority is positively related to group cohesiveness. In other words, the more strongly members are attracted to a group and wish to remain part of it, (i) they conform to the majority view within the group and (ii) will make effort to resolve discrepancies between each other's positions.

There is a danger that highly cohesive teams may be insufficiently critical of innovations they propose or support and fail to give adequate consideration to alternatives. This could lead to deterioration in the quality, though not necessarily the quantity, of innovations produced by the group.

In some organizations, pressures to conform by innovating are observed as the companies have been explicitly built around a philosophy of innovation.

Nystrom (1990) describes one division of the Swedish Chemical Company EKA Nobell where norms for innovation appeared to override all else.

Group decision-making:

Organizational innovation is not wholly a decision process, but it is a process in which decision-making plays prominent part. Groups commonly make decisions about innovations at many points in the process.

- Senior management team of an organization makes decision to introduce a new product.

- A specially constituted project team makes decisions about the design and manufacture of the product.

These or other groups might be responsible for decisions about the testing and evaluation of prototypes and the marketing, distributing and advertising of the final product.

Group polarization:

One area of interest is the phenomenon of group polarization. 'Group polarization' is a more accurate description because what appears to occur is that group decisions become polarized in the direction of the shared values of group members.

In an organization where there is a strong fear of failure, groups may be more cautious than individuals in decisions about innovation. In an organization, which encourages risk and is relatively forgiving of failure in pursuit of it, we might see riskier group than individual decisions.

Commitment:

Another advantage is that if people take part in reaching a decision as a group they are more likely to feel personally committed to it than if the decision is made by a leader and presented to them as a fait accompli.

Group think:

Janis's Work (1972), suggests that groups are most likely to suffer from 'groupthink'. Janis describes the phenomenon of 'groupthink' where members become more concerned about protecting the identity and convivial atmosphere of the group than with coming to optimal decisions.

Groupthink may be combated in a number off ways. Recruiting members with diverse backgrounds and view points will increase the likelihood that a variety of approaches to problems will be considered, although too much diversity may encourage conflict and make it difficult for a consensus ever to be reached. One or more members of the group may be assigned the role of 'devil's advocate', charged with the task of actively seeking weaknesses in innovation proposals.

Social identity:

Social identity theory is a potentially valuable tool for analyzing the role of groups in organizational innovation. The basic proposition of social identity theory is that people seek to achieve and maintain a positive image of themselves. One of the principal ways they do this is by comparing groups they identify with ('in-groups') favorably with those they do not identify with ('out-groups').

Research, examining how specific innovations develop over time has shown that different groups within organizations often have different perceptions of and attitudes towards, the innovation question.

Aydin and Rice (1991), showed that difference in the 'social worlds' of the various occupational groups in a hospital were a major determinant of individual attitudes to a new medical information system. Social identity theory suggests that such differences may constitute an attempt to increase differentiation between In-groups and Out-groups, rather than simply being due to groups having different knowledge about the innovation.

Whether an innovation is resisted or accepted may therefore depend on whether those with whom it is associated are viewed as a negative or positive reference group by other groups. Where identification of an innovation with an out-group causes resistance, management might attempt to reduce it by weakening that identification, perhaps by vigorously promoting the innovation as 'belonging' to the organization as a whole.

It could sometimes be advantageous for managers wishing to facilitate an innovation to downplay its association with one particular group. This strategy is especially likely to be appropriate where the major concern is that a particular innovation is fully implemented with as little disruption as possible. In other situations, strengthening group identities to encourage innovation might be the best strategy. In these organizations implementation is not a major problem.

Minority influence:

In real organizations, status and power differentials within and between groups are the norm and will affect innovation processes significantly. If a minority of one is opposing a proposed innovation at aboard meeting, it makes a considerable difference whether that minority is a relatively junior newcomer to the board or the managing director.

Leadership:

A democratic and participative leadership style is commonly recommended as encouraging group innovation. The rationale is straightforward: it is widely agreed that creativity is facilitated by high levels of discretion (Nicholson and West, 1988) and that people feel more committed to changes if they have participated in decision about them.

A positive association between Group innovativeness and Participative leadership style has been found in several studies, such as those by Farris (1973) with research laboratory teams and West and Wallace (1991) with primary care teams.

The role of the group leader is therefore to provide direction whilst allowing members as much say in decisions and as much freedom to approach tasks in their own way as is practicable.

It should not be assumed that a participative leadership style will always be the most effective for facilitating group innovation or that greater participativeness will always lead to greater innovativeness.

In Farris's (1973) study, for instance, the most innovative teams were not those which were most democratic but those in which the leader exerted a moderate degree of control.

This makes sense when it is recognized that innovation is not just a matter of generating as many creative ideas as possible but of successfully turning ideas into reality. If the leader does not impose some degree of control and direction upon the group then it is easy for the very freedom, which encouraged the initiation of an innovation to make it difficult to form a clear implementation strategy and carry it through to completion.

A rigidly authoritarian style would rarely be optimal. However, different styles are required for different situations as shown in Table 12.1.

Manz *et al.* (1989), considering data on seven major innovations from the Minnesota innovation research program, argue for a contingency approach, as different leadership styles were effective for different stages in the innovation process. Anderson and King (1991) suggested that leaders need to modify their styles over the course of introducing an innovation as different tasks become salient.

Table 12.1 Styles of leadership and innovaton

Innovation phase	Leadership style	Managers' behaviors
Initiation	Nurturing	Encouraging safety and ideas, being supportive, being open minded, ensuring a non-judgemental climate
Discussion	Developing	Obtaining opinions, evaluating proposals, agreeing implementation plans, pushing plans forward
Implementation	Championing	Selling the proposal to all groups affected, gaining commitment, ensuring participation in implementation
Routinization	Validating/modifying	Checking effectiveness, identifying weak links, modifying and improving the innovation

Emergent leaders - Much of the research on leadership and innovation in work groups focuses on formally appointed leaders. However, in many groups an individual assumes a leadership role informally, as a result of personal qualities and intragroup dynamics. This is particularly the case in an autonomous work group, a form of organization, which has risen in prominence in recent years.

Guastello (1995), argued that in groups faced with creativity-related tasks, emergent leaders would not only be facilitative of others' creativity, but would also demonstrate creativity themselves. In a study of groups of university security officers involved in a training programme he found support for both these hypotheses.

Group composition:

Various aspects of group composition have been considered in relation to innovativeness.

Matching people to roles – Margerison and McCann (1990), hypothesize that team effectiveness will be greatest where there is maximal correspondence between the work preferences of individual members and their roles within the team. Where there is a major mismatch, options include redesigning jobs, personal development in less preferred types of work, delegation or reallocation of tasks, or the mismatched person(s) leaving the team.

Homogeneity/heterogeneity – A highly homogeneous group is one in which members have a great deal in common with each other, as opposed to a highly heterogeneous group in which members differ markedly from each other. Similarities and differences may be on many dimensions: age, sex, tenure, professional allegiances, attitudes and so on. High homogeneity may inhibit innovation in some circumstances. A highly homogeneity group is likely to draw on a narrower range of experiences and expertise than a more heterogeneous group and where homogeneity is accompanied by strong attraction to the group, the 'groupthink' phenomenon may lead to poor-quality innovation decisions. It is worth recalling that research on brainstorming groups consistently shows that heterogeneous groups outperform homogenous groups in idea generation.

Conversely, there are possible disadvantages to high heterogeneity. There are more opportunities for clashes of values and opinions in a group with considerable differentiation amongst members than in a more homogeneous one. Even where this does not lead to open conflict, it is likely to be a difficult and protracted task to bring the whole group to consensus on innovation decisions. It may also be more difficult to promote a sense of common purpose, or 'shared vision'– a key facilitator of innovation (West, 1990). Finally, innovation is unlikely to be the only significant function of a group; managers need to consider whether any advantages in terms of innovativeness accruing from heterogeneity will be offset by detrimental effects on other aspects of group functioning. The task of the manager in constituting a group for whom innovation is an important goal is to decide upon the appropriate degree of homogeneity, in the light of the specific requirements and organizational context facing the group.

Diversity - O'Reilly III, Williams and Barsade,(1998), state that 'a group is diverse if it is composed of individuals who differ on a characteristic on which they base their own social identity'. Recruiting members with diverse backgrounds and viewpoints will increase the likelihood that a variety of approaches to problems will be considered and groupthink may be combated. Too much diversity may encourage conflict and make it difficult for a consensus ever to be reached.

O'Reilly III, Williams and Barsade,(1998), looked at the impact of diversity on team innovativeness in a major US clothing manufacturer with a reputation for the successful management of diversity. They found evidence for different effects from different types of diversity.

- Ethnic diversity was associated with increased innovation (through not for all mixes of ethnicity).
- Tenure diversity was negatively diversity was negatively related to innovation implementation, though this seemed to be related to the high levels of conflict associated with high tenure diversity.
- Gender diversity was unrelated to innovation.

Group structure:

The formal structure of a group may influence its innovativeness. The concepts of 'organic' and 'mechanistic' organizational structures developed by Burns and Stalker (1961) are applied to work groups. Organic structures show the following characteristics:

- *Integrative* - An organic group tends to approach tasks in an integrative way, rather than breaking them down into separate subtasks assigned to individual members.
- *Expanding, not rigid boundaries* - Its boundaries of responsibility, authority and influence are not rigidly set, but are to a large extent dependent on the demands of particular situations facing the group.
- *Good communication* - There is a high volume of interpersonal communication, which is characteristically lateral rather than vertical in direction (i.e., between colleagues of similar status, rather than between superiors and subordinates) and supportive rather than directive.
- *Involvement* - There is also a high degree of involvement in decision-making amongst group members. Finally, members of organic groups show strong commitment to the skills and values of their profession, above commitment to the particular organization.

Mechanistic groups have the opposite characteristics, being highly formal, hierarchical and heavily reliant upon rules and procedures.

Meadows (1980) showed that those groups whose tasks involved the highest levels of innovativeness-such as telecommunications research teams-tended to be the most organic, whilst those with a low requirement for innovativeness-such as clerical and stenographic groups-were the most mechanistic.

West (2001) argued that bureaucratic forms of work organization prevalent in the 1950s, 1960s and 1970s stifled the natural innovation potential present in many work groups.

Many of the characteristics of organic structured groups can be seen in autonomous work groups.

These are groups with a high degree of authority and responsibility for the way they conduct their activities, commonly consisting of members of similar status (Guzzo and Dickson, 1996).

Such groups generally make decisions collectively and leadership is participative, often emergent rather than imposed.

Carletta, Garrod and Fraser Krauss (1998) argue that innovation will be facilitated in small autonomous groups. There is better communication within the groups. In larger ones this advantage is not found. They also make the point that organizations can support the kind of communication patterns that enhance innovation by encouraging diverse interactions outside of formally constituted groups.

Carletta *et al.* give the example of the highly innovative 3M company, which has strongly emphasized the importance of interaction outside of immediate work roles, through measures such as multidisciplinary technical forums and a policy of allowing members time to pursue their own ideas.

Group climate:

Climate can be seen as the prevailing atmosphere or mood within a group or organization It has been defined as:

'The feelings, attitudes and behavioral tendencies, which characterize organizational life' (Nystrom, 1990).

The highly important climatic factors that influence innovation processes are discussed here.

Cohesiveness - One aspect of climate, which has been widely considered in relation to group innovation, is cohesiveness-the extent to which members are attracted to the group and wish to remain part of it. There is a strong argument for high cohesiveness having a positive effect on group innovation, as it results in the individual gaining great satisfaction from group achievements, whilst feeling that the group as a whole will share the responsibility for any failures. However such a generalization is not acceptable.

Climate for excellence and participative safety - Studies in organizations tend to show complex relationships between Cohesiveness and Group innovation, in which other variables, such as group size, have an important influence. Recent research has moved on to look at facets of climate other than cohesiveness.

West (1990) proposes 'climate for excellence' and 'participative safety' as two of the four factors in his theory of group innovation. The former refers to a climate in which the quality of decision-making and task performance is highly valued, whilst the latter describes a climate characterized by supportive interpersonal interactions resulting in group members feeling safe to propose and develop radical and risky new ideas.

Group longevity and development:

How do the factors like life span, levels of activity and entrainment affect innovations of groups? We will now examine their influences in detail.

Life span - Whether the length of time that a group has been together influences its innovative performance? Long association leads to less innovativeness. With longevity there may be a genuine problem caused by the hardening of habits of thought and behavior.

Katz (1982), found that R&D teams tended to perform less well the longer they had been together.

For some types of group, restricting the lifespan is not difficult; project teams, for instance, can be set up with the clear understanding that they will be disbanded once the project is completed. Where life span is longer, managers are advised to consider other ways of stimulating innovativeness, perhaps introducing a number of new members to the group or focusing strongly on creativity and innovation in personal and team development activities.

Levels of activity - Group leaders and managers need to recognize that levels of activity in an innovation project will tend to change overtime and that this is not necessarily a reflection of the degree of effort and commitment in-group members.

Conic Gersick'(1989) has shown that groups do not evolve new ideas gradually, but rather undergo what might be termed 'quantum leaps' in their development. In experimental studies she found that groups of fixed longevity when given a simulated project task commonly underwent a significant change in their approach at roughly the midpoint in their life span.

Kelly, Futoran and McGrath (1990) showed that performance effects associated with group deadlines varied according to the kinds of problems they faced earlier. Where groups had encountered 'capacity' problems (i.e., getting work finished on time), they tended to speed up their activities subsequently. Where groups had encountered 'capability' problems (i.e., succeeding in overcoming task difficulties) they subsequently slowed down their performance perhaps to ensure they thought more deeply about their task.

McGrath (1996) suggests that groups which have repeatedly been given inadequate time to complete tasks will tend to become focused on speed rather than quality, with a possible deleterious effect on innovation.

Entrainment - Ancona and Chong (1999) define entrainment as 'the adjustment of the pace or cycle of an activity to match or synchronize with that of another activity'. They argue that group processes in organizations are entrained by a whole range of temporally patterned activities in the wider organization and outside it. These may include such things as planning and financial cycles, seasonal variations in demand and changes in personnel through recruitment and retirement (to name but a few). Such entraining forces can have a major impact on group innovation processes.

Ancona (1990) documents just such an occurrence in a US education department change programme, where innovative teams were constituted in September, but because of the department's cycle of activities were largely unable to begin initiatives until January. The result was a loss of momentum in the programme and consequently of team commitment.

Group norms:

Groups are characterized by the norms their members share. A norm is an attitude, opinion, feeling, or action shared by two or more people-that guides their behavior. The norms of a group regulate and coordinate interactions among its members. If norms were absent, we might refer to the individuals physically assemble in the same place as an aggregate, but not as a group. Traditions, precedents and policies constitute norms that may either stimulate or stifle creativity.

A project group's creativity can be explained by examining the role of norms and traditions operating within groups.

The project team may share certain behavioral regularities: 30-minute coffee breaks, getting started late or waiting for a certain member to read over the plans from the last meeting.

These habits, which are reinforced over time, become the group's norms and traditions. Other norms can center on such operating modes as avoiding conflict so that no member's feathers are ruffled or requiring a majority vote on each idea adopted.

PROMOTING GROUP CREATIVITY

Groups are to be developed into teams by taking the following measures:

- Train the group members.
- Involve all the members in establishing team vision, mission, objectives, tasks and values.
- Set up clear roles for individuals with definition of authority and responsibility.
- Have clear procedures for team involvement in individual tasks.
- Try to maximize the authority of the team.
- Encourage creative conversations and learning by example.

Increasing group creativity is a two-fold task of managing current and future requirements. It involves

(i) **Change management** - Changing the existing paradigms, norms and styles of groups for greater development of innovative potential.

(ii) **Organization interventions** - Safeguarding the styles of creative people whose competencies are matching both current and future requirements.

Change management:

For groups to be creative, they have to reduce conformity and if necessary shift their norms. Although many approaches aimed at reducing the effects of conformity have been developed, the more genuine solution is the one that involves group members.

Reducing conformity:

The following steps can reduce conformity in decision-making:

- The group members have to understand and *themselves counteract* the constraints.

- Brainstorming and other *techniques* that involve "rules" aimed at reducing convergence or conformity effects may be useful.
- Ultimately, however, creativity will be heightened to the greatest extent when members *acquire discussion skills* that enable them to retain independence in the face of pressures.
- When problems and proposed solutions depend on an objective, critical examination of the facts at hand, it is particularly important that group participants be able to monitor and *modify the influence of group norms.*

Shifting norms:

Blake and Mouton (1985) suggest following steps to shifting to norms that better serve innovation objectives:

- *Active involvement* - Organizational members who need to shift their behavior should become active participants in the systematic change process.
- *Identify the prevailing norms* - A first step is identifying the prevailing norms. Group members have to identify the assumptions they make as they work to achieve results with and through others.
- *Manager leads the effort* - The managers responsible for ultimate decisions lead the change effort. If you, the project team leader, are not involved in the process of thinking through the limitations of existing norms, you can't support and approve the development of new, more appropriate norms.
- *Make norms visible* - All the norms are crystal clear. To make them clear, formulate an open, direct and unbiased statement that identifies the problem. Then ask participants what can be done to solve it. Applying this strategy to your project team, you and the team members would discuss dissatisfaction with the low quality of your output and diagnose the problem. Only after the group focuses on the problem can the norm become visible and commitments be made toward solutions.
- *Provide facts* - Facts and data to clear up misconceptions that hold an unproductive norm in place are provided. Free and open exchange of information facilitates the rejection of an old norm and the acceptance of one that square better with the facts in the situation.
- *Provide for ventilation* - Opportunities are provided to ventilate feelings and emotions. In this way negative attitudes that prevent constructive problem solving are dissolved and new norms developed.
- *Remove confusion* - Casual agreements made during the process are crystallized to prevent misunderstandings later on. Clarification, written recordings and repeated communication of group agreements about change prevent confusion from diluting the effectiveness of planned norm shifts.
- *Support* - Follow up is essential to support changes in norms. Because new norms are always weaker than those they replace, people tend to backslide toward the norm that previously prevailed. After the project team has adopted new norms, the manager and team should regularly review them for slippage.

- *Reinforce* - Although the above steps can lead to effective changes in any work group, the best results occur when they are consistent with organization wide efforts to merge attitudes toward productivity with high organizational performance.

Organization interventions:

Organization wide efforts relate to climate, culture and authority structure design efforts of management.

Organization strategy:

The strategy that an organization is pursuing, at any given time, will influence the power of various work groups, which, in turn, will determine the resources that the organization's top management is willing to allocate to it for performing its tasks. An organization's overall strategy, typically put into place by top management, outlines the organization's goals and the means for attaining these goals. Obviously, not all firms pursue innovation.

It might, for example, direct the organization toward reducing costs, improving quality, expanding market share or shrinking the size of its overall operations.

- Innovation strategy may appropriately characterize 3M company but it certainly is not a strategy pursued by Reader's Digest.
- An organization that is pursuing a cost-minimization strategy tightly controls costs, refrains from incurring unnecessary innovation or marketing expenses and cuts prices in selling a basic product. This would describe the strategy pursued by Wal-Mart or the sellers of generic grocery products.
- Organizations following an imitation strategy try to capitalize on the best of both of the previous strategies (Innovation and cost minimization). They seek to minimize risk and maximize opportunity for profit. Their strategy is to move into new products or new markets only after innovators have proved viability. They take the successful ideas of innovators and copy them. Manufacturers of mass-marketed fashion goods that are rip-offs of designer styles follow the imitation strategy. This label also probably characterizes such well-known firms as IBM and Caterpillar. They essentially follow their smaller and more innovative competitors with superior products, but only after their competitors have demonstrated that the market is there.

Authority Structures:

Organizations have authority structures that define who reports to whom, who makes decisions, and what decisions individuals or groups are empowered to make. This structure typically determines where a given work group is placed in the organization's hierarchy, the formal leader of the group and formal relationships between groups.

Formal Regulations:

Organizations create rules, procedures, policies, job descriptions and other forms of regulations to standardize employee behavior. The more formal regulations that the organization imposes on all its employees, the more the behavior of work group members will be consistent and predictable.

Organizational Resources:

Some organizations are large and profitable, with an abundance of resources. Their employees, for instance, will have modern, high-quality tools and equipment to do their jobs. Other organizations aren't as fortunate. When organizations have limited resources, so do their work groups. What a group actually accomplishes is, to a large degree, determined by what it is capable of accomplishing? The presence or absence of resources such as money, time, raw materials? and equipment-which are allocated to the group by the organization-have a large bearing on the group's behavior.

Human Resource Selection Process:

Members of any work group are, first, members of the organization of which the group is a part. The criteria that an organization uses in its selection process will determine the kinds of people that will be in its work groups.

Performance Evaluation and Reward System:

Another organization wide variable that affects all employees is the performance evaluation and reward system. Since work groups are part of the larger organizational system, group members' behavior will be influenced by how the organization evaluates performance and what behaviors are rewarded.

Organizational Culture:

Every organization has an unwritten culture that defines standards of acceptable and unacceptable behavior for employees. After a few months, most employees understand their organization's culture. Members of work groups have to accept the standards implied in the organization's dominant culture if they are to remain in good standing.

Physical work setting

The physical work setting that is imposed on the group by external parties has an important bearing on work group behavior. Architects, industrial engineers and office designers make decisions regarding the size and physical layout of an employee's work space, the arrangement of equipment, illumination levels and the need for acoustics to cut down on noise distractions. They create both barriers as weel as opportunities for work group interaction.

Group Member Resources:

A group's potential level of performance is, to a large extent, dependent on the resources that its members individually bring to the group. A group's performance is not merely the summation of its individual members' abilities. However, these abilities set parameters for what members can do and how effectively they will perform in a group.

The general conclusion is attributes that tend to have a positive connotation in our culture tend to be positively related to group productivity, morale and cohesiveness. These include traits such as sociability, self-reliance and independence. In contrast, negatively evaluated characteristics such as authoritarianism, dominance and unconventionality tend to be negatively related to the dependent variables. These personality traits affect group performance by strongly influencing how the individual will interact with other group members.

However, success does not belong always to the able persons. As the old saying goes, "*The race doesn't always go to the swiftest nor the battle to the strongest, but that's the way to bet.*"

SUMMARY

Creativity for corporations, like vitamins for people, is essential for good health and growth. The task of contemporary managers therefore is fostering creativity in individuals and groups. Some of the factors that have influence on group creativity are: Conformity, decision-making, social identity, minority influence, leadership, group composition, structure, climate longevity and development and norms.

Conformity with the majority is positively related to group cohesiveness. Decision-making process plays prominent part in innovation. . Group decisions become polarized in the direction of the shared values of group members. Janis's work(1972) suggests that groups are most likely to suffer from 'groupthink'. According to social identity theory people seek to achieve and maintain a positive image of themselves. One of the principal ways they do this is by comparing groups they identify with ('in-groups') favorably with those they do not identify with ('out-groups'). If a minority of one is opposing a proposed innovation at aboard meeting, it makes a considerable difference whether that minority is a relatively junior newcomer to the board or the managing director. A democratic and participative leadership style is commonly recommended as encouraging group innovation.

Margerison and McCann (1990), hypothesize that team effectiveness will be greatest where there is maximal correspondence between the work preferences of individual members and their roles within the team. A highly homogeneous group is one in which members have a great deal in common with each other, as opposed to a highly heterogeneous group in which members differ markedly from each other.

Recruiting members with diverse backgrounds and viewpoints will increase the likelihood that a variety of approaches to problems will be considered and groupthink may be combated.

Studies in organizations tend to show complex relationships between Cohesiveness and Group innovation, in which other variables, such as group size, have an important influence. Life span, levels of activity and entrainment affect innovations of groups. The norms of a group regulate and coordinate interactions among its members.

Groups are to be developed into teams by taking the following measures-Train the group members-(i) Involve all the members in establishing team vision, mission, objectives, tasks and values,(ii) Set up clear roles for individuals with definition of authority and responsibility, (iii)Have clear procedures for team involvement in individual tasks, (iv)Try to maximize the authority of the team and (v)Encourage creative conversations and learning by example.

For groups to be creative, they have to reduce conformity and if necessary shift their norms. Organizational interventions in change management relate to the following areas:

Organization strategy, Authority Structures, Formal Regulations, Organizational Resources, Human Resource Selection Process, Performance Evaluation and Reward System Human Resource Selection Process, Performance Evaluation and Reward System, Organizational Culture, Physical work setting and Group member resources.

QUESTIONS

1. Identify the factors that influence group creativity. Explain with examples.
2. How do you promote group creativity in an organization?

EXERCISES

Visit local organizations and inquire about group activity especially the cross-functional teams. First, identify their characteristics. Next inquire the group's innovative thinking and outcomes during the last one or two years. Make a report and submit it to your teacher.

CASE - INNOVATION DELAYS

Arvind Services is an Internet service provider engaged in providing Internet services to corporate and individual clients. The ISP market is neck deep in competition. Product and service differentiation along with a tight rein on costs is essential for survival in this market.

A cross-functional team while focusing on innovation generation came out with an innovation related to customer response process in case a customer loses the Internet access password. The process of providing passwords to clients, in case of loss of password takes at least two days. In addition, the costs in terms of courier cost, manpower cost, overhead cost etc., have to be borne by the company.

The cross-functional team came out with a process innovation, which enabled the company to flash the password on the screen of the client's computer, while ensuring security. The security system designed, related to the verification of the client's identity. This process if implemented, would satisfy unsatisfied needs.

Client needs	Organization needs
1. Immediate availability of password in case of loss. 2. No system down time. 3. Security of password.	1. Reduction in costs 2. Improvement in service to client. 3. Company image differentiation from competitors.

This innovation idea had the making of success. However, after one year of the generation of the idea, the company had still not implemented the innovation.

Questions:

1. What may be the reasons for not implementing the innovation?
2. What will be the likely impact of delay or failure in implementation on group creativity?
3. What do you do to preserve the spirit of innovation in cross-functional teams?

Source: Sanjiv Narang (2001), The Death of Good Ideas, *Human Capital*, June, pp.54-55.

Chapter 13

Managing Creative Employees

Learning Objectives

After you have studied this chapter, you will be able to...

- Appreciate the importance of managing creative employees.
- Understand how much challenging the management of creative employees.
- Explain the characteristics of creativity inducing managers.
- Know the ways of managing creative employees.

Structure

- Introduction
- Significance of Managing Creative Employees
- Challenging Task
- Characteristics of Creativity Inducing Managers
- Initiatives
- Summary
- Questions
- Exercises
- Case : Innovation is Wipro and Wipro is Innovation

INTRODUCTION

Innovators require sensitive human resource management to maximize their potential. The key factor in nurturing innovation has more to do with interpersonal relationships than with facilities or organizational services. Congenial environment, good leadership, meaningful education and training, and attractive stimuli and incentives are needed to unleash the creative talents of individuals and groups. The innovator must be encouraged to be both a generator of new initiatives and opportunistic intervener in each step of the innovation process.

SIGNIFICANCE OF MANAGING CREATIVE EMPLOYEES

As organizations are emphasizing innovation as a key resource, the development and encouragement of creative employees has become important.

Creativity is valued by many firms:

It is true that the value attached to the outcomes of creativity is by no means uniform throughout the world. However, the present trend is in favour of creativity.

Amin Rajan (2001) surveyed over 800 senior executives from 26 countries in all regions of the world and found that far more organizations in Asia and Australia, the Middle East and Africa view creativity as a long-term investment.

Rise in the number of creatives:

Not only are manufacturing companies putting more emphasis on developing gold collar workers, but their numbers are also swelling geometrically in the service sector.

Robert F. Kelley, senior consultant at SRI International, Menlo Park, Calif, and the author of the book —**The Gold Collar Worker** explains:

"The rapid growth of the service industry has created many jobs in management, finance marketing, and computer software. The people attracted to these jobs are smart, motivated people whose goals tend to be different from those of traditional workers."

Competency development needs:

The People Capability Maturity Model (P-CMM) of the Software Engineering Institute, Carnegie Mellon University (1995), emphasized continuous workforce innovation for developing competency at both the organizational and individual levels. Development of creative employees , however, precedes other successful capability enhancement interventions, encompassing all contemporary HR practices. A truly innovative organization qualifies for level-5, the highest level of P-CMM certification.

CHALLENGING TASK

Finding creative people is difficult but it is even tougher to keep them stimulated once they've joined a research organization. Never lose sight of the fact that individuals create, not groups. Traditional managers are aware that their own experience may not yield adequate answers. The task of managing creative employees involves the following:

Spot them carefully:

Management must recognize and foster the creativity, which exists in every person as it is expressed in unexpected ways and at unexpected times. They may look odd and do crazy things. They may look serious and be negligent to operational procedures. But not every crazy and negligent person is creative.

Deal the knowledgeable with empathy:

Moreover, given the fast pace of change today, many mangers have no more expertise—perhaps even less-in specialized areas than the people they supervise, particularly when they're managing "gold collar" workers. As a result, many traditional "top-down" mangers are intimidated by members of this highly educated, creative "company brain trust".

Mr. Kelley says. "They're afraid of what they don't understand; so instead of helping creative people flourish, they clamp down. It's the worst thing they can do."

Protect their independence:

Of all the keys to managing gold collar workers, autonomy may head the list, "the best thing you can do for creative people is just get out of their way. Give them a task and leave them alone," counsels Peter F. Drucker. Most innovators tend to focus on projects or goals and have little patience with the distractions of paperwork, company politics or strict regulations. To these people, work is an extension of themselves and they don't take well to trivial interference," warns Prof. Hakmiller.

3M have developed a project-sponsorship tack that lines up an interested executive with a specific research effort. In theory, the executive's support helps shield the researcher from bureaucratic skirmishes and from the pressure to produce short-term results.

Meet the preferences to challenge:

Cummings *et.al.,* (1997) observed that to ensure the most creative work from employees, managers need to assess the creative potential of each person and place them into work contexts that offer complex job assignments, supportive and non-controlling supervision and competitive co-workers.

They shouldn't be given just any job. Brain trusters should be assigned major projects, but one of their own choosing whenever possible, experts say. A deadline should be imposed, the resources allocated and then-importantly – the supervisor should walk away.

Handle Elitism and troublemaking:

Steve Jobs, chairman of Apple computer Inc., exploited the idea of treating innovators as an elite while developing the Macintosh computer. During breaks, engineers assigned to the project enjoyed a stereo system, video games, and a ping-pong table supplied by the boss. Whether treating certain workers as elite benefits a company is keenly debated. It may have adverse effects. In fact, engineers working on the Apple, II computer grew resentful.

Elitism not only breeds arrogance; it also can undermine authority. Consider the behavior of an employee at Data General Labs.

When faulty air-conditioning at the Data General labs pushed the temperature into the 90s the Eagle engineers walked off the job, refusing to return until it was fixed, "we didn't give management much choice-but it was fixed by morning," chuckles Mr. Guyer.

As a result, old-line managers may view gold collar workers as glorified troublemakers-petty egoists with insubordinate tendencies.

Regardless of how talented or valuable some workers are, like it or not, there are some guidelines they must adhere to," declares 3M's Mr. Krogh.

Exhibit tolerance:

One key to motivating creative workers is tolerance. Sometimes failures take place.

Veterans like 3M's Krogh point out, though, that there must be a reasonable tolerance of failure. "Probably 60% of the things we try don't work, but success takes some gambling," he says.

Develop special ways of handling:

Innovators have different ways of functioning. When encouraged to be on their own they excel. Box 13.1 presents a typical case of employee handling.

Box 13.1 Left free to create

Mead corporation executive Richard Wright recalls that, as a young chemist at another company, he would frequently leave his workstation to ponder problems while walking around the building, then feel guilty about being nonproductive. A boss told Wright, however, that he was doing fine and should continue to follow whatever style best suited him when it came to searching for new ideas.

Wright soon recognized the wisdom of that advice. An assignment relating to analysis of body fluids led to a walk along a riverbank, where he worked out one of his best ideas toward the solution of the problem. He went back to the company, sat down in the cafeteria with a cup of coffee and wrote out the idea on a napkin.

The napkin, he says, is still in the company's files. Whenever it is, it is a symbol of two key factors in the proper approach to creativity. Mangers who recognize that different people need different types of environments in which to stretch their imaginations and workers who can take advantage of these environments, which can range from a well-equipped laboratory to a river bank.

CHARACTERISTICS OF CREATIVITY INDUCING MANAGERS

Employees who demonstrate creativity, initiative and resourcefulness, should be identified, developed and encouraged. Management's role should be to remove roadblocks, expedite effort provide resources and encouragement. Management itself should be innovative and learn how not to impede creative effort. They need to adopt a new approach and develop individual personal relationships with their staff.

Attributes:

Research shows that leaders who encourage creativity have unique behavioral characteristics, which you should consider adopting.

- **Willing to absorb risks taken by subordinates** – Managers who encourage creativity allow subordinates considerable freedom to be creative. One cost of such freedom is mistakes, which are sometimes expensive. In contrast, managers who are afraid of mistakes restrict the freedom of subordinates to experiment, hoping to eliminate most errors.
- **Comfortable with half-developed Idea** – Managers are willing to listen to, and support, "half-baked" proposals and encourage subordinates to press on. Creativity-inducing leaders will not graciously welcome every preposterous idea since they have good intuitive sense about what might work. Yet they are hesitant to discourage the creative flow of ideas or to kill innovation in the bud.
- **Willingness to "stretch" organizational policy** – Creativity inducing leaders do not normally disregard rules and policies, but they do know when the rules need to be stretched for the greater good.
- **Able to make quick decision** – Leaders who foster creativity have good track records in recognizing which half-processed idea is worth betting on. They are also courageous enough to immediately commit resources to carrying it out. The creativity-discouraging manger is predisposed to calling for further studies, or putting the suggested idea in the hands of a committee.
- **Good listeners** – Productive manages listen to their subordinates and build on their suggestions. They seem to have the ability to draw out the best in their people and then add to it. A manager who encourages creativity will listen to an idea and then ask a question such as "how might your idea be applied on an even wider scale.
- **Do not dwell on mistakes** – "Creativity inducing leaders are" willing to begin with the world as it is today and work for a better future." They learn from experience, but do now wallow in it.

Leadership Style

Management style characterized with openness, receptivity, self-confidence and positive appreciation is desirable to encourage employee innovators.

Alfred E.Brown who headed Gillette's Corporate Research Labs (in Michael Wolff, 1979) observed:

The 3M company, for instance attributes its success to heritage of creative leadership, where for years successive CEO's nurtured creative thinking and problem-solving. With a creative atmosphere at the top, you'll find more trust among research people a lot less jealousy, and a willingness to discuss ideas openly rather than play them close to the chest. Information exchange will become habit.

T-shape management:

Morten Hansen and Bolko von Oetinger of the Boston consulting Group call their approach "T-shape management", which relies on a new kind of executive who breaks out of the traditional corporate hierarchy to share knowledge across the organization (the horizontal part of the "T") while remaining fiercely committed to individual business-unit performance (the vertical part).

The successful T-shaped manager, according to Hansen and Oetinger, must learn to live, and ultimately thrive, with the tension created by this dual responsibility. Although this tension is most acute for heads of business units, any T-shaped manager with operating unit obligations must wrestle with it. A typical T-shaped manager, for example, must collaborate in a peer group, connect people from different parts of the company and give or take advice from other business units.

Informal networks:

Karen Stephenson, a professor of management at the university of California, Los Angeles, found in research with the IBM Advanced business unit that informal networks control the daily life of organizations.

A forward-thinking chief executive, for example, might want to test the ground before introducing an innovative new way of working. The gatekeepers would be used to spread the news about the impending change on a semi-formal basis and later the pulse takers would report on the "word on the ground".

At Ispat international, a global steel maker with headquarters in London, the task has been tackled at a strategic level through cross directorships, which require the general manager of every operating unit to sit on the board of at least one other unit. The managing directors of the units operating in Germany and Trinidad, for instance, sit on each other's boards because they both produce "long" steel products, such as rods and other structured materials. The managing directors of all the operating units also have phone meetings each week that last no longer than two hours.

INITIATIVES

The initiatives taken by different managers in different organizations are identified and briefly explained here.

(i) People related initiatives:

The initiatives relating to selection and employment of people include the following:

Select the right people
Give challenging assignments
Provide Job rotation
Allow Freedom at work with right pressures
Encourage Job sharing
Set up Think tank
Establish Peer partnership
Arrange special support services

Select the right people:

Alfred E.Brown advises managers to look for people who are:

Curious	Not necessarily intelligent. But intellectually curious, continually probing with "why?" and "what if?" questions.
Flexible	Flexible, with an open mind that is willing to accept new information. They can put information together in many different ways and reach an acceptable solution.
Sensitive	Highly sensitive to needs, usually spotting them before anyone else. Able, somehow, to put their finger on the real problem, which others have missed and then to define it accurately and clearly. Able to see connections the average person has missed.
Inquisitive	Unorthodox and anti-authoritarian, boldly questioning conventional ideas and established concepts.
Committed	Mentally restless, intense, strongly motivated and completely wrapped up in what they are doing.
Solver	Problem solvers rather than phenomenon studiers. The truly creative problem-solver is normally goal oriented rather than methods-oriented. He is obsessed with achieving an objective and impatient with anything that gets in the way. He never limits himself to available methods, which often hinder new approaches to problem solving.

Give challenging assignments:

Creative people need problems, which are difficult and challenging. Experts advice-.

Use your most creative people on your toughest problems. Don't automatically turn to the resident expert, but recognize that creative people are problem solvers in many different areas. I call them the green thumb people; no matter what they plant, it always seems to come up. They are winners.

Provide Job rotation:

Creative employees should be provided with opportunities to work in different jobs and different people to improve their creativity. However, they should not be disturbed when working on a project. Experts give the following advice.

'Don't make the mistake of keeping creative researchers in one little section or group forever. Expose your bright young graduates and your older creative people,them to the other creative minds in the laboratory by rotating people on a continuing basis. But don't rotate too often; every couple of years should be about right.'

Allow Freedom at work with right pressures:

It is better to let creative employees work at their pace and in their own style. Give creative people lots of freedom. Don't let management hassle the individualist who likes to work in his office with the lights off, or with his shoes off or at irregular hours. "But this doesn't mean there should be no pressure to produce. Pressure can be a great stimulus to creative research production," What kind of pressure? Pressure, says Brown, as simple as "come on, we've got to solve this problem or the company is going to be in trouble."

Encourage Job sharing:

The imaginative use of job sharing is another way of garnering knowledge and ideas. Job sharing has been seen mainly as an equal opportunities measure or a means of recruiting or retaining working mothers or careers with professional skills. What has not always been appreciated is that the close working bond that builds up between sharers often results in the company obtaining two brains for the price of one?

Establish Peer partnership:

One approach is to reorganize into a peer partnership operating in much the same way as a law firm or a partnership of physicians. Ranking scientists and inventors would comprise the partners. Others not yet qualified to be elected as full partners would be junior partners. Technicians and other support personnel would comprise a group of associates. All this would be under the leadership of a director, whose chief responsibilities would be to determine corporate needs, to communicate these to the entire group and to devote himself to expediting his organization's creative effort. He must achieve and maintain a sense of urgency, for, after all, it is a business endeavor, not an academic exercise.

Arrange special support services:

Special support services include assistance in reducing red tape, which produces time delays and tedious reporting procedures, providing market and financial analysis in order to better focus a new idea on the best commercial objectives; access to special skills, facilities or equipment in order to test the feasibility or further needed.

Set up Think tank:

In large companies, creativity flourishes through an internal think-tank group charged with plotting the future and generating ideas for realizing the dreams. Box 13.2 provides a description of how it works.

Box 13.2 Think-Tank

It is small group of employees who are willing to spend extra time on generating new ideas. The group should be quite small, since it should not be difficult for members to meet. The members are the visionaries capable of designing strategies. The people chosen should be interested in creative thinking for its long term corporate impact and internal personal reward, not for possible political gain. Political infighters and climbers are detrimental to any creative group. The people should be at a high enough level to know what is going on in the industry and the company, yet not too oriented to what they view as built-in constraints.

Guidelines – Since meetings are expensive; they should only be called when absolutely necessary. The time spent working on a think-tank project should not detract from a person's normal job hours. The activities of the group members in this job assignment should not be regimented. In managing creativity, the best way to manage it is not to manage it at all.

Expected outcomes – Management should expect a wide range of ideas, some sound, some impractical, some insignificant and some very profound. The ideas in total should represent several functional areas. Management's responsibility is to decide whether to study the idea further. In any case, management should communicate with the group members. Inaction by management at this point is a disruptive demotivator with long-term impact.

Rewards – To truly creative people, being chosen for such a group is an important reward in itself. The interaction with other people with similar characteristics is also a reward. Access to top management to present, and possibly discuss, an idea is an even greater reward and a powerful motivator, regardless of whether the idea is accepted. Recognition by management is the ultimate reward and coupled with a quantifiable expression of satisfaction, results in a very loyal, productive employee.

Limitations – A creative think tank will not work in a highly charged political arena where ideas become political footballs. It will also not work where management is totally interested in the short-term and the bottom-line. In the absence of these constraints, within realistic expectations, a creative group can provide low-cost vitality, with the promise of new ideas rather than no ideas.

(ii) Communication related initiatives:

Interactions serve two purposes (a) to stimulate others and (b) to share information.

Meetings:

Idea interchange sessions provide an opportunity to people to meet with good scientists and engineers on a regular basis. They questioning of established concepts and procedures, will be thought provoking to participants. Similarly, when someone has a very tough problem and is searching for solutions, let him call one of these sessions with six or eight of your most creative people. After he has put forward his possible solutions and the others have put forward theirs, combinations of ideas will often result that nobody saw before.

Open communication:

"Open communication" patterns provide airwaves for innovation, the channels through which ideas can flow freely. In some business units at Wang Laboratories and General Electric, for example, there are rules banning closed meetings; anyone can theoretically attend any meeting. Hewlett-Packard keeps support staffs to reinforce the desire for face-to-face communication in "real time".

Western H. Agor (*Intuitive Management : Integrating Left and Right Brain Management)* gives the following ideas to make interactions effective:

- Where appropriate, keep meeting agendas open and flexible, use no agenda at all, or segment meetings into creative open times. During the open periods, don't allow anyone—particularly left-brain oriented managers –to evaluate proposed ideas.
- Eliminate the interference that interrupts the flow of intuition-tension, anxiety, fear, and other blocks. Foster a relaxed, positive attitude about letting intuition happen. Common mental blocks include: "Everything is fine", "Follow the rules", "To err is wrong", "Playing is frivolous", "That's not my area", "Be practical" and "I'm not creative."

(iii) Ideas related initiatives:

This is the key area of creativity management in any firm.

Welcome new ideas:

In practice it is found that managers fail in their responsibility of encouraging innovators.

In a survey, it is found that the innovation ideas under scrutiny originated by front-line managers or staff. What was revealing was that the greatest challenge these individuals said they faced was not making the idea work but getting it accepted. This suggests that ideas in organizations are like diamonds in the dust lying around unappreciated until a manager has the insight to spot them, pick them up and value them. An intelligent subordinate will be seen, in top-down culture, as a threat to the position of the superior.

Box 13.3 gives the guidelines to deal with idea generators.

Box 13.3 Dealing with Idea generators

Be Receptive - More and better suggestions occur if you offer encouragement. Convince subordinates of your sincere interest by promptly recognizing deserving employees. If you are impatient, too busy or indifferent, a high wall is built between yourself and crew members.

Avoid Premature Criticism - Premature criticism, impatience and saying, "we tried it before" or "it will not work" can easily destroy almost all ideas. A manager should protect creative people from untimely pressures to product results. Ideas should be evaluated on their merits.

Give Credit Freely - Recognizing an employee's contribution to your boss marks you as a good supervisor. Your reward will be worker loyalty, respect and more ideas.

Be Appreciative - Only minor improvement may result from an employee's idea, but even a small improvement is certainly a step in the right direction.

Help prepare suggestions - Some individuals lack the necessary technical, mechanical or writing skills to put an idea on paper. Offer your help in expressing the idea.

Respect an Employee's idea - Any idea is of significant importance to the person who thought it up. Regardless of your opinion about the idea, it is important to someone; show consideration and be courteous.

Look for a Related Idea - A worker's idea may not be practical, but it can reveal another idea, which helps solve a problem. If so, give the employee credit for the alternative solution.

Encourage Suggestions - Your continued support and help will spur employees to think constructively and develop better ways to do their jobs. Build enthusiasm and teamwork by sharing improved work methods.

Explain any Rejection - When an idea is not adopted, the worker deserves an explanation of why the idea will not be used. This may require a careful and thoughtful answer, but you will gain the employee's confidence.

Discussions on ideas - An excellent idea is not automatically transformed into action and results. Bring together workers who have a variety of skills and experiences to create a mix in which creative borrowing prospers. Diversity stimulates the development of new ideas.

Source: Expanded version of Gary K. Himes, Stimulating Creativity: Encouraging Creative Ideas, in *Creativity*, (Ed) A Dale Timpe, Jaico Publishing House: Mumbai, 2003, pp. 98-99.

S.J. Fraenkel has identified twelve actions of managers that kill creativity of employees in his organization and warns them not to use any one of these tactics. Box 13-4 shows them.

Box 13.4 Twelve Ways to kill creativity

1. Drag your feet. Who can argue with the painstaking manager who wants to run it through again?
2. Say yes, but do not do it. This touch of diplomacy leaves almost everyone pleased—for a while.
3. Wait for full analysis. Logic seems to be on your side.
4. Do not follow up. Drop the idea among your associates and let them worry about it.
5. Call many meetings. This will kill time and the interest of others.
6. Put the idea into channels. That way you can forget about it.
7. Boost the cost estimates. A hero's role is guaranteed for saving the company money when the idea is vetoed.
8. Wait for market surveys. They take time –maybe too much.
9. Stick to protocol. Red tape will be around a long time after the dead idea.
10. Worry about the budget. Why spend money when things are going well?
11. Lack a sense of urgency. Your business has existed and will exist for a long time, so why rush?
12. Cultivate the "*not invented here*" syndrome. If a good idea is someone else's, do not be guilty of pushing it.

Adapted from S.J. Fraenkel, "How not to succeed as an R&D Manager," *Research Management*, May 1980, pp. 35.

Ensure People support:

Once a project idea takes shape, potential change masters require a "power tool" – support. They need go-ahead signs from key figures, "blessings" from above, the willingness of peers to cooperate, and the agreement of well placed people to lend their names and reputations to the project.

High innovation companies will have striking features like – high volume of movement and contact. People's careers are likely to take them into a variety of areas. For example, multi-area conferences, meetings, and training programs in such organizations enable people to circulate and to get to know potential supporters and collaborators across corporate space.

Digital Equipment makes it easy for mangers to meet face-to-face by running a regularly scheduled helicopter service to link Northeast facilities. This kind of arrangement made it possible for Heidi Wilson, the corporate manufacturing staff manager, to act on her idea for a rationalized materials flow system.

Encourage Idea champions:

Idea champions are encouraged to carry forward major developments.

Chairman Vincent Learson created this style at IBM during that company's most innovative period. He encouraged different groups to bring forward proposed designs for "performance shoot-outs" against competing proposals. At one time it was, in fact, difficult to find a successful major IBM innovation that derived directly from formal product planning rather than this championship process.

Alastair Pilkington who championed float glass, became chairman of Pilkington Bros – the first person outside the direct lineage of the founder to hold that position. Bell Labs fostered its own breed of Nobel Prize winners and champions (like Shannon, Shockley and Pierce) for various products and causes.

Each system found appropriate ways to reward such champions, sometimes even for extraordinary contributions on projects, which failed in the market place.

(iv) Space related initiatives:

Seating, color patterns, music, and interpersonal communication play an important part in facilitating the flow of right-brain impulses. A research project at the Massachusetts Institute of Technology (MIT) in the late 1980s found that 90% of the ideas that led to product break thoughts were inspired by casual conversations over a cup of coffee or strolling over to a colleague's desk on a sudden inspiration. It also highlighted the barriers that prevented this spontaneous exchange taking place, having to walk to another building, down a flight of stairs or through long corridors or worse still, having to travel to another site.

This kind of research has prompted a number of large organizations to experiment with new workspace designs.

At BMW's R&D centre in Munich, an investigation of how new cars are developed was carried out to discover which members of staff communicate with each other most frequently. As a result, development design engineer responsible for car doors, for example, works next door to the technical planner, who will translate his work into a prototype model. All the **design offices are housed on the same floor** as their model workshop to ensure that staff can communicate with each other easily.

Sun Microsystems became aware that its engineers often gathered in doorways and kitchens, had a chat and then returned to their offices. Realizing that these conversations could have creative value, the company designed spaces called **forums** spreading out from the kitchen area, where people could develop their thoughts in more comfort, other Silicon Valley companies have followed suit.

Cap Gemini Ernst & Young, a leading management consultancy, has established a "**thinking room**" at its Morristown headquarters where staff can sit in isolation booths, put on goggles and think deep thoughts.

(v) Time related initiatives:

Any employee who wants to, regardless of training, position, seniority, etc., be given creative time. Make sure that they either have a reasonable idea to work on or have demonstrated creative talent and will likely generate some ideas, given the time and freedom.

Time off –The 3M Company's approach allows technical people to devote 15 per cent of their office time to working on their own ideas. To make this initiative work better, observe the following guidelines:

- Don't allow everyone to devote (some would say fritter away) 15 per cent of his or her time to creative pursuits. All are not interested, many are not creative and some will abuse the privilege.

- Tangible evidence of participation (a plaque, etc.) should be provided and this should be the same regardless of whether or not their idea became a product.

Time out – As part of the "club working" established at BA's waterside headquarters, the outer area of each department overlooking a landscaped park is reserved for private study, where library rules of silence apply. Scottish Enterprise has "cells" for private study to complement "gives" for joint working and "dens" for team working.

Ricardosemler, of SEMCO an engineering and consultancy company, has provided each employee with a board to signal their need for private space. The boards have three pegs on which employees hang colored flags according to their mood. Green indicates a good mood, when the individual is happy to be interrupted; yellow means "careful"; and red means, "not today, thank you".

Time Away – However, research suggests that despite the good intentions of these initiatives, people prefer to do their most creative thinking away from the office. Nine out of ten of the 120 senior managers interviewed got the inspiration for their best business idea out of the office-on the train, in the car, on the beach, in the shower. This was because when in the office the ability to switch off and "drift and dream" was hampered by the perception that they might be interrupted by some office call.

Given this, some companies have announced sabbatical leave opportunities. To make it effective you may permit up to 15 per cent of your staff to take a creative sabbatical. It allows creative employees the opportunity to set aside what they are doing and work on their new product ideas full time for a year (and more, if needed).

Flexible working hours:

An important provision is flexibility in working hours and conditions. Some companies allow conceptual work at home, during working hours under license and outside working hours at the discretion and volition of the individual.

In a survey, about 85% of the 200 respondent companies indicated they do provide time flexibility. 89% of the respondent companies either budget for unexpected developments or allow engineers and scientists to spend up to 10% of their time on investigations of their own choosing.

(vi) Education and training related initiatives:

Continuing education is a vital component in nurturing the innovator. Companies use both formal and informal approaches.

- Knowledge can be enhanced by sharing at technical meetings and symposia, short refresher or advanced courses as well as study in university and colleges.
- Skill development can be provided through coaching, mentoring and training programs.

Hallmark, a greetings card company runs training workshops for cross-disciplinary product teams with the specific purpose of getting creative and less creative members to work together.

(vii) Motivation related initiatives:

To stimulate creativity, it is important to convince people that you really want it. Putting creative people into high positions is one way, but equally important is to formally and publicly recognize creative contributions.

Intrinsic motivation:

Amabile (1997) states that creativity in all fields including business flourishes under intrinsic motivation – the drive to do something because it is interesting, involving, exciting, satisfying or personally challenging. The rewards gold collar workers want most –even more than money is peer recognition. Indeed, one of the hallmarks of innovating companies is "praise abundance."

Organizations like General Electric's medical operations help instill confidence in their people by fostering the feeling that "we're all winners." Similarly, change masters tend to make everyone involved in their innovation a "hero": everyone shares the credit and the glory.

Special awards:

The trophies and wall plaques and letters of recognition and award breakfasts and late afternoon parking lot ceremonies in high innovation companies are all tools readily available to change masters to say thanks and to motivate people to sign up for the next innovation.

3M, General Electric and Hallmark encourage the most creative workers with additional field trips. To some, being assigned to a special project is an award in itself.

Ideas competitions and awards:

Kvaerner, a Norwegian shipbuilding conglomerate, has had a longstanding internal campaign to increase the volume of ideas circulating around the company and to extend this crusade to front-line staff through competitions and prizes. The winning ideas are highlighted in the company's house newsletters and used as the basis of local press campaigns in the home towns of the individuals.

At Toyota, suggestions that lead to genuine innovations are celebrated in an annual "Ideas Olympics". At a 1996 event, 5,824 ideas were praised under the categories of fun, creativity and recycling. Of these, 139 were paraded publicly in Toyota city in Tokyo's Aichi prefecture.

Recognition to suggestions:

Equally important are measures that ensure that ideas in the suggestions box do not lie there unnoticed or unappreciated. At Hewlett-Pacckard's Asian factories, where ideas boxes are an integral part of a long-standing quality initiative, the performance of line managers and supervisors is appraised, in part, on their ability to demonstrate that they have followed up and actively assessed suggestions from front-line assembly staff.

Intellectual property Awards and Recognition Plan:

Another initiative is the Intellectual property Awards and Recognition Plan, launched in 1996. Benchmark studies in the late 1990s suggested to Nortel that it was successfully registering Gower patents that its principal competitors. The company sees the expansion and protection of its intellectual property rights as a crucial competitive tool. It was therefore keen to explore ways in which the challenge of developing, filing and successfully registering patents for products and technologies could be extended to a broader range of its research and scientific staff.

The aim of the plan is twofold:

- To encourage all research and scientific staff to become actively involved in developing, filing and registering patents for products and technologies developed at its laboratories.
- To publicize successful patent applications in order to emphasize to all staff working for the company the importance of intellectual property.

The plan provides both monetary awards and public recognition for all staff involved in successful patent applications. There are four grades:

- **Patent filing** - This rewards all staff involved in the development of a patent at the point at which it is filed. The award is made at the site at which the work is undertaken.
- **Patent registering** - This rewards staff that has had a patent successfully registered.
- **Cumulative awards** - This rewards staff that has been involved in a number of successful patent applications, usually between five and ten.
- **Significant patent awards** - This rewards staff that has been involved in the successful registering of a patent deemed to be of particular value to the company. Examples include patents that have brought in substantial licensing revenues, that form the basis of an important industry standard, that protect one of the company's core technologies or products or that have received industry-wide recognition.

Staff receives a monetary award and a plaque highlighting their achievement. Presentations for the higher awards are made by a senior manager from the unit's national headquarters in the presence of other patent awardees and take place at sites of scientific or engineering significance.

SUMMARY

Innovators require sensitive human resource management to maximize their potential. The need to manage creative employees is becoming increasingly important because creativity is valued by many firms. There is rise in the number of creatives and competency development is the task of management. Managing creative employees is challenging task for the following reasons: Creativity is difficult to identify, supervisors are less knowledgeable than creative persons and feel intimidated. Creative people are independent and choosy, they prefer challenge, show tendencies of elitism and trouble making and require tolerance and special ways of handling. The initiatives necessary in managing creative employees are:

(i) Manager related (Management style like T-shaped management).

(ii) People related initiatives (Select right people, give challenging assignments, provide job rotation, Allow Freedom at work with right pressures, Encourage Job sharing, Set up Think-tank, Establish Peer partnership and arrange special support services).

(iii) Communication related initiatives (Stimulate others and Information sharing).

(iv) Ideas related initiatives (Welcome new ideas, Ensure People support and Encourage Idea champions).

(v) Space related initiatives (Design. seating, color patterns, music and interpersonal communication).

(vi) Time related initiatives (Time off, Time out, Time away, Flexible working hours).

(vii) Motivation related initiatives (Intrinsic motivation, Praise abundance, Special recognition and rewards, Ideas competitions and awards, Mental muscle, Competitions - Card index, Internal benchmarking exercises and Intellectual property Awards and Recognition Plan).

QUESTIONS

1. Explain the importance of managing creative employees. Why do you consider it challenging?
2. Explain various initiatives a firm can think of in managing its creative employees.

EXERCISES

Evaluate the following conversation - Rewrite to make in positive.

Employee:	I have a new idea to improve our automobile service offer.
Supervisor:	O.K. Shoot. It seems you have a bag of ideas. But will it sell?
Employee:	I think it would really sell. It saves money and time for our customers.
Supervisor:	I don't think time is critical in our service. How much would they be willing to pay for that benefit?
Employee:	I cannot give an estimate of the costs and benefits right now. I have only a feel of it.
Supervisor:	As you know feeling is not enough, you should support your idea with tangible benefits.
Employee:	In that case, I would need your help. Can you spare some time?
Supervisor:	I don' think I have time for this. I have already the pressure of our targets. For the present, you should also mind your targets.

CASE : INNOVATION IS WIPRO AND WIPRO IS INNOVATION

I strongly believe that Innovation is the basis of both survival and success. Innovation is necessary to satisfy new customer needs and create new revenue streams. Innovation is necessary to create higher value for customers. Innovation is necessary to stay ahead of competition - consistently. *Azim H. Premji, Chairman and Managing Director.*

Recognition to innovation:

Over the years, Wipro realized that along with its focus on implementation of quality standards it needed to come out with innovative products and services to gain acceptance in the global markets. It also realized that innovation would provide the company with a platform to differentiate itself from the rest of the players in the industry. In order to come out with innovative products and services, the top management at Wipro committed itself to fostering innovation in the organization and encouraging employees to come out with innovative ideas. The Wipro management identified that innovation would be one of the major growth drivers, especially in the IT field. By 2000, a process to encourage innovation was implemented in all group companies.

Innovation is a purpose:

"Innovation is Wipro - Wipro is Innovation" is our statement of purpose. The challenge this pursuit presents to us everyday is – how does one make Innovation "Purposeful", "Ingrained" and "Deliberate" in our organization. We recognize and nurture "innovative solutions" as one of the four Wipro values. We prioritize focus and resources guided by this value. The Wipro way of Innovation is really about this deliberate sustained innovation.

Our purpose of Innovation is to create higher value for our customers. This continuous thought led us to foresee the benefit of partnering with technology companies to bring value to our customers. Combining these relationships with our strong R&D talent led to the idea of "Lab on Hire" and subsequently to offshore development centers which made offshore outsourcing truly mainstream. Pushing this idea a little further helped us conceptualize the remote infrastructure service model, branded as global command center or GCC to manage the customer's IT infrastructure. Today, we serve our customers with a wide spectrum of services fuelled by the power of innovation.

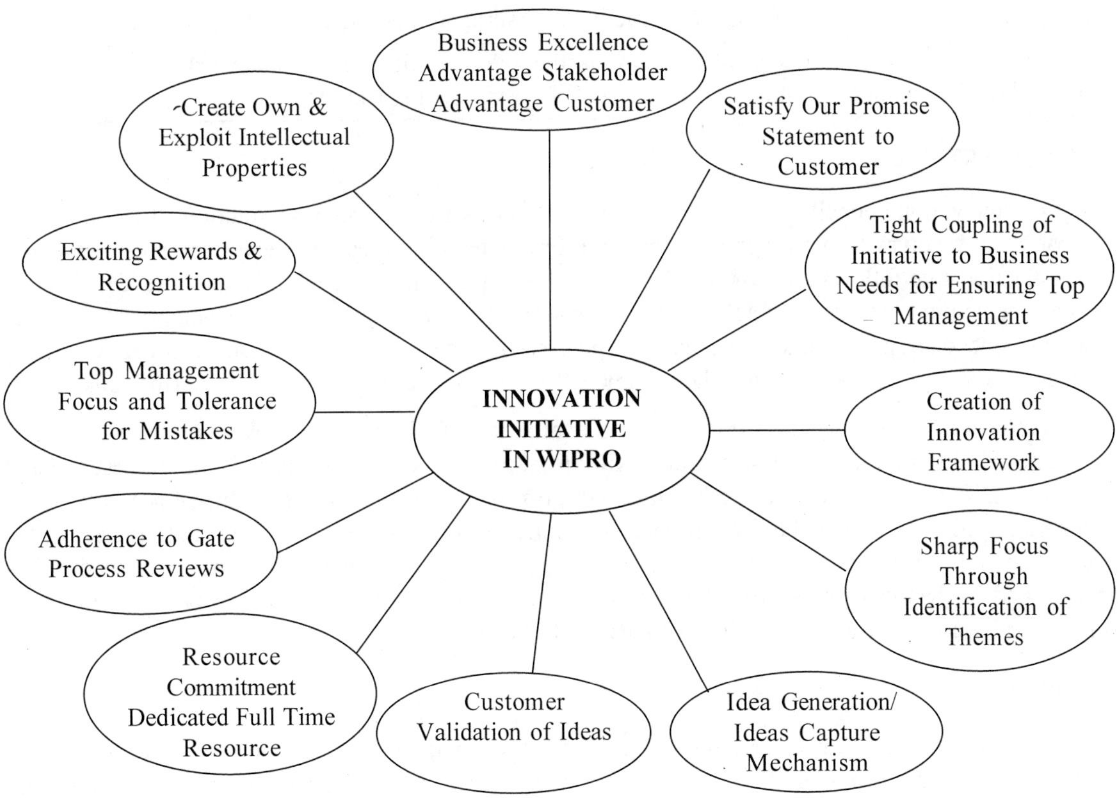

Figure 13–1 Innovation clock at Wipro

Theme Labs:

At Wipro, innovation happens around selected core themes that are strategic to us. Some core themes that we have taken up include.

- Home networking.

- ❖ Knowledge management and collaboration.
- ❖ Content commerce.

Theme based Innovation	Product
Home networking	The Home Gateway Software was the first project under the innovations initiative to be commercialized. It enabled customers to have a networked home. Its applications were virtual private network connectivity, internet sharing, video on demand, IP telephony and home security and surveillance. It comprised comcEngine, Voice Engine and AppEngine software addressing the communication, Voice Over Broadband and Application Service Delivery Infrastructure needs of the Home Gateway devices.
Content Commerce	Flow-brix was a workflow automation framework to provide pre-press workflow solutions for the publishing industry. It also catered to the needs of cross-media publishing and brand asset management.
Collaboration and knowledge Management	i-desk was a web-based employee self-service framework that helped employees to access HR services and programs.

Innovation gates:

Our innovation council is a core team that takes ideas from concept to solution. It has a unique approach that involves 'crossing gates'. Thus, the first gate is the idea gate where the idea originates. The evaluation gate follows this where it is analyzed in depth. Once through this gate, the idea must go through the commitment gate, which allocates resources for the project. At the development gate, the proof of concept is put up and the idea is expected to bring in the first purchase order. Once the product is launched, it goes through the volume gate from where it is absorbed in normal business.

Wipro did not fix any time frame for the evaluation of ideas-it could even stretch over a few months. Said Divakaran, "We don't want to kill any idea at an early state-usually in the first three to four months. That's when we want to be close to a go-no-go decision." The total time for an idea to be commercialized was estimated to be around 18 months. An idea was evaluated from all angles for the first six months. In the next 6-12 months, it was given funds and resources to be developed into a product and in the six months after that, the idea was commercialized-the idea was expected to not only cover its costs but also bring in revenues for the company.

Rewards:

Along with starting the innovation process, the top management at Wipro also realized the role played by rewards and recognition in motivating employees to come up with innovative ideas and framed a detailed rewards policy. The idea generator and the team as a whole, which was accountable for the success of a project, were rewarded and the name, picture and the idea in brief were listed on the company's intranet.

Web support:

The whole innovation process was enabled by Wipro web, which allowed employees to post new ideas on the intranet by just filling in simple questionnaires.

Innovative teams:

In addition Wipro also constituted innovative teams with the aim of generating innovative ideas in line with customer needs and market trends so as to increase customer satisfaction and bring in increased revenues for the company. The marketing team at wipro helped the R&D team know about market demand by exploring the market.

Education forums:

In order to encourage the innovative spirit among employees, Wipro even conducted workshops and brought in external consultants from specialized fields to help employees refine their ideas.

It also gave innovation process guidelines to all the middle level managers and department heads so that they would clearly understand the innovation process.

In addition, Wipro also organized TechForum, an annual technological event at which Wiipro employees were allowed to showcase their new innovative products through paper presentations and demos to portray their competencies to the company's existing and prospective customers. The TechForum was conducted in all Wipro locations in India. Wipro also set up an innovation center in 2001 at Bangalore to encourage business ideas and entrepreneurial skills among employees.

Advisory board:

The corporate vice-president, who innovation center employed around 200 people working on turning people and infrastructure needed to turn their ideas into products and services. Wipro also constituted an advisory board with top academicians consultants and experts from the industry both in India and abroad to guide its innovation initiatives.

Coordination with R&D:

In addition, Wipro also established research and development centers that worked towards meeting future technological challenges. The objective was to have expertise in the new technologies and come up with the products and productive services that could be patented by Wipro. These centers worked with research institutes and also with technology providers like Symbian, Siebel, etc. and provided a platform for the growth of Wipro employees.

Outcomes:

Wipro employees came up with various innovative products such as Flow-BriX, work flow solutions for publishing, I-Desk, the workplace collaboration tool enabling easier HR management by speeding up work process, etc.

Questions:

1. Examine the innovation initiatives at Wipro and comment.
2. Suggest few ideas to Wipro on improving its innovation efforts.

Source: www.wipro.com and www.wiprocorpoate.com and magazines

Chapter 14

Creativity Training

Learning Objectives

After you have studied this chapter, you will be able to...

- Identify the need for creativity training and establish the objectives of training
- Know the creativity testing and development methods
- Understand how to design and organize training programs
- Explain, how to develop intuitive skills of employees
- Appreciate the kind of communication skills required for creativity

Structure

- Introduction
- Need for Training
- Objectives of Training
- Creativity Testing and Development Methods
- Designing Training Programs
- Organizing Training Programs
- Developing Intuition
- Communication Skills for Creativity
- Summary
- Questions
- Exercises
- Case : Mindset Matters

INTRODUCTION

There is a myth that creativity is limited to a few individuals who are naturally creative. In reality, creativity can be learned and applied like any other skill. At the same time, a naturally creative person can through experience learn to raise already high creative output even higher. This realization has led to the organization of training programs on creativity by several enterprises in their quest for becoming creative organizations.

NEED FOR TRAINING

Creativity is not a born quality or skill. It can be developed among people through a process of learning.

Research with fraternal and identical twins supports the view that different abilities to think and to think creatively, are *not* inherited. Thinking and creative thinking are learnable skills like driving a car, swimming or knitting. Some people will be better than others, but, given sufficient motivation, everyone can develop a reasonable amount of skill.

The role of training in promoting creativity can be understood from the following viewpoints:

(i) To change thinking styles:

Problem solving without creative thinking is a garden without seeds: only slugs, thistles, compost, and finely turned soil. Creative thinking will plant a mental garden, which can then be cultivated, weeded, nourished, and harvested. Fortunately, creative thinking can be taught and applied to creative problem solving. As such, training for creativity has to focus on changing the traditional thinking styles of managers, which are barriers to creativity.

- ***Change from Linear to lateral thinking*** - Linear thinking is still common in businesses. Innovative managers believe that the world is complex, chaotic and uncertain. They base their decision-making on modeling of the relationships that exist between People and Organizations, and look for alternatives using an either/or logic; and on the assumption that there are many varied but equally valid routes from A to B.

  Lateral thinking goes beyond the deterministic model. Using flexible approach it seeks to find diverse solutions borrowing from other fields, through both experience and imagination.

- ***Zero-sum game to win–win integration*** - Equally dangerous is the assumption that any decision is a zero-sum game, with winners and losers. This is a product of the Aristotelian principle, deeply rooted in managers with high IQs, that good decision-making means coming up with a winning argument that will triumph over an opponent with a losing one.

(ii) To create confidence for creativity:

We are all naturally creative. When we have confidence, we will explore and manipulate our environment in imaginative ways. Creative coaching can be highly effective in countering these debilitating factors. Indeed, it can actually help to increase our sense of psychological security by equipping us to handle life's uncertainties more effectively.

(iii) To maintain operational excellence:

Organizations are productive and efficient because of standardized procedures, hierarchy, rules and proven techniques. They emphasize on specialization and conformity. Creativity implies experimentation, frequent disregard of established rules and procedures, 'going off tangents', taking off, half-baked ideas and so forth. There is need for mental revolution as Taylor had suggested and improvement in skills for searching excellence and achieving it. Training is required to provide the kind of scientific vigor needed for highly productive operations.

(iv) To keep up with growth opportunities:

Organizations must also keep up with changes in the market and in technology. In order to do this, innovativeness has to be improved. T&D programs help create appropriate skills, knowledge and attitudes for creative approaches and accomplishments.

(v) To sustain vitality during recession:

During an economic recession, the temptation to cut back on all training and development activity should be resisted. Inevitably, some training activities will have to be axed, but those that keep staff up to date with technological advances and market trends should be carefully considered on a case-by-case basis. During an economic slowdown or recession, events such as internal think tanks or benchmarking exercises with close partners, suppliers or industry counterparts, which allow employees to exchange views on can be immensely valuable.

OBJECTIVES OF TRAINING

The overall objectives of training programmes in the present context are to develop employees' awareness of quality, productivity and innovation problems and their ability to judge priorities for attention to problems and opportunities. Creativity training programmes may have the following objectives:

- To expand horizons of knowledge – knowledge of sensing, perceiving and learning the innovation problems/opportunities.
- To improve the competence in systematically analyzing and imaginatively solving the problems.
- To enhance the ability to organize, justify and present the recommendations to the organization for decision and action.

CREATIVITY TESTING AND DEVELOPMENT METHODS

A good majority of studies point to four principal characteristics viz., *problem sensitivity, idea fluency, originality and flexibility*. Experiments have demonstrated that all four of these can be developed to some degree in any individual.

Fluency:

Fluency is the ability to generate many ideas, solutions, alternatives, designs, methods, words, etc. It is the quantitative representation of the ideas in all categories. The total number of ideas give us numerically the measure of fluency. Fluency is of four types: *ideational, expressional, associational and word.*

(i) Ideational Fluency:

It is the generation of ideas where free expression is encouraged and where quality is not evaluated. Table 14.1 gives the number of ways the exercise can be conducted.

Table 14.1 Ideational fluency exercises

Aspect	Instruction	What trainer has to provide
Headings	Write as many headings of a story given below.	Give some short story.
Improvements	Suggest as many ways as you can to improve a given thing.	Say a product or process.(Eg: Pen or writing).
Uses	Write as many uses of a given thing as you can.	Say a product or process(Eg: Pen or writing).
Descriptions	Give many ways to describe an accident.	Say some even (Eg: Strike by employee union or fire accident in a plant).
Topics	Write as many ideas as possible about a work.	Say some work (Eg:driving, managing or selling).
Themes	Write as many words as you can about a given topic.	Give some topic (Eg: Nationality, Industrial democracy).
Thing categories	List the names of things that are ----(Eg: round or that can be called round, Square or pyramidical).	-

(ii) Expressional Fluency:

It indicates production of new ideas to fit a system or logical theories. The ideas can be in the form of sentences, verbal ideas, question responses etc. Tests to measure expressional fluency have been developed (Table 14.2) to show it directly or through other modes, such as simile interpretations, word arrangements etc.

Table 14.2 Expressional fluency exercises

Method	Instruction
Making Sentences	Asking to write sentences using the given alphabets. Eg: Write four word sentences when the first letter of each word is given as w.....c....e....n..... (Answers: We can eat nuts. Willie comes every night. Wholesome carrots elevate nations. Weary cats evade nothing etc).
Simile interpretations	Asking participant to provide similes for a given expression. E.g., Complete sentence that states an analogous idea (say, to friendship.

Method	Instruction
Word Arrangements	Asking to write sentences using the words given. E.g.,Write sentences containing four specified words (say, light, work, make, good) (Answer: Light makes good work, light work makes good, good work makes light, good light makes work, etc).

(iii) Associational Fluency:

It indicates production of ideas or words from a restricted area, i.e., of equal relationships, It requires completion of relations, production of relations, generation of synonyms, analogies, similarities, problems of likeness etc. Some tests to measure associational fluency (Table 14.3) through controlled associations, simile insertions and opposites are given below:

Table14.3 Associational fluency exercises

Method	Instruction
Controlled Associations	Write as many synonyms as possible for given word (say, light)
Simile Insertions	Write adjectival completion for the simile (she is..... like moon: Answers: beautiful, bright, shining etc).
Associations	Write a word that can be associated with two given words(say, chair ....table)
Opposites	Write opposite or nearly opposite of a given word (say, good).

(iv) Word fluency:

It requires only dealing with words. It is generation of words of specifically required epithets. The expressional fluency has a concern only with ideas and sentences whereas word fluency has concern only with words. Thus it is more a test of vocabulary. Tests to measure word fluency include three methods- beginning with a given prefix, suffix or first or last letters of words (Table 14.4).

Table 14.4 Word fluency exercises

Method	Instruction
Prefix	Write words beginning with a given prefix. (say, com.....).
Suffix	Write words ending with a given suffix. (say,......com)
First and Last Letters	Write words beginning and ending with the given letter or letters. (say 'e 'or 'm' and 'r')

Flexibility:

It is the ability to generate a variety of ideas, solutions, alternatives, designs, methods etc.

It indicates in how many distinct different ways an individual can respond to a stimulus. Quantitatively it is a measure of variety. Thus the number of different classes of ideas or things determines the numerical value of flexibility.

It differs from fluency. Flexibility is the representation of categories of ideas whereas the fluency is the number of ideas.. In case of Uses Test, for example, one may give uses of bricks as 'build a house' 'build a school,' 'build a factory' etc. Here his fluency is 3 but flexibility is only 1, as the answers belong to only one category of thought. If the answers were 'make a paper-weight,' 'drive a nail,' 'throw at dog,' 'make powder,' the flexibility would have been 4 as each new response belonged to a different category or class. Flexibility is of two types: *spontaneous and adaptive*. We will now discuss, how can they be measured.

(i) Spontaneous Flexibility:

It is the production of a diversity of ideas in a relatively unrestricted situation. It may include variety of kinds of responses into classes, like number of considerations or properties, attributes or inherent characteristics of problem or product, number of shifts of category responses, versatility etc. It keeps the creator out of rut by jumping from one train of thought to another in thinking of new ideas for some device or product. Some tests used by Thurstone, are described in Table14.5.

Table 14.5 Spontaneous flexibility exercises

Method	Instruction
Cube Fluctuations	Indicate the number of changes in perspective of ambiguous cube.
Windmill Alternations	Indicate the number of alternations from the illusion to another while observing shadow of rotating rectangular blade.
Retinal-Rivalry Reversals	Indicate the number of reversals when a blue field is presented stereoscopically to one eye and a yellow field to the other eye.
Semantic spontaneous flexibility	Indicate 'Uses of Things' (Write a variety of uses of an object ,say 'brick') or 'Alternate Uses' (List different peculiar uses of common object , say, 'paper').

(ii) Adaptive Flexibility:

It is more nearer to originality and like originality it has some divergent transformation quality. The conventional problem solving methods, which have become unworkable, are abandoned to find adaptive flexibility. Thus it involves changes.

All the tests measuring adaptive flexibility suggest several unusual answers to which the original stimulus object can be adapted. The examinee has to make changes of some kind-changes in interpretation of task, in approach or strategy or in possible solutions. Adaptive flexibility thus involves number of detours, freedom to make changes, number of approaches or strategies used in seeking solutions, number of changes of interpretations, changes in direction of thinking etc.

Among various tests used to measure adaptive flexibility are Match Problems, Unusual Uses, Plot Titles etc., as shown in Table 14.6.

Table 14.6 Adaptive flexibility tests

Method	Instruction
Match problems	Indicate several different patterns of matches that can be removed to leave a specified number of squares
Unusual uses	Give different types of uses of 'brick'
Plot titles	Give many appropriate 'titles' for the following story........(Give some story).

Originality:

It is the ability to generate unique off-beat-but appropriate-ideas, solutions, alternatives, designs, etc. It is the measure of quality. When we talk of originality in terms of either figural or verbal or symbolic transformations we designate it as uncommon or unusual. Its main criterion is to be away from the main track.

Some specific tests have been devised where the participant is instructed to produce new ideas, as in Plot titles, Symbol production, Consequences etc. In non-verbal test, the uncommonness of response is the criterion for originality. For example, for a picture of 'sleeping child', the response heading may be 'It is time to retire". Table 14.7 shows the methods of testing.

Table 14.7 Originality tests

Method	Instruction	What trainer has to provide
Plot Titles	Write clever titles for story plots	Give story plots
Symbol production	Produce symbols to represent activities and objects	Give an object or activity
Consequences	List remote consequences of certain changes.	Give a change situation

Elaboration:

It indicates expanding and combining activities of higher thought. It is to provide specification of details that contribute to the development of a general idea. Thus elaboration shows production of detailed steps, variety of implications and consequences, which can be quantitatively measured. The use of contents designates the elaboration as figural, symbolic or semantic etc. Table 14.8 lists some of the elaboration methods

Table 14.8 Elaboration methods

Elaboration method	Instruction
Figural	Add to given lines to produce a meaningful figure
Symbolic	Give as many steps as necessary in planning a play
Semantic	Elaborate the idea: 'A stitch in time saves nine.'

Sensitivity to problems:

It is the receptivity for problems when the creator sees defects, needs, deficiencies, oddities and sees what must be done. Whether the problem is simple or complex, he attacks it from various angles. It is something as Torrance and others (1961) remarked, "Thick-skinned people do no creative thinking." Tests like Apparatus Test, seeing problems, seeing Deficiencies etc. are used to score this ability.Table 14.9 presents three types of tests.

Table 14.9 Tests of sensitivity

Method	Instruction
Apparatus Test	Suggest two improvements for a common apparatus/appliance/machine. (Say, electric heater).
Seeing Problems	List problems that might arise in connection with common object. (Say, bicycle).
Seeing Deficiencies	Point out ways in which a described plan or activity is faulty. Say Employee suggestion system)

Redefinition:

It is close to adaptive flexibility and originality. It requires defining or perceiving the problem in a way different from the usual or established way. It is the ability to rearrange ideas, concepts, people and things, to shift the function of old things or ideas for new purposes. It can be applied to different types of contents in the same way as figural, symbolic, semantic etc., and they can be named with their names as figural redefinition, symbolic redefinition etc. Various tests to test them have been developed. Some of them are given below-first four of figural, next two of symbolic and last three of semantic redefinitions. Three useful methods of testing are given in Table 14.10.

Table 14.10 Tests of Redefinition

Tests	Method	Instruction
Figural tests	Concealed Figure	Indicate which of four complex geometrical figures contains a given geometrical figure.
	Penetration of Camouflage	Locate faces hidden in a given figure.
	Hidden figures	Indicates which of five figures is hidden in a given figure.
	Hidden Pictures	Find human or animal pictures hidden in a scene, as rapidly as possible.
Symbolic tests	Camouflaged Words	Find the game of the sport or game concealed in a sentence.
	Word transformation	Indicate new divisions between letters in a new series of words forming a phrase, to make a new series of words.
Semantic redefinition	Gestalt Transformation	Indicate which of five listed objects has a part that will serve a specified purpose.
	Object Synthesis	Name an object that could be made by combining two specified objects.
	Picture Gestalt	Indicate which object in a photograph will serve a specified purpose.

DESIGNING TRAINING PROGRAMS

Some of the key decision areas in the design of training programmes are discussed here.

Categories of trainees:

Requirements of training differ in their nature and content, for the different categories of programme personnel- facilitators, team leaders and members. Training of programme personnel is usually a chaining process with three successive links. The chain begins with the coordinator or facilitators (s) receiving training from external resources persons. They, in turn, are normally responsible for the training of team leaders. Team members may receive training from team leaders or facilitator(s), or from both.

Team leaders and programme facilitator(s) receive training in the following:

- Training in technical areas and creativity techniques.
- Leadership and team-building skills and group discussion techniques.
- Principles of learning and motivation.
- Communication and presentation techniques.

Communication and presentation techniques are of fundamental importance for teams. A team leader and his team, should be able to effectively present before the management, both orally and through visual aids, the following:

(i) What the problem is?

(ii) How was it identified?

(iii) The suggested methods for solving the problem.

The suggested recommendations must be supported by evidence in the form of well-prepared charts, graphs and tables. They must also be substantiated by proper costing approaches.

Training programmes for the participants in creative work teams, are in addition to other training programmes, which focus on technical and professional work areas. All types and forms, of training activity, are a crucial requirement for an organization's ability to utilize the creative skills and talents of its members.

Team approach to training:

Team approach to creative problem-solving and the training programme for skills up gradation, are mutually supportive.

Team + Creative skills = Creative team

Higher and upgraded skills of the people directly contribute to their capacity for creative work performance. In work of teams, it results in the enhanced value addition to their thinking and doing.

Speakers:

The internal speakers, i.e., speakers from within the company and their presentations include the following:

- *Inventors:* Who describe the creative thinking that went into their discoveries.
- *Innovators:* Who describe how they overcome barriers in bringing new products to market.
- *Professionals:* Who elucidate the importance and value of thinking outside existing paradigms.
- *People from plant and R & D sites:* Who describe creativity teams that meet periodically to tackle problems brought by fellow employees.
- *Members of training center:* Who are skilled in teaching creativity techniques, discuss the concepts and techniques and sometimes lead workshops.

Training programs - content and themes

Various theoretical inputs and associated practical exercises that may be used in training programs are given in Table 14.11. Different themes of training lectures or title for short duration programs are given in Table 14.12.

Table 14.11 Training contents

General principles of creative thinking	Types of thinking, Basic systems thinking, Barriers to creativity Models, semantics, and their influence on mental operations Principles of classification, Shifting between modes of perception Transactions analysis, Self-recognition exercises and Relaxation drills
Specification of problems	Problem typologies, Techniques of identification and analysis Establishing formats, Differentiation: symptoms/root cause generic unique situations localized/system-wide situations
Generating solutions	Field Force Analysis , Morphological Analysis, Check Listing Word Shifts, Brainstorming and Synectics
Selecting an appropriate solution	Principles of making decisions, Establishing criteria, Methods of evaluating, The need to identify the client(s), Recognizing when the time is ripe for a particular innovation
Implementing the solution	Principle of planning, User involvement, Techniques of presentation and persuasion and Monitoring and revision
The influence of the organization	The management climate: positive and negative elements, Patterns of organization, Basics of group dynamics, Resistance to change Scanning for problems/opportunities

Table 14.12 Seminal themes for lectures and seminars

Laughter and Creativity	Managing for innovation	Value of Fables in Reawakening our Imagination
Applied Creativity	Environment for creativity	Creative Problem Solving
Lateral Thinking	Creative Leadership	Creative Techniques
Artistic Visualization	Building the Creative Organization	Creative imagery
Metaphoric Thinking	Creative Blockbusting	Creative Visualization
Odyssey of the Mind	A Framework for speeding Product Development	Software Lateral Thinking Assist
Break Point and Beyond	Intrapreneuring	E-creativity

The training programs organized at Godrej are given in Table15-12 to provide an overall view of how organizations strive to improve the employee skills and knowledge to improve productivity and creativity.

ORGANIZING TRAINING PROGRAMS

Training programs on creativity or innovation management may vary in duration from one day to one week. Exhibit 14.1 gives how a one day training program can be conducted.

Exhibit 14.1

PROGRAMME FOR A CREATIVITY SESSION

Warm-up session
(Creativity exercises: unrelated to the 'main problem')

PROBLEM STAGE

Problem as stated:
'How to'

Description by client

Teams use 'trigger' words to generate new 'How' to's'

New 'How to's' are categorized: realistic, embryonic, implausible

Client chooses a new 'How to': problem as understood

IDEA STAGE

Team splits into smaller groups

Many ideas are generated for tackling the problem: creative techniques

Promising ideas are presented to the client

Client chooses a solution

SOLUTION STAGE

Client paraphrases solution

Team and client list positive, negative and interesting aspects of the solution

Solution checked: new, attractive, feasible?

Next steps: formulation of action plan

Jerry Conrath (1985) divided a training program into six phases and described how it can be organized using exercises that fertilize imagination of the trainees.

Phase One: Warming up:

While some people have had nourishment for their creative thoughts, most have not. Indeed, the rewards in life-school grades, parental praise and job performance appraisals-have usually come from following the rules and getting the "right" answers rather than from examining problems from many angles and exploring many answers.

Ice-breakers:

Use stories, quotations and sermons to warm up the session. Create a climate for active listening and speaking.

For example, you may tell how important time is by giving this quotation on the Bank of Time.

> TIME is a bank that credits your account each morning with 86,400 seconds. Every night it rules off as lost whatever of this you have failed to invest to good purpose. It carries over no balances. It allows no overdrafts. Each day it opens a new account with you. Each night it burns the record of the day. If you fail to use the day's deposit, the loss is yours.

You may inquire the nature of their jobs and how much pressure they have on their routine tasks. Inquire whether they consider routine is more important. De-emphasize routine by telling examples of how routine obsession may lead to failure in the long-run.

You may use the following simple example of - **Slave to routine.** To content oneself with being a "slave to routine" is merely to court disaster.

> Many executives are slaves of routine. They don't seem to realize, as Dr. Guberson points out that the mere fact that something has been done the same way for 20 years is often a sign it is being done wrong. These people remind us of the old army sergeant who was put in charge of a plot of grass in front of administrative head quarters in a camp in Michigan.
>
> The sergeant promptly delegated the job to a back private and told him to watch it grow every day at 5 O'clock. This private did concretionary. One day, however, when there was a terrific thunderstorm, the sergeant walked into the barracks and saw the private doing bank fatigue. "What's the matter with you?" the sergeant bellowed "Its 5 O'clock and you are supposed to be watering the gross!" "But sergeant" the private said, looking confused "look at that thunderstorm."
>
> "So what! Yelled the sergeant "You've got a raincoat haven't you."
>
> Rain or sunshine, same people go about their jobs the same way everyday of the week, every week of the month, every month of the year, never with a single new idea to contribute to their company that might prove in the least worthwhile. These they sometimes wonder why younger," less-talented men (or so they seem to think) go sailing past them into positions higher on the executive ladder that they had been hoping to get themselves.

Now you can say creativity, novelty and variety on the job is important.

You may ask a few questions like:

What does the word 'creativity' suggest to you? The responses are like this, in general.

Being a genius, Making something out of nothing, having a baby, Producing the work of art, thinking beyond, Thinking of totally new ideas, Path breaking-taking a new route,

Make a list of your creative achievements"

Their creative achievement lists may show such items as cooking stew, designing a new form for the office, saving money to buy a car, planning a garden with limited space, inventing stories for children and bringing two hostile employees together. Then, you may ask them to name creative persons, companies and creative products/processes.

Having what their appetites for creative thinking you can now turn to developing their capacity for it. You can tell them stories of creative persons as the one given in Exhibit 14.2.

Exhibit 14.2

Cultivate creative thinking habits

We can learn a lot from the experience of the legendary career of inventor Thomas Alva Edison, who was granted 1,093 patents for inventions ranging from light bulb, typewriter and electric pen to the phonograph motion-picture camera and alkaline storage batter, etc. His work methods reveal that the true keys to unlocking creativity are learned traits – perseverance and an open minded approach to learning. Edison used his creativity not only for developing new inventions but also bring them to market and winning out financially over competitors.

When Edison died in 1931, he left 3,500 notebooks which present a verbal and visual biography of Edison's mind at work they offer fresh clues as to how Edison, who had virtually no formal education, could achieve such an astounding, unrivalled record of invention. The notebooks illustrate how Edison conceived his ideas from their earliest inception and show how he developed and implemented them. The following are some of Edison's creative thinking strategies, which might bend our own mind and thinking.

Edison believed that in order to discover one good idea, you have to generate many. Out of quantity comes quality. He made more than 50,000 experiments to invent the alkaline storage-cell battery and as many as 9,000 to perfect the light bulb. Edison looked at creativity as simply good, honest, hard work. He felt that initial ideas are usually poorer in quality than later ideas. Creative thinking depends on continuing the flow of ideas long enough to purge common and habitual thoughts and produce unusual and imaginative ones.

Edison felt that his lack of formal education was, infact, a "blessing". This enabled him to approach his work with far fewer assumptions than his more-educated competitors, who included many theoretical scientists, renowned Ph.D.s and engineers. He approached any idea or experience with wild enthusiasm and would try anything out of the ordinary.

When experiment failed, Edison would always ask what the failure revealed and would enthusiastically record what he had learned. He had an enormous talent for appropriating ideas that may have failed in one instance and using them for something else.

He relentlessly recorded and illustrated every problem he worked on in his notebooks. Whenever he succeeded with a new idea, he would review his notebooks to rethink ideas and inventions abandoned in the past in light of what was recently learned. He would often jot down his observations of the natural world, failed patents and research papers written by other inventors and ideas others had come up with in other fields. Edison was tireless in his persistence to change a subject into something else through trial and error method until he found the ideas that worked.

(Speech delivered by Mr. Lakshman Prasad, Chairman, Numerators India (P) Ltd, "Making India Inventive: Individuals can make a difference" in *Indian Management,* February, 2000, Vol. 39, No. 2, pp.35-39).

Phase Two: Imagination and Invention:

Imagination is the beginning of creation. You imagine what you desire; you will what you imagine; and at last you create what you will.

In this phase, teach them that they must never impose boundaries on themselves; but instead should think expansively, always pushing beyond the obvious. One-way to get your employees to think expansively is by using the nine-dot exercise below. (For a possible answer see the answers in this chapter).

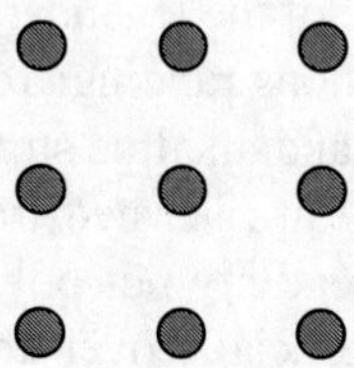

Now you are ready to introduce your staffers to the creative problem solving process itself. There are eight steps to follow:

1. Define the problem.
2. Gather all relevant information.
3. Explore all possible options to solving the problem.
4. Analyze the advantages and disadvantages of each option.
5. Use intuition to help in the process before taking action.
6. Make a decision.
7. Fantasize the worst and the best that could happen with the decision.
8. Implement and evaluate the decision.

Phase Three: Problem Definition:

To get your participants through this difficult first step, ask them to list some irritants, frustrations, or concerns and to turn them into a problem statement. Then examine the results. Problems cannot be solved by thinking within the framework in which the problems were created. [Albert Einstein]. Creativity is less about solving problems than about finding them. We come across two types of problems: Presented and constructed.

Presented problems:

What is a problem? Faced with such a question, most people would probably suggest these answers:

- Something that must be solved (removed/minimized/ignored)
- Something that cannot be solved (removed etc…)
- Something we are set
- An obstacle
- Something that causes pain or stress
- Something we'd rather not have

Presented problems are those, which come to us, or are given to us, or happen to us.

Problems are presented to us by the outside world. Examples would include:

- A piece of machinery breaking-down
- A target set us by somebody else
- Being stuck in a traffic jam
- A sudden shift in interest rates

Thus, a presented problem is a discernible gap between Initial conditions and Goal conditions.

. *Constructed problem:*

For the same question – what is the problem, thinking further, some people might add:

- Something we set ourselves
- A challenge
- Something that gives us the opportunity to do better
- Something that can be solved

Constructed problems are problems that we make for ourselves. There may not be anything specifically wrong; but we are interested in the possibility of improvement or change or doing something different. Examples would include:

- Gaining a qualification
- Improving our performance
- Innovating a new product
- Increasing market share
- Improving an existing procedure or service
- Working out a long-term strategy

A problem is chance for you to do your best. [Duke Ellington]

Thus a constructed problem is the created gap between Current conditions and a Potential future.

Presented problems arise out of a tension between what is and what ought to be. Constructed problems include a tension between what is and what might be.

Tensions:

When a problem arises, people experience two types of tensions - Emotional tension and Creative tension. Emotional tension is like the tension between two jammed machine parts: a stress that threatens to cause damage. It is unwelcome, unpleasant and exhausting. It can be relieved in only two-ways: by applying pressure; or by separation. We can seek to overcome the problem, or avoid it: fight or flight.

Creative tension is like the tension in a taut rubber band, stretched between current reality and our vision of the future. It is potential energy: it is exciting and energizing and provokes movement.

Problem statement:

The first step in tackling a problem creatively is to transform it into a constructed problem. Exhibit 14.3 shows what is not a problem definition. The easiest way to do this is to cast it as a 'how to' statement.

- A piece of machinery breaking-down.

  How to repair the machinery?

- A target set by somebody else.

  How to meet the target?

Exhibit 14.3 Problem definitons:

Not problem definition	Examples
A statement of an irritant or concern is not a definition of a problem and does not open the problem itself	Statements such as "I'm too busy," "I need a new car," or "My typewriter is too old" are merely statements-not problem definitions
Symptoms or information indicating that a problem exists must not be taken for the problem itself	"This typewriter is missing 13 letters" is not a problem definition but merely a symptom of a problem.
A definition must open up the problem solving process, not leap to a conclusion or decision.	"Should I have a cup of coffee?" is not a problem definition because it doesn't open up the problem solving process but leaps to a conclusion or decision.
A definition must be specific to the solver and enable the individual to be involved in the problem solving process through implementation.	"How do I streamline my work habits in order to get the work done on time?"

Other examples of good definition are:

How do I save enough money to purchase a new car?

How do I convince my manager that a new typewriter is necessary?

Using these examples as guides, help your employees to work through their statements to design clear, open problem definitions.

Phase Four: Exploring options - The second and third steps in decision-making are, gathering all relevant information and exploring all options to solving the problem. This requires participants to go beyond the obvious.Give some warm-up activities to help them get started. For example ask them:

Think of as many possible uses as you can for some object in the room that they can all see.

The goal is not to come up with only eight or ten uses but with 20 to 30. This will put participants in the mindset of expansive, exploratory, creative thinking. Giggling should be allowed for we giggle when we warm up to jog, too. And remember: Success comes from quantity, not quality, at this step of the process. Here is another good warm up activity that will help employees go beyond the obvious.

Count the squares in the figure given below:

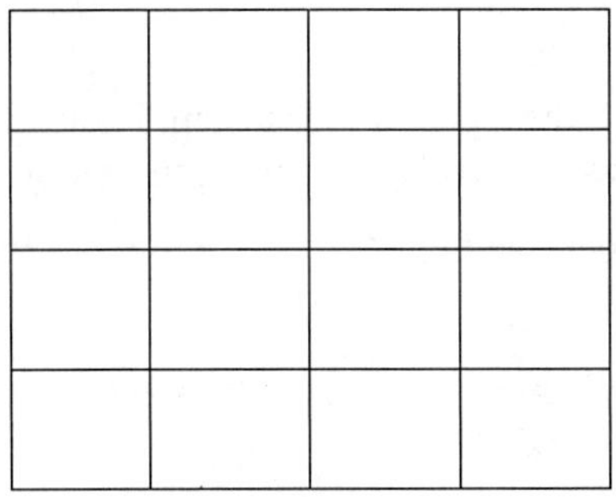

What usually happens is that half the group settles on 17 squares puts pens down, them waits impatiently for a halt to what appears to be a very simple task. When the supervisor walks around the room looking at answers and giving no feedback, pens are picked up again, exclamations of discovery are heard, and new numbers are added. After 10 to 12 minutes, about one-quarter of the group settles on 30 squares while most people wrestle with 26, wondering what the big deal is. By the time the activity is stopped, some more people come up with 30. The reason: Training tells people there are 17 squares, because they were taught to count. Perception tells them there are more- that is, 30.

After performing this exercise, your trainees should be ready to refocus on solving their problem. Arrange them in groups of three or four and ask each to explain his or her problem definition and important information about the problem. Them have each group come up with as many options as possible to solving the member's problem. No one should be allowed to make such comments as: "My boss wouldn't let me do that," "It's too expensive," and "I've tried that before, it didn't work," for such judgments kill creative thinking. If adequately warmed up, your groups should buzz with ideas-solid, bizarre, routine, imaginative, funny and traditional ones.

Phase Five: Synthesize and Analyze:

The fourth step in creative problem solving is analyzing the advantages and disadvantages of each option. One way to develop employees' skill in this area is to have them practice synthesizing-combining the strengths of two different things to produce something new.

For example, choose two items, such as a ballpoint pen and a clock, and ask employees to combine the strengths of each into a new invention. In one instance, someone came up with the idea of putting a timing device on a pen to record the time actually spent on a letter or a report.

Now have your staffers return to the list of options they previously developed and ask them to analyze the advantages and disadvantages of each potential solution. For a one-day training seminar, it's sufficient to spend only a few minutes on step five (intuitive thinking), step six (decision-making), and step seven (fantasizing the worst and best that could happen with a decision).

Ask employees to take a break from analyzing their options and to try not to consciously make a decision based on them. Instead, tell them to let their intuition go to work-it will. Then, for example, if they have trouble choosing between two options, suggest that they flip a coin. If disappointment pops up over the result, tell them to go with the other option. Obviously, their intuition is telling them something their analysis did not reveal. Finally, tell them to make a tentative decision and quickly explore the worst and best consequences of that decision. It's helpful to prepare for the best and perhaps to rethink the decision if a worst possible case is too ugly.

Phase Six: Identify the bottlenecks:

To help your trainees handle the eighth and last step, implementation and overcome any barriers they may have to solving problems creatively, give them the following exercise:

List the creative thinking blocks and put a "p" next to those that are personal and an "o" next to those that are organizational.

Then explore with them strategies for overcoming both types of barriers so that everyone will leave the session with a solution to a problem.

DEVELOPING INTUITION

Here are some guidelines for enhancing intuitive capabilities. Of course, they are only illustrative and one may try those which are suitable to himself or herself.

(i) Make a log of all the moments when you might have been using intuition during one day. Which were the most significant? How might you act on your insights?

(ii) When was the last occasion when intuition would have been helpful but it didn't happen? What was in the way? Check. Try to overcome it.

(iii) Allow your intuition to make minor decisions for you; deciding what to wear for an appointment; ordering at a restaurant; buying a small gift for a friend.

(iv) Make predictions about everyday events: who is on the phone when it rings; who will a sports fixture; tomorrow morning's newspaper headline; a colleague's first words when you meet tomorrow; this week's sales figures. Betting is not recommended!

(v) Turn the sound down during a TV soap or sitcom and work out what the story is. You may need a friend to watch with you, wearing headphones, to verify your description; alternatively, tape the section you are watching and play it back.

COMMUNICATION SKILLS FOR CREATIVITY

Good communication skills are necessary to the trainees for effective participation in group discussions and presentations. Here are some tips and exercises, which are very basic for expressing views to others during discussions.

Oral expressions

Giving advice My advice is (would be) You might consider I would advise you Why don't you	**Suggesting** Suppose we do What about leaving I think I suggest I've got an idea. I am sure. A suggestion What is we do Would it help if? Be better if? Let's think Why do n't we Could n't we. We could try testing	**Persuading** You ought to (should) You better I would large you to
Seeking advice Could I ask your advice on one point Would you advise me on Can you please tell us how can we Do you think we should	**Agreeing** Great! Good idea! Fine. Right. Ok. All right then. I think you are right. I agree with Agreed. I agree up to	**Dissuading** You ought n't to You should n't You should consider carefully.
Reaching Consensus That's no good because I do not thank that would work because I disagree I am against because I do n't know about that	**Disagreeing** I'd like to raise question In my opinion I feel very strongly that I should like to show attention to I fail to understand I submit that My final argument is against /in favor of I suppose the view /motion that May I ask- I strongly oppose the view I suppose On the contrary I disagree I firmly reject	**Advice** The first thing we have to do is Next After that We must n't forget to I think we should It's important to We need to We ought to I don't think
Know I know that I am sure that I am told that I believe that	**Wish** I had love to I wish we could If only we could I have always wanted to I'd really like to	

Types of Critical Questions:

1. *Questions of clarification:*

   Examples — Could you give me an example?

   —Is your basic point ___ or ___ ?

2. *Questions that probe assumptions:*

   Examples — You seem to be assuming ___

   — How would you justify taking this for granted?

   — Is this always the case?

3. *Questions that probe reasons and evidence:*

   Examples — How could we go about finding out whether that is true?

   — Is there reason to doubt that evidence?

4. *Questions about viewpoints or perspectives:*

   Examples — How would other groups or types of people respond? Why? What would influence them?

   — How would people who disagree with this viewpoint argue their case?

5. *Questions that probe implications and consequences:*

   Examples — What effect would that have?

   — If this and this are the case, then what else must also be true?

6. *Questions about the question:*

   Examples — To answer this question, what questions would we have to answer first?

   — Is this the same issue as ?

Door openers:

Some questions are "door openers" leading to conversation. Some questions seem to "close the doors" you'd like to open. Study the following questions and check those that open up conversation and tick them.

1. Is something wrong?
2. How do you feel about this?
3. Do you like me?
4. Why did you say that?
5. Oh! Really.
6. Would you explain that to me?
7. What did you do today?
8. What would you have done?

9. How was the meeting?

10. For instance.

(*Answer:* The odd numbers are door-closers usually answerable by one or two words. The even numbers call for thoughtful response).

Wordsmanship

How to win at wordsmanship? Philip Broughton developed systematic Buzz Phase Projector. It employs a lexicon of 30 carefully chosen buzzwords. Think of any three-digit number. Then select the corresponding buzzword from each column.

For instance, number 257 produces "systematized logistical projection'' a phase that can be dropped into virtually any report with that ring of decisive, knowledgeable authority. No one will have the remotest idea of what you are taking about; says Boughton "but the important thing that they are not about to admit it".

Column 1	Column 2	Column 3
0 Integrated	0 Management	0. Options
1 Total	1 Organizational	1. Flexibility
2 Systematized	2 Monitored	2. Capability
3 Parallel	3 Reciprocal	3. Mobility
4 Functional	4 Digital	4. Programming
5 Responsive	5 Logistical	5. Concept
6 Optimal	6 Transitional	6. Time-phase
7 Synchronized	7 Incremental	7. Projection
8 Compatible	8 Third generation	8. Hard work
9 Balanced	9 Policy	9. Contingency

Ordering:

(i) Arrange the following words associated with eating on a scale

Bite ________________________________Gorge

Gobble, nibble, hog, feast and gormandize

(ii) Check whether the arrangement based on person's build is in order?

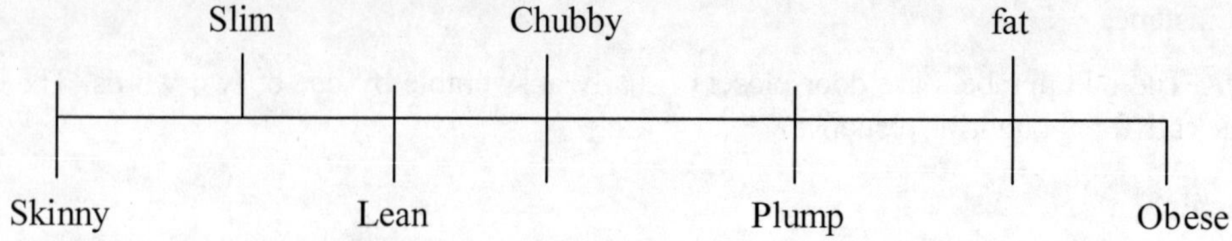

SUMMARY

The belief that creativity is a skill that can be learned and applied like any other skill has led to the organization of training programs on creativity. The importance of training in promoting creativity can be understood from the following viewpoints: (i) To change thinking styles, (ii) To create confidence for creativity, (iii) To maintain operational excellence, (iv) To keep up with growth opportunities and (v) To sustain vitality during recession.

Creativity training programmes may have the objectives such as expanding horizons of knowledge, improving the competence in systematically analyzing and imaginatively solving the problems and enhancing the ability to organize, justify and present the recommendations to the organization for decision and action.

A good majority of studies point to the following principal characteristics- Fluency, Flexibility, Originality, Elaboration, Sensitivity, Redefinition and Curiosity.

First coordinator or facilitators (s) receive training from external resources persons. They, in turn, are normally responsible for the training of team leaders. Team members may receive training from team leaders, or facilitator(s), or from both. Team approach to creative problem solving and the training programme for skills up gradation, are mutually supportive.

Training program may be divided into five phases: warming up, imagination and invention, problem definition, exploring options, synthesize and analyze and identify the bottlenecks. Maintaining a log of intuitions, analyzing them and using them can develop intuition. Good communication skills are necessary to the trainees for effective participation in group discussions and presentations.

QUESTIONS

1. Substantiate the need for creativity training and establish the objectives of training.
2. Explain the creativity testing and development methods known to you.
3. Describe the steps in designing training programs.
4. Explain, how to develop intuitive skills of employees?
5. What kind of communication skills are required for creativity?

EXERCISES

(a) Reading Quiz:

1. Read everything before doing anything.
2. Put your name in the upper right hand corner.
3. Circle the word name in sentence # 2.
4. Draw five small squares in the upper left hand corner.
5. Put an X in each square.
6. Sign your name under the title.
7. After the title write yes, yes, yes.
8. Put a circle around each yes in sentence #7.
9. Put a 'Y' in the lower right hand corner.
10. Multiply IIII X IIII
11. Write the numbers from ten to one backwards.
12. If you have followed the directions carefully, write, I have:
13. Now that you have finished reading carefully, write 'finished'

Follow the directions. You have only 3 minutes.

(b) Riddles:

(i) I have no hands and no legs.
But I have a long tail
I have one eye
Who am I? (Needle)

(ii) I am a box
I have no mouth
But I talk
I have no ears
But I hear.
Who am I? (Telephone)

(iii) Until I am measured
I am not known,
Yet how you miss me
When I have flown.
What am I? (Time)

(c) Quizzical questions:

1. What do the numbers 3,7,8,40,50, and 60 have in common that no other whole numbers have?
2. What letters will you never find in the alphabet?
3. What word is spelt wrong in every dictionary?
4. Name ten parts of the body that are spelt with three letters.
5. What is it that the Pope has but does not use it; your father has it but your mother also uses it; nuns don't need it; and your sister's husband has it but your sister also shares it?
6. There are 9 hens and 8 boxes. What you have to do is, fit the 9 hens in the 8 boxes. Is it mind-boggling? Try, you will find it very easy.

Answers:

(a) Nine dot exercise

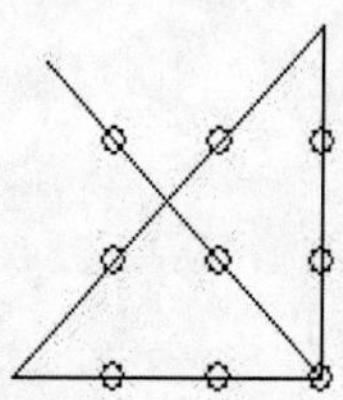

(b) (i) Needle (ii) Telephone (iii) Time

(c) 1. When they are spelled out, they each have five letters.

2. The ones in the postbox

3. The word 'wrong'

4. Eye, Ear, Leg, Arm, Toe, Rib, Jaw, Gum, Lip, Hip

5. A surname

6. Draw nine boxes diagram and put the alphabets (N-I-N-E-H-E-N-S) – one in each box.

CASE : MINDSET MATTERS

In the early 1980s, I became General manager of P&G's Greek subsidiary, in the Middle East division, different to the rest of Western Europe. We were due to launch *Always*, a sanitary napkin brand, along with Western Europe. This was simultaneously being test marketed in the south of France. Western Europe decided not to go ahead at that stage. It subsequently did so, some five years later, with great results. The issue the Greek subsidiary was faced with was whether to postpone, as Western Europe had or to try to go ahead on its own.

It would have been easy to adopt a limiting mindset, in line with the overall company mood of not being ready. There were many issues regarding the brand on which one could adopt a limiting mindset and find all the reasons to postpone. But, in fact because of the business situation in Greece, we were almost forced to adopt a powerful mindset to help make the project work.

The Greek subsidiary had historically relied heavily on a large detergent business. But the outlook for this was not good: it was subject to severe government price controls and restrictive government procedures for introducing new products. The only option for the Greek subsidiary was to diversify. We had to adopt a positive mindset about making projects like *Always* work, because we couldn't build a profitable subsidiary from our detergent base.

The mindsets, which would lead to the project not working, were all reasonable. For example:

- ❖ The product category couldn't be advertised on Greek television, for reasons of taste.
- ❖ The Always product couldn't significantly premium priced versus local competitive brands, particularly in view of the low per capita income in Greece.
- ❖ It would be difficult to get Greek women to change from their traditional habits and brands they would stay with current practices rather than trying something new.
- ❖ The new Always top sheet would be rejected by traditional Greek women and they wouldn't try it.
- ❖ The Greek subsidiary couldn't go it alone on the brand without the support of simultaneous work going on in other western European countries.

Once such limiting mindsets were adopted, there would have been plenty of data to select to support them and to postpone the project. Instead, for each limiting mindset a more powerful one was adopted and different, more enabling action steps were identified:

- If we could breakthrough the problem of the ban on sanitary napkin advertising, advertising the product advantages of Always would make a huge impact on the Greek consumer. The brand group did get the TV authorities to agree to always advertising, first by agreeing to advertise after 9 pm, then by getting agreement to superior absorbency demonstrations without the physical pad being shown and finally getting agreement to advertising without these constraints.
- If we could find a way to make premium pricing versus local competitors acceptable, the project would be profitable and viable. The brand group did manage to make premium pricing acceptable after all, the actual usage of sanitary napkins is relatively low-they are only used for one week a month. The actual premium cost of using always for those occasions, versus a competitive brand, was less than the price of a cup of coffee a month. The better absorbency and protection of always more than made that worthwhile for the Greek consumer.
- If we could find a way to get Greek women to experience the superior performance of Always, they would be prepared to change from their current products. The brand group found effective ways to sample the new always product going door-to-door and giving the correct size samples for each woman in the household, making always a product they would jointly consider and try.
- If we could find a way to help traditional consumers consider the feel of the top sheet in an acceptable way, they would appreciate its superior performance. The brand group invented a new term for the top sheet, Alveonet, which helped bring connotations of the dry feeling the consumer experienced with it.

- If we could find a way to attract staff group and expert resource from other countries to help Greece, it wouldn't matter that Western Europe was postponing. The brand group found that visiting Greece could be made one of the more enjoyable business experiences for any staff group or helpful expert.

In the end, by adopting powerful mindsets instead of accepting limiting ones, the Always project was made to work for Greece. The brand was launched nationally and become one of the biggest successes of Always in any country, anywhere in the world.

Questions:

1. Analyze significance of mindsets based on the case.
2. How can positive mindset be developed among employees, especially key decision-makers?

Source: John O'Keeffe (2005), *Business Beyond the Box*, Magna Publishing Company Ltd, Mumbai. pp.162-165.

Chapter 15

Creative Thinking

Learning Objectives

After you have studied this chapter, you will be able to…

- Distinguish between Traditional and Creative thinking processes
- Know the right and left brain thinking approaches
- Explain linear and non-linear thinking processes
- Discuss intuition as a thinking approach

Structure

- Introduction
- Traditional Vs. Creative Thinking
- Left and Right Brain Thinking
- Linear Thinking Processes
- Nonlinear Thinking Processes
- Creative Thinking Process
- Intuition
- Summary
- Questions
- Exercises
- Case : Electronic Game Industry is Dead, Say Designers

INTRODUCTION

Humans are intellectual animals. They are distinguished by their ability to think in myriad ways. Different thinking patterns are identified by psychologists, which range form linear to non-linear ones. The non-linear thinking processes, which facilitate creative thinking, should be developed among the employees to make an organization innovative.

TRADITIONAL VS. CREATIVE THINKING

Table 15.1 draws the differences between the Traditional and Creative thinking processes.

- Traditional thinking is concerned with search and discovery; creative thinking is concerned with imagining and experimentation.
- Traditional thinking is orderly and sequential; creative thinking is disorderly and parallel.
- Traditional thinking is based on rigorous logical analysis and unambiguous judgment in the form of yes/no, right/wrong, true/false; while creative thinking generates and accepts plural possibilities without judging or evaluating them in their inception phase.
- Traditional logical thinking operates in terms of dichotomies, polar categories and contradictions, in order to arrive at a judgment, conclusion or choice. Creative thinking, on the other hand, embraces both sides of a contradiction or dichotomy in order to design a new way forward. It is oriented towards searching through very large spaces of possibilities for identifying broad parallel and plural alternatives.

Table 15.1 Traditional Vs. Creative thinking

Basis	Traditional thinking	Creative thinking
Concern	Tries to find absolutes to find relationships; is concerned with stability	Tries to find new ways for looking at things; is concerned with change
Thinking Process	Linear, orderly, sequential and vertical. Convergent. Seeks continuity by logically progressing from one step to another.	Non-linear, disorderly, associative, parallel and lateral. Divergent. Attempts to introduce discontinuity by making illogical (free associations) jumps from one step to another.
Idea generation	*Approach* critical. Limited in idea generation. Analyses ideas to determine why they do not work and need to be rejected.	Generative. Analyses ideas to determine how they might be used to generate new ideas. Imagines to go beyond. Uses intuitive and heuristic approaches.
	Focus on solution. Selectively chooses what to consider for generating ideas; rejects information not considered to be relevant. Progresses using the established patterns; considers the obvious.	Welcomes chance intrusions of information to use in generating new ideas'; considers the irrelevant. And progresses by avoiding the obvious.

Basis	Traditional thinking	Creative thinking
Idea screening	Seeks *yes or no* justification for each step. Tries to find what is right.. Applies rational intelligence based on rigorous logical reasoning methods.	Uses *yes, and* approach. Avoids looking for what is right or wrong. Tries to find what is different. Applies emotional intelligence based on feelings and hunches along with rational methods.
Idea evaluation	Objective in analysis. Operates in dichotomies, polar possibilities and contradictions to conclude. Calculative. Uses probabilities in estimating risk involved in the choice.	Subjective in analysis. Operates with plural possibilities to move forward. Also experimental- considers possibilities of solutions in knowing risk involved in the choice.
Idea selection	Prefers unambiguous judgment Solution. The prevailing view is: there is one definite answer to the problem. You can pronounce death sentence to the not so useful ones.	Uses suspended judgment. Does not hurry for a solution Any solution is only *an answer* The guiding principle is: You can defer an idea but cannot terminate its life.
Brain	Left brain, verbal and reasoning	Right brain, visual, richness in reasoning. Novelty

Source: Modified version of De Bono, E. *Lateral thinking: Creativity Step-by-Step*, New York: Harper & Row,1970 and de Bono E. *Six Thinking Hats*, Boston: Little Brown, 1985.

In an activity like problem solving, both kinds of thinking are important to us. First, we must analyze the problem; then we must generate possible solutions; next we must choose and implement the best solution; and finally, we must evaluate the effectiveness of the solution. As you can see, this process reveals an alternation between the two kinds of thinking, critical and creative. In practice, both kinds of thinking operate together much of the time and are not really independent of each other.

LEFT AND RIGHT BRAIN THINKING

How people think depends on the hemisphere of the brain activated. Figure 15.1 shows the thinking styles based on position and side of the brain.

Position	Side	
	Left	**Right**
Upper	**Problem solver** Mathematical Technical Analyzer Logical	**Conceptualizer** Synthesizer Imaginative Holistic Artistic - *Creative*
Lower	**Planner** Organizational Controller Conservative Administrative	**Talker** Musical Emotional Interpersonal

Figure 15.1 Thinking styles

Henry Mintzberg observed:

The left side of the brain has dominated strategy formulation, with its emphasis on logic and analysis. Overly structured, this creates a narrow range of options. Alternatives, which do not fit into the predetermined structure, are ignored. The right side of the brain needs to become part of the process with its emphasis on intuition and creativity.

Organizations are therefore advised to hire heterogeneous teams, to have variety in thinking. The rule:

Hire a person who is unlike you and with whom you are uncomfortable.

Who brings problems; who brings ideas; who differs; who argues.

Here are eight simple devices for a person to help engage the right brain as well as the left:

1. Use color.
2. Use pictures.
3. Use metaphors and analogies.
4. Appeal to emotion.
5. Use your gut feel.
6. Use stories as well as data.
7. Use picture words as well as jargon.
8. Use mind maps instead of lists and notes.

LINEAR THINKING PROCESSES

Psychologists have examined the process of thinking by individuals and developed different explanations. Logical thinking is one.

Logical thinking is a learned mental process, that uses reasoning consistently to come to a conclusion. Problems or situations that involve logical thinking call for structure, for relationships between facts and for chains of reasoning that "make sense". Logical thinking is based on the following:

Premises - These are the assumptions the argument is built on; or to look at it another way, the reasons for accepting the argument. The premises of an argument are often introduced with words such as "Assume…" "Since…" "Obviously…" and "Because…"

Inference - In inference, you start with one or more propositions, which have been accepted; you then use those propositions to arrive at a new proposition. If the inference is valid, that proposition should also be accepted. Inference steps are often identified by phrases like "therefore…" or "…implies that…"

Conclusion - The conclusion is the result of the final step of inference. The conclusion is said to be affirmed on the basis of the premises and the inference from them.

The ladder of inference:

Chris Argyris has pictured mental processing as a ladder (Figure15.2). At the bottom of the ladder is observation; at the top, action.

- From our observation, we step onto the first rung of the ladder by selecting data.
- On the second rung, we add meaning from our experience of similar data.
- On the third, we make assumptions that generalize those meanings.
- On the fourth, we construct mental patterns (beliefs or 'theories') out of those assumptions. The mental patterns dictate our actions.

We travel up and down this mental ladder all the time. So skilled are we at climbing it, that we can actually leap all the rungs in a matter of seconds. Such 'leaps of abstraction' substitute generalizations for observation of reality and treat these generalizations as 'facts'. Our mental patterns can help us to leap down the ladder by dictating what to select in future (what William Isaacs has called 'a reflexive loop'). This is a *mindset* in operation.

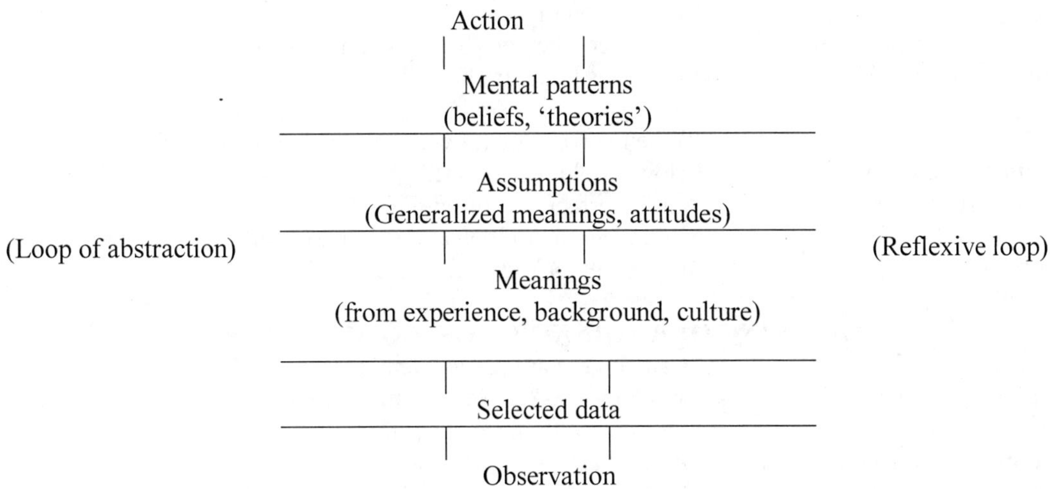

Figure 15.2 Ladder of Inference

We can use the ladder to serve three purposes as shown in Figure 15.3

- Make our thinking more visible to others.
- Ask others about their thinking.
- Offer our own thinking for examination, by others and ourselves.

MAKE THINKING MORE VISIBLE	
Action	This is what I think we should do.
Mental patterns	I think that, in general… (beliefs and theories) This is what every one says….
Assumptions (generalized meanings, attitudes)	I've made this assumption, because… I consider this as …..
Meanings (from experience, background, culture)	Let me give you an example.
Selected data	This is what I've been looking at.
Observation	
ASKING OTHERS ABOUT THEIR THINKING	
Action	"What leads you to suggest this?" (avoid "Why?") "What makes this a good plan?"
Mental patterns (beliefs, 'theories')	"Can you take me through your thinking?" "How does this relate to that?" "I'm lost on this stage."
Assumptions (generalized meanings, attitudes)	"I wonder whether you're assuming…?" this seems to contradict…" "have you considered…" "When you say that, I wonder whether it means that…?"
Meanings (from experience, background, culture)	"How would this affect…?" "Am I correct you're saying…?"
Selected data	"What led you to look at this in particular?"
Observation	"Have you looked at…?"
OFFERING OUR THINKING FOR EXAMINATION	
Action	"Can you see any flaws in my reasoning?"
Mental patterns (beliefs, 'theories')	"Would you organize this stuff differently?" "Do you see things differently?"
Assumptions (generalized meanings, attitudes)	"Are my assumptions valid?" "In what circumstances?"
Meanings (from experience, background, culture)	"You must remember I see it like this because…" "Do you interpret it in some other way?"
Selected data	"Is my observation correct?"
Observation	"Have I missed anything?"

Figure 15.3 Purposes in Ladder of inference

Five-Part Method:

The thinking process is a five-part method for enabling anyone in any kind of organization to determine.

- What to change?
- What to change to?
- How to execute the change?

Composed of five logical trees, the thinking process provides a structured way to "navigate" complex change.

- **What's the problem?** The current Reality Tree reveals the root causes of the undesirable effects in any system—the constraint preventing improved performance.
- **What do we do about it?** The "Evaporating Cloud" (a conflict resolution diagram) identifies and resolves overt and hidden conflict. Breaks chronic conflict perpetuating root causes of undesirable effects. Helps create new solutions.
- **What would happen?** The Future Reality Tree verifies validity of proposed solutions before resources are invested in them. Identifies possible adverse side-effects of the proposed solution and ways to prevent them.
- **How do we make it happen?** The Prerequisite Tree uncovers obstacles to implementation of solutions. Helps develop ways around the obstacles and time sequences the actions required to overcome them.
- **How do we execute it?** The transition tree builds a step-by-step implementation plan for each facet of the change and provides the rationale for persuading people to follow it.

NON-LINEAR THINKING PROCESSES

Approaches to nonlinear thinking are many and probably baffling to the novice.

Dr. Edward de Bono, who coined the term "lateral thinking," teaches techniques that jar normal thought patterns in problem solving and shift them to new starting points. These techniques (which can be found in his 1992 book, *Serious Creativity*, HarperCollins) lead to provocations and alternative approaches to the problem.

Lateral thinking is defined as "seeking ways to solve problems by apparently illogical means." In science, many major discoveries have come about through a chance observation, accident or mistake that led to non-obvious ways of perceiving things.

Non-linear thinking processes are not rational and vertical. They use emotion (feelings and intuitions) along with paralogical and systems approaches. They go beyond the obvious. They expand the horizons of knowledge by taking a holistic view. They defy logic and traditional reasoning methods.

Paralogical thought – This is the kind of thinking that leaps out beyond the boundaries of logical, linear thinking and begins to imagine the bizarre and otherwise unthinkable solutions to a problem. The advantage of entertaining this kind of thought is that otherwise overlooked possibilities are at least considered, no matter how absurd they appear on the surface and no stone is unturned in the consideration of resolution.

Emotional thinking – Carl Jung, developed this two-stage model of mental process into two sets of paired complementary functions: sensations and intuition; feeling and thinking. Jungians understand sensation and intuition as functions of perception and feeling and thinking as functions of judgment (Figure 15.4)

First-stage thinking is concerned with perception. We recognize something because it fits into some preexisting pattern. We encode experience to make it easier to deal with. We name an object or event; we translate complex activity into an equation; we simplify a structure by drawing a diagram. Intuition helps us to see that reality that lies beyond what our senses tell us: the deeper meanings, relationships and patterns. "Intuition," says Jung, is "perception of the possibilities inherent in a situation.

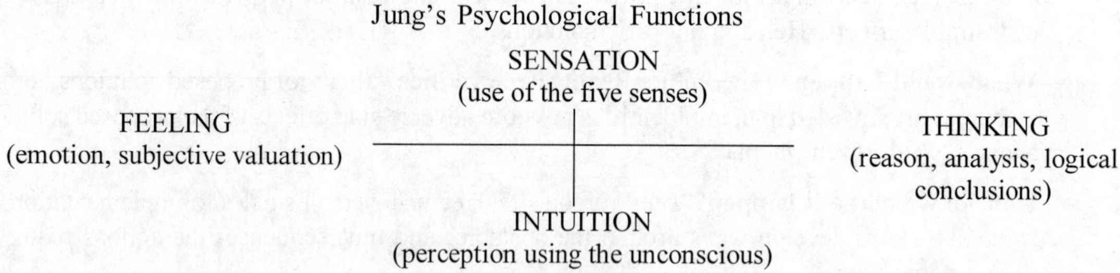

Figure 15.4 Jung's Model of Mental Process

Second-stage thinking involves judgment. We identify and define problem. Then make judgments about the data by manipulating the code-language and mathematical symbols. We 'reason' using logic, analyze and categorize, argue, debate and construct watertight channels of cause and effect. We evaluate using critical thinking to decide whether something is good or bad, moral or immoral, 'correct' or 'incorrect'.

For instance, a manger has perceived a downturn in sales as 'a marketing problem. Then he uses market intelligence and research, past experience and critical scrutiny of the marketing department to judge how best to solve it. He feels that promotion is less effective and guesses that use of celebrity advertising in TV channel could be the right solution. However, he will proceed to the next stage of thinking. The second-stage thinking is highly sophisticated. He may even use computers to do it for him.

Indeed, for most of us, 'thinking' is second stage process. "The first stage is taken for granted", says Edward de Bono, "and often assumed to be there at all". People are not nearly so skilled at first-stage thinking. There are virtually no techniques or tools to help people stop and examine their perceptions. If one wants to become more skilled in first-stage thinking, Jung's model suggests two courses of action:

- Sharpen the five senses.
- Develop intuition.

Sharpening the senses is not essentially difficult, though seeing or hearing clearly may be hampered by emotion, conflict, fatigue or sheer noise. Developing the intuitive skills, on the other hand, requires training the mind.

Dialectical thinking - Kant had distinguished two kinds of logic:

Logic type	Source of understanding	Understanding about
Analytic logic	Through sense-experience	Natural phenomenal world
Dialectical logic	Beyond sense-experience	Transcendent world-Infinite or whole

Paradoxical thinking - Paradox is a statement that is seemingly contradictory or opposed to commonsense as yet is perhaps true. A true paradox presents a perceptual enigma to the mind. What appears to be real cannot be, and yet it is? To study paradoxes allows the mind to reach beyond what appears to be obvious. Reaching beyond the obvious is the essence of creativity. Paradox is all around us and permeates our daily experience more than most people are aware. Yet, we all have a general tendency to shy away from paradox, assuming at first glance that there are irreconcilable opposites involved and the twain shall never meet.

Some paradoxes we face are:

Do more with less; Improve quality and reduce cost; operate the business successfully and ethically; be competitive, yet collegially.

The paradox process by Derm Barrett is a thorough study of the concept of paradoxical thinking. The heart of his theory is that thee are three major types of paradoxical thoughts:

Contrarian thinking - The test of a first rate intelligence is the ability to hold two seemingly opposed ideas to mind at the same time. Contrarian thinking involves imagining and reasoning the opposite position. For instance, "You can complain because roses have thorns or you can rejoice because thorns have roses."

Contrarian thinking is seeing black when others see white, opportunity instead of failure.Great companies and organizations need diversity, not "group think."

Janusian thinking – Janusian thinking is named after the Roman god *Janus* who looked four ways simultaneously. It suggests that information processing is paradoxical. Instead of ruling out alternative hypotheses, *Janusian* thinking calls on us to embrace contradictions - "brings two opposites together in your mind, holding them there together at the same time, for considering their relationships, similarities, pros and cons.

Even old proverbs take on new meaning: one can "look before you leap" and at the same time understand that "he who hesitates is lost." *Janusian* theory discusses both principles simultaneously.

Hegel's Thinking – When you visualize how to fuse, combine, mingle, integrate or synthesize two opposites to produce a third entity, it is known as Hegelian thinking.

Newspaper photographs consisting of black and white dots through their interplay produce a cohesive picture.

CREATIVE THINKING PROCESS

Creative thinking process involves apparently the divergent and convergent processes. Figure 15.5 shows the two stages of creative thinking.

- **Convergent thinking** - The second stage judges the new ideas found and brings them back into the world as something of use. It evaluates and judges them, using convergent or focused thinking: logic, categorization, measurement and analysis, comparison against objectives.

First stage	Second stage
Soft **Divergent**	**Hard** **Convergent**
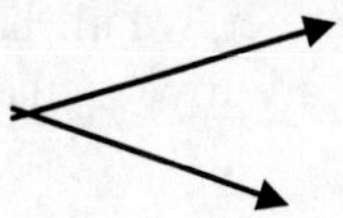	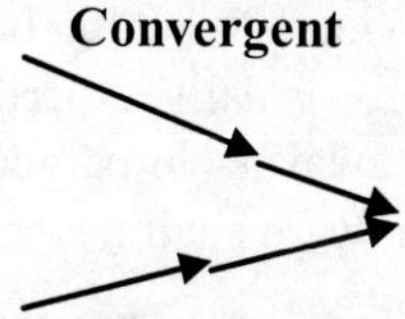
'Find something new'	'Get something done'
What if? Why not? What associations can we find? What rules can we break? What assumptions are at work? What is this like? What analog could we use? What metaphor suggests it? Suppose the problem were a solution?	Will it work? Can we do it? Has it been tried before? Does it fit in? Have we got the resources? Is the timing right? Who can help? How much will it cost? Suppose it fails?

Figure 15.5 The two stages of Creative Thinking

Divergent thinking:

This is also termed as diffuse thinking. It involves moving away from a problem or situation (*parallel* or *Para-logically*) in order to explore and investigate its potential or radiant thinking. It is imaginative. Perceptions are widened by questioning assumptions (*contradictions*), by looking at material in new ways (*paradox*) or by making random relations (*juxtapositions*) with unrelated ideas. It involves obtaining a new insight, seeks previously unsuspected relationships, adopts new frames of reference and makes some critical choices.

The purpose of this unconventional thinking is to find something new. The critical steps in the thinking process can be outlined as below. They are iterative making the process circular or spiral.

- *Problem definition by analysis* - Identifying the key components and concepts we can develop a working definition of the problem. First the problem boundaries are defined. Then the problem is factored to understand it in depth.
- *Solution finding by exploration* - Divergent thinking directs one's thinking away from the narrow confines or limits of a given problem. It allows thoughts to wander into other related areas. Search involves exploration avoiding premature evaluation.
- *Redefine the problem* - Based on the new knowledge gained, challenge the boundaries of the problem. Restate or refine the constraints. Reinterpret or relax them. Eventually develop new perspectives that help define problem in a different way.
- *Solution finding by imagination and intuition* - Think unconventionally and unsystematically. Go beyond. Allow your mind imagine with logic and gut feelings and work out a solution.

Convergent thinking:

Convergent thinking or optimal thinking consists of those steps, which enable one to reach a right solution to problems, which mostly have one right solution.

- *Problem definition by intelligence* - It involves classification or categorization. Listing the components/elements of a problem, using analogies, making comparisons and classifications, and displaying the situation through tables, charts and diagrams.
- *Problem analysis to find solution* - It involves – (i) breaking down or factoring a problem into sub-problems, (ii) seeking relationships among components, (iii) establishing relative priorities or importance of elements or relationships and (iv) making cross classifications, identifying methods/procedures to a possible solution. Analysis may involve working backward from a solution.
- *Synthesis for modeling situation with problem* - It is concerned with seeing patterns among components or elements and involves aggregation and juxtaposition of elements in terms of their similarity, proximity, consistency, relationships and so on. It also attempts to use a broad conceptual model to organize facts and information.
- *Optimization to create problem-free situation* - It is essentially concerned with refining a solution. It may hence involve substitution of parts, addition of components/elements, and deletion of superfluous items in creating anew frame-work or model without a problem. .

INTUITION

It refers to making decisions listening to the inner voice. It may be whispering secrets to success. Such whispers have no scientific or logical bases.

Definitions:

Intuition is a voice within, mystical and not easily defined. But here are a few definitions.

- An inner-way of knowing.
- Apprehension without the intervention of any reasoning process.
- Wisdom communicated subliminally.

Growing recognition:

More than ever before, management experts and psychologists encourage mangers to trust their intuition, tap creativity and rely on 'flashes of insight".

Henry Mintzberg (HBR, 1976) wrote: "The evidence here is that a great deal of the mangers inputs are soft and speculations-impressions and feelings about other people, hearsay, gossip and so on. Further more, the analytical inputs-reports, documents and hard data in general–seem to be of relatively little importance to many managers."

John Naisbittt (Megatrends, Warner Books,1983) observed: "Another shift I see that really impresses me is a new respectability for intuition incorporate settings. Now people are willing to say," I just feel this is going to work.

Robert Bernstein, Chairman of the Board at Random House, New York maintained: "Only intuition can protect you from the most dangerous person of all–the articulate incompetent."

Some Indian managers in a round table conversation for The Management Review of IIM-B, reported that they would recommend the use of intuition along with rational thinking. For instance, Kiran Mazumdar (Chairman & MD, Biocon India, Biocon Quest India, Biochemizyme India) observed:

"Of course rationale and intuition go hand in hand. You can talk about intuition being extremely emotive but you're backing it up with facts."

N. Pani (Senior Editor, Times of India) provides a caution in using intuition. He maintained:

"Coming to intuition, we must be careful not to privilege intuition at the expense of rationality. The real question is to find out whether you can talk about an area for rationality and an area for instinct. If you take a view that I will only use my intuition where there is no rational answer available, I would go along with that. But to position intuition as something that is above rationality can be dangerous."

Reliability of intuition:

Despite the growing recognition of intuition as a way of decision-making, its reliability continues to be suspected. Why are so many research managers, trained in logical and analytical thinking, so uncomfortable with the idea that this elusive language of the mind, intuition, could be a vital factor in successful innovation? We will discuss the reasons for doubting the value of intuition.

- **Conceptual ambiguity** - Some research managers claim it's because they cannot find a satisfying definition for the word. Others say they hesitate about considering intuitive skills as an important resource because they don't know-how to measure it.
- **Trust in analytical approach** - In general, organizations are driven by the values of judgment-measurement, rationality, systematic procedures and finding 'the right answers'. Use of intuition as a thinking tool is not encouraged. It is almost embarrassing for executives to talk about the power of intuition.
- **Complementary role** - Some managers use intuitions but do not totally depend on it. Intuitive thought actually complements rational thinking when pure logic and reasoning aren't enough. Intuition, is a supplemental resource to buttress the rational findings.
- **Special skill of some people** - Some technologists consistently come up with important, innovative breakthroughs. The reason they cite was intuition. However, others, often with superior academic and intellectual credentials, rarely (if ever) get success. Is it because successful ones are endowed with intuitive skills? If yes, then intuition is a born skill of some people. They had a "sixth sense," an extra dimension of thought, so that they knew when to question analytical data, statistics, literature information, or supervisor's advice when making certain technical decisions. They seemed to instinctively realize just what was needed to bring about positive results from situations of uncertainty.

Consultant Philip Goldberg (The Intuitive Edge: Understanding and Developing Intuition, Jeremy P. Tarcher Inc, 1984) cites a study in which 83 per cent of the scientists surveyed admitted to having assistance from their intuition. However, only 7 per cent of the scientists said that their intuition is always right. Other estimates ranged from as high as 90 per cent to as low as 10 per cent. Thus as a tool for success, intuition is still and probably always will be, more an art than a science. Managers should listen to their inner-voices, but heed them judiciously.

Use of intuition:

Intuition as a tool for success is still and probably always will be more art, than a science. Even the idea of "expert intuitives," those with *exceptional* intuitive skills in aiding decision-making is gaining credibility.

Companies like DuPont, Lockheed, Viacom, General Foods and others are beginning to think so too. They're utilizing intuition consultants in their training courses on creativity and leadership skills. A new journal, *Intuition*, has recently been launched and the Intuition Network grows, now under the auspices of the Institute of Noetic Sciences.

Levels:

Weston H. Agor (Intuitive Management-Integrating Left and Right Brain Management) suggests that executives receive intuitive flashes on four different levels.

- *Physical-Intuitive* awareness comes as bodily sensations. E.g.: Headache indicates stress.
- *Emotional-Intuitive* signals are transmitted in the form of feelings. E.g.: Instantly we like or dislike a person.
- *Mental-Intuitive* cues come from a pattern or order from seemingly unrelated facts.
- *Spiritual-Intuitive* awareness goes beyond self and organizations to world outside.

Developing intuition skills:

Intuitive powers can be identified and improved. The development process involves the following steps:

1. Self-evaluation of intuitive skills.
2. Know the inhibiting factors.
3. Strengthening intuition.

1. Self-evaluation:

The first step in developing intuition is self-evaluation. It is necessary to understand one's own intuitive powers.

Ask yourself: Am I intuitive? If yes, when and how does it come, in respect of what issues and with what outcome?.

Weston H. Agor of the University of Texas (El Paso), developed a test instrument for measuring and scoring intuition. One can use it to measure intuition of employees in their organization.

Table 15.2 gives a simple checklist to evaluate your intuitive powers and habits.

Table 15.2 Self-evaluation Check list of Intuition

Aspect	Question	Response
Incidence	Have you ever tried to be intuitive? What did you do? Did it work?	
Timing related to problem	When do intuitions come to you? When you are closely involved in the matter? Shortly after taking a break from it? While engaged in some other activity?	
State of mind	What is your general state of mind when they arrive? Relaxed, at rest, even sleepy? Distracted? Concentrated?	
Facilitating time in a day	At what time of day do you seem to be most intuitive? On waking? Late at night?	
Type of arrival	Are your intuitions sudden or gradual? Do you need time to ponder?	
Trust	Do you trust your immediate reaction?	
Context	Are you more intuitive about somethings than others? About technical problems or dealing with people? Making decisions or sizing up a situation?	
Facilitating activities	Are there any activities that seem to be conducive to intuition? Cooking? Washing up? Gardening? Playing or listening to music? Walking? Swimming? Meditation? Daydreaming?	
Type of message	What is the basic message? An insight (that something is true)? An instruction (to do something or avoid doing it)?	
Form of intuition	In what form did it come to you? Verbally? Visually? Physically (a 'gut feeling')?	
Strength	How strong was it? Vivid? Vague? Sudden? Prolonged? Has it been repeated? If so, has any part of it changed?	
Emotional reaction	How does the intuition make you feel? Exhilarated? Relieved? Depressed? Warm? Certain?	
Rational reaction	What do you think about it? How logical is it, in hindsight? How reasonable? How appropriate?	
Novelty	How surprising is it? How unlike custom or the dictates of authority?	
Acceptability	What is your overall reaction to it? Are you inclined to accept or reject it?	

Source: Alan Baker (1997), *Creativity for Managers*, Excel Books, New Delhi. pp.16-17. A modified version.

2. Know the inhibiting factors:

The factors inhibiting intuition can be personal as well as situational.

- ***Recognize inhibiting factors in yourself*** **-** Low self-esteem, an excessive need for security, fear of failure, fear of change, an intolerance of uncertainty, an urge to keep control, dishonesty, stress and boredom are some of the inhibiting factors.
- ***Recognize situational factors*** - Lack of time, other people's feelings/desires/opinions/ arguments, intermediate targets, and resistance in the wider culture of the organization, etc.

  The most powerful factor inhibiting the use of intuition may be the corporate culture in which you operate. If an organization is internally competitive or strongly conformist, you will probably not find much encouragement to exercise your intuition. If colleagues or senior mangers demand 'hard' justifications for every decision, you may find yourself compelled to dress up your intuitive insights in 'data clothes': exhaustive cost benefit analyses, resource management plans and market research.

3. Strengthening intuition:

Alan Baker (1997) suggests the following actions to strengthen intuitive powers:

- Train the mind to produce intuitions.
- Examine and test the intuitions.
- Use and promote intuitions.

We will now elaborate the three steps helpful in promoting intuition.

Train the mind to produce intuitions:

With practice, one can become more familiar with your intuitions. They are unlikely to appear if we are stressed or if we feel likely to appear when the circumstances are relaxed, co-operative and open. The following guidelines if followed would make one's mind capable of producing intuitions.

- **Open the door** - We cannot command intuition to work for us; like Aladdin's genie, it may initially appear by accident. We can, though, make ourselves available for it to visit. Philip Goldberg (1983) observed:

  If we issue an open invitation and make intuition feel that visits are welcomed at any time, it can become a perfect guest, showing up on all the right occasions, dressed properly and bearing felicitous gifts.
- **Learn how to manage stress** - Loss of clarity, 'treadmill thinking', lack of concentration and mild frustrations are symptoms of stress. Take a break and remove the stress.
- **Seek quite times** - Try to build quite periods in to your timetable.
- **Balance mental stress with physical stress** - Take up a regular physical activity; try yoga; go for a brisk walk.
- **Practice flexibility in your thinking** - Look for the ambiguities, the vague or awkward information. Seek new perspectives on what you're doing; examine your emotional or physical responses to ideas or events.

- **Improve exposure** - Expose yourself to a wider range of experience. Do something, read something and go somewhere – different.
- **Lighten up** - Try not to take matters too seriously. Humor is one of the great indicators that intuition is at work.
- **Focus on ends, not means** - Clarify your goals. Try to imagine unique, perfect solutions to problems. Ask: "what's the real problem?" recognize when you are becoming obsessed with processes and targets.

Examine and test your intuitions:

Intuitions are valuable only when they have relevance and practical validity.

- **Defend your insight logically** - A good insight can be defended rationally, even if the process of having it is irrational.
- **Look at it from all sides** - List its positive features, its negative features and its interesting features, in that order.
- **Examine consequences** - Work through the implications and consequences of the intuition. What else would be true if this were true? Does the intuition explain other evidence? Who would be affected if you acted on it? How? When? How might they respond?
- **Test it** - Find a way to test your intuition as safely as possible. Conduct an experiment or some gentle research. Try something out.
- **Subject it to criticism** - Talk about it to somebody else. This may be one of the best ways of exposing the intuition to the light of day. We become clearer about the true content of an intuitive insight when we explain it to others; and a fresh pair of eyes can provide a new perspective.

Use and promote intuition:

Without intuitives, the world would surely be a poorer and more desolate place. Albert Einstein said, "the really valuable thing is intuition," and Emily Dickinson stated it poetically, "I deplore those who have only the facts but not the phosphorescence."

The key considerations in using and promoting intuitions are:

- **Acceptance at workplace** - Know-how your organization responds to intuitive ideas. Some organizations foster an aggressive attitude to problem solving. They believe that for every problem there must be a single, perfect solution; making decisions quickly is seen as a sign of strength and delay is interpreted as weakness. The response to problem solving may be different at different levels of the organization. Decisions at the highest level are often made on the basis of very narrow, second-stage thinking.
- **Acceptance by colleagues** - Know-how your colleagues react to intuitive ideas. How might you make the use of intuition more acceptable in your team or among your colleagues? If your colleagues show resistance to using intuition, ask why? Encourage them to use their intuitive powers by sharing your intuitions with them.
- **Encourage others** - As managers, we may even be able to encourage others to offer their own intuitions: to indicate by our own example that we value intuition as a part of the decision-making process.

SUMMARY

Humans are intellectual animals. They are distinguished by their ability to think in myriad ways. The two hemispheres of brain left and right are sources of logical and creative thinking. Organizations are therefore advised to hire heterogeneous teams, to have variety in thinking.

Linear thinking is the process in which one uses reasoning consistently to come to a conclusion. Chris Argyris suggested a ladder of inference. There are different versions. One is 5-part method (What's the problem? What do we do about it? What would happen? How do we make it happen? How do we execute it? Another version is 3-part method (Identify the problem, identify the cause and remove the cause).

The linear thinking process can be improved by following the axioms: tolerance to ambiguity, look before you leap, pause and notice; wait and see, insightful thinking and systems thinking.

Approaches to nonlinear thinking are many and probably baffling to the novice.

Dr. Edward de Bono, who coined the term "lateral thinking," teaches techniques that jar normal thought patterns in problem solving and shift them to new starting points. Paralogical thought. Emotional thinking, systems thinking, metaphoric thinking, positive thinking, dialectical thinking, juxtapositions and paradoxical thinking (Contrarian, Junasian and Hegelian thinking types) are other non-linear thinking processes.

The creative process consists of cycles of divergent and convergent thinking. Divergent thinking (radiant thinking) involves moving away from a problem or situation (*Parallel* or *Para-logically*) in order to explore and investigate its potential. Convergent thinking or optimal thinking consists of those steps, which enable one to reach a right solution to problems, which mostly have one right solution. Traditional and creative thinking differ in many respects. Traditional thinking tries to find absolutes to find relationships and is concerned with stability. Creative thinking tries to find new ways for looking at things and is concerned with change. It refers to making decisions listening to the inner-voice. It may be whispering secrets to success. Such whispers have no scientific or logical bases.

Alan Baker (1997) suggests the following actions to strengthen intuitive powers: train the mind to produce intuitions, examine and test the intuitions and use and promote intuitions.

QUESTIONS

1. Explain left and right brain thinking of humans.
2. Elaborate the linear thinking process using one of the models known to you. Distinguish between Creative and Traditional methods of thinking.
3. Briefly discuss some of the nonlinear thinking methods.
4. Explain the divergent and convergent thinking processes.
5. What is intuition? Is it reliable? How do you promote intuition?

EXERCISES

1. Multiple uses test:

The purpose of this exercise is to identify as many things as possible for which you could use a paper clip.

Step 1:

Give yourself one minute exactly and write down all the things you can think of for which you could use a paperclip. Write them here, now:

Count how many you came up with.

Step 2:

Now give yourself another minute and write down all the things you can think of for which you could not use a paperclip. Write down everything that comes to mind, even if subsequently you could think of a way you could use a paperclip for that purpose.

2. Association test:

Take any word at random in the dictionary and find another word to which your brain can't make any connection from the first word.

3. Creative addition:

Add up all the numbers 1 to 100. What's the answer?

4. The numbers exercise:

(a) How do you turn six into seven by adding one line?

(b) How do you turn IX into six adding one line?

5. The letters exercise:

Cross out six letters from the following sequence, so that the remaining letters, without altering their sequence, spell a well-known word:

BSIANXLAETNTAERS

6. The Glasses exercise:

There are three empty glasses next to three full glasses. By moving just one glass, how could you arrange the glasses such that no empty glass is next to an empty one and no full one next to a full one?

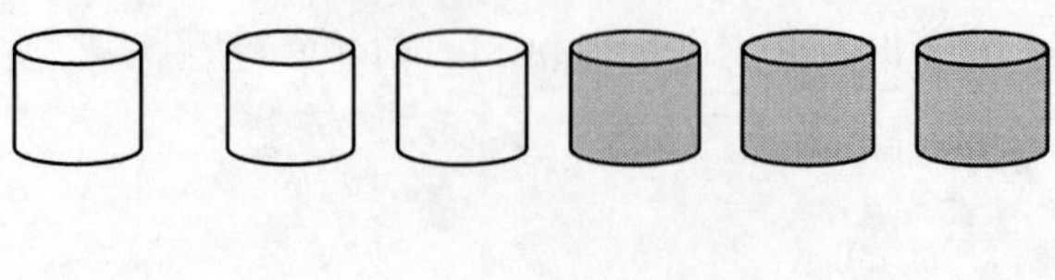

7. Series:

What's the next letter in this series? WTNLIT

8. Eleven:

The matches below signify the number six. Add just three matches to equal eleven.

VI

9. Counters:

Consider the following arrangement of counters. Move one counter only to end up with two lines each containing four counters.

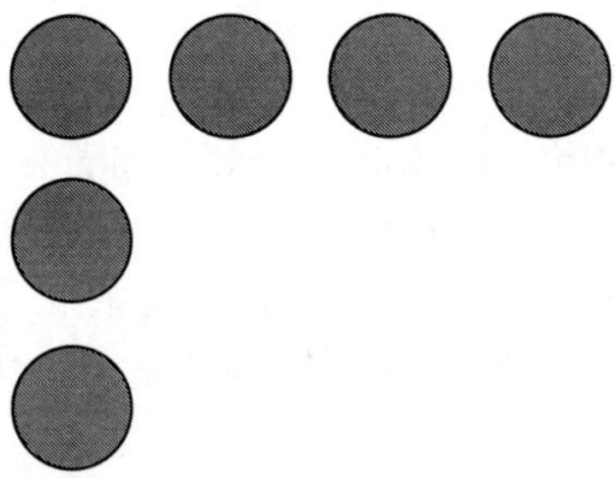

10. Swimming pool:

A man has a swimming pool in his garden situated between four splendid oak trees, as shown below:

He is rather disappointed with the size of the pool and wants to double its size but keep it square. On the other hand, he doesn't want to cut down any of the oak trees. Can it be done?

Answers and comments

What can we learn from this exercise?

(1) Multiple uses test:

Step 1 is often a largely incremental exercise. You think of things that are an extension of the way you currently use a paperclip, e.g., it can be used as a hairclip; unravel it for a tooth pick etc.

Step 2 is different. As you try to think of things you couldn't use a paperclip for, your mind almost automatically does a 'quality check' to see if that is really true. It scans the imagination to see if there could be a connection. For example, you might have thought you couldn't use a paperclip as a hat. But then your mind will realize that you could flatten and thin down a giant paperclip until it was like a sheet of foil and once you has a sheet of foil, of course, you could fold it and make a hat, of sorts.

In step 2, you set up the impossible and then can challenge your mind to see if there is a way to make it possible. This generates far more ways to use a paperclip than the incremental approach in Step 1. and far more different uses that would never have been devised by your mind under an incremental approach.

2. Word association:

It's impossible. Some or other association we can find. Setting up the impossible and challenging your mind to find a way to get there from where you are is the secret of why setting step change goals gets great results.

3. Creative addition:

There are several ways to do this. Write them down and do simple though lengthy additions; use a calculator; use a computer.

A simple solution was first developed by Gauss as an answer to the question posed to him in a classroom. Write down the numbers 1 to 50 one way. Write down the numbers 51 to 100 in reverse order underneath. Then add them.

1	2	----	49	50
100	99	----	52	51
----	----		----	---
101	101		101	101

The answer is clearly 50 × 101 = 5050. It's simple when you know-how .

4. The numbers exercise:

(a) Write six in roman style. (VI). Add a single line to make it Seven (VII).

(b) Put a horizontal line through IX and invert it.

IX = VI

Alternatively add a single curved line S and make it SIX

In this numbers exercise,we generally think of Arabic numerals (6 and 7). Think outside that box (in Romans) and the solution is relatively easy. The difficult bit is to get outside the box.

5. The letters exercise:

(i) One answer is BANANA. You get it by removing the letters SIX LETTERS from the sequence.

(ii) Another answer is LETTER. You get it by choosing six letters and removing them each time they appear in the sequence. By choosing XIANBS, you end up with the word LETTER.

In this exercise, the box is thinking that six individual letters are to be crossed as a group like first six or next six and so on. Think outside the bunch other alternatives appear, such as crossing out any six individual letters, each crossed out each time they appear.

6. The glasses exercise:

Take the middle full glass, pour its contents into the middle empty glass and return it to its place.

In the glasses exercise, the box is thinking that the solution comes from moving the position of any one glass. It should, however, quickly become apparent that thinking in this box would not generate a solution. This may trigger thinking out of the box. The answer lies in moving the contents of one glass, rather than the position of a glass.

7. Series:

The answer is 'S'. The letters are the first letters of the words in the question.

In the series exercise, it is thinking that there is a numerical or pattern relationship between the letters themselves.

8. Eleven:

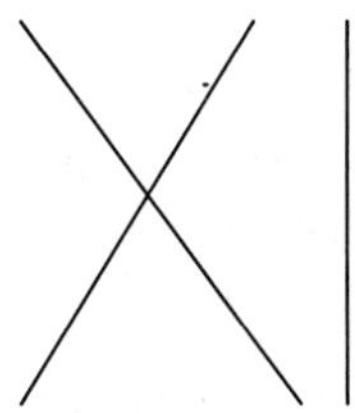

Add inverted VI to the number VI to make it XI.

In this exercise, previous patterns also form a box of thinking. The tendency is to think of adding matches to form an equation. Or the experience of the first mind-opener (six) may trigger the alternative of trying to spell the word eleven. But both these are boxes of previous experience. To get the answer you have to think outside of these boxes.

9. Counters:

Pick up the end counter in the row of four and place it on top of the counter in the corner, making two rows of four.

In this exercise, the box is to think of moving counters on a flat surface. However, you need to think in a different dimension to get the answer.

10. Swimming pool:

Yes. By stretching like the one as given here.

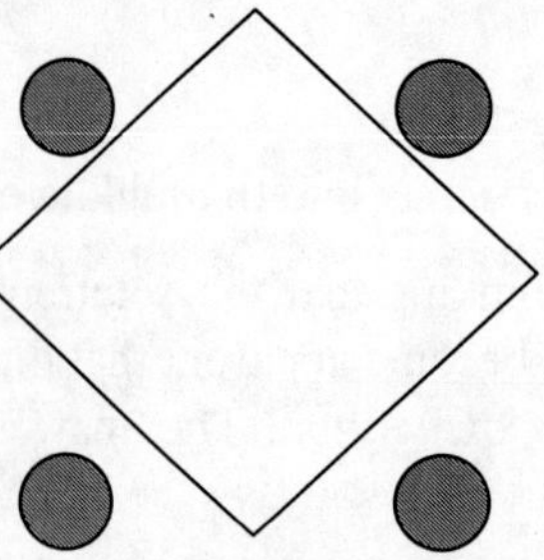

In this exercise, the box is to maintain the orientation of the pool in the pattern established. Once you go in different directions and stretch you get the answer.

CASE : ELECTRONIC GAME INDUSTRY IS DEAD, SAY DESIGNERS

The electronic game industry is dead, veteran computer software designers lament in the heart of Silicon Valley. Chris Crawford, whose experience in creating electronic games dated back to when he went to work for Atari in 1979, sounded a death knell for the industry during a gripe session at the Game Developers Conference in San Jose. "Nothing better can be done about the game industry, because it is dead," Mr. Crawford said. "It is a body that has a beating heart, but is essentially brain dead."

Interactive story telling was the future. "Games are about things, while story-telling is about people." The game designer and author told an audience of 500 persons during a session titled "*Burn baby burn –Game developers brand.*" Many in the audience of game designers and enthusiasts challenged Mr. Crawford, while others agreed and suggested ways the industry might be resurrected.

A game developer with creative Artist Agency contended a lack of business sense by game developers was killing creativity because it left them relying on corporate publishers to market their ideas. "We have great ideas," he said. "What's happening is that we don't make a good business around the ideas. Think about money and consider how the audience is going to purchase independent games," The game industry should be more like the movie industry where daring independent films such as Broke back Mountain have a chance of being made.

Other panelists blamed a lack of innovation for the dying game industry. Jonathan Blow, an independent game designer, argued that most new games are just old games but with different graphics.

Question:

What in your view, would be the new turns of the game industry?

Chapter 16

Directed Creativity

Learning Objectives

After you have studied this chapter, you will be able to...

- Define creativity and describe the process of creativity
- Discuss the principles behind directed creativity
- Understand the influence of time factor on thinking processes
- State the heuristics for effective creative thinking.

Structure

INTRODUCTION

In a hypercompetitive and dynamic world, sustainable competitive advantage can be achieved only through creative managers, creative teams and creative business processes. Responding to day to day challenges, continuously thriving for 'more and better for less', require managers who are creatively agile and ambidextrous in strategic and operational decisions. Creativity has the potential to enable managers to cope with these extreme situations and gain competitive advantage by tapping their own as well as their team's inherent creative abilities. Creative tools and techniques facilitate this process by using a systematic approach.

DECISION-MAKERS REQUIRE CREATIVITY

Each business situation is different. But for each situation there is an optimum window between spending too much time creating alternatives and not taking enough time to think of enough alternatives. In the same way, there is an optimum window for deciding between the alternatives, which you've created and not doing this too early or too late. John O'Keeffe (2005) describes how action orientation and thinking when rushed can cause problems. Figure 16.1 presents the four trouble areas of decision-makers

Too fasting closing options

Premature panic	Burning bridges ahead of you
Paralysis by analysis	Inertia

Too slow in closing options

Too much option seeking Too little option seeking

Source: Modified version of Karl Albrecht, *Brainpower* cited in John O. Keffe (2005), *Business Beyond the Box,* Magna Publishing Co Ltd., Mumbai, p.121

Figure 16.1 Trouble areas of decision-makers

Inertia - This is the trouble area. You don't spend enough time to generate enough alternatives. Also you take too long time choosing between the few choices you've created. In other words, you are too inactive and indifferent to problem solving.

Paralysis by analysis - Otherwise known as *para analysis*. There is so much discussion on what to do without a desire to arrive at a decision. This is also never going to get great results. At best it produces incrementalism.

Premature panic - This is also a trouble area: not spending enough time creating alternatives and then deciding too fast. This is a typical area for many action-oriented people and organizations.

Burning bridges ahead of you - This fourth trouble area is just as bad having generated a good number of alternatives, you still decide between them too soon; when there is no need to nor any advantage in doing so. It may be far better to 'sleep on it', 'to hold your fire' and see what happens.

Decision-makers frequently get into situations covered by the action zone trouble areas. The reasons for their getting into problems can be many. Mindset is one causal force. We find so many proverbial advices- that are sometimes controversial – influencing our attitudes in a particular situation. Table 16.1 presents some of them which have potential to misguide a decision-maker.

Table 16.1: Axioms that may misguide

Activity	Axiom	Explanation
Choosing options	A bird in the hand is worth two in the bush.	This drives a mindset of closing down options. Adopting it broadly, in too many situations, will push you to premature panic and burning bridges ahead of you. It won't lead to breakthrough results.
	Beggars can't be choosers.	This drives a reluctant acceptance that you have no more than one option. Adopted too broadly, this will push you towards premature panic and business collapse.
	Hobson's choice.	This describes not liking either of two options again, too often in this area and you are nowhere near breakthrough results.
Action	Any action is better than no action.	This drives an early decision between early options.

Guidelines:

How to keep away from the traps?

Understand the problem – Force yourself to write a description of the exact problem. Don't leave it vague. Ensure that people make a decision on the scope of the problem or opportunity they are trying to tackle. It is not enough just to be sure that you are in the action zone, it has to be the action zone of the right problem.

Keep focused on the problem -When you're up to your neck in alligators, it's difficult to remember that the original objective was to drain the swamp.

We create 'alligators' ourselves by focusing energy and talent on relatively minor problems which divert your attention. Things can get so bad that people have to go 'off-site' to get any quality time to do any quality thinking. So insist on the value of doing these: write the right problem in the zone. Zone in on the right problem. Act in the action zone, on the right problem.

Look before you leap - Having identified and kept focus on problem, think for solution. Obvious solutions may be related to the symptoms and not to the problem. They only bring back the problem or create new problems. The real enduring solution is difficult to get. It is here,creativity is essential. Box 16.1 presents a situation which emphasizes the need for creativity in decision-making.

Box 16.1 Facing competition

Your competitor has lowered the prices. If sales are disappointing your sales force may tell you it's because competitors have dropped their prices. You clearly can't afford to let competition buy your business away. Sales are disappointing so you feel you can't simply *do nothing.*

You bosses will be asking you what action you're taking. An obvious action is to drop your prices. This will almost certainly cause your sales to strengthen. So you will have appeared to take tough action to solve the problem. However, sometimes this is premature panic. Dropping prices is difficult to reverse and terminally hurts profits and so you really need to be sure that's the best option. Consider some other alternatives:

- Is it a definite fact that competitors have dropped prices? If they haven't and you drop yours, you will be starting a profit-eliminating spiral, not them.
- If they have changed pricing, is it a temporary promotion or a permanent move? Your action should be different, based on whichever it is.
- Is there any other explanation for disappointing sales, e.g., a product reason that you should be taking action on that you won't take if you assume the problem is pricing?
- Finally, ask yourself what the problem. Is that you are trying to solve when you drop prices: probably the problem of disappointing sales? Is this the right problem to be tackling? Isn't the problem that declining sales mean declining profit? Are you really going to be more profitable by dropping prices than by holding price and finding other ways to boost sales?

Thinking in different directions, helps one to look for unusual and creative solutions

PRINCIPLES BEHIND DIRECTED CREATIVITY

Broadly speaking, when you need to be creative, pay attention to things in new ways, escape your current mental patterns associated with the topic and keep moving in your thinking to avoid premature judgement and satisfying. Critically examining the essential requirements of creativity one would find three principles behind the tools of directed creativity. They are related to creativity process stages in Table 16.2.

(i) Attention.

(ii) Escape.

(iii) Movement.

Table 16.2 Principles of creativity

Principle	Creativity stages	Osborn's model
Attention	Preparation	*Orientation:* Putting up the problem. *Preparation*: getting pertinent data. *Analysis:* breaking down the relevant material.
Escape	Imagination	*Ideation*: Piling up alternatives by way of ideas. *Incubation:* letting up, to invite illumination.
Movement	Development and action	*Synthesis*: putting the pieces together. *Evaluation:* Judging the resulting ideas.

Figure 16-2 captures the three basic principles and provides a quick checklist of things to consider.

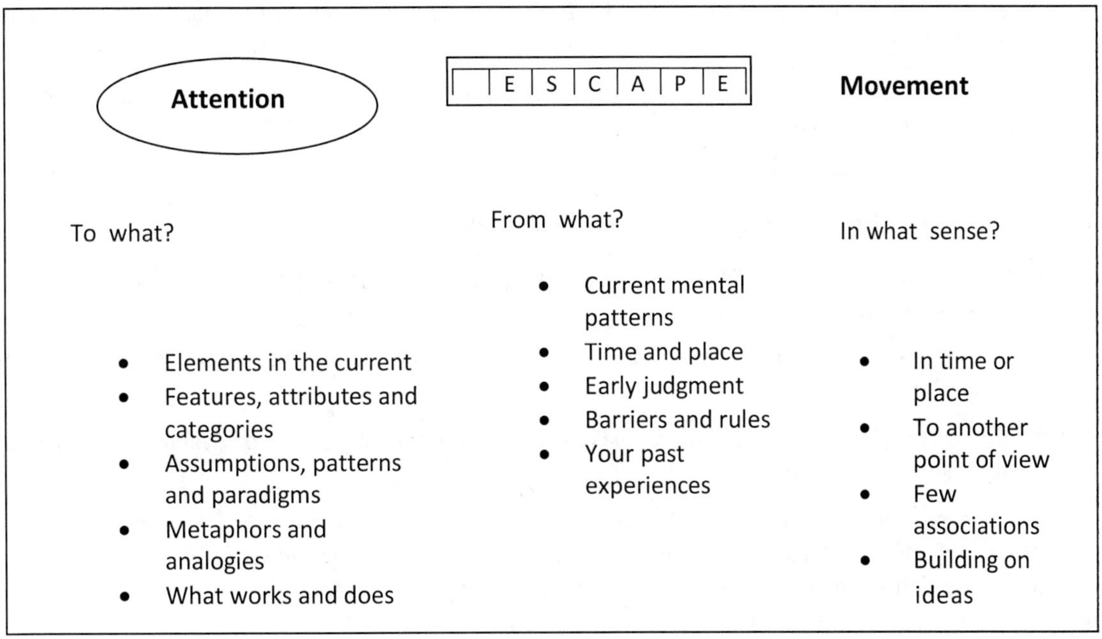

Source: Paul E. Plesk, *Creativity, Innovation and Quality*, Prentice-Hall of India Ltd, New Delhi, 1998.

Figure 16.2 Principles behind the methods of directed creativity.

Attention:

Preparation is primarily about the *principle of attention.* When we come into contact with the reality, we sense the world. Sensory stimulus comes to us with a great deal of information. Our observation can be either on purpose or by chance.

We may purposefully look at, for improving services of a hospital, the services of banks, educational institutions and a manufacturing firm. We may by chance notice ATM of a bank and pause to think about its application in a hospital.

Our observation is focused.

We generally sense only a part of the reality. We do not really care about things that are not of immediate concern. Our perception processes tend to be too focused and over summarize information. While focus is good, it also means that most of the information that comes to our senses is quickly discarded as not being relevant to the matter on hand. The discarding process is good because it helps prevent information overloads; but it limits our knowing and minimizes the chance of creative surprises.

Here we give examples of those benefited by attention.

- George De Mestral, the inventor of Velcro, noticed the mechanism by which sticker burrs attached themselves to his pants leg when he walked through the woods.
- Stock brokerage firms began offering electronic trading services when they noticed that many of the rich investors are also users of computers.
- Akio Morita walking around saw some one jogging who said, 'it's so boring'. I wish I could get a small music system that I could afford. Akio Morita developed product at an affordable price.

Creativity requires focusing on something that we have not focused much attention on before. Tools include writing, drawing and making a movie.

The guidelines therefore are:

❖ Set a goal of purposefully noticing one thing each day.

❖ Carry a handbook and a pencil or lap top computer or call your own voice mail, to record the message.

❖ Record the essence of the situation, positives, negatives and extracted concepts. Also any other thoughts you have.

❖ You can also try to draw a picture, make a slow motion mental movie or explain it to some one and listen to yourself.

Preparation is an essential part of directed – creativity cycle. It is naïve to think that you can just walk into a brainstorming session and emerge with several breakthrough ideas effortlessly. Creative preparation is a deliberate act. It is about expansive thinking. It is blend of generative and analytical thinking.

Escape:

While the preparation phase was primarily about creative attention and some escape, the imagination phase of the directed creativity cycle primarily utilizes escape and movement. When mental escape breaks the bonds of the current reality, mental movement finds another place to settle. If we direct our mental movement towards novel connections, we end up with creative ideas.

In other words, having focused our attention, on the way things are currently done, we have to mentally escape from our current patterns of thinking. The means of escape are an outrageous idea, a good night's sleep, walk in the woods, etc. Keep exploring and connecting thoughts in the new lines of thinking tools include brainstorming. Analysis in this phase is concerned with clarifying concepts, finding associations and memorizing the observed phenomenon. Here are some approaches to divergent thinking.

(a) Seeing other points of view:

- **Read** - Absorb material from books and journals from many different fields.
- **Conversations** - Talk to strangers, your customers, your competitors etc.,
- **Role play** - Purposely try to think like some one else.

(b) Refocusing a topic:

- **By word play** - Van Gunaly's (1992) two-word method. Select key words from your original statement of the issue. Alternatively, either consult the sources for substitutes or put the words together in random combinations.
- **By hierarchy** - Nadler and Hibino (1994) suggested this tool. Develop statements of the purpose relating topic and arrange them in a hierarchical order.

(c) Looking closer and analyzing:

Traditional analysis is concerned with evaluative questions and seeks to find right and wrong answers. Creative analysis is concerned with asking expansive questions and seeks to explore many more possibilities.

- **Questioning** – 5W's and H list by Kepner and Tregoe (1963, 81) Who? What? Where? When? Why? and How?
- **Multimode thinking** – Six thinking hats by Edward de Bono (1986).
- **Component analysis** – Make a list of assumptions, paradigms and rules.
- **Grid analysis** – FCB grid by Richard Vaughn (1978) – Think and feel aspects of topic in relation to high and low involvement levels.

(d) Searching for analogies:

The dictionary defines analogy as the inference that if two or more things agree with one another in some respects, they will probably agree in others. Identify analogies and generate creative thoughts from them. When using analogies focus on common areas between proposed analogy and your topic, don't let the differences excite premature judgement that rejects the analogy.For identifying the analogies, go for excursion and Synectics.

(e) Creating new worlds:

The basic approach involves constructing a detailed future or idealized scenario and then thinking about what you would do if such a scenario were true. Senge *et.at.,* (1994) out line the steps for creating scenarios.

- Have clear sense of purpose – a focused, but broad topic.
- List the driving forces in the situation.
- Divide the forces into two groups – predictable and uncertain.
- Create two or four detailed scenario descriptions by combining the predictable forces with several possibilities for unpredictable forces.

- Each such scenario creates a new world. Walk around in these new worlds and think about what you would do.

The key idea behind this method is escape. We escape time and effort by simply leaping over to a new future. The exploration of these virtual worlds will give us innovative ideas that we might be able to adapt to the real world of today.

Peter Johnson (1988), the head of Banne'ville power Administration, created a 'phantom super – computer' – an outrageously idealized organization that could accomplish anything – and then challenged himself and his organization to keep up with it.

Ratan Tata declared that one lakh car would be introduced by Tata Motors and placed a challenge to his organisaiton. Nano, described as an engineering marvel was brought out as a result of it.

(f) Playing within Vs. with boundaries:

Identifying boundaries and playing with them rather than within them can help identify areas where it might be possible to take right decision and action. Its certainly true that: *'If you don't know where you're going, you'll end up someplace else.'* But it's also true that: *'If you always know exactly where you're going, you have no chance of discovering someplace else'*.

Movement:

After the exhilaration of imagination, the ideas require examination for enhancement and evaluation.

Harvesting Judgment is needed to harvest promising innovation from among the virtually infinite array of possible mental associations. Liberal harvesting policy is advised because several of the ideas initially selected will not make grade on the final evaluating; other ideas will end up being combined or streamlined.

Harvesting - may be done by a relatively large group of 12 to 20 people. Majaro (1988) has developed a nine-cell screening matrix that can be helpful at a final harvesting meeting. Figure 16.3 shows the grid based on subjective ratings for attractiveness and compatibility.

- Attractiveness refers to the idea's impact on the internal and external customers or the public at large.
- Compatibility refers to our assessment of the ease with which we could implement the idea.

Typical questions are:

Will it get noticed?

Will people like it?

Can we do it?

Obviously, ideas falling in 1, 2, and 4, cells are chosen for enhancement.

Compatibility \ Attractiveness	High	Medium	Low
High	1	2	3
Medium	4	5	6
Low	7	8	9

Figure 16.3 Nine-cell screening matrix

Enhancement:

Enhancement is the process of critically evaluating an idea with an eye toward making it even more attractive. Tools used in the earlier phase can be adopted here. Box 16.2 gives a list of questions adapted from Debono (1992). The tasks in the list are meant to be taken together. Start any where on the list and consider multiple questions at the same time. Keep evaluating and reevaluating until you think you are done. Then go through the list one final time to make sure you have not missed anything.

Box 16.2 Enhancement questions

1. **Shaping** - How can we modify the idea to address objections that would otherwise cause rejection?
2. **Tailoring** - Can we modify the idea to even better fit our needs?
3. **Strengthening** - How can we increase the power or value of the idea?
4. **Reinforcing** - What can we do about weak points?
5. **Looking towards implementation -** What can we do to the idea to enhance the probability of implementation? Who must be involved?
6. **Comparison to current -** How does the idea compare to what it is replacing? Should we do further enhancement, expand or scale back the idea?
7. **Potential faults or defects -** What could possibly go wrong with this idea? What can we do?
8. **Consequences -** What are the immediate and long-term consequences of putting the idea into action?
9. **Testability and Prototyping -** How can we try the idea on a small-scale?
10. **Pre-valuation -** How can we further modify the idea to meet the needs of those who will evaluate it next?

We now need to document and communicate our enhanced ideas. Formats may range from relatively informal, one-page summaries to full-scale business plans. They can be supplemented with discussions; role-plays, simulations, models and prototypes. Box 16.3 gives the important contents of the idea presentation.

Box 16.3 Instructions for documenting an idea

The Idea - Explain the idea in two to three clear, informative, compelling paragraphs. Attach flowcharts and other supporting details.

Benefits and Positive Aspects - Describe three to 10 key benefits of the idea. Consider benefits to multiple customers both internal and external.

Negatives and Potential Downsides - Demonstrate your objectivity by identifying potential objections, negative points and consequences here.

Supporting Information - Use this section to report facts and the numbers. How much will it cost in staff time and money? How many tangible benefits can we expect to get in terms of increased customer satisfaction, revenues, cost savings, reduced cycle time and so on? What data exist to further support the notion that this is a good idea? Just summarize here; use attachments to provide the details of any analysis.

Intuitive Conclusion - In one or two sentences or phrases, tell us how you really feel about it. Use emotive, descriptive, metaphorical language. Communicate how excited or unexcited you are. Use the following examples as guides for communicating various shades of feelings that you might have.

"This idea is a home run!"
"Wow! What are we waiting for"?
"We really think customers will like it".
"A solid idea, we should do it; but we won't win any prizes for it."
"It's better than doing nothing".
"Perhaps this idea's day will come later".
"All things considered, not worth the effort".

Implementation - Creative ideas have no value until they are put into action. The idea is accommodated in the real world through change process. Implementation, in essence, is change management. While plans help implementation, effective human resource management smoothens the process by involving people. Generally, people resist change. There are five Is for overcoming resistance: Incentives, Information, Intervention, Indoctrination, and Involvement.

The following techniques will be helpful to overcome informal fears:

- Write down the worst thing that could happen. (Often you find that it is not so bad).
- Ask yourself, "If I wait, how much better will things be"?
- Break big tasks down into smaller pieces and start tackling them.
- Reverse-prioritize to say no to less important tasks that you might use as an excuse to avoid pushing ahead with your innovation.
- Set deadlines for yourself and share these commitments with others.
- Use the broccoli-first principle: Do the part you hate most first to get it out of the way?
- What ever you chose to do, be proactive and open?

HEURISTICS

The following heuristics help us in different phases of creativity:

H-1: Be sensitive:

To be creative, you have to look around using all the five senses. In addition, use sixth sense. Thus receive more stimuli from the environment and beyond.

H-2: Look around:

Live in the world and go about your daily activities. Observe the reality. Pause and think. What is going on there? What is it? Why? Then dwell on it long enough to find a new mental concept and to store away. There is no need to act on your observation right away.

H-3: Pause and notice:

Make it a habit to purposefully pause and notice things. Nearly every expert includes advice to this effect. For example, Perkins (1981) suggests that 'we make use of noticing". McGartland (1994) maintains that the creative person is capable of "receiving new information and seeing new distinctions and Fritz (1991) advises to "practice objectively observing current reality".

Pausing and noticing means thinking for just a moment about the positive, negatives and concepts presented in a new experience. But why pause and notice? Is it beneficial? Yes, in many ways. Specifically, the benefits are:

- You perceive freshly.
- You have more analogies and metaphors to apply.
- You spot new associations and trends much earlier than others.

The benefits to the firm are:

- Makes possible continuous bench-marking and quality improvements.
- Improves strategic planning.

H-4: Enrich memory by focusing on a few topics over a limited period of time:

If creative thinking is the novel association of existing concepts in memory, then it follows naturally that it is useful to create a storehouse of concepts. They will be available for further linking to issues that need creative thought. Memory is a mental rut. The more frequently we access the stream of thought, the deeper the rut. The deeper the rut, the more automatic is our thinking. One should try to access different ruts to be creative. Focus on a particular topic overtime that our mental valleys associated with it will become richer and more complex. One can explore more novel linkages with other concepts. Have deadlines for your creative project. End times are helpful in bringing closure to one cycle of creative thinking and preparing for the next. It is important that the predetermined time be subject to revision, to avoid premature closure.

H-5: Redefine your problem, broaden it and gain more insights:

Adams (1986, 115) warns "*more specific problem statements lead to quicker solutions, but less conceptual creativity than more general statements*". Systems approach helps moving from small subsystem to larger system and gives a broader definition to the problem. A potential pitfall is that the need to address bigger issues can keep us from taking any action all.

H-6: Make novel associations to come up with original and useful ideas:

- Select a random word and connect it some how to the situation of interest, being attentive to novel concepts.
- Look for different mental associations by listening to other's train of thought.
- Practice interrupting, stepping slowly through and redirecting your trains of thought in search of novel associations.

H-7: Use humor to unlock creativity:

Many scholars of creativity assert that humor is one of the purest forms of creativity. Therefore, laughter in considered as the most reliable clue that we are on something creative. Ask individuals or groups to purposefully generate at least one totally outrageous but humorous idea along with their other ones.

The major obstacle in using this heuristic is that, typically, laughter is considered out of place in work settings. Serious, straight – laced people often believe that humor is an unproductive waste of time.

H-8: Develop flexibility in thinking:

Recognize that your streams of thought and patterns of judgment are not inherently right or wrong; they are just what you think now based primarily on patterns from your past. Our notions of what is right or wrong, acceptable or not, sensible or eccentric are just relics of some of one else's past judgment. The rules, assumptions, background and criteria of success are ever changing. There is no absolute right or wrong in most of the areas of business and daily work. Learning to view all things as being subject to change is key in unlocking the imagination. The personality trait of flexibility will be an asset in this context. *Every trip of imagination is a temporary journey only. One should return to where he was.*

- Seek out the opinions and ideas of others, particularly children.
- Abandon the notion of "*the only right way*" to do something.

H-9: Relax well to think well:

Idea generation is a hard mental work. When your mind is tired, it will tend to settle into a comfortable thinking pattern – the way it has always been, the status – quo, the un-novel. Two hours of idea generation will not be as productive as four 30 – minute sessions with breaks in between.

H-10: Select a few ideas for development; save the rest:

Select the ideas that you think will be successful. Make a preliminary feasibility study of the ideas and screen them for further development. Save the rest for latter creative processes.

H-11: Evaluation is inherently an intuitive process:

Do not expect to be right all the time in your evaluation.

Evaluation is the process of choosing the right innovation to implement. Eventually, all creative ideas must face the test of cold, hard evaluation – the final step in the development phase of the directed creativity cycle.

H-12: Look before you leap:

This encourages avoidance of premature panic or burning bridges. A bias for action misleads you and you make the mistake of closing out your options too early. This way you'll never get discontinuous results. *You'll miss out on the 'big play'.*

H-13: In implementation involve people and set up deadlines:

Fritz (1991, 300) advocates the use of deadlines to organize your actions, build energy and momentum and position yourself for your next creations. Make sure that your deadlines do not rush things unproductively. Thy should contribute positively to the goal of innovation by giving you and the concerned people healthy pressure to push on to implementation.

H-14: Remember creeping complacency is the enemy of creativity:

Begin continuous improvement and prepare for the next cycle. One should keep an eye on the innovation in use and try to seek further improvements in it by modifications. In the spirit of continuous learning, we should also reflect on our experiences in the past round of the directed creativity cycle prior to embarking on the next round.

SUMMARY

Creativity involves looking beyond the boundaries of our normal thinking and experience. The stages in creativity process are: preparation, saturation, deliberation, incubation, illumination, verification and accommodation. The three principles behind directed creativity are: attention, escape and movement. Each business situation is different. But for each situation there is an optimum window between spending too much time creating alternatives and not taking enough time to think of enough alternatives.

Heuristics helpful indifferent phases of creativity are: be sensitive, look around, pause and notice, enrich memory by focusing on a few topics over a limited period of time, redefine your problem, broaden it and gain more insights, make novel associations to come up with original and useful ideas, use humor to unlock creativity, relax well to think well, select a few ideas for development; save the rest., evaluation is inherently an intuitive process, do not expect to be right all the time in your evaluation, look before you leap, involve people in implementation and set up deadlines and remember creeping complacency is the enemy of creativity.

QUESTIONS

1. Define creativity and describe the process of creativity.
2. Discuss the principles behind directed creativity.
3. Discuss the influence of time factor on thinking and analyzing processes.
4. State the heuristics for effective creative thinking.

EXERCISES

Collect 4 research papers or books on creativity and prepare a note on creative processes and principles. Based on the write up interview 3 executives who are heading a branch or division to improve the theory with practical problems and measures taken.

CASE : CREATIVITY FOR AGENCIES

With clients demanding greater value for money and brands losing steam in a tough market, advertising agencies are trying to be more than mere creative shops. Helping them move closer to their clients are hot new tools to monitor brands and their health.

Says Ram Sehgal, President Rediffusion DY&R Brand Communications (2000-01 capitalized billing: ₹ 75 crore):

"There is immense pressure on ad agencies to add value to their clients' brands and, therefore, add value to their thinking process. Clearly, clients want us to partner them in brand structuring and integrated communication".

Put another way, companies want agencies to almost become extensions of their marketing arms, giving them end-to-end service. Tarun Rai, Senior vice-president and general manager of Hindustan Thompson Associates (HTA) (billing: ₹ 207 crore), sees his agency as a "brand custodian" for clients. "For HTA, life begins much before the creative brief."

Euro RSCG (billings: ₹ 30 crore) has also decided to go national with its Sales Machine division, which specializes in direct marketing and promotional activities apart from providing marketing strategies. The agency has adopted the concept of a Central Business Idea to create brand communications. An agency official says:

"As an agency, we can think laterally. We are aware of market and consumer categories and so, instead of giving the client just a creative, we work out a business idea that can generate sales".

Analytical Tools for Every Use

LEO BURNETT

Brand Belief System: Separates customers into four categories – Believers, who exhibit behavioral loyalty and attitudinal affinity for the brand, Captives (buyer without attitudinal affinity), Wannabes and Non-Believers. A brand's strength depends on its number of believers.

Brand Stock: A tool which helps identify the best growth prospects for a brand by giving actionable inputs or by identifying the structural barriers inhibiting brand adoption.

FCB ULKA

Chess Team: A competitor-centric tool that helps a client understand a rival brand's possible game-plan and evolve counter-strategies. A qualitative too, it focuses on in-depth interviews with people who know the competitor well, giving one on insight into the company's internal thinking.

Mind & Mood: A research tool to understand consumer segments better and to help with creative development. It helps read the minds and moods of consumers. E.g., Woman Mood, Youth Mood.

Relationship Monitor: Still to be brought into India, it measures the quality of a brand's customer relationship through quantitative techniques. It tells a company whether it is at a base level or at a fairly evolved stage as far as consumer relationship is concerned.

REDIFFUSION DY& R

Brand Asset Valuator: Tool for building and managing brand equity. Maps brands in the consumer's mind. Interview-based techniques asks set of 8-10 questions taking into account four important parameters for evaluating brands – differentiation, relevance, esteem and knowledge.

O&M

Brand Scan: Quantitative tool to track the "six equalities" of a brand – Product, Image, Customer Relationship, Channel, Visual and Goodwill – separately. Helps focus client spending in areas of weakness.

Brand Audit: Complements Brand Scan with a qualitative focus, by giving pointers to a brand's emotional connect with the consumer. Samples are usually small – around 20-25 – but go deep into consumer's thoughts and feelings on the brand.

Questions:

1. Do you think new tools will serve the purpose of improving service to and satisfaction of clients?
2. What type of creative orientations do you think is necessary for modern ad agencies ?

Source: Shweta Jain, An Old dog Learns New tricks, *Indian Management*, October, 2000, Vol. 41, No. 7, p.44.

Chapter 17

Individual Creativity Techniques

Learning Objectives

After you have studied this chapter, you will be able to...

- Explain creative problem solving and mind processes
- Know-how mindsets inhibit creativity and how they can be changed
- Describe various creativity techniques

Structure

INTRODUCTION

Creativity is a process of generating new ideas for improving products and processes of Organizations. An awareness of the methods and techniques of creativity will help foster and utilize creative talents of its human resources. The creative thinking process requires the right mind and systematic methods. Several methods are developed which help stimulate and generate creative solutions to problems.

TRAINING MIND PROCESSES

Minds are like parachutes: They only function when open. (Charles Mingus). Man's mind stretched to a new idea never goes back to its original dimensions. (Edward De Bono).

How the mind facilitates creative thinking can be understood by the following explanation:

Step-1 Define: Define the problem carefully to make sure you are solving the real problem and to help engage your unconscious and conscious minds to the problem.

Mind Focus	Ask why the problem exists. This may lead to a broader statement of the problem. Try to subdivide the problem into smaller problems. This may lead to a narrower restatement of the problem.
Mind Grip	Write down at least three two-word statements of the problem objective. Select the combination of words, which best represents the precise problem you want to solve. Use this to write a new, more optimal and effective restatement of the problem.
Mind Stretch	List the goals, objectives and/or criteria, which the solution of the problem is to satisfy. (Think of the obstacles, which must be overcome.) Then stretch each goal, objective or criterion and write down any ideas, which are stimulated.

Step-2 Open: Write down the most optimal statement of the problem. Open yourself to consider many diverse solution ideas. Delay judgment on ideas generated until the identify step. First, list any ideas which are on your mind.

Mind prompt	Ask other people with diverse backgrounds, knowledge and intelligence for solutions to your problem. Use their solutions as prompters for your own ideas.
Mind Surprise	List ridiculous, laughable ideas. Use them to trigger more reasonably, possible usable solutions to your problem.
Mind Free	Stimulate fresh ideas by forcing similarities between your problem and things, which aren't logically related to your problem. 1-Write down the name of a physical object, picture, plant or animal. 2-List its characteristics in detail. 3-Use the listed characteristics to stimulate insights into and ideas for the solution to your problem.

Step-3 Solution: Then circle the best ideas generated during the Define and Open steps. Identify the best solution to your problem and modify it until you are satisfied and put into action.

Mind Integrate	Review your goals; objectives and/or criteria then trust your own gut-level feeling to select the best idea from the already circled ideas.
Mind Strengthen	List the negative aspects of your idea. Be vicious. Then modify the solution to reduce the negative aspects.
Mind Energize	Exaggerate the worst and best potential consequence, which might result from your solution. Modify your solution to minimize bad consequences and maximize good consequences.

Step-4 Action: Carefully write down a statement of your final solution idea. Transform your solution idea into action. Use the DO IT process and catalysts again to help creatively solve the problem, which you now have of "How to transform your solution idea into action?"

CHANGING MINDSETS

Creativity will help us to solve problems when:

- There is no single identifiable cause.
- The cause(s) cannot be removed to the satisfaction of all concerned.
- The information is inadequate or too much.
- The information is ambiguous.
- There is no precedent to follow.
- The variables are difficult to measure.
- Time is limited.
- The decision-maker wants to do something different.

In such cases, decision-makers have to move from the cycle of routine to the creative cycle: leaving behind the old routines and habits of thinking for a while. Then they explore new possibilities by thinking beyond.

A mindset is a fixed way of looking at things. We all have mindsets, some of them helpful but many of them limiting. People and organizations have mindsets without realizing it.

Success depends more on how we set our minds than on how good our minds are in the first place. This is true for individuals, for groups and for organizations. Often, however, we set our minds in a remarkably blinkered way. For example, adopt the mindset 'this is going to be a bad day' and your mind will find all sorts of examples and reasons to support that point of view and cement that mood. By contrast, ask your mind to address the question 'How can we make this a great day?' and it will create great ideas to achieve that. By changing mindset many organizations have succeeded in making products and profits. Box 17.1 presents the success cases.

However, changing mind set is not that easy. That is why supposedly very intelligent people and very smart organizations, can still be extremely limited and can be described by phrases such as:

- They have a closed mind on this.
- They have a very blinkered attitude.

- They just can't see it.
- Their heads are in the sand.
- They have a blind spot on this.
- They are narrow minded on this.
- Their bias is unshakeable.
- They are turning a deaf ear to it.
- They can't see the light of day.

Unlearning is necessary for new learning. It is not enough to learn or adopt a new mindset for the future. For breakthrough results, you need to get rid of the limiting ones you are carrying. Hamel and Prahlad made this point in *Competing for the Future.*

Why do children learn new skills much faster than adults? It is partly because they have less to unlearn. Music teachers and sports coaches put emphasis on the early development of right habits, because they know that learning is easier than unlearning.To create the future, a company must unlearn at least some of its past. We are all familiar with 'the learning curve', but what about "the forgetting curve? The rate at which a company can unlearn those habits that hinder future success. The more successful a company has been, the latter it's forgetting curve."

Box 17.1 Industry transforming mindsets

Running/track shoes- For athletes to all. "we're not in the business of supplying athletics shoes to athletes; we're in the business of supplying leisure shoes to everyone. Everyone should wear our trainers as leisure shoes'.

Watches - a Recall what happened to the watch industry when someone chose a new mindset: 'we're not in the business of selling timepieces; we're in the business of selling fashion accessories.' This change of mindset transformed the fortunes of Swatch and the Swiss watch industry.

Restaurants traditionally tried to gain a competitive edge through the caliber of their staff-excellent chefs and excellent service. McDonald's changed it by selling ambience.

Cars used to be built by bringing in different teams of workers to a static position where a car was being built. Ford changed all this after visiting a meat packing line. It adopted the mindset of bringing the work to the workers and so invented the assembly line.

Retail shops traditionally brought goods to the customer. The first supermarket decided to bring the customer to the goods.

Television news programs used to have the mindset that news had to be transmitted in relatively short edited bursts at fixed times in the evening. The mindset was to compete only via the caliber and personality of the newscasters. CNN adopted a different mindset-that people would be interested in news as it breaks, whatever time of day.

Banks always had the mindset that all customers wanted personal attention. ATMs challenged this and made the opposite mindset work.

INNER-CREATIVITY TECHNIQUES

Creative mind is always present in that interval or gap between a Conditioned ego response and a Spontaneous self-aware intuitive moment. Dive into the gap headfirst; allow your heart to follow. When you emerge your whole psyche will be cleansed and clarified and a bit of spontaneous joy will leave its mark on your mind. Inner-creativity is only a moment away. We will now discuss some common methods of sparking inner-creativity.

Meditation
Self-awareness
Light heartedness
Diversion
Dreamscape
Lucid dreaming
Creativity period
Creativity focus
Future memory
Creative triggers
Doodling

Meditation:

There are many forms of mediation and they don't all involve sitting alone in some quiet place. Meditation is closing the eyes, still the chattering mind and focus on one specific thought, sound (via mantra) or enter complete stillness in the void. If meditation appeals to you there are many varied methods, you can seek out which works best for you. Meditation puts your brain into an alpha or, when you become proficient a waking theta state. In this altered state the gap will open and creative mind emerges.

Self-Awareness:

The practice of self-awareness runs through all the great religious and philosophical disciplines. Buddhism, Zen, Sufi Mystics, Christian Mystics, Hindu Yogis and Taoists practice the art of mindful self-awareness. This is a non-judgmental form of watching one's daily actions and thoughts in the present moment in a detached frame of mind. When learned and applied, this can create the necessary gap between the Ego and the Self and great clarity of mind unfolds.

Light-heartedness:

This is an excellent frame of mind to enhance creativity. When we see the humor in everything, we perceive the intuitive and original moments that otherwise go unnoticed. Humor embellishes the absurd and unusual, and this is where creativity springs.

Diversion:

Dalls Dudley Lynch believe that the left side of the brain can be repressed by such techniques as playing soft, rhythmic music while gazing at a glass coffee pot onto which a series of colored lights are projected.

Dreamscape:

Michael Michalko (1991) describes this as a tool for idea generation. Dreams consist of memory streams that are somewhat randomly stimulated and linked together while we sleep.

- Recall and record the dreams.
- Link those memory streams to the topic in focus.

Dreaming is the language of the mind during our nightly sojourns. It stands to simple reason that this time could be used wisely. Personal creativity is greatly increased by utilizing the information gleaned from the subconscious mind in dreams. It is also possible to learn to control your dreams, adding a whole new dimension to the sleeping experience. If you recall your dreams upon waking, you can take the symbols, images and adventures you experienced and discover what is going on at deeper levels of your psyche. This is incredibly valuable information that will improve creative potential immensely.

Lucid Dreaming:

Lucid dreaming is an excellent way to harness creative mind and use its power to the ultimate. When you become aware in a dream that you are dreaming and that you have the power to control the outcome of the dream, you have unlimited power. This is the basic definition of having a lucid dream.

Example, if you are having a dream in which you are being chased or victimized in some way, you become lucid and realize that this is a dream, you then turn upon your attacker, face the problem squarely and resolve it fearlessly. Perhaps this is something you are reluctant to do in waking life. If you can remember to do this in a dream, then the next time a similar challenge presents itself in waking life you will be able to turn and face it without running. This is how lucid dreaming can improve our waking emotional balance and creative imagination.

Creativity period

Alyce M.Green and Elmer Green, theorized that the critical period is the few moments before one drifts off to sleep at night (hypnogogic state) and few moments before one awakens in the morning (hypnopomic state). These states can be clearly identified on electroencephalogram machines by the predominance of theta brain waves with some alpha waves. In contrast, individuals when alert are producing mostly beta waves, when day dreaming mostly alpha waves and when sleeping delta waves. One has to achieve and prolong the theta state for stimulating creative ideas.

Creative Focus:

All creative work is the result of clarity and the expansion of focused intent.

Professor Eugene Gendlin suggested that a person could reach a theta state and remain there indefinitely through a process akin to self-hypnosis. There are two kinds of focus: hard and soft.

- Hard focus is the willful concentration of attention on a single point or idea to the exclusion of all else.
- Soft focus is the purposeful expansion of awareness to include the whole environment, without singling out any one part and being aware that you are aware.

After you have concentrated on what the problem is and searched for known solutions, allow yourself the ability to do a soft focus before you determine a solution.

Soft focus begins with a relaxation of the mind and visual field. You become aware of all that is around you simultaneously, but acutely aware that you are aware. Mediators can relate to this idea fairly quickly, as this is the purpose of many eastern meditations.

- Relax the body wherever you are. This can be at work, home or traveling. (Though not advised when driving a car).
- Neutralize your emotional state. Allow yourself to become passive to your environment.
- Open your mind. Look out to something quite neutral in your environment. The sky is a good place. A white wall. Anything that won't distract is a passive focus.
- Imagine the space that surrounds you. Imagine that you are that space.
- Imagine that you are expanding out into the empty space around you. Imagine yourself as a blue feather that is floating on the wind. Float away for a time from all your prejudices, assumptions, needs and limitations towards the project or problem you are addressing. There is no destination, no time, no obstacles, just a free-floating feeling. You are aware that you are floating freely with no place to go and no time to be anywhere. Just be and enlarge into that sense of freedom and expansion.
- Allow a feeling of expansion to permeate your mind. Allow yourself to become aware that your aware but without boundaries.
- You can close your eyes if you need to, but after awhile you can do this with eyes open.

Future Memory:

To remember the future you need to reorient your relationship to how you experience 'time'. Though the concept of memory is usually applied to the past it can also be applied to experiencing the future before it has occurred.

P.M.H. Atwater (Future Memory) fairly sums up the essentials of learning to remember the future with the following quote. "The true art of memory is the art of attention (directing the mind) and intention (exerting the mind)."

- Attention is the key to concentrating and focusing your mind to a particular place or time.
- Intention is the act of willing yourself to participate in whatever you are focused upon.

Being mindful of these two key elements in your everyday life will measurably enhance not only your creativity but also your ability to experience greater realities.

- Allow yourself to relax and see your environment in its infinite detail.
- Allow your imagination to penetrate the details of your environment in a probative way.
- Be conscious of the way you process information. Be aware of how you categorize, catalogue and pattern your sensual experience. Be mindful.
- Begin to keep record of your experience. When you sit and mindfully examine your environment, keep a journal of what you see and what you feel?

- ❖ Begin to imagine what the current scene will look like in the future.
- ❖ Imagine a current problem you have and see it solved. Imagine that you are remembering how you solved it?
- ❖ Realize that what you are doing is real? Allow your belief system to expand to accept your new relationship to time.

Creative Triggers:

The technique is a combination of biofeedback and memory of the *aha* experience. Biofeedback is the complete awareness of a bodily function and the conscious regulation of that function. The trigger will take you out of associated memory and circular thought patterns. Psychologists are familiar with the term state-dependent memory. Memory of a meaningful and powerful event can reintroduce the same physical, emotional and mental conditions that were present during the initial event. By recalling this exact event and the feelings present, you can change your current relationship to those feelings. This is the procedure.

- ❖ *Choose a personal trigger* - It can be putting your index finger and thumb together or touching your forehead or placing your hand over your heart, etc. The particular signal isn't important, but the signal needs to be something you will remember and you can do even in a public place.
- ❖ *Focus* - Sit back, close your eyes, relax and vividly remember a time when you had a difficult problem to solve.
- ❖ *Recall* - Remember the room you were in, the time of the day, the exact surroundings and what the problem was that you needed to resolve. Then remember the moment the solution came to you. As you remember this exact moment of revelation concentrate on the feeling. Be very clear that you are immersed in the feeling of elation and relief you felt when the insight appeared and the problem was solved.
- ❖ *Personal trigger* - Associate it solely with this specific memory. For example, as soon as you vividly remember the moment of resolve, touch your forehead and hold that feeling. As you repeat this exercise a few times each day, the act of touching your forehead should elicit an exact feeling of resolved insight.
- ❖ *Use personal trigger* - When you use the trigger the *aha* experience will be immediately recalled. When this experience is evoked you have set the stage for a repeat performance from your subconscious mind.

Doodling:

Doodling essentially allows our intuitive feelings to express themselves in pictoral symbolic form. Interpreting these symbols can help to unveil meanings that are not apparent to our linear mind. A symbol conveys an entire thought in one image. Language depends upon a linear procession of symbols to convey a thought. While doodling, words may form themselves and these should be accepted. But, for the most part, doodling allows the unconscious to come to the surface without judgment or critical analysis from the conscious mind. To practice the art of doodling do the following:

- Focus on something that you are attempting to create or resolve. Hold the initial idea or desire in the mind and allow yourself to go into a blank stare or soft focus, preferably on a neutral background (the sky, a white wall, neutral carpet). As ideas and feelings come to the mind simply doodle them onto a piece of clean white paper.

- Allow yourself to focus exclusively on an idea and discuss it with a friend. While you are discussing it, doodle on a piece of clean white paper. Continue to doodle as you talk and listen. Don't interpret or inhibit what you are drawing.
- While doodling just allow your hands to follow your impulse. It's best if you can go into a mild trance and disengage the conscious mind. In some disciplines this is called automatic writing. The difference is that automatic writing tends to focus on words in sequence. Here we simply want to the engage the unconscious mind in an imaginary way and record the images that are brought to the surface.
- When you finished doodling set the paper aside for a period of time. When your mind is fresh look at what you've drawn. You will begin to get feelings or ideas. You may even see actual structures in the doodles. You may have unconsciously drawn the solution to your problem as a structure.

Doodling can also include numbers. Numbers are far more than a convenient measure of the physical world. Some people are prolific doodlers when they are talking on the telephone, sitting at a meeting, attending a lecture or sitting in any passive environment.

DIRECTED CREATIVITY METHODS

Directed creativity methods are those that help individuals to sense, perceive and learn new ways of looking and thinking at the problems and discovering solutions.

Evolution:

This is the method of incremental improvement. New ideas stem from other ideas, new solutions from previous ones, the new ones slightly improved over the old ones. The evolutionary method of creativity is based on the principle: *Every problem that has been solved can be solved again in a better way.*

Many of the very sophisticated things we enjoy today developed through a long period of constant incrementation. Making something a little better here, a little better there gradually makes it something a lot better—even entirely different from the original.

For example, look at the history of the automobile or any product of technological progress. With each new model, improvements are made. Each new model builds upon the collective creativity of previous models, so that over time, improvements in economy, comfort and durability take place. Here the creativity lies in the refinement, the step-by-step improvement, rather than in something completely new.

Revolution:

Sometimes the best new idea is a completely different one. No way comparable to the existing ones.

A professor, adopting an evolutionary approach asks:, "How can I make my lectures better and better?" A revolutionary idea might be, "Why not stop lecturing and have the students teach each other, working as teams or presenting reports?"

For example, the evolutionary technology in fighting termites eating away at houses has been to develop safer and faster pesticides and gasses to kill them. A somewhat revolutionary change has been to abandon gasses altogether in favor of liquid nitrogen, which freezes them to death or microwaves, which bake them. A truly revolutionary creative idea would be to ask, "How can we prevent them from eating houses in the first place?" A new termite bait that is placed in the ground in a perimeter around a house provides one answer to this question.

Reapplication:

Look at something old in a new way. Go beyond labels. Move from fixation, remove prejudices, expectations and assumptions. Try to discover how something can be applied for different purposes or situations.

For example, a paperclip can be used as a tiny screwdriver if filed down; paint can be used as a kind of glue to prevent screws from loosening in machinery; dishwashing detergents can be used to remove the DNA from bacteria in a lab; and general purpose spray cleaners can be used to kill ants.

Changing Direction:

Many creative breakthroughs occur when attention is shifted from one angle of a problem to another. This is sometimes called creative insight.

A classic example is that of the highway department trying to keep kids from skateboarding in a concrete-lined drainage ditch. The highway department put up a fence to keep the kids out; the kids went around it. The department then put up a longer fence; the kids cut a hole in it. The department then put up a stronger fence; it, too, was cut. The department then put a threatening sign on the fence; it was ignored. Finally, someone decided to change direction, and asked, "What really is the problem here? It's not that the kids keep getting through the barrier, but that they want to skateboard in the ditch. So how can we keep them from skateboarding in the ditch?" The solution was to remove their desire by pouring some concrete in the bottom of the ditch to remove the smooth curve. The sharp angle created by the concrete made skateboarding impossible and the activity stopped. No more skateboarding problems, no more fence problems.

This example reveals a critical truth in problem solving: the goal is to solve the problem, not to implement a particular solution. When one solution path is not working, shift to another. There is no commitment to a particular path, only to a particular goal. Path fixation can sometimes be a problem for those who do not understand this; they become over committed to a path that does not work and only frustration results.

Transformation:

This is the use of simple questions to trigger creative thinking and offer alternative solutions. In this strategy, one begins with an already existing object or idea and searches for ways it can be altered to provide possible solutions to a problem. Some of the transformational of manipulative verbs that can be used to activate creative thinking are:

abstract	adapt	animate		
combine	concretize			
divide	distort	disguise	dissect	
eliminate	elaborate			
integrate				
magnify	minify	multiply	manipulate	modify
rearrange	restate	repeat	reverse	
substitute	subtract	simplify	standardise	
transform	transmute	translate	transpose	
unify				

Association:

Everyday we are used to associating the things with each other: bread and butter, salt and pepper, paper and pens. Accepted associations make life comfortable and predictable, but they can also dull one's ability to discover and produce something new.

So as to break-up the pattern of repeated associations, try to practice mentally linking-what-doesn't-usually-get-linked. For example, when pen is associated with black board, whiteboards and marker pens were born.

The little game of new associations can unleash their creativity and produce unique ideas.

Suppose the problem is described as that of "getting something from one place to another via a powered vehicle." The important dimensions are:

- the type of vehicle (cart, chair, sling, bed);
- the medium in which the vehicle operates (air, water, oil, hard surface, rollers, rails);
- the power source (pressed air, internal-combustion engine, electric motor, steam, magnetic fields, moving cables, moving belt).

Imagination to structure different combinations in a variety of ways led to cart-type vehicle powered by an internal-combustion engine and moving over hard surfaces - the automobile.

Synthesis:

With this method, two or more existing ideas are combined into a third, new idea. Combining the ideas of a magazine and an audiotape gives the idea of a magazine you can listen to, one useful for blind people or freeway commuters.

For example, someone noticed that a lot of people on dates went first to dinner and then to the theatre. Why not combine these two events into one? Thus, the dinner theatre, where people go first to eat and then to see a play or other entertainment came into existence.

Attribute listing:

Crawford has summarized the principles of attribute listing as follows:

- Creation is not inspirational alone-it is largely adaptation and experimentation.

- Creation it not mechanical combination of different ideas. It is useful modification.
- In trying to modify the current attributes of the product or object, it is desirable to search for concrete alternatives.
- Move from closely related attributes to the far reaching ones.
- Creation is a long range on going modification process.

As an example take telephone. It has attributes like: communication from a fixed point, heavy, large in size, monotony of one ring tone, no caller identity, cannot respond to or record a call, etc. Now consider modifying attribute-handling convenience-for that alternatives are cord less phone and mobile phone. .

Check list method:

In this method series of questions are asked inquisitively as to what can be done to the phenomenon that we want to improve or recreate. Some questions are: Can we Add? Subtract? Alter? Rearrange? Adapt? Magnify? What are the opposite properties? Minify? Other uses? Other new ways of utilizing it? Alternative ways of producing it? (ASARAMOMONA).

Consider cell phone-Add extra features like camera, TV, computer, internet etc. Subtract or reduce weight. Minify the size. Magnify the voice and light. Other uses – It can be useful as a gift article, useful communicating device to individuals, groups and offices.

Morphological analysis:

Morphology means structure. The method involves identifying the structural dimensions of a problem and examining the relationships among them.

Les us take an example.

Imagine that you want to create a new lamp. The starting point for this might be to carry out morphological analysis. Properties of a lamp might be power supply, bulb type, light intensity, size, style, finish, material, shade, etc.

You can set these out as column headings on a table, and then brainstorm variations:

Power Supply	Finish	Bulb Type	Light Intensity	Material	Size	Style
Battery	Metallic	White	Very high	Metal	Very large	Black
Gas	Enamel	Colored	High	Glass	Large	Antique
Mains	Terracotta	Daylight	Medium	Wood	Medium	Modern
Solar		Halogen	Low	Plastic	Small	Concrete
Generator			Variable	Stone		Roman
Crank				Earthen		Ethnic
Oil/petrol				Fabric		Natural
Flame				Ceramic		

Interesting combinations might be:

- Solar powered/battery, medium intensity, daylight bulb-possibly used in clothes shops to allow customers to see the true color of clothes.
- Large hand cranked arc lights-used in developing countries or far from a mains power supply.
- A ceramic oil lamp in Roman style-used in theme restaurants, resurrecting the olive oil lamps of 2000 years ago.
- A normal table lamp designed to be painted, wallpapered or covered fabric so that it matches the style of a room perfectly.

Some of these might be practical, novel ideas for the lighting manufacturer. Some might not. This is where the manufacturer's experience and market knowledge are important.

A variant to this is attribute analogy chains in which for each attribute analogies are developed to find new ideas.

Random stimulus:

In each random creativity technique the user is presented with a random stimulus and explores associations that has a potential to bring novel ideas. In this method first state the job to be done (JTBD). Then look around and pick up at random something and use it as an input for developing ideas for developing a solution.

Random Word technique is the simplest technique of this class where a randomly picked word is used to generate new associations. To pick up a word, you may use a dictionary. Open a page and locate a word at random. Use the word for ideas.

For example the job to be done is: designing a car tyre. You picked a word- shoe. Now generate ideas based on attributes of shoe.

Shoe	Car tyre
Should not tear-off	Should not puncture
Know its condition by touch	Monitor on dash board showing amount of tyre wear on the wheel
Variety of colors	Multicolored
Soft, spongy cushion	Semi-solid tyres: half air, half sponge/thick rubber.

In random picture technique, choose pictures which have a theme(not be pictures of individuals). Allocate at least 5 random pictures per group.

A picture will appear on the screen and one of your team members has to come and start a story with the picture as stimuli. He will speak to the audience with his back to the screen. After a minute, change the picture on the screen without informing the speaker. The speaker is not allowed to look back to see the new picture. The other members of his group have to link the story to the new random picture. As soon as someone from the team volunteers to continue he can stop the present speaker and replace him. This will continue with 5 different pictures for the same group. The theme provides associations to the job to be done.

SUMMARY

The creative thinking process requires the right mind and systematic methods. Several methods are developed which help stimulate and generate creative solutions to problems. Creative mind is always present in that interval or gap between a conditioned ego response and a spontaneous self-aware intuitive moment. It can be learned.

Changing your mindset is a form of creative and logical thinking. A mindset is a fixed way of looking at things. People and organizations have mindsets without realizing it. Success depends more on how we set our minds than on how good our minds are in the first place. Changing mindsets will help solve problems easily. It moves one from old to new perspectives.

Inner-creativity is only a moment away. The basic approaches to inner creativity are meditation, self-awareness, light-heartedness, diversion, dreamscape, lucid dreaming, creativity period, creative focus future memory, creative Triggers and doodling. Directed creativity methods include: evolution, revolution, reapplication, changing direction, transformation, association and synthesis.

QUESTIONS

1. What is mindset? How is it important? Explain, how mindset to be changed.
2. Explain creative problem solving and related mind processes.
3. Explain any four of the following methods of developing creative methods (i) evolution, (ii) revolution, (iii) reapplication, (iv) changing direction, (v) transformation, (vi) association and (vii) synthesis.
4. Describe directed creativity methods .

EXERCISES

The cotton textile industry began facing competition from others like China and Taiwan who could produce at a lesser cost. Competing with them purely on a price basis was just impossible. So, the National Institute of Design (NID) was approached for help. It conducted a survey among over 5,000 exporters and buyers and made a presentation to manufacturers in the cluster. Undertake a small study of 20 buyers and make a presentation in the classroom.

CASE : PRODUCT INNOVATIONS IN INDIA

One of the important reasons for the failure of many products in India is the direct and insensitive adoption of product forms, which have been popular elsewhere. Over the past several decades, whole string of brand names have turned out to be failures or have had very difficult times during the market entry phase. Examples are Rothmans cigarettes, which was once a coveted brand, English Leather and Yardley cosmetics, Rayban sunglasses, Reebok shoes, Maxwell House coffee and so on. Brooke Bond, a major player in the beverages market, had repeatedly attempted to launch a different flavor of coffee in South India and failed. Brooke house is one such brand that comes to mind. Lipton's launch of a range of noodles with a very British sounding brand name, supermum, which too sank without trace, is yet another instance.

Sometimes the product concept itself may be irrelevant to the vast majority in the country. For a long time this used to be the case with deodorants and convenience foods although the situation is changing since liberalization and the emergence of an affluent class of consumers in the 1990s. Even if the product form is relevant and useful, it could be before its time which is one of the most frequently quoted reasons for the disastrous failure of some very good ideas such as Hindustan Lever's Hima range of dehydrated foods back in the early 1970s.

The Amalgamations group in the South launched a small truck under the Ford brand name which has an unusual feature of a tilting cabin. The project had to be abandoned when the product met with severe customer resistance from the traditional truck drivers besides several other reasons of unacceptability to the market. Yet another difficulty faced especially by entrepreneurial managers of the market is the lack of adequate data of the market structure and size. Many have entered into supposedly vast markets such as detergents, toilet soaps, ready-made garments, wristwatches, women's cosmetics and so on, only to find that brand success is a mirage that always eludes them. Underlying this apparent paradox is a misconception that there must be a potential for any good quality product at a reasonable price if heavily advertised and aggressively promoted.

Question:

Is it possible to arrive at some tentative generalizations in respect of innovation? Conduct a brainstorming session for suggesting a framework for creating future innovations.

Chapter 18

Group Creativity Techniques

Learning Objectives

After you have studied this chapter, you will be able to...

- Explain the characteristics and benefits of small groups.
- Describe various group creativity techniques based on discussion.
- Explain creativity methods of groups that use writing techniques.
- Employ writing techniques for creativity.

Structure

- Introduction
- Group Techniques
- Writing Techniques
- Techniques Based on Pictures, Maps and Networks
- Summary
- Questions
- Exercises
- Case : Excellence Sans Struggle

INTRODUCTION

Innovation and creativity do not happen in a vacuum or in a predictable manner. However, it is essential for growth and survival of the organizations. For it to happen, there are no panacea or magic formulae. It requires the courage and hard work of people, the employment of right kind of processes and techniques. In any organization small groups are of paramount importance by presence and contribution. Making small groups productive and creative is a major challenge for managers.

GROUP TECHNIQUES

Small groups have fewer than 20 or so members, making it easier for people to actively participate. They meet as small gatherings or as breakouts of large meetings and offer many opportunities for creative, flexible interchange of ideas and lively, meaningful participation. Small groups offer many benefits.

- **Participation** – They encourage broad participation and promote a sense of equality among members.
- **Interaction** – They foster interaction between participants. People are encouraged to speak frankly and openly. Open and fair meeting processes promote give-and-take and interaction.
- **Outcome** – Small group techniques offer a strategy for achieving a meeting goal. They help keep conversation on track or establish a step-by-step process for handling discussion. They help develop consensus or an action plan.

Several methods have been identified for producing creative results. Here are some popular ones.

Off The Wall Thinking:

OTW thinking is like brainstorming. While brainstorming prohibits negative thinking OTW thinking encourages Janusian thinking - seeing both sides of an idea, both positive and negative. When you understand why an idea doesn't work, you can then focus on how to make it work?

The process of OTW thinking is as given under:

- Selecting a facilitator.
- Knowing the rules of the game.
- Independent thinking –No talking.
- Group discussion.
- Group priority.

Each group selects a facilitator. The role of the facilitator is very simple but very important.

- Facilitate a meaningful discussion. NOT to be the boss.
- Make sure everyone feels safe to participate.
- Seek clarification of ideas. NOT to judge the ideas or the people.
- Make sure all ideas are written on cards and taped on the wall.
- Most important task is to keep the flow going – creativity happens in a flow.

The following rules are followed:

Each person writes his own cards	Put the Header number on the front of the card
Answers should be 3-5 words in length (captures ideas)	Only use a Sharpie pen. Answer each Header as often as you want, but only one idea per card
Write with the card in a horizontal position.	No right or wrong answers. Just ideas for discussion

Round One – No Talking:

- The "Headers" (or key questions) are written on blue cards and taped side-by-side across the top of the wall area. Each Header has a number in the lower right hand corner to signify the column number.
- Once the Header cards have been posted, the Facilitator reviews each Header with the group to make sure every person understands what each Header means.
- The participants are given a handful of yellow 3×5 index cards and a sharpie pen.
- Each person writes his/her ideas or answers to each question.
- The answers are taped in a row underneath the appropriate Header.

It is important that there be no group discussion during Round One. The "No Talking" round allows each person to put their true thinking on the cards without being influenced by stronger personalities or more articulate members of the group.

Round Two – Group Discussion:

- After all cards have been taped to the wall, the Facilitator leads a group discussion.
- Begin with the first Header column and read the cards aloud.
- The role of the Facilitator is to get the group discussion started.
- Once the group begins the discussion, the Ideas will begin flowing. The key is to ask a "probing question" – one that gets a response; for example :

  Are there any ideas missing here? Is there a card in this row that someone doesn't understand? What did you mean by this? Is there a card here that anyone disagrees with? Is there a card that shouldn't be here?
- All Ideas generated during the group discussion are written on cards and taped on the wall.

Round Three – Group Priority:

- Once the group discussion has been completed, the Facilitator then tells the group that they need to reach consensus on the most important ideas in each column.
- They can select two to three of the cards as the most important ideas in that column. This forces them to focus on what is most important to them.
- Put a large "X" on the cards selected in each row.
- Cards can be added or ideas re-phrased to best capture their priority thoughts.

OTW Thinking is a proven way to deliver better ideas and build consensus. Its chief merits are as follows:

- Uses your brain and your eyes to think.
- Can see relationships between ideas?
- Everyone is using a common thinking process, so group creativity is enhanced.
- Allows everyone to participate equally.
- Ownership is achieved only through participation.

Brainstorming:

Alex F. Osborn (Applied Imagination,1952) a principal of New York ad agency Batten, Barton, Dustine and Osborn found that instead of one mode of thought, each person actually had two.

- One, freely associative, was the idea generator.
- Two, which worked in a step-by-step logical fashion, acted as a filter.

Osborn employed 'brainstorming' to generate ideas. The method worked. Instead of five or six ideas just an hour session had once produced, the group of seven people could now produce upto 150 at a sitting.

Brainstorming sessions are held when a company needs a lot of ideas.

- Form a group of six to ten people. It is not a good idea to include too many experts in the group, because they tend to look at a problem in a rigid way. The problem should be specific.
- Hold the sessions, preferably in the morning.
- The duration maybe, about an hour.
- The chairperson starts with, "*Remember, we want as many ideas as possible—the wilder the better and remember, no evaluation.*"
- Experts announce their ideas. The ideas start flowing, one idea sparks another and within an hour over a hundred or more new ideas may find their way into the tape-recorder.

For the conference to be maximally effective, Osborn laid down four guidelines:

- *Criticism is ruled out:* Negative comments on ideas must be withheld until later. All criticism is forbidden to allow for free exploration of any and all ideas.
- *Freewheeling is welcomed:* "Freewheeling" is encouraged with zany ideas welcomed, as it is easier to later refine ideas than to make them more unique. The wilder the idea, the better; it is easier to tame down than to think up.
- *Quantity is encouraged:* The greater the number of ideas, the more the likelihood of useful ideas.
- *Combining and improving ideas in encouraged:* Participants should suggest how ideas of others could be joined into still newer ideas to get the best solution.

Brainstorming is a technique for finding alternatives, which can be used at all stages in the creative problem solving process. As it is entirely a divergent thinking strategy, convergent thinking must be provided at a later point within each stage.

Reverse Brainstorming:

This process involves listing ways of achieving a goal opposite of the one actually desired. What is most interesting about this process is that the ideas proposed using this technique are very often the ones currently in practice?

Synectics:

Synectics is a Greek word meaning "the fitting together of seemingly diverse elements". William J. J. Gordon, an executive of Arthur D. Little Inc., Cambridge, Massachusetts, developed this creativity process. He felt that Osborn's brainstorming session produced solutions too quickly, before a sufficient number of perspectives had been developed.

The Synectics theory is built on the premise that success in problem solving is increased by using non-rational thought to lead to rational solutions. The process, therefore, involves making the strange familiar and the familiar strange. Synectics relies heavily on analogical and metaphorical thinking.

For instance, scientists had long assumed that internal gases caused infection until Louis Pasteur concluded that it came from external microorganisms. Pasteur formed his discovery after observing that grapes would ferment only when the skin was broken.

There are three types of analogies commonly used:

1. Fantasy:

Children think of fantastic, way-out and perhaps ideal solutions to a problem: these can lead to creative yet workable ideas.

For example, How to move a sleeping cow from the adventure playground? Make it fly.

2. Direct analogy:

Children think of parallel problem situations in real life, faced by people or nature.

For example, the problem of moving the sleeping cow might be compared to how cranes carry heavy loads.

3. Personal analogy:

This requires children to place themselves in the role of the problem itself.

Imagine you are the sleeping cow in the adventure playground. You want to move to another place where it's quieter, without losing any sleep. What would you do?

He further observed that every problem requiring creative solution actually contained at its heart an essential paradox.

For instance, one of the assignments was to compress potato chips into a small space. The paradox was the fact that while potato chips could be compressed, they would be destroyed in the process. Having determined that paradox, the creative group was asked to find an instance in which nature had solved this problem. The group found an analogy in leaves. Although fragile, they noted leaves were found compressed and undamaged. How? They are moistened. Thus arose the idea of shaping potato chips while moist. The client subsequently sold the idea to Proctor & Gamble, which introduced Pringle's chips in a can.

The synectics sessions would last a minimum of three hours, for Gordon believed that fatigue played an important role in unlocking ideas. Gordon described five principles underlying the synectics method:

- *Deferment* – Look first for viewpoint rather than solutions.
- *Autonomy of object* – Let the problem take on a life of its own.
- *Use of the commonplace* – Take advantage of the familiar as a springboard to the strange.
- *Involvement/detachment* – Alternate between entering into the particulars of the problem and standing back from them, in order to see them as instances of a universal.
- *Use of metaphor* – Let apparently irrelevant, accidental things suggest analogies that are sources of new viewpoints.

Dialectic approach:

In this method the members of the group evaluate the alternatives of solutions for a problem by taking *for and against* stands. By such diametrically opposing approaches they generate arguments that cover all the aspects of an alternative and go deep in its evaluation.

Many problems that groups face are complex and ambiguous and there are several alternative solutions that might be adopted. They need a thorough examination of the assumptions and inferences that underlie them and their solutions. In this kind of situation, two useful techniques are: dialectical inquiry (debate) and devil's advocacy.

Dialectical inquiry:

Here is a basic outline of procedures for preparing and carrying out a dialectical debate:

1. Divide your group into two advocate subgroups.
2. Have one subgroup develop a set of recommendations for solving the problem. Make sure to keep list of all key assumptions and facts that underlie them. Give a copy of this list and the recommendations to the other subgroup.
3. After receiving the first group's list of key assumptions, the second group should develop another set of plausible counter-recommendations whose assumptions contradict those of the first group.
4. After both groups have catalogued their key assumptions about the situation developed their plans for solving the problem, structured debate between the two subgroups is ready to begin.
5. Have someone state the problem.
6. Elect an advocate from each of the subgroups to present orally and in writing all key facts, data and assumptions to the other group.

7. After each side has had a chance to make their presentation, the subgroups should then debate both plans, the goal being to expose hidden and/or faulty assumptions.
8. Once the debate is completed, the group should agree on which assumptions are most plausible and develop and/or fine-tune their commendations based on these surviving assumptions.

Devil's advocate:

The following procedures will help you and your team prepare for round of devil's advocacy:

1. Divide your team into two subgroups, one of which will serve as devil's advocate.
2. The subgroup that is not devil's advocate should develop a plan to solve the problem, making sure to write down all key assumptions and facts that support them.
3. The first subgroup then submits their commendations and a list of the assumptions that underlie them to the devil's advocacy group.
4. The devil's advocate group subjects the plan to an intense evaluation, trying to uncover everything that is wrong with the recommendations and inaccurate with the assumptions.

The first subgroup then goes back and adjusts their recommendations based on the valid criticisms of the devil's advocate group.

Thinking Hats Method:

Debono suggested the method. Hat in this context means a particular state of mind. Wearing a hat means the thinker should focus on a given problem exclusively in terms of the state of the mind denoted by the hat concerned.

Hat	Mental orientation
White	Hard facts, figures and information
Red	Hunches, feelings and emotions
Black	Negatives, logical faults, errors, inadequacies or risks
Yellow	Positives, values and benefits, hopes, dreams and wishes
Green	New ideas and concepts
Blue	Synthesis, summaries, overviews and conclusions

White hat thinking - We only look at facts and what information is available.

- White Hat thinking is neutral and objective.
- Only facts and figures are listed. We can subdivide facts into first class facts, which are checked and proven or second-class facts, which are believed to be true.
- White hat identifies information that is missing and lists suggested sources for that information.

Red hat thinking - Simply asks for emotional reaction. This is given without any necessity for justification or explanation—aspects which usually restrict expression of emotions. This is the hat, which encourages intuitive thinking. Feelings are simply stated without any judgment or need for clarification.

Thus Red Hat thinking is:

- Legitimizing your emotions and feelings.
- About fears, likes and dislikes, love and hate.
- The opposite of objective information.
- Given without the necessity for justification or logical reasons.
- Allows exploring of others feelings.

Black hat thinking - Looks at what is wrong with this situation or idea? It directs the users attention at negatives or dangers. It is especially necessary where the initial reaction is one of optimism.

Thus Black Hat thinking is:

- Critical or negative judgement.
- Looks at the risks.
- Points out dangers and potential problems.
- Points out faults.
- Caution is the objective-not argument.
- Logical reasons must be given.

Yellow hat thinking - Here attention is directed only at the benefits or good points. This is especially effective where the initial reaction to a concept is negative. It compels the user to look from an objective viewpoint and consider all points of view.

Thus Yellow Hat thinking is:

- Positive and constructive.
- Explores for value and benefits.
- Seeks logical support.
- Looks at why this will work.
- Looks at the good points only.
- Logical reasons must be given.

Green hat thinking - is used where alterative explanations or solutions are required. It encourages an open mind, which is probably the most important thinking disposition.

Thus Green Hat thinking is:

- Symbolic of fertility and growth.
- Creative thinking.
- The search for alternatives.
- Does not have to be logical.
- Movement from one idea to another. Replaces judgment.
- Generates new concepts and perceptions.

Blue hat thinking - This is the hat, which decides what thinking, will be done? It is the planning process. At the end it is used to redirect the thinking if there is any drift.

Thus Blue Hat thinking is:

- Controls the thinking process.
- Organizes the thinking.
- Thinking about what thinking is needed.
- Calls for the use of other hats.
- Maintains focus.
- Provides summaries, overview and conclusions.

Nominal group technique:

NGT is a structured group approach used to develop ideas.. It works best in small groups of 8-12 people. NGT sessions may last 1½ to 3 hours and deal with only one question.

NGT is similar to brainstorming, except that it is based on the understanding that certain group goals can be best achieved *by writing rather than by discussion.* Each expert has an equal chance because discussion is accommodated in sequential order. The guidelines for conducting a Nominal Group Technique session developed by Andrew Vande Ven and Andre Delbecq are as follows:

Group meets – Select the NGT leader; make sure he or she knows exactly how the method works and completely understands the issue to be addressed. Select the team members- Usually from seven to ten participants (never fewer than five). Prepare materials on relevant aspects of the problem and give it to group members. Members may be randomly chosen or assigned because of their specific talents. Select a meeting spot that will be available for one to two hours. It should be comfortable, private and free from any possible distractions. Ideally members should be seated around a table, where they can easily see one another, the leader and the chalkboard or flipchart. Give paper and pencils necessary for the participants' ideas and 3 by 5 cards needed for the voting process.

Ideas – The leader (not a group participant) hands out pencils and paper, at the top of which is printed the question under consideration. State an open-ended question ("what are some ways we could encourage participants to car pool?").

Members write out their responses. 10 to 15 minutes should be allowed for this step. Have each person spend several minutes in silence individually brainstorming all the possible ideas and jot these ideas.

Reflection – Ask each person to note down his or her own views or reflections. Eg "List three best and three worst aspects of the course", "what is the most important aspect to be changed?" Allow only a few minutes.

Sharing – Using a round-robin approach, go round the group and ask everyone for his or her first idea. Do not discuss. The recorder writes all the ideas on a flip chart or chalkboard.

Then ask each person for their second idea and so on, until all ideas are recorded. Cluster similar items together but do not discuss issues. (The idea generation and recording generally take about a half-hour.) The facilitator reads each idea and asks if there are questions, interpretations or explanations.

It's a good idea at this point to number the ideas. No criticism is allowed, but clarification in response to questions is encouraged.

Discussion – The group discusses each idea as listed, in sequence. No ideas are deleted although they may be combined or expanded. The leader hands out the 3 by 5 cards and instructs the group members to identify the five most important ideas on the master list and write them down on their cards. Then the members are asked to rank-order the ideas (5 points for the highest-ranked, down to 1 point for the lowest.). It takes few minutes.

The facilitator asks each person how do they feel. Let people know that feelings are OK. Summarize feelings as well as content — *"Joe, you seem to be disturbed about something."*

Solutions - Suggest ways to reach conclusions. Clarify the decision the group needs to reach so people don't waste their time on other things. Let members know when it may be time to move on to the next problem or agenda item.Try to break big problems up into workable pieces and deal with each part separately.Periodically summarize what has happened and what has been decided. Be sure to restate the decision made.

Voting – Have each person evaluate the ideas individually and anonymously vote for the best ones. Allow each person to allocate six votes to cover their views. They can give all six votes to the item they feel most strongly about or they could give one point to each of six items or four points to one item and two to another, etc. Thus identify items with high scores and those with low scores from many people.

Reporting – Put people into groups to discuss the most significant items. Share votes within the group and tabulate. A group report is prepared, showing the ideas receiving the most points. Allow time for brief group presentations on their solutions.

Delphi Method:

The Delphi method gets its name from the ancient Greek oracle at Delphi, who was said to be able to look into the future. Essentially, it is survey of experts. Expert opinions are pooled concerning a given problem domain. It works this way.

1. A panel of experts (located at different places) is constituted.
2. For the first round, each expert is usually given (through mail method) a short written explanation of the problem and is asked to prepare an anonymous opinion about a focused problem domain.

   For example, one problem could be to estimate when air cargo revenues of XYZ airline would equal its passenger revenues.
3. The expert opinions are collected and compared. Summary of the results highlighting common points and differences in views is prepared.
4. For the second round, each expert is given a summary of the results of the first round and is asked to make a second (still anonymous) estimate on the same issue based on the additional information and reasons provided in the summary of the preceding anonymous opinions. Knowing how the other experts responded, an expert may stick to or change his or her initial answer.

5. Step 2 is repeated two or more times and then a final summary is prepared. By this point, all extreme estimates will have been deleted and those that remain will converge on a narrow range of answers.

The Delphi method has three important features:

1. *Anonymous response* - Because opinions are obtained anonymously, the danger that the response of one expert will bias another is removed. For example, a top executive will have no influence on a subordinate who may be part of the group.
2. *Controlled feedback* - Through a controlled set of rounds, the Delphi method allows each expert to rethink any previous answers in light of the anonymous feedback received from other experts.
3. *Statistical group response* - The final opinion of the experts is an aggregate of each expert's response in the final round.

The Delphi method has two main limitations:

- First, experts often lack the necessary knowledge on which to base their final judgment. The problem could be one of communication.
- Second, poorly designed questionnaires have been known to be less than effective in developing an understanding of the complexity of the problem domain.

WRITING TECHNIQUES

The following techniques use cards, slips or boards for writing ideas:

Brain writing:

In this method, ideas are not discussed openly but written on a piece of paper and then passed, minus the writer's name, to another individual, who builds on those ideas and passes the paper on once again. North Carolina's center for creative leadership believes that idea generation is only a small part of creative problem solving and thus devotes 90% of its session to the logical dissection of ideas.

Story writing:

When we try to get to grips with an ill-structured problem we set about obtaining information that will increase our familiarity with the problem. Story writing (see Van Gundy, 1988) is a technique, which helps this process along and at the same time helps to use the information to generate ideas.

Writing a brief story that is somewhat related to the problem generates ideas. Information in the story is then studied and is used for idea stimulation. The procedure is as follows:

1. A fictional story about the problem is developed (less than 1000 words). One should avoid writing directly about the problem and the story should be highly imaginative.
2. The story should then be examined closely and major principles, actions, characters, events, themes; expressions, objects, etc. should be listed.
3. This data should then be used as a basis for suggesting problem solutions.

Crawford slip writing:

The idea was originated by C.C. Crawford in the 1920s and the variation here is that suggested by Charles C. Clark (1978). The procedure is given below:

1. Each person in a group (which can be several thousand people) receives a stack of at least 25 3" × 5" slips of paper.
2. A problem is presented verbally to the group using such expressions as: How can we…? Or How to…?
3. Members of the group are required to record one idea on each slip of paper without thought being given to its relative importance.

Story boarding:

Story boarding was originally a technique used by Disney to help manage the production of their animated features. The point is to be able to glance at the board and quickly see what is going on and how you can add to it. You can use it to immerse yourself and your group in a problem and then to plan, brainstorm ideas, create communications and organize.

- Get several packs of three-by-five cards and bright markers.
- Assemble key people in a room with a corkboard or a board you can tape things to, and then select a topic.
- Write the topic on one of the three-by-five cards and post it on the board.
- On the board sort cards into three categories: Topic Card (for the main topic you'll be storyboarding); Header Cards (for general points, categories) and Sub Cards (for ideas that fall under the headers: details, ideas that develop).
- Cards might look like this stacked vertically on a board:
    - TOPIC CARD
    - Header Card
    - Sub-card
    - Sub-card
    - Sub-card
    - Sub-card
- The idea is to piggyback off each other's ideas and look for interconnections among them. Consider every idea as relevant.

Structure the story boarding into two sessions: The first is for creative thinking (no criticism allowed! The second is for finding solution.

TECHNIQUES BASED ON PICTURES, MAPS AND NETWORKS

Goman(1989) notes that visual aids in various forms can be used to boost creativity.

Pattern Diagrams:

Pattern diagrams use associative thinking to help us clearly see the overall picture. By emphasizing the links between ideas in a field, they encourage us to think more freely and display the shape of our thinking simultaneously. The common patterns in use are:

- **Sequences** - PERT diagram shows sequence of activities.
- **Cycles** - Working capital cycle (Cash- Raw material – Finished goods-Cash).
- **Maps** - Force filed map of Kurt Lewin.
- **Processes** - Production process, marketing process, etc.

The process of making a pattern diagram is as given under:

- Take a plain of paper: as large as possible and in landscape format (long side horizontal).
- Put a visual image of the idea you are considering in the middle.
- Write down anything that comes to mind in association with that word or image.
- Write single words, in block letters, along lines radiating from the central word or image.
- Single words have more free 'hooks' to associate with than groups of words.
- Every line must connect to another line.
- Look for themes and details. Themes are words expressing bigger ideas, which will tend to be placed nearer the centre of the diagram. Details are those that expand the idea. Connect them to themes as twigs to branches.
- Look for words, which connect to the senses: seeing, hearing, touch, taste and smell. Look, too, for words to do with movement.
- Use color, images and symbols throughout the diagram: to highlight structure, stimulate your imagination and bring your pattern diagram to life.
- Give each branch a boundary line, which 'hugs' the branch and gives it a unique shape.
- Keep going. Your brain is able to generate ideas far more quickly than you can write but only if you leave it as free as possible to do the job. If a word occurs to you, do not analyze it; note it down and look for the connections it triggers. Order and structure will take care of themselves. If your pencil stops moving, you are thinking too hard.

They will help you to break free of mindsets, see new connections and generate ideas. Pattern diagrams help you to see and develop the shape of your thinking.

Visual metaphor:

The idea behind the visual metaphor (Majaro, 1991) is to have people represent a problem and how they see the problem solved in a pictorial form. Drawing skill is unimportant and has no bearing on the use of the technique. The steps involved are as follows:

- **Everyone draws the picture of problem** - People participating in the exercise draw a picture of what they consider to be the problem with which they are concerned. Words should be avoided when drawing the picture.
- **Everyone draws the picture of solution** - A picture of the solution to the problem is next drawn. The instruction is to simply portray the situation, as it would appear if the problem had been solved.
- **Everyone notes differences between the two** - People are then asked to note individually how their solution picture differs from the problem picture. Once all the changes are noted each person has then to interpret these into analogous steps, which could be taken to solve the problem in real life. They have to do this without conferring.
- **Group Interpretation** - The group is then asked to interpret each person's problem and solution picture.
- **Group Solution** - In the last stage of the exercise, the group discusses and collates each person's suggested steps for reaching a solution to the problem. There are usually two or three definite measures that can be taken.

Mind-Mapping:

Goman (1989) describes a form of 'visual thinking' called 'mind-mapping' (Figure 18.1). Mind mapping is a lot like storyboarding, except you don't use the cards.

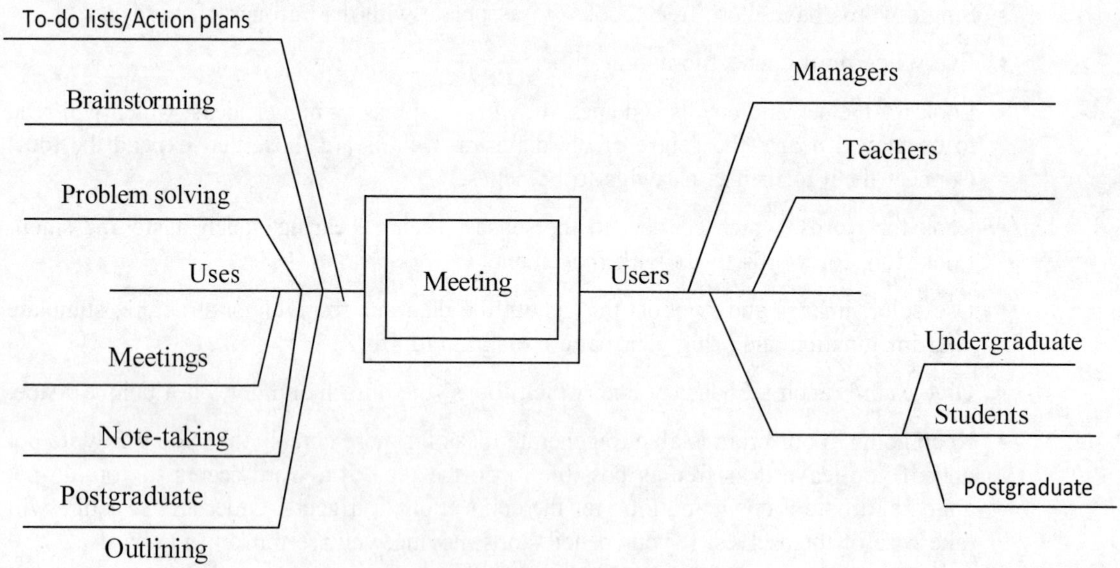

Figure 18.1 Mind-mapping

Mind-mapping was invented and developed by Tony Buzan. It is best approached in the following way:

- Turn the page sideways.
- Put a picture or symbol in the middle of the page (access to right brain) to represent what you want to think about.

- Use several colors (also helps access the right brain).
- As your thoughts come, draw a branch out from the center. Put one word on the branch. Add a picture or visual clue. Use different colors for different branches.
- As ideas come, add them, as secondary, smaller branches on the main branches, like a tree.
- Link ideas and thoughts between branches using connecting arrows, asterisks, symbols, numbers, colors, underlining or whatever.
- As you do a mind-map different linkages will occur to you, different themes, different ways to approach the subject. You can always do another mind-map using these new branches or linkages if it helps you sort things out in your mind.

Mind-mapping is hugely powerful technology for your cranial computer. It can bring breakthrough effectiveness in thinking about the problem, in summarizing your thoughts or knowledge, as an *aide memoire* for a presentation instead of notes or a written script.

Fishbone diagram:

The cause & effect diagram is the brainchild of Kaoru Ishikawa, who pioneered quality management processes in the Kawasaki shipyards, It is also known as the fishbone diagram because it was drawn to resemble the skeleton of a fish, with the main causal categories drawn as "bones" attached to the spine of the fish. It is used to explore all the potential or real causes (or inputs) that result in a single effect (or output). It can be used by individuals or teams; probably most effectively by a group.

Drawing of a diagram on a blackboard by a team leader involves the following tasks:

Figure 18.2 depicts a typical fishbone diagram.

- ❑ **Defining the problem** - clearly and precisely (in quantitative terms) Leader places the problem under consideration in a box, which denotes the shape of head of the fish.
- ❑ **Identifying the causes** - Taking the views of group members identify the causes and categorise them. Generally four to six categories of causes are identified. Table 18.1 shows typical classifications. Leader asks for assistance from the group to determine the main causes, which are subsequently drawn on the board as the main bones of the diagram. List every possible cause of the problem at the extremities of the bones and at 45 degrees to the backbone of the fish.
- ❑ **Identifying the specific causes** - The specific causes can be pooled through brainstorming. Leader attempts further breakdowns of the causes. Places them on additional branches of the bones running at 45 degrees to the backbone.
- ❑ **Establishing the most important causes** - Once the diagram is completed the group uses it as a discussion vehicle. It is customary to look at the points it raises in ascending order of complexity, startling with the simplest relationships.
- ❑ **Suggesting solutions** - The team assists by making suggestions and, eventually, the entire cause and effect diagram is filled out. Once the entire fishbone is complete, team discussion takes place to decide what are the most likely root causes of the problem. These causes are circled to indicate items that should be acted upon and the use of the tool is complete.

An example:

A firm is facing the problem of absenteeism.

The two broad categories and subcategories of causes are: Personal and work related (Management, environment, machines and workers).

The possible specific causes are:

- **Workers:** lack of interest in work, difficult job.
- **Management:** bad boss, low wages, substandard raw materials.
- **Machines:** poor machines.
- **Environment:** too hot, dirty, foul smell, etc.
- **Personal:** family problems, moneylenders' harassment.

Again, which one is first? Priorities are set for discussion. Say, machine is the first priority. Then the suggestions taht follow are replacing with new one, improving maintenance, training workers in maintaining the machine, subcontracting such production, etc.

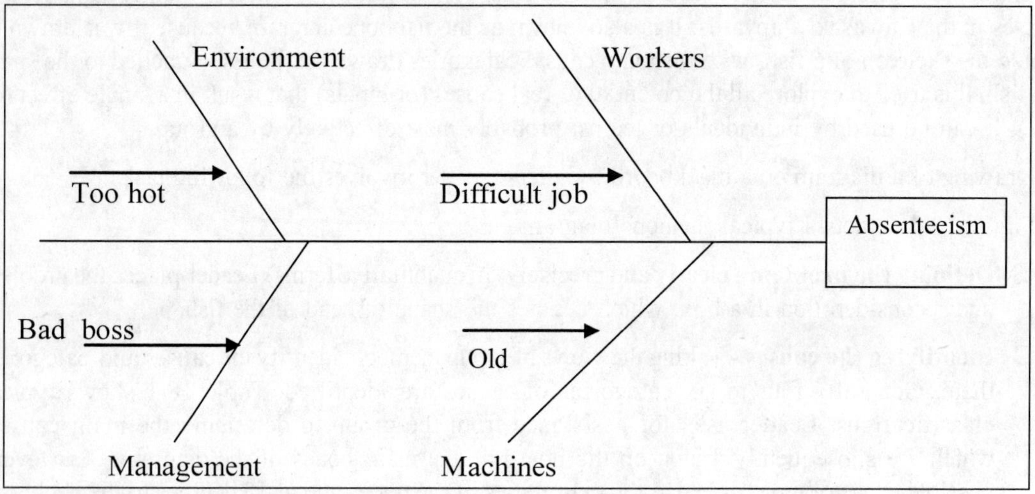

Figure 18.2 Fishbone diagram

Tree or Systems flow diagram:

It is a mapping technique. The steps involved are:

- Define the goal.
- Disaggregate it into related sub-goals.
- Design the specific paths and processes required to resolve the problem.
- Identify the factors which account for the existence of a given problem.

The procedure can be as follows:

- Take cards and a flip chart.
- The central issue card is placed to the left of the table or flip chart.
- The ideas/tasks cards are placed to the right of central issue card. Ideas are generated with the questions like: In order to achieve, what must happen or exist? What has caused the effect? If we do, will it lead to the accomplishment of the goal/task? The ideas are coded as follows:
    - Possible to carry out.
    - More information is needed to consider it.
    - Impossible to carry out.
- The entire diagram is reviewed to ensure that there are no gaps in sequence or logic.
- Other groups may be involved in reviewing the relevant inputs and making revisions where necessary.
- The group is allowed to write for upto 10 minutes. At the end of this time the slips are collected in.
- Another group of people then sort the ideas written on the slips into piles according to their frequency of occurrence or degree of usability.
- Once the ideas have been sorted, the best ones are then developed into workable proposals.

They can also be drawn as free diagrams, resembling a tree turned on its side. From a single outcome or trunk, branches extend that represent major categories of inputs or causes that create that single outcome. These large branches then lead to smaller and smaller branches of causes all the way down to twigs at the ends. The tree structure has an advantage over the fishbone-style diagram. As a fishbone diagram becomes more and more complex, it becomes difficult to find and compare items that are the same distance from the effect because they are dispersed over the diagram. With the tree structure, all items on the same causal level are aligned vertically.

Force field analysis:

Force field analysis facilitates the graphic representation of a problem in terms that are readily understandable and that can lead to the production of good solutions (Figure 18.3). In any problem situation, there are two types of forces.

- **Driving forces** - Those working in favor of a solution, which can be harnessed, to good effect in producing a solution. The idea is to make it easier for these forces to work.
- **Restraining forces** - Those working against the implementation of a solution to a problem. The idea is to lessen the impact that these forces have over a situation and the problem it contains.

The forces are first identified and then ranked for their degree of importance in relationship to the problem under analysis. Priority has to be given to altering the impact of high priority forces on a problem.

Driving forces	Importance	ACTUAL	DESIRED	Importance	Restraining forces
Staff have experience	1 →			← 4	Everyone under time Pressure
Staff want to succeed	4 →			← 1	Ideas not rewarded
Staff are hard-working	3 →			← 3	Bosses resistant to change
Staff are resourceful	2 →			← 2	No resources to develop Ideas
Increase					Decrease
How to make use of experience of Staff?					How to reward ideas?
How to make use of resourcefulness of Staff?					How to lessen resistance to change?
Etc.					Etc.

Figure 18.3 Force field analysis

Quality Circles:

It is small group of employees in the same work area or doing similar type of work who voluntarily meet regularly for about an hour every week to identify, analyze and resolve work related problems. The important objectives of Quality Circles (QCs) are:

- To improve quality of products/services, productivity and reduce cost of production per unit of output.
- To satisfy the workers' psychological needs for participation, recognition etc.
- To utilize individual imaginative and innovative skills through problem solving techniques etc.

Quality Circle consists of the following people:

- **Members:** The activities of the members include - attending meetings without fail, participating actively in the meetings and contributing ideas/views in the problem identification and problem solving discussions and developing useful solutions to the problem.
- **Leader/Deputy Leader:** The circle members elect The QC leader. Generally the line manager acts as the leader of the quality circle for conducting meetings and acting as link between Members and Facilitator in problem solving techniques.
- **Facilitator:** Facilitator takes responsibility for training members, initiating the setting up of QCs, acting as an evaluator and reviewer of QC operations and programmes and providing feedback to the Steering Committee about the proceedings.
- **Steering Committee:** It is an apex body made up of the departmental heads from every major function like production, finance, material management, engineering and other service areas headed by the Chief Executive of the plant. They provide budget for QC activities and make QC activities as part of the organizational goals.

Suggestion Systems:

Suggestion schemes can motivate employees and contribute to the management of change. Highly developed suggestion schemes typically aim to collect ideas from operational-level employees in order to improve standardized procedures and raise quality.

The concept of a suggestion scheme is simple. Dunn and Lloyd (1997) offer the definition.

A suggestion scheme is a formal mechanism, which encourages employees to contribute constructive ideas for improving their organization.

Both the public and the business sectors of the economy have adopted suggestion schemes as means of facilitating innovation and service improvements. The system has following personnel to administer the scheme:

- Scheme administrators are responsible for processing suggestions and for the overall administration of the scheme.
- Evaluators are individuals within the organization with the necessary specialist knowledge to assess the merits of suggestions.
- Award Panels are responsible for the final approval of evaluations, suggestion implementation and the level of awards.
- Implementing managers are the people who will be responsible for implementing the suggestion if it is to be adopted.

Suggestion schemes operate in the following way:

- Employees are encouraged to submit description of existing problems, a detailed account of the proposed solution and a list of potential benefits to the company. They are advised to review previous suggestions for guidance and to eliminate duplicates.
- Most organizations stress that suggestions should ideally be submitted through the natural hierarchy of the organization. Since line managers are prone to manipulate or even block ideas, the only safe way to submit suggestions is directly to the scheme administrators.

- Once received, suggestions are logged and screened to remove duplicate and 'out of scope' suggestions.
- If an idea is accepted, it goes to a suitable evaluator who then supplies the scheme administrator with an assessment of its benefits and feasibility.
- Successful suggestions earn a reward for the suggester.
- They are passed to an implementing manager for further work. In some schemes, the sugggester is actively involved in all the stages, thus improving transparency and the suggester's sense of ownership of the idea.
- If a suggestion is rejected, the suggester receives a full explanation. There may also be encouragement to resubmit the idea in a different or more developed form.

SUMMARY

Small groups have fewer than 20 or so members, making it easier for people to actively participate. They include special activities or formats that help interest and engage people. They encourage broad participation and promote a sense of equality among members. Several methods have been identified for producing creative results. The popular ones are: Off The Wall Thinking, Brainstorming, Synectics, Dialectic approach, Thinking Hats Method, Nominal group technique, and Delphi Method. Writing techniques include Brain writing, Story Writing and Crawford slip writing. Techniques based on pictures, maps and networks, Pattern Diagrams, Visual metaphor, Mind-Mapping, Fishbone diagram, Tree or Systems flow diagram, Force field analysis, Quality Circles and Suggestion systems.

QUESTIONS

1. Explain the characteristics and benefits of employing small groups in creativity.
2. Describe the following techniques of creativity: (i) Off The Wall Thinking, (ii) Brainstorming, (iii) Synectics and (iv) Dialectic approach.
3. Explain the creativity techniques given below: (i) Thinking Hats Method, (ii) Nominal group technique and (iii) Delphi Method.
4. Examine the use of writing techniques in creativity.
5. Explain any four of the following creativity techniques: (i) Pattern diagrams, (ii) Visual metaphor, (iii) Mind-Mapping, (iv) Fishbone diagram, (v) Tree or Systems flow diagram and (vi) Force field analysis.
6. Explain the merits and demerits of suggestion systems and quality circles as creativity techniques.

EXERCISES

Create next generation products:

1. "Herman Miller, Inc designed Equa chair to flex in response to the person sitting in it and permits one to recline while keeping one's feet flat on the floor. Herman Miller say that most

people did not make use of all the adjustments and knobs on office chairs that are supposed to make them more comfortable. They needed chairs that would be comfortable without manipulating knobs. "Therefore, we set out to design a chair, to solve that problem," says Armstrong, the vice-president. .

2. Microsoft will bring to the marquee its digital music player Zune, the first challenger for the iconic apple ipod. The launch of Apple ipod in 2001 was a significant development in the global digital music entertainment industry and saw the loyalties of consumers shift from the Walkman to a much sophisticated and advanced musical offering from Apple. For five years, ipod has been the undisputed king, gaining a significant 76 per cent share of the US market. But now for the first time, the leader's throne will be under threat! What will challenge Zune?

CASE : EXCELLENCE SANS STRUGGLE

Rashtriya Ispat Nigam Ltd (RINL), the public sector Steel giant in India is located on the coast of Bay of Bengal, 16 kms off the South West of Vishakhapatnam Port.

Vision:

The vision of the Company is articulated, as 'RINL shall be a self-supporting, growing Company with continuous improvement in productivity, quality and customer satisfaction'. The core values that support the Vision are commitment, customer satisfaction, continuous improvement and care for the environment. in order to support its vision, RINL has taken TQM as the corporate initiative from February 1997 on wards. The top management's commitment, enthusiasm of trade unions, positive attitude of employees was responsible for its success during the infancy period.

TQM a comprehensive management strategy:

It focuses on process and customer satisfaction through employees' involvement. The TQM strategy is adopted in the Company in four phases.

Phase I: Warming-up:

It is done to ensure that all employees think and talk alike when quality is referred.

Phase II: Formation of Cross-Functional Quality Action Teams (QAT):

QAT recognizes that quality improvement takes place in organizations through teamwork. It rests on three pillars: technical competence, teamwork and administrative structures.

Phase III: Creating a Value Employee Index:

It is done through the survey method. The HR department conducts regular survey on employee satisfaction, motivation, morale, commitment to the organizational etc. A consultant conducted the first survey in 1993 as part of the restructuring process and since then it is done on regular basis. They have resulted in various initiatives like team building across all middle levels, the establishment of corporate business information forum and even a top management retreat. Organizational research is also systematically made to understand specific shop floor situations. The data so collected is analyzed to make inferences.

Phase: IV: Exposing Workmen:

The executives who have already been trained in TQM are given the responsibility of educating the workers.

Quality circles:

In order to encourage the employees to participate more enthusiastically in TQM programme, RINL has launched various employee involvement schemes like Quality Circles (QCs) and Suggestions Scheme. Quality Circles were fist introduced in the Company in April 1990 to facilitate the employee to discuss the work-related problems and come out with suitable solutions. During 1998-99, 3250 QCs solutions were implemented leading to a savings of ₹ 12 crores to the organization. In 1999-2000, 3350 QCs suggestions were implemented which fetched ₹ 9 crores to the Company. In 2000-01, about 3400 QCs suggestions were implemented with a savings to the tune of ₹ 9 crores to RINL.

Suggestion scheme:

In order to increase efficiency, productivity and all round progress Suggestion Scheme was first introduced in the Company on January 1993. A Revised Suggestion Reward Scheme, 'Srujan Vikas' was introduced in 1996 in order to motivate the employees through recognition and helps the plant by way of substantial savings. During 1998-99, RINL employees generated 22,110 suggestions resulting in a saving to the tune of ₹ 19 crore to the Company. Similarly, in 1999-2000, 23,260 suggestions were generated which resulted a savings of ₹ 7.92 crore and during 2000-01 about 25,000 suggestions were received which fetched the Company a savings or ₹ 8 crore.

Problems:

Through TQM programme was started with great enthusiasm on part of both the executive and non-executives, it suffered from a relative slow-down or stagnation after a few moths of its exercise. This can be attributed to the following reasons:

- The departments of non-executives of the non-works (like Finance, Personnel etc.) were a bit skeptic about the concept of TQM.
- Employees are not sufficiently empowered to participate in decision-making in their work areas.
- The employees of the non-works departments do not assume the required personnel responsibility for TQM implementation, which is very crucial.
- Majority of employees through practiced TQM, but do not show the required commitment and involvement for TQM.
- Many organizational hierarchies stifle the initiatives of the employees and enhance the cycle time.

Despite all the above limitations, it is interesting to find that most of the employees (both executives and non-executives) express their confidence for the success of TQM in the organization.

Questions:

1. Prepare a brief report on implementation of quality circles.
2. How do you solve the problems identified in the case?

Chapter 19

Product Innovations

Learning Objectives

After you have studied this chapter, you will be able to...

- Explain the necessity of product innovations and classify them
- Identify the target market for disruptive innovation and current trends in FMCG sector
- Describe the technology strategies for innovation and new product development process
- Know the innovations in packaging and positioning
- Discuss the factors influencing the causes for product failures.

Structure

- Introduction
- Significance
- Types of New Products
- Target Market for Disruptive Innovation
- Product Development Strategies
- Dynamically Continuous Innovation Strategies
- Technology Strategies for Innovation
- Packaging Innovations
- New Product Development Process
- Beyond Product Innovation
- Positioning Innovations
- New Product Failures
- Summary
- Questions
- Exercises
- Case : Consumer Oriented Innovations

INTRODUCTION

Marketers will often find themselves against a wall and may be tempted to believe that the only way to get to the other side is to break the wall with their head. A company's product line may be doing badly; competitors may have launched hot products and end may seem nigh. Under such circumstances, innovation and creativity of marketers can salvage the situation.

Today product obsolescence has become a major threat and opportunity for companies.

Obsolescence can be either technological (Compact discs rendered cassettes outmoded) or style or fashion (old versions of automobile replaced by new ones). Planned obsolescence has become a major program for dynamic companies seeking to stay ahead of the other companies in the run for market gains. They are developing strategies to shorten product life-cycles and focusing on new product development.

SIGNIFICANCE

In recent years, the ability of firms to innovate is creating significant differences between the Best and the Rest.

A study of over 200 companies entitled "Winning New Products" conducted by the Kellogg Graduate School of Management shows that successful innovation firms were more likely to generate growth rates of 20 per cent or more compared with less successful ones. As Robert Cooper points out in product Leadership: Creating and Launching Superior New products (Oxford University Press), while 46 per cent of resources are spent on unsuccessful products, the best 30 per cent of companies have a success rate of 80 per cent.

As Steve Jobs once pointed out "innovation distinguishes between a Follower and a Leader." For FMCG companies, innovation is no longer a luxury; it holds the key to survival.

TYPES OF PRODUCT INNOVATIONS

Product innovations can be categorized in different ways using perspectives of marketer and consumer.

Change in Product line based:

Four levels of innovations can be identified as given in Table 19.1.

Table 19.1: Categories of New Products

Categories	Description	Examples
New-to-the-world products	New both to the company developing them and to the marketplace using them	Zipper, photocopy machine, computer, digital camera internet etc.
Line extensions	New to the marketplace but not to the company.	Colgate tooth powder, tooth paste, mouthwashes etc.
Me-too products	New to the company but not to the marketplace.	Detergent powders like Rin, Wheel and others.
Product modifications	Existing products that have been slightly modified.	LCD projectors-VPL-FE 40SXGA and VPL-FX 40XGA.

Change in customer habits based:

Innovations can be of three types, on the basis of the extent of change they cause in consumer's existing habits.

1. Discontinuous innovations.
2. Continuous innovations.
3. Dynamically continuous innovations.

Discontinuous innovations - Discontinuous innovations by their very nature are discontinuous to every customer segment, since they comprise new to the world products only. These new products are so fundamentally different from products that already exist that they reshape markets and competition. Successful new to the world products are pure technological innovations which serve a very strong latent need. They change customer habits totally.

The idea of mobile connectivity did not cross our minds because we believed that it was in realms of infeasibility. But as soon as the relevant technology came forth to enable the mobile connectivity, customers lapped it up.

Electrotherm India Ltd, an Ahmedabad-based induction furnace technology company, has launched a range of battery- powered two-wheelers in Gurjarat. These vehicles are unique as they neither require registration and payment of road tax, nor do they require a driving license to drive them. The company expects good demand for the 'YO' Bikes.

Electrotherm has also developed a battery-powered three-wheeler auto rickshaw in collaboration with the National Institute of Design. In addition, the company is working on battery-powered buses and has developed the prototype of a 14-seater bus.

Continuous innovations - Continuous innovation is the other extreme where an existing product undergoes marginal changes, without altering customer habits. For the company, it is a process of differentiation in its brand name, fragrance, color and packaging. There should be a 'Just Noticeable Difference' (JND). They change customer habits marginally.

For example, improvements in laser jet printers, digital TVs, shaving razors, or changes in call plans (Airtel, Cell One) are continuous innovations.

Dynamically continuous innovation - Dynamically continuous innovation falls between the Discontinuous and Continuous innovation. The changes in customer habits caused by this type of innovation are moderate.

The progression from a manual to an electronic typewriter and the advent of cable and satellite television, the walkman giving way to the portable CD player or the pager giving way to the cell phone.

igate offers Business Service Provisioning (BSP) unlike other vendors who undertake outsourced processes, it undertakes an outsourced corporation. A set of tasks forms a process. A set of processes forms a corporation. Igate does not look only at one process or two. In BSP, Igate owns the technology as well as the process frameworks. Its billing is based on each transaction.

TARGET MARKET FOR DISRUPTIVE INNOVATION

Developing countries are ideal locations for disruptive innovation to take place for two reasons:

- First, disruptive innovators compete against non-consumption. The product or service that emerges out of disruptive innovation serves people who were either not served earlier or were used to poor service. So the customers welcome disruptive innovation that offers a simple and modest version of the product in the high-end market. Also, new businesses do not have to compete with established players when they enter comparatively unserved markets (developing countries).
- The second reason why developing markets are a good location for disruptive innovations is that business models designed for low-income markets can be successfully employed in other markets, but business models developed for high-income markets cannot be applied to low-income markets.

PRODUCT DEVELOPMENT STRATEGIES

There are eight strategies that a company can follow as shown in Table 19-2:

1. **Facelift** - Minor changes are made in the product with little or no change to the rest of the marketing mix or target market.
2. **Inconspicuous technological substitution** –The Company brings major technological changes with little or no changes in marketing mix. The technological change is not brought to notice of customers by advertising profusely. Brand loyalty is retained through major technological processes and product changes with little attempt to highlight these changes through advertising.
3. **Remerchandising** – It is a modification of name, promotion, price, packaging and distribution while maintaining the basic product.
4. **Relaunch** – Both the product and other marketing mix elements are changed.
5. **Conspicuous technological substitution** – A major technological change accompanies by heavy promotional and other marketing mix changes to stimulate awareness and trial.
6. **Intangible repositioning** – The basic product is retained but other marketing mix element and target customers change.
7. **Tangible repositioning** – Both the product and target market are changed.
8. **Neo innovation** - It brings out fundamental changes in the technology of the product.

Table 19.2 Types of Product innovations

S.No.	Innovation	Product	Marketing mix	Market	Technology
1	Facelift	Minor changes	Little or No Changes	Little or No Changes	
2	Remerchandising	Minor changes	Changes		

S.No.	Innovation	Product	Marketing mix	Market	Technology
3	Relaunch	Change	Change		
4	Intangible repositioning		Change	Change	
5	Tangible repositioning	Change		Change	
6	Conspicuous technological substitution		Change		Change
7	Inconspicuous technological substitution				Substantial Change
8	Neo innovation				Radical change

DYNAMICALLY CONTINUOUS INNOVATION STRATEGIES

For many of FMCG companies' new product development has become synonymous with mere product extensions or variations. The critical success factor for innovation in FMCG companies is not the technological breakthrough it represents-this is limited by nature in any case.

1. Belief that variety pays:

Eager to put consumer-responsiveness at the heart of a company's operations, too many resources are typically funneled to product variations that brand managers can easily fit in their portfolio or which are in their comfort zone. Since these objectives are harder to reach with radically new products, these projects inevitably suffer or are relegated to background.

2. Limited R&D:

Unlike product industries such as pharmaceuticals, automotive or chemicals, the R&D function plays a limited role in the innovation process with in FMCG companies. What matters is the degree to which the entire organization can be aligned to make the innovation a success? It means getting the linkage between Product development and the Supply chain right, since that is where speed-to-market is achieved or destroyed.

Innovation becomes a holistic issue focused on building the company-wide capability to develop a constant stream of innovative products and bringing them to market faster. One way of achieving this is to create a structured process involving cross-functional teams with distinct phases built on the themes of strategy, execution and capability building.

3. Customization:

The effort of marketers is directed to customization. The growth of middle income groups and the emergence of youth and career woman as powerful buying force has encouraged marketers to adopt product customization strategy.

For example, fairness creams and grooming products, which were hitherto limited to female segment have entered male segment and customized products are offered to them. Today we have shampoos and hair oils for different income groups and different hair types.

TECHNOLOGY STRATEGIES FOR INNOVATION

A company's technology strategy may choose the following strategies:

New technology - It can invest in R&D and replace an older generation of technology with a new one. This is called breakthrough approach. This is a linear, step-by-step strategy of technology substitution.

The vacuum tube was replaced by semi-conductors.

Hybrid technology - It can work to combine existing technologies into hybrid technologies. Fusion of unrelated technologies will dramatically increase the degree of innovativeness of products. This is technology fusion approach. It is non-linear, complementary and cooperative process. It combines incremental technical improvements from several previously separate fields to create revolutionary products.

Fiber-optics communications systems are results of fusion of optics and electronics.

A company's technology strategy should combine both breakthrough and fusion approaches. Relying solely on breakthroughs is risky because it focuses the R&D too narrowly and ignores the possibilities of improvements with existing technologies. Companies that hope to gain competitive advantage should follow the following three principles of technology fusion.

Modular designs:

Modularity is building a complex product from smaller subsystems that can be designed independently and can function together as a whole. Modular designs can increase the rate of innovation. Innovations in modules must fit in the design of the complete product.

Through widespread adoption of modular designs, the computer industry has dramatically increased its rate of innovation.

By breaking up a product into subsystems or modules, designers can gain tremendous flexibility. Different companies can take up responsibility for separate modules. Companies, which operate in industries where modular designs prevail, have to make a strategic choice.

- **Architect:**

A company can compete as an architect creating the visible information or design rules for a product made up of modules or it can compete as a designer of modules that conform to the architecture, interfaces and test protocols of others. For an architect, advantage comes from attracting module designers to its design rules by convincing them that this architecture will prevail in the marketplace.

- **Module maker:**

For the module maker, advantage comes from the mastering of hidden information of the design and from superior execution in bringing its module to market. Sometimes module makers may have enhanced the performance of the modules to such an extent that attractiveness of the product is governed by the presence of their modules in the product.

Intel and Microsoft have become such powerful makers of modules in the computer industry.

PACKAGING INNOVATIONS

Packaging innovation today is an integral part of making brands stand out in a crowded marketplace, as also in ensuring that products are delivered to consumers in the condition they would like to use them. Recognizing the important role that packaging plays, HUL traditionally has invested and is consistently strengthening its packaging development capability, both through dedicated in-house teams and in partnership with its vendors. Box 19.1 presents the innovations in packaging.

Box 19.1 innovations in packaging

Hindustan Unilever Limited (HUL) has bagged 20 prestigious India Star awards and three Asia Star awards for outstanding innovation in packaging concepts and systems across its Foods and Home & Personal Care brands. The awards, given every two years by the Indian Institute of Packaging and the Asian Federation of Packaging, were presented yesterday at a function in Mumbai. The 23 awards that HLL has received reflect leading edge innovation being done by HLL in meeting these objectives.

The award winning HLL packaging innovations are for Brooke Bond Taj Mahal, Brooke Bond 3 Roses, Bru Instant Coffee and Deluxe Green Label Roast & Ground Coffee, Bon Oval, Kissan Ketchup, Annapurna Chapatis, Viennetta, Pond's Talcum Powder, Pond's Cold Cream, Fair & Lovely Perfect Radiance, Pears Face Cleanser, Close-up and Sunsilk.

For the Brooke Bond Taj Mahal Topatiner pack, for the first time a vaccum toptainer has been incorporated with a hinged polypropylene lid. It extends the vacuum pack benefits of better aroma and moisture barrier to consumers of one kg packs. The recloseability feature ensures that it becomes an in-use pack at the consumer's home, eliminating the need to transfer the tea to any other container.

The Kissan Multiplayer Ketchup bottle provides good visibility, and yet, unlike glass, is not breakable. Squeezability helps optimum consumption, while the cap ensures better closing and less spillage.

Fair & Lovely launched the Perfect Radiance range of 12 high-technology products with premium packaging, resulting in outstanding visibility and shelf appeal and therefore high off-take. Similarly, all the other innovations by HLL ensure both outstanding visibility on the retail shelf and also distinct consumer benefits.

NEW PRODUCT DEVELOPMENT PROCESS

The development of new products typically occurs in seven stages. A brief description is given here.

1. Idea generation.
2. Idea screening.
3. Idea evaluation.
4. Business analysis.

5. Product development and testing.
6. Market testing.
7. Commercialization.

I. Idea generation:

A large number of ideas can be generated using different sources as shown in Table 19-3 and different methods of idea generation.

Table 19.3 Idea sources

Source	Benefits
Customers	Express their requirements
Scientists and R & D	Do basic and applied research
Competitors	New products and modifications
Sales People	Competitive and customer intelligence
Top management	Entrepreneurial thinking, intelligence and intuition
Media	Success and failure stories of products

There are several methods by which the existing product can be manipulated to generate a new one.

Subtraction - The subtraction method works by removing components, particularly those that seem desirable or indispensable like removing legs of a chair or cover of a pen. The effort first should be to see if the product could function without the component.

Multiplication - The multiplication method makes one or more copies of an existing component and then alters those copies in some important way.

For example, the Gillette double bladed razor features a second blade that cuts whiskers at a slightly different angle.

Division - The *division method* divides an existing product into its component parts. The integrated product can now be assembled from modular components. Each of the modular components may have different variants and customers can customize their product by choosing any variant of each of the modules.

Today the home stereo has modular speakers, tuners and CD and tape players, which allows customers to customize their sound system.

Unification - The *task unification method* involves assigning a new task to an existing component of the product. Two or more tasks are unified in a single component.

An example is the defrosting filament in an automobile windshield that also serves as radio antenna.

Association - The *attribute dependency method* alters creates the dependent relationship between a product and its environment.

By creating a dependent relationship between Lens color and External lighting conditions, eyeglass developers came up with a lens that changes color when exposed to sunlight.

Benchmarking - For example, banks have maintained limited time for interaction with their customers. Customers could mostly transact with the bank during day hours but there have always been establishments like restaurants, which have dealt with customers during night hours. Take another instance. Pen and pencils have different benefits and features. It is possible to endow one with the features and benefits of the other and vice versa.

Reapplication - Best innovators systematically use old ideas as the raw materials for one new idea after another. The old ideas are used in new places, new ways and in new combinations. The essence is to take an idea that is commonplace in one area and move it to a context where it is not common at all.

Junk is source of ideas:

Some companies believe in Edison's dictum, "to invent, you need a good imagination and a pile of junk."

Designers at IDEO are obsessed about learning about material and product they have no immediate use for. They constantly remind themselves of old ideas by visiting hardware stores and junkyards. They capture ideas by doing focused work on specific problems. They collect related products and writing on these products. They observe users in their own setting. They invite experts and executives from diverse industries to talk about ideas for products.

Boeing's operation technology center keeps idea flowing by holding company wide technology forums.

Old is gold:

Innovative companies do not let themselves forget ideas by keeping around them products in which those ideas are embedded. Designers can look at them, touch them and play with them.

IDEO has made a science of accumulating junk. Designers put plastic parts, toys, prototypes, drawings and sketches on display in their offices. They also bring eclectic assortment of items to brainstorming sessions to inspire new designs. The designers constantly talk about the products they have collected and discuss how they might be used.

The steam engine was used in mines for seventy-five years before it was used to propel boats.

2. Idea screening:

The aim is to spot and drop poor ideas. Idea generation stage leads to creation of a large number of ideas. In screening stage, the available many ideas are reduced to a few attractive propositions. In this stage, a company must avoid two types of errors

- A drop error – when a company dismisses good ideas by mistake.
- A go error – when a company decides to develop a poor idea.

Product ideas are evaluated by various methods. The popular ones are Check-list method and Rating method.

3. Idea evaluation:

The aim is to find the degree of consumer acceptance and technological feasibility for the new ideas. This is a critical stage in NPD. It involves bringing together two separate elements into accord: customer acceptance and technical feasibility. Crawford refers to this process as creating a protocol or agreement.

(a) ***Customer acceptance testing*** – A product concept is a detailed description of the idea expressed in terms of design, operations and benefits. *Product positioning maps* may be used to clarify the different and unique features the perceived product can offer. Concept testing can be done using the following techniques:

- ❑ Customer opinion survey on ideal attributes.
- ❑ Conjoint analysis of product attributes.

(b) Technical feasibility – Technological aspects set limits to marketing expectations. Engineers are concerned with the production aspects of the ideas. Their evaluation considers

- ❖ Technological design and process requirements.
- ❖ Costs and profitability as expected by firm's criteria.
- ❖ Quality and other features as required by marketers.

4. Business Analysis:

The aim is to assess economic viability. Business analysis focuses on investment, profits, costs, outputs and price aspects of the product as shown in Table 19.4.

Table 19.4 Business Analysis

Analytical tool	Measures
Sales forecasting	Estimating first time sales Estimating replacement sales Estimating repeat sales
Breakeven analysis	Determining costs and output levels Estimating revenues and profits
Capital budgeting	Computing Return-on-investment at different risk levels Finding Pay-back period
Intuition	Success

5. Product development and Testing:

The aim is to design right physical product. A product idea that passes the business test moves to R & D and/or engineering to be developed as a physical product. Pilot production creates one or more prototypes of the product. The prototypes are subjected to two types of tests

- ❖ Functional tests.
- ❖ Consumer tests.

The *functional tests* are conducted under laboratory/workshop conditions. *Consumer tests* may be conducted by display and demonstration of the physical and functional features of a product. The venues of display can be one or more of the following:

- ❖ Company's own premises.
- ❖ Consumer firms.
- ❖ Exhibitions.
- ❖ Dealer/distributor showrooms.

To test a new design for safety, BMW had to build expensive physical prototypes. Data from crash tests arrived late and their findings could not be incorporated in the early stages of product development and designs had to be reworked at a later stage to incorporate the results of the crash test. But now these tests are conducted virtually on powerful computers quickly and cheaply. It is possible to try many combinations of configurations and see which one is best. Designers can in corporate the feedback from experiments in their later versions of designs and can commit to a design early.

6. Market testing:

The aim is to test the product under actual conditions. If consumer evaluations of product performance are positive, then the product is ready for marketing. However, some companies may prefer market testing, to make sure of its success. Firms under time pressure to introduce new products may either by pass this or reduce the amount of testing. When research (testing) expenditure is viewed high compared to the benefits of information (test results) testing maybe dropped.

Experimentation is crucial in the innovation process. It helps in realizing potential faults early, reinforcing new knowledge, reducing costs or preventing fatal errors later.

7. Commercialization:

The aim is to market the product and generate sales and profits. It involves two important decisions as shown in Table 19.5

Table 19.5 Commercialization Decisions

Design factors	Focus Options	Decisions/dilemmas
Production Program	In-house production	Building/renting capacities Creating an effective supply chain Preparing production plans and schedules Setting up ways for quality controls
	Outsourcing	Identifying number of sources Evaluating them based on their supply capabilities Establishing quality criteria Contracting for timely deliveries

Design factors	Focus Options	Decisions/dilemmas
Marketing program	Coverage	Full Vs. limited
	Timing	Launch along with or before the competitor
	Geography	Single or multiple regions
	Target market	Demographic or psychographics Segmentation
	Positioning	Emotions or rational benefits
	Marketing mix Strategy	Product, price, promotion, place and people.

The approach that companies choose in commercializing their ideas is the most important factor in deciding the success or failure of a new product idea. There are three approaches companies can choose as explained here.

Integrator approach - In approach, companies manage all the stages of the innovation process by which they turn ideas into profits. These companies control and integrate each link in the chain.

The integrators believe that this is the least risky approach, but it requires manufacturing expertise, marketing skills, cross-functional cooperation and a big up-front investment to succeed.

Intel invested $4 billion in semiconductor research in 2002, manufactured its products almost entirely at company owned facilities and managed the marketing branding and distribution of its chips.

Orchestrator approach – In the orchestrator approach companies draw on the assets or capabilities of partners and the orchestrator's own assets and capabilities contribute only a small part of the process.

The success of Handspring depended on the company's relationships with IDEO, which designed its devices and Flextronics which manufactured them.

This approach adopted when a company wants to launch products quickly or reduce its investments. But this approach is difficult to manage and is riskier than integration. Companies have to be adept at managing projects across organizations and skilled at developing partnerships. They must also know how to protect their intellectual property rights because the flow of information between partners increases the risk of knowledge theft and piracy.

Licensing approach – This is used in industries like biotech and information technology where the pace of technological change is rapid.

IBM earns substantial royalty from products and technologies they let other companies take to market.

Companies use licensing to profit from innovations that do not fit with their strategies. Licensors ask for equity stakes in the ventures that commercialize their technologies. That allows the innovator to retain an interest in the new products future. It maybe tough to sell off innovations because of the attachment of the people who developed them but it should be done if it makes a financial sense.

Choosing the right approach:

This is a very critical decision. We will now discuss the merits of each approach in different situations. Table 19.6 shows the factors influencing the choices.

Table 19.6 Commercialization approaches and influencing factors

Approach	Company position	Market position
Integrator	Product enjoys a patent protection. Company has the financial, human and physical assets necessary to manufacture the new product quickly Can invest heavily in physical assets.	Potential partners are not developed.
Orchestrator	Company skilled at managing projects across several different organizations. New product requires lot of complementary products and infrastructure support. Breakthrough innovation is not related to core business Product life-cycles are very short like that of disk drives. Value attached to brand is high. Time to market is critical.	Supplier base is sophisticated
Licensing for royalty	Company has ability to protect intellectual property rights and structure the right long-term deals. Strong intellectual property protection is available. The market is new to the company. .New brand is not critical for success of the company. Technical risk of not functioning well.	Customer acceptance doubtful, even if it functions well.

BEYOND PRODUCT INNOVATIONS

Product is key to disruptive innovations. As discussed earlier, strategies like Facelift, Relaunch, tangible repositioning and Neo-positioning have focus on product. The other ones, like Inconspicuous technological substitution, Remerchandising, Intangible repositioning are innovations supportive to existing product. Box 19.2 provides an example of increasing sales through focusing on new segments.

Box 19.2 Colgate and GSK war

The premium segment of the toothpaste market of Colgate consisted of a lot of players like Colgate's very own Sensitive, Pepsodent's Sensitive, Miswak and a few more players who were already charging a premium price – a premium of around 30 per cent than the other toothpaste variants present in the market. A few months back GSK's Sensodyne entered into this market and decided to occupy a place into a smaller niche segment and took the competition to an all new level.

The pricing of Sensodyne ₹ 42 for 40 gram tube and ₹ 75 for a 80 gram tube which was priced to directly take in the then leader in the sensitive tooth market Colgate Sensitive which was priced at ₹ 42 for 40 grams and ₹ 75 for 80 grams. Colgate is charging a price of ₹ 70 for a 40 gram tube and ₹ 120 for a 80 gm tube which is an increase of 66 per cent in the price of Colgate Sensitive Pro-Relief over the price of Colgate Sensitive Original.

GSK launched Sensodyne with a positioning statement that it helps to fight the problem of sensitive teeth within a week. This fact was then accentuated by the company by using Dentist's in their ads who were shown recommending use of Sensodyne to fight the problem of sensitive teeth.

We will now discuss positioning as a strategy of enhancing value of a brand.

POSITIONING INNOVATIONS

The USP positions a brand strongly in the mind of the consumer and also creates a strong differentiator, creating a "partition" for the brand among competing brands in the respective category. Contrary to the popular perception that only price points are the key to success at the lower ends of the market, a brand could provide value at a higher price point and establish success.

- Reynolds charged a premium of 50 per cent to 100 per cent over the unorganized sector and the brand's success was based on value-good design and smooth writing.
- Fevistick (adhesive in the form of a stick) had convenience as its USP (though it was several times more expensive than regular gum).

Wider availability, association with certain products and desirable features/ingredients make positioning successful.

- Vim scouring powder from HUL was introduced in the year 1904. It was convenient to use and effective on stubborn particles deposited on vessels. During the seventies, a number of regional competitors introduced scouring powder when a major chunk of consumers were using ash for cleaning vessels. Vim, which was expensive more than six time the regional/ local brands, reformulated the powder and positioned it a "Vim leaves nothing but a sparkle."
- Dhara (NDDB) launched a sunflower oil variant in 1992 at a time when the category was registering growth. It also got good volumes. Sweekar and sun drop, the competitive brands were positioned on the health platform. Positioning edible oil against entrenched aspect of "children-father relationship" — children considered "my daddy strongest".After that the brand registered a notable growth.
- Zodiac brand was introduced in 1960 as neckties. It was also one of the earliest readymade shirt brands launched in India. During the eighties, a number of premium brands like Park Avenue, Van Heusen and Louis Philippe built themselves in the premium end of the market. The "bearded man" of Zodiac who provided the brand with a distinctive personality to convey the "classic business statement" positioning.
- Colgate Total was initially launched as toothpaste that prevents several problems associated with dental care. The brand did not take off and was relaunched as toothpaste, which offers a '12-hour' protection (though the initial USP is still printed on the package). The brand has made significant progress after the relaunch.

Successful brands develop associations over a period of time in a focused manner. A brand like Raymond's started with a benefit association but has since strongly consolidated its association with an emotional proposition. Building a brand differentiator and sustaining it is a major marketing challenge in today's context. Box 19.3 describes how the positioning of *Liril* was developed. Table 19.7 shows some examples in the Indian context.

Table 19.7 Associations of Major Brands

Brand	Association
Titan	Gifting and warmth
Pepsi	Young, vibrant and fun-loving
Close -up	White teeth, freshness and confidence
Pepsodent	Germ fighting action
5-Star	Energy and fun
Bajaj	Value for money
LG	Value through innovative features
Videocon	Bring home the leader
Esteem	The ultimate in luxury

Box -19-3 Liril – The freedom soap

But when you are into mass communication like advertising, say *Liril* Soap, which is within the reach of most Indians, the target group could be anything up to 200 million. Women would be my first target group. But women in small towns don't even go out to jobs. In that case, I must appeal to women who stay at home, doing jobs for their families, cooking, cleaning and scrubbing. The only time they get to themselves is the 10 minutes in the day, when they close the bathroom door to have a bath. So this is the time their imagination is allowed to flower. And one of the best thinking times that you have in the day, is your bath. When water relaxes you and frees your mind, if you allow it, to float around.

What does the Indian housewife daydream about, during the 10 minutes of freedom that she gets? We did some research and we found out that she day dreams about escape – escape from this world of drudgery, where she is working for everyone else. In fact some of them even fantasized and said they dreamt of Amitabh Bachchan – remember I am talking of 25 years ago, when Amitabh was a young man – coming on a white horse and carrying them away. Astounding, because we thought the Indian woman was so traditional!

So, if that is what here secret life was in the bath, then the bath is more than just cleaning herself, it was a time for refreshing herself. It was like going on journey or having a holiday – a 10-minute holiday – and coming out feeling, 'Ah, now I can face all my jobs and responsibilities'. Now how could we help her with a soap? Soap is such a mundane product. It's for lather, for perfume, and so on, and sometimes they have cold cream in a soap. But basically, a soap is a soap is a soap. But no, a soap is not a soap, is not a soap.

I had a marketing director in Hindustan Lever, who was a very down to earth person, but he said one thing I will always remember. He said, 'A bar of soap, is a bar of hope'. In other words, it is not just a practical thing, it has an imaginative avatar. In a sense, soap is a very sensual experience. You rub your body with the lather and it relaxes you, just as a good massage would relax you. With this caressing and this free floating of their thoughts, we thought, now how can we give them the sense of freedom? a sense of being without cares, 'bindaas' (lovely, Hindi filmy word). That was how the idea of the water sprite, or the young girl bathing in the waterfall was born: a Raj Kapoor kind of fantasy. Fantasies sell not just products, but ideas of social change as well. Though *Liril* says it is freshness soap, it is really freedom soap. This was borne out in 1998, when a very big company, a rival of Hindustan Lever, did a survey among housewives in Punjab, asking them what quality they associated with each well-known brand of soap. Lifebuoy, they found, was associated with 'health', Rexona with 'good skin', and Lux with 'glamour'. But when they gave them *Liril,* they did not say 'freshness', they said 'freedom'.

Source: P.N.Thirunarayana (2001) Alyque Padamsee: A Sense of Wonder, *IIMB Management Review,* March, Vol.13, No. 1

NEW PRODUCT FAILURES

New products may fail for several reasons. But some innovative companies created markets by their persistence and intelligent communications with target audience.

(i) Difficult brand name:

A difficult brand name is potentially dangerous, especially in heterogeneous India.

Petit Beurre, the 150 years old brand *in* France, was a biscuit launched by Britannia in 1990. It meant "little butter," The name tripped uneasily over the tongues of both consumers and retailers.

Another food company with another tongue-twisting name was wiser. Initial ads of *alpenliebe* were devoted to saying the name over the over again, in different tones and cadences, till consumers were all trained into pronouncing it correctly.

(ii) When better substitute is available:

The *real value vaccumizer* was supposed to keep *namkeens* fresh. It was a clunky, expensive equipment that sat on the housewife's crowded kitchen counter. It failed because *ziplock* kept *namkeens* fresh just as well.

(iii) When ahead of customer readiness:

Timing is everything. If new product launch is too early, consumers do not see a need for it and if it is too late, the competitor races ahead. If the company is aware that its product is way down on the diffusion curve and will need a huge amount of persuasion to swing over early adopters, then it should have a marketing and distribution plan to influence customers.

Milkfood yoghurt, Burn Philp cake mixes, Maggi Tonite were products that foresaw the move to processed foods, but the introductions were too early.

Indians are not used to flaunt hair in shades of auburn or burgundy. L'oreal convinced them that it was the trendy thing to do. It achieved this feat by taking over the salon market and peppering the media with images of models with streaked hair.

(iv) When customer habits are hard to change:

Reckitt launched dishwasher tablets called *Finish* in 2006.The number of dishwashing machines is minuscule in India even in 2006. In 2000, when dishwasher tablet *calgonit* was launched, the number of dishwashers was abysmally low. So, the potential for *calgonit* dishwashing tablets was an infinitesimal percentage of the detergent market that was used by the tiny percentage of dishwasher users. Nothing fundamental has changed in the Indian market in the last six years. It was not worth launching dishwasher tablets in India even in 2006.

Kellogg had waited more than a decade in India to convert a nation of hot-breakfast eating Indians, to having cold milk on crispy cereals.

In the early 90s, Ariel managers were disturbed with the archaic Indian practice of scrubbing clothes with bars. "Not required, just soaking in the powder would do", they said in an ad, which dramatically showed middle class households chucking unused bars. Yet, the Indian housewife continued to use bars to get rid of the 'ring-around-the-collar,' and P&G had to make a bar to cater to this habit.

(v) When customers feel uneasy about the product:

Amul came up with *Amul slim scoop*, a healthy ice cream with isabgol. Consumers eat ice cream to feel good about themselves. They eat isabgol to create some internal lubrication. Combining the two is unappealing. This cannot be a desirable differentiation. The product died a quiet death.

SUMMARY

Today product obsolescence has become a major threat and opportunity for companies.

They are developing strategies to shorten or lengthen product life-cycles and new product development. As Steve Jobs once pointed out "innovation distinguishes between a follower and a leader." For FMCG companies, innovation is no longer a luxury; it holds the key to survival.

Innovations range from radical new technologies to incremental product modifications- Product line based or changes in customer habits based. There are eight product replacement strategies: face lift, inconspicuous technological substitution, remerchandising, relaunch, conspicuous technological substitution, intangible repositioning, tangible repositioning and neo-innovation.

There are five methods by which the existing product and its immediate environment can be manipulated-subtraction method, multiplication method, division method, task unification method and attribute dependency method. Dynamically continuous innovation falls between the Discontinuous and Continuous innovation. The changes in customer habits caused by this type of innovation are moderate. The helpful methods for this type of innovation are bench-marking and building on old ideas. Best innovators systematically use old ideas as the raw materials for one new idea after another.

Developing countries are ideal locations for disruptive innovation to take place for two reasons- (i) target against non-consumption and (ii) employability of business models in other markets. Today FMCG sector is becoming more innovative delivering new promises and new product variants. On one side innovation is limited to marginal variations in products and on the other customization to meet customer specific demands. New product development process involves seven stages-idea generation, idea screening, idea evaluation, business analysis, product development and testing, market testing and commercialization.

Packaging innovation today is an integral part of making brands stand out in a crowded marketplace, as also in ensuring that products are delivered to consumers in the condition they would like to use them. Positioning by USP places a brand strongly in the mind of the consumer and also creates a strong differentiator, creating a "partition" for the brand among competing brands in the respective category. Successful brands develop associations over a period of time in a focused manner.

New products may fail for several reasons-(i) Difficult brand name, (ii) When better substitute is available, (iii) when ahead of customer readiness, (iv) when customer habits are hard to change and (v) when customers feel uneasy about the product.

QUESTIONS

1. Explain the need for different types of product innovations in FMCG sector and trace the current trends.
2. Describe the technology strategies for innovation and new product development process.
3. Explain the trends in packaging innovations.
4. Examine, how in recent times product positioning is used to gain competitive advantage.
5. Name any two product failures and state the factors influencing the causes for product failures.

EXERCISES

Select a company or product category and collect data on product innovations and obsolescence. Predict new product development possibilities for the company or product category.

CASE : CONSUMER ORIENTED INNOVATIONS

HUL believes that creative application of technology is critical to delight consumers. Most big companies assume that developing products for poor consumers requires less strategic flexibility, less marketing inspiration and less expensive R&D than developing products for rich consumers. Hindustan Unilever has learned that, in fact, the opposite is true. It takes a genuinely creative company that is filled with highly imaginative product developers to reach the poorest of the poor.

Hindustan Unilever's mission is to meet everyday needs for nutrition, hygiene and personal care, with brands that help people feel good, look good and get more out of life. HUL's Research & Development base, one of the largest in Indian industry, helps achieve this mission, with novel products and new processes. The company has over 380 patents, demonstrating its leading edge in consumer-relevant R&D.

The Hindustan Unilever Research Centre (HURC), with facilities in Mumbai and Bangalore and global technology centers in India have over 200 highly qualified scientists and technologists, many with post-doctoral experience acquired in the US and Europe. Set up in 1958, HURC's aim is to develop new products and processes, improving benefits and quality of existing products and optimal use of resources Major innovations have taken place, down the decades, in every category in which HUL is present. From Home Care to Personal care, Beverages to Foods.

Better cleaning, lesser water consumption:

Consider for example, HUL's development of a water-saving technology for its detergents. One of the most severe problems that India faces today is shortage of water. Water scarcity affects one in every three Indians. In a typical Indian home, at least 20% of the water consumed goes behind washing of clothes. HUL decided that it would be of immense benefit to an Indian household, if a technology could be developed, which would help reduce water consumed in washing of clothes. HUL's scientists have innovated a path-breaking technology - it reduces water consumption and time taken for rinsing by 50%. The technology has already been introduced.

World's most advanced water purifier:

People in cities and towns spend enormous amounts, either in fuel or devices, to ensure safe drinking water. HUL's scientists have developed a breakthrough device, called "Pureit", which purifies water as safe as boiled water, providing 100% protection from all water-borne diseases; it also removes pesticides that may be present in drinking water. Its operation does not require electricity, running tap water and plumbing or expensive maintenance. It thus provides water at a cost of just ₹ 1 for every six litres - or less than 20 paise a litre.

Iodine In Salt – the vital ingredient:

Iodine, it is well-known, is important for the mental development of young children. Iodised salt is a well-accepted mode of ensuring appropriate iodine intake. Yet Iodine added to salt is lost in transport, storage as well as in the process of cooking. HUL scientists have developed a patented breakthrough technology to stabilise iodine in salt, following work on the stability of iodine under Indian conditions of storage and cooking. The technology has made it possible to actually realise the purpose of iodised salt that people get appropriate iodine intake through the food they eat.

Skin lightening:

Research in the biology of skin pigmentation has led to the formulation of a product like Fair & Lovely Skin Cream and Lotion. The product has been periodically updated through new patented actives. It has now become a global success through exports to over 30 countries. The product is equally used by the local population of these countries, apart from those of Indian origin.

Hair care:

Consider Indian women and their hair. India is home to 16% of the world's population but also home to 28% of the world's hair, thanks to the long tresses that Indian women maintain throughout their life. In a culture in which many poor women still avoid any appearance of self-indulgence, hair grooming is often their one luxury. Even women with faded saris and little jewellery rarely leave home with a hair out of place.

Which means that women look for unexpected opportunities to care for their hair. This insight led to two product-development strategies. One reinforced a prevailing consumer habit, that of using soap for hair and body wash. Just over half of consumers, especially low-income consumers, use soap to wash both their hair and their body everyday, Unilever's research shows. Rather than fight it, marketers decided to create an opportunity. Two years ago, Hindustan Lever marketers thought of testing a prototype hair soap. But that development still didn't acknowledge the fact that consumers use one soap because it's more convenient and because it costs less.

So came the idea for a low-cost soap that cleans the body and the hair. Product developers spent a year in the lab before finding the right formula. Marketers had already built a strong beauty brand in Breeze, a discount soap. Now marketers could build the Breeze brand even further. The new soap is called Breeze 2-in-1, and distribution is targeted at smaller towns and rural areas. "It's an example of product marketers piecing together insights from the field and stretching their imaginations," says Mukul Deoras, 38, head of the personal-wash business.

It's also an example of how Lever gets consumers to buy higher-quality products, or how it gets them to buy "up the value chain," as company executives say. Deoras acknowledges that this brand may cannibalize users of Unilever's other discount soaps and shampoos. But, he says, "even if there's cannibalization, it's okay. Consumers are buying a value-added product, which is likely to increase loyalty."

The other strategy targeted women who weren't even willing to try shampoo, because they thought that it was too harsh. Marketers decided to tackle the harshness issue head on. An ad campaign showed a straw broom (what happens to hair with soap) alongside soft tresses (the benefits of shampoo). Coupled with this campaign, the company developed a sachet of Lux shampoo. It capitalized on the Lux-soap brand, and it cost less than any other sachet: just 50 paise compared with two rupees. The visual cues and sachet size were so powerful that in the test state of Andhra Pradesh, volume sales of shampoo jumped by 50% in just three months.

It promises to pay-off with more premium products too. A woman named K.M. Bhagilakshmi used to use soap-nut powder, a local crop near her town of Dabospet in the state of Karnataka. "But the dandruff would still be there," she says. After seeing advertisements for Clinic All Clear, Unilever's premium antidandruff shampoo, on the vernacular cable channel, she bought a sachet for 2.50. Now she and her husband buy a sachet (7 milliliters) once a week.

This combination of consumer insight, advertising, and product development is part of Hindustan Unilever's recipe for success in habit building. One-third of India's 60.6 million pounds of shampoo sales in 2000 came from sachets in rural India. Unilever claims 70% of those rural sales. Already half of its $1.02 billion sales in soaps and detergents come from rural markets. The potential to build an even larger market with more regular consumers is mind-boggling — if companies are prepared to do the hard R&D work that is required to deliver on that potential.

New products – New principles:

"We need to apply top-class science and technology in order to solve simple problems for a reduced cost to the consumer," says Dr. V.M. Naik, 53, Deputy head of Hindustan Unilever's Research Laboratory in Bangalore. Naik, who spends about 70% of his time in the lab, is not just refining high-end shampoos. He is the primary scientist behind recent mass-market products such as low-cost ice creams and low-cost soaps. "Technology that liberated consumers before can be a constraint for new innovation," says Naik. "New products require new principles."

Questions"

1. Do you accept the view that HUL is successful in making innovations consumer oriented?
2. What kind of orientation changes, you would consider, necessary for HUL to be the market leader?

Chapter 20

Process Innovations

Learning Objectives

After you have studied this chapter, you will be able to...

- Explain the concept, characteristics and types of processes.
- Know the different process design approaches.
- Appreciate process improvement methods.
- Discuss the emergent innovation methods like BPR, TQC and benchmarking

Structure

- Introduction
- Types of Process Innovations
- Process Improvement
- 5W2H
- Work Simplification
- Kaizen
- Stretch Goal
- Six Sigma
- Business Process Reengineering (BPR)
- Total Quality Management (TQM)
- Benchmarking
- Summary
- Questions
- Exercises
- Case : HUL's Manufacturing Renaissance

INTRODUCTION

Process innovations have changed the course of life of individuals and societies. The printing press, for example, was the start of universal education; Bessemer's steel process provided the world with its most important construction material and gunpowder ended the feudal system of medieval world. The Internet created a global village and the mobile phones made connectivity simple. Since the power of innovation is so great, the support to technological innovation is of strategic importance to any society.

TYPES OF PROCESS INNOVATIONS

Process innovations can be continuous or discontinuous.

The internet itself can be categorized as a discontinuous/radical innovation and a process innovation in specific since it alters the internal operations of a firm, changes their mode of transaction with the various stakeholders-customers and suppliers-and modifies their responses to the market forces-industry and competition.

In marketing in addition to the user role, marketers introduce innovations for the buyer and payer roles as well.

- Mobile phones are innovations for user communication process.
- Debit cards (which have a cash reserve against which a merchant draws the amount for the current purchase) or prepaid phone cards are innovations for the payer role.
- Shopping on the internet or by computer are innovations for the buyer role.

PROCESS IMPROVEMENT

Process management is primarily about the prevention of errors. It provides a foundation for building quality into production by eliminating errors at source. This is a major criterion, covering a great deal of ground. It starts with the conversion of customer requirements into design features and then winds its way through process-quality assessment and control and the quality of support services and suppliers.

Naturally, there are many stops along the way to check for continuous improvement. The principles, tools and techniques for process control can be found in almost any quality control handbook. For many processes, these techniques are quite straightforward and obvious. However, in the case of complex services such as education, healthcare and consulting, whose services are often more complex and often less, amenable to quantitative analysis (and benchmarking) than are manufacturing processes, the path to control becomes less distinct.

Why this disparity? Manufacturing processes are often more measurable. Interaction with customers is a much more predictable affair. The transformation of raw materials is sequential and routinised. In services such as consulting, by contrast, processes constantly fluctuate in response to new information. Can we consider five bad parts per million in advertising, insurance or banking? Nevertheless, it is possible to set up tolerance variables against which to measure the acceptability and quality of a service, even if such measurement is based only on the subjective perceptions of customers (such as customer satisfaction and dissatisfaction).

Improvement should be a proactive task of management in a competitive world. The process improvement has started way back in 1900s when Taylor announced his scientific management principles. One of the principles states: Science, not a rule of thumb. Science is a body of knowledge evolved by inquiry. Process improvement methods and approaches are many and some of them are given below:

5W 2H

Questioning old ways lead to new ideas. The simple approach to questioning is – 5W 2H

What is being done?

Why is this necessary?

Where is it being done?

When is it done?

Who is doing it?

How is it being done?

How much does it cost now?

The question of how can work be simplified, had led a seventeen-year-old Lynn Hunt to window technique in her typing work. Box 20.1 explains the improvement.

Box 20.1 Window technique in typing

Lunn Hunt takes high school commercial courses mornings and works as a typist in downtown Cleveland, Ohio, afternoons. One day, her office manager noticed she was tucking a slip of green paper behind the sandwich of carbon-treated invoices she was rolling into her typewriter. The slip had an odd-shaped window cut in it.When Lynn was finished, the manager picked up the green slip and found an addressed envelope behind it. She smiled. “Beautiful! You can type addresses on the envelopes at the same time as the invoices!”

“Well”, said Lynn Hesitantly, “I... want to keep up.”

“You will.”

Adaptations of the window techniques followed. Sometimes it was a matter of tucking small, odd shapes of carbon paper behind particular spot on the stack of letterheads. Whatever the typing chore, Lynn learned to address the envelopes at the same time she typed the forms and soon became the fastest worker in the office. A small thing, perhaps, but on-the-job inventiveness speeded the entire office’s typing practices and earned her a raise.

WORK SIMPLIFICATION

Work Simplification is defined as the use of equipment, ergonomics, functional planning and behaviour modification to reduce the physical and psychological stresses on the body of activities at home or work. Work simplification techniques range from low-tech (such as using no-scrub cleaners) to high-tech (such as using voice recognition software for typing).

Low tech methods include-Using an automated can opener instead of the manual version, Using pre-pressed clothes that eliminate the need for ironing and Sliding heavy objects or using a wheeled cart to avoid lifting.

Work simplification is achieved by gathering and organizing facts about the work and displaying them so that they can be questioned and improved by knowledgeable people. Improvements include eliminating entire processes or portions of processes that are unnecessary, combining tasks, changing the sequence in which tasks are accomplished, changing the location where they are done, changing the people doing them and changing how they are done.

In a "full" process chart, where all symbols are used, it is common to chart the process from the "viewpoint" of the material being processed, the worker carrying out the work or, less commonly, a piece of equipment. These process charts present processes and make the opportunities for improvement so apparent that changes can actually be made.

The common symbols (of which there are only five) were first promulgated by the American Society of Mechanical Engineers and have become known as the ASME symbols. Figure 20.1 shows the symbols.

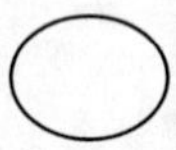	**OPERATION:** A main step, where the part, material or product is usually modified or changed.
	**INSPECTION:** Indicates a check for quality or quantity.
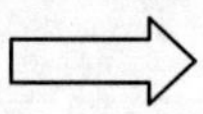	**TRANSPORT:** The movement of workers, materials or equipment.
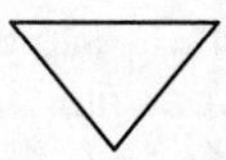	**STORAGE:** Controlled storage in which material is received into or issued from a store or an item is retained for reference purposes.
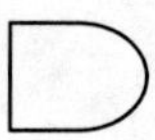	**DELAY or TEMPORARY STORAGE:** Indicates a delay in the process, or an object laid aside until required.

Figure 20.1 Symbols in process chart

KAIZEN

The word Kaizen means "continuous improvement". It comes from the Japanese words ("kai") which means "change" or "to correct" and ("zen") which means "good". Kaizen requires an understanding of operating practices and total involvement of people.

- **Improvement** - The Kaizen philosophy is to "do it better, make it better, and improve it even if it isn't broken, because if we don't, we can't compete with those who do." It focuses on small, gradual and frequent improvements over the long-term with minimum financial investment.
- **Continuous** - Kaizen is a system of continuous improvement in quality, technology, processes, company culture, productivity, safety and leadership.
- **People involvement** - Kaizen is a system that involves every employee - from upper management to the cleaning crew. Everyone is encouraged to come up with small improvement

suggestions on a regular basis. This is not a once a month or once a year activity. It is continuous. Japanese companies, such as Toyota and Canon, a total of 60 to 70 suggestions per employee per year are written down, shared and implemented.

- **Tools** - Quality circles, automation, suggestion systems, just-in-time delivery, Kanban and 5S are all included within the Kaizen system of running a business.

STRETCH GOAL

To inspire results that make an impact, setting S-t-r-e-t-c-h Goals is crucial. Setting Stretch Goals that motivate you and inspire your team to achieve extraordinary results is a worthy but difficult task.

Stretch goals are not used to reach ordinary short-term objectives, but to drive achievement and results to a new level currently viewed as impossible. Stretch goals must cause people to move beyond their current way of thinking. As Einstein said,

"The significant problems we face cannot be solved at the same level of thinking we were at when we created them."

When setting a stretch goal, remember that it must be sufficiently difficult to cause people to think, "We can't accomplish this by doing things the same old way and we are going to have to do things differently." However, the stretch goal can't be so difficult that people give up, thinking the task is absolutely impossible.

Stretch goals provide the following benefits:

- **Achievement** - The more difficult the goal, the greater the sense of achievement.
- **Buck the ordinary** - Setting Stretch Goals causes you and your team to think and act differently. If you don't demand something out of the ordinary, then you will continue to achieve the same results you've always achieved.
- **On Target** - Commitment is highest when you and your team see the goal as important and are convinced that significant progress is possible.
- **Trailblazing** - Setting Stretch Goals means embracing the need for change and a break away from old traditions and habits.
- **Out of the Box** - Setting Stretch Goals causes you to think differently.

Use these components in setting Stretch Goals:

- Are to be both specific and difficult to lead to the breakthrough performance?
- Should be focused on long-term meaningful objectives.
- Should not be too difficult to achieve as to de-motivate yourself and others.
- Must be linked to your overall strategy.
- Must clearly articulate why this goal should be achieved.

SIX SIGMA

Some companies like Motorola use defects per unit as quality measure throughout the company. For instance, the goals are set in different areas as follows:

- Improve product and service quality ten times by the end of next year.
- Improve product and service quality at least 100 times by the end of second year.
- Achieve a culture of continuous improvement to assure customer satisfaction.
- Achieve ultimate goal of zero defects in everything done.

Six Sigma simply means a measure of quality that strives for near perfection in any process-from manufacturing to transactional and from product to service. It aims at eliminating defects in the observed process. Pioneered by GE it got world wide attention.

It is a disciplined, data-driven statistical approach. The statistical representation of Six Sigma describes quantitatively how a process is performing. A Six Sigma defect is defined as anything outside of customer specifications. A Six Sigma opportunity is then the total quantity of chances for a defect. To achieve Six Sigma, a process must not produce more than 3.4 defects per million opportunities.

With the advent of globalization, many companies in India adopted Six Sigma methodologies. Box 20.2 presents how Six Sigma philosophy spread across industries. .

Box 20.2 Wipro and Six Sigma

The quality movement had in fact found its biggest evangelist in GE CEO Jack Welch. Welch himself announced that he was "nuts about" Six Sigma, so sold on it that he encouraged company secretaries to get Six Sigma trained. The joke goes that even the simple task of letter drafting became another project that was put through the rigours of Six Sigma to minimise errors. Of course, once GE reported millions in bottom line benefits through its Six Sigma implementation, it didn't take long for several other large companies, like AlliedSignal and Texaco, to buy the quality dream.

Indian companies, eager to benchmark themselves against global standards, adopted it.. According to Suresh Lulla, founder & director Qimpro, one of the country's first dedicated quality consulting firms, quality tools like Six Sigma are actually rather well-suited to services industries because wherever a process is highly dependent on human interaction, the chances of variability are high.

Wipro was the first to adopt Six Sigma. It was 1995 and Wipro Systems was a relatively small company with a focus on software products and launched its global software and R&D services divisions. Catapulted onto the global market, chairman Azim Premji felt that Wipro needed to upgrade its understanding and practice of quality in order to compete and despatched teams to study methods adopted by Japanese, European and American companies. Finally it was the company's association with General Electric (GE) that nudged it towards Six Sigma, a rigorous methodology that used data and statistical analysis to improve a company's operational performance by identifying and eliminating defects. In 1998, Wipro's Mission Quality journey began. "We decided this was the way we were going to do business in Wipro - the Six Sigma way," said Jagdish Ramaswamy, Chief Quality Officer, Wipro.

BUSINESS PROCESS REENGINEERING (BPR)

The term is also known as "Process re-engineering": Business Process Redesign (BPR) is the study, analysis and redesign of fundamental business processes to reduce costs and/or improve value added to the business. Clearly BPR is an on-going process critical to an organization's succession competitive market place.

Improving business processes is paramount for businesses to stay competitive in today's marketplace. Here are some arguments to justify the view.

- Over the last 10 to 15 years companies have been forced to improve their business processes because we, as customers, are demanding better and better products and services. And if we do not receive what we want from one supplier, we have many others to choose from.
- New technologies (like the internet) are rapidly bringing new capabilities to businesses, thereby raising the competitive bar and the need to improve business processes dramatically.
- Another apparent trend is the opening of world markets and increased trade. Such changes bring more companies into the marketplace and competing becomes harder and harder.
- In today's marketplace, major changes are required to just stay even. It has become a matter of survival for most companies. Moreover, companies want breakthrough performance changes, not just incremental changes and they want it now.

As a result, companies have sought out methods for faster business process improvement.

Many companies have benefited by the process of reengineering. There is saving of time, effort and money along with increased efficiency. Box 20.3 explains the case of IBM credit corporation.

Box 20.3 BPR of IBM Credit Corporation

IBM Credit Corporation cut the process of financing IBM computers, software and services from seven days to four hours by rethinking the process. Originally, the process was designed to handle difficult applications and required four highly trained specialists and a series of hand offs. The actual work took only 1 to 5 hours; the rest of the time was spent in transit or delay. By questioning the assumption that every application was unique and difficult to process, IBM Credit Corporation was able to replace the specialists by a single individual supported by a user friendly, computer system that provided access to all the data and tools that the specialists would use.

Steps in reengineering:

Figure 20.2 presents one view of process reengineering. The focus is mostly on customer and value addition to the customer. Viewing the material transformation process in terms of those activities tied to transforming material into something of value to the customer is a process view. Such a view examines inventory in terms of customer value, not internal economies.

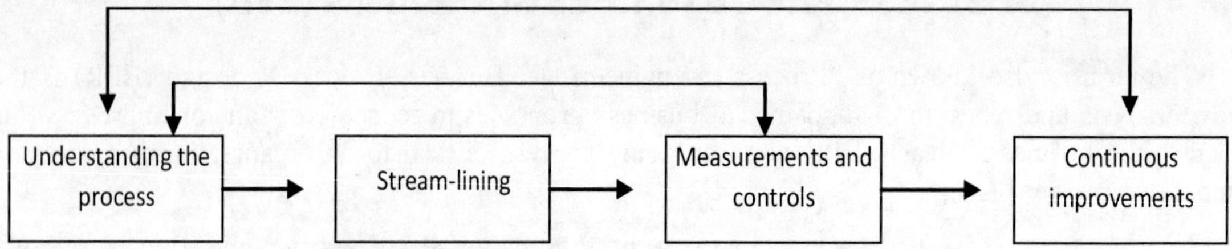

Figure 20.2 A view of process reengineering

Source: Michael J. Stahl, "*Total Quality Management in the Global Environment*", First Indian Edition 2000, Infinity Books, p. 503.

Essential requirements:

Reengineering requires focusing on critical processes, often using cross-functional teams, information technology, leadership and process analysis. These are explained in the following paragraphs:

Critical processes - The emphasis of reengineering should be on core business processes, rather than functional departments such as purchasing or marketing. By focusing on core processes, managers may spot opportunities to eliminate unnecessary work and supervisory activities. Reengineering should be reassured for essential processes, such as new product development or customer services because of the time and energy involved.

Bell Atlantic, for example, reengineering processes. After five years of sustained effort, it cut the time to connect new customers from 16 days to just few hours. The changes caused Bell Atlantic to lay off 20,000 employees, but the company has become decidedly more competitive.

Strong leadership - Senior executives must provide strong leadership for reengineering to be successful. Otherwise cynicism, resistance ("we tried that before") and boundaries between functional areas can block radical changes. Managers can help overcome resistance by providing the clout necessary to ensure that the project proceeds within a strategic context. Executives should set and monitor key performance objectives for the process. Top management should also create a sense of urgency, making a case for change that is compelling and constantly refreshed.

Cross-functional teams - A team consisting of members from each functional area affected by the process is charged with carrying out a reengineering project. Reengineering works best at high-involvement work places, where self-managing teams and employee empowerment are the rule rather than exception. Top-down and bottom-up initiatives can be combined – the top-down for performance targets and the bottom-up for deciding how to achieve the targets.

Information technology - Information technology is a primary enabler of process reengineering. Most reengineering projects design processes around information flows such as customer order fulfillment. The "process owners" who will actually be responding to events in the market place need information network and computer technology to be more effective in their jobs. The reengineering team must think through and find answers to questions: who needs the information, when they need it and where.

Clean slate philosophy - Reengineering requires a "clean slate philosophy" that is starting with the way the customer wants to deal with the company to ensure a customer orientation, teams begin with internal and external customer objectives for the process. Teams often first establish a price target for the product or service, deduct profits desired and then find a process that provides what the customer wants at the price the customer will pay. Reengineers start from the future and work backward, unconstrained by current approaches.

Process analysis - Despite the clean slate philosophy, a reengineering team must understand things about the current process: what it does, how well it performs and what factors affect it. Such an understanding can reveal areas in which new thinking will provide the biggest pay-off. The team must work at every procedure involved in the process throughout the organization recording each step, questioning why it is done and then eliminating it if it isn't really necessary. Information on standing relative to competition process by process is also valuable.

TOTAL QUALITY MANAGEMENT (TQM)

The 'Total' part of TQM emphasizes that it is an all-round excellence effort and is not about one aspect of the company. The 'Quality' part of TQM emphasizes upon not only quality product but also quality services. Quality is operationally defined under TQM as meeting or exceeding customer's expectations. The 'management' part of TQM implies that, this is a management approach, not just a narrow quality control or quality assurance function.

The techniques of TQM include, Kaizen, Stretch goals, Six Sigma, 5S and others.

5S – It describes a workplace organization method (five words that begin with S–Sorting, Straightening or Set in order, Shining, Standardising and Sustaining) in which the worker is continually making their workstation efficient by ensuring its cleanliness, order and standardization.

Implementation of all these TQM techniques and the accompanying changes in the organizational structure and processes bring large-scale transformation in an organization. A comparative picture of the nature of work organizations before and after TQM implementation is presented in Table 20.1

Table 20.1 Work Organizations-Before and After TQM

Focus/Processes	Before TQM	After TQM
1. Business goal	Increased production and profitability	Customer orientation, improving quality and reducing cost.
2. Definition of quality	Conformance to "customers' requirements"	Achieving "customers' delight and exceeding 'customers' expectations"
3. Major constituencies	Customers (external), employees, entrepreneurs, stakeholders	Customers (both external & internal), stakeholders, entrepreneurs, employees and suppliers
4. Quality plan	Quality planning for inspection and testing	Strategic quality planning and objective
5. Quality design	Design to meet customers' requirements-in terms of cost, quality and reliability	Design for robustness and customer satisfaction

Focus/Processes	Before TQM	After TQM
6. Quality responsibility	Responsibility of quality specialist	Responsibility of all-may be done by using the design of experiments, concurrent engineering, re-engineering techniques etc.
7. Role of Management	Formal authority and top-down	Participative and informal
8. Role of employees	Emphasis on work related targets and less involvement in improvement	Team-based work and total employee involvement in production and quality
9. Organization structure	Mechanistic, hierarchical & tight structure	Organic, lateral/flattered and flexible structure
10. Nature of interpersonal relationship	Competitive (win-loss)	Collaborative (win-win)

BENCHMARKING

Benchmarking means measuring one's performance against that of one's competitors.

Two simple definitions of benchmarking are:

Benchmarking is the continuous process of measuring products and services against the toughest competitors or those companies recognized as industry leaders.

Benchmarking is the search for industry best practices that lead to superior performance.

Importance - Competitive benchmarking is gaining importance in the light of increasing global competition. Setting one's priorities and being certain that those priorities are consistent with the needs of the market place are essential. The top five competitive priorities in Europe, Japan and the United States, in 1992 were as given in Table 20.2.

Table 20.2 Competitive priorities

Priority	Europe	Japan	United States
1	Conformance quality	Product reliability	Conformance quality
2	On-time delivery	On-time delivery	On-time delivery
3	Product reliability	Fast-design change	Product reliability
4	Performance quality	Conformance quality	Performance quality
5	Delivery speed	Product customization	Price

Benchmarking is to ensure continuous improvement and is only one of the means of achieving this. Competitive benchmarking provides a means of learning from one's competitors.

Types of benchmarking - Analysts have observed four types of benchmarking.

- **Product benchmarking** - refers to the practice of tearing down a competitor's product to see what can be learnt from its design and construction (also known as Reverse Engineering).

- **Functional benchmarking** – Focuses on the process rather than on the product. Typical processes might be order entry, assembly, test, product development and shipping.
- **Best practice benchmarking** – Is similar to functional benchmarking except that it focuses on management practice rather than on specific processes. Best practices might consider factors such as the work environment and salary incentives for employees in firms with exceptional performance.
- **Strategic benchmarking** – Has a goal of considering the result of other benchmarking comparisons in the light of the strategic focus of the firm.

Phases in benchmarking – The steps involved in bench marking can be stated under four distinct phases as given below:

(i) Planning phase:

(a) Identify, what is to be benchmarked – which process? Why?

(b) Identify comparable companies – the local competitor or the leader or the industry best globally.

(c) Determine data collection methods – On-site observation or survey or secondary data collection methods.

(d) Collect data – decide data presentation and analysis techniques (flow-charts, tree diagrams, graphs, tables etc.

(ii) Analysis phase:

(a) Determine the current performance "gap" – analyze data to compare actual with standards.

(b) Project future performance levels – identifies the desired levels of performance of your company in future.

(iii) Integration phase:

(a) Communicate benchmark findings and gain acceptance from top management and people concerned.

(b) Establish functional goals – for accomplishment by concerned staff without ambiguity.

(iv) Action phase:

(a) Develop action plans – prepare schedules, budgets and procedures for implementation.

(b) Implement specific actions – assigns tasks and supervises. Get feedback from-to-time.

(c) Monitor progress – keep an eye on targets and achievements. If necessary chase the progress.

(d) Recalibrate benchmarks – Based on experience revise benchmarks. For this obviously return to phase 1, step 1.and repeat the exercise.

Focus and guidelines:

The focus of benchmarking is generally narrow addressing particular process in an organization. Table 20.3 below provides guidelines.

Table 20.3 Guidelines to Benchmarking

Type	Focus	Team	Info Guidelines
Product	Dissecting the products	Designers, engineers and supervisors	Secondary data sources or surveys
Process	Manufacturing	Engineers, supervisors and specialists	On-site observations
Best practices	Management	Management staff	All sources
Strategic	Management	Top management	Selective sources. Rarely on-site observation.

Illustration of bench marking

Dawn Iacobucci and Christie Nordhielm developed a flow chart shown in Figure 19-3, which shows the steps involved in booking and occupying a hotel room. As the chart makes clear, an astute hotel manager will look far beyond the hospitality industry for models of excellence to emulate.

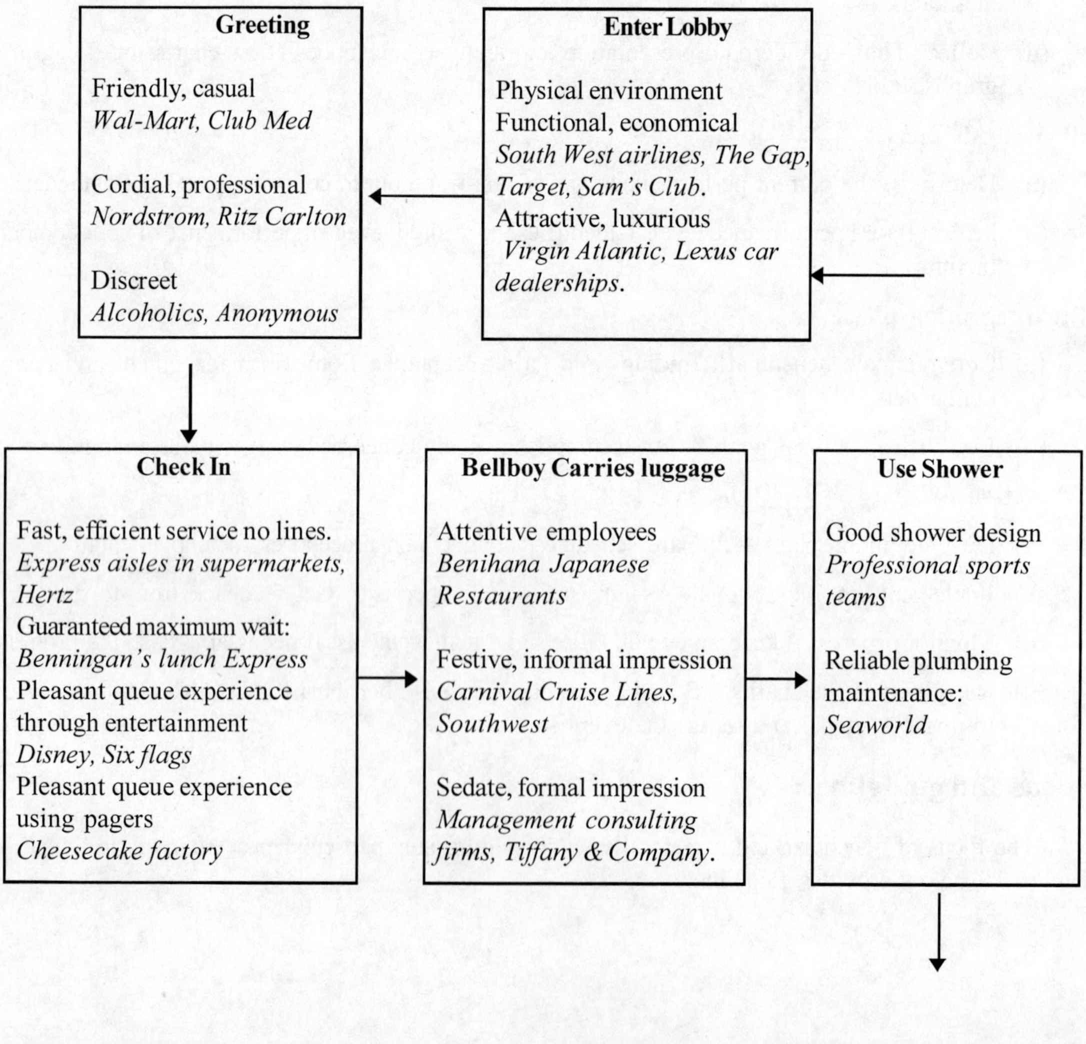

Get Advice on Restaurants

Intelligent agents who know restaurants
Electronic agents. Yahoo!

Employees
Travel agents

Agents who know their customers
Nordstrom

→

Breakfast

Room service food arrives promptly, at appropriate temperature: *delivery pizzerias*

Courteous delivery personnel:
UPS

→

Check-Out

Quick, seamless departure
TV checkout software:
Sega children's games, intuit's Turbo Tax

↓

Choose Hotel

Awareness and familiarity recall
Mc Donald's Pepsi
Competitive advantage price
Crown Books, Gateway computers, Old Navy
Quality:
Barnes & Nable, Nerman Marcus, Hewlett-Packard

→

Make Reservation

Availability, yield management
Airlines, Wal Mart

Flexible pricing
Priceline sprint
Telephone customer service
Coca-cola, FritoLay
On line access
EBay, Amazon, American greetings.com

→

Travel to Hotel

Easy access send map with confirmation:
Hertz airport kiosks, MapQuest.com
Convenient site location:
Interstate gas stations, *McDonald's*
Access any time of day
On-line banking, 7 eleven, Taco Bell

↓

Look Around room

Nice ambience
Set designers: Hollywood, Broadway retail: Crate & Barel, IKEA systems

Plush surroundings,
generous amenities resorts and health spas

Minimalist environment
Harvard college dormitories monastery retreats

Top security
Secret service, banks, jewellery stores, shopping malls.

→

Require Assistance of a Hotel Employee

Quick attention to minor problems
On star cellular One Coca-cola's 800 numbers, Xerox.

Quick attention to major problems
Hospital emergency rooms, Johnson & Johnson (e.g. Tylenol)

Customized, tailored service
Amazan, Nordstrom

→

Call Home

Fast, friendly hotel-operator assistance
Lands End 800 number

Smooth call-center management
911, Home shopping Network, infomercials.

↓

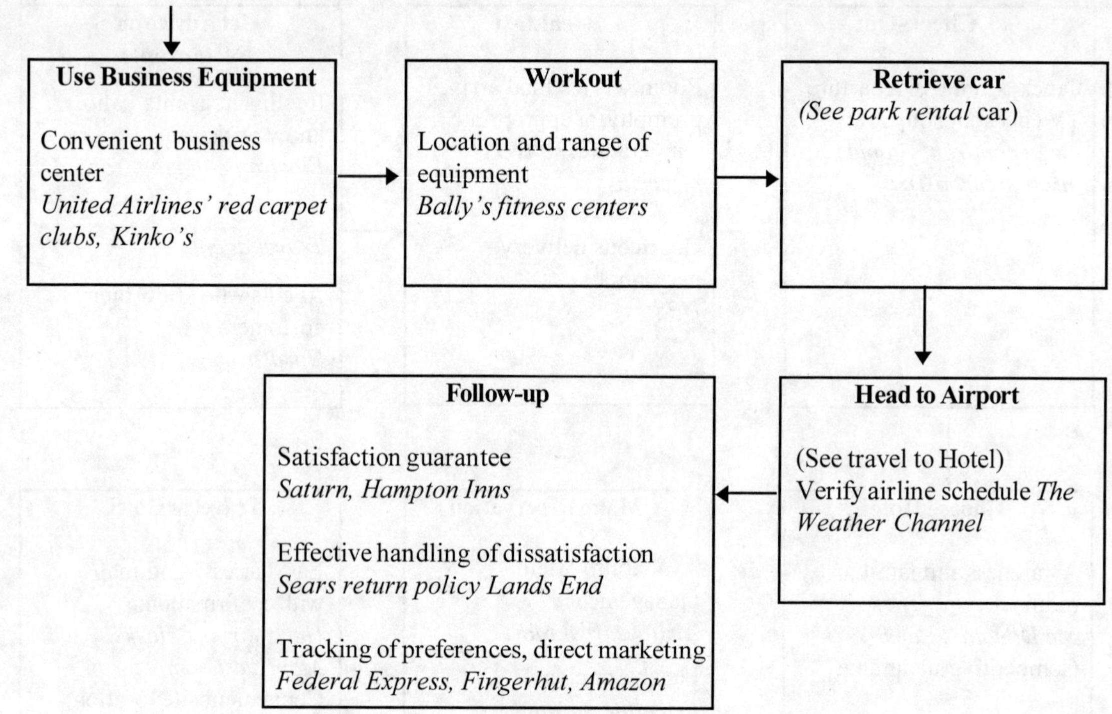

SUMMARY

Process innovations can be continuous and discontinuous. Process improvement methods include: 5W 2H,Work simplification, Kaizen, Stretch goal, Six sigma,BPR, TQM and benchmarking.

QUESTIONS

1. Explain the concept of process. What are the approaches to new process design?
2. Discuss the use of design tools like 5W 2H,work simplification and Kaizen.
3. What is Six Sigma approach? How does it improve quality?
4. Elaborate the process of business process reengineering.
5. With the help of cases, explain the application of TQM.
6. What do you understand by benchmarking? Give an illustration.

EXERCISES

Take a service or production process of your choice and redesign it with improvements for more efficiency and effectiveness. Use presentation diagrams and logical thinking methods.

CASE : HUL'S MANUFACTURING RENAISSANCE

Ever since the mid-1990s, the ₹ 11,000 crore FMCG juggernaut has been moving relentlessly forward to squeeze out costs from every possible area. Once seen as the breeding ground for union troublemakers, Hindustan Unil manufacturing locations have become laboratories for worker empowerment, innovation and cost efficiency. How?

TPM concept:

The answer lies in three letters: T-P-M. That's shorthand for total productive maintenance, a concept pioneered by the Japan Institute of Plan Maintenance (JIPM), Tokyo, for operational excellence. What TPM does is help companies achieve high levels of productivity by developing self-managing abilities in workers and managers, which, in turn, improves skills and work practices. In the process, companies can benefit by cutting costs and raising production simultaneously. Gurdeep Singh, director (HR and Technology) of Hindustan Unil Ltd (HUL) and a TPM enthusiast, puts the benefits simply. "TPM", he says, "is the only business initiative where our returns have been eight to 12 times investment." The reason why this happens is explained succinctly by Singh. Before TPM, the worker was seen as having just a pair of hands. After TPM, he acquires a head as well. He can think creatively.

TPM' s 8 PILLARS
Autonomous
Kobetsu-Kaizen
Planned maintenance
Quality maintenance
Development management
Education & training
Safety, health & environment
TPM in offices

Organization:

On the factory floor, says Vikram Agarwal, General factory manager at HUL's Daman and Silvassa units, every worker belongs to at least one TPM circle. In the Silvassa detergents factory, for example, there are around 20 circles, each with its own distinct identity and name ("Panther" circle, for example). Each circle has a leader, usually an officer of HUL. At the next level are the pillar heads, usually managers, focusing on the "eight pillars of TPM" (which deal with issues such as "autonomous" maintenance, quality, education and training and office TPM). Above this we have a group comprising the technical heads of HUL, the corporate quality assurance and TPM head and factory managers. At the apex is the corporate TPM steering committee headed by the HR director. While the factory level circles meet weekly (usually twice), pillar heads meet monthly and corporate-level meetings review progress once a quarter.

Training:

Mentoring and training permeate all activities in a TPM initiative. Says Uttam Chatterjee: "The officer (heading a pillar) is a coach to an extent. When he does autonomous maintenance (the first of TPM's eight pillars) along with workers in his area, if he finds abnormalities he has to tag it and come up with one-point lessons (kaizens). These lessons are initially written by circle leaders. The lessons are 20-seconders which explain why something is right, wrong and the know-why. In course of time, the officers encourage others to write such one-point lessons and the writers become teachers."

Change approach:

If all this suggests that TPM at HUL is a bottom-up or middle-up approach, one is wide-off the mark. Given the usual mistrust between Unions and Management, HUL does not waste too much time trying to convince everybody about the utility of TPM even though it is the worker who benefits most from the additional safety of machine operations, reduction of physical effort and improved opportunities to learn new skills. In the initial days, the unions typically saw TPM as another bargaining lever. What will you give us if we agree to raise productivity by so-and-so amount?

HUL sidesteps all attempts to links TPM to wage settlements and bargaining by asking managers to take the leadership role in initiating new practices. As dictated by JIPM norms, they first identify the model lines and machines, which need improvement. At this stage, says Chatterjee, "your achieve results through managers; you don't take help form workers. That cuts down all the discussions and ensuing problems. Then we start implementing the training programme. After seeing visible changes in the model lines, some workers start joining those groups. Others are also willing to start the process in their line. That's a demand pool created. The people start reinforcing this when they see the capability and creativity of a worker stretched by this tool (TPM) which he enjoys."

Modified JIPM Model:

While HUL works within the framework prescribed by JIPM while implementing TPM in its factories, it has also made innovations on its own to adapt to local conditions. Broadly speaking, any manufacturing unit has to go through two phases to implement TPM – the preparatory phase and an implementation phase. The two are punctuated in-between with a "kickoff" ceremony. However, the word "preparatory" is a bit of misnomer. For, a substantial bit of implementation actually begins even in the preparatory phase. Chatterjee, in fact, lists at least 21 steps that a factory needs to take before kickoff. These include items like clearing an annual budget, awareness training, communication with employees and unions, creation of a TPM organization and secretariat, initiation of 'autonomous' maintenance on model machines by managers, documentation of improvements made during the preperatory phase and achieving significant results in terms of loss reductions. To make sure that factories don't treat TPM lightly, they are barred from kickoff unless they are able to show a minimum 30 per cent improvement in Operating Equipment Efficiency (OEE). One major area where HUL has stumped its JPM auditors is by shortening the implementation time for achieving the excellence award.

Knowledge management:

The reason why HUL is able to implement TPM faster is that it now has its own pool of around 70-and-odd TPM instructors who are effectively in-house consultants. In fact, one of the Japanese auditors visiting an HUL factory is reported to have remarked that the company has effectively "created a TPM University". It is this in-house pool that enables HUL to make intelligent deviations from the JIPM norm to suit its factory conditions.

Five geographical hubs have been created in five regions covering 25 strategic sites, with each hub having a lead factory with considerable TPM experience and one facilitator. Quarterly meetings are held in various regional factories to make sure that learning experiences and kaizens of one factory are quickly transferred to another.

Says Chatterjee: "We have set up a website where the design changes (kaizens, etc) are available. As a result, to some extent we are unfair to those factories, which developed those kaizens. The Japanese say that it is not a question of stealing with pride. It becomes a crime if you don't replicate it (good practice). Very recently, we set up seven-eight knowledge management teams (equipment-wise). For example, for the form-fill-seal machines used in Chhindwara, Rajpura and Mangalore, we picked one guy from each factory to form a KM team to replicate fast. We want to eliminate time lapses in replicating a good development and to standardize it."

Achievements:

As things stand today, HUL has four units, which have already received the JIPM Excellence Awards – Sumerpur, Chhindwara, Yavatmal (personal products) and Silvassa (personal products). Sumerpur, which provided HUL with its first learning in TPM, is now poised to move one step ahead to the Consistency Award in level one. When Sumerpur in Uttar Pradesh was first chosen by Unilever as a TPM candidate in 1994, it didn't appear as though the management was throwing its full weight behind the proposed transformation. The net result was slow learning: Sumerpur took five years from the time it started dabbling with TPM to its first excellence award. But the next three factories – Chhindwara, Yavatmal (PP) and Silvassa (PP) managed it in four years or less. The future hopefuls may do it in three years or even two.

Enthused with the business results achieved so far, the HUL management decided in August 1999 that TPM would be implemented at all strategic sites, and all new factories. Some 30 factories of HUL including Unilever factories in the region are at various stages in rolling out TPM.

What is clear is the accelerating nature of the rollout? This is likely to happen for three reasons.

- Total top management commitment. Something that was lacking when Sumerpur experiment started.
- The last eight years have helped HUL create over 70 trained TPM instructors, enabling it to operate a virtual "university" on TPM.
- Institutionalizing knowledge management in TPM. To speed up the process of TPM implementation in the organization, a TPM Community Of Practice (COP) was set up in June 2000.

The TPM movement is also being extended to other parts of the supply chain. Some of HUL's suppliers who want to cater to Unilever factories worldwide see TPM as the way to gain recognition as quality suppliers. Quite clearly, the TPM movement at HUL and its extend supply chain is spreading like a virus. As factories within HUL compete internally to outdo one another on kizens and efficiency improvements, employees are being driven to higher levels of motivation and creativity. When last heard of, workers at Sumerpur were busy downloading quick machine changeover tips from a nearby cyber café. That should offer one clue on which way HUL's shop floor revolution is heading.

Questions:

1. Explain the concept of TPM and its application in HUL.
2. From the success story of HUL, what lessons do you draw for other organizations?

Source: Prasad Sangameswaran and R. Jagannatham, HUL' s Manufacturing Renaissance, *Indian Management*, Vol. 41; No. 8, pp. 30-43.

Chapter 21

Innovation Diffusion

Learning Objectives

After you have studied this chapter, you will be able to...

- Explain the concept of innovation diffusion and impact of innovation
- Understand diffusion as an integral of innovation strategy
- Identify the different diffusion types
- Describe innovation diffusion theory and factors influencing diffusion
- Know the characteristics of innovation adopters and role of opinion leaders
- Discuss, how individuals and organizations and countries adopt innovations.

Structure

- Introduction
- Concepts
- Diffusion Orientation in Innovation
- Innovation Diffusion Theory
- Factors Influencing Diffusion
- Attributes of Innovation
- Characteristics of Adopters
- Consumer Adoption Process
- Role of Opinion Leaders
- Marketing Strategies
- Innovation Adoption by Organizations
- Summary
- Questions
- Exercises
- Case : Innovation Adoption

INTRODUCTION

Innovations are an essential element of the dynamic societies and modern organizations across the world. It is the critical activity of R&D institutions, innovative groups and marketers. As new and better products or processes are developed, they are launched in the market place and the users through their purchase or rejection of them determine their fate. Since innovations are becoming expensive and their chances of success are becoming slim over the years due to heavy competition, it is important to know the nature of innovation adoption and the strategies of innovation diffusion.

CONCEPTS

It is a process through which an innovation spreads throughout a social system overtime. It involves special types of communication methods or system to help diffuse changes in practice, as well as changes in knowledge or attitudes. Thus, diffusion is the process of closing the gap between what people do not know and what they can effectively put to use. The process is complete when:

- A sufficient number of customers are using the innovation to pay back the amount used to develop it.
- It starts to make a profit.
- A system is in place for assessing the need for changes to ensure the longevity of the technology.

Customer response to these new products and services is referred to as innovation adoption. It may be defined as the set of successive decisions an individual person or organization makes before accepting an innovation.

The internet has grown much faster than previous media innovations like telephone, television, radio and the cable, Morgan Stanley Dean Witter Technical Research states that it has taken radio 38 years to reach 50 million users; television, 13 years; cable, 10 years and the Internet just 5 years.

The diffusion process refers to the spreading of an innovation's acceptance and use through a population.

DIFFUSION ORIENTATION IN INNOVATION

Innovation is to be viewed as an integral part of the innovation process, rather than a discrete activity that takes place after the development of the technological innovation as shown in Table 21.1. The benefit of such orientation is significant.

- **A longer life** - Is certain if the innovation meets a well-defined customer need that the seller understands. The seller must remain aware of any changes in customer needs and modifications that would meet those changing needs.
- **Renewal of the technological innovation** - Diffusion cycle requires a continuous program for reassessing the needs of customers, competitive and regulatory threats, opportunities to serve industries that have not been served and imaginative tailoring of the technology to meet new needs.

Table 21.1 Innovation Process with Diffusion

Process steps	Tasks	Diffusion perspective
Preparation	Top management establishes innovation climate of expectations and responsibilities.	Identification of unfulfilled needs in society.
	Defining problem in terms of ideas and research projects.	Imagination on products and services.
Saturation	Collects complete information on various aspects.	Potential of existing technologies and new directions for research.
Deliberation	Examining ideas available and generating new ideas.	Open market innovations. Ideas from consumers, suppliers and retailers.
Incubation	Carrying unconscious and involuntary work on the problem.	-
Illumination	Striking at an idea unexpectedly.	-
Verification	Examining real life application of the idea.	Prototypes. Consumer tests. Test marketing.
Development	Full scale development of product. Lab to world.	Linking the basic scientist's work to the applied scientist's work and the world outside the laboratory Improving the linkage between R&D and marketing.
Communication	Positioning to make Unique Selling Proposition clear. Developing communication strategy.	Highlight benefits to consumer. Also inform precautions in using the product.
Launching	Place the market in retail outlets.	Feed-back. Word-of-mouth advertising.

How can the consumers be involved in different stages of innovation development?

Creativity stages:

During this phase problem definition can be done with the help of market research. Potential consumers can be involved in giving their ideas for creating new products or services. In the verification stage, either the concept or prototype can be tested involving a panel of potential users or through displays in exhibitions or select retail outlets.

Development stage:

Diffusion at development stage involves linking the basic scientist's work to the applied scientist's work and the world outside the laboratory through the comprehensive diffusion perspective. Applied scientists have a responsibility to keep abreast of consumer problems that need solution. Basic scientists need to describe their findings in ways that allow applied scientists and marketing people to visualize market possibilities. Many successful basic research scientists take the opportunity to visit the field to see what is going on.

Improving the linkage between R&D and marketing is highly related to successful – continuous and timely-diffusion efforts. Lack of communication can cause many problems.

An inventive scientist may develop a new way of making bricks and constructing houses from the fly ash of thermal plants, but may not get feedback about the market's acceptance of the idea. The lack of feedback may cause him even to leave the company and abandon his idea.

Communication stage:

Prelaunch activity marks the beginning of this stage as a small-scale pilot test gets under way and the first customer trials begin. The next major activity is the launch of the innovation trails. During such trails, the organization can assess technology acceptance, alter methods of transfer, check manuals for ease of understanding and the like.

Communication activities are the next major events. The marketing department develops a description of the attributes of the new technology, selects channels for its marketing message, and begins development of a promotional program. Marketing next assesses the target market segment to identify the potential adopters that should be influenced first.

Launching stage:

This is the last stage of a comprehensive innovation/diffusion process. It includes a search for a wider range of potential markets, new industries new geographic regions, new market segments that have not been explored and new ways to couple the innovation with other innovations.

The way that electronics and computers have diffused throughout the industry and the world is a prime example of full -scale diffusion.

INNOVATION DIFFUSION THEORY

Some inventions 'take the world by storm' (archetype: the Sony Walkman). Others seem to fail, lie dormant for decades, but when 'their time has come', their use grows quickly, even explosively (archetype: the fax machine). Most achieve slow penetration at first, then their adoption grows more quickly, but later slows down again.

A broad social psychological / sociological theory called Diffusion Of Innovations (DOI) explained by Rogers (1962) describes the patterns of adoption. We will discuss its major tenets.

Diffusion Process:

The diffusion process is the manner in which innovations spread throughout a market. The term spread refers to purchase behavior in which the product is purchased with some degree of regularity. The market can range from virtually the entire society (for a new soft drink, perhaps) to the students at a particular high school (for an automated fast-food and snack outlet). For most innovations, the diffusion process appears to follow a similar pattern over-time; a period of relatively slow growth, followed by a period of rapid growth, followed by a final period of slower growth. This pattern is shown in Figure 21.1. However, there are exceptions to this pattern.

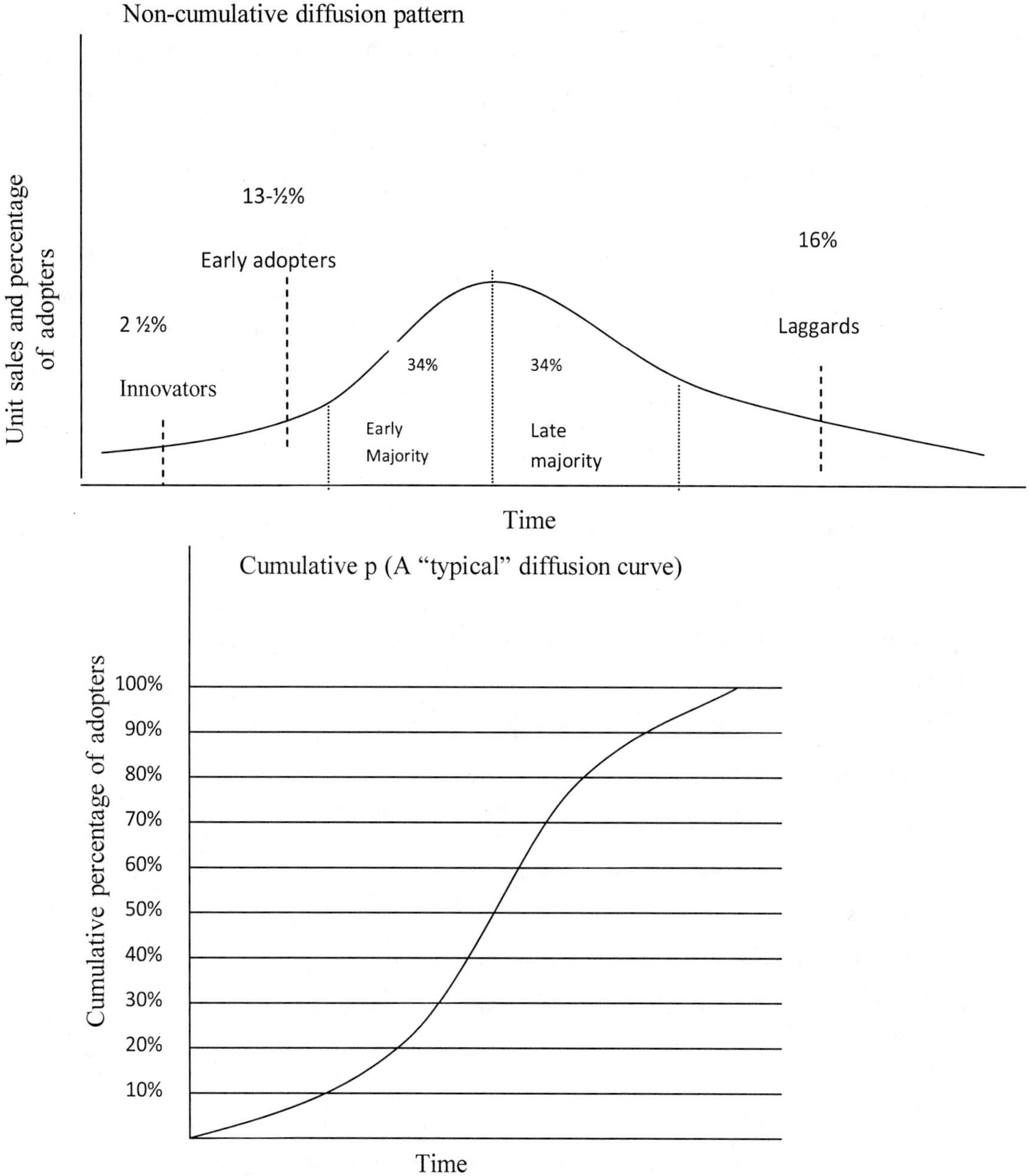

Figure 21.1 The diffusion process

Adopter categories:

Different adopter categories are identified as given under:

- **Innovators** (venturesome) – Innovators (2.5%) are the first to buy a new product. These people are venturesome, willing to be daring and different.

- **Early adopters** (Respectable) – Early adopters (13.5%) closely follow innovators are somewhat less adventurous. Many characteristics of the innovator group are also found among them.
- **Early majority** (Deliberate) – They (34%) deliberate on innovation and consider innovation some time before adopting. They legitimize new ideas for others.
- **Late majority** (Skeptical) – They (34%) yield only because of economic necessity or social pressures.
- **Laggards** (Traditional) – Laggards (16%) make up the last group to adopt a product.
- **Non-adopters** (Indifferent) – No matter what the innovation, there are always some individuals among laggards who never buy the new product or adopt the new style. These people are known as non- adopters.

Important roles in the innovation process include:

- **Opinion leaders** - who have relatively, frequent informal influence over the behavior of others.
- **Change agents** - who positively influence innovation decisions, by mediating between the change agency and the Relevant social system.
- **Change aide** - who complement the change agent, by having more intensive contact with clients, and who have less competence credibility but more safety or trustworthiness credibility.

The change agent functions are:

- To develop a need for change on the part of the client;
- To establish an information-exchange relationship;
- To diagnose the client problems;
- To create intent to change in the client;
- To translate this intent into action;
- To stabilize adoption and prevent discontinuance;
- To shift the client from reliance on the change agent to self-reliance.

Stages:

The stages through which a technological innovation passes are:

- **Knowledge** (exposure to its existence and understanding of its functions);
- **Persuasion** (the forming of a favorable attitude to it);
- **Decision** (commitment to its adoption);
- **Implementation** (putting it to use);
- **Confirmation** (reinforcement based on positive outcomes from it).

Early knowers generally are more highly educated, have higher social status, are more open to both mass media and interpersonal channels of communication and have more contact with change agents. Mass media channels are relatively more important at the knowledge stage, whereas interpersonal channels are relatively more important at the persuasion stage.

Innovation decisions may be classified as given under:

- **Optional** – where the person or organization has a real opportunity to adopt or reject the idea.
- **Collective** – where a decision is reached by consensus among the members of a system.
- **Authority-based** – where a decision is imposed by another person or organization, which possesses requisite power, status or technical expertise.

FACTORS INFLUENCING DIFFUSION

Developing diffusion strategy involves a number of activities and many people.

Organizational climate:

An important factor related to successful diffusion is an organizational climate that supports diffusion and innovation objectives.

Studies of successful diffusion show that one of the most consistent features is the presence of dedicated people who persist in their efforts. Such people are called "*technology champions*" or "*change agents*".

Next is the climate. Organizations with flat, organic structures and participative style of decision-making are more supportive of innovation and diffusion of innovations.

Technology Champion:

Within the organization the change agent should provide communications between the Marketing and the R&D organization. In market driven organizations, the main directions for technological innovation come from marketing. R&D's reaction comes in the form of guidance on what is technically feasible and ideas from scientific circles.

A technology driven organization offer a market contrast, as R&D drives the stimulus and marketing officials must find applications. These efforts can help create new markets by applying technological breakthrough to largely unperceived needs.

When introducing a new technology to potential customers outside the organization the change agent must explain the need for the technology. Demonstrations, films, or other techniques can help the customer to become aware of the need for the new technology. The change agent must show real interest in the user's problems and prove it in his or her behavior.

Opinion Leaders:

Opinion leaders influence opinions and actions in informal ways. They are people or institutions whose information and opinions are sought on subjects in which they are considered experts. They are technology gatekeepers and feel qualified to evaluate a technology and market gatekeepers who feel qualified to describe what people want to buy.

A good example is the position that various individuals and organization took towards C-DOT's switching technology.

Communication Strategy:

Developing a communication strategy is one of the major tasks of the diffusion process. To achieve successful communication, the organization must relate the innovation's attributes to customer needs. The company's message must also prove its reputation for reliability, honesty and thoughtfulness about the innovation.

For example, Motorola, a US based semiconductor and communication company to introduce cellular technology in India, advertised extensively in the media portraying it as a technology for development of rural India.

Attributes of the Innovation:

It is widely recognized that five general attributes of innovations are useful in preparing messages: (i) relative advantage, (ii) compatibility, (iii) complexity, (iv) testability (trialability), (v) visibility (observability) and (vi) cost. To convey these attributes to potential adopters, the change agent must discover what the customer seeks, thinks and feels.

Diffusion types:

Different types of innovations require different diffusion efforts.

- **Breakthrough innovation** - If the technology is new to both the market and the company, adopters of the technology have to be educated on its use. Diffusion efforts may have to overcome resistance to the complexity of the technology (as with fibre optics) or social or cultural barriers (birth control devices).
- **Improvements** - In contrast, if the technology is a modification or improvement of an existing technology (Example: energy saving process), diffusion efforts must stress the superior attributes of the new technology

ATTRIBUTES OF INNOVATION

The six general categories of attributes are only a sample of those available for use in structuring messages to potential adopters. A firm can run into problems if it uses these categories without careful thought about how they apply to the company's technological innovation.

Relative advantage:

The factors that affect the perception of the relative advantage include:

- The innovation's comparative cost.
- The savings in time or effort it provides.
- How soon it is available (most companies want it as soon as possible).
- Perceived risk.

Companies can reduce the perceived risk of trying an innovation by offering performance guarantee (like yield for a new process). Social factors may also affect the customer's perception of relative advantage.

For example, the oil crisis increased interest in energy saving technologies for automobiles, power generation etc. Water contamination has raised demand for water purifiers. Frequent power cuts necessitated the introduction of long life batteries for mobile phones.

Compatibility – is the degree to which potential adopters see an innovation as consistent with their values, experiences and needs. The organization should see if the new technology suits the current or evolving customs or beliefs, symbols of acceptance and status, and previously introduced ideas.

For example, many organizations that have traditionally been in the low technology engineering sector are diversifying into high technology computers and communication areas as these are supposed to have a higher status in the business world today.

Complexity – is the degree to which an innovation is relatively difficult to understand and use. Organizations seeking to introduce technologies that are difficult to use or understand must concentrate their efforts on developing simple how-to-use and how-to-understand explanations.

The computer industry's emphasis on developing user-friendly menu driven software technology is one example of efforts to overcome user's resistance to perceived complexity.

Testability – Trialability or divisibility is the degree to which potential adopters can experiment with an innovation on a limited basis. Development of such opportunities is an important diffusion activity.

For example, modular switching technology not only facilitates absorption it also allows for testing the basic building blocks. This in turn facilitates decision-making on acquiring technology for larger units.

Visibility – Observability or communicability refers to the conspicuousness of the innovation. It is the degree to which the results of a new technology are apparent to others. New products that are highly visible will be communicated most readily to other adopters.

When digital technology was first introduced for telephone communication the users could clearly perceive a significant difference in the quality of the call; and the adoption of digital technology by telephone companies proceeded at a rapid rate.

Cost – refers to the magnitude of financial resources required to obtain and operate the innovation. Innovations in high cost would be expected to diffuse more slowly. However, one study indicates that cost does not appear to be significantly correlated with rate of adoption.

CHARACTERISTICS OF ADOPTERS

There are different ways of looking at society and adopters can be broadly categorized on the basis of how they act. Table 21.2 presents them.

Table 21.2 Innovation adopter categories

Locus of control	Adopter categories	Behavior
Inner-directedness (20% in society)	Innovators (venturesome)	Show initiative. Seek new experiences and like to explore. Motivated by an innate curiosity and is likely to be among the first to try anything new, often for the fun of it.
Outer-directedness (80% in society)	Early adopters (respectable)	Motivated primarily through the direction of others. These folks generally wait to try something new until they've seen others do something for long enough they feel its safe and accepted, for them to try it too.
	Early majority (deliberate)	
	Late majority (skeptical)	
	Laggards (traditional)	

What are characteristics innovators? According to scholarly research in the field, these are the characteristics of innovators.

Innovators – Being venturesome:

They are the customers most confident about thinking for themselves and most likely to deviate from their local community's established way of doing things. As might be expected, members of this group are likely to be younger and better educated than the average consumer. They come from well-established families and are cosmopolitan having friends outside the family. They are generally higher-income buyers or financially stable individuals. They have adequate risk capital (both material and social) and can afford to take calculated risks.

Early adopters – Following the lead:

To be an early adopter often requires the income, self-confidence and education to use a product that has still not gained wide acceptance. A major difference, however, is that unlike innovators, who adopt the product during the introduction stage of the product life-cycle, most early adopters buy the product during the growth stage.

Early adopters are relatively large in number. They tend not to be different in age but to have many more year of education, higher social status and upward social mobility, be in larger organizations, have greater empathy, less dogmatism, a greater ability to deal with abstractions, greater rationality, greater intelligence, a greater ability to cope with uncertainty and risk, higher aspirations, more contact with other people, greater exposure to both mass media and interpersonal communications channels and engage in more active information seeking.

They read more magazines than the average person and have high usage rates in the product category in which the innovation falls. Although members of this group follow the lead of the innovators, they are more integrated into their local communities. Early adopters are conceived of as opinion leaders, who help to determine which new products later adopters will find acceptable. They contribute greatly to a new product's progress. Developers of new products therefore spend considerable time and resources in identifying and reaching this group. They are a significant target for advertisements and other promotions aimed at creating a market where none existed before.

Early and late majorities – Riding the bandwagon:

The early and late majorities, taken together, constitute approximately 68 per cent of the overall group that adopters a new product. They make up the mass market on which many products depend. The two halves of this market are seen as having similar characteristic in differing degrees.

The early majority is usually made up of solid, middle-class consumers, who are more deliberate and cautious in making purchasing decisions than are early adopters. Once this group adopts a new product, late in the growth stage, the product's acceptance and its diffusion throughout the social system are well established. In general, members of the early majority are of average socioeconomic status.

As time goes by and more consumers adopt an innovation, it is perceived to be less risky. At this time, the product has reached maturity, and the late majority adopts the innovation. Members of the late majority are slightly less educated and financially stable than members of the early majority. They also are older, more conservative and more traditional. They tend to be skeptical about new product ideas and reluctantly adopt innovations only when the products no longer carry the risk associated with newness. Social pressure also may force late adopters to purchase a product.

Laggards – Bringing up the rear:

These people see a need for the product but for economic, social or educational reasons have been slow to accept it. Innovations are not welcome to this older group, which is lowest in socioeconomic status. Laggards resist challenges to past fashion and traditions. The laggard group is especially easily identified when the product in question is clothing. Frequently, laggard group begins to wear the style at a time when all other consumer groups start dropping it.

Driver – Rider – Dragger classification:

Another way to look at any society facing change is by looking at three distinct personalities. There are drivers (early adapters), who drive new innovations and thinking. There are the riders (middle adapters) who will eventually ride along with new trends. There are always the draggers (late adapters) who are still grousing about using word processing and the fax machine.

Together, these three main groups create a bell curve of innovation diffusion. The amount of time it takes for an innovation to diffuse across society can vary based on many factors.

Widespread use of the telephone took 25 years, fifteen years for personal computers, seven years for widespread use of the fax machine and five years for widespread use of the World Wide Web.

The most effective means of motivating other-directed personalities (middle to late adapters) to accept new thinking and change is by "Tom Sawyerism," demonstrating satisfaction from tangible benefits without direct advocacy.

You might know the story, by Mark Twain, where Tom is whitewashing a fence and specifically avoids asking his friends for help while making it look like he's having a great time. Eventually his friends convince him to accept items in trade in return for his letting them in on the fun. Tom knew better than to be direct, he instead showcased the benefits for all to see.

While in this case Tom really didn't want to be whitewashing the fence and succeeded in enticing his friends to do his work for him, the point here is that often indirect advocacy through showcasing the benefits is more effective than preaching about the benefits. Strategies will be required, not to tell folks what they should be doing, but to unobtrusively lead them to the discovery of what they can do for themselves. (Tom Sawyerism)

Measuring innovativeness:

Table 21.3 and Box 21.1 gives methods of measuring innovativeness.

Table 21.3 Measuring innovativeness

Factor	Agreement scale				
	Very much	Much	Somewhat	Less	Very less
Risk taker/Venturesome	5	4	3	2	1
Variety seeker	5	4	3	2	1
Individualistic and independent in thinking	5	4	3	2	1
Initiative or desire to be among the firsts	5	4	3	2	1
Not tradition bound	5	4	3	2	1
Dislike for status-quo	5	4	3	2	1
Younger					
Well educated	5	4	3	2	1
Large income	5	4	3	2	1
Better social status	5	4	3	2	1
Higher occupational status	5	4	3	2	1
Integrated with community	5	4	3	2	1
Friends outside	5	4	3	2	1
Greater participation in friendship and organizational groups/Socially mobile	5	4	3	2	1
Read magazines and newspapers	5	4	3	2	1
Cosmopolitan	5	4	3	2	1
Has favorable attitudes toward new products	5	4	3	2	1

Box 21.1 Innovativeness

(Yes or No or a five-point agree/disagree scale)

1. I like to take a chance.
2. I like to try new and different things.
3. When it comes to taking chances, I would rather be safe than sorry.
4. I like to wait until something has been proven before I try it.
5. If people would quit wasting their time experimenting, we would get more accomplished.
6. When I see a new brand on the shelf, I usually pass right by.

7. In general, I am the first (last) in my circle of friends to buy a new—when it appears.
8. I like to buy new—before others do.(Note: Items 3,4,and 5 are negative items. Score them in reverse)

Source: Compiled by Jagdish N. Seth and Banwari Mittal (2003), *Customer Behaviour: A Managerial Perspective*, Thomson Asia Pte Ltd Singapore. p. 146.

CONSUMER ADOPTION PROCESS

The adoption of innovation by the users follows a pattern often referred to as purchase process model. Let us consider the following four stage model for explaining the behavior of adopters:

- Awareness/Uncertainty.
- Insight/Adoption.
- Internalization/Adaptation.
- Enlightened Expectations

Awareness/Uncertainty:

Lack of adequate knowledge and skills in knowing and using the product lead to perceiving risks in adopting it. Incase of technical products, techno fear and related ego-protecting excuses, are strongest at this stage.

For the individual at the "uncertainty" stage, it is important to keep the instructional tasks very simple with short step-by-step, mastery learning format such that there is no failure, only success. Easily obtainable objectives are necessary to build confidence, as well as encouraging messages whenever possible.

In case of Internet, at this first stage people often experience acute self-doubt and self-depreciation as to whether they will be able to master the basic computer, internet, typing and written skills. A very shallow understanding of the potential benefits is common at this stage, though there is the general impression that there are advantages. Manuals with simple explanations, demonstrations and short duration training programs will be helpful to the adopters. Upon proving to them they can communicate online, there is often a surge of optimism and confidence.

Insight/Adoption:

Self-confidence begins to build through hands-on experience. As the adopters use the product they identify its benefits and problems. They learn to reap the benefits without inhibitions and encounter the problems without fear.

At the "insight" phase people accept that telecommunications skills are not beyond reach and begin to see an increasing number of ways to benefit. They "adopt" use of the Internet and begin to gain a broader of idea of what it has to offer them.

Internalization/Adaptation:

Usage falls into a pattern of purposeful use and becomes a routine and transparent. There will be occasions of experience sharing. As others observe the use, they become enthusiastic and learn from the adopter. Ultimately they gain confidence to buy and use the product.

The "internalization" stage is achieved through regular use when people begin to view the online skills as merely an extension of one's self. Use of Internet begins to be adapted to meet personal needs in an increasing number of ways. At this point "being online" is no more threatening than making a voice telephone call.

Enlightened Expectations:

The fourth stage, "enlightened expectations," begins after people internalize the innovation. Imagining new original uses begins to occur once the experience and satisfaction become regular. Users become masters and think proactively about the future developments of the product.

At this stage, there is a growing acceptance that the Internet has even greater potential benefits. People begin to make an internal commitment to pursue their full potential for new uses of the Internet. This may be a year or more after initially going online. Willingness to serve as an online resource person, to tutor others online, or even to teach others online are indications to one has arrived at this "enlightened" stage.

ROLE OF OPINION LEADERS

Innovators and early adopters may become opinion leaders. Opinion leadership is the giving of information and advice, leading to acceptance of the advocated position by the recipient of the opinion.

This definition has two implications:

- First, not only must information be given, but also it must be accepted frequently or by a majority of those who receive the opinion.
- Second, the information given by the opinion leader must pertain to a recommended action, and the recipients of the opinion must act on the recommendation.

Opinion leaders have two qualities, both necessary for their success:

(i) **Expertise** - It is possessing knowledge about the innovation that is not yet common knowledge. Since a person cannot be an expert on everything, opinion leadership is by necessity interest-area specific.

(ii) **Trustworthiness** - It refers to the perceived benevolence and dependability of the opinion giver. It is founded on the requirement that the opinion giver has no vested interest in promoting a position.

Box 21.2 presents some illustrative measures that customer behavior researchers recommend for measuring opinion leadership and innovativeness.

Box 21.2 Illustrative Measures of Opinion Leadership and Innovativeness

1. Compared to your friends, are you more likely to be asked, less likely to be asked, or about as likely to be asked about——?
2. During the past six months, how many people have you told about—?

   a) Told no one (b) Told a number of them.
3. In your discussions with your friends and neighbors about—, are you more likely to

   a) Give information/receive information?

   b) Be used as a source of advice/not used as a source of advice?
4. My friends and neighbors often ask my advice about— (Agree/disagree).
5. I influence the types of —— my friends buy (never/sometimes/often).
6. I look to my friends for advice on——.

Source: Compiled by Jagdish N. Seth and Banwari Mittal (2003), *Customer Behaviour: A Managerial Perspective*, Thomson Asia Pte Ltd., Singapore. p. 146.

Innovators and opinion leaders are just as important among business customers. Marketing expert Eric von Hippel calls them "*lead users*." Lead users use the products of today in ways that predict how those products should be modified to meet the needs of tomorrow. Thus, lead users use existing products to their maximum capacity with some unmet needs. Marketers can study these users and their needs and can implement innovations in those products.

Von Hippel cites the example of college students as the lead users of personal computers. The students had access to time-sharing terminals linked to mainframe computers at the university; these terminals were functional equivalents of what would be later known as personal computers. By studying their usage, marketers could have predicted the future popularity of desktop-based computer games among college youth.

MARKETING STRATEGIES

The significance of the adoption process to the marketer is twofold:

1. Not all innovations may be successful to gain adoption by consumers.
2. Not all consumers pass through the adoption process with the same speed-some move swiftly, while others proceed more slowly.
3. The marketer's communication forms vary in their effectiveness over the different stages in the adoption process.

Several factors that may lead to an incomplete adoption process are listed in Table 21.4 The marketer should take care to minimize the marketing problems leading to consumer failure to complete the adoption process.

Table 21.4 Causes for adoption failure

Process stage	Marketing-organization causes	Consumer causes
Awareness	Poorly used or too little communication.	Selective exposure. Selective perception.
Comprehension	Communication hard to understand.	Selective retention.
Attitude	Communication not persuasive.	Complacency. Suspended judgment.
Legitimating	Poor source effect of communications.	Peer-group pressure against adoption. Low regulating use of innovation.
Trial	Behavioral response not specified in communications.	Alternative equally good innovation not available.
Adoption	Failure to develop new products and improve old products.	Replaced by another innovation.

Source: Gerald Zaltman and Ronald Stiff, "Theories on Diffusion", in Scott Ward and Thomas S. Robertson (eds) *Consumer Behavior :Theoretical Sources*, Engle wood Cliffs: Prentice-Hall, p. 451.

These points can be important in assisting the marketer to develop an effective promotional program.

Strategies based on adoption stages:

Figure 21.2 shows the consumer adoption model and the related purchase process model.

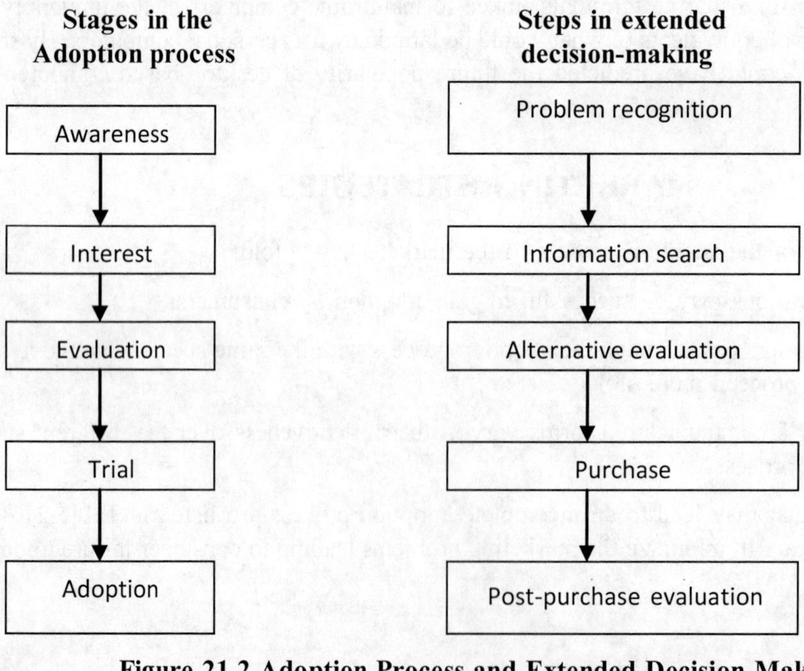

Figure 21.2 Adoption Process and Extended Decision-Making

For early stages of the adoption process, the marketer would design awareness and interest generating messages. Mass media appear to be most effective in creating awareness. At later stages to help consumers in evolution, marketers may use personal sources of information. Marketer would desire to have effective personal selling and word of mouth communications at these points.

Strategies based on product attributes:

Table 21.5 provides a framework for developing strategies to enhance the market acceptance of an innovation. The critical aspect of this process is to analyze the innovation from the inhibitors point of view.

Table 21.5 Strategies based product attributes

Diffusion Determinant	Diffusion Inhibition	Diffusion Enhancement Strategies
Compatibility	Conflict	Emphasize attributes consistent with normative values.
Relative advantage	Low	Lower price. Redesign product.
Complexity	High	Distribute through high service outlets. Use skilled sales force. Use product demonstrations. Undertake extensive marketing efforts.
Observability	Low	Use extensive advertising.
Trialability	Difficult	Use free samples to early adopter types. Offer special prices to rental agencies. Use high-service outlets.
Perceived risk	High	Document success. Highlight endorsement by credible sources. Provide guarantees.

Source: Del H.Hawkins, Roger J. Best and Kenneth A. Coney (2003), *Consumer Behaviour: Building Marketing Strategy*, Tata McGraw-Hill Company, New Delhi, p. 254.

Strategies based on Target market:

Marketing strategies should be based on characteristics of target market and innovator adoption categories. Table 21.6 shows the characteristics of the markets and the potential strategies.

Table 21.6 Characteristics of the markets and the potential strategies

Determinant	Inhibitor	Strategy
Marketing effort	Limited	Target innovators within group. Use regional roll out.
Nature of group	Conservative	Search for other markets. Target innovators within group.
Felt need	Weak	Use expensive advertising to share importance of benefits.

Determinant	Inhibitor	Strategy
Innovator and early adopters	Lack of awareness and credibility	Stress excitement of ownership. Explain, how product is new and revolutionary. Use sophisticated or technical messages and cosmopolitan appeals. Use publicity for new product announcements. Use highly credible spokespersons. Employs narrowly targeted special interest and prestige publications. Appeal to "enthusiasts"—those highly involved in product category. Use pioneering advertising in specialized mass media. Distribute trial size of product to homes. Use "event marketing" to introduce new products to media and trade.
Early majority	Lack if rationale for purchase	Use mass advertising to build brand preference. Stress benefits and compare brands in ads. Use demonstration-oriented advertising and house party personal selling. Rely on peer pressure to overcome deliberateness. Use price-oriented ads to gain market share. Employ sales promotion tools such as coupons and trial sizes sold in stores. Run dealer promotions to get them to stock and display the product. Feature opinion leaders in ads and use testimonials.
Late majority	Skepticism	Overcome skepticism by using guarantees and seals of approval such as Good Housekeeping. Underwriters Laboratory, etc. Demonstrate product in store. Use on-package coupons. Stress extended warranty protection and service/repair centers. Use value-marketing approach in advertising stressing high quality for a low price. Employ straightforward appeals. Use mass advertising to support dealers of the brand.
Laggards	Lack of interest	Spend little on promotion because interest in product is disappearing.

Source: David L. Loudon and Albert J. Delta Bitta (2002), *Consumer Behaviour*, Tata McGraw-Hill: New Delhi, p. 279 and Del H.Hawkins, Roger J. Best and Kenneth A. Coney (2003), *Consumer Behaviour: Building Marketing Strategy*, Tata McGraw-Hill Company, New Delhi. p. 254.

Strategies Based on Innovation Resistance:

Innovation adoption is a slow process of overcoming resistance crated by two factors – habit and perceived risk. When habits are hard innovation adoption will be doubtful.

Similarly when perceived risk is high, innovation adoption takes long time for less venturesome people. Based on the combination of the two factors, four types of innovation resistance can be found, as depicted in Figure 21.3.

Habit \ Risk	Low	High
Weak	**No resistance innovations** (New and improved versions of established products; fads and fashions)	**Risk resistance innovations** (Discontinuous and replacement innovations)
Strong	**Habit resistance** (Continuous and replacement innovations)	**Dual resistance innovations** (Social programs)

Figure 21.3 A Typology of Innovation Resistance

Source: Jagadish N. Seth (1981), Psychology of Innovation Resistance, *Research in Marketing*, (4), pp. 273-82.

Habit resistance innovations:

Many innovations face this resistance. Adoption requires unlearning old practice and learning ones. Without incentives one would not take the trouble of new learning.

Cars that work on electric power rather than gas and that would require consumers to recharge their batteries regularly. For consumer to learn this new habit, they would need substantial incentive, such as the prospect of significant savings in the costs of energy.

Risk resistance innovation:

The more the risk associated with trying an innovation is the slower the diffusion will be risk can be financial, physical or social. Perceived risk is a function of three dimensions:

- The probability that the innovation will not perform as expected.
- The negative consequences due to failure.
- The possibility and cost of reversing negative consequences.

Consumers feel a need for the benefits offered by laser eye surgery and view the probability of its working successfully as being quite high. However, they perceive the consequences of failing as being extreme and irreversible and therefore do not readily adopt this innovation.

Consider consumers switching to solar-energy home-heating systems. Once installed, using one or the other system entails no physical action, so habits do not come into the picture. But there is risk that the solar system may not work. Documentation of risk-free performance of new technology is required before rational consumers can be expected to adopt these innovations.

Dual resistance innovations - Finally, there are innovations that entail overcoming old habits as well as high risks. These are the hardest for consumer to accept.

Examples include social program in developing countries, such as contraception practices. Consumers in these societies perceive health risks in the use of contraceptives and using them requires learning new routines.

Marketers should reengineer these innovations to minimize both the learning of new habits and the perceived risk. A classification of marketing strategies to overcome different barriers to innovation adoption is provided in Table 21.7.

Table 21.7 Marketing strategies to overcome barriers

Type	Barrier	Strategies
Functional	Usage barrier	Develop a systems perspective (e.g, packaging). Integrate innovation with preceding activity (packaging). Emphasize on market development.
	Value barrier	Improve product performance (modification and development.). Improve product positioning. Reduce price by lowering costs.
	Risk barrier	Use a well-known brand name. Elicit endorsements and testimonials. Facilitate trial (increase market exposure).
Psychological	Tradition barrier	Educate customers. Use change agents. Understand and respect traditions.
	Image barrier	Borrow good image (brand name. Make fun of negative image. Create a unique image.

Source: A modified version of David L. Loudon and Albert J. Delta Bitta (2002), *Consumer Behaviour*, Tata McGraw-Hill, New Delhi, p. 282.

INNOVATION ADOPTION BY ORGANIZATIONS

The characteristics of the innovation itself are of critical importance in determining whether or not it will be adopted.

Credibility:

Innovations are more likely to be adopted if they originate within the organization. This is based at least partially on the perceived credibility of the source of the innovation.

Compatibility:

The more compatible an innovation is with the existing system, the more likely it is to be adopted. This, of course, implies that organizations are likely to be conservative in their innovations or technological policies, since what is compatible is unlikely to be radical. In some cases, an innovation is worthwhile only if it is adopted at a particular time or a particular sequence in the organization's operations.

Power politics:

The economic conditions and the internal politics of the organizations involved affect how the innovations are adopted. Organizations are characterized by power struggles. The outcome of these struggles, together with organizational characteristics determines whether or not a particular change will be made.

Internal policies:

If an innovation or technological policy is likely to be disruptive to interpersonal relationships, it is less likely to be adopted. This refers to the fact that some innovations, small changes in an organization's structure, can have the effect of paving the way for such additional actions.

The adoption of one innovation or the development of a technological policy is likely to lead to the capacity to involve the organization in additional such actions.

Innovativeness:

Adoption of management innovation tends to trigger the adoption of technological innovations more readily than the reverse.

SUMMARY

Since innovations are becoming expensive and their chances of success are becoming slim over the years due to heavy competition, it is important to know the nature of innovation adoption and the strategies of innovation diffusion. Innovation diffusion is a process through which an innovation spreads throughout a social system overtime. It involves special types of communication methods or system to help diffuse changes in practice, as well as changes in knowledge or attitudes. Customer response to these new products and services is referred to as innovation adoption.

The diffusion follows a bell curve. On this curve, the first adopters are called innovators and normally constitute 2.5 per cent of the population. They adopt independently of other people. Those who adopt later are imitators; namely, early adopters (13.1%), early majority (34%), late majority (34%), and laggards (16%) in that order. The development of a corporate strategy for diffusing innovations to target consumer segments around the world requires an integrated approach.

Factors influencing diffusion strategy include: organizational climate, technology champion, opinion leaders and communication strategy, attributes of the innovation and characteristics of adopters. Internalization of innovation involves four stages: Awareness/Uncertainty, Insight/Adoption, Internalization/Adaptation and Enlightened Expectations. In organizations the characteristics of the innovation itself are of critical importance in determining whether or not it will be adopted. Generally, credibility, compatibility, power politics, internal policies and innovativeness are the organizational determinants of innovation adoption. Two important trends in Indian society encouraging innovation are youth, the change agents and learning, anew way of life.

Innovators and early adopters may be opinion leaders. Marketing Strategies and the Diffusion Process.Two points important in assisting the marketer to develop an effective promotional program are: (i) Not all consumers pass through the adoption process with the same speed-some move swiftly, while others proceed more slowly and (ii) The marketer's communication forms vary in their effectiveness over the different stages in the adoption process.

QUESTIONS

1. What is innovation diffusion? What is its impact on society?
2. Identify the different diffusion types. Explain diffusion as an integral of innovation strategy.
3. Describe innovation diffusion theory and factors influencing diffusion.
4. Know the characteristics of innovation adopters and role of opinion leaders.
5. Discuss, how individuals and organizations and countries adopt innovations.

EXERCISES

From the magazines, newspapers and Internet collect information about how a new product / brand was launched by a company and how it gained market acceptance. Conduct a survey to know the views of innovators and early adopters.

CASE : INNOVATION ADOPTION

To the global design and R&D centers. Most of these relate to modifying and customizing products according to Indian needs. For instance, based on research provided by Samsung India, the following modifications are introduced.

- Washing machines for the Indian market now include a "sari wash" course.
- TVs now come with higher sound output, given the Indian preference for loud sound quality.

Samsung India's two software development centers, in Noida and Bangalore, are building solutions for virtually all products that use software: from the latest LCD and plasma TVs, mobile phones (the current focus is on 4G, WCDMA and multimedia), digital cameras to printers and IT products. In fact, the Bangalore centre has filed over 145 patents based on its software development work. Besides, about 30 Indian engineers work closely with their Korean counterparts at the Samsung headquarters in Seoul, particularly on customizing phones and developing software for Indian needs (regional language menus, for instance).

The effort at the global design centers hasn't gone unnoticed. Last year, Samsung won five Industrial Design Excellence Award (IDEA)- making it the first Asian company to win more awards than any European or American rival. Since 2000, it has won 33 top design contests and earned about 100 citations at top design contests in the US, Europe and Asia.

Thanks to the design and innovation drive, Samsung's brand value has risen dramatically in western markets, particularly in the US, in the past couple of years. The recent fifth annual Business Week\interbrand ranking of the 100 most valuable global brands named Samsung as the fastest growing global brand over the past five years with a 186 per cent surge in brand value. This year, at the 20th position, Samsung was the leading consumer electronics brand, above Sony at 28 and LG at 97.

The attention to product design is winning the company approval even in India. Says National Institute of Design Executive Director Darlie Koshy.

The work done at Samsung is rather unique because of the multidisciplinary approach it follows-the focus is not just on the look and feel of the products, but also to observe their performance in an experiential performance in an experiential space and then identifying the areas where they can be enhanced.

Designs on the Indian market:

Samsung in India is hoping to build upon this value and repeat its increasing success in global markets in the country. Will it be able to do so in an extremely price-sensitive market, particularly when it is targeting its growth mainly form the premium market and not the mass market?

Says Harminder Sahni, principal at retail consultancy KSA Technopak.

In a developing consumer products market like India, no company can choose to focus only on one end. There are huge numbers of consumers across segments and they are jumping over the fence all the time. Companies have no choice but to straddle many segments until such time as market segments mature.

For his part, Zutshi believes that is already happening-the market in India is upgrading by leaps and bounds. He points out that the market in Bihar has seen tremendous increase demand for flat panel TVs. Similarly; Samsung's twin-door frost-free refrigerators have sold beyond expectations in Punjab and Uttar Pradesh.

"If you are able to deliver the latest technology at an affordable price, the consumer will not be willing to go back to outdated technology," he says.

Moreover, says Zutshi:

"We do have products that sell in smaller towns. But even these offer value and include the current technologies. For instance, all our flat TVs incorporate a recently introduced DNIe picture enhancing technology, which usually comes with LCD and plasma TVs. That's perhaps the reason why many of products are not priced as low as that from some of our competitors."

The consumer electronics and home appliances market in India is hugely segmented, making it difficult to point to a clear leader. Nevertheless, for sometime now, LG Electronics has been the number one player in many categories. LG's strategy has been remarkably simple: it has kept prices low while targeting the mass market. That's helped it bring in the numbers. It's been offering a range of feature-acked but economically priced products. The company's kept its focus firmly on increasing its penetration in the rural and semi-urban mass markets.

For its part, Samsung claims it's never been a price warrior-its focus has always been on the premium market, which is why it has remained a steady No. 2 or No. 3 player in most product categories. Will sticking to that strategy now help it achieve its ambitious targets? Zutsoli thinks so.

"It takes time to ensure your supremacy in market share. Once you get your brand perception right in the minds of the consumers as a brand that delivers the best technology and gives you value for money, then ultimately market share goes up."

On target:

But has Samsung been able to get that message across to potential customers. How many customers actually pay attention to differentiation on the basis of technological innovations such as DNIe or Silver Nano(for refrigerators and washing machines) or even one based on design?

Sales staff training - KSA's Sahni agrees, adding that in many cases, the sales staff at the showrooms are not able to point out the key differentiators. That's one issue Samsung's already been tackling. Last year, the company started the Samsung Marketing Academy, which conducts regular training programmes to educate the sales forces, shop-owners and company employees on the company's technology and design, how it is different from what competitors are offering and how to better explain the difference to the consumer. By equipping the salespeople to sell knowledge-oriented lifestyle products, the company is hoping to provide customers a more informed buying experience, which will translate into higher sales.

Showrooms for experience - Keeping its target customer in mind, the company has also created a network of over 80 exclusive showrooms comprising Samsung Digital Zone (focusing on high-end digital audio-video products such as MP3 players, camcorders and LCD/plasma TVs), Digital Worlds and Homes (where the emphasis is on creating an experiential zone for consumers to "feel" the product) and Plazas (which are relatively smaller).

It's also ensuring a presence in most big malls and multiplexes; even in the multi-brand outlets, the focus is to create a shop-in-shop atmosphere. The new, "Imagine" ad campaigns focuses on products like LCD TVs and cell phones that reflect the lifestyle positioning. Samsung India's got ambitious designs on the Indian market.

Questions:

1. What should be the focus of innovation – design or promotion?
2. Suggest appropriate measures to Samsung to achieve its goals.

Chapter 22

Legal Aspects of Innovations

Learning Objectives

After you have studied this chapter, you will be able to...

- Know the concept of intellectual property rights, .
- Understand legal provisions in India relating to their protection
- Recognize the provisions at international level

Structure

- Introduction
- Safeguarding Innovation
- Concept of IPR
- Historical Background
- What can be Protected?
- Significance
- Benefiting from Patents
- Indian Patents and Designs Act, 1991
- IPR in International Setting
- Patenting Trends and Challenges
- Summary
- Questions
- Exercises
- Case : New Waves

INTRODUCTION

Patents play an increasingly important role in innovation and economic performance. During the last decade there is rise in patenting activity. The increasing use of patents to protect inventions by business and public research organizations is closely connected to recent evolutions in innovation processes, the economy and patent regimes. Scientific and technological advances have created new waves of innovation, notably in Information and Communications Technology (ICT) and biotechnology.

SAFEGUARDING INNOVATION

Innovators have to be careful in maintaining the secrecy and proof of their innovations.

Documentation:

Patent notebooks are used to provide legal protection for inventions.

The basic Bell patents for the telephone were defended in court and the survival of Bell Telephone was ensured by a few crude notes made by Bell on the back of an envelope which (luckily) had been properly signed, witnessed and dated.

Documentation can have many other useful, complementary functions: a recorder, a reminder, a source of ideas, a means of ensuring project continuity and a way to communicate with yourself and within a project group.

A physicist learned of the invention of the electron microscope and, not knowing the principle used, worked out 3 different ways by which it could be built. Later he checked the patent and found it used one of his methods, but another of his methods was superior and made the original patent obsolete.

In documentation, neatness is not essential, but clarity and conformance to legal standards is critical. Other things that should be recorded: sources, questions, what doesn't work, things to try. A truly effective, comprehensive patent requires planning, teamwork and iteration: invite everyone to participate in finding ways around your patent claims or to break them or improve on them. A one page summary sheet of the important procedures and checkpoints should be included inside the front cover of every patent notebook issued.

An example of a World Class Patent Strategy at General Electric merits attention. Box 22.1 provides a brief of it.

Box 22.1 GE documentation Procedure

GE uses a very powerful "standard optimizing procedure" in preparation for filing a patent: A brief patent disclosure is circulated within the company before any formal patent application is prepared. Everyone is invited to find ways to improve upon, extend or "break" the patent. All the relevant ideas are then incorporated into the formal patent application(s) and all contributors become co-inventors. There are many important advantages to this approach: It results in more "industrial strength patents" that are more valuable, more comprehensive, more likely to stand up in court and hence more profitable than the initial submission.

- If a new product results from the patent, it will have more "parents" or "champions" eager to work, fight and solve problems to ensure its ultimate success.
- The increased communication and critical reviews may result in radical new approaches and solutions to the problem.
- The review process encourages more people in the company to be aware, supportive and active in the patent process.

Secrecy:

It is essential that you do not tell anyone anything at anytime, if you want to patent - disclosure will mean the information is released into the public domain and you will lose your right to protect. Even a chat at a conference can be disclosure.

Confidential Information:

It is sometimes more appropriate to keep information secret or confidential rather than formally protecting it. Secret means not telling anyone, and confidential means people may be told, but must agree not to tell others. The confidential relationship must be established before the information is handed over, preferably in writing so that you can prove it existed if necessary.

Anyone who breaks a confidentiality agreement is liable in damages. It is a good idea to regard all-important information as confidential and to mark all documents as such.

Registration:

Patent can be registered, by making an application at the Patent Office of a country. The application must be accompanied by a description of the subject matter and will be subjected to a rigorous examination to identify any 'prior art' (existing knowledge).

The usual procedure for securing international patent protection begins with an informal application to the Patent Office. The next stage is to file an international application, which will again be the subject of rigorous examination and search. A complicated series of examinations take place at this stage and costs can reflect the amount of work undertaken!

A patent is finally granted up to four years from the initial application stage. Patents last for 20 years and must be maintained annually by maintenance payments. Depending on which countries the patent is held in, the cost can amount to tens of thousands of pounds over 20 years.

CONCEPT OF IPR

Traditionally intellectual property is divided into two groups like:

(i) Industrial property, which includes inventions, industrial designs and marks and trade names to distinguish goods.

(ii) Copyrights broadly include literary works, musical works including any accompanying words dramatic works, pantomimes and choreograph works, pictorial, graphic and sculptural works; motion picture and other audiovisual works; sound recordings and architectural work.

Today , IPR embraces mainly four items:

(i) Patent, (ii) Trademarks, (iii) Industrial designs and (iv) Copyright.

HISTORICAL BACKGROUND

The practice of defining intellectual property started in Italian city-states. First patent was granted to Filippo Bruncelleschi in the Republic of Florence in 1421. He was given a three-year monopoly for his invention concerning special hoisting gear used in barges. An ordinance relating to patents was enacted in Venetian law of 1474. In England, domestic producers granted a series of patents to encourage foreign inventors to import their inventions and to stimulate inventions. In India, it was introduced by enacting the act on protection on inventions in 1856, which was based on the British patent law of 1852.

Patents:

A patent is a property right granted by the state to a patentee, excluding others, for a limited period, from using the patented invention without the proper authorization of the owner of the patented invention.

Patents can be of two categories:

1. Process patents.
2. Product patents.

The process patent means that the process of the manufacturer is patented and nobody can manufacture any product by that process without the consent of the patent holder. On the other hand, product patent means that nobody than the patent holder can legally manufacture the particular product.

SIGNIFICANCE

Patenting provides a strategy for protecting rights and benefits of inventions.

Monopoly Rights:

By grant of patent, protection by way of a monopoly is extended to the inventor for a limited period for:

(i) Inventing a new and useful article.

(ii) A new process of making an article.

(iii) An improvement of an existing article, which has an industrial application.

Benefits:

Patents can prevent any body from benefiting from the protected technology without a proper license from the patentee.

Thus, patenting helps in encouraging research and development and safeguarding the interests of the researchers. In granting patents, there is a trade-off between the costs incurred by the country granting the patent due to monopoly pricing and the gains accruing to it due to encouragement to innovative efforts. This represents an indirect welfare/loss to Indian consumers because of higher prices associated with introducing product patents.

WHAT CAN BE PROTECTED?

Similar to patents we have facility to protect original works and commercial goods.

Trademarks:

It is another form of intellectual property rights, which distinguished the goods and services of an enterprise from those of competitors. Trademark typically identifies individual enterprises as the origin of marked goods or services. The practice of using trademark in India is very old. As long as 3,000 years ago, Indian craftsman used to engrave their signature on their artistic creation before exporting.

Trademarks are any device, logo, legend, label, word or container that are associated with goods or services and distinguish those of one supplier from another. A trademark can be registered, but does not have to be.

You can use the symbol ® if the mark is registered and ™ if you wish to indicate proprietary rights. Trademarks are registered with the Trade Mark Registry, initially for a period of ten years. Before you adopt a mark, it is expedient to have a search undertaken to ensure you are not infringing anyone else's trademark.

The main aspects of trademarks activities are:

- Selection of trademarks.
- Obtaining protection for trademarks and subsequent maintenance and monitoring the trademark activities of competitors.
- For getting a trademark legally protected, a trademark has to be registered in the trademark register of the industrial property office of the country in which protection is sought. A registration of the trademark is always granted for a limited period but it can be renewed in perpetuity. Any sign cannot be registered as trademark. There are certain legal requirements to be met for getting a sign registered a trademark. If it is not used for any reason, then it may be struck-off from the register. The international classification of goods and services for the purposes of the registration of marks established under the Nice agreement is used by more than 110 countries.

Industrial designs:

Industrial design refers to the creative activity of achieving a formal or ornamental appearance for items produced industrially. Design rights apply to an article which has aesthetic qualities, i.e. not merely functional. The design applied in an article must have an appearance, which is capable of visual judgments.

For protecting an industrial design it must be new and original. It is usually protected against unauthorized copying or initiation. The usual criteria for registration are shape, configuration, pattern or ornament.

The protection period is usually for five, ten or fifteen years.Like a patent but unlike a trademark, an industrial design cannot be renewed, for indefinite period. The owner of an industrial design can prevent any one else from infringing the registered designs.

- **Registered Design Rights:**

A representation (set of drawings or photographs) of the article is lodged at the Patent Office and court action can be brought against anyone who makes an article to that design. Registered design rights give a monopoly right, which lasts for a maximum of 25 years and can be sold, hired or licensed. It is much cheaper to register a design than to apply for a patent.

- **Unregistered Design Rights:**

This is similar to copyright, but also applies to articles made industrially. This right protects against piracy and counterfeiting but does not last very long – ten years at the most. A design right occurs automatically and does not need to be registered. It is important to claim it however by labeling 'Design Right' together with the date and name of the author on the article.

Copyrights:

Copyright is an automatic right that subsists in all original writing, drawing, computer programs and music and drama regardless of artistic merit. To be protected by copyright law the author's work must be original. However, to qualify for protection, the work is not required to pass a test of imaginativeness or inventiveness. Question of applying for protection does not always arise since copyright comes into force without registration or other formalities. But registration is required for enforcing the right when the third party has copied a particular work, which is always done in secret. Where possible the ownership should be indicated with the legend, accompanied by your name, your organization and date. Always ensure you are not breaching anyone else's copyright. Copyright lasts for the lifetime of the author plus 60 years.

The copyright laws of almost all countries provide for the protection of the types of works like (i) literary works, (ii) musical works, (iii) artistic works, (iv) maps and technical drawings, (v) photographic works, (vi) motion pictures or cinematographic works and (vii) computer programs.

The practical value of copyright law depends on the extent to which they are effectively implemented. It serves as an incentive to authors and their assignees to create and disseminate knowledge.

Trade secrets:

Inventors may prefer to maintain an idea or process as confidential and to sell or license it as a trade secret. Occasionally, it is inventor who alone knows the secret of invention. Today, there is a tendency to entrust innovation projects to employee teams. Employees involved in creating the invention are supposed not to reveal the trade secret to competitors. Ethically, it is considered wrong to make such revelations. Though employees are asked to sign a confidential information agreement but it is not possible to enforce it legally. Unfortunately, legal action can be taken only after the secret has been revealed.

BENEFITING FROM PATENTS

An inventor may gain benefits by giving rights to others to market his invention. Licensing and franchising are the two approaches to share the property rights with others.

Licensing:

Licensing may be defined as an arrangement between two parties-licensor and licensee. Licensor has proprietary rights over some information, process or technology protected by a patent, trademark, or copyright. Licensee is one who obtains permission to utilize the property right held by licensor and agrees to pay a royalty or some other specified sum in exchange.

Licensing has significant impact on business.

- When inventor lacks resources to expand sales of his invention, as a marketing strategy, licensing helps grow the business in new markets.
- For entrepreneurs who wish to start a new venture by imitation of an existing invention, licensing paves way for using an attractive invention.

A patent license agreement may be of two types:

- Only marketing rights with a different label in a new market. The licensor may decide to be the manufacturer of the product and give the licensee the rights to market it under their label in a new market (i.e foreign market).
- No change in label. The licensee may decide to manufacture and market the patented product under its own label only. Licensor has to sell the product under the label of inventor.

Franchising:

Franchising is an agreement where by the inventor gives exclusive rights of distribution to an independent retailer in return for payment of royalties and conformance to standardized operating procedures. The person offering franchise is known as franchiser. The person who purchases the franchise is called franchisee.

INDIAN PATENTS AND DESIGNS ACT, 1991

The fundamental principle of patent law is that a patent is granted only for an invention, which must be new and useful, that is to say it must have novelty and utility. The following are the salient features of a patent:

(i) The patent must be in respect of invention and not a discovery.

(ii) In respect of one single invention there must be one single patent.

(iii) Patent may be in respect of a substance or in respect of a process.

(iv) It is not possible to bifurcate a patent and state that one relates to the substance and the other to the process.

(v) In order to have a complete patent, the specifications and the claims must be clearly and distinctly mentioned.

(vi) It is the claims and claims, alone which constitute the patent.

When a patent is granted and is in force in respect of either the article or the process it is called "patented article" and "patented process" respectively. The person in whose favor the patent is granted and who is entered on the register of patents as the grantee or proprietor of the patent is called "patentee".

Patentee - True and first inventor:

A patentee is a true and first inventor. True and first inventor is a person who first made the invention and applied for the patent. If two persons have independently made the same invention and neither has used or disclosed it to the world, them one who applies first for the patent will be considered in law the tend first inventor although the other might have made it earlier in point of time [Bombay Agarwal Co. Vs. Ramchand AIR 1953 Nag. 154]

The patentee during the period of the patent holds exclusive monopoly right to manufacture the new article invented or to manufacture an article according to the invented process. The patentee can prevent any other person from using the patented invention. After the expiry of the patented period, anybody can make use of the invention. There is an obligation cast on the patentee to work the invention on a commercial scale either by himself.or through licensees.

What inventions are not patentable?

The following inventions are not patentable as they are not considered inventions:

(a) An invention which is frivolous or which claims anything obvious contrary to well established natural laws.

(b) An invention the primary or intended use of which would be contrary to law or morality or injurious to public health.

(c) The mere discovery of scientific principle or the formulation or an abstract theory.

(d) The mere discovery of any new property or new use for a known substance or the mere use of a known prices, machine or apparatus unless such known process results in a new product or employs at least one new reactant.

(e) A substance obtained by a mere admixture resulting only in the aggregation of the properties of the components thereof or a process for producing such substance.

(f) The mere arrangement or re-arrangement or duplication of known devices each functioning independently of one another in a known way.

(g) A method or process of testing applicable during the processes of manufacture for rendering the machine, apparatus or other equipment more efficient *error the improvement or control of manufacture.*

(h) A method of agriculture or horticulture.

(i) Any process for the medicinal, surgical, curative, prophylactic or other treatment of human beings or any process for a similar treatment of animals or plants to render them free of disease or to increase their economic value oar that of their products.

(j) An invention relation to atomic energy falling within sub-section (1) of section-20 of the Atomic Energy Act, 1962.

How to apply for patents?

A true and first inventor, his assignee or legal representative can apply for a patent for an invention. Application should be filed at appropriate office of the patent office. Appropriate office of the patent office shall be the Head Office of the patent office or the branch office, as the case may be, within whose territorial limits—

(a) The applicant resides or has his principal place of business or domicile.

(b) If the application is made jointly in the names of two or more persons, the applicant whose name is first mentioned, resides or has his principal place of business or domicile.

(c) If the applicant or the party in a proceeding has no place of business or domicile in India, the address for service in India given by the applicant or party is situated [Rule 4].

With a view to the fulfillment of a treaty, convention or arrangement with any country outside India which affords to applicants for patents in India or to citizens of India similar privileges as are granted to its own citizens in respect of grant of patents and the protection of patent rights, the central government may, by notification in the official gazette declare such country to be a convention country.

Every application for a patent shall be for one invention only and shall be made in the form prescribed in second schedule to the patent rules, 1972 and filed in the patent office with the fees prescribed in first schedule to the rules.

An application for a patent is required to be accompanied by a provisional or a complete specification. A specification, whether provisional or complete shall contain-

- Description of the invention.
- A title sufficiently indicating the subject matter to which the invention relates.
- Name, nationality and address of the applicant.
- Signature and date at the end.

If the complete specification is not filed within 12 months, the application will become invalid. The controller may permit the complete specification to be filed at any time after 12 months but within 15 months from the date of filing an application. The time is intended to provide an opportunity for making a precise expression of the invention.

Where an application is accompanied by a complete specification, a declaration as to the inventor ship of the invention shall be furnished in Form 5 with the complete specification or at any time before the expiration of three months from the date of filling of the complete specification.

Applicants have to supply, if the controller requires, drawings for the purposes of any specification, whether complete or provisional. [Rule 14(3)]. Models or samples shall be furnished only when required by the controller.

Where an application is made for a patent in respect of any improvement in or modification of the main invention, the controller may grant the patent for improvement or modification as a patent of addition [Sec.54(1)]

When the complete specification is filed in respect of an application for a patent, the application and the specification are referred by the controller to an examiner for making a report in respect of the following matters:

(a) Whether the application and the specification relating there to are in accordance with the requirements of the act and of any rules made thereunder.

(b) Whether there is any lawful ground of objection to the grant of the patent.

(c) The result of investigations made to ascertain the prior claim of the invention.

(d) Any other matter, which may be prescribed.

The examiner shall ordinarily make the report to the controller within a period of 18 months from the date of such reference. The examiner shall make an investigation to ascertain:

- *Prior publication*: Whether the invention claimed has been anticipated by publication in any document before the date of filing of the complete specification by the applicant.
- *Prior claim of any other specification*: Whether the invention is claimed in any prior claim of any other specification.

If there is any objection, the controller may allow a period of two months from the date of its publication for removing the objection. The period of two months may be extended by controller on application made to him in Form - 4, but the total period shall not exceed six months [Rules 21-26].

On the acceptance of complete specification, the controller shall give notice thereof to the applicant and shall advertise in the official gazette the fact that the specification has been accepted. The application shall be accorded a serial number , which shall be the number of the patent.[Rule 32].

Rights of patentees: [Sec. 48]

The patent granted shall confer on the patentee, the exclusive right by himself his agents or licensees to make, use, exercise, sell or distribute such article or substance in India. Where a patent granted is for a method or process of manufacturing an article or substance, the patent shall confer on the patentee, the exclusive right by himself, his agents or licensees to use or exercise the method or process in India.

Rights and obligations of co-owners of patents: [Sec. 50]

Rights and obligations of co-owners of patents shall be determined by an agreement between them. Subject to such an agreement in force, the rights and obligations of co-owners of patents shall be regulated as under:

- Each of the co-owner shall be entitled to an equal undivided share in the patent.
- Each of the co-owner shall be entitled by himself or his agents, to make, use, exercise and sell the patented invention for his own benefit without accounting to the other person or persons.
- A license under the patent shall not be granted and a share in the patent shall not be assigned by one of such persons except with the consent of the other person or persons.
- Where a patented article is sold, the purchaser and any person claiming through the co-owner of the patent shall be entitled to deal with the article in the same manner as if a sole patentee had sold the article.

Term of patent: [Sec. 53]

The term of every patent granted shall—

- In respect of an invention claiming the method or process of manufacture of a substance, where the substance is intended for use, or is capable of being used, as food or as a medicine or drug, be 5 years from the date of sealing of the patent or 7 years from the date of the patent whichever period is shorter.
- In respect of any other invention, the term shall be 14 years from the date of the patent.

IPR IN INTERNATIONAL SETTING

There are large numbers of agreements and treaties related to intellectual property rights. These are such as the World Intellectual Property Organization (WIPO), World Trade Organization (WTO), agreement on Trade Related aspects of Intellectual Property Rights (TRIPs), Budapest treaty, biodiversity convention, Geneva Convention and trademark law treaty etc.

The World Intellectual Property Organization (WIPO):

WIPO a specialized agency of United Nations came into force in 1970. All members of the United Nations are its members. Over the years, governments have negotiated and adopted multilateral treaties in the various intellectual related fields each of which establishes a 'Union' of countries which agree to grant people residing in the other countries of the union the same protection as they grant to their own people.

The World Trade Organization (WTO):

WTO came into existence in 1995 by an international treaty signed by the members of GATT (General Agreement on Tariffs and Trade). The highest authority of WTO is the ministerial conference. It constitutes the representatives of all member countries usually trade ministers. It has other subsidiary bodies which carryout day-to-day activities. General council is one of the body which delegates its responsibility to three other bodies such as: (i) the council of trade in goods, (ii) trade in services and (iii) Trade Related aspects of Intellectual Property Rights(TRIPs).

The TRIPs agreement, which is binding for all WTO members, came into force on January 1995. This agreement makes protection of intellectual property rights an integral part of the multilateral trading system as embodied in the WTO.

In order to apply the provisions of TRIPs agreement, in addition to the transition period of one year, developed countries were granted a delay of further period of four years from the date of application of agreement (that is until 1st January, 2000). Developing country like India was given an additional period of 5 years (2005) to extend product patent protection to types not previously patentable. Least developed countries are not required to apply for the period of 10 years from the general date of application of agreement.

The term "intellectual property" in TRIPs agreement refers to copyright, neighboring rights trademarks, geographical indicators, industrial designs patent, layout designs (topographies) of integrated circuits and undisclosed information. All members, even those availing themselves of the larger transitional periods, are required to comply with obligation a national treatment (equal treatment for foreign and domestic individuals and companies) and most favored nation treatment (non-discrimination between Foreign individuals and Companies) as stipulated in the TRIPs agreement.

PATENTING TRENDS AND CHALLENGES

Between 1992 and 2002, the number of patent applications filed in Europe, Japan and the United states increased by more than 40%. More than 850 000 patent application were filed in Europe, Japan and the United states in 2002, against about 600 000 in 1992.These figures reflect the growing importance of patents in the economy.

Growth in patenting corresponds to the following factors:

❖ A new organization of research that is less centered on the individual firm and more based on knowledge networks and markets.

❖ Innovation processes have become increasingly competitive and co-operative.

❖ Market mechanisms have become key in technology diffusion.

❖ Businesses have been demanding more and more patents to accommodate these new conditions.

❖ Patent regimes themselves have experienced major changes that have encouraged an increase in patenting. New types of inventions-software, genetic, and business methods been deemed patentable by some patent offices.

❖ The ability of patent-holder protect and enforce their rights has also increased, leading many to call the past two decades a pro-patent policy era.

The patent system has been instrumental in the recent waves of innovation, which have occurred in the fields of biotechnology and ICT.

Challenges:

This strengthening of patent systems in the European Union, Japan and the United States has however, raised new concerns and exacerbated old ones.

There have been numerous claims that *patents of little novelty or excessive breadth have been granted*, allowing their holders to extract rents from other inventors and from customers. This has been of particular concern in software, biotechnology and business methods, where patent offices and courts have had most difficulties in responding to rapid change, building up institutional expertise, evaluating prior art and determining correct standards for the breadth of granted patents.

Patenting might *hamper the diffusion of knowledge* - and therefore innovation. Other concerns have been raised about access to basic technologies, and research tools, which seems to have been hindered sometimes by patent-holders exercising their right to exclude. As universities are becoming more likely to patent and commercialize their own inventions, exemption for research use of existing inventions are under threat.

In the near future, the patent system will be facing even greater challenges than those it has confronted in the past two decades, including increased globalization, the overwhelming use of internet as a vehicle of diffusion and expanded innovation in services. Well-informed and more global policies will be needed to prepare the patent system to meet these new challenges, so that it can continue to fulfill its role of encouraging innovation and technology diffusion.

SUMMARY

Today, intellectual property rights embrace mainly four items. (i) Patent, (ii) Trademarks, (iii) Industrial designs and (iv) Copy right. Patents play an increasingly important role in innovation and economic performance. Patenting experienced a sizeable boom in the last decade. It is sometimes more appropriate to keep information secret or confidential rather than formally protecting it. Trademark typically identifies individual enterprises as the origin of marked goods or services Industrial design refers to the creative activity of achieving a formal or ornamental appearance for items produced industrially. Design rights apply to an article which has aesthetic qualities, i.e. not merely functional. Inventors may prefer to maintain an idea or process as confidential and to sell or license it as a trade secret. Unfortunately, legal action can be taken only after the secret has been revealed.

Patent notebooks are used to provide legal protection for inventions. Patent can be registered, by making an application at the Patent Office of a country. The application must be accompanied by a description of the subject matter and will be subjected to a rigorous examination to identify any 'prior art' (existing knowledge).

The TRIPs agreement, which is binding for all WTO members, came into force on January 1995. This agreement makes protection of intellectual property rights an integral part of the multilateral trading system as embodied in the WTO.

Growth in patenting corresponds to factors like- new organizations of research, competitive and co-operative innovation processes and efficient market mechanisms for technology diffusion and expansion of the list of patentable items. The patent system has thus been instrumental in the recent waves of innovation, which have occurred in the fields of biotechnology and ICT.

Two major concerns are – (i) there have been numerous claims that patents of little novelty or excessive breadth have been granted, allowing their holders to extract rents from other inventors and from customers and (ii) patenting might hamper the diffusion of knowledge and therefore innovation.

QUESTIONS

1. What do you understand by intellectual property rights? Explain their significance.
2. Describe the legal provisions relating to patenting.
3. Elaborate the significance of patenting in the context of globalization.

EXERCISES

Prepare a list of three patents, which have become controversial in recent years and identify the reasons for such controversy. Discuss it in classroom.

CASE : NEW WAVES

Although the R&D movement in India is still in its early stages, the country has the potential to grow into a global R&D hub. Donn Szaro, *Global Director, Health Services Industry Srevices, Ernst & Young*, Florida voices his views to P N V Nair of *Pharmabiz.com* on the state of the industry, the challenges and successes.

What is the growth perspective for the industry in India and across the world?

The industry has become increasingly global and the need to identify strategic partners across the globe has never been more prominent.

From your discussions with some key players in the biotech, pharma and the health services sector, what is your assessment?

It's clear that India has had success in the industry with its expertise in reverse technology, its support at the state government level with the emergence of biotech parks and incentives to develop business and the natural competitive advantages of language, low costs and an ever-expanding educated workforce. The IT boom of the last decade also will help in attracting foreign direct investment in the future.

In international rating where do the Indian pharma / biotech companies stand?

At this point in time, India's biotech and pharma industries constitute a modest proportion of their respective global markets (in value terms). Nevertheless, they have the potential to become strong players in the coming 5-10 years. Indian pharma and biotech companies have already started making their global presence felt. Dr Reddy's and Ranbaxy's achievements are well known. Biocon has captured a 10% of the US cholesterol lowering drug market with Lovastatin, in less than 6 months of its launch. WHO certification for Shantha Biotechnics' indigenously developed hepatitis-B vaccine last year is also a significant achievement.

Will Indian patent law be sufficient enough to attract MNCs for their R&D set up and introduction of their patented products?

This is the main issue facing the Health Sciences industry in India now. Will the 2005 patent protection laws and subsequent policies offer the proper level of enforcement to nurture the industries' development in India? It is the main premise behind the question; will the future of India be Imitation or Innovation? The government needs to ensure that India will be a place safe for foreign direct investment and for the development of the entire drug discovery process (i.e., new drugs, R&D and clinical trials, etc). If all elements are there in the laws, policies and enforcement, then yes I believe this will undoubtedly be a major milestone in the development of India's role in the Industry.

What are the areas where Indians stand to gain in the future?

(If all things are in place...) by 2005 then India stands to gain from more direct investment by MNCs, new focuses for the Indian biotech/pharma companies in brand development and an expansion of India's role in the global marketplace; especially in research, clinical trials and production.

Do you think strategic alliances and mergers will help the industry?

The title of our biotech report is "Beyond Borders" and the title of our latest report on the pharmaceutical industry is "Partners with Vision." Partnering on global level is more pertinent now in meeting the challenges of the industry than ever before. With the cost of bringing a new drug from discovery to market at over $700m (US) and rising, alliances are crucial. Companies are cross-leveraging their core competencies across the globe and India stands a lot to gain in this respect because it is such an appealing market because of the stability, culture, cost and educated workforce.

Ten years from now, what will be the scenario in the pharma industry?

Biopharmaceutical companies will increasingly face the challenge of having to continuously produce new drugs, keeping their pipelines flowing, monitoring the regulatory environment, while keeping focus on their bottom-line.

The innovation that created successful pharmaceutical companies seems to be waning. Present day pharma companies will continue to experience consolidation in the market by acquiring new companies, forming alliances with other companies that can lead to mergers (like Pfizer/Warner Lambert for example), and potentially get acquired themselves, all in an effort to meet the challenges of today's industry. Nevertheless, the marketing and distribution infrastructures, developed and refined over decades, will continue to be a key strength.

Pharma industry is one of the highly regulated industries. Have you got any proposal to make it less cumbersome?

In the US the appointment of a Food & Drug Administration head has been key to getting the organization back on track of more efficient approval processes. I believe there needs to be harmonization of the various regulatory authorities standards and protocols.

Is there any way to reduce the cost and time frame from discovery to marketing the drugs?

The most critical challenge for the global pharma industry is the increasing cost of drug discovery and development and the increasing time to market. This can be attributed largely to the declining R&D productivity (high attrition rates and cost of failures) and increasing regulatory demands of the USFDA (in terms of higher number of patients in clinical trials) for drug approval.

The application of new age technologies like high throughput screening, genomics, combinatorial chemistry and bioinformatics are capable of significantly bringing down the attrition rates and addressing the productivity problem. However, competitive advantage would go to firms that best control clinical trial costs, which alone account for a third of the total cost of drug development and almost half the time taken. Many pharma majors are meeting this challenge by conducting clinical trials for their drugs in developing countries like India, where costs are one seventh of that in the US or EU. The need to reduce the time and cost also explains the increasing trend towards outsourcing research to specialized CROs (Contract Research Organizations) and partnering and alliances between Pharma-pharma and Pharma-biotech for joint research and development.

What are your suggestions to make the healthcare delivery system more effective and affordable to the common man?

The rising cost of healthcare delivery and limited access to life saving drugs have become issues of global concern. Though member nations of the WTO have clearly approached the issues on Intellectual Property from different perspectives, there is broad recognition that differential pricing could play a key role in ensuring access to existing drugs at affordable prices, particularly in the poorest countries.

In India, roughly 60% of the total health expenditure is met from the self-paid category while the Government's contribution covers 25-30%. A majority of private hospitals are expensive for a normal middle class family. The opening up of the insurance sector to private players is expected to bring down the costs of healthcare delivery. Currently, in India only about 2 million people (0.2% of total population of 1 billion) are covered under medical insurance schemes whereas in developed nations like USA, about 75% of the total population are covered under such schemes.

The Government has an onerous responsibility to improve the primary healthcare infrastructure in the country. Higher investments in the health sector, well-directed policy initiatives to improve the quality and safety standards and fiscal incentives to encourage higher private sector participation seem to be the right prescription. The private sector should come up with business models that can render an acceptable level of quality and wholesome healthcare to the masses at affordable costs. The success story with recombinant hepatitis B vaccine, where a couple of indigenous companies have been able to bring down the price by almost ten fold is a pointer towards this trend.

You say that India has everything it needs. What is required to be done to seize the opportunity?

Yes, I reiterate that the Indian pharma and biotech industries have everything they need to be globally competitive - low cost of innovation, established prowess in manufacturing, adequate government support and highly skilled scientific personnel. Here is my prescription for seizing this opportunity:

- Develop and strengthen the base of scientists through training them in world-class drug discovery skills.
- Embrace the role of IPRs in kick starting innovation.
- Increase interaction between Industry and Academia.
- Pay attention to quality and leverage the global recognition you have earned for your IT skills.
- Lastly, take the path of collaborative growth through global partnerships and alliances.

Questions:

1. Make a SWOT of Indian R&D (innovation) system.
2. Do you agree with the suggestions given by Donn Szaro? What additional measures do you have to recommend?

Chapter 23

Innovation and Entrepreneurship

Learning Objectives

After you have studied this chapter, you will be able to...

- Identify the characteristics of entrepreneur
- Know that a manager has to be an entrepreneur
- Explain, how entrepreneurial management can be made effective
- Highlight the role of intrapreneurship in organizations.
- Suggest guidelines for successful intrapreneurship

Structure

INTRODUCTION

Today, in all sectors of global economy, large corporations are found developing new products and services and creating innovative technologies and systems. India needs entrepreneurs. It needs them for two reasons: to capitalize on new opportunities and to create wealth and new jobs. As such it is important to know-how entrepreneurs can be innovators and managers. It is also necessary to know how entrepreneurship can be made effective

CHARACTERISTICS OF ENTREPRENEURS

Every truly creative individual is a minority of one. There is no one else like him or her. It is difficult to group such persons into neat descriptive categories. The stimuli, traits and skills commonly observed in entrepreneurs are given in Figure 23.1.

Stimuli	Traits	Skills
Dream to realize A strong need to achieve A strong desire for money A need for power A need for affiliation	Perseverance Patience Self-confidence Willingness to take risks Good physical health	Good technical skills Ability to get along with employees Ability to lead effectively

Figure 23.1 Profile of an entrepreneur

We will now discuss the motivations and traits of an entrepreneur.

A big dream to realize:

Entrepreneurs are a sort of dreamers. They dream to visualize their future and strive to succeed. Reader's Digest was born by the dream of Dewit Wallance. Box 23.1 gives the details.

Box 23-1 Dream realized

Dewit Wallance was wounded in First World War. In the hospital for months together he used to read for 15-16 hours a day. Still the reading material like books/periodicals, letters, etc. used to get piled up. He could not complete them. So he had a constant DAY-DREAM to start a monthly magazine carrying digested articles/short stories/novels etc. He continued to develop his DREAM. He prepared 'dummies' for 6-8 months' issues of his magazine—'READER'S DIGIET'. Ultimately people were convinced about his project and first issue of Reader's Digest was issued in February 1922 with a borrowed capital of US $ 1300.After that Dewitt Wallance has not to look back. He continued the publication and now Reader's Digest is number one magazine throughout the world, published in many languages including Hindi and commands a very high circulation.

Strong need to achieve:

As their desire to achieve is stronger, they endure criticism. A lot of now famous people endured criticism when they first suggested an idea of theirs. It's a good thing to have open minds, but closed ears when it came to critics of the new ideas like Edison, Bell, the Wright brothers and virtually thousands of others. The story of Wrights and Edison in Box 23.2 substantiates this view.

Box 23.2 Desire to achieve

The Wrights faced nearly unending ridicule after they suggested a self-propelled heavier than air contrivance could fly. Experts and non-experts had a great time being pompous on the possibility of flights. There was professor Simon Newcomb, a respected American astronomer, who took delight in saying the Wright brothers were wasting their time and money. There is no known combination of substances and machinery and forms of force (that) can be united in a practical machine. Which man shall fly long distances through the air," said Newcomb. They had critics not only amongst scientists, but in the clergy, too. Bishop Milton Wright said, emphatically, "Flight is reserved for angels and to think anything different is blasphemy." Long after the Wright brothers had succeeded and airplanes were being built by dozens of companies, the doubters persisted.

Edison and his light bulb fought an uphill battle, even after he had proven it was not only feasible, but a tremendously useful item. His detractors, nevertheless, continued to voice the opinion, "It will never work." Henry Morton, the president of Steven's Institute of Technology, said of the light bulb: "Everybody acquainted with the subject will recognize it as a complete failure." Had Edison listened to his detractors someone else would have invented the light bulb.

Perseverance:

Rarely is an idea marketable as it is first conceived in someone's mind. It generally takes some research, refining and a lot of hard work. Sometimes, it takes years of hard work. The zipper, took literally decades to go from idea and crude model to common usage. Yet today it is used in everything from clothing to keeping artificial turf on sporting fields together. Box 23.3 provides an account of the effort.

Box 23.3 Relentless effort for Zipper

Whitcomb Judson invented the zipper in 1891 when he grew tired of having to lace his shoes. Along with his partner, Lewis Walker, they set up a factory to produce zippers in 1894.They soon learned it was easier to design a zipper than to produce one. Equipment capable of making zippers couldn't be found. They made numerous attempts to build their own machinery. All ended in failure. Discouraged, Judson abandoned his partnership and left the company. Walker, on the other hand, became even more committed to the zipper. He hired a Swedish engineer, Gideon Sundbeck, who eventually did create a machine for manufacturing zippers cheaply and in large quantities. In 1921, Goodyear Rubber produced rain galoshes using Walker's and Sundbeck's zippers. The public loved them. By the end of the decade, zippers were being used in a variety of garments. It had taken nearly three decades for an idea to become a reality and another 10 years before the product found common usage.

Patience to get lead:

Innovators may not be able to come up with success in a short time and with limited funds. They have to experiment repeatedly and need sponsors to support their ventures. The story of Carlson shows how innovators persist with their ideas. Box 23.4 presents the account.

Box 23.4 Persist to win

Around 1935, Mr. Chester Carlson, former carbon chemist, printer and patent lawyer, was working in the patent office of Mallory Company. He was disturbed by the cost and errors involved in typing and copying patterns for transmission to outsiders. Carlson began to work nights and weekends, at home and in the public library, to create a copying process. He experimented with various photoelectric plate surfaces and adhering black powders. Working with very simple equipment and a part-time employee in a rented room, Carlson got his first image in October 1938. With a crude demonstration device, he agonizingly went from company-to-company seeking development support. But there was no significant copying business then. By 1942, Carlson had obtained patents on basic concepts in the process. But by then Carlson was, in his words, "in desperate straits" financially, although he only had some $ 3,000 invested in the process. Finally, in 1944, a "vest pocket" division Battelle had set up to sponsor new ideas agreed to use some of its own money for development in return for a share in potential royalties.

In 1947, as a result of seeing a write-up of one of Carlson's patents, a small company named Haloid investigated and agreed to license and develop the process. The company's existing products were stagnating and its president, Joseph Wilson, was willing to take risks to develop an entirely new market. Although xerography became one the of the great success stories of all time, it was not profitable until the early 1950s, thirteen to seventeen years after its conception.

Willingness to take risks:

Entrepreneurs are undaunted by rejections. They prefer to go on their own instead of giving up. Charles Darrow developed the game Monopoly and met Parker Brothers Inc for marketing it. When they refused to do so, he marketed them on his own. Box 23.5 presents a brief account of his success story.

Box 23.5 Confidence rewarded

In 1932, Charles Darrow invented the game Monopoly. He created the game on his kitchen table and tried to sell the idea to Parker Brothers Inc. They turned him down. Supposedly, experts at Parker Brothers told him the game was too complicated and took too long to play. They recommended numerous changes. If he made those changes, they agreed to take another look at the game. Darrow, on the other hand, liked his game the way it was and chose to leave it alone. Instead, he began selling it door-to-door and then through a Philadelphia department store. Sales were so good that the experts at Parker Brothers decided to take another look at it. They bought the rights to Monopoly and paid Darrow a royalty on every game sold. The game is now being sold virtually unchanged from the way Darrow designed it, except for the foreign versions where street names have been changed to reflect native streets and locales.

Millions of people in the United States, Canada, South America, Europe and even Asia loved Charles Darrow's idea. It made him a lot of money.

Self-confidence:

When they have an idea for a way to do something better, faster, more cheaply or more productively, entrepreneurs go ahead. However, they may make mistakes in their judgments and miss the opportunities. Box 23.6 tells now Edison , Henry Ford and Westinghouse misjudged opportunities.

Box 23.6 Mistaken judgments

Edison made mistakes about the value of a good idea. Edison invented the phonograph and is credited with inventing the motion picture projector, too. Yet after trying to create talking motion pictures he gave up, rationalizing his failure by saying of talking pictures, "They are a hopeless novelty the public will not support."

Henry ford was assured by Alexander Dow of the Dow Chemical Co. that the internal combustion engine would never work out as a means of propelling automobiles. "Electricity is the coming thing." Dow told Ford, "but gasoline-no."

George Westinghouse, on the other hand, was called a fool by Commodore Vanderbilt when he tried to sell the idea of airbrakes to the railroad magnate. Vanderbilt couldn't grasp the concept of rubber hoses and air pressure replacing mechanical, hand-set brakes on trains. It was not because Vanderbilt was stupid. It was more a case of "we've done it this way for years." Or "don't confuse me with facts, my mind's made up."

ENTREPRENEUR AS MANAGER

The entrepreneur as a manager looks different. It is generally observed that where there is management, there is order, no chaos. But in case of entrepreneur we find different approaches (James Brian Quinn, 1979).

(a) Planning:

The entrepreneur operates is an uncertain environment and tries to work with an undefined process.

- **Multiple competing approaches** – For every success there are hundreds of failures. It implies that an innovation project has many contenders. Different ideas and different approaches make the decision-making complex.
- **Chaos acceptance** – The inventor/entrepreneur is not bound to formal plans or PERT charts of progress. Progress on a new innovation typically comes in spurts among unforeseen delays and setbacks. He accepts and even enjoys the essential chaos of development. He does not have to waste time explaining his progress or lack thereof to a board or legislature with less commitment and with false expectations concerning the speed and orderliness of progress.
- **Long time horizons** – The inventor/entrepreneur is undeterred by the seven to fifteen years that typically elapse between Invention and Financial success. He does not make detailed financial calculations of such matters. He defines success as of the time of exploitation and he provides a continuity of interest and support for the entire development cycle.
- **Incentives/risks** – The individual inventor/entrepreneur can satisfy his personal desires for money, achievement or recognition and is motivated to do so. Because he is a committed expert in the field, he perceives the risk as less than any review group would. He does not panic when others might. This becomes especially important when risking money on very large-scale systems.

(b) Operations:

The effort made by entrepreneur through trails and error to complete the project of innovation will be characterized by the following features:

- **Flexible financial support -** The inventor/entrepreneur is not dependent on any single financial source. If one source will not satisfy, others may. At crucial times there are specialized venture capitalists used to taking "one out of twenty" development risks.
- **Low early costs -** Because the inventor/entrepreneur works out of his own home, his overhead cost is minimal. He invents to avoid costs. He uses sweat capital instead of capital for materials or equipment. As a result, failure cost is low and not publicly visible. Although many failures occur, there are no formal inquiries when the entrepreneur is wrong. Future progress is not inhibited by past failure or fear that such failure could be represented as a fraud against the public or stockholders.
- **No detailed controls -** In the early stages, detailed market estimates are costly, inaccurate, and perhaps misleading. Early estimates of such things as computers, xerography and metal skis were all misleading. No market existed for such products. Consequently, market estimates both seriously understated potentials and entirely missed the products 'opening market niches'.

When the first jet planes started to fly, the best market research pointed out that there were not even enough passengers for all the transatlantic liners then in service or being built. Five years later, the transatlantic jets were carrying fifty to one hundred times as many passengers each year as had ever before crossed the Atlantic.

MAKING ENTREPRENEUR MANAGEMENT EFFECTIVE

Entrepreneurs cannot be successful managers for various reasons. The broadest area of the thinking skills and styles of pursuing goals of entrepreneurs can be codified as given below. Entrepreneurial employees are referred to as intrapreneurs.

Marsha Sinetar (1985) identified the following characteristic features of entrepreneur that make them less fit to be managers:

- They are easily bored and would rather move into untried areas.
- They are comfortable with ambiguity, at least when it comes to work.
- They are neither risk-averse nor troubled by ambiguity.
- They may be uninterested in social matters and thus may not be socially "well-rounded."
- They need to use their minds to solve difficult, personally fulfilling problems.
- The healthier their personalities, the more likely it is that they experience their work as a calling or dedicated vocation.

How does the Pioneering Innovative (PI) entrepreneurs succeeds? The following decisions are taken by them to make the progress profitable:

- Opts for markets or market segments where there is first mover advantage.
- Utilises powerful learning strategies such as going in for pilot projects before scaling up and doing in-house R&D.
- Masters personally the entire process of operating in a new market or market segment before product launch.

- Places experts on the board.
- Makes extensive networking.
- Enters into joint ventures only after a good deal of homework and capability development.
- Professionalizes their management as their units grew larger.
- Contributes to social causes (altruism),
- Emphasizes product quality and customer service.

Professionalizing management in the venture implies developing a risk taking culture, market focus, strategic controls and networking.

Risk taking culture:

Entrepreneurial organizations make a clear departure form traditional type of organizations. Table 23.1 shows the departures.

Table 23.1 Organizational Culture: A comparison

Dimension	Traditional organization	Entrepreneurial organization
Strategy	Status quo; conservative	Evolving, futuristic
Productivity	Short-term focus, profitability	Short and long-terms, multiple criteria
Risk	Averse, punished	Emphasized, rewarded
Opportunity	Absent	Integral
Leadership	Top-down, autocratic.	Culture of empowerment
Power	Hoarded	Given away
Failure	Costly	OK. Teaches a lesson
Decision-making	Centralized	Decentralized
Communication	By the book, Chain of command	Flexible, facilitates innovation
Structure	Hierarchical	Organic
Creativity	Tolerated	Prized and worshipped
Efficiency	Valued, Accountants are heroes	Valued if it helps realize overall goals

Source: I. Cornwall and B. Periman, *Organizational Entrepreneurship*, (Homewood, Illinois: Irwin, 1990).

Focus on the markets:

Identification of new markets and/or exploring new opportunities in the existing market is an important task of entrepreneurs.

New products-Anything genuinely new creates markets that nobody before even imagined.

No one knew that he needed an office copier before the first Xerox machine came out around 1960; five years later no business could imagine doing without a copier.

New uses - A product designed for one specific use, especially if scientific or technical, often stays with the market and the end use for which it was designed; but not always. The innovator has limited vision. In fact, he has tunnel vision. He sees the area with which he is familiar to the exclusion of all other areas.

An example is DDT. Designed during World War II to protect American soldiers against tropical insects and parasites, it eventually found its greatest application in agriculture to protect livestock and crops against insects.

The Dupont Company never thought of automobile tires as a major application for the new Nylon fiber it had developed. But when one of the Akron tire manufacturers showed interest in trying out Nylon, Dupont set up a plant. A few years later, tires had become Nylon's biggest and most profitable market.

To be market-driven, the new venture should be willing to experiment in new markets or in new uses in the existing market.

- Provide free samples to people in the "improbable" market to see what they can do with it, whether they can use the stuff at all or what it would have to be like for them to become customers for it.
- Advertise in the trade papers of the industry; indications of interest may come from unexpected quarters.

Networking:

Today's entrepreneurs are deeply embedded in networks, partnerships, alliances and collectives. Businesses are motivated to participate in formal networks or joint-venture formation in order to:

- Increase internal capabilities and protect resources (internal motivation):

  Entrepreneurs usually have a wide range of friends, acquaintances and business associates. They are able to make use of these informal network relationships to obtain resources and opportunities for their firms.

- Strengthen strategic position and competitiveness (external motivation). These networks provide them with information about their environment and they enable entrepreneurs to build reputation and credibility for themselves and their firms.
- Develop long-term strategic advantages that increase future flexibility (strategic motivation) The networks themselves can be sources of sustainable competitive advantage as well as a means of procuring other resources that can be a source of sustainable competitive advantage.
- Further social concerns and values of entrepreneurs (social motivation) Networking, the process of enlarging the entrepreneurs' circle of trust is a socialization process.

Strategic outlook and controls:

Prudent strategic management is possible when entrepreneurs adopt right approaches and tools. One of the latest tools, which is comprehensive in evaluating the financial as well as other aspects of business is Balanced Score Card (BSC) shown in Figure 23.1.

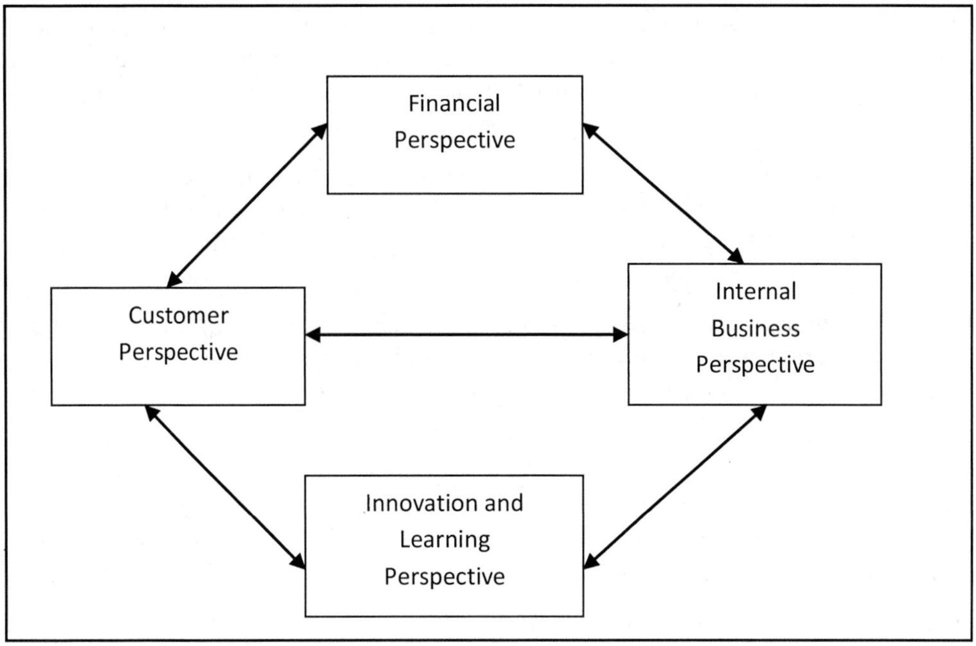

Figure 23.1 Financial and Operational Measures in BSC

The Balanced Score Card (BSC) is a systematic management process that generates objectives, activities and measures for organizational performance. The balanced score card is a set of measures that gives managers a fast but comprehensive view of their business. A good balanced score card has 15 to 20 different measures derived from the four basic dimensions of entrepreneurial performance:

- Financial dimension (How do we look to our investors?)
- Customer dimension (How do we look to our customers?)
- Internal operating dimension (What must we excel at?)
- Innovation and learning dimension (Can we continue to improve and create value?)

Because the entrepreneurial venture's existence is characterized by change and growth, these measures can be fine-tuned to reflect changing circumstances. When the environment of the venture changes rapidly, old criteria can be discarded and new measures can be implemented. This system is called "balanced" because it helps the entrepreneur balance:

- *The Long-term vs. the Short-term* - Some of the criteria measures will capture a 3 to 6 month period's activity. Others will attempt to drive the organization to longer-term goals, 3 to 5 years out.
- *Lagging indicators vs. Leading indicators* - Some criteria measure what has happened in the past, like financial performance or manufacturing productivity. These are the lagging indicators and they tell the entrepreneur about the past. Other measures are leading indicators and relate to the future. Such measures and capital investment, training, new hires and research intensity capture the venture's current activities in anticipation of a future payoff.

- *External performance expectations vs. Internal performance expectations* - Some of the measures deal with how the company is managing its relations with the external environment. Examples would be customer or vendor relations. Other measures deal with internal operations such as manufacturing efficiency and employee skill acquisition.
- *Financial performance vs. Nonfinancial performance* - The balance between these two is critical. Too much emphasis on financial results can choke growth as the entrepreneur seeks to maximize short-run opportunities. Too much emphasis on nonfinancial measures (such as "eyeballs" captured in Internet scenarios) risks running out of money and willing investors.
- *Driver measures of future performance vs. Financial measures of past performance* - The drivers are critically important because they indicate that a company is building the capabilities and acquiring the intangible assets it needs for future growth.

The benefits of using the balanced score card have been shown for many established companies over the years, and the same lessons apply for new ventures. Organization performance must be integrated and balanced. However, there are some other advantages to using the balanced score card approach since it is not only a measuring tool, but also a system of managing. Many companies have used the BSC to:

1. Clarify and gain consensus about strategy.
2. Communicate strategy throughout the organization.
3. Align goals (departmental and personal) to strategy.
4. Link strategic objectives to long-term targets and annual budgets.
5. Identify and align strategic initiatives.
6. Perform reviews (both periodic and systematic).
7. Obtain feedback to learn about and improve strategy.

INTRAPRENEURSHIP

Becoming a creative business person, not merely a manager, requires a relentless pursuit of innovation. It means prioritizing ideas, placing them at the center of work, not getting distracted by day-to-day concerns and creatively bringing value to the firm. In business, being an innovator will be the next core competency- the essential capability for success.

Concept of intrapreneurship:

Large corporations create ventures, too. This phenomenon is called "intrapreneurship," with the prefix intra denoting "inside" the organization. Intrapreneurship is defined by Dollinger, 2003) as follows:

- Entrepreneurship within an existing business.
- The development within a corporation of internal markets or autonomous or semi-autonomous business units that produce products, services or technologies in a unique way.
- An opportunity for corporate managers to take initiative and try new ideas.
- An Internal Corporate Venture (ICV).

Entrepreneurship Vs. Intrapreneurship

On comparison, we can draw some differences between Intrapreneur and Entrepreneur (Pinchot, 1985; Knight, 1985, and Hill, 1987). Table 23.2 shows them.

Table 23.2: Differences between Intrapreneur and Entrepreneur

Basis	Intrapreneur	Entrepreneur
Seek autonomy and freedom and have long-term perspective	Yes.	Yes.
Sensitive to hierarchy	More. Has to counter politics. Utilizes support system.	Yes.
Finalizing project	Approval from top. Have to sell ideas.	Self-confidence and own decision.
Resource acquisition for innovation	Search within organization	Search in markets
Ownership and control	Separated. Sometimes leaves an organization.	Not separated. Can carry on projects?
Status symbols	Organizational	Social and organizational

Skills of intrapreneurship:

Annette Moser-Wellman (See Rajat Gupta, 2001) suggested a framework of some of the most powerful skills in the intrapreneurship and called them the five faces of genius:

- **The seer : Visionary skills** – When painters begin to paint, they have an image in their minds eye-an internal picture they "see". Bill Gates said that the original vision for Microsoft was "a PC on every desk and in every home." It was the image that created the future.
- **The observer** – Observers pay attention to small things and get big ideas from those details. Former Sony President Akio Morita developed the Walk-Man when he got the idea from a small thing he noticed. During a party for one of his teenagers, he saw that kids were lugging heavy stereo equipment from one room to the next. Morita asked himself, "what if music was portable?" and the Walk-Man was born.
- **The alchemist** – The "alchemist" uses the world around them to come up with new ideas. Physicists, for instance, find breakthrough theoretical ideas by creating analogies of the natural world. Marlboro cigarettes were a brainstorm of advertising guru, Leo Bunett. Burnett was flipping through a magazine and stumbled on a retrospective of the American cowboy. He connected the need to reposition the cigarette with the love of the cowboy. It was through this connection that the icon of one of the world's biggest brands was born.
- **The fool** – The "fool" is one of the most powerful creative skills. The "fool" knows how to invert problems, persevere when the going gets tough and isn't afraid to pursue absurd solutions. Oprah Winfrey is arguably the most powerful business woman in the world. She built her

empire with a "fool" strategy. When she began her talk show, other talk show hosts were featuring people's problems and making fun of each other. Oprah turned the model upside down and started focusing on the strength of the human spirit. She created a book club, a magazine and programs that featured the positive power of humanity.

- **The sage** - Seers take complicated information, synthesize it quickly and then come up with a great ideas. A perfect example would be the business genius of Michael Dell. Prior to Dell computers, you had to buy a computer at a retail store. A low-margin business, fraught with tangled problems, Dell simplified the route to market. His idea in effect went straight to the heart of the problem and revolutionized the way we buy computers.

The Process of Intrapreneurship:

There are five recognizable stages in the process of intrapreneurship or corporate venturing (Cornwall and Periman, 1990):

Problem Definition - Stage 1 begins with problem definition. Problem or alternatively, opportunities- may come from sources within the company or industry. The key to recognizing intrapreneurial opportunities is to be sensitive to change and open to surprise.

Coalition Building - Stage 2 requires coalition building. The intrapreneur must develop relationships within the corporate bureaucracy that help support the innovative project throughout its early development. This parallels the entrepreneur's search for legitimate partners and supporters.

Resource Mobilization - Stage 3 calls for resource mobilization. In the early stages of resource acquisition, the intrapreneur may be "borrowing" resources that are officially assigned to others in the corporation. As the project gains momentum and resource needs mount, official and formal recognition of the Internal Corporate Venture (ICV) is needed. This will occur when the ICV passes the test of the corporation's internal capital market and receives its official budget.

Project Execution - Stage 4 is the actual execution of the ICV. It is paralled to an entrepreneur's official launch of a new venture, except that there are multiple levels of managers with different degrees of experience.

Venture Completion - Stage 5 is the venture-completion phase. If the ICV has been less than a success, it can be dismantled and its resources reabsorbed by the corporation. If it has been successful, it can be continued and additional investment can be made.

Benefits of intrapreneurship:

Intrapreneurship offers several benefits to the organizations. According to Zahra (1991) the following benefits can be identified:

- Intrapreneurship provides large corporations the opportunity to adapt to the increasingly dynamic, hostile and heterogeneous environment businesses face today.
- It also enables the corporation to diversify from its core business through internal processes. Many companies have an aversion to trying new technologies and products that were "*not invented here.*"
- Intrapreneurship gives the corporation the ability and opportunity to conduct market experiments.

- If the corporate and economic environment is receptive to the mutation, it is "selected" and may grow into a large and profitable division or company.
- It can be used as training ground for new managers. Corporations can develop future leaders by monitoring the progress of these intrapreneurs. Managers who can succeed in the new venture have much to offer the "mother" firm.
- Also, intrapreneurial activities help to open new channels of distribution. Finally, established corporations use intrapreneuring activities to augment their bottom-line. They do this primarily through direct investment in entrepreneurial companies.

GUIDELINES FOR SUCCESS

Realizing the significance of intrapreneurship, several companies today are encouraging it in different ways.

At 3M, any young engineer can pitch a new business or product idea to top management and be appointed head of the project if it is approved. The projected new venture is then set up as a separate business. The innovative product is assigned a project manager, who remains in charge of the venture until it is successful or abandoned. The project manager can mobilize all the skills and resources necessary for the product's development. The incentives for the new business team are aligned with the project's success-members of the team are rewarded and promoted as the business grows.

Intrapreneurship does not work without radical changes in the thinking of corporate managers and their stockholders.

Look into the future - In fact, in most situations, we have our heads in the sand. We are ducking the issue of the rate of change around us, because we don't want to face up to it. We have almost 'retired on the job'. We take solace in concepts like: 'It's served us very well for a number of years. Your mind is a brilliant personal cranial computer but most people don't know how to operate it. Warren Bennis has rightly observed: The major challenge for leaders in the Twenty First Century will be how to release the brain power of their organizations.

Incrementalism is not enough -The rate of change is now so high that incrementalism will not work. Simply decide from now on to spend only 50 per cent of your time on incremental activities and to invest the remaining 50 per cent in a applying the methods and strategies for breakthrough results.

For example, Nokia, the hugely successful finish mobile phone company, identifies and then attacks a concept of 'NOYRYYS', a Scandinavian term referring to complacency. It insists on 'no mediocracy'. Or as Toyota admits: '*Kaizen is not enough*', Michael Hammer reminds us that nowadays: '*If you think you are good, you're dead.*'

Aim big:

Future requires vision and aspirations. What do many companies aspire to? 'Become market leader'. That's powerful.

In the early 1960s Philip Morris had only a 10 per cent market share in cigarettes and held a poor sixth position in the marketplace. Nevertheless, it gave itself a word picture to aim for when it set our to 'become the General Motors of the tobacco industry'. It did.

Make the terminology in your goal statements inspirational.

Consider what do most No.1 brands say is their objective? You'll get answers like: 'Stay No.1. 'Defend the position successfully'. 'Maintain it'. These are not thrilling, nor do they inspire great actions.

Some 'round numbers' in word pictures are more magical, help drive whole-brain activity and are good for step change goals. They are not however, inspirational. Draw a word-picture, or use metaphors and analogies, to help describe what it would look like.

Here is a comparative picture of number word examples

Numbers –not inspirational	Words –inspirational
➢ Double profit in two years ➢ Reach a million-dollar turnover ➢ Get to 50 per cent market share ➢ Cut costs in half	➢ Make this brand like Coca-cola ➢ Have a 'speed boat' organization rather than an 'ocean liner'. ➢ Go paperless ➢ Make our nation proud

RIGHTS OF INTRAPRENEUR

Pinchot (1985) and others have suggested the following rights for promoting successful intrapreneurship. The rights when granted will help remove barriers to intrapreneurship and give innovation benefit to organizations:

1. *The right to appoint oneself as an intrapreneur* - Intrapreneurs cannot wait for the corporation to discover them and then promote them to an intrapreneurial position. People must have the right to take initiative themselves.

2. *The right to stay with the venture* - Corporations often force the originators of ideas and projects to discontinue their creations, as they require additional resources, expertise and become better developed and bigger. Intrapreneurs need the right to continue with the project and see it through.

3. *The right to make decisions* - Intrapreneurs need the right to make the important decisions that affect the future of the venture. If decision-making has to follow the hierarchy principle, it may go to people who don't care.

4. *The right to appropriate corporate slack* - In large bureaucracies, managers control resources so tightly it is often impossible to redeploy them to more productive uses. Intrapreneurs need discretion to use a percentage of their budgets, time and physical resources to develop new ideas.

5. *The right to start small* - Large corporations have a home-run philosophy. They prefer to have a few well-planned large projects going. Intrapreneurs need permission to create many smaller, experimental ventures and let natural selection processes produce the winners.

6. *The right to fail* - Intrapreneurship cannot be successful without risk, trial and error, mistakes, and failures. False starts are part of the process. If intrapreneurs are punished for failure, they will leave the organization and others will be reluctant ever to take chances again.

7. *The right to take enough time to succeed* - The corporation cannot set unrealistically short deadlines for intrapreneurial efforts to succeed. They must be patient with their investment.
8. *The right to cross borders* - Intrapreneurs often must cross organizational boundaries to put together the resources and people needed for the project. Corporate managers resist incursions on their turf. Intrapreneurs need passports and the freedom to travel.
9. *The right to recruit team members* - Intrapreneurs need the freedom to recruit for the cross-functional teams they must assemble for the project. The team must be autonomous and members should have first allegiance to the team, not their former department.
10. *The right to choose* - Independent entrepreneurs can choose among many suppliers, financial sources, customer groups and personnel. The intrapreneur must not face internal corporate monopolists who constrain the choices for procuring resources. The intrapreneur needs the freedom to choose from external sources when they are superior.

SUMMARY

An entrepreneur seeking innovative business will exhibit the following important characteristics: endures criticism with a desire to create, perseverance-invention takes time, a willingness to tolerate uncertainty and patience, self-confidence and self-reliance and a strong need to achieve – even after failure. The entrepreneur as a manager looks different. It is generally observed that where there is management, there is order, no chaos. But in case of entrepreneur we find different approaches: (i) Chaos acceptance, (ii) Low early costs, (iii) No detailed controls, (iv) Incentives/risks, (v) Long time horizons, (vi) Flexible financial support and (vii) Multiple competing approaches.

Intrapreneurship refers to entrepreneurship inside the organizations. Research has shown that intrapreneurs have the ability to use all five skills of seer, observer, sage, alchemist and fool. For fostering intrapreneurship in organizations are: look into future, Incrementalism is not enough and Aim big. If rights are granted to intrapreneur some of the barriers can be successfully overcome.

QUESTIONS

1. Identify the characteristics of entrepreneur. Trace the differences between a Manager and an Entrepreneur.
2. Explain, how entrepreneurial management can be made effective.
3. Highlight the role of intrapreneurship in organizations.
4. Suggest guidelines for successful intrapreneurship in organizations.

EXERCISES

Assess the entrepreneurial attitudes of your colleagues using this instrument.

Instruction:

In order to assess what you believe to be important entrepreneurial abilities, and to what extent you possess them complete the following quiz. Write the number that represents your assessment on a scale of 1 to 5 as described below against each characteristic.

Importance scale: 5-Very important 4-Important 3-Neutral 2–Less important 1-Least important.

Possession scale: 5-Very much 4-Much 3-Uncertain 2–Less 1-Very less

Characteristics	Importance	Extent I possess
A strong need to achieve.		
A need to associate closely with others.		
An ability to get along with employees		
A willingness to tolerate uncertainty		
Good physical health		
A high level of energy		
A willingness to take risks		
Self-confidence		
Innovation		
Ability to lead effectively		
Patience		
A strong desire for money		
Being well organized		
A desire to create		
A need for power		
Self-reliance		
Desire and willingness to take the initiative		
Competitiveness		
Versatility		
Perseverance		

Now that you have rated the importance of entrepreneurial characteristics and the ones you possess suggest a suitable action plan for developing entrepreneurial.

CASE : ENTREPRENEUR INCARNATE

"Women are not on the rise. They have already risen" is perhaps the best way one would define Tomoyo Nonaka, Chairman, Sanyo Electric Company Ltd. (a leader in consumer commercial electronics), who is one of the most influential woman entrepreneurs in Japan!

Competencies and credits:

Hearing Tomoyo converse might make one purport that she is a fervent environmentalist, talented with great oratory skills. To top it all, as a woman who qualified with a master's degree in the Graduate School in Humanities and obtained a degree in journalism from the Faculty of Humanities of Sophia University in Tokyo, to view Tomoyo simply based on her educational degrees, can only but mislead. More so, if you were only to know that she started her career in 1979, working as a rookie anchor in a TV programme of Japan Broadcasting Corporation called Kaigai Weekly (taking almost thirteen years to become the main newscaster for another World Business Satellite program in TV Tokyo).

But entrepreneurship is what Tomoyo has become an incarnate of in Japan and even across the globe, especially given the most hitting fact that she is the first woman, in highly male dominated social order, to lead the massive Japanese Group, streamlining Sanyo's business offerings and rebuilding its global image. In 2005, the Fortune magazine placed her in the list of World's 50 most powerful women. In the same year, Time magazine listed her as one of the *Top people to watch in international business*.

Having served as a member for several advisory and discussion councils – such as the ministry of finance, the ministry of public management, Home affairs, posts and Telecommunications and the Ministry of education, culture, sports, science and Technology-and defining her nation's future, perhaps has given her much more happiness than professional accolades. Currently, she is a member of the council on the Financial system of the ministry of finance and the Council on Science & Technology. But it was in the year 1996, after quitting the broadcasting profession, that Tomoyo started joining government advisory committees and corporate boards (Sanyo being one of the notable ones, which she joined in 2002). After having served as a director in Sanyo's board for three years, the world was astounded when Tomoyo, with no past electronics experience, was appointed Chairman of Sanyo in April 2005.

Entrepreneurial initiatives:

Soon after taking charge as chairman, she undertook various audacious initiatives.

- Cutting of costs.
- Downsizing of the employee strength.
- Focusing the business on environment friendly products.

She notably launched the '*Sanyo Evolution Project*' (a project which has been developed to execute the think GAIA vision that focuses on environment friendly and energy related products). She affirms:

"My main emphasis has been on promoting Sanyo as an earth friendly company." "Our company has diligently worked on its research and development to innovate technologies that would safeguard the global environment."

Under Tomoyo's prescience, the company developed various environment friendly products with the help of latest technologies that have the potential to solve environmental problems, faced across the world. Tomoyo discloses,

"Our company wants to be a provider of solutions which would offer values that benefit the environment such as solar batteries which use the power of sunlight for the generation of energy, CO_2 compressors that would be helpful in preventing global warming, products such as rechargeable batteries like the Eneloop which would help the user to recharge batteries over 1000 times which is phenomenal for the consumer."

But how does India fit into all these plans? Tomoyo champions that India is a very important market in Sanyo's global journey and that Sanyo will contribute towards the prosperity of India by providing environment and energy-related products to the market. She proffers:

"As the Indian economy grows and energy consumption increases, Sanyo, through its long-term commitment to business in the Indian market, aims to provide solutions to the future demands of a mobile active life-style".

While Tomoyo does admit to the growing eminence of Korean giants such as Samsung and LG in the global markets, she is quite confident about Sanyo's uniqueness.

"I believe our research and development is one of the best in the world and that makes us stand out in competition. We have spent approximately $1 billion for our R&D".

Tomoyo is credited with bringing in the most dramatic change within Sanyo's six thousand strong R&D team, a change that rewrote Sanyo's product development initiatives. She divided the team into three sets:

1. Blue planet Team, which was given the responsibility to create products that would protect the earth's environment.
2. Genesis III team, which would provide solutions for clean and sustainable energy.
3. Harmonious Society team, which would bringing newer lifestyle technologies into the market.

When questioned on her employee orientations, Tomoyo strongly supports the adage, *"Failures are stepping stones to successes!"*

Mirroring this philosophy, soon after taking over as the chairman, she had propagated within her employees.

"There is a difference between aiming to achieve a 0% failure rate and a 100% success rate. We should not be afraid of failure... we should passionately work towards achieving success."

Leading a global enterprise can be quite taxing yet exciting and her smile widens when she shares.

"I believe in a participative style of leadership with a very strong R&D in place."

According to her, employees in return should make sincere efforts to display the technological prowess of Sanyo to the customers across the globe. But Tomoyo's business acumen, despite her environmental and leadership advisories, is quite ruthless and competitive. The lady outlines her mission:

"To translate our technologies into services and offerings for our customers across the world, which would in turn create greater business opportunities for us."

A New age businesswoman:

While Tomoyo is all geared up to make Sony recover its lost legacy, the lady, like a true Japanese, is completely bound to and bonded with her family. She's as much a wife, if not more, to her husband, as could be the best woman in contention. She emotionally shares that her husband, Tomoyasu Ozeki, who is a renowned consultant in international business, has aptly provided her supporting her efforts... words that resound supremely with a belonging that only the deepest of cultural values can bring.

Truly, Tomoyo personifies the definition of the new age businesswoman, perhaps more so because she belongs to Japan, a country where woman reaching the top, is a brilliant rarity. Her conviction to benchmark performances and technological excellence notwithstanding, if there were one reason that this empress of Sanyo still rules the hearts of not only the Japanese, but also the global community, that would surely be the fact that the world now sees a radically transformed paradigm of what it takes to be a leader... Tomoyo Nonaka remains, with effervescence, our entrepreneur incarnate!

Questions:

1. What makes Tomoyo an entrepreneur of repute?
2. What kind of challenges she has in the competitive market and how she can overcome them?

Source: Edited by Meena Shukal & R. Prasad (2006), Entrepreneur Incarnate, *Business & Economy*, Vol. 2, Issue XII, 15 December –28 December, pp. 84-85.

Chapter 24

Innovative Society

Learning Objectives

After you have studied this chapter, you will be able to...

- Explain, how innovation causes social development
- Evaluate the spirit of innovation in India
- Discuss the factors favorable and unfavorable to innovation in Indian society
- Explore the prerequisites and measures to be taken to make India Inc. an innovative nation

Structure

INTRODUCTION

Innovation is creating and introducing new ways of doing things, better use of goods and more efficient services and systems. Innovation is an essential ingredient for today's social and economic growth. It improves our quality of life, raises our standard of living and enables our organizations to grow and prosper. The challenge before government and corporate managers therefore is how to build a creative society for innovations.

CHARACTERISTICS OF CREATIVE SOCIETY

A creative society respects the best traditions and carefully records them for posterity because they are inheritances of past creativity. At the same time, every tradition is questioned for its contemporary or future relevance and here is continuing search for new forms of human expression. A creative society is an economic necessity especially for poor nations. The characteristics of creative society are as follows:

1. **Open society** – A creative society is open to fresh ideas. It receives information from different sources and disseminates it to different sections of people.
2. **Achievement orientation** – Creative society is not a mere challenge meeting one; it is a challenge seeking one. Stress is on becoming; not on being.
3. **Autonomy** – Free access to cultural media; freedom to experiment with resources and share new thoughts with society.
4. **Resources availability** – Availability of physical means for better quality of life and availability of language for expression.
5. **Collaboration** – Sense of mutuality and sharing, for bigger achievements.
6. **Self-identity** – High level of self-awareness among individuals; criterion of growth is progress towards self-determination.
7. **Diversity** – Existence of differences in people and practices.
8. **Recognition** – Incentives and awards for creative effort.
9. **Knowledge base** – Emphasis on learning and use of knowledge in problem solving.
10. **Crisis** – Existence of turbulent environment leading to doubt and challenge.

INDIA AS A CREATIVE SOCIETY

The society in India is characterized by openness, diversity, equality and flexibility.

Open society:

Indian society has opened up as traditional barriers are broken by social and economic changes.

- **Liberated family** - The traditional nuclear family has been superseded by a mixture of alternative configurations – married couples, unmarried couples, single parents, same-sex partners and extended families. The impact on household structures has been quite remarkable.The heterogeneity of social structures has been matched by equally vibrant diversity in the economic, technological and educational spheres.

- **Equal opportunities** -The spread of democratic values and social revolution that accompanied freedom fight has led to emancipation of minorities and weaker sections and led to eradication of untouchability and reduction in removal of gender discrimination. The share of economically active women has risen by half since the 1980s.

Achievement orientation:

In this knowledge society, youth have become the key change agents and technology leaders. Through social media, there is lot of information exchange and youth are promoting new values of achievement, life-styles and adventure.

Competition is keen on innovations. Going by the trends of post economic liberalization, it is clear that as competition has increased, new product activities by firms that have a strong intention of remaining competitive have shown an increase.

Indian companies are the most active innovators as compared to their counterparts in the major Rapidly Developing Economies (RDEs). This is indicated by the fact that India filed 1,018 US patents between 1999 and 2003, followed by Russia with 1,000, China with 980, South Africa with 566 and Brazil with 525. Dr Reddy's Laboratories and Ranbaxy are high R&D spenders and have licensed molecules to global pharmaceutical firms for clinical trials.

Autonomy:

Indian government has promoted autonomy to community organizations, many higher educational institutions like IITs, IIMs, Universities, scientific organizations and regulatory bodies like All India council for Technical Education, University.

Grants commission and so on. There are many journals on research which publish research based papers without any inhibitions. Individuals can share their knowledge through publications or participation in seminars, workshops and conferences.

Resources availability:

The last half-century witnessed a proliferation of choice in goods and services. A multitude of scientific and technological breakthroughs have widened the spectrum of possibilities in such areas as medical treatment, communication, information, energy, transport and housing beyond anything most people ever imagined fifty years ago. Leisure activities and self-expression have also flourished as educational attainment has improved and the number of nonworking hours over a lifespan has increased for many people.

The patronage to different languages in the country and their promotion has led to free sharing of views and knowledge. A good number of channels on TV offer social and cultural programmes that promote cultural diversity and integration.

Collaboration:

Indian industry and academia are tapping the invaluable experience and contacts of expatriate Indians who have been an important part of the innovation businesses abroad. The innovation experience of the expatriate Indians can be gauged from the fact that over 30% of Silicon Valley start ups are backed/founded by Indians.

Self-identity:

Going hand in hand with these changes within the society has been the emergence of an even more colourful kaleidoscope of values, cultures, religions and spiritual beliefs. Particularly pronounced has been the spread of "postmodern" values, implying not only greater concern for quality of life and tolerance, but also a greater attachment to individual self-expression and individual value systems.

Diversity:

India's great societal diversity, be it language, ethnicity or culture, makes for a heady combination for the cross-pollination and fertilization of ideas that breed innovation. Blending indigenous knowledge with modern science has the potential to develop new technology/products. For instance, there is great scope to develop pharmaceutical products, environment friendly technologies based upon appropriate blends of traditional wisdom and modern science.

Recognition:

There are institutions that continuously encourage and award innovations by different classes of people. For instance, the Department of Science and Technology (DST) India helped establish the National Innovation Foundation (NIF) - India, with the main goal of providing institutional support to grassroots green innovations. NIF awards innovatons and provides support in patenting. Box 24.1 profiles an award winner.

Box 24.1 NIF award winner

Harkesh Kataria (21), a student from Gurgaon has deviced a rain protector, which withdraws the clothesline to prevent clothes hung for drying from getting wet in rain.He is studying for the final year B.A. and part time working in the PCB design departmentof ASTI Electronic India Pvt. Ltd. for the last six months. He was still a student when he submitted his entry for NIF's competition.

One has to always run to collect clothes hung out for drying during monsoons if it rains. Harkesh's idea was to devise a system through which this could be done automatically.This is a motor driven and moisture sensor based system (Pat app. No 158/del/2012) which withdraws the clothesline into shade when it starts to rain, thereby preventing the clothes from getting wet..

Source: http://6award.nif.org.in/awardprofile-all.php

Strong knowledge base:

Learning has become a way of life for Indians. Traditional education has been historically slow to change, as have rural communities. In the past, many have taken pride in their dedication to traditional ways of doing things, but today, this attitude can bear an unwelcome heavy price. It's a fact, that with technology changing with accelerating speed, our society is changing faster all the time as a direct result.

Recent data compiled by The National Association of Software and Services (also known as Nasscom), The Economic Times Intelligence Group and other sources suggest that India has over 21 million graduates, of which around six million are science graduates, around 1.3 million with engineering degrees and over 600,000 are doctors. There were additional 2.4 million graduates, including 26,000 doctors and around 600,000 science graduates added in the year 2004 alone to the overall numbers of graduates in the country. India has a huge talent force, which gives the country a solid footing and advantage over its peer group in the research and development (R&D) sector.

Crisis:

Some of the crisis factors in the context of Indian society are:

- **Individualism** - The emergence of individualism, is negatively viewed. Many people see the future of societal change mainly in terms of disintegration and polarisation.
- **Unemployment** - Also the prevailing view is that society has failed in certain aspects to meet the expectations of increasing population. The exceedingly high unemployment rates for underqualified young people, even many years after leaving school is one major concern.
- **Inequalities** - Concern is also mounting about uneven access to new technologies across society, particularly to IT and use of the internet. It is reported that 10% of the poorest households own computers, compared with nearly 70% in the top income bracket. As for internet use, it ranges from 3% in the lower half of the income distribution to 32% in the top 10% of income earners.
- **The low-end market** - In '*The Innovator's Dilemma*' Clayton Christensen proposes that disruptive innovations invariably take place at the low end of the market or in a new market that never existed before. India scores heavily on this count, as the huge market in India is essentially low-end with customers (70% of population in rural areas and 80% of demand is to come out of middle or lower segments). Companies can disrupt at the low end of the market through low- cost business models.

ACHIEVEMENTS AND STRENGTHS

India has made significant achievements in some fields and progressing to become the R&D hub in near future. The notable achievements are as follows:

Destination to outsourcing - The huge pool of highly educated scientific talents, lower wages, lower research cost, the relatively easy access to participants in clinical trials (for pharmaceutical companies) and reforms in India's patent regime providing more protection to intellectual properties will encourage more foreign companies to either set up their own R&D centres in India or outsource their R&D activities to an India-based company.

Successful R&D accomplishments - India has done a remarkable job of diffusing knowledge and technology, especially in agriculture. As a result of the "green revolution," India has transformed it self from a net importer to a net exporter of food grains. India's "white revolution" in the production of milk has helped it to achieve the twin goals of raising incomes of rural poor families and raising the nutrition status of the population. In manufacturing sector also several companies are focusing on R&D and are doing well (Box 24.2).

Box 24.2 Leading R&D companies

Companies including Tisco, Indian Oil Corporation, Bharat Electronics and HMT have bagged the Department of Scientific and Industrial Research (DSIR) national awards (2001) for outstanding achievements in Research and Development (R&D). Indian Oil Corporation, Faridabad bagged the DSIR award in the chemical and allied industries sector; Bharat Electronics, Bangalore in electronic industries sector; Tratec Engineers Pvt. Ltd, Gurgaon, HMT Machine Tools Ltd, Hyderabad and Kweng Alloys Pvt. Ltd, Billimora in mechanical engineering sector; TISCO in new materials sector; Gujarat Narmada Valley Fertilisers Company Ltd, and Narmadanagar & Engineers India Ltd, New Delhi in the area of pollution control & environmental protection; SK Dynamics Pvt. Ltd, Roorke in technology exports; Vatanu-Cool Rotaryvanes Ltd, Pune in technology absorption; and Mohana Orthotics and Prosthetics Centre, Chennai for successful commercialisation of public funded R&D.

Expansion in R&D Infrastructure - To its credit, India has been taking bold steps to strengthen its R&D infrastructure, developing technological innovations and altering the mind set of its people toward better creation, acquisition and use of technology. It is endowed with a critical mass of scientists, engineers and technicians in R&D and is home to dynamic hubs of innovation, such as Bangalore and Hyderabad. It also has vast and diversified publicly funded R&D institutions, as well as world-class institutions of higher learning, all of which provide critical human capital.

Growth in patentable research - An increasing trend is discernible in the number of patents granted to companies by the Indian Patent Office, indicating greater awareness of the importance of knowledge and the value of protecting it through patents. Among Indian patents, it is the drugs and electronics industry that has shown a sharp increase in patenting in recent years.

The focus of research is shifting to patentable innovations, indicating better conceptualization of research. The recent amendments to the Indian Patent Act adopted in a move toward adhering to the intellectual property norms under Trade-Related Aspects of Intellectual Property Rights (TRIPs) has also boosted confidence among international players. Patents granted to India are rising.

Emerging as a major global R&D platform - The outsourcing of high-end R&D to India is yet another new trend that is evident from the large number of established R&D outsourcing centers in India, from IT and telecom to automotive and pharmaceuticals sectors.

- According to the Government figures currently, more than 155 international companies are already doing R&D in India. The pharmaceuticals, automobiles and IT sectors are leading the way.
- About 100 multinational companies (MNCs) have already set up R&D centers in the country, leading to the deepening of technological and innovative capabilities among Indian firms. Microsoft, Motorola and Intel have all increased their R&D facilities in India.
- Many America-based companies are designing auto parts and consumer electronic items in India by either outsourcing or setting up their own design centers in India.
- Several Indian companies, such as Ranbaxy and Dr. Reddy's Laboratories have also started forming R&D alliances with global firms.

Such collaboration presents several benefits for Indian industry.

- The linkages among local firms, universities and research institutes and the worldwide R&D network of multinationals further integrate India into global technology development.
- Useful in inculcating a commercial culture among scientists and helping them to apply knowledge for productive ends.

Developing Partnerships:

India is also developing public-private partnerships to harness the potential of traditional knowledge to meet health and welfare needs and to reduce poverty.

Increased R&D spending:

Indian companies in the past have had a very bad track record on R&D spending; they spent less than one per cent on R&D, but now things are changing, and the situation is different as the companies have realized the benefits of spending more on R&D. Most of the Indian executives state that their companies would increase spending on innovation in the near future. They also feel that generating organic growth through innovation has become essential for success in their industry.

In pharmaceuticals, automobiles and software, the Indian industry has started responding to global challenges and upped investments on R&D. Among the top 10 companies spending on R&D are Dr. Reddy's Labs, TELCO, Bharat Heavy Electricals Ltd, Reliance industries, Ranbaxy Laboratories, Oil & Natural Gas Corporation (ONGC), Mahindra & Mahindra, ITI Ltd., Steel Authority of India Ltd. and Bharat Electronics Ltd.

Ranbaxy (the pharmaceutical giant) spends around seven per cent of its sales revenue of US$ one billion on R&D and Dr. Reddy's Laboratories spends around 14 per cent of its annual sales of around US$ 446 million on R&D. The increased spending on R&D has started to deliver results for both the companies in the auto sector in India. This will only encourage the domestic as well as foreign automobile companies based in India to spend more on R&D.

FAILURES AND WEAKNESSES

Despite the above notable achievements the following weak points merit attention in evaluating the performance and progress.

Ranked low in patenting – India still languishes at a despairing 63rd rank in terms of global competitiveness. Patent output is an indicator of the innovative ability and by this measure India has not been the most innovative. India's share of global patenting is small.

The total number of international patents filed by India's top 20 organizations (in terms of patents filed) in a period of five years is less that MIT's patent output for the same period. Even more noteworthy, obscure organizations like General Hospital Corporation in the state Massachusetts has a patent output more than the total number of patents filed by India's top eight organizations. The per capita patenting output of India is highly insignificant when compared to countries like Taiwan.

R&D spending is relatively low - The levels of R&D expenditure India *vis-à-vis* countries such as Taiwan, Singapore, Israel and Korea is very low.

- ***Low private sector spending*** – In India, about 70 per cent of R&D is performed by the central and state governments, an additional 27 per cent by enterprises (both public and private sector industries),and less than 3 per cent by universities and other higher education institutions.

  In contrast, inmost countries in the Organization for Economic Cooperation and Development (OECD), the private sector finances 50-60 per cent of R&D, because it increasingly has the finance, knowledge and personnel needed for technological innovation.

  About 86 per cent of the country's joint stock companies, out of the total of 8,334, do not depend on R&D at all. Even among the relatively big investors on R&D, there are only seven Indian firms, which spend more than ₹ 50 crore per year, while there are about 463 companies spending less than ₹ 1 crore.

  Firms play a bigger role in R&D in Ireland, Japan, Korea, and Sweden. Universities also undertake research to a much larger extent in developed countries and have stronger linkages with the corporate world.

- ***Defence orientation*** – In the case of Government funded R&D, defence sector continues to garner maximum funds with 60 per cent of the total R&D allocation. There is a diminishing investment in industrial R&D with the belief that the corporate sector has to take up the responsibility.

Rampant Piracy:

The scale of intellectual property piracy is massive. There are both economic and social consequences of IP piracy. Without a favorable climate that will safeguard the investment in IP, not many corporates will risk their capital by investing in India. This is one reason why the amount spent in R&D by private companies as a proportion of the government spending on R&D is les compared to other nations.

Skewed educational system:

Plain data suggests that India is sitting upon the second biggest scientific pool (*Source:* CSIR, India) and its university system is pumping out engineers and scientists in large numbers. But the patenting and R&D output of Indian firms is very low. The reasons are:

- The course syllabi at the school and undergraduate level tend to be unremarkable without a focus on knowledge that is of practical value to the student. There is a greater emphasis on learning by rote.
- Indian Universities are heavily dependant on government grants for their research funding, which, with few exceptions, have not produced desired results. Successful interactions between Academia and Industry are few.
- Indian academicians also are not as focused on pure research as their western counterparts, for whom the research output is a key performance parameter. The quality of Ph.D.s churned out of the Indian universities fare poorly in comparison to their western counterparts. This can be attributed to the fact that only a small fraction of the Ph.D.s get absorbed in the industry and the vast majority has to enter the teaching profession, which, in the absence of consulting projects is a low paying activity.

Poor in Knowledge dissemination:

Regarding scientific and technical articles in mainstream journals (per million people), India matches the performance of China, but the contributions of both countries are very low compared with developed countries.

Lack of data on innovations:

Innovation and the resultant product are brought to the market after detailed analysis of consumer data and repeated test marketing. Only when businesses are able to correctly define market segments and are able to position their products appropriately for the target market, will the products connect with the consumers. Unlike in western countries, the databases in India are limited. The data collection methods are skewed to urban respondents who do not reflect the true face of India.

Lack of risk capital:

Availability of venture capital is also rather limited in India, but some signs of vibrancy are evident, and a notable venture capital investment market is emerging. The economist cites the ready supply of risk capital as a prime reason for the success of Sillicon Valley. There are four levels of financing in the US that provides entrepreneur funding, right from seed capital to multi billion-dollar funding.

1. Seed financing:

Friends, family and/or the local high net worth individuals provide it. This is probably the most crucial source of funding because most ideas could just die out at this stage for want of finance.

2. Venture funding:

- Half to a couple of million dollars is provided by small boutique of local VC funds.
- A couple of million dollars to ten million or more is provided by a large VC fund.
- Stock markets and banks fund the venture with equity and debt.

Traditionally in India, Financial Institutions (FIs) and banks were the only sources of capital for an entrepreneur. Like other large FIs, they used to be very conservative in their lending. The lending parameters were based more on the pedigree of the applicant than the quality of the business idea. There was a lack of an institutional framework that could assist in lending to entrepreneurs planning to set shop on the basis of a new technology idea.

Low FDI:

Foreign Direct Investment (FDI), although increasing, is also rather low by global standards. Also there were sectoral caps on the amount of foreign direct investment (FDI) coming in, and even now not all sectors can avail of FDI. The majority of the R&D related inward FDI in India materialized only after the economy had been liberalized. This FDI, however small, has been creating a new competitive advantage for the country, especially in the IT domain and in industries, such as automotive.

Limited Industrial Clusters:

Innovation is heavily influenced by clusters – a regional concentration of a group of related an supporting firms. Clusters characterized by the presence of suppliers, customers and skilled resources are great promoters of innovation. After the number of firms in a cluster reaches a critical mass, owing to cross industry linkages, the degree of innovation grows exponentially. India has experienced limited cluster development, with a few exceptions of isolated clusters in Kanpur (leather), Ludhiana (hosiery) etc. It's only in the last decade that technology clusters like Bangalore have come up.

The Government plays a key role in enabling the development of clusters. The creation of Silicon Valley in California, owes a lot to the liberal California laws, which valued individual enterprise and easy creation of spin offs. The creation of clusters, as a matter of state policy, by creating Special Economic Zones (SEZ) and giving them tax-free status is a recent development in India.

Low risk appetite for intangibles:

Indians exhibit exceptional ingenuity in making things work or adapting them to suit the Indian environment, but have not demonstrated the same facility in the creation of new products and services. This can be attributed to the low risk appetite of the average Indian. Specifically, Indians lack the appetite to invest in intangibles owing to an inherent disregard of their value. India has supplied raw materials and other factors of production to the world rather than finished products.

Founder Led Businesses:

Professional managers, often find it difficult to push innovation that may seem counter intuitive to other people in the organization. The founder led and family owned businesses in India, are ideally suited to drive innovation because they can go in for long-term initiatives without being unduly perturbed on packaging their initiatives for the approval of the board or the financial markets. The success of Tatas and Ambanis can be attributed to the combination of family control and professional managers.

MEASURES TO BE TAKEN

India has to take a number of policy, corporate and social initiatives to remove impediments to building its innovation capacity and be competitive at a global level. They comprise steps like developing communication and other infrastructure for R&D, and creating an attractive environment to motivate R&D investments, including favorable tax and other incentives.

Build innovation infrastructure:

Establishing science and technology parks to encourage industry-university collaboration. Such parks might attract R&D work from both foreign and domestic firms if the parks are situated close to reputable academic institutions. Paying adequate salaries and creating a proper working environment for scientists and engineers that provides them with access to capital equipment, instruments and other infrastructure needed for R&D. Failure to compensate researchers adequately and lack of a supportive environment will only exacerbate the problem of brain drain

Institutionalize innovation:

There is a steady stream of innovations in US. It is not because the Americans are any smarter than the Indians. It is because the US society, academia and industry have institutionalized innovation. Arindam Banerji emphasizes the need for institutionalizing innovation in India. He cites his own experience and that of another scientist to show how innovative thinking is discouraged in India (Box 24.3).

Box 24.3 Discouraging environment

When asked a question on the possibility of building engine cylinders of non-circular cross-section, the decrepit professor (in IIT) jeered at the suggestion. Chastened, I never bothered to find out the truth until I ran across a magazine article describing the use of elliptical engine cylinders in some high-performance German cars.

Abhas Mitra, at the Bhabha Atomic Research Centre (BARC) in Mumbai, was perhaps the first and the only scientist, who openly challenged Stephen Hawking of Cambridge University, who is regarded by many as the modern-day Einstein. Naturally, Mitra now feels vindicated following Hawking's own admission two weeks ago at a conference in Dublin, Ireland, that there isn't a black hole 'in the absolute sense'.

Hawking's about-turn has vindicated Mitra. But, in retrospect, he feels sad about the treatment he got at home while trying to take on Hawking all by himself. Too 'embarrassed' to be associated with a man who challenged Hawking, even Mitra's close colleagues avoided him and he became an outcast. To add insult to injury, BARC authorities removed Mitra from the theoretical physics division on the excuse that this division was meant only for those doing 'strategic research'.

Create Incentives to innovation:

At individual level, recognition and remuneration are important in prompting and sustaining innovation. People cannot be expected to develop their innovative skills if they believe their efforts will not be appreciated. People will go to great lengths to solve problems, but only if they know that their solutions will bring them recognition.

At company level, apart from the commercial advantages of innovation, support from government in the form of incentives like subsidies and tax exemptions are expected. Such incentives will encourage risk taking by corporates.

Governments with future tax revenues in mind may provide support to business and industry for R&D as well as commercializing new idea. Unfortunately, however, government is willing to provide financial assistance only at research and development levels, believing that little else is required to ensure the commercialization of an idea. In fact, research investment is only a small portion of the total cost to create a new industry, bring out a new product or improve our standard of living.

Promote World class practices:

In India, where large disparity exists between the most and least efficient producers in any sector, considerable economic gains can also be harnessed from moving the average domestic practice to the best domestic practice, not to mention best international practice. This will require a host of efforts, including improving the system for technical norms and standards such as product quality, work safety, and environmental protection that can facilitate the proper diffusion of know-how.

The growing stock of global knowledge can be tapped more effectively by providing incentives for international technology transfer through trade, FDI, licensing and personnel movements, along with informal means through imitation, reverse engineering and spillovers.

Encourage Knowledge enhancement:

India should thus take steps to improve its innovation system further, not only by taking advantage of new knowledge created at home, but also by tapping knowledge from abroad and disseminating it for greater economic and social development. It should also improve the efficiency of public R&D and increase private R&D, as well as encourage greater university-industry linkages. Confederation of Indian Industry suggested the increase of knowledge partnerships (Box 24.4).

Box 24.4 Knowledge Partnerships

To help bridge the R&D gap, the confederation of Indian Industry organized an "Industry-Institute Networking Forum" in Delhi. It was intended to drive knowledge partnerships for mutual benefit.

Speaking at the seminar. R Chidambaram, principal scientific advisor to the Government of India, said the Indian industry should establish long-term relationships with science leaders for the technological development of the country. According to him, the current barriers between Industry and Institutes were partly cultural, in that scientists saw their mission as generating new knowledge while companies preferred to focus on making money. Added to this was the perception that increased industry interaction would damage the quality of science. He called for a change in the mindset.

H.R.Bhojwani, Emeritus Scientist at the Council for Industrial and Scientific Research (CISR), gave examples of successful industry-industry partnerships, Bhojwani said that 14 projects, involving 110 institutions and worth ₹ 100 core, had taken-off in the past two years, setting a new trend in terms of global thinking.

N.Srinivasan, Deputy General, CII, said that the focus of Indian corporates should be on R&D and not only for commercial purposes. Despite having the fourth largest population of scientists and engineers, the DSIR estimates that there are only 1,140 in-house corporate R&D units. Partnerships between Industry and Institutes have miles to go before they can make a real contribution to our global competitiveness.

Strengthen Industry – institute interaction:

The following initiatives are suggested to improve industry-institute interaction:

- Allowing national research institutes to collaborate with domestic and foreign firms to forge closer links with industry. One way of encouraging scientists to work closely with industry and in so doing improving linkages between Technology development and Application would be to provide incentives such as bonuses and a share of royalties from products created through their research.
- Using the savings to strengthen university-industry programs by means of matching grants and other initiatives, including encouraging academics to spend sabbaticals in relevant industries so that their research meets the needs of the productive sector.
- Restructuring and modernizing universities and publicly funded R&D institutions by giving them flexibility, freedom of operation and financial autonomy.
- Increasing the intake of students into science and engineering, given the competition for recruitment of trained personnel; this may require adding colleges and universities (such as IITs or others modeled after them).

- Developing entrepreneurial skills and management training for S&T professionals to encourage them to undertake business activities.

Encourage NRI Participation:

Encouraging members of the Diaspora and renowned expatriates to contribute further to innovative activities by appointing them to the management boards of national research institutes, universities and so on to facilitate the design of university programs that better suit corporate requirements. Motivating scientists and engineers from India working in the United States and other developed countries to enter into alliances with multinational companies and establish firms or labs to undertake R&D on a contract basis in India.

Provide several Sources of Funding:

There should be continuous supply of capital for innovative efforts.

- Auditing and monitoring S&T efforts and institutional performance to identify what works well and then redeploying resources to programs that have a proven track record of success.
- Finding alternative sources of funding for R&D, especially as the government reduces its budgetary support for research programs. In some countries such as China, academic institutions are launching commercial ventures of their own or in collaboration with the corporate sector.
- Encouraging the private sector to invest in R&D. Strengthening R&D by companies so that they can have a more demand-driven and market-oriented approach with closer collaboration among researchers, partners and customers in developing new products and services that can be speedily brought to the market.
- Encouraging venture capital, which can also be used as an incentive for commercialization of research.
- Promoting a national fund to support grassroots innovators, with the aim of building a national register of innovators, converting innovations into viable business plans and disseminating knowledge of indigenous innovations, especially for job creation.

Activate Public relations:

Effectively enforcing and implementing PR to create confidence among domestic and foreign innovators on protection of their innovations in the country is highly important. .

SUMMARY

The essentials for a creative society are: favorable climate in a society characterized by –openness, achievement orientation, autonomy, resources availability, collaboration, self-identity, diversity, recognition and environment of change or crisis. Then there should be government support and corporate initiatives for innovation.

There are two views that describe the state of affairs in India. It is doing well because it is ranked well in the world, has strong knowledge base, becoming destination to outsourcing, has to its credit successful R&D accomplishments, making expansion in R&D Infrastructure, achieved growth in patentable research, is emerging as a major global R&D platform, entering into partnerships with lead companies and increasing R&D spending.

There is also a feeling that its performance is not up to the mark. The reasons cited are:

It still languishes at a despairing 63rd rank in terms of global competitiveness. The levels of R&D expenditure India *vis-à-vis* countries such as Taiwan, Singapore, Israel and Korea is very low. Unfortunately, India has still many unfavorable factors. They are: protected economy, tradition bound, disregard for intellectual property, rampant IP piracy, skewed educational system, poor in knowledge dissemination, lack of data on innovations, lack of risk capital, low FDI, limited industrial clusters and low risk appetite for intangibles.

Can India produce billion-dollar innovations? Yes, if the following measures are taken:

Institutionalize innovation, encourage knowledge enhancement, promote world-class practices, establish global linkages, build innovation infrastructure, strengthen Industry-institute interaction, encourage NRI participation, provide several sources of funding and activate public relations.

QUESTIONS

1. Explain, how innovation causes social development.
2. Evaluate the spirit of innovation in India.
3. Discuss the factors favorable and unfavorable to innovation in Indian society.
4. Explore the measures to be taken to make India Inc. an innovative nation.

EXERCISES

Form a team of researchers. Examine the curriculum and instruction modes in select schools, colleges and universities to gauge the spirit of innovation in the learning systems in India. Make a paper for discussion in classroom.

CASE : INNOVATIONS FOR SOCIAL DEVELOPMENT

The IBM India Research Lab (IRL) lab aims to advance information technology through research in software and services. It seeks to provide leadership by delivering innovations to its clients and IBM's operations in the region and globally. It has been working closely with the research community, industry, government and academia. It has significant initiatives in services and sciences, information management, user interaction technologies, e-Commerce, life sciences, distributed computing and software engineering. The lab has over 100 researchers and aims to grow IBM's interests in the region. It focuses on core technologies in the solutions and services space.

IBM's focus on innovation is deep rooted. Innovation is not just essential but imperative to IBM's very existence and growth in the global market place. Many of the lab's technologies have made their way into major products and solutions from IBM and are on the threshold of making a major difference to its services organizations. The lab is busy not only inventing, but also applying those inventions for real customer benefit. Examples range from the highly technical to activities that directly touch ordinary people.

For instance, the India lab has created a new 'e-Coupon' technology. This automatically tracks the coupons owned by a customer, prompting the user to redeem them at the right time. This eliminates the need for customers to carry them to the store, remember what coupons are applicable to which products and adhere to the validity period. This technology is now a part of IBM's websphere commerce suite of software products and is being implemented by IBM's clients.

At the more technical end of the spectrum, technology created in the lab is being incorporated into the Tivoli systems management software. This will help CIOs and IT managers handle database administration better. This is part of IBM's overall focus in the area of 'autonomic computing.' Here, computing systems are being made more self-healing, self-configuring and self-managing to reduce their cost and complexity. Hence, even small and medium business can take advantage of their capabilities to link more tightly with their customers and suppliers in what is known as an 'on demand' mode of operation.

The India lab is focused on not just the creation and patenting of new technologies, but also on the innovative application of those technologies.. They will help customers transform the way they do things. A recent initiative the lab has undertaken, along with other groups in IBM India, is a study to understand how IBM can improve India's education and health care systems through IT. The report helps as a roadmap to integrate IT in education and healthcare systems.

IBM has strong capabilities in the eGovernance area. IBM Inida is working with over 15 Governments on projects, including Gujarat, Karnataka, Uttaranchal, Chandigarh, UP, West Bengal, Andhra Pradesh, Pondicherry, Maharashtra and Kerala. Uttaranchal and IBM India have signed two Memorandums of Understanding (MoU) for a statewide e-Governance and University program initiative. This will provide the Uttaranchal Government with a plat form to leverage IBM's application development methodologies. It will reduce the development time to build applications to deploy e-Governance initiatives in the State. While IBM will act as program manager, it will also assist the Governemet of Uttaranchal in conceptualizing G2G (government-to-government) projects based on platform-independent and open standards.

IBM's education initiative is aimed at select colleges. The primary objective of this program is to train engineering and technically qualified students to become IBM certified professionals. IBM will also provide an opportunity for the faculty and students of the identified colleges to design world-class curriculum, aligned to industry needs.

Questions:

1. Comment on the innovation spirit of IBM India.
2. Based on your experience, suggest the role to be played by any one Indian company in making India superpower.

References

1. Adizes, Ichak (1979), Organizational Passages-Diagnosing and Treating Life Cycle Problems of Organizations, *Organizational Dynamics*, Summer, pp3-25.

2. Allen, Thomas J. (1971): "Communication Networks in R&D Labs," *R&D Management* 114-21.

3. Amabile, Teresa M., Constance N. Hadley, and Steven J. Kramer (2002), "Creativity Under the Gun," *Harvard Business Review*, August 57.

4. Amabile, Teresa M. (1998), "How to Kill Creativity," *Harvard Business Review*, September-October 77-87.

5. Ansoff H, and Stewart J. M. (1967): Strategies for a Technology based Business, *Harvard Business Review* 45(6), 71-83.

6. Bagchi,Suboto,(2006) Innovations Real Test, *Business Standard*, February,21, Strategist-supplement, p.3.

7. Baker, Norman R. Stephen G. Green, Alden S. Bean(1985), How Management Can Influence The Generation Of Ideas, *Research Management*, Industrial Research Institute Inc.

8. Banerji , Arindam(2003),Can India Produce Billion-dollar Innovations, ,*Indian Management;* Vol. 41, No. 5, August, p 14. (arindam_banerji@yahoo)

9. Barron F. (1975). The Disposition Towards Originality, in Calvin W. Taylor and Frank Barron's *Scientific creativity*.

10. Berkshire, S D. (1995). *Critical Behaviors in Innovative and Creative Decision making and Problem-solving Work Groups (group process).* Proquest Dissertation abstracts.

11. Bhattacharya, Arindam and Abheek Singhi(2006), A Formula for Innovation, *Business Standard*, March,21, Strategist-supplement, p.3.

12. Bhattcharyya, Dipak Kumar(2002), Managing Innovation and Creativity, *Indian Management,* Vol. 41, August, pp 22-23.

13. Bhattacharya P. S. (1982), in *Creativity in Education.* National Psychological Corporation, Agra.

14. Board, et.al., (1971) cited in Hussain, S. (1988). *Creativity: Concept and Findings.*: Motilal Banarsidass., Delhi.

15. Booz-Allen, Hamilton (1968): *Management of New Products*, New York, Booz-Allen Hamilton Inc

16. Bowenfeld. (1952). Cited in Hussain, S. 1988. *Creativity: Concept and Findings.* Motilal Banarsidass, Delhi.

17. Bulchandani, K.R. (2002), *Business Law for Management*, Himalaya Publishing House, Mumbai.

18. Butcher H. J. (1970). *Human Intelligence, its Nature and Assessment.* Buttler and Tanner. Great Britain.

19. Chan Kim ,W. and Renee Mauborgne(2000), "Knowing a Winning Business Idea When You see One," *Harvard Business Review*, September-October , 129-136, 138.

20. Clark, Kim and Steven Wheelwright (1992), *Revolutionizing Product Development*, Free Press, New York

21. Clegg, Brian and Paul Birch(2004), *Crash Course in Creativity*, Kogan Page India Ltd, New Delhi.

22. Coleman J. C. (1969). *Psychology and Effective Behavior.*, Scott, Foresman and Company, Glenview, Illinois.

23. Cooper, Robert G. (1985), "Selecting Winning New Product Projects," *Journal of Product Innovation Management*, February 35.

24. Cooper, Robert G.(1990), "Stage-Gate Systems: A New Tool for Managing New Products," *Business Horizons*, May-June, 45-54.

25. Cornwall. and B. Perimain(1990), *Organizational Entrepreneurship*, Irwin, Home wood Illinois.

26. Dale Timpe, A(ed)(2003), *Creativity*, Jaico Publishing House, Mumbai.

27. Daniel, John D, Robels Fernando (1981): The Choice of Technology Export Commitment: The Peruvian textile industry. *Journal of International Business Studies. 13*(1), Spring-Summer.

28. Darrell Rigby and Chris Zook (2002), "Open Market Innovation," *Harvard Business Review,* October, 80-89.

29. Dasgupta, S. (1977). *Creativity in Education,* National Psychological Corporation, Agra.

30. Dasgupta , Jayatri,(2004), Innovations in Rural India, *Effective Executive*, September, pp.61-71.

31. David,Fred R.(2003), *Strategic Management: Concepts & Cases*, Pearson Education, New Delhi.

32. Dawn, Lacobucci and Christie Nordhielm (2000), Creative Benchmarking, *Harvard Business Review,* November-December, Pp 24-25.

33. Debono, Edward(1992), *Serious Creativity*, Profiles Books Ltd.,London.

34. De Bono, E. (1967). *Use of lateral thinking*. Penguin Books. London.

35. ——. (1972.) *Po: Beyond yes and no*. Penguin Books. London.

36. ——. (1985). *Six thinking hats.* Penguin Books. London.

37. Dollinger Marc, J. (2003), *Entrepreneurship: Strategies and Resources*, Pearson Education Pte Ltd., Delhi.

38. Drucker, P F (1998), The Discipline of Innovation, *Harvard Business Review,* 149-157.

39. Drucker, Peter F (1985), *Innovation and Entrepreneurship*, Harper & Row, New York,

40. Drucker, Peter F. (1986) *Innovation and Entrepreneurship: Practice and Principles,* Affiliated East-West Press Pvt Ltd., New Delhi.

41. Drucker, Peter F. (1970).*Technology, Management, and Society* ,: Harper & Row, New York .

42. Dubrin(1982), *Applied Management*, Texas, Business Publications, pp 50-59.

43. Dutta, Sanjib and Anil Kumar Kartham (2004), Disruptive Innovation: Making it Happen in Organizations, *Effective Executive*, April, pp.22-30.

44. Etzel, Michael J..Walker, Bruce J and William J.Stanton (2004), *Marketing* Tata Mc Graw-Hill Publishing company Ltd., New Delhi.

45. Fellers,G ary (1996) *Creativity for Leaders*, UBS Publishers 'Distributors Ltd, New Delhi.

46. Fenichel, O. (1945). *The Psychoanalytical Theory of Neurosis*. Norton & Company Inc. New York.

47. Foster Richard, (1986). *Innovation: The Attacker's Advantage*, Summit Books, New York

48. Freud, S. (1960). Civilized sexual morality and modern nervousness in Collected Papers, Vol. II Summarized by M.I. Stein and S.J. Heinze in *Creativity and the individual.* The Free Press of Glencoe, Chicago

49. Gomez, Henry and Davila, Carios (1995), *Management Innovation in Developing World*, International Management Network, Geneva

50. Himes, Gary K(1982). Stimulating Creativity Encouraging Creative Ideas, *Supervision*, The National Research Bureau Inc.

51. Jantz, Alfred H.(1975) The Encouragement of Employee Creativity and Initiative *Personnel Journal.*

52. Glickman, Rosalene(2005) , *Optimal Thinking*, Manjul Books Pvt. Ltd., Bhopal.

53. Goldberg, Philip (1983) *The Intuitive Edge*, Tarcher.

54. Glaser, Milton A. 1993), Intuition: A Newly Recognized Factor for Innovation in R&D, *R&D Innovator*, Volume 4, Number 12,December.

55. Grossman, Stephen R., Bruce E. Rodgers and Beverly R.Moore(2003), *Unblocking Creativity at Workplace*, Jaico Publishing House, Mumbai.

56. Gupta, Rajat(2001), *India Today*, February 12.

57. Hage, J (1980), Innovation – Japan Races Ahead as US Falters, *Science*, 210: 751-54.

58. Harnessing creativity to improve the Bottom line, *UK Chartered Institute of Management Accountants*, September 2001.

59. Hill, I.(1987) An Intrapreneur Turned Entrepreneur compares both worlds. *Research Management,* Vol.30, May/June, pp 33-37.

60. Hodgetts, R.M. F.Luthans. and S.M.Lee. (1994)"New Paradigm Organizations: From Total Quality to Learning to World Class." *Organizational Dynamics*. Winter. pp.4-19.

61. Homby A. S. (1974): Oxford Advance Learner's Dictionary of Current English, Oxford University Press, Oxford, p.288.

62. Howkins, John(2005) , Enhancing Creativity, *Seminar*, September,pp29-32.

63. Huff V.E. (1992). Creativity and TA in Sidney. J. Parnes (ed). *Source Book for Creative Problem Solving*, Creative Education Foundation Press. Buffalo, New York

64. Hurssey, David (1976): *Corporate Planning: Theory and Practice*: England; Pergamon Press. P. 35.

65. Hussain, Sabiha (1999), Shotgun on the Move, *The Economic Times*, 15,June.

66. "Inspiring Innovation", *Harvard Business Review*, August 2002, 49

67. James, M.and Jongeward D. (1971). *Born to win*. Canada, Addison Wesley.

68. Jarial G. S. and Sharma A.K. (1980). Creativity and its components as affected by intelligence, personality and their interaction. *Asian Journal of Psychology and Education,* 6(21), 26-32.

69. Jonas,Salk, (1985) The *Anatomy of Reality*, Praeger, New York.

70. Jongeward, D., Sayers, P. (1973). *Everybody Wins: Transactional Analysis Applied to Organization*. Reading. Addison – Wesley.

71. Kanter, Rosabeth Moss(1982), "The Manager as Innovator," *Harvard Business Review*, July-August, 95-105.

72. Kanter, R.M. (1983). *The change masters: Innovation and entrepreneurship in the American corporation,* Simon& Schuster :New York

73. Katz ,Ralph (ed)(1979) *The Human Side of Managing Technological Innovation,* Oxford University Press, New York,.

74. Kavanagh, Eric *When Unconventional Wisdom Prevails: The Power of Contrarian Thinking*, ontact him at ekavangh@tdwi.org

75. Kazmi,Azhar (2003), *Business Policy and Strategic Management* ,Tata Mc Graw-Hill Publishing company Ltd., New Delhi.

76. Khandawalla, Pradip.N.(1984), *Fourth Eye*, A.H.Wheeler &Co Ltd., Allahabad

77. Kimberley, J R (1981), Managerial Innovation. Paul, et. al, *Handbook of Organization Design,* Vol. 1, , Oxford University Press. New York

78. King, Nigel and Neil Anderson, *Managing Innovation and Change*, (2003), Thomson Learning, Singapore.

79. Kotler, Philip (1994): *Marketing Management Analysis, Planning, Implication and Control,* New Delhi: Prentice-Hall, p.171

80. Kotler, Philip (1988): *Principles of Marketing*, Prentice-Hall of India, New Delhi, and p.152.

81. Kripa Raman, (2006), Out-of-the –Box Thinking, *Business Line –e-World*, March 13, p.1.

82. Kriquir, R.(1989) Technological innovation in Canada; A Comparison of independent entrepreneurs and corporate innovators, *Journal of Business Venturing*, pp 281-288

83. Krishnamacharyulu C.S.G & Lalitha R.(2006), *Industrial Marketing*, Jaico publishing House, Mumbai.

84. Lakshmana Prasad, (2000), Making India Inventive-Individuals can Make a Difference, *Indian Management*, February, pp.35-39.

85. Leifer, Richard, Christopher McDermott, Gina Colarelli O'Connor, Lois Peters, Mark Rice, and Robert Veryzer, (2000), *Radical Innovation* , Harvard Business School Press, Boston.

86. Leonard, Dorothy and Susaan Straus(1997), Putting Your Company's Whole Brain To Work, Harvard business review, July – August, pp.111-116

87. Lloyd, Spencer and Andrzej Krauze, *Hegel for Beginners*, Icon Books.

88. Luckenbach, Thomas A.(1986)),Encouraging "Little C" and "Big C" Creativity *Research Management*, Industrial Research Institute Inc. ,

89. Nanda,Ashish,(2005) Innovate or Perish, *Business Standard*, October ,25, Strategist-supplement, p.3.

90. Narayanan, V.K (2005), *Managing Technology and Innovation for Competitive Advantage,* Pearson Eduction (Singapore) Pte. Ltd. Delhi.

91. Newman, Warren and Summer(2003), The Process of Management, Prentice-Hall of India, New Delhi.

92. O'Keeffe, John.(2005) , *Business Beyond the Box*, Magna Publishing Co Ltd., Mumbai.

93. Peters, T J and Waterman R H (1982): *In Search of Excellence,* Harper & Row. New York

94. Pethe, S. And Gupta, P.K. (1997). The cutting edge. *Indian Management*, 36 (8).

95. Petty, Geoffrey (2005), *How to be better at ...Creativity*, Kogan Page India Pvt Ltd, New Delhi.

96. Pinchot, G.(1985), *Intrapreneurship*, Harper & Row, New York.

97. Plesk,Paul E., *Creativity, Innovation and Quality*, Prentice Hall of India Ltd.

98. Prasad, T.S.V.K,(1999), Innovative Management, *JIMS 8M*, January-march, pp.11-13

99. Quinn, J B (1992), *Intelligent Enterprise*, The Free Press, New York.

100. Robbins S. P. (1980). The Administrative Process. Prentice Hall. Eaglewood: NJ

101. Robbins, Stephen P. and Mary Coulter (2002), *Management,* Pearson Education (Singapore) Pte. Ltd., New Delhi.

102. Robbins, Stephen P(2003). *Organizational Behavior,* Prentice Hall of India, New Delhi, pp. 648-51

103. Rubinstein, Gwen (1985), Whole Brain Management , *Association Management*, American Society of Association Executives, New York

104. Robert D Hisrich, Michael P Peters, Dean A Shepherd (2007), *Entrepreneurship*, Tata McGraw-Hill Publishing Company Limited, New Delhi. Pp 161-174

105. Rogers E.M (1962), *Diffusion of Innovations*, The Free Press, New York

106. Roy, Rothwell, (1992): Successful industrial innovation: Critical factors for the 90s, *R&D Management* 22(3), 221-39.

107. Rudnitsky, H. (1996) "One Hundred Sixty Companies for the Price of One," *Forbes,* February 26, pp.56-62.

108. Russ, Sandra W. (1993), *Affect and Creativity*, Lawrence Erlbam, Hillsdale, NJ

109. Sage, Lee A., (2000) *Winning the Innovation Race*: John Wiley & Sons, New York.

110. Sandhya U.(2006) Open Innovation Brings Advantages to All, *The Hindu :Opportunities,* November, 8, pp.1 &8

111. Schoonhoven, Bird Claudia, et al (1990): Speeding products to market: Waiting time to first product introduction in new firms. *Administrative Science Quarterly*, 35, 177-207.

112. Senge P.M. (1990) *The Fifth Discipline: The Art and Practice of Learning Organizations,* Doubleday, New York.

113. Shah,K.M.(2000),Centralized Campus Recruitment-An Innovative Approach, *Indian Management*, March, pp.28-31.

114. Shapiro, Albert (1985)."Creativity and the Management of Creative Professionals," *Research-Technology Management*, March.

115. Sharma K. N. (1979). *Dynamics of creativity*. National Psychological Corporation. Agra.

116. Srivastav,A.K.,M.P.Chowdiah and K.B.Akhilesh(1994) (ed)*R&D Management*, TMH Publishing Company Ltd., , New Delhi.

117. Studer, Gary A(1982) . Working Creatively, *Management World*, Administrative Management Society.

118. Supriya, M.V. (2001). The Intuitive Knowledge Management Process: Implications for Competitive Edge in The E-Millennium, *JIMS 8M*, July-September, Pp 31-34.

119. Syrett, Michel and Jean Lammiman (2004), *Successful Innovation*, Profile Books Ltd, Hatton Garden, London.

120. Torrance E. P. (1962). *Guiding Creative Talent*, N.D., Prentice Hall of India Ltd, Delhi.

121. Torrance E. Paul. (1965). *Rewarding Creative Behavior*. Prentice-Hall. Englewood Cliffs, N.J:

122. Tripathi S.N. (1996). *Talent and Creativity*. National psychological Corporation. Agra.

123. Tushman ,Michael L. and Charles A. O'Reilly III, (1997) *Winning Through Innovation,* Harvard Business School Press, Boston.

124. Vajayan.K.(2001), Innovative Strategies for Market Leadership, *JIMS 8M*, July –September, pp.10-12.

125. Vasantha Kumar (2004), Innovation Begins at School, Business World, November,p.7.

126. Vittal.N.(2001), Managing Innovation for Excellence in Knowledge Management , *JIMS 8M*, October –December, pp. 4-7.

127. Watson, Gregory H. (1993), Strategic *Benchmarking,* John Wiley & Sons, New York, pp. 149-167.

128. Wellman, Annette Moser (2006),The Five Faces of Genius, The Strategist, *Business Standard*, 7 March, ,p.3.

129. Wheeler, Elmer(2002), *How to make your day-dreams*, Wilco books, Mumbai.

130. Wheelen L.Thomas and J.David Hunger(2003), Concepts in Strategic Management, Pearson Education,New Delhi.

131. Wissema J.G., H.WVanderpol and H. M.Messer, .(1980) Strategic Management Archetypes, *Strategic Management Journal,* January,p.43.

132. Yamanouchi, T (1995), *A New Study of Technology Management*, Asian Productivity Organization, Tokyo, Japan.

133. Zaltman G. Duncan, R L Johny H (1973), *Innovations & Organization*, Wiley Inter Science. New York.

Bibliogrphy

Arieti, Silvano. Creativity: The Magic Synthesis (New York: Basic Books, 1980).

Austin, James H. Chase, Chance, & Creativity (New York: Columbia University Press, 1978).

Bosticco, M. Creative Techniques for Management (New York: International publications Service, 1972)

Dauw, Dean C. and Fredian, Alan J. Creativity and innovation in organizations Dubuque, IA: Kendall/ Hunt Publishing Company, 1971.

Drucker, Peter F. Technology, Management, and Society (New York: Harper & Row, 1970).

Hare, A.P. Creativity in Small Groups (Beverly Hills, CA: Sage Publications, 1982).

Maier, N. R. F. Problem solving and creativity in Individuals and Groups (Monterey, CA: Brooks/Cole, 1970).

Osborn, Alex F. Applied Imagination (New york: Charles Scribner's Sons, 1952)

——, Your Creative Power (New york: Charles scribner's Sons, 1972)

Steiner, Gray A. Creative Organization (Chicago: University of Chicago Press, 1965).

Taylor, C.W. Climate for creativity (Elmsford, NY: Pergamon press, 1972)

Agor, W.H. 1989. Intuition in organizations: leading and managing productively. Newbury Park, Callif: Sage Publications.

Amabile, T.M. 1983. The social psychology of creativity. New York: Springer-Veralg.

——, 1989. Growing up creative: Nurturing a life of creativity. New York: Crown.

Arieti, S. 1976. Creativity: the magical synthesis. New York: Basic Books.

Atkinson, P.E. 1990. Creating culture change: the key to successful total quality management. London: IFS Ltd.

Basdur, M. 1995. The power of innovation: How to make innovation a way of life and put creative solutions to work. London: Pitmann Publishing.

Bower, J.L., and C.M. Christensen. 1995. Disruptive technologies: catching the wave. Harvard Business Review 73, no. 1: 43-53.

Carr, C. 1994. The competitive power of constant creativity. New York: AMACOM.

Clark, C.H. 1958. Brainstorming: How to create ideas. North Hollywood, Calif. Wilshire Book Company.

Crawford, R.P. 1954. The techniques of creative thinking. Burlington, Vt. Fraser Publishing.

——, 1964. direct creativity with attribute listing. Burlington, Vt. Freser Publishing.

Csikszentmihalyi, M. 1988. Society, culture, and person: A systems view of creativity. In the nature of creativity, edited by R.J. Sternberg. Cambridge: Cambridge University Press.

Davenport, T.H. 1993. Process innovation: Reengineering work through information technology. Boston: Harvard University Press.

De Bono, E. 1967. Use of lateral thinking. London: Penguin Books.

——. 1972. Po: Beyond yes and no. London: Penguin Books.

——. 1985. Six thinking hats. London,: Penguin Books.

——. 1992. Serious creativity. New York: Harper Collins publishing.

Fiero, J. 1992. The Crawford slip method. Quality progress 25, no. 5:40-43.

Foster, R. 1986. Innovation: the attacker's advantage. New York: Summit Books.

Fritz, R. 1991. Creating. New York: Fawcett.

——.1993. Creating minds. New york: Basic Books.

Getzels, J. and M. Csikszentmihalyi. 1976. The creative vision: A longitudinal study of problem finding in art. New York: Wiley.

Ghiselin, B. ed. 1952. The creative process. Berkeley, calif: University of California press.

Gordon, W.J.J. 1961. Synectics: The development of creative capacity. New York: Harper & Row.

Guilford, J.P.1950. Creativity. American Psychologist 5, no. 9: 444-445.

Haefele, J.W.1962. Creativity and innovation. New York: Van Nostr and Reinhold.

Hall, G.J. Rosenthal, and J. Wade. 1993. How to make reengineering really work. Harvard Business Review 71, no. 6: 119-131.

Harrington, H.J.1991. Business process improvement. New York: McGraw Hill.

Higgins, J.M. 1994. 101 Creative problem solving techniques. Winter park, Fla: New management publishing Company.

Holyoak, K.J. 1990. Problem solving. In an invitation to cognitive science: Thinking, vol,3 edited by D.N. Osherson and E.E. smith. Cambridge, Mass: MIT press.

Isaksen, S.G. and D.J. Trefflinger. 1985. Creative problem solving: the basic course. Buffalo, N.Y: Bearly Publishing.

Kanter, R.M. 1983. The change masters: Innovation and entrepreneurship in the American corporation. New York: Simon& Schuster

Krone, R.M. 1990. Improving brainpower productivity. Journal of Quality and participation(December): 80-84

Langley, P., and R. Jones, 1988. A computational model of scientific insight. In the nature of creativity, edited by R.J.Sternberg. Cambridge: Cambridge University press.

Leboeuf, M. 1980. Imagineering: How to profit from your creative powers. New York: McGraw-Hill.

Majaro, S. 1988. The creative gap: Managing ideas for profit. New York: McGraw-Hill.

McGartland, G. 1994. Thunderbolt thinking: Transform your insights and options into powerful results. Ausin, Tex: Bernard-Davis.

Michalko, M.1991. Thinker toys: A handbook of business creativity for the 90's. Berkeley, calif: Ten speed press.

Morris, J. 1992. Creative breakthroughs: Tap the power of your unconscious mind. New York: Warner Books.

Nadler, G, and S. Hibino. 1994. Breakthrough thinking. 2d ed. Roklin, Calif: Prima.

Osborn, A. 1953. Applied imagination. New York: Charles scribner.

Parnes, S.J. 1992. Source book for creative problem solving. Buffalo, N.Y.:Creative Education foundation press.

Pearson, A.F.1979.Communication, creativity, and commitment: A look at the collective notebook approach. In proceedings of creativity Week, I 1978, edited byS.S. Grryskiewicz. Greensbor., N.C.: Center for creative leadership.

Perkins, D.N. 1981. The mind's best work. Cambridge, Mass: Harvard University press.

Prince, G.M, 1970. The practice of creativity. New York: Harper & Row.

Ray, M.L., and R. Myers. 1986.Creativity in business. New York: Doubleday.

Rowan, R. 1986.The intuitive manager. New York: Little, Brown & Co.

——, Ed. 1988. The nature of creativity. Cambridge: Cambridge University press.

Sternbrg,R.J., and T.I.Lubart. 1995. Defying the crowd: Cultivating creativity in a culture of conformity. New York: Free Press.

Tardif, T.Z, and R.J. Sernberg. 1988. What do we know about creativity? In the nature of creativity, edited by R.. Sternberg. Cambridge, England: Cambridge University Press.

Tatsuno, S.M.1990. Created in Japan: from imitators to world-class innovators. New York: Harper & Row.

Tempe, A.D, ed. 1987. Creativity: Volume 4 in the facts on file series on the art and science of business management. New York: KEND publishing.

Torrence, E.P. 1987. The blazing drive: the creative personality. Buffalo, N.Y.: Bearly limited.

Utterbeack, J.M. 1994. Mastering the Dynamics of Innovation. Boston: Harvard Business school press.

Van Gundy, A.B,. 1987. Creative problem solving. New York: Quorum books.

——, 1992. Idea power. New York: American management association.

Von Hiple, E. 1988. The sources of innovation. New York: Oxford university press.

Wallace, D.B. and H.E. Gruber. 1989. Creative people at work. New York: oxford University Press.

Weisberg, R.W. 1993. Creativity: Beyond the myth of genius, New York: W.H. Freeman.

Wonder, J., and P. Donovan. 1984. Whole brain thinking. New York: Ballantine.

Wyckoff, J. 1991. Mind mapping: Your personal guide to exploring creativity and problem solving . New York: Berkley.